MW01040296

Tiptoeing Through

The Classics

A GUIDEBOOK FOR CITIZEN-SCHOLARS

BOOK 1, VOLUME 1: CHRONOLOGICAL
SECOND EDITION

A project of faith and philosophy
for and by
students and faculty of Valor Christian High School
Highlands Ranch, Colorado

Valor Christian High School
3775 Grace Boulevard
Highlands Ranch, CO 80126
www.govalor.com

Ordering Information:
Quantity sales. Special discounts are available on quantity purchases by corporations, associations, and others. For details, contact Valor Christian High School at the address above.

Tiptoeing through the Classics: Book 1, Volume 1 / —2nd ed.

Preface

The Dilemma of a Classical Education

I'S JUST TOO MUCH. The term "classical education" has been used in Western culture for centuries, with each era modifying the definition and adding its own selection of subjects. The original goal of a classical education was audacious: to provide a systematic framework to teach all human knowledge—all truth—certainly an impossible task in today's world of knowledge explosion and specialization.

A classical education would embrace a study of the basics: reading, writing, oral delivery, grammar, arithmetic, geometry, algebra, history, geography. It would then move forward into advanced study: literature, poetry, drama, art, music, mathematics, logic, philosophy, natural philosophy (science), languages and theology.

In the 20th and 21st centuries the term "classical education" is used to refer to a broad-based study of the liberal arts and literature, as opposed to a practical or professional program (i.e., earning a living, putting bread on the table, vocational topics), which today some might call STEM (science, technology, engineering and math), plus law, business, accounting, and the like.

In the 1950s **Mortimer J. Adler** (1902–2001) and **Robert Maynard Hutchins** (1899–1977) set forth ***The Great Books of Western Civilization*** as "center stage" in the curriculum for a classical education. Their magnificent opus produced a set of 60 volumes covering 161 authors and classic works produced over 33 centuries (from Moses: 1300 BC to Aleksandr Solzhenitsyn: 2008 AD). Thank you Messrs. Adler and Hutchins for your gift to all humanity.

But it is still simply too much. We are mere high school students. There aren't enough hours in the day to tackle your massive undertaking. We doubt that many college students could or would embark on such a task either. These volumes represent a lifetime of study, and they are worthy of it.

Our compromise then is to revert to reductionism, to whittle down these massive volumes into that which can be joyfully mastered in four years at Valor Christian High School. We have in effect created the *CliffNotes* or the *SparkNotes* to *The Great Books of Western Civilization*. We call it *Tiptoeing through the Classics* (TTTC).

Some people say, when they hear about this book, "Hasn't that been done before?" The answer is no, not in this unique way with these particular purposes. The motivations driving the work began with the desire to encapsulate the thinkers Adler chose for the Great Books series to provide a panoramic, chronological view of the history of philosophical ideas of the world since the beginning of written records. The book provides a big-picture history as well as indicating the importance of each individual in definitive bullet points, key works by the writer, a short biography, and key words clarified. Framed by historical markers that give perspective to the time periods, the subjects range from philosophers to scientists, historians to poets, statesmen to storytellers. As the book has developed over a period of years, important people not on Adler's original list were added, and extended definitions for understanding the language of philosophy, government, and economics became part of the Appendices. Since TTTC includes a review of both authors and events, there is a vast amount of information (again, it's too much!). Nonetheless, this remains a dynamic document that our students and faculty can review, challenge, and add to over the years. This book is growing organically.

The Goal of *Tiptoeing through the Classics*

- Create a beginning point for <u>a lifetime of continuing study</u> of the classics,
- Facilitate an <u>economy of student effort</u> (60-fold more efficiency, less work),
- Show the "big picture" of the classics (the good, the bad and the ugly),
- Allow college students to focus on vocational learning (earning a living) while pursuing a lifetime study of the classics via self-study,
- Understand the value of man's muddling, struggles, confusion, flourishing, and depravity,
- Display the never-ending tumult over the generations of invading armies, roadway bandits, might makes right, tyrants, plagues, slavery, castes and classes … The Reformation … The English Civil War … The American Revolution … The French Revolution … The American Civil War … The Russian Revolution … WWI … Hitler … WWII … the fall of civilizations … teenage hormones … plus man's rebellion against wisdom.
- Create an appreciation for the gift of the Bible versus the brilliance and folly of these classics.

The "Dot Point Writing Style"

The principle mechanism by which we <u>simplify authors to their essence</u> is the "Dot Point Writing Style." All of our lives can be described rather well as a series of 15–30 dot points, like these:

- Was born in Omaha, Nebraska, of modest means
- Wrote over 120 plays in the course of his life, but only 7 survived
- Lived as a devoted Roman Catholic
- Graduated Magna Cum Laude from the Columbia School of Journalism
- Was active in the Socialist Party of America
- Worked as Editor of the Los Angeles Times
- Had her ashes scattered on the grounds of the Augusta National Golf Course

We have found this writing style allows us to quickly and effectively: cut to the chase, crystallize the hard facts, strip away excessive vocabulary, and delineate the real historical subject. Please let us know if we have missed the mark.

Our Additions and Enhancements

We have found that creating summaries has been helpful in exposing <u>cross-millennial comparisons</u> such as Plato vs. Hume, revealing <u>voids</u> such as the absence of political expression from Cicero to Hobbes, and presenting <u>counter theses</u> like America vs. Socialism-Marxism-Communism-Progressivism.

In our enthusiasm for this task, for a variety of reasons we could not help but add several dozen more authors and important personalities to the Adler/Hutchins list of the classics. We also added numerous historical time-markers to bring context to these authors. To differentiate our entries from the original Adler/Hutchins list, we include the ◊ symbol in the Table of Contents and title for those people or topics added by Valor.

Technical Considerations

Tiptoeing through the Classics is designed for readability, to express the essence of a topic for maximum comprehension. Recognizing that, we have adopted certain stylistic guidelines to eliminate distractions within the material itself. Primarily, we have chosen to list references in Appendix C, rather than within or following each entry. We also do not include specific citations within the text itself. While we acknowledge that rigorous scholarship cites one's sources, we determined that too many in-text citations interrupted the material's flow. In-text citations prove to the reader that the source material is reliable, but they do this at a cost of distracting the reader—in violation of the book's purpose. Presenting the essence of an idea or historical figure is our sole concern; we do not need to continually remind our readers that the content is trustworthy. Additionally, *Tiptoeing through the Classics* contains no index, as the entire work is practically an index itself. Besides, we entrust our modern readers with the gift of discovery, encouraging them to search on their own for related terms and references when confronted with topics of interest.

The designers of this compendium believe that through this summary students will see philosophical thought as it relates to religion, science, etc., in a way they've never seen before. The hope is that a short, accessible entry will provide a student with context of events and people in an intellectual timeline as well as pique his interest for additional study of the classics. Browsing other authors will prompt them further. The creators of the book have no doubt about the students' abilities to be freethinkers who can evaluate what they read in today's society to develop their own ideas about what is good. The creators regard the classics as superlative resources for culturally literate students, who will make good college students and citizens.

Due to the scope and dynamic nature of this project, *Tiptoeing through the Classics* is written in multiple narrative styles. Acknowledging its provenance from dozens of contributors, the book necessarily inherits from these authors varying conventions for expression and exposition, including first-, second-, and third-person narrative styles (while maintaining third-person style for strict academic review). We consider these variances in voice, tone, and expressions to be a positive acknowledgment of the work of so many dedicated researchers.

Why Two Books?

Unusually, *Tiptoeing through the Classics* is substantially one set of content expressed in two sequences:

> **Book 1** is in the author's <u>date of birth</u> sequence with a few exceptions, which clusters noted authors of a period. This sequence offers numerous historical interludes to add context for the reader. Volume 1 comprises all of the individual entries interspersed with historical signposts for context. Volume 2 consists of the various supporting appendices. The material is separated into two volumes solely to accommodate the page-count limitations of the printing process.

> **Book 2** is categorized by author date of birth <u>within major subject matter</u>—i.e., literature, philosophy, STEM (science-technology-engineering-math), economics, history, religion, America's intellectual foundation, and Socialism/Communism. This "subject matter sequence" brings considerable clarity, focus and simplicity to each subject. A glossary is added to the chapter on philosophy, as word meanings are the

essence of philosophy. Chapter 4 on Economics offers a primer to "jump-start" student understanding, and Chapters 7 and 8 offer breakthrough historical insights.

Both sequences have their own usefulness. Enjoy.

Why College? Why a Classical Education?

Putting all the distractions aside (i.e., the party life, athletics, and hormones) there are just two reasons to go to college. They are to:

- Learn a Vocation—that is to feed your family, put bread on the table, gain career skills, learn about science, technology, engineering, math, medicine, the law, teaching, business, accounting, and other marketable talents. To acquire a trade and prosper.
- Study the Classics—that is, to grasp the meaning of the Good Life: to be happy, gain wisdom, enjoy life, and reap the fruit of the Spirit. To learn: how then shall we live?

In these modern times secular colleges have all but given up on the latter, leaving but one reason to go to college—to learn a vocation.

Oddly, the Classics and the Bible serve parallel purposes in teaching about "How then shall we live?" The Bible is spiritually discerned, and the Classics are mostly secular. The Bible is clearly superior to the Classics in teaching the Good Life, but they both have their place.

This modern world we live in is all about Pleasure (accomplishment, popularity, self, sex, money, and power). These are good things if pursued properly, though most people do not. But, no amount of Pleasure can make you Happy. Happiness is attained by pursuing truth, compassion, goodness, work, and creativity.

Given the deplorable state of Classical Education in higher education, we suggest you use your time to learn a vocation. Studying the classics may better be a "lifetime of self-study."

Freethinking

Good ideas (positive and life-enhancing ideas) keep us on track for what is "profound and enduring," and will make us happy. **Bad ideas** (negative and life-destroying ideas), on the other hand, will set us back.

How will we determine what is a good idea and what is a bad idea?

In studying classic figures, note that Charles Darwin's father, Roger Darwin, claimed to be a "freethinker." The meaning of that claim suggests that every one of us owes it to himself to be a "freethinker." How can any educated person not be a freethinker? Isn't that the first stipulation of what it means to be "educated?" The 19th-century British mathematician and philosopher William Kingdon Clifford perhaps best describes the premise of freethought:

> " It is wrong always, everywhere, and for anyone, <u>to believe anything upon insufficient evidence.</u>
>
> —"Clifford's Credo"

This credo applies to everyone—religious people and scientists and atheists and Marxists and socialists and progressives alike. Salty one-liners and emotion-filled appeals are <u>not evidence</u>, even though they facilitate debating victories.

Reading the lives and works of the classic authors gives us cause to question if all of them had wisdom. Virginia Wolff, for example, was chronically depressed and committed suicide. What can we learn from her? Perhaps we can learn <u>how not to live</u>; we can learn from the mistakes of others. Is that what Adler and Hutchins had in mind when they placed Virginia Wolff among the great classics? Karl Marx's ideas failed miserably. What can we learn from him? Bertram Russell had numerous affairs and was married four times. So, too, with Friedrich Nietzsche and … <u>well, no one is perfect</u>. We are all <u>deeply flawed</u>. If we remain committed to freethinking, we must search for all kinds of evidence.

HOW TO READ (THIS) BOOK

WHAT EXACTLY IS THIS BOOK that you now hold in your hands? There are several ways to answer this question. For one, it is a crack at the thinkers placed by Mortimer Adler in the Encyclopedia Brittanica's *Great Books of the Western World* series from the 1950s. Adler's list there, including 129 philosophers, historians, theologians, scientists, and creative authors who have shaped Western culture and thought is by no means exhaustive. In fact, this book contains more than those original 129 authors (which notably included very few poets). We also used another list of Adler's that he placed in the appendix of his classic work *How to Read a Book* and have added a few more authors that Adler excluded yet we feel are vital (Jonathan Edwards, Aldous Huxley) and a few others of whom Adler would not have been aware or would not have been in a position to judge their historical legacy (C.S. Lewis, J.R.R. Tolkien, Milton Friedman, Jacques Derrida, etc.). At the same time, we cannot claim an exhaustive list for ourselves and will likely add thinkers in future additions.

For another, this book is the product of hundreds of hours of research and writing over the course of a few years by dozens of students and teachers at Valor Christian High School. This is a truly collaborative effort. For another, it is our meager appreciation of the depths of Western culture and the intellectual, philosophical, historical, scientific, and literary heritage that has helped shape the world we inhabit. For yet another, it is likely a Christian interpretation of the classics. The article there is important—this is "a" Christian interpretation, not "the" Christian reading of the classics. Even within the project itself there is no unified voice. Each of us wrote from our own perspective and our own reading of the thinkers under our consideration. There is therefore an important multiplicity of voices and worldviews present even under the umbrella of *Tiptoeing Through the Classics*. We love that feature of this work and have resisted the impulse to smooth over these differences and make every entry adhere to a certain tone and style. But if this is the case, and there is no single, unified voice, is the text you are holding simply the opinion of a bunch of high school students likely confronting many of these figures for the first time with the oversight of a few faculty members?

The purpose of this chapter is to answer that critical question of whether or not you can trust the analysis that follows in this hefty book. In order to best move toward an answer to that question, there are a few things that need to be discussed: the best way to read a figure from the past, the best way to write about a figure from the past, and the way we intend our audience to read and use this book.

How to Write: Critical Objectivity, Uncritical Acceptance, or Overly Critical Rejection?

One of the things that will help you read this book is some insight into how it was written, specifically regarding the principles and ideas that animated the authors as they wrote. When confronting the magnitude of something as vast and diverse as the entire Western tradition and canon, we are unavoidably confronted with some less than savory characters. There are people who did bad things, believed bad things, and wrote bad things. What do we do when we encounter a figure from the past who we would just assume not deal with? Who, if we were to meet them in our personal lives, might have some firm phrases we would use about them and/or their ideas?

Because Adler's goal in compiling this list of authors and their famous primary texts was not to create a 2,500-year-long running tally of the best people to grace the West. The catalogue of names in the *Great Books of the Western World* are not interchangeable with the catalogue of saints. In my classroom I have banished the word "interesting" as a descriptor of texts. "What did you think about *x* character in *y* book, student?" "Oh, he was interesting." It is a filler word, a non-word. There is a similar word that we can use about each of these thinkers and authors in the series: each was *influential*. Influential is a word that tells us one thing—their ideas, texts, theories, etc.—moved people in some way, while refusing to place any sort of value judgment on the nature of that influence. By the standard of the bare word influential, Jesus of Nazareth is influential as is Adolph Hitler; or, to use figures from the series, Aquinas and Heidegger are both influential figures.

But as Christians, we must judge what we read by the standards and worldview of our faith. To refuse to do so is to refuse, in some manner, our calling to be both salt and light in the world. We cannot in our reading treat Nietzsche the same way we treat Augustine. So, then, the question we addressed as we worked through this book was how to treat a figure like Nietzsche or Marx or Freud or others whose work is inimical to the Christian faith?

It is a question that inspired much debate and not a little arguing as we worked through (and continue to work through) our analysis of these texts. In order to help you understand our process I want to say a few things about three types of reading—critical objectivity, uncritical acceptance, and overly critical rejection—and then give a few test cases of what the bullet point "facts" featured in this book might look like depending on the reading lens we use.

In order to illustrate these three ways of reading, let me use one example of a potential bullet point fact on Karl Marx, an "influential" figure if ever one existed.

Critical Objectivity

Lived much of his life in extreme poverty in London. Two of his children died in infancy; a third died at age eight.

Uncritical Acceptance

Rejecting the trappings of wealth that he derided in his writings, Marx voluntarily lived in extreme poverty in London, even losing three of his children.

Overly Critical Rejection

A freeloader who refused, despite his education, to find consistent employment and chose a life of poverty alleviated only by the charity of his friends. His "heroism" cost the lives of three of his children.

Those are three radically different ways of saying virtually the same core fact: Marx was willingly poor. The problem with the uncritical acceptance take is obvious—it makes an intense value judgment that Marx was noble and living out his ideals in the way he rejected the accumulation of wealth. It makes the loss of his children seem like the unfortunate byproduct of his strict adherence to his own principled code. The problem with the overly critical rejection take runs the other way. It turns Marx into a nineteenth century welfare-queen, living off the largess of his wealthier and presumably gullible benefactors. It discounts entirely that wealth acquisition might not have been his most prominent goal.

But is the critically objective take the best way to think about Marx? Is it sympathetic to his life? Condemning of his choice to live a life of poverty? This is harder to say. Without saying that the poverty was voluntary, are we making Marx look noble? By tying his London poverty to the death of his children are we making him complicit in their deaths? This is a fraught question. None of us are ever entirely objective. Historical knowledge, as the theologian N.T. Wright maintains, always involves interpretation. There is no such thing as a bare fact that doesn't require interpretation. How we feel about Marx or economics more generally, before we even begin reading Marx, will determine what we think is the best way to present this biographical fact. What the historian of events or the historian of ideas must decide is to what degree he allows his preconceptions, biases, and own cultural milieu to influence his interpretation of an event, figure, or school of thought.

Let's leave biography aside for a moment and think more in the realm of ideas. The reason Marx is in the series is not because of his neat life story, but because the things he wrote came to profoundly influence and inspire generations of political dissidents. Below is an example of one of Marx's ideas stated in the tone of pretended objectivity:

- Believed in the primacy of material and physical conditions over spiritual ideas: your environment and conditions of your life determine what and how you think

This *is* very nearly what Marx actually says. The substance of his critique of religion is that it causes people to focus on the life-to-come rather than the life-right-now. If we are promised eternal splendor and joy, it makes us more willing to accept brutal and inhumane treatment in the present life. Therefore, religion numbs us, like an opiate, to the real problems of the world, which we exchange for the solutions of the next world. We are free, and as a Christian I certainly do, disagree with this notion, but it is what Marx believed and the idea has animated his followers in the ensuing nearly two centuries. But let's take a moment to put the pretended objective version of the bullet point into its two other potentials. First, uncritical acceptance:

- Boldly freeing humanity from enslavement to centuries of religious oppression, argued that the material and economic conditions we live under are more influential than any childish notions of spiritual realities

And now overly critical rejection:

- Undoubtedly motivated by his own atheism, argued that religious believers are the equivalent of opium-using saps who are not smart enough to see that true enlightenment lies in rejecting God and focusing on the here-and-now

The differences between the two is profound. Both lose objectivity quickly. Both heap up judgmental adjectives and reveal as much about the writer as they do about the thinker being examined. Personally, I lean more towards the interpretation of the overly critical rejection. However, my biases as a person of faith and therefore a believer in the ultimate spiritual truths of Christian doctrine incline me to fall in with that interpretation *more than* a straightforward reading of what Marx actually wrote would allow.

This is more than academic hairsplitting. The way we wrote this book will largely dictate the way that you read and respond to this book. Our method of composition is hugely practical for you as a reader.

I trust that it is clear from the two examples above that, despite the impossibility of ever completely abandoning bias, the critically objective (another way to say this might be *studied* objectivity) comes the closest to presenting the philosopher, scientist, author, theologian, or historian in the plainest language and the language most recognizable to that thinker. In the way that we wrote these entries, one of the first principles was whether or not the thinker under our microscope would recognize himself or herself in what we have written. In order to pull this off it required that we read each author—whatever our preconceptions might be—with an open mind and a charitable intention[1]. This idea can be called many things, but we like to think of it as the hermeneutic of love.

The Hermeneutic of Love

This is not our own term and requires some unpacking. Hermeneutic simply means our, *your*, way of reading. Do you come to the text under one of the ways of writing listed above—uncritical acceptance, overly critical rejection (before you've even read), or critical objectivity—or read in some other way? We promised a couple of paragraphs ago that we would not get into academic hairsplitting and we will do our best in what follows to keep our word, but the way we read these thinkers will inevitably influence the way we write about them and therefore the degree to which you can trust our interpretation.

In recent decades a certain way of reading—a hermeneutic—has come to dominate university literature and philosophy departments. It is called the hermeneutic of suspicion. The hermeneutic of suspicion believes that we can trust neither the author as an arbiter of meaning, nor the text as having one proper interpretation, so it is really all up to us as readers to come up with our own interpretation of a text. Author intention—what the author intended to communicate—is either meaningless, unknowable, or oppressive to the reader and need not be bothered with. The text itself is simply a repository of the cultural assumptions and systems of oppression that governed that culture and therefore the text, too, cannot claim our fidelity to its plain words[2]. One of the first and most famous advocates of this theory of reading was a French philosopher named Jacques Derrida (see our Derrida entry in Chapter 7). Derrida was principally concerned with liberation of the reader from what he saw as bondage to the author and the text. He believed that strict adherence to an author or a text "totalized" the reader's interpretation and was totalitarian in that respect. It restricted our readerly freedom. In place of objective analysis, Derrida encouraged us to "play" with the text. While Derrida's ideas, actually applied to texts, lead to interpretive anarchy, his ideas are so broadly influential that they need to be understood. In many ways, humanities departments at universities today are broadly Derridaean.

Kevin Vanhoozer shows, though, that the linchpin of Derrida's philosophy is the death of God. If there is no lawgiver, no objective standard in the universe, no plan beyond chaos and entropy, then Derrida's

---

[1] Indeed, one of the highlights of this project for those who worked on it was the capacity to be *surprised* by what we found. Many thinkers, from Plato to Gibbon to Spinoza, were simply different than each writer thought they would be when they sat down to work on the project. This is one of the highlights of philosophical research more broadly. Finding out our own gaps in knowledge or incorrect assumptions or finding delight in a previously unimagined source is both serendipitous and humility-inspiring. What else do we miss when we read with blinders on?

[2] This is a very brief and almost criminally incomplete view of what is, in truth, a complex and at times appealing theory of reading. For better work on the subject, please consider the following sources: Kevin Vanhoozer, *Is There a Meaning in This Text?*; N.T. Wright, *The New Testament and the People of God.*

rejection of author and text and descent into utter subjectivity makes more consistent philosophical sense. However, as Christians we steadfastly reject Derrida's first principle. If the universe is governed, as we believe, by a benevolent God, then there are things that are knowable. There are real intentions when an author sets pen to paper that through the nearly magical quality of writing we can discern. In other words, Christians believe in the author because we believe in the Author. We believe in the written word because we believe in the Word.

So, on to the hermeneutic of love. As I mentioned above, this is a borrowed term. We borrowed it from N.T. Wright, the eminent New Testament scholar and former Bishop of Durham in the Church of England. In his book, *The New Testament and the People of God*, Wright talks about the hermeneutic of suspicion that has come to cloud even his field of Biblical history. While ultimately rejecting the extremes of Derrida and others, Wright concedes that protests against "postmodern readings" are going to be "ineffectual" unless a "better epistemology" is put forward that provides a "better account of what happens when a text is being read."[3] Wright also acknowledges that all reading is subjective in certain ways. No matter how close a reader gets to the author's intention in a text, he will still be reading the text through a particular lens.

In the end of his analysis, Wright names his own theory of historical writing *critical realism* (what I have called critical objectivity). There is a reality (the realism part) that actually happened and we can know it or at the very least know part of that reality. However, we must be critical readers and not uncritically accept every text we have from antiquity as gospel truth or, on the other hand, overly critically reject everything as having no meaning for our own time. Branching away from the unartful term, critical realism, Wright labels this position the *hermeneutic of love*.

Vanhoozer, in his book *Is There a Meaning in This Text?*, takes up the project suggested by Wright of providing a better epistemology than the postmodern readings allow. After laying out the ideas of Derrida and his forebears and disciples, Vanhoozer makes a case for the author, the text, and a more humble place for the reader. In his introductory chapter, Vanhoozer commends what he calls an "Augustinian hermeneutics." Augustine's famous statement, *credo ut intelligam* (I believe in order to understand) is a way of attaining the hermeneutics of love, especially directed at readings of the Bible, that Wright attempts through his own reading of Scripture. Vanhoozer describes Augustine's credo as "the critical stance of the believing reader as well as the proper epistemological stance for human beings in general." There is a type of reading that can only be done out of love, that emanates out from initial belief.

Once we read in this way, once we read Christianly, we can reject the cynicism and suspicion and deconstructionism that has taken over literary theory and philosophy in the past 40 years. In place of suspicion, we can put love. Vanhoozer calls Augustine's "chief hermeneutical maxim" to "choose the interpretation that most fosters the love of God and neighbor." In competing interpretations—and there will be competing interpretations—this is the line the Church Father commends that we hold. It is, according to Augustine, the first principle of the Bible.

Further distancing himself (and us, I hope) from the hermeneutic of suspicion, and reading a text in love, Augustine also states that even when reading texts outside of Scripture it "is most honorable to

---

[3] Wright, 61

believe that the author was a good man, whose writings were intended to benefit the human race and posterity." Such a belief might eventually be proven wrong, but our starting place should not be doubt, suspicion, and antagonism. A starker antithesis to the latter pages of my *Norton Anthology of Literary Theory* could hardly be imagined.

Wright's hermeneutic of love can do no better than Vanhoozer's Augustinian hermeneutic. As if often the case, sometimes the best way forward is a return to the past.

What This Means for This Book

Now that you have read more about literary theory than you ever hoped, the question remains: what does this mean for our book? Did we always read every thinker under a hermeneutic of love? Would Augustine, N.T. Wright, and Kevin Vanhoozer line up to give us high-fives?

The short answer is … probably not. However, having this as an ideal guides the way we mess up. Hopefully our falling short in this is not detrimental to your experience as a reader. It is a high standard: to read people, even people with whom you disagree vigorously, with love requires an almost supernatural effort. Here is why we find this nearly impossible standard worth shooting for, even if our aim is not always true: ***as we get out of the way as readers and writers about the classics and confine ourselves to a critically objective reading of the texts and present that critically objective reading in this book, we allow you to read, wrestle with, and think deeply about these thinkers.*** The book you hold in your hands now is one designed to help you do the hard work of analyzing and contemplating what the great contributors to the Western tradition have written. This book is not a definitive take on the classics that tells you what you ought to think about each work, but a springboard to a lifelong personal reading of these great works. If we come out swinging with an overly critical rejection of a thinker or if we encourage slavish, unthinking devotion to another, we forestall your ability as a reader to think about each thinker on his or her own terms.

Our audience is primarily high school students who are past the point where they can be, or should be, spoon-fed beliefs. Our passion at Valor Christian High School is the long-term spiritual health and growth of our students. In order to achieve our lofty aims as a school, we need to cultivate students capable of engaging with ideas that even run contrary to their faith. Because unless our students remain hermetically sealed within a Christian commune their entire adult lives, they will face these thinkers. Even if they do not face a figure like Nietzsche directly, they will face situations and institutions and schools of thought governed, implicitly or explicitly, by the ideas of Nietzsche.

It is not enough to tell our students that our faith is true or give them tidy apologetic lessons that may or may not stand-up under scrutiny; we need to equip them to confront the big ideas in our culture and stand for the supremacy of Christ.

In order to best achieve this aim, we need to present the thinkers as they were and let students do the hard work of reaching conclusions on their own. In *Interpretive Acts*, William Harris writes: "We read with two purposes: to understand what the author means, and to relate that meaning to what we know, believe, seek to know, or might believe." This is precisely the type of reading we wish to foster. First, that the reader would pursue true understanding of the author's intention in the text. Second, that they would then make a judgment about how to relate those ideas to their own lives. These activities have to come in this order if one is to read with the hermeneutic of love. If we blow past what the author intends to our own conclusion or view of significance, we have not actually read the text. At the same time, if we stop merely with comprehension of the author's intent and do not seek to apply what is written to our own view of the world, we have either merely checked some cultural literacy box or, what it worse, opened ourselves up to uncritical acceptance by not doing the work of criticism. Any interpretive foot on the gas on our part will encourage students to cede control to our interpretation and not do this work on their own.

Woe to those who call evil good and good evil. . .

But is this enough? If we step out of the way and let students do the wrestling and interpreting, what if they do it wrong? What if a student reads our analysis of Nietzsche and decides that he sounds awesome? Are we ignoring the scriptural warning against those "who call evil good and good evil" (Isaiah 5:20)? Rather than strengthening the faith of our students are we setting them on a course of destruction?

This is a vitally important question for a Christian school to address. Since this book has been written primarily with a Christian high school audience in mind, it is worth taking a moment to address this issue.

First of all, we are not making any effort to portray Marx or Nietzsche or Heidegger or Sartre as good. To return to our example about Marx's belief about the primacy of the material over the spiritual, notice that we never agree with Marx. We are only relaying on to our students what he actually believed. There are similar cases with other thinkers. We are not baptizing these pagans, as Augustine did with the Greeks, but stating as accurately as we can what the substance of their beliefs were.

Second of all, this is not primarily a work of commentary but a work of introduction to the classics. I mentioned above that the goal is not to forestall discussion of the classics because now they are explained, but for this text to function as a springboard into the deep ocean of writings available to our students. If we were writing a commentary on *Thus Spoke Zarathustra* or *The Communist Manifesto*, this text would read differently. We had neither the space nor the intention to do so.

Thirdly, as argued above, the average high school student is at an age where they need to be thinking for themselves, deciding whether the Christian worldview is something they will ultimately adopt or discard. For the student on the fence about beliefs, coming down with too strong of a take—calling something evil without adequately explaining *why*—runs the risk of turning them away from the larger project of this work.

Finally, this work is intended for classroom use. As much as we desire *Tiptoeing* to be a springboard to lifelong reading, we also desire it to be a springboard to discussion within the high school classroom. Within that classroom, once we have established the "just the facts, ma'am" reading of an author, we are then free to interpret together. So, if we were teaching a unit on Marx and we read the critically objective take on his beliefs about the primacy of the material over the spiritual, we would certainly feel free to do our part to call an evil idea evil *within the context of the classroom*. And, within the context of discussion within that classroom. And, in response to the earlier comments of engaged students. A text that cuts off all debate is unlikely to be fruitful in convincing anyone to engage these ideas. It becomes, then, a matter of preaching to the choir.

Ultimately, our hope is to demystify the classics. Too often we can approach ancient or revered texts with trepidation. We want students to believe that they have the intellectual capacity to read the best and most influential texts in the history of Western culture and *be able to submit those texts to the authority of Christ. By* writing this book in a critically objective manner, our hope is that students will respond by examining the primary texts themselves for more clarity, more discovery, and a deeper and more provoking spiritual and intellectual challenge.

Great texts reward deep reading. Deep reading helps form habits of mind that are of great value in the faith formation of a young man or woman. We pray that this text, in some small way, contributes to the cultivation of profound spiritual depth in the life of its reader.

Because we want you to read well so that you can think well so that you can argue well so that you can defend truth well.

The end goal is not simply to read Marx with love but to be able to disagree with Marx (or anyone else) from a fundamental position of understanding rather than caricature. John Milton, the English poet, once wrote the following about truth: "Let Her and falsehood grapple; who ever knew truth put to the worse in a free and open encounter?" As Christians, we believe that the truth is powerful enough that in a fair and open contest it will always beat falsehood. This is not to say that lies do not ever win and take root within a people, only that they do so not because truth was beaten in a fair fight but because truth was ignored. As Christians, we need fear no idea, because no matter how glittering the falsehood we know that the deep beauty of truth gleams more brilliantly.

More recently, Bret Stephens, a columnist for *The New York Times*, gave a speech at a press club in Australia called "The Art of Disagreement." In this remarkable speech about the death of disagreement in our contemporary political and social culture, Stephens said the following:

> Most importantly, [disagreements] are never based on a misunderstanding. On the contrary, the disagreements arise from perfect *comprehension*; from having chewed over the ideas of your intellectual opponent so thoroughly that you can properly spit them out.
>
> In other words, to disagree well you must first *understand* well. You have to read deeply, listen carefully, watch closely. You need to grant your adversary moral respect; give him the intellectual benefit of doubt; have sympathy for his motives and participate empathically with his line of reasoning. And you need to allow for the possibility that you might yet be persuaded of what he has to say.

Stephens sounds like a modern Augustinian. Is he counseling open-minded subjectivity? Not in the least. What Stephens advocates here, and what he goes on to do in the speech, is to note that for any disagreement to be worth having it must first begin from a place of sympathy, respect, and careful comprehension of your opponent's ideas. In the remainder of the speech he calls out some ways in which we have lost this vision in the West and the consequences we suffer under for the loss.

Along with the hermeneutic of love, then, we also want you to read under the hermeneutic of truth. Once you have understood Nietzsche, we want you to debate Nietzsche, get mad at Nietzsche, laugh at Nietzsche. We want you to submit Nietzsche to the cross of Christ and the sacred texts of our faith and let truth reign over falsehood. If we give you a caricature, an uncritically accepting or overly critically rejecting take, of a figure in this book we will send you out into the world with a flawed notion of who Nietzsche really was. When you meet and debate someone who knows what she is talking about, she will destroy you in the debate because your position comes from a flawed starting point. However, if we equip you with a book written under the hermeneutic of love and within the classroom you learn to read under the hermeneutic of truth, you will in turn be well equipped to face any intellectual or spiritual adversary you may face in this world.

That, indeed, is our prayer as you begin this journey.

Toby Coffman, faculty

CONTENTS

CHAPTER 4: THE RENAISSANCE AND REFORMATION   137

Chapter 1
The Ancients to Caesar

Man: A being in search of meaning.

—Plato

THE GREAT INVENTIONS AND DISCOVERIES, 9000 BC–2000 AD

THIS CONCURRENT EVOLUTION OF INVENTIONS is presented as a matter of interest, as a parallel observation to better understand that while civilization has evolved technically, human nature has not.

Consider the advance of our tools, and especially the importance of writing within them: Oral tradition, fire, the stone cutting edge, the wheel, agriculture, horses, the metals, writing (as collective learning), the lever, the ship, concrete, the printing press (as affordable writing), gunpowder, electricity, the battery, the generator, the light bulb, the telegraph, gasoline, the engine, the automobile, the tractor, the airplane, the radio, penicillin, pasteurization, the computer, and the internet (as both ubiquitous writing and ubiquitous junk).

Today this list grows faster than ever, yet without writing, without recording ideas—whether via the printing press or the internet—there would no universal persistence of wisdom and knowledge. No Adler, no Hutchins, no collective learning, no education, no classics, no Bible, no Renaissance, no enlightenment, no government of the people.

Writing is the "Mother of all Inventions," the keeper of all truth, and the repository of all falsehoods and lies.

And its elevation started with *The Epic of Gilgamesh*.

THE EPIC OF GILGAMESH ◊ 2800 BC, *The First Great Writing*

> " Combines the power and tragedy of the *Iliad* with the wanderings and marvels of the *Odyssey*. It is a work of adventure, but is no less a meditation on some fundamental issues of human existence.
>
> —Tzvi Abusch, Brandeis University

- Is an epic poem from Mesopotamia
- Was possibly drawn from five separate Sumerian poems about Gilgamesh
- Is a single epic pieced together from two versions—Old Babylonian tablets from 18th century BC (incomplete), and 12 late-Akkadian tablets from 13th–10th century BC
- Was discovered in 1853 and first translated in 1870
- Depicts the central character of Gilgamesh, whose existence has been verified by artifacts
- Is part of a collection in the Sulaymaniah Museum, in the Kurdistan Region of Iraq

Gilgamesh, although the main character of an epic, is thought be a historical person documented by ancient inscriptions about him and other characters. He is, in fact, the Sumerian King listed in the Sumerian King List, and ruled the city of Uruk for 126 years some time between 2800 and 2500 BC. He and his son Urlugal were credited with rebuilding the goddess Ninlil's sanctuary in her sacred quarter of Nippur known as Tummal.

The *Epic of Gilgamesh* is considered the first great work of literature. The first half of the poem tells the story of Gilgamesh and his clashes with Enkidu, a wild man the gods created to stop him. Later when the two become friends, they together take down Humbaba, the monster guarding Cedar Mountain. When Gilgamesh turns away from the attentions of a goddess, she sends the Bull of Heaven to destroy him. Gilgamesh and Enkidu are able to defeat him as well, after which the gods show their disapproval by killing Enkidu. In the second half of the epic, Gilgamesh sets out on an extended journey to find the secret of eternal life. He encounters Siduri, a wise woman who attempts to discourage Gilgamesh on his search for immortality and to be happy with the simple things. She directs him to Utnapishtim, who had been given immortality because he had trusted the gods when they warned him of an imminent flood. Utnapishtim advises him to give up his search. Finally Gilgamesh learns that death is inevitable for man and is the result of man's own hands.

The *Epic of Gilgamesh*, discovered in 1853 by Hormuzd Ramssam, was written in a dialect of Akkadian sometime between 1300 and 1000 BC. The Standard Akkadian version begins "He who saw the deep" while the older version begins with the words "Surpassing all other kings." The word "deep" points to the wisdom Gilgamesh learns and brings back from Utnapishtim. Gilgamesh is revered because of his many building projects and his accounts of what he had learned from Siduri and Utnapishtim.

HEBREW BIBLE / OLD TESTAMENT, 2200–460 BC, *God Reveals Himself*

> Hear, O Israel: The LORD our God, the LORD is one. You shall love the LORD your God with all your heart and with all your soul and with all your might. And these words that I command you today shall be on your heart.
>
> —Deuteronomy 6:4–6 ESV

The Patriarchs, 2166–1859 BC

The age of the three Biblical Patriarchs: Abraham, Isaac, and Jacob. The nation of Israel stems from these forefathers.

Exodus, 1446–1250 BC

The LORD delivered the Israelites from Egyptian slavery through his servant Moses. Before Pharaoh allowed them to leave, Egypt experienced 10 plagues, the last of which was the death of the first-born son. In this plague, the angel of death passed over each Israelite house that had lamb's blood on the door, marking the beginning of the Passover celebration. Led out of Egypt by a cloud of smoke and a pillar of fire, the Israelites crossed through the Red Sea on dry land and, when Pharaoh's army gave chase, the Egyptians were drowned.

Judges, 1375–1050 BC

The period of the judges occurred after Joshua's death and consists of 15 judges who rose up to lead and deliver the Israelites from various threats.

United Monarchy, 1050–931 BC

The name given to the Israelite kingdom during the reigns of Saul, David, and Solomon when the 12 Israelite tribes were unified under one ruler.

Kingdom Divided, 931 BC

After Solomon's death, the Kingdom of Israel divided into two separate nations. The 10 northern tribes called themselves Israel and placed their capital in Samaria, while the two southern tribes, Benjamin and Judah, retained their capital in Jerusalem.

Assyrian War and Exile, 721–701 BC

Sennacherib, the king of Assyria, seized the Samarian capital of the northern kingdom and led the Israelite people into captivity. When Hezekiah, northern Israel's ruler, refused to pay tribute to Assyria, Sennacherib laid siege to Jerusalem. However, on the night of Passover, 185,000 Assyrian soldiers died from a plague, rendering Israel victorious.

Babylonian Exile, 597–538 BC

Nebuchadnezzar, the king of Babylon, following typical Mesopotamian practices, took the prominent Jews, such as professionals, priests, and the wealthy, back to Babylon to become slaves. Among these slaves was Daniel, who refused to cease prayer to the God of the Bible; he was thrown into a den of lions, but was unharmed.

Persian Repatriation, 538–142 BC

After Babylon was overtaken by Persia, Persia's king, Cyrus, allowed almost 50,000 Jews to return to their homeland of Israel and rebuild their temple and wall.

Author Identification

The authors and dates of the Hebrew Bible are widely debated amongst scholars. This chart reflects the traditionally accepted authorship of each book, but includes both the conservative and liberal estimates.

Author	Book	Composition Date Range
Moses	The Torah	1446–1260 BC
David	The Psalms	1446 BC–538 BC
Samuel	Judges	1003 BC
	Ruth	1010 BC
	1 and 2 Samuel	Late 10th century BC
Solomon	Proverbs	10th century–after 539 BC
	Ecclesiastes	971–931 BC

	The Song of Solomon	960–931 BC
Obadiah	Obadiah	850–400 BC
Amos	Amos	793–739 BC
Hosea	Hosea	753–687 BC
Micah	Micah	750–687 BC
Isaiah	Isaiah	740–681 BC
Unknown	Job	Early seventh century BC–538 BC
Nahum	Nahum	664–612 BC
Habakkuk	Habakkuk	640–609 BC
Zephaniah	Zephaniah	640–609 BC
Daniel	Daniel	605–536 BC
Ezekiel	Ezekiel	593–571 BC
Joshua	Joshua	Late second millennium–539 BC
Joel	Joel	Ninth–fourth century BC
Jeremiah	1 and 2 Kings	539–330 BC
	Jeremiah	550 BC
	Lamentations	587–516 BC
Haggai	Haggai	520 BC
Zechariah	Zechariah	Fifth century BC
Ezra	1 and 2 Chronicles	400 BC
	Ezra	433–424 BC
	Nehemiah	433–424 BC
Malachi	Malachi	Mid-fifth century BC
Unknown	Esther	485–464 BC

John Reid II, researcher

The Three Periods of Greek History

The Ancient Period, 1300–510 BC

Comprising 800 years from the growth of self-governing colonies to the victory over the Persians.

- Beginning of Greek culture because of their architectural advances, writing system, and establishment of religious rites
- Early beginnings of scientific inquiry, philosophy, and mathematics
- Movement from monarchies to republics toward democratic rules
- Institution of laws
- Pottery and sculpture and the first minted coin

The Classical Period, 510–323 BC

Spanning the 187 years from the Greek naval victory at Salmis over the Persians to the death of Alexander the Great—The Golden Age of Athens.

- Notwithstanding the Peloponnesian Wars, a period of relative peace and prosperity
- Greece becomes a superpower with a strong navy
- Pericles had the Acropolis built
- Attained greatness in almost every field of learning
- Great artist and thinkers flourished
- Democracy was established for males over 20
- The scientific method was established
- Conversations about the origin of life, the universe and philosophy
- Mathematics becomes a discipline
- Architecture, art, and sculpture revealed human emotion and beauty
- Peloponnesian Wars ended with Athens and Sparta ruined and then united under Macedonian rule

The Hellenistic Period, 323–31 BC

Encompassing 292 years from the time of Alexander's empire being divided at his death to Roman troops taking over the last of the territories.

- Greek ideas and culture spread from the Eastern Mediterranean to Asia
- Hellenistic states were monarchies whose rulers desired riches
- Made connections with other countries, importing a great variety of luxurious items from great distances
- Built elaborate palaces and decorations, museums, zoos, libraries, and universities
- Philosophy turned inward to discover what was best for the individual

BABYLONIAN TABLET, 1700 BC

Around 1922, an American archeologist and diplomat named Edgar J. Banks (perhaps the inspiration for Indiana Jones), found a clay tablet in southern Iraq, near a site corresponding to the ancient city of Larsa. George Plimpton, a publisher, bought the tablet from Banks, and when he died, his estate, including the tablet, went to Columbia University. The tablet, which was dated to approximately 1700 BC, became known as Plimpton 322.

Plimpton 322 contains four columns and 15 rows of numbers. The fourth column is the row number, 1–15, and the middle two columns are completely visible and unbroken. The edge of the first column, however, was broken off and mathematicians have had to extrapolate to figure out what the missing digits could be. The tablet's meaning baffled mathematical experts until 2017 when researchers at the University of South Wales, Australia, proved it is a trigonometry table. In all likelihood, ancient architects used it to build temples, palaces, canals and other structures. The tablet proves that the Babylonians beat the Greeks to developing trigonometry by a century and a half.

Babylonian mathematics used a base 60, or sexagesimal system, rather than the 10 which is common in the modern era. Because 60 is far easier to divide by three, experts studying the tablet found that the calculations are far more accurate. The tablet, according to Dr. Daniel Mansfield of UNSW's School of Mathematics and Statistics, "describes the shapes of right-angle triangles using a kind of trigonometry based on ratios, not angles and circles." He calls the tablet a work of "undoubted genius" and the only completely accurate trigonometric table. The accuracy stems from the very different Babylonian approach to math.

Thus, a 3700-year-old artifact made of clay has great relevance for today's world, including possible practical applications in surveying, computer graphics and education.

THE ANCIENT PERIOD, 1300–510 BC

Greek Religion and Mythology

Greek mythology is the body of myths and teachings that belong to the ancient Greeks concerning their gods and heroes, the nature of the world, and the origins and significance of their own cult and ritual practices. It was a part of the religion in ancient Greece.

Virtually the first thing the reader comes upon in studying the ancient Greeks is religion and mythology—comic-book-like religion. But a much more sophisticated view unfolds when one studies Socrates, Plato and Aristotle.

Many Greeks recognized the major gods and goddesses: Zeus, Poseidon, Hades, Apollo, Artemis, Aphrodite, Ares, Dionysus, Hephaestus, Athena, Hermes, Demeter, Heracles, Hestia, Asclepius and Hera. This despite philosophies such as Stoicism and some forms of Platonism using language that seems to posit a transcendent single deity.

The oldest known Greek literary sources, Homer's epic poems *The Iliad* and *The Odyssey*, focus on the Trojan War and its aftermath. Two poems by Homer's near contemporary Hesiod, the *Theogony* and the *Works and Days*, contain accounts of the genesis of the world, the succession of divine rulers, the succession of human ages, the origin of human woes, and the origin of sacrificial practices. Myths are also preserved in the Homeric Hymns, in fragments of epic poems of the Epic Cycle, in lyric poems, and in the works of the tragedians of the fifth century BC.

The Oracle at Delphi

Delphi was believed to be the center of the Universe—not just another holy site or shrine, but the place where the physical world and the spiritual worlds met. Like the Olympics, the oracle of Apollo was open only to Greeks. In the fourth century the Sanctuary of Apollo at Delphi was at its height of popularity, as pilgrims, poets, politicians, and kings all sought the advice of the Oracle, said to be the voice of Apollo. Leaders wanting to know if this was the time to go to war asked the Oracle. Many times the answer was vague and open to interpretation.

It worked as follows. A priestess of Apollo, called a pythia, entered a trance after breathing fumes that came through a hole in the earth. She then spoke in riddles, with priests interpreting her words. Cities brought bountiful offerings, so that over time Delphi amassed great wealth. As the Greek world grew, Delphi, a separate entity owing allegiance to no particular city-state, became a mediator in disputes between the city-states and Greek colonies. Even more, Delphi shaped policies, settled border disputes, and authorized the founding of new colonies. Because of the competitive nature of the Greeks, disputes were common not only among individuals, but among communities and city-states as well.

The Spartans

Greek citizens, who were subjugated by the invading Dorians, united as a group around the 10th century BC. By 650 BC the ruins of Sparta can be found in the southeast Peloponnese, just outside the modern Greek city Sparta. Sparta became an important Greek city-state in which the citizens depended on the farm workers (helots), and constantly feared an uprising by them. The helots gave some of their produce to the masters, the spartiates, but had no rights themselves. As a result the Spartan citizens felt the need to become strong warriors. Each male citizen was made to be a soldier, a hoplite, who sported a bronze helmet, an armored breastplate, leggings, and a red cloak. Every hoplite carried a shield, spear, and swords or bows and arrows.

All the strongest babies were the property of the state; the weakest were abandoned. All 7-year-old boys were forced to live in military barracks, where they trained for war by learning discipline and experiencing austere living conditions, such as having just one tunic per year and enduring whippings to become accustomed to pain. A Spartan man became a soldier at 20 and served until 60. Although women had no voting rights or importance in the government, girls were given exercise and freedom in order to become strong mothers, who would give birth to warriors.

The government of Sparta, also demanding, was in control of kings. Death was the punishment for any rebellion against the government. Under the kings, a council of elders and a general assembly, along with a board of five ephors who were elected annually, did city-state business in secret. Their main goal was to succeed at war.

As a result Sparta emerged as a dominant military force in ancient Greece. At first they fought beside Athens, but later became fearful of Athens's growing power. In Sparta's most powerful period between the eighth and fourth centuries BC, they went to war with Athens in a number of battles, known as the Peloponnesian Wars. Sparta defeated Athens in 404 BC, but weakened all of the city-states in the process. Subsequently Sparta fell to Macedonia, and declined until they prospered again under the Romans, only to be defeated by the Goths in 395 AD.

Now the word "spartan" calls up a person of discipline and courage as well as describing something that is simple and rugged.

The Athenians

The primary rivals of the Spartans were the Athenians, founded by Theseus around 1300 BC. Theseus hailed from the city of Troezen, across from the Saronic Island of Poros, and was said to have been born from the union of Aegeus, king of Athens, and the daughter of Troezen's King. At the age of 16 Theseus was tasked with lifting the heavy stone where his father had put a sword and sandals. Successful in his efforts, he walked to Athens to find his father, defeating monsters and evil along the way. After arriving in Athens as a hero, he volunteered to go to Crete, where King Minos had been demanding a sacrifice of young men and virgins to a monster called the Minotaur. Theseus defeated the Minotaur and returned to Athens, although he forgot to remove the black sail of death from the ship. His father, King Aegeus, thinking his beloved son dead, hurled himself into the sea, giving the Aegean its name.

Upon his return Theseus abolished the monarchy, declared Athens a democracy, and unified the scattered villages of Attica. He made it a policy to give aid to the weak and helpless. His exploits also included adventures with Hercules, Jason and the Argonauts, the Amazons, and even a journey to the underworld. Later he was overthrown and then murdered while exiled on the island of Skyros. Whether fact or fiction, the meaning behind these stories is what is important to the Athenians; Theseus embodies all they stand for. The Athenians of the fifth century used his deeds as the standards to measure themselves and their democracy. Theseus was to the Athenians what George Washington is to Americans today.

King Solon reformed the Athenian democracy in 594. Solon was to Athens what Lycurgus was to Sparta, and his reforms paved the way out of a volatile period and into the Golden Age. The sixth century was a time of social strife, and to keep society from falling apart the Athenians elected Solon, a poet and statesman. His role was to mediate between the various conflicting groups and reform the system of economics in Athenian society, a system with an enormous disparity between those who were well off and those who were not. Under Athenian law, if you could not pay your debt, the person you owed could seize you and your family and sell you as slaves to get his money back. Solon's economic program was called the seisachtheia (shaking off of burdens), because it released the lower classes from the burden of debt to those in the wealthy classes. By canceling and reducing debts and abolishing a system of mortgage that had turned many poor landowners into slaves, Solon made a more level playing field. He wanted even the poor to take part in Athenian government, and he formalized the rights and privileges of the four social classes whose access to public office now depended on how much property they had instead of by birth. The lowest class was called the thetes (laborers) who could take part in the general assembly, but they could not run for office. The other economic groups, from the bottom up, were the Zeugitai (Yeomen), Hippeis (Knights), and the Pentakosiomedimnoi (those with over 500 measures of wet and dry produce).

Solon's economic reforms led to the future prosperity of Athens. He banned the export of all agricultural products, with the exception of olive oil, which was as valuable to the ancient Greeks as it is to modern ones. By offering citizenship he attracted some of the finest craftsmen of the Greek world to Athens. He discarded the Athenians system of weights and measures in favor of the more widely used one from Evia, enabling the Athenians to more easily trade with the other Greeks in the Aegean. He made being unemployed a crime. He created a supreme court, made up of former Archons (rulers or chief magistrates) of Athens, and another legislative body of 400 to debate laws before putting them before the people for a vote.

Though Solon's reforms did not cure the ills of Athenian society overnight in the way that Lycurgus had done with the Spartans, the long-term effect was to solidify the rule of law, and eventually led to Athenian democracy. After committing these laws to writing, Solon left Athens to avoid being continuously asked to interpret his laws. He wanted Athenians to self-govern.

Solon journeyed to Egypt, where he started (but never finished) a story about Atlantis, a place he had learned about from the Egyptian priests. After he left, the Athenians began fighting among themselves again, and for two years the city was a leaderless anarchy—that is, they were without an archon, a leader.

The Tyrants

Athenian politics comprised three groups, which corresponded to the different areas of the Attica peninsula: the Men of the Shore, the Men of the Plain, and the Men from Beyond the Hills. In 561, Pisistratus, the leader of the Beyond the Hills faction from eastern Attica and a remarkable orator, showed up in the agora with his clothes ripped and bleeding and told the Athenians his enemies had attacked him. He was given permission to protect himself with bodyguards. With these men he seized the Acropolis and tried to make himself ruler. He was driven out. Three years later he tried again by marrying a young girl from another leading aristocratic family but she left him for not fulfilling his matrimonial duties, and Pisistratus left for Thrace where he focused on amassing more wealth by digging for silver and gold. In 546 he returned with his riches and a six-foot-tall woman whom he dressed as the Goddess Athena and had her drive him into Athens on a chariot. Apparently this worked, because his followers defeated his opponents at the Battle of Palini, and Pisistratus became the ruler of Athens. Though the word tyrant in our culture brings up images of Nazis, secret police, and torture chambers, it actually means a leader who was not restrained by law or constitution nor was he elected, chosen or born into power. In other words, it did not mean that someone had ill intent, but rather that he could do whatever he wanted, because there was nothing above or below that could stop him.

The period of Athenian history under Pisistratus was one of peace, and his rule was a positive step in the establishment of democracy, perhaps more so than Solon. It was under his rule that the Dionysian and Panathenaic Festivals turned Athens into the cultural center of the Greek world while the sculpture, and pottery of this period raised the bar to a new level. By establishing relations with other Greek tyrants and annexing the island of Delos and its sanctuary of Apollo, he created prosperity as well as a sense of Athenian identity that brought the people of the city together and an end to the infighting that had been the cause of so much stagnation. Unfortunately his sons, who assumed power after his death in 528, were not quite up to the task and were tyrants in the sense of the word that we are familiar. Hipparchus was assassinated in 514 and Hippias was expelled from Athens in 514, returning in 490 BC when the Persians (unsuccessfully) invaded Attica.

After another period of instability following the expulsion of Hippias, two aristocratic leaders, Cleisthenes and Isagoras, emerged as the leading contenders for rulership of Athens in 510. When Isagoras called on the Spartans to help him assume power and banish the family of Cleisthenes, the Athenians rejected the outside interference and Isagoras himself. Cleisthenes became archon. He redrew the political map of Athens in a way that broke the power of the old aristocracy and gave all the Athenian people a voice in politics. His reforms included the annual rotation of power (so no single group or person could become dominant) and the splitting up of the four tribes of Athens into 10 new tribes, which were then broken up into smaller demes (municipalities or precincts), which were then spread around so that it was more difficult for the old families to organize into a political faction. The Athenians embraced this and identified so strongly with their deme that when asked his name he would give his first name, the name of his father, and his deme.

HOMER, 800–701 BC, *The Greek Muse*

> " I have taken away the mist from your eyes, that before now was there, so that you may well recognize the god and the mortal. Therefore now, if a god making trial of you comes hither do you not do battle head on with the gods immortal, not with the rest; but only if Aphrodite, Zeus's daughter, comes to the fighting, her at least you may stab with the sharp bronze.
>
> —*The Iliad*

- Was a Greek storyteller and poet
- Attributed human characteristics to the Greek gods

- Remains a mystery: almost nothing is known about him, and both his date of birth and birthplace are speculations
- Was thought to be blind, because the bard Demodocus in The Odyssey is a blind poet
- Is attributed as author of *The Iliad* and *The Odyssey*, although this is often questioned
- Had *The Iliad* and *The Odyssey* first written down around 700 BC, although they had been recited orally for years
- Could have been the author of the *Homeric Hymns*
- Focused on heroism and social status
- Immortalized Bronze Age Greece in his poems
- Had shrines christened in his honor by some Grecian cities during the Hellenistic Period in the third century BC

Key Works

The Iliad, c. 762 BC
The Odyssey, c. 700 BC

Biography

In ironic contrast to the great detail with which Homer wrote, few details are known about his life, including whether the Greek poet even existed. He is the attributed author of *The Iliad* and *The Odyssey*, believed written in the eighth century BC, two works that have become pillars of Classical Greek epic poetry and the Western tradition itself Masterfully synthesizing drama with narrative form, the poems were composed in the oral tradition. The poetry was formulaic, often repeating set phrases and epithets, creating a rhythmic quality whose cadences helped listeners latch on to audible patterns to create spontaneous verses. Harnessing the history of the Bronze Age, Homer often employed historical anachronisms, adorning his characters with the tools and equipment of his own time. His writing embraces archaic mythology and recounts a time when the gods freely interacted with humanity.

The Iliad

The Iliad is an epic poem about the Greek hero of the Trojan War, Achilles. Homer begins the poem by invoking the muse to "sing the rage of Peleus's son Achilles, / murderous, doomed, that cost the Achaeans countless losses." It is set in Troy, or Ilium, the land from which the poem takes its name. Reared by his mother, the sea-nymph Thetis, Achilles fights as a ferocious demigod against the Trojans under his captain Agamemnon. *The Iliad* focuses on the last years of the 10-year Trojan War. The poem begins with Achilles and Agamemnon quarrelling over their prizes of war: the women Chryseis and Briseis. Achilles asks Agamemnon to return Chryseis to her father, a priest of Apollo, because he fears Apollo's wrath will destroy their campaign. Upset over his loss of Chryseis, Agamemnon avenges himself by robbing Achilles of Briseis. Achilles then refuses to serve any longer under Agamemnon, which devastates the Greek war effort. Achilles, guilty over bringing suffering to his comrades, yet too self-important to fight alongside Agamemnon, agrees to a plan devised to help Greece's cause. Achilles allows his friend Patroclus to pose as Achilles himself in battle. Hector, son of the Trojan King Priam, kills Patroclus in battle, inspiring Achilles to rejoin the conflict. He obtains new armor from Hephaestus, the god of fire and crafts, and avenges Patroclus's death by killing Hector, then drags Hector's body by chariot for nine days until the gods agree that Hector must be allowed proper funeral rites.

The Iliad is significant for its emphasis on choices and Greek life. When Patroclus is killed, Achilles faces the monumental decision to return to war or to keep safe from harm. His grief ultimately prompts him to return, where he secures eternal glory but also an untimely and tragic death. *The Iliad* also holds great cultural value because it cemented the place of the Trojan War as a defining event in Greek history. The apocryphal events of Homer's Trojan War are part of the foundation on which the Greeks built their collective identity, and the values, ethics, and narrative of Homer's *Iliad* form its basis. For instance, *The Iliad* demonstrates the Greek mindset of when and why to go to war. Homer portrays the justification of both sides of the Trojan War, legitimizing the conflict. In Greek thinking, some wars are necessary and, as shown in *The Iliad*, must be fought in order to defend honor and courage.

The Odyssey

A continuation of *The Iliad*, *The Odyssey* is an epic poem of adventure, named for its protagonist, Odysseus, who is trying to find his way home to Ithaca from Troy. For 10 years after the conclusion of the Trojan War, several of the gods keep Odysseus from going home. Eventually, Odysseus is granted permission to return to Ithaca, where he is king and where his wife, Penelope, is dutifully waiting. However, the decision to return home does not come without a cost. If Odysseus chooses to remain with the nymph Calypso, who is desperately in love with him and on whose island Odysseus has been living for seven years, he is guaranteed eternal life. Ultimately deciding that a mortal life in the home he loves is worth more than an immortal life on a remote island, Odysseus chooses his mortality and his home and begins his journey. *The Odyssey* is the first of many stories—Dante's *Inferno*, *The Wizard of Oz*, even the more recent film *E.T.*—to attempt to capture the sentimental value of "home" and what it means to find one's way back to it. Not only is *The Odyssey* a telling exposé on the importance of finding home, but it is also an exploration of mortality—what it means to live and to die.

Just as Achilles in *The Iliad* is a man of outstanding physical strength, Odysseus is a man of superior discretion and cleverness. In *The Iliad*, Odysseus is in part responsible for the reconciliation between Achilles and Agamemnon. In *The Odyssey*, however, Odysseus uses his wisdom not to pacify wronged leaders but to escape captors and other obstacles on his journey—Calypso, the Lotus Eaters, Polyphemus the Cyclops, Circe, the Sirens, the realm of Hades, and the sea demon Scylla. Once he reaches Ithaca, disguised by Athena as a beggar, Odysseus seeks help from his old swineherd, Eumaeus. He remains in disguise until he encounters his son Telemachus, with whom he formulates a strategy to violently oust Penelope's suitors and reinstate himself on the throne.

Like *The Iliad*, *The Odyssey* is significant for its impact in unifying Greek culture. Whereas *The Iliad* focuses more on warfare and large-scale cultural issues, *The Odyssey* relates more to personal conflicts affecting the daily lives of individuals. It deals especially with spiritual growth, loyalty, and perseverance. Odysseus's spiritual growth is seen as he battles against temptation—the temptation to remain with Calypso in immortality or to give in to the alluring song of the Sirens. Loyalty can be seen in the character Eumaeus, who helps Odysseus despite his long absence and, initially, his convincing disguise. Loyalty can also be seen in the behavior of Penelope, who resists her many suitors and faithfully waits over a decade for her husband's return. Perseverance is the most prevailing virtue in *The Odyssey*. It is his ultimate desire to be at home in Ithaca, reunited with Penelope, that prompts Odysseus's journey, and it is perseverance that motivates Odysseus to complete his trek.

Universal Weakness

Throughout the plots of *The Iliad* and *The Odyssey*, Homer demonstrates that all beings—gods, rulers, and peasants alike—are fallible, and no one, regardless of individual status, is immune to the struggles of life. His characters are always subject to an inescapable weakness, whether physical or emotional. For example, Achilles is infamous for his mortal (Achilles') heel, a deadly weakness that leads to his downfall. Even the gods and demigods exhibit weaknesses of character; although not physically flawed, many of the gods have flawed temperaments, impulses, or rationales. They often act impulsively or irrationally. The weaknesses of the goddesses are mainly of the heart: lust, infidelity, jealousy, and vanity. Many take on human lovers, which routinely brings downfall and suffering. By humanizing his divine characters as well as his mortal ones, Homer depicts weakness as a universal trait and shows the dangers of self-indulgence through his characters' downfalls. Weakness, although apparent in everyone, is to be guarded against. One must not allow weakness to compromise judgment or encroach on morality. Ultimately for Homer, weakness is a fact of nature that always comes at a cost.

The Strength of Intelligence

Homer believed that having intelligence is more useful than having brute strength. In *The Odyssey*, Odysseus and his men are able to escape the Cyclops, Polyphemus, because of Odysseus's plan to blind Polyphemus and then disguise themselves beneath the sheep to escape the cave. While Polyphemus is obviously much stronger, a clever trick blinds him and frees Odysseus and his men, showing that cleverness outstrips burliness. Throughout his whole journey, Odysseus uses his cunning to receive aid from people and deities alike. It is through the tales of his heroes in *The Iliad* and *The Odyssey* that Homer emphasizes that while strength is useful, wit is what will save the hero in the end.

Heroism

Today heroes wear tights and capes, but Homeric heroes cloak themselves with *kudos* (glory), *kleos* (fame), and *timē* (honor). Although Homer presents a number of fierce warriors in his epic tales, the true heroes govern the council room as well as dominate the battlefield. Heroes stand out from the rest in their excellence as "speakers of words and doers of deeds." Especially seen in the struggle between Achilles and Agamemnon in *The Iliad*, a hero legitimizes his authority through external confirmations of his power, such as reputation and gifts. Driving the plot of *The Iliad*, both heroes argue over who should keep a spoil of war, a girl named Briseis. For Homeric culture, this is not an issue of love but of honor—Briseis is a symbol of authority. These two characters clash because of the origins of their authority and because of the arenas of their excellence. As King, Agamemnon inherited his power and governs well in the council room; as a great warrior, Achilles earned his standing and fights more bravely and effectively on the battlefield. Both the inherited and the earned authority hold legitimate sway with Homeric audiences. Eventually, Agamemnon loses his credibility by demonstrating his inability to successfully lead his men, and Achilles confirms his heroic merit by choosing to pursue honor against his better judgment. Explaining the hero's plight, Achilles outlines the dilemma before him:

> For my mother the goddess, silver-footed Thetis, telleth me that twofold fates are bearing me toward the doom of death: if I abide here and war about the city of the Trojans, then lost is my home-return, but my renown shall be imperishable; but if I return home to my dear native land, lost then is my glorious renown, yet shall my life long endure.
>
> —*The Iliad*

To seek eternal glory and to defend his friend's honor, Achilles returns to the battle to lay down his life. The Homeric hero receives homage not only through the spoils of war, like Briseis, but also through the enduring *kleos* of epic poetry. As the ultimate hero, Achilles gets the girl, as well as the glory—death.

Rachel Jeffries, 2015

AESOP ◊ 620-560 BC, *Greek Slave and Master Story Teller*

" Do nothing without regard to the consequences.
—"The Two Frogs," *Aesop's Fables*

- Was born in Greece, possibly Thrace
- Was chronicled by Aristotle, Herodotus, and Plutarch, even while details of his life are based in legend
- Has yet had no actual writings discovered, although 94 fables are attributed to him
- May have been a freed slave
- Was fictionalized in *The Aesop Romance*, where he lacks the power of speech but is given the gift of story-telling by a priestess of Isis
- Suffered mockery in the *Romance*, because of his ugliness and the sound of his voice
- Had his fables collected and recorded in prose and poetry in Greek and Latin
- Wrote often about talking animals and plants; the fables presented morals and lifelong truths
- Has had his stories rewritten and translated in many cultures for centuries: the fables of today do not mirror the earliest of the Aesop fables
- Has been described differently by various painters, writers, and playwrights: African, neither ugly nor a slave, a hunchback, a dwarf, and a beggar
- Is sometimes compared with Br'er Rabbit in modern times, as they share the themes of oppression and the hero's cleverness in the face of danger
- Continues to be depicted in the 20th century, in novels, plays, and television shows

Key Works
Aesop's Fables, 620–560 BC

Biography
Fables are fictions that point to truths. *Aesop's Fables* is a collection of fables credited to Aesop. The Greek historian Herodotus mentioned in passing that "Aesop the fable writer" was a slave who lived in Ancient Greece during the fifth century BC. Even Plato, while he was in jail awaiting execution, put some of Aesop's fables to verse.

Of diverse origins, the stories associated with Aesop's name have descended to modern times through a number of sources. They continue to be reinterpreted in different verbal registers and in popular as well as artistic mediums. Aesop couldn't possibly have written many fables attributed to him, yet the storytelling tradition is what has allowed his fables to be told and retold to this day.

One exemplary fable, "The Goose That Laid the Golden Egg" creates an idiom used to demonstrate an unprofitable action motivated by greed. It refers to one of Aesop's Fables, number 87 in the Perry Index (a list of 575 such fables.)

> A cottager and his wife had a Hen that laid a golden egg every day. They supposed that the Hen must contain a great lump of gold in its inside, and in order to get the gold they killed it. Having done so, they found to their surprise that the Hen differed in no respect from their other hens. The foolish pair, thus hoping to become rich all at once, deprived themselves of the gain of which they were assured day by day.
>
> We should set Bounds to our Desires, and content ourselves when we are well, for fear of losing what we had.

The English idiom, sometimes shortened to "killing the golden goose," derives from this fable. It identifies a shortsighted action that destroys the profitability of an asset.

Throughout history, thinkers have revered the value in Aesop's universal lessons. Apollonius of Tyana, a first-century-AD philosopher, said, "Like those who dine well off the plainest dishes, he made use of humble incidents to teach great truths." Unlike poets, who "do violence to their own stories in order to make them probable," Aesop "told the truth by the very fact that he did not claim to be relating real events."

With the use of the printing press, chroniclers and translators of Aesop influenced people from Italy to Germany, fortified by the testimony of Christian writers—including Martin Luther:

> Moral teachings, if offered to young people, will contribute much to their edification. In short, next to the Bible, the writings of Cato and Aesop are in my opinion the best.
> —Martin Luther, *Works*

AESCHYLUS, 524–456 BC, *Father of Tragedy*

> It is an easy thing for one whose foot is on the outside of calamity to give advice and to rebuke the sufferer.
> —*Prometheus Bound*

- Was a Greek dramatist, one of the big three Golden Age Greek tragedians, along with Sophocles and Euripides
- Focused on the relationship between Greek gods and man
- Introduced second and third actors in plays as well as the chorus
- Acted in his own plays, which was uncommon at the time
- Wrote over 90 plays; however, only seven are preserved
- Fought in the Greek war against the Persians; his tombstone mentioned only his military service, not his literary contribution
- Won five Greek playwriting competitions at the festival of Dionysus throughout his life

Key Works

The Persians, 472 BC
Suppliants, 469 BC
Seven Against Thebes, 467 BC
Agamemnon, 458 BC
Oresteia, 458 BC
Prometheus Bound, 415 BC

Biography

Although he did not invent tragedy, Aeschylus certainly immortalized it on stage. Aeschylus was considered the first tragedian, writing over 90 plays throughout his life. Born in 524 BC into a noble Athenian family in the small city-state of Eleusis, Aeschylus claimed that, when sent to watch grapes ripen as a child, he fell asleep and Dionysus, the Greek god of the harvest and wine, came to him and commanded that he write tragedies. He wrote his first tragedy at the age of 25, but had to take a respite from theater after he was called to fight in the battle of Marathon, the Greek defensive against Persian invaders. After the battle, he returned to writing with a grasp of the potential of plays, introducing multiple actors and the chorus that would become hallmarks of Greek theater. Many of his plays were focused on the gods of Greek mythology and their interaction with humankind, specifically those interactions involving evil and treachery from the gods. He continued to write successful plays throughout his life, and won every play competition he entered until he was 50 years old, when he began to compete with Sophocles. The popular theory about Aeschylus's death in 456 is that a turtle's shell dropped by an eagle fell on his head; however, the story can't be substantiated. Though his life ended abruptly, his work continues to capture audiences today. Aeschylus will forever be remembered as one of the great Greek playwrights who revolutionized the dramatic tragedy.

Hubris

Hubris, the state of excessive pride, is an element of many of Aeschylus's tragedies. In *The Persians*, hubris is seen in the character of Xerxes, the king of Persia. Xerxes desires to surpass his father's reputation, a selfish ambition growing to the point of sacrificing everything else. With misdirected values, he throws away the lives of thousands of warriors. A messenger in *The Persians* tells the Persian people of the battle, in which "never in a single day has such a large number of [Persian] men died." Having gone so far as to compare himself to the gods during his campaign, Xerxes in his arrogance brings about the downfall of his army. Aeschylus uses the destruction and death of Xerxes's men to show the consequences of hubris-inspired decisions.

Agamemnon, another of Aeschylus's plays, shows hubris in a different light through Clytemnestra, the queen of Argos. Her pride expands while her husband Agamemnon is away fighting the Trojans. While Agamemnon tries to avoid overwhelming pride, stating, "I am a mortal, a man; I cannot trample upon these tinted splendors without fear thrown in my path," Clytemnestra urges him to forsake his humility in favor of a lavish and extravagant return that would be fit for a god. She is disappointed by his return and her loss of power. He goes on to humbly say, "I tell you, as a man, not god, to reverence me." Agamemnon properly asserts his kingship and its requisite respect, but he is still a man and deserves no higher treatment than such. Clytemnestra's hubris causes her to taint her husband's reputation and act unfairly toward him. In the end her pride causes her to slay Agamemnon so that she may enjoy the power of the sole remaining monarch. By juxtaposing humility and pride in his stories, Aeschylus shows how hubris corrupts.

Justice

Another key element in Aeschylus's work is justice. *Prometheus Bound* focuses on the myth of Prometheus and his punishment enacted by Zeus for giving humans the gift of fire. Throughout the play, the disputed concept of justice recurs in the ideals of the three main characters, Prometheus, Zeus, and Io, a mortal woman whom Zeus transforms into a cow. Judith A. Swanson writes that Aeschylus uses these characters as conduits to express three separate concepts of justice: pity in justice, principled justice, and accountability in justice. Pity in justice occurs when the judge pities the offender and decides that mercy is the best verdict, as Zeus will eventually have pity on both Prometheus, to free him from his enchainment on a boulder, and Io, when he ends her suffering and wandering around the Earth.

Prometheus's character presents the second concept of justice, principled justice, which sets down principles and laws and punishes those who break them. Prometheus knowingly breaks the gods' laws by providing mortals with fire and so must be punished.

Aeschylus uses Zeus's character to show accountability in justice. However, punishing those with a skewed perception of morality would be cruel, so Aeschylus criticizes Zeus's character by depicting Io continually wandering the Earth and attempting to discover what she did to experience such torture. These three concepts are combined to offer a complete picture of justice. While imprisoned, Prometheus prophesies that Io's descendant in her family's 13th generation will free him, telling her, "Fate has determined that it be one of your descendants." It is through this prophecy that Aeschylus assimilates his three concepts. Zeus will have to pity Prometheus in order to free him, but Prometheus must endure his punishment because he broke the law (principled justice) and he knows that what he did was wrong (accountability of justice) while he waits for the 13 generations. Swanson writes that Prometheus's prophecy "symbolizes the hope that all three notions of justice will be harmonized." This justice includes a punishment, a willingness to serve the punishment, and mercy—the collaboration that forms Aeschylus's ideal form of justice.

Cole Baker, 2012
Ryan Russell, 2015
Remington Swingle, 2016

THE CLASSICAL PERIOD, 510–323 BC

The Age of Pericles

With the threat from the east gone, Athens began a 50-year period under the brilliant statesman Pericles (495–429 BC), during which time the Parthenon was built on the Acropolis and the city became the artistic, cultural, intellectual, and commercial center of the Hellenic world, attracting all sorts of smart and interesting people and taking command of the other Greek states. Continuing their war against the Persians, they liberated the Ionian Greek cities of Asia Minor and the Aegean islands.

In 478 Athens and its allies on the island of Delos, the sacred island of Apollo, formed the Delian League. After swearing an oath, these Greek city-states, some who were forced to join by threats, began to rid the land of the last remaining Persians and freed the seas of piracy. But as enemies became fewer and members of the league wanted to devote their resources to peaceful endeavors, Athens became more powerful and forced other members do what was best for Athens. This took the form of payments, supposedly for the maintenance of the fleet, from the other members. The funds were used to build the temples and monuments of the city of Athens. When the island of Thassos rebelled against this payment, Athens attacked them. In 454 the treasury of Delos was moved to the Acropolis for "safe-keeping."

The Fourth Century BC

From 396 to 387 BC the Greek states were in revolt against Sparta. Led by Corinth, and fueled with funds that came from Persia to keep the Greeks fighting amongst themselves, peace finally came to all the Greek states for the first time in what was known as the Peace of Antalcidas. In 398 the Athenians reformed the Delian league and once again became the leading power in the Aegean world. In 371 the Thebans defeated the Spartans in the Battle of Leuctra. Sparta was then invaded and the Messenian helots emancipated. Hemmed in on all sides, Sparta would never again be the power it had been. Thebes under Epaminondas became the most powerful city-state, though not powerful enough to unite the others. The soldier-writer Xenophon witnessed much of this period. In fourth-century Athens, sculptors like Scopas and Lysippus explored the beauty of the human form. The playwright Menander introduced a style of drama known as New Comedy, akin to today's situation comedy. Aristotle was busy collecting data on everything to develop his theories of the visible world, while Plato focused on the spiritual with his theory of forms—which would influence Christian mysticism. Meanwhile the speeches of Demosthenes and his rival Aeschines were asking the critical question of the time, how to deal with the rising power of Phillip of Macedon.

The Olympic Games

From 776 BC through the Golden Age, until the Roman Emperor Theodosius finally banned them in 393, every four years men from all over the Greek world came to the town of Olympia to compete in the Olympic Games. Though there were other games in classical Greece, the Olympics were the most important. During the period of the games a sacred truce was in effect so competitors could pass through hostile territories to get to Olympia. The games were held on the second full moon of the summer solstice and were not restricted to athletic events. There were also feasts, competitions between orators, poets, prayers, and sacrifices, appropriate since it was a religious festival dedicated to Zeus. The games were held for Zeus's enjoyment, to foster the Greek love of competition, and to promote the Homeric value of *arete* or excellence—perhaps the most important quality of the Greek heroes of *The Iliad*. Athletic fanaticism was yet another gift of the ancient Greeks, and by the second century even the priests in Jerusalem were spending more time practicing the discus then they were on their priestly duties. The Olympic and other Panhellenic games were open only to Greeks, and one's Greekness was confirmed by his inclusion in the games. By Herodotus's definition, to be a Greek meant to share blood, language, religion, and customs, but eventually to be considered a Greek meant to live and act as a Greek, particularly by engaging in competition with other Greeks. Those who competed were not seeking riches but undying glory, or *cleos aphthiton*, for themselves, their families and their community. Poets like Pindar turned their victories to prose so that even today we know their names and exploits. While the Greeks who competed at these games did not see themselves as a nation they did see themselves as a culture united in language, blood, religion, and especially the spirit of Homeric competitiveness as they cheered on the athletes who modeled themselves on Homer's heroes.

THE GRECO-PERSIAN WARS, 499–449 BC

In the early fifth century BC, the Achaemenid Empire of ancient Persia sought to extend its power westward across the Aegean Sea, where east met west. Against them stood a handful of Grecian city-states determined to maintain their autonomy in the face of foreign encroachment. What followed were a series of battles over half a century in which the Greeks—sometimes narrowly—claimed victory over their Persian aggressors, safeguarding the greater European continent from Asian invasion.

The ancient Greeks can be considered the seminal cradle of Western civilization, though they almost weren't. The Persian Empire constituted one of the biggest, most important empires of the ancient world, at this time larger than even China—a formidable opponent indeed. Yet the Greeks held their ground, secured their sovereignty, and went on to cultivate a culture that would come to guide and shape the modern world as we know it. Without the Greeks everything would be different, and without the Grecian victories against Persia there might have been no Greeks.

The Greco-Persian Wars started when the borders of the Persian Empire merged with the collection of city-states that constituted Greece. The smaller isolated cities that were closest to their Persian neighbors fell first, each succumbing to the sheer number of Persian soldiers. As each city and its people were enveloped, they only added more strength to the Persian military. In 522, Darius took control of the empire, setting out to strengthen and enlarge Persia.

Notable Battles

The Battle of Marathon, 490 BC

The turning point of the first Greco-Persian War, and some would say Western civilization.

In 490, Darius focused on his neighbors to the West, and invaded Greece with an army exceeding 25,000 soldiers. The Greeks, preemptively aware of the invasion, gathered their forces in preparation. Many city-states sent their soldiers, but the most militant of the city-states, Sparta, did not come to the aid of its neighbors. Sparta's absence left a Greek army of 10,000 to fight a force more than twice its size.

Despite the disparity in troop size, the Greek army managed to beat back the attack and send Darius ignobly back to Persia. The combined forces and tactics of Athens and Plataea proved sufficient to rout and drive out the significantly larger Persia army, postponing further Persian entanglements in Europe indefinitely until the death of then-emperor Darius I.

This battle has retained a spot in ancient lore as being the birthplace of the Marathon. After the battle turned in favor of the Greeks, Pheidippides, a messenger, ran from the battlefield of Marathon to Athens to tell of the great victory. Legend has it that shortly after arriving and announcing the victory, Pheidippides died from exhaustion. Every marathon run since that day has been in his honor.

The Battles of Salamis and Thermopylae, 480 BC

A decade later, Darius's heir, Xerxes, arrived back on Greek shores to attempt conquest yet again. The battle of Thermopylae is probably the most well-remembered battle of the second Greco-Persian War, immortalized as one of the first great "last stands" in history.

Xerxes landed his force near the pass of Thermopylae, a narrow pathway walled by a cliff face on one side and a sheer drop to the sea on the other. The Spartans were the first to react this time, marching to Thermopylae and, despite being outnumbered by the Persian forces, holding back the armies of Xerxes for two days in order to impede the enemy's progress. Although the immediate result of this battle was a Greek defeat, it granted the other city-states time to prepare a proper counter-attack.

Following their defeat at Thermopylae and a disastrous retreat from Artemisium, the Greeks gathered their remaining naval forces by the island of Salamis, just off the coast of Greece. The superior Persian forces, overseen by the Persian King Xerxes himself, attempted to box in the Greek fleet, only to find their overwhelming numbers made it difficult to maneuver the comparatively tight straits. The Greeks seized upon the opportunity and managed a decisive victory. This time it was King Xerxes' turn to retreat, with most of his army in tow. Although the Persians made a few more token attempts at conquering Greece, they were no longer the threat they once were.

This effort and sacrifice on the part of the Spartans allowed the other city-states to gather their full force and prepare for Xerxes. On the third day a Greek traitor showed the Persians a secret path around the pass, allowing the Persians to surround the Greek army. The majority of the Greeks fled, but 300 Spartans and a handful of other brave soldiers stayed behind and fought to their death. The Persians marched on, pillaging and burning their way through Greece. Athens was evacuated before being burned by the Persians, an event which marked the high mark of the Persians' attack. A combined army of Spartans, Athenians, and Tegeans fought the Persians on land while Themistocles of Athens fought the indomitable Persian navy at the naval Battle of Salamis. Overcoming the odds again in defense of their homeland, the Greeks defeated the Persians and sent them back to their lands.

Small skirmishes continued on the borders of the two nations for the next 30 years, but the era of all-out invasion was over.

SOPHOCLES, 496–406 BC, *Playwright of Humanism*

" Many are the wonders of the world, but none is more wonderful than man.

—*Antigone*

- Had a strong career, winning the Dionysus festival 24 times
- Wrote over 120 plays in the course of his life, but only 7 survived
- Based his plays off Greek mythology, like other playwrights at the time
- Focused on characters over plot
- Was attuned to the problems that women were facing during his time
- Introduced scene paintings, a third actor, and a larger chorus to Greek drama, all building off the innovations of Aeschylus
- Expressed themes of fate, irony, and free will, mainly

Key Works
Ajax, 450–430 BC
Antigone, 443–441 BC
Oedipus the King, 435–410 BC

Biography

Son of Sophilus, Sophocles was born to a wealthy family in Colonus, a city-state near Athens, in 496 BC. Throughout school Sophocles grew fond of Homer as well as other Greek lyric poets. Near the beginning of his career, around age 28, he entered his work in the Festival of Dionysus, a celebration in honor of the god of wine, which included a drama competition. He defeated Aeschylus and won his first of 24 victories, never placing lower than second. According to Plutarch, "there were three periods in Sophocles's literary development: imitation of the grand style of Aeschylus, use of artificial and incisive style, and use of the best style and that which is most expressive of character." He made many changes to Greek drama that differentiated his work from the work of others; it is said that he "found tragedy in the clouds and brought it down to earth." By the end of his career Sophocles had written over 120 plays, although only seven have survived. Never leaving Athens, he died in 406 BC at the age of 90.

Fate over Free Will

Although Sophocles's focus is similar to that of other playwrights of his era—mythology, the hubris of his characters, etc.—he incorporated many new themes into his work. Among these are the idea that fate punishes the prideful, the conflict between man-made law and the law of the gods, the importance and redemptive quality of love, sympathy for the plight of women, and hardship resulting in knowledge and dignity.

Sophocles contributed to contemporary theater by introducing fate as an inescapable force. Plays before Sophocles didn't suggest a power higher than that of the gods, but many after him include fate as a character. The inescapable nature of fate also challenges his theme of free will. Though Sophocles's characters strive to be unrestricted, they cannot run from fate. Perhaps best known, Oedipus's father's efforts to avoid the prophecy of his son killing him and marrying his widowed wife cannot be averted. Likewise, Oedipus's own attempts to subvert the prophecy of the Delphic oracle lead him right into fulfilling the decree of fate. No amount of strategy can fight the power of Apollo's oracle throughout the play—fate proves too strong for anyone to change.

Dramatic Irony

Dramatic irony runs rampant throughout all of Sophocles's plays. Each of his characters' lives is a brutal gauntlet of excruciating circumstances that lead him to curse his own existence and the gods. Dramatic irony is seen regularly today in horror movies when the audience knows where the killer is waiting but can do nothing but watch as the characters in the movie walk right into the killer's clutches—this is Sophocles's trademark. Sophocles uses dramatic irony in his *Theban Trilogy* by allowing the audience to know more than the characters. Here, in *Oedipus the King*, Oedipus finds out the horrible details of his life:

> O god—
> all come true, all burst to light!
> O light—now let me look my last on you!
> I stand revealed at last—
> cursed in my birth, cursed in marriage,
> cursed in the lives I cut down with these hands!

As Oedipus tries to escape his destiny, he runs straight into the hands of fate. Meanwhile, Sophocles has foreshadowed this moment for the audience from Oedipus's birth. Similarly, in the *Theban Plays*, Sophocles builds dramatic momentum throughout each story until reaching a single dramatic moment. The climax allows for a satisfying resolution of the irony strategically set in motion in each play.

From Myth to Man

Instead of writing new tales, Greek writers based their plays on ancient myths. This method ensured that their audience already knew the plot so that the playwright could focus on bringing it to life with character development. Sophocles was no different, drawing his inspiration for his most famous play, *Oedipus*, from the ancient myths of the dark King of Thebes. However, Sophocles surprised his audience by creating empathy for Oedipus, who had his life uprooted in *Oedipus the King*, the first of his trilogy. Sophocles alters the story in other ways as well, making Apollo the central force rather than the Furies. The Furies, known as great seekers of justice, would have made Oedipus out to be someone who rightly deserved punishment. By withholding the Furies and dramatizing the role of fate, Sophocles was able to change the audience's view of the well-known myth of King Oedipus.

Sophocles changed the culture of Greek drama, introducing elements that altered both the atmosphere and the message. Mechanically, he introduced scene paintings, a third actor, and a larger tragic chorus. But of most importance, he took the simple, individual man and changed him into a complex, passionate character.

Savannah Cressman, 2011
Trisha Rouleau, 2015

HERODOTUS, 484–425 BC, *The Father of History*

> " Of all men's miseries the bitterest is this: to know so much and to have control over nothing.
>
> —*The Histories*

- Was born in the Greek colony of Halicarnassus, and later exiled for participating in a revolt against a local tyrant
- Grew up with a fascination in the Greco-Persian war
- Spent significant time understanding and describing the Persians: their beliefs, behaviors, customs, and other aspects of their culture
- Was considered by some to be the father of anthropology
- Revolutionized historical documentation as he inquired about history through man's actions alone, rather than through myth and the inner-workings of the gods
- Emphasized the importance and significance of the diversity of life
- Had only one eye, due to an accident in his youth

Key Work

The Histories, c. 450–420 BC

Biography

Little is known of Herodotus's life, as he rarely recorded his personal story or ideals, but it is believed he was born around 484 BC in Halicarnassus. Historian Landauer writes, "Though far from the center of Greek culture, residents [of Halicarnassus] spoke Greek, considered themselves Greek, and followed Greek customs, religion, and politics." It is believed that his family was prominent in the social structure of Halicarnassus, as Herodotus clearly was the beneficiary of an aristocratic education. His ability to travel indicates that he was a man of some means. Later in life, Herodotus was exiled to the island of Samos for playing a role in a revolt against a local tyrant. After writing and revising *The Histories*, Herodotus is believed to have finally settled in the "panhellenic colony of Thurii in southern Italy," where he died, possibly of the plague, around 420 BC.

The Father of History

Using his unique approach to historical inquiry, Herodotus traveled around the Mediterranean documenting history as he saw and heard it from witnesses. The Greco-Persian Wars fought during the first half of his life fascinated him. It was based on his research of these conflicts and the two competing civilizations that he began writing his famed work, *The Histories*. In his time, the gods or demigods were principal characters in the record of most historical events. Herodotus created a different approach, which his successor Thucydides emulated, that characterized history as the story of man, rather than stories of the gods. Throughout his travels, he was known for meticulously recording the life and culture of every place he visited, and is notable for lacking national prejudice and for seeking a variety of cultural perspectives in his understanding of other nations and Greek states. Because of his passion for documentation, Herodotus is often referred to as the "Father of History."

Despite his belief in accurate documentation, Herodotus also received criticism for a lack of veracity in his *Histories*, garnering him the moniker "Father of Lies." His trustworthiness has been doubted both in ancient and modern times, given "the inherent defects of his character, his credulity, his love of effect and his loose and inaccurate habits of thought." The description of Babylon is a prime example of Herodotus's questionable historical accuracy. He claimed vast dimensions for the city, arguing that it was a perfect square with 15-mile-long sides, with an "eighty three feet thick and three hundred thirty feet high wall," accessed by a hundred bronze gates. Subsequent archaeological exploration has shown that Herodotus dramatically exaggerated the scope of the great city. This kind of exaggeration leads to the conclusion that his account was "based on hearsay, rather than a personal visit, even though Herodotus writes as though he visited the site himself." His tendencies throughout *The Histories* of relying on secondhand accounts and his penchant for personal opinion may detract from his authority, but his diligent and innovative documentation style firmly secures his vital place in history.

Herodotus's descriptions of the two centuries preceding his life still serve as modern history's primary source of information concerning the politics, culture, and history of the ancient Greeks and Persians during that time. Moreover, his explanations of navigation, scientific discoveries, and geography have provided historians with an impressively accurate assessment of the state of Greek science and technology of the fifth century BC. Herodotus remains a compelling historian whose empirical and anthropological approach revolutionized the documentation of world history.

Nate Kosirog, faculty
Nathaniel Whatmore, 2015

" Of all things upon earth that bleed and grow, a herb most bruised is woman.

—Medea

- Was born in Athens to a wealthy, powerful family, and began producing plays as a young adult
- Participated in the City Dionysia festival, an annual event celebrating plays, and won first place four out of 22 times
- Often worked on his plays on the island of Salamis, where he sat in a cave, looked out to sea, and wrote
- Focused his plays heavily on women, the nature of the relationship between passion and reason, and a reduced role of the gods
- Disagreed with the participation of Athens in the Peloponnesian War
- Was one of the three great Greek tragedians, following Aeschylus and concurrent with Sophocles
- Incorporated more vernacular language than other playwrights, while keeping his plays in the genre of Greek tragedy
- Gained a considerable amount of recognition after his death, despite being mocked by Aristophanes

Key Works
Medea, 431 BC
Electra, 420–416 BC
Bacchae, 406 BC

Biography
Euripides was born c. 480 BC to what historians believe was a wealthy Greek family in Athens, Greece. The details of his childhood and young adult life are virtually unknown, but he resurfaces in the historical timeline when, as a young adult, he began to produce his plays at competitions, particularly at the City Dionysia festival in Athens, celebrating theatrical works. Despite claiming victory only 4 of the 22 times he competed, his plays were among the most widely produced in the ancient world. While a mere 19 of what are assumed to be in excess of 92 plays remain intact, the works of Euripides are among the most studied of all ancient poets. Many of the women in Euripides's stories are vengeful, cruel, and unfaithful, leading many to believe that these were based on his own experience. However, scholars have found evidence of only one marriage, which produced three sons. Euripides continued writing tragedies until his death.

Classical Greek Tragedy
Euripides was one of the three great Greek tragedians whose plays have survived throughout the centuries. His work, while structurally similar to the work of his contemporaries—Aeschylus and Sophocles—was radically contentious and continues to be influential today. Tragedies always involved traditional myths and some sort of religious facet. Great tragedians made the audience feel separate from the characters in a specific situation yet related to them with common emotions, ambitions, and desires. For example, Euripides innovated increased singing roles for the actors and used emotionally resonant music. The audience could thus identify with his characters' concerns. Euripides also chose a simple vocabulary for his plays and gave his characters problems that the audience could directly relate

to. For instance, Euripides used the heroes of Greek mythologies but gave them contemporary attitudes and problems. His characters were not the infallible subjects that were so often portrayed by his contemporaries, but rather mortal, earthly creatures. Most of his innovations became more famous after his death, because during his lifetime his criticism of Athenian culture and abruptly realistic portrayal of human nature made him a contentious voice.

Medea

Euripides's most widely studied work is *Medea*: a play that focuses heavily on the role and nature of women in Greek society, as well as the interaction between the warring forces of passion and reason. Medea tells the story of the Greek hero Jason after his successful quest to recover the Golden Fleece. While on his journey, he meets Medea, a beautiful princess and sorceress who aids him in recovering the Fleece, and marries her. Several years after settling in Corinth, Jason decides to divorce Medea, subsequently marrying the princess of Corinth. In a jealous rage, Medea kills Jason's new wife and the king, the princess's father, with a poisoned cloak. Amidst this cataclysm, Medea orates on the nature of the suffering of Greek women, lamenting that "[women] bid the highest price in dowries just to buy some man to be dictator of [their] bodies. … How that compounds the wrong!" Afterwards, she takes her sons into her home and kills them to further spite Jason. Medea's shocking murder of her sons is an egregious overreaction to their father's actions, prompting her nurse to accuse her of "mak[ing] the sons share in their father's guilt." After killing her children, Medea flies away with their bodies on a chariot drawn by dragons, leaving Jason alone and miserable.

Traditionally, women in Greek society were put down, seen as inferior to men, and given little power. While a woman could not divorce her husband without a legitimate reason and help from a male citizen, a husband could divorce his wife at any time he wished. Medea, crazed by her husband's betrayal, rebels against this system. In addition, the play shows the relationship between reason and passion. In the heat of her anger, she makes the decision to kill her sons to spite her husband. While her rational mind tells her that killing her sons is wrong, her anger in the heat of the moment causes her to carry out the deed despite her reservations.

Jeff Culver, faculty
Cole Watson, 2018

SOCRATES, 469–399 BC, *Founder of Western Philosophy*

" The unexamined life is not worth living.

—At his trial for impiety

- Was a key figure during classical Athens' peak of political, artistic, intellectual, and military greatness
- Worked as a stonemason; his father was a stonemason and sculptor; his mother was a midwife
- Compared his teaching to his mother's midwifery: not pregnant with wisdom himself, but guiding students to give birth to the wisdom with which *they* are pregnant
- Served as an infantry soldier during the Peloponnesian War; courageous in battle, with great physical endurance

- Taught philosophy to the brilliant young military commander Alcibiades; when Alcibiades was wounded in retreat, Socrates stayed behind and rescued him; Alcibiades received the prize for bravery, but urged Athens to give it to Socrates; Socrates refused it
- Defended reason over power, justice over might, essentially inventing political philosophy
- Lived (and died) by his principles: wisdom is the highest good; philosophy ("love of wisdom") is the happiest human life; better to suffer injustice from others than to be unjust yourself
- Defied the unjust orders of the Thirty Tyrants who ruled Athens at the end of the Peloponnesian War
- Did not write his teachings; is known to us because Aristophanes satirized him in *The Clouds* when Socrates' reputation was growing, and later because Plato (his most famous student) and the historian/philosopher Xenophon recounted or recreated many of his mature conversations
- Believed the first step to gaining wisdom is to accept your ignorance, reject assumptions and preconceptions; no one will *seek* knowledge until he admits he *lacks* it
- Taught in an ironic, question-and-answer style now known as the Socratic Method, designed to expose and weaken unsupported beliefs; the student learns the need for philosophy in seeking true knowledge
- Shifted the focus of philosophy from materialist physics to ethics (the conduct of life and care for the soul)
- Prepared young men for life as virtuous citizens by teaching that their intellectual and moral lives were more valuable than material and political gain; wisdom more valuable than power and fame
- Intuitively sensed the existence of a monotheistic God, a natural moral law, and a spiritual after-life in the midst of the polytheistic Greek culture
- Was skeptical of democracy, concerned about the danger of mob rule by the passions, rather than reason
- Was charged, at age 70, with impiety and corrupting the youth of Athens; was convicted and sentenced to death by drinking hemlock; had an opportunity to escape but refused, citing respect for the rule of law

Biography

Although he was born into an average, middle class family, Socrates's life and path were anything but average. He lived at the height of Athens when the city-state was in conflict with other neighboring principalities over land and power. Socrates fought bravely and courageously for Athens as a foot soldier in the Peloponnesian Wars between Athens and Sparta. Later, he married a young woman who has been described as difficult of temperament and with whom he fathered two boys. Although he tried to make a living as a stonemason, Socrates spent most of his time in the public square, breaking principles into smaller questions to stimulate thought with citizens, mostly young aristocrats. Socrates influence on two of these young men became a part of the government's specific complaints against him. Although scientists had educated him, Socrates was dissatisfied with their focus and sought to discover moral truth using philosophy. This path directed not only his daily life, but also statements he made about democracy and about his own destiny.

Socrates's two foundational beliefs formed the basis for Plato's philosophies and a profound change in the philosophic study: (1) Happiness can be attained by living a good and moral life. (2) All good comes from knowing oneself and purpose throughout life; it follows that virtue is knowledge, and moral virtual is teachable. Socrates encouraged his followers to think for themselves by asking questions, a method that came to be known as the "Socratic method," and "dialectic," characterized by considering possible consequences of a statement.

After Sparta's victory in the war, Athenians were ruled by an oligarchy for eight months. The Thirty Tyrants in power were so brutal that the citizens rejected the "rule by a few" and struggled to maintain a weakened democracy. Always a social critic, Socrates praised Sparta and questioned democracy as an effective government; both ideas may have brought about a growing criticism directed toward him.

Socrates demonstrated his personal desire to examine his own life and actions when he was ordered by the Thirty Tyrants to show his support for their government by taking Leon of Salamis from his home for an unjust execution. Socrates refused and was saved from retribution himself only when the Thirty Tyrants were overthrown. Later, with the proof that he had influenced two important young men, Critias and Anytus, as well as lack of support for the democracy, Socrates was brought to trial for "corrupting the youth" and "not believing in the gods of the state."

Socrates was described by Plato as a "gadfly," who, as a fly incites a horse to movement, Socrates stimulated thought and examination toward justice and virtue in all things including politics. His paradoxical thinking has been revealed through the writing of Plato, Xenophon, and Aristophanes. Among the most famous of these writings, the dialogue *Phaedo*, Plato recorded Socrates delivering an unapologetic speech to his accusers at his trial and then speaking to his trial visitors about the immortality of the soul. Many other dialogues by Plato reveal Socrates's discussions and possibly some of Plato's own thoughts. Plato describes Chaerephon's question to the Oracle at Delphi, "Is anyone wiser than Socrates?" The Oracle says there is no one wiser because Socrates claims to have no wisdom. Realizing one's absolutely ignorant state is true wisdom, according to Socrates.

Xenophon, an Athenian soldier, also wrote his memories and reflections in three nonfiction writings: *Memorabilia*, *Symposium*, and *Apology*. *Memorabilia* tells of Socrates's life as a teacher, one of moderation and willingness to talk with everyone about important issues. *Symposium* shows Socrates as a relaxed, convivial banquet guest, and records his remarks about the value of spiritual love. *Apology* is Xenophon's version of Socrates's defense at his trial.

Later Aristophanes wrote the satiric comedy *Clouds*, which presents Socrates differently, portraying a character who runs "the Thoughtery." Aristophanes mocks Socrates by depicting him as a Sophist (one of a group of professional teachers of rhetoric) who accepts money for leading students to pursue answers to foolish questions.

Found guilty, Socrates was sentenced to drink the poison hemlock, and despite the pleadings of his friends, refused to submit to the accusations or escape to freedom. Socrates appeared to welcome his death as its own escape. His methods and ideas focused his disciples on writing and creating schools of philosophy that influenced Aristotle, Alexander the Great, and generations to come.

Daren Jonescu, advisor

THUCYDIDES, 460–399 BC, *The Warrior Historian*

> War takes away the easy supply of daily wants, and so proves a rough master that brings most men's characters to a level with their fortunes.
>
> —*The Peloponnesian War*

- Led Athenians as a general in the Peloponnesian War, and was exiled for his failure to reach Amphipolis before the Spartans
- Remained a loyal Athenian even while in exile, even though he condemned certain aspects of Athenian democracy and culture
- Wrote firsthand accounts of human nature as it relates to war and to history
- Was the only surviving source of the Peloponnesian War
- Believed that war was like a harsh schoolteacher on the human condition
- Was the first to write with the sole intention of documenting history instead of providing philosophical or dramatic vignettes
- Gathered information from both sides of the war: despite being Athenian, he interviewed and studied the Spartans as well

Key Work

The Peloponnesian War, 431 BC

Biography

Not much can be stated with certainty about Thucydides, as records detailing his biography are inconclusive. He was born around 460 BC in Athens and lived with his father Olorus. Eventually he was promoted in Athenian society until he was given the rank of general within the Athenian army. During his ascension in the military, Thucydides began keeping notes on the outbreak of the war as well as the social life of the time—specifically regarding the plague in Athens, which he had contracted and recovered from before the war. As the Peloponnesian War began, Thucydides kept an account of the events that transpired. In 423 BC, however, he was banished from Athenian society after failing to reach the Athenian colony of Amphipolis in time to rescue it from the Spartans. During his exile, Thucydides dedicated his life to documenting the war and its exact history, specifically traveling throughout the nations and documenting both sides of the war and its effect on society and its people. While Thucydides lived to see the end of the war, his documentation stops abruptly in 411 BC, 11 years before the war's end. It is believed that upon the war's conclusion in 399 BC, he returned to Athens and died soon thereafter.

The Role of History

Even though his work is incomplete, Thucydides is considered a significant historian for a number of reasons. His historical method is distinguished by the large variety of documentation supporting his accounts, illustrating a break from the traditional embellished Greek mythologies and oral interpretations of his time. While Thucydides offered a detailed narrative of significant historical events, he also interpreted these events in consideration of human nature. He appeals to our passions, judgments, the role of chance, and emotional needs in order to emphasize the importance of behavior and feelings in determining the trajectory of both individuals and societies. In this way, he not only described what occurred, but presented also the reasons and incentives that formed the foundation of historical decisions and outcomes.

By including the role of human nature in shaping societal values, Thucydides allows the reader to have a richer understanding of history. Thucydides also made a political argument regarding the worth of democratic institutions as a successful system of governing. By the time he began to document the war, the view that political deliberation was the result of the elite advancing their own interests without any regard for the well-being of society was growing. Thucydides emphasized the importance of historical and political education and the proper limits of political leadership. Although some have interpreted him as hostile to the democratic process and arguing against its efficiency, Thucydides characterized a democratic polity as being the most well-equipped political system to answer society's problems; he thought democracy was capable of cultivating informed and free citizens who are guided by a careful understanding of the past. Because of his highly detailed and comprehensive description of history, Thucydides is often referred to as the co-founder of history alongside the historian Herodotus.

Nate Kosirog, faculty
Danni Malinski, 2018
Nathaniel Whatmore, 2015

HIPPOCRATES, 460–377 BC, *The Father of Medicine*

" Medicine is of all the Arts the most noble.

—The Law of Hippocrates

- Traced his lineage back 18 generations to Asclepios, the Greek god of medicine
- Started a school of medicine on the Island of Cos
- Led to a transition in medicine from being religiously dominated (theocratic medicine) to rational medicine
- Believed that the physician (*iatros*) should be a lay person with medical knowledge, acting with God's help
- Created the *Hippocratic Oath*, which has been used since then as a basis for medical ethics
- Received credit for a wide body of writings compiled in his *Hippocratic Corpus*, although true authorship is generally attributed to his students
- Believed that the role of physician was to be nature's helper in addressing the needs of those fighting disease
- Focused on an ancient form of holistic health, addressing the entire patient and his environment
- Developed the theory of the four humors, which proposes that man is composed of four basic elements: blood, mucus, lymph, and gall

Key Work

Hippocratic Corpus, 400 BC

Biography

As with nearly all of the ancient Greeks, information about Hippocrates is inconsistent and lacking in credibility. What is known is that Hippocrates was a Greek physician born on the island of Cos in the Aegean Sea around 460 BC. A medical school existed there, which some attribute to Hippocrates. It is believed that Hippocrates was originally born to a physician who claimed to have been a descendant of Asclepios, the Greek god of medicine and the son of Apollo. To separate the early connection between medicine and religion, Hippocrates became known as "The Father of Medicine." However, it is clear from the various writings attributed to him that he did not see the practice of medicine as completely separate from religious belief. He saw physicians as lay people, outside of the priesthood, with medical knowledge acting as aids to God. He also believed that God's help was necessary for physical health. Still, Hippocrates focused his medical practice and teachings on the empirical, using observation and experimentation to draw rational conclusions on how to address disease and treat patients. In the end, Hippocrates developed a method of medical care that was holistic, emphasizing scientific knowledge, emotional compassion and prayer, and physical exercise.

Influence on the Medical Field

The accepted medical practices of the time assumed issues of health and disease to be curable only by divine intervention, usually in the form of priests acting as magicians or healers. Rather than relegate health purely to the religious world, Hippocrates believed that health was a more natural process and could be understood using reason. He theorized that illnesses and ailments could be understood and cured by applying empirical knowledge and rational thought to their treatment. This theory surfaces in *The Oath* when Hippocrates emphasizes that a physician "will follow that system of regimen which … [he] consider[s] for the benefit of [his] patients." Therefore, the physician must use discernment in choosing right treatment. This reliance on empirical fact and rationality vastly altered medical understanding and practice.

In the famous *Hippocratic Oath*, Hippocrates begins to define a medical ethic and commitment for all medical professionals:

> I swear by Apollo, the Physician and Aesculepius and Hygeia and Panacea and all the gods and goddesses, making them my witnesses, that I will fulfill according to my ability and judgment this oath and this covenant:
>
> To hold him who has taught me this art as equal to my parents and to live my life in partnership with him, and if he is in need of money to give him a share of mine, and to regard his offspring as equal to my brothers in male lineage and to teach them this art—if they desire to learn it—without fee and covenant; to give a share of precepts and oral instruction and all the other learning to my sons and to the sons of him who has instructed me and to pupils who have signed the covenant and have taken an oath according to the medical law, but no one else. I will apply dietetic measures for the benefit of the sick according to my ability and judgment; I will keep them from harm and injustice.
>
> I will neither give a deadly drug to anybody who asked for it, nor will I make a suggestion to this effect. Similarly I will not give to a woman an abortive remedy. In purity and holiness I will guard my life and my art. I will not use the knife, not even on sufferers from stone, but will withdraw in favor of such men as are engaged in this work.

Whatever houses I may visit, I will come for the benefit of the sick, remaining free of all intentional injustice, of all mischief and in particular of sexual relations with both female and male persons, be they free or slaves.

What I may see or hear in the course of the treatment or even outside of the treatment in regard to the life of men, which on no account one must spread abroad, I will keep to myself, holding such things shameful to be spoken about.

If I fulfill this oath and do not violate it, may it be granted to me to enjoy life and art, being honored with fame among all men for all time to come; if I transgress it and swear falsely, may the opposite of all this be my lot.

The Four Humors

Hippocrates also developed a set of practices based upon his concept of the four humors—a system likely influenced by early philosophers such as Thales, Anaximenes, and Empedocles. These individuals developed the theory that the world was composed of four elements: fire, earth, air, and water. Hippocrates knew this understanding of the world, and as a result, developed the four humors as the necessary framework, using the elements of blood, lymph (phlegm), gall (black bile), and mucus (yellow bile) as the foundational elements. These elements were thought to be the primary body liquids with correspondence to the elements of air, water, earth, and fire. Maintaining balance was considered necessary for good health.

His discussion of the humors, along with his *Aphorisms* and most other works attributed to him, are compiled in his *Hippocratic Corpus*, which depicts healing philosophies and practices. These philosophies and practices regularly reference the four humors as foundational knowledge in understanding how to approach medicine. Also through these writings, Hippocrates began to set the stage for the advancement of medicine as a scientific discipline, creating a scientific method for studying the human anatomy and its ailments. Hippocrates prompted an era of advancement for humanity through his care for mankind, through his methods, and through his ethical obligation to perform with purity and goodness the job of aiding human health.

Nate Kosirog, faculty
Nathaniel Whatmore, 2015

ARISTOPHANES, 455–380 BC, *The Old Comedian*

" Full of wiles, full of guile, at all times, in all ways, are the children of Men.
—*The Birds*

- Was arguably the most successful practitioner of Greek Old Comedy
- Wrote during Athens's war with both Persia and Sparta
- Supported an impossible peace between Sparta and Athens
- Transformed theater and satire into a powerful means of political persuasion
- Made an enemy of Cleon, the most powerful politician during his lifetime

- Was asked to host a second performance of his work, *The Frogs*, an honor rarely granted to any playwright in ancient Athens.

Key Works

The Frogs, 405 BC
The Clouds, 423 BC
The Knights, 423 BC

Biography

Aristophanes grew up at the height of the Golden Age of Athens. In a career that lasted over 40 years, he produced over 40 plays, of which only 11 currently survive. They covered a wide range of subjects, though Aristophanes placed special emphasis on politics and education. Although popular with the public, his biting satire—especially of Cleon, the most powerful politician of Athens—earned Aristophanes political threats and Cleon's lasting enmity.

Aristophanes radically shaped theater, comedy, and politics for both Athens and the world. Where once the political sphere was governed by the rhetoric of politicians, the officials of Athens were forced to reconsider and reshape their images in light of Aristophanes's new, theatrical critique. Aristophanes achieved a degree of political influence previously unheard of, reaching crowds in a manner and quantity unachievable by Athenian senators. Until his death in 380 BC, he harbored the dream of a unified Greek state that would transcend the differences between rivals Athens and Sparta.

Old Comedy

Aristophanes worked in a style known as Greek Old Comedy. Old Comedy was characterized by elements of the fantastic, and often resorted to satire as a means of commentary on popular religious, ethical, and political beliefs. This style tended to be "informal, and even bawdy, with numerous references to bodily functions." In addition to its use of satire, Old Comedy often employed a Chorus, a body of individuals—often times depicted as animals or mythical beings—who acted as "outside" commentators that interact with the audience on the events of the play. This challenge for audience interaction, called "parabasis," also explicitly conveyed the playwright's opinions.

Politics

Aristophanes wrote during a tense period in Athenian history, riven by the Peloponnesian Wars. In the heat of the conflict, Aristophanes repeatedly urged the citizens of Athens to seek peace. He quickly realized his influence as a playwright and took it upon himself to persuade the people of Athens politically. According to Sommerstein, he was "very conscious that the intellectual had a social responsibility. He felt that responsibility strongly himself: he was … the only comic dramatist who openly prided himself being, through his plays, a benefactor of the Athenian people."

Aristophanes called for peace in a number of his works, including *The Peace* and *The Acharnarians*. Arguably his most influential political work was *The Lysistrata*, a vision of peace between Athens and Sparta that was procured by the women of both nations, who refused to have sex with their husbands until a treaty was signed. Aristophanes did not intend his story as an actual solution for the war. It would have been regarded at the time, arguably more so than now, as a laughably unrealistic occurrence. Aristophanes intended his piece to be fantastical so that his audience would receive the more subtle idea of peace within his play. *Lysistrata* depicted the importance of family as the primary reason for peace between Athens and Sparta. In the opening of the play, mothers from both nations yearn for peace because of the loss of their husbands and sons. Both Athenians and Spartans were Greeks, members of a single family. As such, the shared loss of their children seemed senseless, especially since the war seemed to favor only foreign Persia, who loomed in the background, ready to strike the weakened victor of the war.

Education & Attack on Socrates

Aristophanes was a master of satire, using parody and unabashed ridicule to critique, dismantle, and highlight Athenian cultural and political problems. Of particular interest for Aristophanes was education. In his play, *The Clouds*, he discusses the shortcomings of both the "old" and "new" styles of education present during his life. The old education focused on the poetry of Homer and aimed to develop a balanced individual who spoke eloquently and was physically fit. In contrast to this holistic and traditional approach, the new method, often called "sophistry," imparted showy and extravagant logic that, while persuasive, was neither ethical nor sound.

Aristophanes did not find the old manner of learning to be perfect, but he preferred it to the new. In *The Clouds*, Strepsiades enrolls his child, Pheidippides, into Socrates's new "Thinkery," hoping that his son will be able to swindle the courts out of his debts. Before sending Pheidippides to the school, however, Strepsiades enrolls himself. Upon arriving, Strepsiades sees various students bent over, studying the ground. According to the students, this method allows them to simultaneously study the ground with their eyes and the stars with their behinds. After meeting the students, Strepsiades meets Socrates himself, who is found hovering over the school in a sort of hot air balloon, "suspending" his judgment. Through these two satirical images, Aristophanes ridicules the new education, which he finds nonsensical. This is made clear through the depiction of Socrates, who literally has his head in the clouds.

At his school, Socrates studies the "just and unjust" arguments—representative of the old and new models of education—seeking how to overcome the just argument with the unjust argument. The unjust argument was morally deficient but rhetorically superior in comparison to the just. Through it, one could gain an advantage over his opponents with craftiness and deceit. Aristophanes was very critical both of this new method and of Socrates personally, and so described the philosopher as one "who was a thinker about the things up above … and made the worse argument the better." After failing to endure the "thinkery" himself, Streidippides enrolls his son, who becomes a successful student of the unjust argument. Though Streidippides manages to sidestep his debts, his son becomes a monster because of his education. At the end of the play, Pheidippides justifies any action, and so begins beating his father without remorse. The play closes with Streidippides burning Socrates's school.

David Eschrich, researcher

THE PELOPONNESIAN WAR, 431–404 BC, GREEK CIVIL WAR

A brutal civil war among the Greek city-states, principally Athens and Sparta, the Peloponnesian War was fought in three waves over 25 years.

Following the defusing of the Persian situation, the Grecian city-states unfortunately fell into infighting, shoring up into two factions: the Delian League (lead by Athens) and the Peloponnesian League (lead by Sparta). The war concluded with a Peloponnesian victory, but the cost was considerable: Athens, formerly the most prominent, most powerful city-state in ancient Greece, was reduced to a shadow of its former self, while the march of Sparta's war machine, though victorious, left its allies impoverished. The fledgling democratic ideals of Athens, too, were crushed.

This war reshaped the ancient Greek world. Athens, with its democracy and the strongest city-state in Greece prior to the war, was reduced to a state of near-complete subjection; while Sparta, the military oligarchy, became established as the leading power of Greece.

The war marked the end to the fifth century BC and the Golden Age of Greece.

XENOPHON ◊ 430–354 BC, *A Historian of the Peloponnesian Wars*

66 A person should "consider what sort of a creature he is for human use and get to know his own powers."
—remarking on Socrates, *Memorabilia* IV.ii.25

- Was a soldier, historian, and memoirist
- Wrote in an engaging, understandable style
- Recorded his teacher Socrates's life and beliefs very differently than did Plato
- Emphasized the virtue of self-control in his writings as a moral philosopher

Key Works

Hiero, c. 380–370 BC
Memorabilia, 371 BC
Anabasis, 370 BC
Apology, c. 370 BC
Education of Cyrus, c. 370 BC
Symposium, c. 365–360 BC
Agesilaus, c. 360 BC
Hellenica, c. 360 BC

Biography

Xenophon, known as Xenophon of Athens, was a Greek historian, soldier, mercenary, and student of Socrates. Born on a rural estate near Athens during the Peloponnesian War, Xenophon lived at a time of great civil unrest. His education prepared him as an equestrian, a farmer, and a soldier. At age 29 he joined Poxemus as a mercenary in a border protection exercise against Persia. It resulted in the death of Cyrus the Younger and the execution of the participating generals. Xenophon took charge and rescued the leaderless group. Upon his return to Athens, Xenophon joined a Spartan military group and was exiled from Athens as a result. The Spartans honored him by giving him a beautiful estate in Elis, where he wrote in his 23 years of semi-retirement with his wife and two sons. When Sparta was defeated, Xenophon moved to Corinth.

Importance

Xenophon is thought to be the originator of a variety of new writing genres including the first personal memoir, the continued history, and the biographical novel. Xenophon wrote history to recount his own times, the late fifth and early fourth centuries, as an Athenian citizen. He wrote about the end of the Peloponnesian War in *Hellenica* (a continued history) which follows Thucydides's record the *History of the Peloponnesian War*. Xenophon also wrote *Anabasis*, a history of the time in his life (a memoir) when he joined Cyrus the Younger in an effort to defeat Persia.

Xenophon's association with Spartan generals in the Persian campaign is just one indication that he admired the Spartans. Several of his writings, such as *Agesilaus* and *Constitution of Sparta*, show a pro-Spartan bias.

Besides Plato, Xenophon is the most knowledgeable about Socrates. Xenophon learned at the feet of the master himself, and he wrote several biographies about him. In 399 BC he wrote several *Socratic Dialogues* and an *Apology* about Socrates's trial and death.

Xenophon wrote with such clarity and brevity that he was well-known for his writing during his lifetime, recorded by Diogenes Laertius in his *Lives of Eminent Philosophers*. Xenophon wrote in Attic Greek, the dialect of Attica, most similar to later Greek, and was described as the "Attic Muse" because of the pleasing phraseology he used.

Moral Philosophy

We learn from his admiration of Socrates, Xenophon's strong moral values:

1. Self-control, moderation, restraint of appetite, balance
2. Importance of hard work for warding off temptation, good health, and building character
3. An ideal of service that means offering help, life advice, and moral guidance to friends and strangers
4. Practicality which brings the most benefit to the most people
5. Egalitarianism demonstrated by a wife's side-by-side work with her husband, a general eating with his men, a king working in his garden

Nate Kosirog, faculty
Nathaniel Whatmore, 2015

PLATO, 427–347 BC, *The Father of Philosophy*

> " And at first he would most easily discern the shadows and, after that, the likenesses or reflections in water of men and other things, and later, the things themselves, and from these he would go on to contemplate the appearances in the heavens and heaven itself.
> —*The Republic*

- Born to a wealthy, powerful family; as a young man aspired to be both a politician and a poet
- Sold into slavery and later freed

- Converted to philosophic life by Socrates, who became the chief protagonist in most of his public writings
- Owned a small garden in a public space called *Academia*; used this garden as a school of philosophy; Plato's "Academy" often considered the first formal educational institution in the West
- Established philosophy as a formal discipline and program of study; Aristotle was among his students
- Wrote his ideas indirectly through philosophical dialogues (at least 36), rather than treatises; taught his full theories at the Academy, but the lectures were private, for advanced students only
- His dialogues present questions and possible answers about a vast range of subjects, including metaphysics, logic, ethics, rhetoric, religion, art, education, political theory, love and friendship, and mathematics
- Does not appear as a character in his dialogues; the philosopher's role is filled by a man Plato describes in a letter as "a Socrates made beautiful and new"; hence, impossible to know which "Socratic" views are Plato's, which belong to the historical Socrates, and which are just thought-provoking hypotheses
- Also, intuitively sensed the existence of a monotheistic God, a natural moral law, and a spiritual after-life in the midst of the polytheistic Greek culture
- Stood aloof from Greek polytheism; saw a higher unifying principle, "the Good" or "the One"
- Used mythological language to describe the immortal soul's fate in the afterlife
- Described philosophy as "practicing for death," i.e., separating soul from body; but insisted (in *Phaedo*) that suicide is immoral and impious
- In *The Republic*, argued that philosophers (lovers of wisdom) are the only men who find no personal advantage in practical power; hence, the most just rulers would be "philosopher-kings"
- Attempted to train a young tyrant to become a "philosopher-king," but failed; accepted the unlikelihood of bringing theoretical ideals into practical reality, becoming political philosophy's first "conservative"
- Hypothesized that *learning is recollection*, i.e., *rediscovering* the ideas our souls knew before birth by observing imperfect representations of these ideas in everyday life; this, for example, is how we can "learn" the idea of a *circle*, although in the material world we have never seen a perfect circle
- Believed that the highest knowledge is not empirical (scientific), but that it comes (if it comes) from a rational "intuition" of unchanging Forms or Ideas (ergo: anti-David Hume, 1711 AD)
- Defined a hierarchy of reality in the Allegory of the Cave, in which the immaterial, intelligible world is the truest, like the world of sunlight outside the cave, while the material, sensible world is like dim shadows in the cave, barely knowable at all; everyday opinions (the cave) are subject to social influences and indoctrination, whereas the world of Ideas (sunlight) is eternal and unchanging
- Developed metaphysics; proposed the "Theory of Forms (or Ideas)," in which natural objects (e.g., a man) acquire their identity by "participating" in the higher reality of separate, immaterial Forms (e.g., Man)
- A kind of dualist, often contrasting body and soul as prison and prisoner; described philosophy as the soul's effort to escape from the body (i.e., from appetites and emotions which obscure reason)

> " Reason is, and ought only to be the servant of the passions.
>
> —David Hume 1711–1776, Scottish philosopher

> " Passions are, and ought only to be the servant of Reason. (paraphrased)
>
> —Plato 427–347 BC, Greek philosopher

This debate between reason and passion characterizes much of mankind's struggles.

Key Works

Euthyphro, 380 BC

Gorgias, 380 BC

Meno, 380 BC

Crito, 360 BC

Phaedo, 360 BC

The Republic, 360 BC

Timaeus, 360 BC

Biography

Plato is arguably the most famous mind in all of ancient philosophy. He is credited with "inventing" philosophy as a discipline; bringing together topics such as ethics, epistemology, and political theory; and giving them "a unitary treatment." He was born to parents Ariston and Perictione into one of the wealthiest and most politically active families in ancient Athens. From a young age, he engaged in athletics and the arts and became the most famous student of Socrates. Socrates was a remarkably influential figure in Plato's life; he formed the basis of Plato's philosophy and is the constant protagonist in his dialogues. Through works like *The Republic*, *The Apology*, and *The Euthyphro*, Plato introduced novel ideas in the areas of justice, love, equality, and religion. He is known also for founding the Academy, thought to be the first school in the West. Plato furthered the future of philosophy and thought, not only through his own works but also through those of his students, the greatest of whom was Aristotle.

Plato versus Socrates

Because Plato wrote dialogues with his teacher, Socrates, as the main character, it is frequently difficult to tell which ideas are Plato's and which ideas are from Socrates. There are debates about this topic, but most people think that in Plato's early work, he's probably recording what Socrates actually thought, while in his later work, we see more of Plato's views as different from Socrates.

Trial of Socrates

The trial of Socrates is the central, unifying event of the great Platonic dialogues. Because of this, Plato's *Apology* is perhaps the most often read among them. In the *Apology*, Socrates tries to defend himself against charges of disbelief in the gods and corruption of the young. Socrates insists that long-standing slander will be the real cause of his demise, and says the legal charges are essentially false. Socrates denies being wise and explains how the Oracle at Delphi launched his life as a philosopher. He says that his quest to resolve the riddle of the Oracle put him at odds with his fellow man, and that this is the reason he has been mistaken for a menace to the city-state of Athens.

In his defense to the Athenian jury, Socrates describes himself as a "gadfly": one who nips at the side of Athens—just as a fly would a horse—so as to waken it to its blunderings. However, while Socrates rejects the answers of all those around him, he rarely, if ever, provides any answers of his own. Socrates's "ignorance" is likely his most notable quality. He boldly declared that he was the wisest man because he knew that he knew nothing.

Allegory of the Cave

The "Allegory of the Cave" is probably the most popular illustration of Platonic philosophy. In *The Republic*, Socrates tells his companions that there is a strong divide between appearance and reality. The objects and world people perceive is not, in fact, the "really real." Rather, all aspects of reality are, in essence, captured in the realm of thought and reason, a realm of which most are unaware.

To capture this idea, Socrates asks his companions to imagine a cave, broken into three levels: a ground level occupied by chained prisoners, a roadway, and a final level containing a fire. The fire on the top level casts shadows on the wall in front of the prisoners as it strikes two-dimensional cutouts of objects like trees, girls, and houses. The prisoners on the floor are chained in such a way that they can only look forward at the wall in front of them, and they've been positioned this way their entire lives. As a result, they confuse the shadows for actual trees, girls, and houses, because they have not seen these figures in their true form. The shadows, for them, are reality.

Having set this scene, Socrates suggests that one of the prisoners breaks free from his chains wanders and out of the cave. Upon exiting the cave, the prisoner is blinded by the brilliance of the sun and is in pain. Once his eyes adjust to the new light, he is amazed by the textures, tones, colors, and overall beauty of the world around him. Enamored by this newfound reality, the former prisoner journeys back into the cave to tell the others about his discovery. When he describes the world and the light, however, the prisoners mock and shun him, as they refuse to believe in any reality beyond the shadows in front of them.

Theory of Forms

The idea that there is a distinction between shadows and reality leads us to Plato's Theory of Forms. This typically refers to the belief that the material world—the world of matter and energy—is not the real, primary world, but only a copy of it—an image or spirit. In some of Plato's dialogues this is expressed by Socrates, who spoke of forms in formulating a solution to the problem of universals. The forms, according to Socrates, are archetypes of the many types of things, and properties (characteristic, but non-essential qualities) we feel and see around us that can be perceived only by reason. In other words, Socrates was able to recognize *two worlds*: the apparent world (of matter and energy), which constantly changes, and an unchanging and unseen world of forms (ideas, rules, spiritual beings), which is the cause of what is apparent.

In the *Republic,* the highest form is identified as the Form of the Good, meaning truth, compassion, work and creativity. It is the source of all other forms, including spiritual beings, and could be known by reason. The source of all things, in virtue and meditation the soul has the power to elevate itself to attain union with the One. Platonism had a profound effect on Western thought, and the Christian Church, which understood Platonic forms as God's thoughts, adopted many Platonic notions.

Justice and the Good Life in The Republic

Plato is particularly famous for his ideas concerning justice and the good life. In *The Republic*, Socrates questions many common definitions of justice. In the opening of the dialogue, he speaks with an elderly gentleman who defines justice as keeping promises and returning what one owes. Socrates responds with an exception to this definition, arguing that it would be unjust for a man to return borrowed weapons to their owner if the owner is a madman. This initial definition and counter argument—what is referred to as the "dialectic" or "Socratic method"—begin a long debate over the true meaning of justice, in which several characters offer their thoughts.

In *The Republic*, Socrates provides a defense of the just life and its essential connection to happiness. According to Socrates, justice is a virtue. As such, it promotes the well-being of the soul, just as a good diet and exercise promote the well-being of the body. The soul flourishes when it forms community and unity, and "justice produces unanimity and friendship." Contrarily, "injustice produces factions, hatreds, and quarrels." Socrates provides an understanding of justice as the highest of virtues, which allows for the flourishing of one's soul. Consequently, he argues for the superiority of the just life through example. He provides a picture of the just soul by comparing it to a thriving city.

The Three Parts of the City

The thriving city, like the just soul, has three parts. In the city, society is broken down into three social groups: the producers, the auxiliaries, and the rulers. The producers are members of the working class and are concerned with the production and trading of material goods. The auxiliaries are warriors concerned with fighting, bravery, and honor. The rulers govern the whole of society and decide the best ways to address the needs of the city. When each part of this society performs its own function and avoids responsibilities outside its order, the city functions well. Also, the producing and auxiliary orders best perform their functions when they serve the needs of the rulers.

The three divisions of the ideal city correspond to Socrates's three divisions of the soul. He states that the soul is composed of an appetitive, a spirited, and a rational element. The appetitive element concerns the base desires for material pleasures (money, in particular). The spirited element is concerned with emotional and honor-driven pleasures. And the rational element is concerned with philosophical pleasures. According to Socrates, the individual thrives when the two lower elements— the appetitive and the spirited—perform their respective functions inasmuch as they serve the ultimate desire of the rational element.

Thus, like the ideal city, the just soul is governed by a just *philosopher king*. This is the source of Plato's famous quote, from *The Republic*:

> Unless … either philosophers become kings in our states or those whom we now call our kings and rulers take to the pursuit of philosophy seriously and adequately … there can be no cessation of troubles. … Nor, until this happens, will this constitution which we have been expounding in theory ever be put into practice within the limits of possibility and see the light of the sun.

In summary, Plato believes that "justice belongs to the highest class [of good]" because a just individual is a virtuous individual, and a virtuous individual is a truly happy individual. As stated, virtues are habits that fortify and heal the soul, and one achieves a virtuous and just life by participating in and contemplating the Forms. To Plato, as he illustrates in his Allegory of the Cave, most individuals live their lives mistaking shades of truth for whole truths in themselves. In order to live well, "we must break away from the confining assumption that the ordinary objects of pursuit—the pleasures, powers, honors, and material goods that we ordinarily compete for—are the only sort of goods there are." Rather than confuse these shades with reality, people must "transform [their] lives by recognizing a radically different kind of good—the Forms—and we must try to incorporate these objects into our lives by understanding, loving, and imitating them, for they are incomparably superior to any other kind of good we can have."

Cloie Dobias, 2015
Jackson Howell, 2015
David Eschrich, researcher
Daren Jonescu, advisor

DEMOSTHENES ◊ 384–322 BC, *Statesman and Orator*

> Inter omnis unus excellat. (He stands alone among all the orators.)
>
> —Cicero

- Had his life recorded in Plutarch's *Parallel Lives*
- Received a large inheritance at age 7 upon his father's death; his guardians took it
- Learned effective speaking strategies while fighting (successfully) to regain his inheritance in court
- Was hired as a logographer (speech writer) due to his skill
- Made his first political speech to apprise the Athenians of the Persian threat, suggesting that Athens remain independent and proposing tax revisions to raise money for ships
- Aroused rancor toward his opponents in his speeches
- Made influential orations condemning Philip II of Macedon, the dominant ruler of the period; the term "philippic," meaning a fiery speech denouncing someone, derives from these orations
- Became controller of the navy
- Accused Philip and his son, Alexander the Great, of treachery carried out with the help of their agent, Aeschines—Demosthenes' lifelong rival
- Was convicted of bribery, resulting in exile; was rescued a year later by the Athenians
- Committed suicide when Alexander's successor sent men to kill him to end his public influence

Key Works

On the Navy Boards, 354 BC
On the Crown, 354 BC
The Phillippics, 351 BC, 344 BC, 341 BC
Olynthiacs, 349 BC
On the Peace, 346 BC

Biography

Demosthenes was born the son of a wealthy sword maker who left him an inheritance when he died. He was motivated by the greed of his guardians, who took most of what was due to Demosthenes. So when he didn't have the means to participate in the traditional gymnastic education, Demosthenes began to work on his oratory skills, with the goal of suing his transgressors. In *Parallel Lives* Plutarch wrote about Demosthenes's rigors to study rhetoric and delivery to overcome a speech defect.

Although his efforts to regain his inheritance weren't very successful, he became skilled in rhetoric, which inspired wealthy men to hire him as logographer (speech writer). He worked for his clients at the same time he was involved in a struggle with Philip of Macedon. His first speech before the Assembly moved the Athenians to fortify their navy as a show of readiness to the Persians, who posed a threat. He encouraged Athens to allow the Persians to attack first so that allies would join them. The theme for Athens of protecting freedom by staying independent, while maintaining a willingness for alliances when in danger, resounded with the adult male citizens of the Assembly.

This began a focus on Athenian foreign policy for Demosthenes. He soon became the leader of a political party, which mistrusted other Greek city-states. The Athenian Assembly, sometimes numbering 6000, allowed Demosthenes the floor even though they had been known to shout down or laugh away an orator they didn't like. He was a tough personality with a biting tongue, unafraid to call down his opponent in an effort to persuade the audience to think critically. A methodical student of history, Demosthenes asked the Athenians to think about their history, and used parallels from the past to drive his point home. He reminded them to remember their love of democracy and hate for tyrants.

While Athenians worried about a threat from the East, Philip from the north in Macedonia was grabbing southern Greek cities. As Philip continued aggressively south, the Athenians tried to close off the pass at Thermopylae. Philip changed the direction to avoid conflict, and the Athenians weren't sure of Philip's intentions. Demosthenes presented the "First Philippic," which was the beginning of a 29-year opposition to Macedonia's imperialism. He called upon the Athenians to take charge of their own destiny and defy Philip. Yet the speech failed to do the trick and Philip continued on to Olynthus. Demosthenes reinforced his position with three speeches (the *Olynthiacs*), but failed to rally Athens to strengthen their position. At last Philip and the Athenians came to an agreement, the Peace of Philocrates. Demosthenes didn't like the terms, but he encouraged the signing nonetheless. Philip and Demosthenes were at odds for years, as Demosthenes challenged Philip's honor and Philip continued to incite the city-states against one another. Demosthenes, as a result of his "Third Philippic," was made controller of the navy, a position through which he could bring about the naval reforms he had advocated and bring together an alliance against Philip. In the ensuing war, Athens was dominant at sea, but Philip ruled on land. At last Philip defeated the allies at Chaeronea.

Philip was assassinated in 336, bringing to the throne his son Alexander. The Greeks hoped for peace, but Alexander destroyed Thebes after a rebellion, and proved to be a formidable leader. Alexander left Athens alone as he started his campaign in Asia.

In a continuing debate with his foe Aeschines, an orator who had been at odds throughout the conflict with Philip, Demosthenes debated publically his opinion of Aeschines's behavior over the last 20 years. He called Aeschines "an agent of the Macedonians," using historical detail to persuade the jury to convict and exile Aeschines.

Demosthenes endured a similar fate. He was accused of stealing, then fined and imprisoned, after which he escaped and fled. When Alexander died the following year, the Athenians repatriated him. But as Alexander's successor came near, the orator had to flee again. When the Athenians decided again to sentence Demosthenes, he killed himself with poison. Some historians believe that the vagaries of Athenian loyalty reveal the decline of Athenian democracy. The *Alexandrian Canon* by Aristophanes and Aristarchus praised Demosthenes for his oratory skill. Longinus described him as "a blazing thunderbolt."

Nate Kosirog, faculty
Nathaniel Whatmore, 2015
Daren Jonescu, advisor

ARISTOTLE, 384–322 BC, *The Philosopher*

> " It is the mark of an educated mind to be able to entertain a thought without accepting it.
> —*Nicomachean Ethics*

> " Anyone can get angry, or give and spend money—these are easy, but doing them in relation to the right person, in the right amount, at the right time, with the right aim in view, and in the right way, that is not something anyone can do, and it is not easy.
> —*Nicomachean Ethics*

- Hailed from Stagira, but lived most of his adult life in Athens as a non-citizen
- Studied and taught at Plato's Academy for many years
- Established his own school in Athens, the Lyceum; tutored Alexander, the son of Philip II of Macedon (later Alexander the Great)
- Was a polymath: wrote world-changing works in physics, metaphysics, psychology, music, rhetoric, politics, government, ethics; wrote the *first* major works in literary criticism, biology, zoology, logic, linguistics
- Produced diverse writings: dialogues, facts gathered scientifically, and systematic accounts of original ideas
- Was treated by medieval Christian and Muslim thinkers as the chief pre-Christian authority on issues of cosmology, ethics, and science for centuries; called simply The Philosopher by Catholic thinkers, even today
- Defended a geocentric cosmology that was not disproven until Galileo, in 1615 AD
- Criticized many of Plato's theories, including the "Theory of Forms," believing that forms (ideas) reside in individual substances, not in a separate intelligible world; famously wrote about his criticisms of Plato's Academy, "We must love our friends, but we must love truth more"
- Systematized the principles of logical thinking, analyzing the structure and rules of the syllogism (e.g., "All men are mortal. Socrates is a man. Therefore Socrates is mortal.")
- Was the first major thinker of the West to attempt to categorize and relate all the separate sciences of the day
- Defined four kinds of causes in all things: *material* (e.g., flesh and bones), *formal* (the idea "man"), *efficient* or "moving cause" (parents who bring the human into being), and *final* (goal or purpose, "manness")

- Argued that the cosmos is moved by a hierarchy of unmoved movers: eternal, immaterial, thinking beings which cause the motions of the cosmos as objects of thought and desire (i.e., final causes)
- Asserted that the first unmoved mover (Prime Mover) is the ultimate object of thought and desire; is implied as the final answer, beyond the limits of scientific thinking, in Aristotle's physics; stands on the edge of his psychological theory, as the divine mind illuminating human thought (God as the "light" of the intellect)
- Divided being into ten categories, sorting words and reality into ways of existing, including substance (e.g., "man"), quality (e.g., "brown"), quantity (e.g., "many"), relation (e.g., "on the left"), etc.
- Explained ethics as the study of *eudaimonia*, "happiness," meaning a virtuous life: *moral virtue* is the habit of choosing "the golden mean" between excessive and deficient emotional responses, as courage is a mean between rashness and cowardice; *intellectual virtue* encompasses mature practical and theoretical reasoning
- Made friendship central to his ethics, and analyzed it into three types from lowest to highest: friendships of *utility, amusement,* and *virtue* (good character); true friends are "one soul in two bodies" who think together
- Perhaps failed to grasp the highest form of friendship, military bonding, Semper Fidelis

Key Works

Metaphysics, 350 BC
Nicomachean Ethics, 350 BC
On Poetics, 350 BC
On the Soul, 350 BC
Organon, 350 BC
Physics, 350 BC
Politics, 350 BC
Rhetoric, 350 BC

Biography

Aristotle expanded Hellenistic thought, building upon the work of Plato on a variety of writings on logic, purpose in nature, division of the soul, natural categories of masters and slaves, and ethics. At 17 he began his course of study at Plato's Academy, where he studied logic and metaphysics. He expressed his theories in dozens of books, though only his lecture notes remain to us.

In 343 BC, King Philip of Macedon asked him to come to Pellas, the capital city, to tutor his son, Alexander, who would become Alexander the Great. Aristotle stayed in Macedon for two years and eventually returned to Athens in 335 BC. He then created the school, *Lyceum* or *Peripatetics*, where he perpetuated his system of thought. In 323 BC, he left Athens because of anti-Macedonian rebellion and, as he said, he didn't want Athens to make the same mistake of killing philosophers twice. He went to the island of Chalcis where he died only one year later. Aristotle revolutionized intellectual inquiry, and his works drastically impacted medieval theology as well as modern mathematics. He bridged the gap between philosophy, the arts, and science.

Aristotelian Logic

Logic is the systematic study of arguments. Though Aristotle was not the first person to *use* logic, he was the first to formalize it into an official discipline. One of his most famous innovations was the syllogism, a deductively valid argument in which if the premises are true, the conclusion *must* be true. The most basic syllogisms consist of two premises that lead to a conclusion. This is one of the most famous:

" All men are mortal.
Socrates is a man.
Therefore, Socrates is mortal.

The first two statements are premises, or propositions, which guarantee the conclusion, "Socrates is mortal," by virtue of being true.

Not One Cause, but Four

The concept of a substance is central to Aristotle's view of what is ultimately real. A substance is any individual thing. It's a combination of matter and form, whether a bronze statue, a fork, a penguin, or a king. The substance is what remains constant through change of characteristics or form. When a green leaf turns red in the fall, the substance that is the leaf has lost the characteristic of being green but gained the characteristic of being red.

Why do things (substances) change? Aristotle thought there were four different types of explanations for change, and these are called Aristotle's "four causes." These are the material cause (the matter the makes up something), the formal cause (such as the shape of a chair), the efficient cause (what triggers the process) and the final cause (the purpose for something).

Type of Cause	Definition	Example
Material Cause	What something is made of	Yarn
Formal Cause	The arrangement, shape, or form of something	A sweater's shape
Efficient Cause	"The source of the change"—what starts the process	The person who makes the sweater
Final Cause	Why something is made or the purpose of its existence	To wear

Happiness, the Golden Mean, and Friendship

Aristotle's premier work on morality, *The Nicomachean Ethics*, begins by discussing the purpose of human beings. Considering the ultimate reason behind every individual's actions, Aristotle concluded that the "end," or purpose, of humanity is to be happy. Aristotle's term for happiness, *eudaimonia*, translates as *human flourishing*. Unlike all other ends "which we choose for something else," happiness serves no ulterior purpose. It is the final goal of every human action, and it must be chosen for its own sake. Happiness is an "activity." It is the product of a virtuous life, and virtues are excellences, or states of being that are worthy of praise. Thus, for Aristotle, happiness is being an excellent human.

Aristotle lists many examples of virtues. Each of these excellences—courage, justice, self-control, or any other—is the middle point between two extremes of behavioral deficiencies and excesses. For example, the virtue of courage stands as the middle point between being shamefully fearful and senselessly bold. Aristotle called this middle point the golden mean. Aristotle's person of virtue, who has become virtuous by doing the proper actions over and over until they become like "second nature," enjoys being virtuous and finds it both easy and pleasant.

Vice (defect)	Virtue (mean)	Vice (excess)
cowardice	courage	rashness
sloth	ambition	greed
stinginess	liberality	extravagance
drunkenness	self-control	abstemiousness

Aristotle thinks that the moral life is closely related to friendship, and therefore in his writings on happiness and virtue Aristotle discusses different types of friendship. He argues that everyone both desires and needs friends, and he thinks there are three main reasons why we're attracted to different types: friendships of usefulness, friendships of pleasure, and friendships of goodness or virtue. According to Aristotle, most people have friendships of utility and pleasure. A friendship of utility is one in which one individual uses another to achieve his needs. For example, Tom has a friendship of utility with Jerry since he associates with Jerry only in order to utilize his membership with an exclusive club. A friendship of pleasure is one shared by one or more individual(s) who enjoy one another's company. In a friendship of pleasure, one may find some degree of happiness, but she does not form close bonds with the individual(s) with whom she shares this kind of friendship. By contrast, one who engages in a virtuous friendship, or a friendship of the good, enters into a relationship of mutual respect and admiration, wherein each member desires the good of the other, as she desires good for herself.

Politics

To Aristotle, a consideration of ethics leads directly to politics. Since the aim of each human being is happiness, the aim of the ideal state, or political organization, is creating a social environment that best fosters happiness. In his *Politics*, Aristotle considers various forms of *polis*, or state, distinguishing states based upon their number of rulers and their effectiveness (in regard to promoting happiness). He discusses states that have one ruler, states that have few rulers, and states that have many rulers. Depending upon the success of each, Aristotle derives two categories of state. If a state adequately promotes human flourishing, he labels it "correct." If not, he labels it "deviant."

	Correct	Deviant
One Ruler	Kingship	Tyranny
Few Rulers	Aristocracy	Oligarchy
Many Rulers	Constitutional Republic or Polity	Democracy

Regarding the three correct states, Aristotle determined the best option according to the degree of "distributive justice" offered by each. The happiest people live in a state that dispenses justice well, and a proper dispensation of justice entails treating people fairly. Of course, each form of government operates on a unique understanding of fairness with regard to human equality. While the oligarchy prizes the worth of the rich over the poor, a democracy values everyone equally, regardless of merit. Consequently, the democrats believe that justice yields equal distribution to all, whereas the aristocrat will take for granted that the best citizens are entitled to more than the worst. Aristotle concludes that a constitutional republic, or what he calls a "polity," is usually the best form, since it blends oligarchy and democracy, and results in more long-term stability.

The best political state seeks human flourishing as its ultimate aim and employs liberty only insofar as it achieves this aim. This is not human flourishing for all, though. Aristotle famously thought the categories of master and slave were natural categories; some people are slaves because they were captured in war, but others are naturally born slaves.

Cloie Dobias, 2015
Jackson Howell, 2015
David Eschrich, researcher
Nate Kosirog, faculty
Daren Jonescu, advisor

ALEXANDER THE GREAT ◊ 356–323 BC, *A Military Genius*

" In the end, when it's over, all that matters is what you've done.

- Was tutored until age 16 by Aristotle
- Became King of Macedon at age 20 upon his father's assassination
- Inherited a mighty kingdom and army and the generalship of Greece
- United the Greek city-states and led the Corinthian League
- Committed to carry out his father's Panhellenic project to capture Persia
- Defeated Persian King Darius III after 10 years of aggressive campaigns
- Gained control of an empire stretching from the Adriatic Sea to the Indus River
- Desired control of the land all the way to "The Great Outer Sea"
- Made plans to conquer Arabia
- Turned back because of his troops' demands in a battle for India in 326 BC
- Died in Babylon in 323 BC with the reputation of being one of the greatest commanders throughout history

Biography

Alexander (from the Greek "defend" and "man," meaning "protector of men") III of Macedon, commonly known as Alexander the Great, was born in Pella, Macedonia in 356 BC as part of the Argead dynasty of Philip II of Macedon. Aristotle was his tutor. As a teen Alexander became a soldier and helped his father unite the Greek states into the Corinthian League. Philip was in control of a strong kingdom and army when he was assassinated. Alexander reacted to his father's death by working hard to take over the army and gain the support as leader of the Corinthian League and then the Greek city-sates. In the tradition of his father's ambitious expansion plan, the Panhellenic Project, and with his new role as general of Greece, Alexander spent the next 10 years seeking and conquering Persia, which resulted in the death of King Darius III and control over the Achaemenid Empire. Next he went after Egypt and created the city of Alexandria for a commercial center. Then he conquered eastern Iran and began an attack in northern India. The audacious military strikes took his troops to Asia and northeast Africa. Alexander was never defeated in battle, which not only grew his empire to something never seen before—from Greece to Egypt and India, but also earned him the reputation of a remarkable military leader. Alexander didn't stop and continued to go to the "ends of the world and the Great Outer Sea," by way of an attack on all of India. His troops forced him to go back, though. He died of malaria just three years later, unable to finish his plan to make Babylon his capital city and to invade Arabia.

The young king's military campaigns lead to three significant developments: the destruction of the Persian Empire, its replacement by Alexander's own empire, and the spread of Greek culture, language, and ideas—a new Hellenistic Age—throughout the affected regions. The influence of traditions and language brought by Greek colonists endured through the Byzantine Empire of 1600 and generations to come, becoming more than just "Greek," and marking the proper birth of Western culture.

Alexander is also an example of the Greek hero in the tradition of the legendary Achilles. He has become the standard for military leadership and tactical wisdom.

THE CONQUESTS OF ALEXANDER THE GREAT, 335–328 BC

Notable Battle

The Battle of Gaugamela, 331 BC

Also called the Battle of Arbela, this was the decisive battle of Alexander the Great's invasion of the Persian Achaemenid Empire. Alexander's army of the Hellenic League met the Persian army of Darius III near Gaugamela, close to the modern city of Erbil (Iraqi Kurdistan). Despite being heavily outnumbered, Alexander emerged victorious due to his superior tactics and army. It was a decisive victory for the Hellenic League and led to the fall of the Achaemenid Empire.

THE HELLENIC PERIOD, 323–31 BC

The Hellenistic period was a time of great change to Greece. After Alexander the Great's death, Greek influence spread with the divided kingdom. A united Greece ended as Alexander's four generals divided the empire, providing the impetus for migration and, as a result, culture building. Cassander, Ptolemy, Antigonus, and Selecus were the *Diadochi*, rival generals fighting over succession. Ptolemy founded the Ptolemaic Dynasty in Egypt; Selecus reigned over the Seleucid Empire of Mesopotamia, Anatolia, and some of India. The citizens intermarried, too, as they founded new cities, often drawing inspiration and resources from many parts of Greece, including the new colonies. Kingdoms with a more centralized power replaced the old city-states. Growing culture meant improvements:

architecture, selfless donations to benefit the majority, more celebrations, and creation of libraries. The fruits of literature, theatre, architecture, science, exploration, and philosophy flourished. Aristotle (father of modern sciences), Epicure (the moralist), Menander (playwright of comedy), Euclid, Archimedes, and Polybius contributed to the remarkable progress of the Hellenistic period. The combination of varying language gave rise to a common language, Koine Greek, which came to be used throughout the Hellenistic world. This time of prosperity ended with the Roman conquest in the Battle of Actium in 31 BC.

EPICURUS, 341–271 BC, *Ancient Greek Hedonist and Materialist*

" Is God willing to prevent evil, but not able? Then he is not omnipotent.
Is he able, but not willing? Then he is malevolent.
Is he both able and willing? Then, whence cometh evil?
Is he neither able nor willing? Then why call him God?"

—The Epicurean Paradox

- Developed Epicureanism, one of two major philosophical schools (along with Stoicism) of the Hellenistic period
- Taught in "The Garden," at his home on the outskirts of Athens, where his students, including women (like Plato's Academy, but not common in ancient Greece), met and practiced philosophy
- Had nearly all his writings destroyed by Christian authorities, who thought them ungodly
- His philosophy focused on two related positions: atomism and hedonism
- Believed the world is made of "atoms" (Greek for "indivisible") that collide and stick to one another in various forms to produce our sensory world (materialism)
- Believed all knowledge is rooted in the evidence of our senses, against Platonic idealism
- Hedonism: happiness equals pleasure; therefore, the highest pursuit of man should be his own pleasure
- Epicurus's hedonism does *not* mean undisciplined "pleasure-seeking"; defines pleasure as the absence of pain, so pleasures that lead to pain (physical or emotional) are inconsistent with the goal of reducing pain
- Believed feelings of serenity and tranquility give the most pleasure with the least pain; hence, an extremely moderate life is happiest—basic shelter, clothing, and food are sufficient for happiness
- Believed that gods exist, but are unconcerned with, and therefore irrelevant to, human life and purposes
- Defined justice as an agreement of mutual non-harm (to cause and receive no pain)

Theodicy in a Nutshell

The vindication of divine goodness and providence in view of the existence of evil.

Consider the Epicurean Paradox, quoted just prior. By logical extension, how can a good God allow anything negative at all, even a child's minor injury?

What is good or bad or *evil?*

- Good is that which is positive or life-enhancing, in the long-term.
- Bad is that which is negative or life-destroying. And,
- *Evil* is that which is negative or life-destroying due to **intent or free will**, human or Satanic.

No **ill-intention**, no free will, **no Evil.**

- Weeds and earthquakes and cancer are *bad but not evil.*
- Murder and rape and child abuse are both *bad and evil.*
- Pulling an impacted wisdom tooth is good because in the long-term it is positive and life-enhancing.

The key to answering the Epicurean Paradox lies in these simple definitions of good, bad and evil with particular focus on the word **_ill-intent_**. Only humans and Satan (with their free will and selfish nature) are capable of evil. And, God does *not interfere* with free will.

Earthquakes and cancer and natural disasters are the result of the nature that God also created for good. Techtronic plates create earthquakes, which create mountains, which create weather …

> … in all things God works for the good of those who love him…
>
> Romans 8:27

It is instructive to observe that the amount of our suffering is directly proportional to the amount of love involved. That is: no love, no suffering; great love, great suffering.

Love is the yeast, the catalyst, the magnifying glass of pain and suffering.

Epicurus was clever, but wrong.

> Woe to those who call evil good and good evil…
>
> Isaiah 5:20

Key Works

Letter to Herodotus, c. 305 BC
Letter to Pythocles, c. 305 BC
Letter to Menoeceus, c. 300 BC
Principal Doctrines, c. 300 BC
Vatican Sayings, c. 300 BC

Biography

Epicurus, born in 341 BC, grew up in the Athenian colony of Samos on an island in the Mediterranean Sea with his mother, Chairestrate; his father, Neocles; and his three brothers. He studied Plato but rejected his theories and followed the philosophies of the materialist Democritus. He moved to Athens in 306 BC, where he founded his Garden—the place where he taught and practiced the Epicurean philosophy with his close friends until his death from kidney stones in the year 271 or 270 BC.

However, his philosophy did not die out with him. Epicureanism continued to be a central philosophical movement during the Hellenistic period until the rise of Christianity.

Physical Theory

Through sensation and experience, Epicurus sought to gain knowledge. Nevertheless, he based many of his conclusions about the scientific and mathematical world on the research of ancient atomists; of these, Democritus became his favorite. He also believed that motion at the atomic level obeyed different laws than motion at the level of the everyday objects we can see with our eyes, even though the everyday objects are made up of the infinitely small, atomic particles. In a letter to his colleague, Herodotus, Epicurus defines these particles—modernly referred to as atoms—as the most minuscule structure of all matter, "vary[ing] indefinitely in their shapes," in "continual motion through all eternity," and supplying energy to the universe at all times. By examining the world around him, Epicurus determined that every existing atom comes from another existing atom: objects cannot be created out of nothing. He claimed that since he was able to study the world through his senses, they were all he needed to study the universe. "We must by all means stick to our sensations," he argued, because these sensations constituted a reliable way for him to learn. Epicurus's primary belief was that in an infinite universe the most important thing to do was appreciate the mystery and pleasure of being alive, forgetting the fear of an inevitable death and allowing pleasure to bring peace. Only by learning to "trust the evidence that [nature] provides" while acknowledging our insignificance in the universe will any human be able to truly appreciate the gift it is to find happiness.

Pleasure and Pain

Epicurus's conception of the physical theory of atoms and void aids his explanation of the soul, which he viewed as wholly material. Soul atoms scatter amongst the body atoms, giving sensations of pleasure and pain. These sensations of the soul are habitual and often times irrational. Using this materialist conception of the soul, Epicurus hoped to eliminate what he considered an irrational fear of punishment in the afterlife, which causes anxiety and in turn "extreme and irrational desires." He explains, "when we are, death is not come, and, when death is come, we are not. It is nothing, then, either to the living or to the dead, for with the living it is not and the dead exist no longer." Thus, the fear of death is empty. For neither the body nor the soul may exist without the other. A body without a soul becomes inanimate; a soul without a body becomes insensible. By eradicating anxiety, people could be free to pursue natural pleasures, rather than get lost in the perverse irrational pleasures prompted by fear.

According to Epicurus, there are two types of pleasure: the moving pleasure and the static pleasure. Additionally, there are three types of desires: the natural and the necessary (food), the natural and the unnecessary (a certain type of food), and the unnatural and the unnecessary (power). To this hierarchy of pleasures, Epicurus adds a subordination of the fleeting and the supremacy of the lasting.

In Epicureanism, the lessening of pain is more desirable than heightening of pleasure; that is, a painless life is more desirable than a life of immense pleasure and pain. For Epicurus, pleasure is "the absence of pain in the body and of trouble in the soul." Pain often obscures one's ability to feel pleasure. Physical pleasure and pain come directly from the present, but mental pleasure and pain come from the past, present, and future. The greatest pains often come from anxiety and fear of the future, especially that of death. Therefore, Epicurus propounds rational desire as the means of pursuing pleasure because irrational desire leads to fear and pain or to the pursuit of some immediate pleasure, which only leads to more pain later. This kind of hedonism suggests that a fulfilling life comes from the static pleasure of the natural and the necessary: "those that look to happiness, physical well-being, or life itself."

Social Theory

Although the main witness for Epicurus's views on the evolution of human society is Lucretius's poem, his concepts regarding the interactions between humans are primitive and simple. His theory suggests that humans began with no intellectual or social advantage over any other being on the earth, that they only survived because they were physically hardier than their modern descendants. However, humans quickly started realizing the natural wonders of the world around them that them apart from any other species: the discovery of fire, the ability to come together for protection, and the utilization of natural resources. During this time emphasis on family developed, as well as a greater sentiment and appreciation for relationships. With these advancements, a way to communicate became necessary for survival—the invention of language allowed people to establish friendships and alliances, which granted more security. Since sharing was essential for survival, they naturally did not withhold any items from others in their community. However, an inevitable accumulation of wealth created a struggle over these goods: the people with the most wealth became the most powerful because they had what everyone else needed. By manipulating this power, they eventually became leaders and even kings. While people tried to overthrow the rich tyrants, the period of violent anarchy that followed brought society to the conclusion that it was wiser to live under the rule of law. Though submission to the law brought fear of punishment, it was here that justice was born. When facing the argument that humans didn't need justice to bring them happiness, Epicurus responded that it is still virtuous to live justly because the anxiety that comes with the possibility of being discovered will "diminish happiness and tranquility," two things that he referred to as the ultimate goals in life. This ties into Epicurus's most fundamental philosophy that the greatest pleasure is "to be free of pain" and that the "removal of … pain is the limit of the magnitude of pleasure." Epicurus encouraged people to return to their roots of seeking pleasure only in natural desires; the best way to achieve this should be through living wisely and honorably in every aspect of a simple life.

On Friendship

Epicurus states thus in *Vatican Sayings*: "Friendship goes dancing round the world, announcing to all of us to wake up to happiness." He founded The Garden with the intention of not only teaching his philosophies but also practicing them with his friends. Located on the outskirts of Athens, The Garden secluded the Epicureans and gave them a place of tranquility and simplicity to live hedonistically. Based on his social theory, humanity began as asocial, but eventually the "capacity for friendship arose out of need, [and] once the capacity for such feelings was acquired, feeling them came to be valued in itself." He highly valued friendship because of its instrumental value for creating pleasure—the purpose for all mankind. Epicurus "understood the task of philosophy first and foremost as a form of therapy for life, since philosophy that does not heal the soul is no better than medicine that cannot cure the body." Though it may seem egotistical to promote friendship for the sake of one's own pleasure, "Epicurus held that a wise man would feel the torture of a friend no less than his own, and would die for a friend rather than betray him, for otherwise his own life would be confounded."

Briauna Schultz, 2013
Daren Jonescu, advisor

EUCLID OF ALEXANDRIA, 325–265 BC, *Father of Geometry*

" The laws of nature are but the mathematical thoughts of God.

- Wrote five axioms and five postulates of mathematics and geometry
- Studied mathematics at the Platonic Academy in Athens, Greece
- Associated with Plato's friends, Eudoxus of Cnidus and Theaetetus
- Wrote *Elements*, a geometry textbook that survives to this day
- Responded, "There is no royal road to geometry," when asked by Ptolemy if there was an easier way to do geometry
- Proved 465 propositions, starting from his small set of axioms and postulates
- Created the basis of all Euclidean geometry with his proofs
- Included diagrams and instructions for his students to easily understand the subject

Key Works

Data, c. 300 BC
Division of Figures, c. 300 BC
Elements, c. 300 BC
Optics, c. 300 BC
Phaenomena, c. 300 BC

Biography

All that is known about this Greek mathematician and philosopher is found in the commentaries of Proclus from the fifth century AD. According to these records, Euclid taught in Alexandria, Egypt, under the rule of Ptolemy I Soter. He studied mathematics at the Platonic academy in Athens, and then moved to Alexandria during the rise of its great library. While there, Euclid wrote several mathematical works, including his most famous work, *Elements*, which created the foundation of Euclidean geometry. He defined geometry for 2,000 years to come, and his insistence on proofs being founded on logic and reason has influenced mathematics for millennia.

Elements

Euclid's crowning achievement was the writing of *Elements*, still the most popular mathematics textbook of all time. In its 13 volumes, he proved 465 propositions from a starting point of 23 terms, five axioms, and five postulates. These terms are basic definitions of a point, a line, and other fundamentals needed to work with math at any level. The axioms are common-sense notions that, while obvious, were so crucial to all of mathematics that they had to be listed. The postulates, finally, are the basic concepts for geometry. He included clear and accurate proofs of his propositions, all of which survive to this day and are used in all geometry classes. His first six books comprised the rules and techniques of plane geometry, while the next four presented his ideas on number theory, and the final three discussed three-dimensional geometry. All of them included easy instructions for students, such as how to construct a line through a perpendicular plane, and many presented new theorems, such as Book X's 115 propositions on irrational numbers.

Jack Beebe, 2012
Jeff Culver, faculty

ARCHIMEDES, 287–212 BC, *Father of Modern Physics and Calculus*

> " Eureka! Eureka!
> —Upon making his most famous discovery regarding volume

- Developed the Archimedes principle for measuring volume
- Designed many war machines to help the city of Syracuse, at the time under siege by Romans
- Made revolutionary advances in physics, hydrostatics, static mechanics, and pycnometry (density measurement)
- Is considered the "Father of Calculus" and the "Father of Mathematical Physics"
- Wrote about plane equilibriums, the parabola, the sphere and cylinder, spirals, conoids, spheroids, floating bodies, measurement of a circle, pi, and the method of mechanical problems in *The Archimedes Palimpsest*
- Defined the laws of levers

Key Work

The Archimedes Palimpsest, c. 250 BC

Biography

Archimedes was born around 287 BC in Syracuse, Sicily, but he studied in Alexandria, Egypt. According to historians, he designed one of his most significant inventions there, known simply as Archimedes' screw, a mechanical device for raising water from the Nile River into canals for irrigation. After finishing his studies in Alexandria, he returned to Syracuse to continue his work in science and mathematics. Around 214 BC Romans attacked Syracuse and laid siege to it for more than two years. During this time, Archimedes invented war machines and weapons that helped to defend the city. Unfortunately for Archimedes, his own inventions did not protect him, as he was killed by Roman soldiers in 212 BC while working on a mathematical problem in the sand.

Father of Physics

Archimedes, the greatest intellect of antiquity, is modern to the core and a man who transcended his own time—many of his ideas and principles are still in use today. Some people regard him as the "Father of Modern Physics," a title he earned by being among the first to do mathematically reliable work. Archimedes's pulley system led to many innovations; he moved heavy objects with levers, and he used the mechanical advantage of the screw to move water and other heavy objects. In his groundbreaking work with levers, Archimedes is reported to have said, "Give me a place to stand and I will move the earth."

The Archimedes principle is taught in many physics courses today. According to legend, Archimedes had been challenged by the idea of finding the volume of an irregular object, like the measurement of a solid gold crown. One day he observed how the water level rose when he entered his bath. He reasoned that since water is incompressible, a body immersed in water would displace its volume in water. It is said that Archimedes was so excited upon his discovery, he ran from his bath, naked, into the streets exclaiming "Eureka!" With this pivotal discovery he was able to measure the volume of the king's crown and could therefore judge if it were of pure gold. Many applications derive from the Archimedes principle: floating boats, diving submarines, rising hot air balloons, and sinking hydrometers all owe a debt to Archimedes.

Father of Calculus

Archimedes is often given the title the "Father of Calculus," and is thought to be one of the greatest mathematicians that ever lived. His approach to the problem of calculating the area under an irregular curve was to divide the area into many rectangles to fill the original area, then add up the area of the rectangles while making more and more of them smaller and smaller. This approach is still introduced to all beginning calculus students and is the starting point for Newtonian Calculus. Archimedes is also credited with the computation of pi: "the value that represents the ratio of the circumference of a circle to its diameter," which is certainly one of the most important ratios in science and math.

Inventions

Archimedes was recognized in his own time for his unique and useful inventions. He invented the compound pulley, the lever, the iron claw, and burning mirrors. The compound pulley, a mechanical device with a series of wheels and rope used to transmit force from one object to another, was a momentous innovation in the movement of large objects. One of his wartime inventions, the iron claw, had a talon that attached to the underbelly of an enemy ship, tugged it upwards, and either caused it to sink entirely or land on its side. Another wartime invention of Archimedes was the idea of "burning mirrors." He discovered that it was possible in maritime warfare to strategically position large mirrors on ships in such a way that the sun's rays could be reflected and focused onto enemy ships, causing them to catch fire. His two wartime inventions greatly aided the Syracusans during their skirmish with the Romans.

Brady Weisner, 2016

Chapter 2
The Romans

*I found Rome a city of bricks
and left it a city of marble.*

—Augustus

ARCHAEOLOGICAL EVIDENCE shows a human occupation of the Rome area from at least 5000 BC, but the dense layer of much younger debris obscures Paleolithic and Neolithic sites. Evidence of stone tools, pottery, and stone weapons attest to at least 6,000 years of human presence. The power of the well-known tale of Rome's legendary foundation tends also to deflect attention from its actual, and much more ancient, origins.

Legend of Rome

Rome's mythological origin story begins the political power struggles that ensued much later. Romulus, the first ruler of the city, and his twin, Remus, were sons of the God Mars and raised by a she-wolf. The two brothers argued until Romulus killed Remus, after which the survivor named the city after himself and invited citizens of all classes to make up Rome's population. All slaves and freemen came and were provided with wives, women abducted from nearby settlements in what came to be known as the Rape of the Sabine Women. Romulus fought a war against the Sabines, but made their king equal in his power. Then he named 100 noble men to advise him as part of the new Roman senate. Six more kings followed from 750–550 BC, to rule the many colonies in southern Italy, (Cumae, Napels, Reggio Calabria, Crotone, Sybaris and Taranto) along with a portion of Sicily.

ANCIENT ROME 753–31 BC, ROMULUS TO AUGUSTUS

753 BC	Mythical Romulus and Remus founded Rome
509 BC	Creation of the Roman Republic
390 BC	The Gauls sack Rome
356–323 BC	Alexander the Great conquers the East
264–146 BC	The Punic Wars (Rome versus Carthage)
247–181 BC	Hannibal, Great General from Carthage
146 BC	Rome conquers Greece and Carthage
146–44 BC	Social and Civil Wars
44 BC	Julius Caesar assassinated
44–31 BC	Power struggle between Marc Antony and Octavian (Augustus)

Roman Republic

Rome became a republic in 509 BC. Their power came from their conquests and from their labor force. Before its transformation Rome, like many ancient powers, was a dictatorship. The Republic used a complex unwritten constitution to guide their government. Its purpose was to impose checks and balances on the various groups that held power in Rome. Due to the constant struggle and alterations of power, the constitution was amendable, and the Romans took advantage of this and improved it often. During the Republic, the Senate—a group of mostly wealthy men who discussed the important topics of the day—had the most power. Although city magistrates were not required to follow the Senate's decisions, they rarely ignored them. The Senate also did not have strict control of the military, but through their advice to magistrates they could control large portions of it. Throughout the time of the Republic, the Nation of Rome grew into the entire peninsula of Italy, and took over Greece, North Africa, and France. This enlargement of Rome led to a need for more positions of power and a more complex government, sufficient to deal with the city itself, the many nations that were a part of the budding Roman Empire, and each of their representatives. The large amount of responsibility wielded by the Roman government gave some people more power than others.

On the home front in 494 BC, the plebian class (the least wealthy commoners) rebelled in the first of three struggles for their political rights. They demanded voting rights equal to the rights of the Aristocratic patricians, who were delineated in the census by their ability to buy a horse for military campaigns and provide leaders for government and the military. The plebians continued to make inroads, eventually getting written laws (The Laws of the Twelve Tables) to protect themselves. The next achievement was The Lex Canuleia, which allowed patricians and plebians to intermarry. Finally the Ogulnian Law increased the number of legislators, requiring the new positions be plebeians. As factions continued to argue, the Roman Constitution was codified.

THE PUNIC WARS, 264–146 BC, ROME VS. CARTHAGE

Rome's influence and territory increased with their triumph in the Punic Wars from 264–146 BC.

Following the death of Alexander and the division of his empire, two new groups would come to vie for power over the Mediterranean. South of the sea was the city of Carthage, whose influence in the region was tremendous, thanks to its maritime trade and naval prowess. To the north was Rome, which would eventually rise to take Carthage's place as the preeminent power of the west.

The Punic Wars constituted the largest military conflict of the Western world at the time, and one of the largest of all antiquity. Sparked over Rome's desire to expand its influence over the Isle of Sicily, these three wars would end with the complete destruction of Carthage, and the foundation of the Roman legacy that would last well into the fifth century AD.

Notable Battle

The Battle of the Metaurus, 207 BC

Having successfully crossed the Alps, Carthaginian general Hannibal hoped to crush Rome. Unfortunately for him, his reinforcements (led by his brother) were crushed by the Romans at Metaurus, stranding Hannibal in Italy, cutting off Carthage from one of its most important military leaders. Rome's victory here effectively crippled Carthage, leaving the Mediterranean ripe for further conquest. Although this loss did not mark the end of Carthage's military clashes with Rome, it was the point past which they faced the prospect of increasingly diminished returns.

Roman Expansion Continues

Population expanded as Italian farmers moved to the city because of massive, slave-operated farms (latifundia). Sicily, Sardinia, and parts of Spain were part of the acquisition. Roman military took advantage of the weakening, yet admirable, Greek civilization, and in just 50 years took over the mainland of Greece. Corinth and Carthage followed. Rome was powerful and rich because of the spoils of war.

Inside Rome, though, the Republic experienced discontent: the Social War between Rome and its allies, coupled with the Servile Wars (slave uprisings), necessitated changes in policy for allies and subjects.

THE CRISES OF THE ROMAN REPUBLIC, 133–27 BC

With the Mediterranean effectively under Rome's control, the Roman Republic entered into a period of on-and-off civility and civil war, eventually culminating in the "Destruction" of the Roman Republic and the establishment of the Roman Empire. This span of a hundred years provided a brutal testing ground for the political values of the Republic, which ultimately (in this case) failed and gave way to autocracy.

Notable Battles

The Battle of Pharsalus, 48 BC

Julius Caesar, full of his Gallic triumph, attacked Rome, and with his victory took the power to rule for four years—the beginning of the end of the Republic.

The seminal battle of the seventh Roman Civil War was also known as "Caesar's Civil War," after Gaius Julies Caesar, who battled with his former ally Pompey Magnus. Pompey fought for the sake of the Republic, with a significantly larger army at his disposal, but was forced by his backers in the Senate to withdraw after the continued survival of Caesar's forces month after month. Although this battle did not mark the end of the Civil War, it was at this point Caesar's victories started to garner him more popular and political support, whereas Pompey's began to dwindle. Ultimately Caesar would defeat Pompey and return to Rome with his head held high to establish himself as a dictator, only to be stabbed to death by a group of senators.

He was assassinated in 44 BC, and with that act Marcus Antonius and Octavian disbanded the republic despite the support of Marcus Junius Brutus and Gaius Cassius Longinus.

The Battle of Actium, 31 BC

Marc Antony and Octavian fought from 44–31 BC for control of Rome. The decisive naval confrontation of the 12th and final war of the Roman republic, waged between Octavian and Mark Antony. Octavian's victory over Mark Antony and his Egyptian allies allowed the former to consolidate his power and popularity over the Roman public and rise to the position of First Citizen, and later Caesar—his imperial title, derived from the late Caesar's name. This constituted the official end of the Roman Republic and the beginning of the Roman Empire.

Octavian finally triumphed in 27 BC and became Emperor, gaining more power than Julius had. The Republic was no more, and would never have the chance to regrow. The legacy of the Roman Republic can be felt still today in democracies around the world.

Roman Empire

44 BC–14 AD	Augustus establishes the Roman Empire
64	Great Fire of Rome during Nero's rule
69–96	Flavian Dynasty; building of the Coliseum
284–337	Diocletian and Constantine; building of the first Christian basilicas
312	Battle of the Milvian Bridge; Constantine the Emperor
330	Constantine makes Constantinople the new capital of the empire
395	Definitive separation of Western and Eastern Roman Empire
410	The Goths of Alaric sack Rome
455	The Vandals of Gaiseric sack Rome
476	Fall of the final emperor Romulus Augustus

At its most powerful and the largest city in the world, Rome had about 2,000,000 residents. Its beauty and architectural magnificence was improved upon at the hand of Augustus and his successors. Even the Great Fire of Rome led only to further enhancement. Then after the second-century peak, 2,000 people died each day from the plague. Marcus Aurelius, emperor at that time, is the last of the "Five Good Emperors" of the Pax Romana, a time of peacefulness and little expansion. His son Commodus marks the beginning of the decline of the Western Roman Empire.

The third century saw the encroachment of barbarians and less safety. Emperor Aurelian had a huge wall built around the city in defense. Then Rome's position changed as the western emperors ruled from elsewhere and Constantine I moved the capital to Constantinople. The Bishop of Rome became the Pope through the Edict of Thessalonia, which emanated from Constantine's conversion. Yet those in power continued to honor the role Rome had played in history, through the last wave of architecture: Maxentius built the basilica in the Forum, Constantine the Arch of Constantine, and Diocletion the greatest baths. As patron of the Christian buildings, Constantine bestowed the Lateran Palace on the Pope and saw the construction of the magnificent St. Peter's Basilica.

Despite Constantine's strong, growing faith, Paganism still thrived as the belief of the aristocrats and the senators.

From 410–476 Rome was sacked by their enemies and some Roman troops (mostly barbarians). Until that time, they hadn't been defeated for 800 years.

APOLLONIUS OF PERGA, 262–190 BC, *The Great Geometer*

> Moreover, apart from such usefulness, they are worthy of acceptance for the sake of the demonstrations themselves, in the same way as we accept many other things in mathematics for this end and for no other reason.
>
> —*Treatise on Conic Sections, Book IV*

- Innovated with early work on the conic sections (circles, ellipses, parabolas, and hyperbolas)
- Is revered next to Archimedes as the most illustrious of the Ancient Greek geometricians
- Had a majority of his life and work lost to history
- Coined the names of the conics, excluding the parabola, which was attributed to Archimedes

Key Works

Treatise on Conic Sections, 8 Volumes, c. 230–200 BC
Cutting of a Ratio, c. 230–200 BC
Cutting of an Area, c. 230–200 BC
Determinate Section, c. 230–200 BC
Tangencies, c. 230–200 BC
Inclinations, c. 230–200 BC
Plane Loci, c. 230–200 BC

Biography

Almost nothing that was written about the life and times of Apollonius of Perga remains today. He was born in Perga, Pamphylia, in what is now Antalya, Turkey, in roughly 262 BC, and he studied in Alexandria under the successors of Euclid. Scholars know only that he was a revered geometer of the Alexandrian School that worked about 40 years after Archimedes. What has survived of his works is meager and untrustworthy. The most well-known of his works is *Conics*, which was originally eight volumes. Books I–IV of those survive in the original Greek, while Books V–VII remain in only Arabic translations. Book VIII is lost, but some idea of its contents can be gained from the lemmas to it given by Pappus. Through this work, Apollonius provided a systematic textbook on the elements of conics, which effectively eliminated the work of his predecessors.

Conics

Apollonius's greatest surviving discovery is the conic system. A conic is a curve that is created by cutting two circular cones, one atop of the other, with a plane (see figure). The forms created from this cut include parabolas, hyperbolas, ellipses and circles. A parabola is a curve that is formed with a cut through the base of one cone through the side of the same cone (4) Graphically, a parabola is the set of all of the points on a graph that are the same distance from a fixed point (focus) and a fixed line (directrix). Graphically, an ellipse is the set of all points on a graph in which the sum of two fixed points (foci) are the same. An ellipse is created when a cut is made through the center of the cone (2 and 3). The circle is classified as a specific type of ellipse (2). A circle is formed by cutting a circular cone with a plane perpendicular to the symmetry axis of the cone. A hyperbola is created by cutting a circular cone with a slanted plane (5). Graphically, a hyperbola is the set of all the points in which the difference of two fixed points (foci) are the same. These shapes appear extensively throughout nature, engineering, art, and architecture.

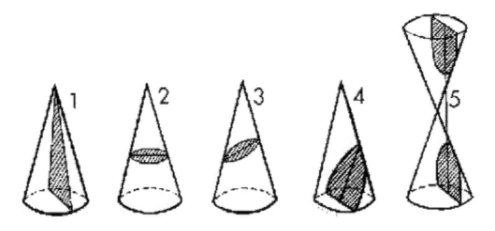

Appolonius's Conic Sections: straight lines, circle, ellipse, parabola, hyperbola

Legacy

Geometric proofs for all the conics have helped mathematicians for centuries. Apollonius's work on parabolas transcends time, and parabolas are now used for everything from satellite and radar dishes to microphones in recording studios. Ellipses mimic planetary travel and allow shockwaves to make some surgeries obsolete. Hyperbolas are now used in architecture, engines, and are seen in the paths of particles. On top of this, Apollonius developed methods of multiplying large numbers, and he was the first to make astronomical observations on the principles of geometry.

Brady Weisner, 2016

CICERO, 106–43 BC, *Believer in Reason and the Goodness of Man*

> This, then, ought to be the chief end of all men, to make the interest of each individual and of the whole body politic identical. For, if the individual appropriates to selfish ends what should be devoted to the common good, all human fellowship will be destroyed.
>
> —*De Officiis*

- Lived in the Roman Empire around the time of Julius Caesar
- Praised the glories of the Republic as a notable lawyer and politician
- Wrote mostly in the form of dialogue
- Held that man is basically good, but is corrupted by desire and pleasure
- Asserted that the search for truth is valuable only when it is practical and beneficial to the human condition and society
- Argued against man's greed and lust for power, suggesting that both should be kept in check by reason
- Was influenced by Greek thought and the Stoic philosophy of reason and cooperation
- Opposed the Epicurean philosophy of pleasure
- Contended that reason is the ultimate defining attribute of humanity
- Articulated the concept of Natural Law
- Espoused "The consent of the governed" philosophy, which is foundational to American government

- Was assassinated for his opposition to Marc Antony after the assassination of Caesar
- Partially inspired the Renaissance and Enlightenment humanist movement

Key Works

Orations, 63 BC
De Republica (The Republic), 51 BC
De Legibus (On the Laws), c. 50 BC
De Finibus Bonorum et Malorum (On The Ends of Good and Evil), 45 BC
De Amicitia (On Friendship), 44 BC
De Officiis (On Duties), 44 BC
De Senectute (On Old Age), 44 BC

Biography

Marcus Tullius Cicero was born in 106 BC to a landholding family without noble roots, near the end of the Roman Republic. In his youth, Cicero's family placed significant importance on learning and Cicero quickly distinguished himself as a strong student and orator. Likely, his innate abilities and the importance of the legal profession and politics led him in those directions later in life. Once becoming a lawyer, Cicero quickly proved his ability by winning several important cases. After proving himself, Cicero moved on to pursuing politics and eventually rose to the position of consul, the highest elected position in the Roman republic. His heightened reputation as a politician came soon after rising to this position as he brought a charge against his previous political rival, Catiline, eventually leading to condemnation of the latter and the execution of his supporters. Along with being a strong orator, he dedicated himself to the translation and explication of Greek texts and ideas so that the general populous could understand. He also championed the then-dwindling Republic as the right form of government and disseminated writings, participated in debates, and chose political allies promoting this belief. While he and his writings were generally respected, his advocacy of the Roman Republic made him powerful enemies such as Julius Caesar and Mark Antony. It was his opposition to Antony that eventually led to his assassination in 43 BC.

Cicero and Stoicism

Stoic philosophy significantly influenced Cicero's views on ethics and the nature of reality. Fate, according to the Stoics, ruled over all life. Since fate would deny any action harmful to nature, everything that happened was considered good for the world as a whole. Because of this belief, any personal harm was embraced as a component of the greater good; this explains why in modern times the word "stoic" is applied to someone who does not display emotion. The Epicureans, who were the largest group opposed to the Stoics, held instead that the pursuit of pleasure was the ultimate purpose of life and all choices were to be made so as to maximize personal pleasure. It is important to understand both Stoicism and Epicureanism in order to understand Cicero because he spent significant time responding to the Epicureans in *On the Ends of Good and Evil* and Cicero's stoicism significantly influenced his political philosophy exemplified in *De Officiis*.

Nature of Man

Cicero held the nature of man to be inherently good but corruptible if self-focus became primary. He also distinguished between men and animals, identifying man's ability to reason as the major difference between the two as well as man's connection to the "supreme god" (*De Legibus* I.22). Cicero stated that mankind had to possess a characteristic that separated him from the rest of the animal kingdom. He observed that "every species of living creatures [had been created] with the instinct of self-preservation," an inexplicable desire to survive (*De Officiis* I.11). After further examination, Cicero decided that beasts "adapt [themselves] to that alone which is present at the moment; while man—because he is endowed with reason … perceives the causes of things … draws analogies, and connects and associates the present and the future—easily surveys the course of his whole life and makes the necessary preparations for its conduct" (*De Officiis* I.11). This points to Cicero's belief of man being inherently good, having the ability to reason and thus discern right and wrong for himself and society. Still, Cicero did not dismiss the corruption of man and went on to claim that, for the most part, people could be led to wrong-doing in an effort to secure some personal end—that man could be corrupted by his "appetites," desires that benefit the individual such as wealth, happiness, and power. While prone to selfishness and the pursuit of pleasure, Cicero believed that man was created for all humankind—that "[man is] not born for [himself] alone, but [his] country claims a share of [his] being, and [his] friends a share; … and as men, too, is born for the sake of men, that they may be able mutually to help one another; to contribute to the general good … and thus by [their] skill, [their] industry, and [their] talents to cement human society more closely together, man to man" (*De Officiis* I.22). All of this underscores Cicero's conception of man as inherently good and that, guided by reason, he purposed to benefit his fellow man and humanity as a whole.

Natural Law

Founded on his belief regarding the nature of man and consistent with his application of stoic thought, Cicero articulated one of the first arguments for natural law. He goes about this especially in his *De Legibus (On the Laws)*, by differentiating between Civil Law, law that is primarily used in the safeguarding of interests and ordering of discourse, and natural law, law resulting from the nature of man. Cicero most concerns himself with natural law, and he traces its origins to mankind's "being begotten by the supreme god" who created them in a spectacular way as to "share in reason and reflection" with that god, unlike the animals. This shared reason created a "primary fellowship" between god and mankind and pointed to the unity that could be established through the law of nature and rational law established by man. From this he concludes, "we have been born for justice and that right has been established not by opinion but by nature." He draws this out further when he states that we have been made to "participate in the right," and that "those who have been given reason by nature have also been given correct reason, and thus law, which is correct reason in ordering and forbidding."

This concept of natural law was much more of an ideal than the law codes that existed in the days of Cicero. Most civil codes of Cicero's time emphasized *jus gentium* (law for nations) and *jus civile* (law for citizens)—an overall focus on conforming to the expectations of nation states, rather than focusing on the ideal code of law, which is the pursuit of natural law. This law is unique in that it was "conceived to be valid for all men, not merely as citizens of some state or other but as rational beings sharing in the divine reason that rules the universe." As a result of this, and consistent with his understanding of human nature, Cicero draws the conclusion that each individual can grasp what is right innately and that the application of this is what makes a man virtuous.

Influence on Humanism

Although Cicero worked in the time of the Roman Republic, his philosophies greatly influenced the Humanistic movement to follow. It is said that "it was he who formed the very concept of 'humanism,'" for Humanism is founded "on the basis of human rationality—the ability to make and understand decisions, to grasp connections and consequences, and to draw sensible conclusions." Here Cicero's emphasis on reason is evident. Additionally, Cicero's fundamental beliefs in the nature of man and the natural law encapsulate Humanistic qualities–that man is created to better himself and his fellow man. Cicero also articulated in *De Officiis* that within man "there is an added hungering as it were, for independence … from this attitude comes greatness of soul and a sense of superiority to worldly conditions." This statement articulates a core value of Humanism: the idea that man is an individual who, when he comes to terms with this individuality, achieves a "greatness of soul and a sense of superiority to worldly conditions," which in turn shows man's superiority to the world and develops a more Humanistic approach to life. Cicero's defining influence on Humanism can be found in *De Legibus* in his dialogue with Atticus Pomponius, and Quintus as he talks about the value of man and his reason:

> It [mankind] alone, of all kinds of natures and animate beings, has a share in reason and reflection … moreover what is more divine than reason–I will not say in a Human Being but in the entire heaven and earth? … Therefore, since nothing is better than reason, and since it [is] in both Human Being and god, the primary fellowship of Human Being with god involves reason … since that is law, we should also consider human beings to be united with gods by law … [and] among those who have a sharing in law, there is a sharing in right … so that Human Beings are held to be in "blood relation" and "race" of the gods.

Here Cicero indicates that man is related to the gods through his ability to reason. Due to this relation, Cicero concludes that man should share the ability to discern what is morally wrong or right (natural law), an ability that should be used to better himself and his fellow man. Cicero thus began to formulate the idea of man being within equal standing of reason with god, and within this standing, man should rationalize within his own mind, not a god's. Thus, Cicero began to plant the seeds of humanism in the world through his belief in man's nobility and reasoning.

Matt Horn, 2015
Nathaniel Whatmore, 2015
Nate Kosirog, faculty

TITUS LUCRETIUS CARUS, 99–55 BC, *The Shrouded Poet*

> All religions are equally sublime to the ignorant, useful to the politician, and ridiculous to the philosopher.
>
> —*De rerum natura*

- Was an accomplished Roman poet
- Was an Epicurean philosopher who disliked violence, although his merit as philosopher is under debate
- Has mysterious and relatively unknown origins, though he may have had a wealthy upbringing
- Denied the existence of any deity or afterlife, based on his world model of the void and atomic particles

Key Work

De rerum natura (On the Nature of Things), 50 BC

Biography

Despite the significance of his epic poem, *De rerum natura (On the Nature of Things)*, remarkably little is known about Lucretius. The only facts historians know for certain are that he was an accomplished Roman poet during the first century BC and that he adhered to Epicurean philosophy. This lack of information may be due to pious Roman Christians seeking to suppress "the poet's anti-religious sentiments and materialist blasphemies." St. Jerome even claims that Lucretius met his end at his own hand after being driven to insanity by his books. There is no evidence to back up this claim. Although a few historians believe the poet to have been a former slave and freedman of the aristocratic family Lucreti (hence his name), most hold that he was a member of the family from birth. The elegance and style of his writing speaks to a wealthy upbringing. Furthermore "the easy and natural way (friend to friend, rather than subordinate to superior) in which he addresses Memmius, his literary patron and the addressee of the poem," indicate that he grew up on equal status with the aristocrat (Simpson). Despite his apparent status, Lucretius was a reflective man who hated the violence and political upheaval that engulfed Rome during his life.

Epicureanism

Though his status as an originator of any school of philosophy is suspect, Lucretius was certainly a great expander of the school of thought known as Epicureanism. Outright, Lucretius states that his primary goal is to make Epicureanism more comprehensible for the reader. Since the philosophy can "seem too grim" for the uninitiated, he intends to "explain the system in sweeter music." Indeed, Lucretius says that "nothing is more sweet than full possession of those calm heights, well built, well fortified by wise men's teaching, to look down from here at others wandering below." Lucretius believed Epicureanism alone could provide this relief.

As its central tenet, Epicureanism emphasizes the disposal of needless anxieties; foremost among these inessentials is belief in divinity. According to Lucretius, religion causes men to "lay foully grovelling on earth, weighed down by grim Religion looming from the skies." The specter of religion creates fear in humans, causing them to "foully grovel" upon the earth. Furthermore, religion often "mothers crime and wickedness" and creates bloodshed and fear that is unnecessary. For example, it was religion that led to the sacrifice of Iphianassa to Artemis in Aulis. Additionally, it is "priestly rant" that "overturn[s] your sense of logic, muddle[s] your estates by fear." Lucretius argues that similar anxiety and wickedness are also the result of religion; therefore, if religion is disregarded and ignored, such evils will end.

Furthermore, Lucretius argues that fear of death is equally worthless. He points out that fear of death makes men greedy. Since without religion there is no afterlife, "we cannot be wretched in nonexistence," "we have no cause for fear," as "death alone has immortality." Death itself is inevitable, for only death is immortal. Therefore, there should be no fear of death as it does not bring eternal punishment nor can it be evaded.

Science and Religion

In *On the Nature of Things*, Lucretius intends "to demolish religious belief and banish superstitious fear." Doing so required Lucretius to portray a materialistic and independent universe. As he wrote in his poem, "nature has no tyrants over her, But always acts of her own will; she has no part of any godhead whatsoever."

Lucretius's godless, spiritless universe was based on the idea of atoms and the void. Essentially, tiny particles make up all material in the world. Lucretius declared that the wind, smells, and even drying laundry were proof that such particles exist. Even the mind or soul was made up of atoms according to the science of Lucretius. These atoms were simply composed of a finer substance than those of the body. All atoms in the Lucretian universe were accompanied by the void, "completely empty space without particles in it." This void allowed for motion because without it, atoms would have no space to move about. Furthermore, the void permitted objects to have different densities.

Atoms and the void composed the entire world for Lucretius, and every substance could be broken down into particles and empty space. There was no spirit or soul and thus no afterlife in his philosophy. Not only was there no afterlife, but also there was no divine intervention in his worldview. There was no creation event because matter could not be miraculously created from nothing. According to Lucretius, "if things could spring up from no seed, men would grow out of the sea or fish from the ground, the seasons would be meaningless and ageing spontaneous (from boy to man in an instant); that doesn't happen, so things must have fixed seeds." Likewise, Lucretius believed that matter could never be completely destroyed, although he was among the first to postulate that all things, from stars to mountains, decay over time. He argued that living creatures came to be when the "fertile young earth naturally sprouted with life forms, and the organisms thus generated were innumerable random formations. Of these, most perished, but a minority proved capable of surviving." Thus, Lucretius prefigures much later evolutionary thought.

Throughout his works, Lucretius seeks to explain matters in a simple, logical way so that the common man may understand him. His elegant, yet simple, style of writing is what sets him apart from many other philosophers.

Matt Horn, 2015
Nathaniel Whatmore, 2015
Nate Kosirog, faculty

VIRGIL, 70–19 BC, *Rome's Prophetic Poet*

" The descent into Hell is easy.

—*Aeneid*

- Wrote the *Aeneid* to celebrate Roman life and explore human nature
- Used a Greek name for the *Aeneid* to acknowledge Homer, the Greek writer of *The Iliad* and *The Odyssey*
- Asked Augustus, when Virgil was dying, to destroy the manuscript of the *Aeneid* because it was unfinished, but Augustus ignored the request and had the epic published
- Coined the first use of the phrase *e pluribus unum*, in his poem "Moretum"
- Had the *Aeneid* attacked by some as Augustan propaganda
- Thought that human behavior, especially under the influence of the gods, was important to understanding Roman life

Key Works

Eclogues, 39 BC
Georgics, 29 BC
Aeneid, 19 BC

Biography

Like many figures from antiquity, legend comprises Virgil's history. In 70 BC he was born into a lower class family in northern Italy and grew up as a farm boy with a childhood that provided no glimpse of his later greatness. However, after Virgil became the national poet of Rome, writers crafted fantastical stories about his birth, striving to prove that he had always been destined for greatness. After publishing *Eclogues*, a pastoral poem praising the Italian countryside, Virgil moved to Rome and made connections with courtiers of Augustus. He published his second major work, *Georgics*, in 29 BC, which was extremely popular and made him "the most respected and imitated writer in the Roman world." Next, he began his final and most popular work, the *Aeneid*, at the urging of Augustus. He spent 11 years working on it until he fell ill and died in 19 BC. Virgil's dying wish was that the *Aeneid* would be burned because it was unfinished, but Augustus could not bear to destroy such a beautiful piece of writing. Instead it was slightly edited and a published shortly thereafter.

The Aeneid

The *Aeneid*, Virgil's masterpiece, stands as one of the most well-known and most-studied classics of literature. Drawing inspiration from Homer's epics *The Iliad* and *The Odyssey*, the ever-meticulous Virgil "licked the verses out" and created a poem using Roman history to convey the gamut of human experience—anger, tragedy, war, love, and sacrifice. To this day, the *Aeneid* connects with its audience and transplants readers from the modern world back to the Roman Empire. With its tales of unpredictable gods and glorious Roman history, the *Aeneid* captures the imagination through its striking imagery and informatory verse.

The epic poem begins at the end of the Trojan War with Aeneas and his men sailing for Italy, barely escaping their burning city of Troy. While fleeing, Aeneas encounters a storm and lands in Carthage. There he falls in love with Dido, who commits suicide when Aeneas leaves her to settle Rome. On his journey, he encounters many divine obstacles, including a visit to the underworld that reignites his passion to establish the city of Rome. He eventually lands on the coast of Latium. There, the gods yet again interfere, causing war to break out between the Trojans and the Italians. Eventually, Aeneas kills Turnus, the Italian leader, with his sword, and so ends the *Aeneid* with a victorious Aeneas.

Although the *Aeneid* is focused on Rome and its founding, the scope of the epic broadens out. The *Aeneid* is both history and oracle. Virgil studied the entirety of Roman history, including his present day Rome, forging the tales together as one story, one reality, so that he could create an epic that reflects all of Roman life. According to literary critic Helen Conrad O'Brien, "The *Aeneid* was written to explore the source and meaning of Roman life"; it was a "tool of divine providence," in which Virgil uses past mythologies and traditions to justify and legitimize Rome's reign. And yet "Virgil wrote an epic not just for Rome but for humankind." R.D. Williams also reflects on the universality of the epic: "Virgil, however, is one of those poets who used aesthetic skills not only for their own sakes, but in order to explore human behavior in its most crucial aspects." Virgil lionizes Rome and Augustus, but more significantly, the *Aeneid* delves into human nature—its weaknesses, its strengths, its finitude, and its fortune.

Some attack the *Aeneid* as a work of Augustan propaganda, justifying the horrors of war and condoning Augustan atrocities during the civil war, while others defend it simply as an evocative work of epic poetry. While the work did consolidate Roman identity and revive traditional Roman virtues and morals, what has given the poem its lasting fame and place on high-school syllabi is the beauty of the work.

Samantha Sherwood, 2015
Lauren Wood, 2015

HORACE, 65 BC–8 BC, *The Republican Poet*

> " The aim of the poet is to inform or delight, or to combine together, in what he says, both pleasure and applicability to life.
>
> —*Ars Poetica*

- Coined the phrase "Carpe Diem" (seize the day) in his *Odes*
- Was a slave for part of his life, and later a leading Roman poet in the age of Augustus
- Studied at Plato's Academy in Athens
- Served under Brutus in the Roman military after the assassination of Julius Caesar
- Achieved the military rank of Tribunus Militum (Military Tribune), a high rank in the Roman Army that often led to a Senate Seat
- Satirized many things in Rome, including himself
- Had his poetry known as "the common currency of civilization"
- Mastered the art of writing poems inspired by the classical Greek in Latin

Key Works

Odes, 23 BC
Ars Poetica, 10 BC

Biography

Quintus Horatius Flaccus, known to the English-speaking world simply as Horace, was born on December 8, 65 BC, in the Samnite region of southern Italy. Historians speculate that his father was captured in a war of rebellion against Rome, and thus for at least part of his life Horace was a slave. Horace's father managed to gain his freedom, and improve the family's social position enough so that Horace could attend school. After being educated in Rome, Horace left to complete his education in Athens at Plato's Academy, where he was engulfed in the fallout from the execution of Julius Caesar. Horace joined ranks with Brutus, who came seeking support in Athens, and fought with him when Octavian (Augustus) and Marc Antony put down the rebellion at the Battle of Philippi in 42 BC. Granted clemency by Octavian, Horace returned to Italy destitute, after his father's estate had been confiscated. His friend Maecenas gave him a farm in 32 BC, securing some degree of financial stability and it was in these years that he began publishing his poetry. He published the first book of his *Satires* in 35 BC, the second in 30 BC. His *Odes* were published as a unit in 23 BC. Failing to make a splash with the *Odes*, he published his first book of the *Epistles* in 20 BC. The second book, which includes the famous *Ars Poetica (Art of Poetry)*, appeared as late as 10 BC. Still seen as one of the greatest lyrical poets of all time, Horace died at only 56 years old. Through odes, lyrical poems and satire, Horace portrayed life in Rome and essences of his poetry style still are observed in more modern poetry from people like Robert Frost. He is most famous for his synthesis of the classical Greek style of poetry and the Latin language. His *Odes* have been imitated and translated by everyone from Milton to Lowell, and his self-deprecatory style and autobiographical focus are standard features of much contemporary poetry.

Knowledge of the Ancients

To progress in poetry was to learn from the masters. Several times throughout *Ars Poetica*, Horace commends a deep reading of the classics. It is imperative for those who wish to be poets to immerse themselves in the classic masters who have charted the way. He encourages a young poet, "Ye [who are desirous to excel], turn over the Grecian models by night, turn them by day." In part, a foundation in the classics will help the poet to discern his own poetic vocation. Horace charges the young poet, "You who write, choose a subject that's matched by / Your powers ... / ... Whoever chooses rightly / Eloquence, and clear construction, won't fail him." The poet gets the good sense required to choose his subject well from the classics, and once the subject is well-chosen, familiarity with the classics helps one to write well.

The Poet and Real Life

This knowledge gained by books is insufficient, though, for the poet. In the words of Pritchard, "he who would write must go to the same fountain whence these masters who wrote books drew their own inspiration, life itself." Horace writes, "I'd advise one taught by imitation to take life / And real behavior, for his examples and extract / Living speech." Imitation is required for discovering the beauty of form and the accomplishments of the great poets that have preceded your era, but the beating heart of poetry is still drawn from real life. Great poetry also displays a mixture of natural talent and hard work. He writes, "Whether a praiseworthy poem is due to nature / Or art is the question: I've never seen the benefit / Of study lacking a wealth of talent, or of untrained / Ability: each needs the other's friendly assistance." For those who argue that poetry is a divine gift, Horace would respond that while talent is undeniable, talent alone will not blossom into poetic maturity apart from hard work. Moreover, the notion that "talent" was a greater blessing than "poor old technique" has led many poets to act insane so that they can be called geniuses. The important thing is to be excellent in your poetry, a consideration that has a practical side as well: "mediocrity in poets, no man, god or bookseller will accept."

The Purpose of Poetry

In *Ars Poetica*, Horace makes the following claim for the duty of the poet, "[t]he aim of the poet is to inform or delight, or to combine together, in what he says, both pleasure and applicability to life." The best poetry ought to be able to do both. This definition of poetic aim has been adopted, adapted, and denied for centuries. Philip Sidney, writing during the Renaissance, seized on Horace's declaration and modified it so that the duty of the poet is to instruct *and* delight. Sidney thus highlights a moral, virtuous component to poetry that was latent for Horace. Early in *Ars Poetica* he says in this vein, "[i]t's not enough for poems to have beauty: they must have / Charm, leading their hearer's heart wherever they wish." Horace seems to be in some sort of middle ground between a moral definition of poetry—like Aristotle's—and the modern conception of art for art's sake. Daniel Jacobson has argued that Horace missed the boat: "Horace conspicuously lacks the earnestness of both ideological critics and the champions of 'Art for Art's Sake'—loosely speaking, moralists and formalists." While he takes the formalist approach somewhat seriously, arguing that "who can blend usefulness and sweetness wins every vote," his aesthetic approach is a bit undercut by his emphasis on such a blend being the most financially successful way to write poetry.

Kenny Bottoms, 2015
Toby Coffman, faculty

LIVY, c. 59 BC–17 AD, *Chronicler of Rome*

> " This above all makes history useful and desirable: it unfolds before our eyes a glorious record of exemplary actions.
>
> —*Praefatio*

- Was a Roman historian who worked on a history of Rome throughout his life
- Lived during the time of civil war and the power-hungry dictators in Rome
- Wrote with the goal of bringing the Roman people back to the initial glory of Rome (*Ancient*)
- Is believed to have also written philosophical writings, but none have survived
- Is famous for the boldness and scope of his project, but is not classified as one of the major historians
- Wrote with the colorful language of poetry even while maintaining historical accuracy

Key Work

Ab Urbe Condita Libri (The History of Rome), c. 9 BC

Biography

Livy, or Titus Livius, was born in Patavium—modern day Padua—around 59 BC. Not much is known of the early stages of his life, but it is believed he was born to a wealthy Roman family and received an education like any wealthy boy growing up at the time. Within Patavium, a strong sense of traditional virtues emphasized respect of the gods, patriotism, and self-control, all which influenced Livy's emphasis on each. Livy is believed to have taught rhetoric and philosophy, although not as well known as his other pursuits. In 30 BC, he moved to Rome and began his project documenting the entire history of Rome. Living in Rome during a period of civil wars, the fall of the Republic, and power struggles between dictators, Livy was disappointed in Rome's current condition and sought to write a history of Rome that would redirect people to the glories of its beginning and what it could be. He spent the rest of his life devoted to this work, producing almost four books annually on his history of Rome. In the end, Livy died in Patavium around 17 AD after completing his life's work, a compilation of the events from the origin of Rome to near his death.

Livy's history is the only surviving history of Rome through that time period. Although only one third of his writing remains, some of it not completely accurate, Livy has been praised for the ambitious effort and focus.

Nate Kosirog, faculty
Nathaniel Whatmore, 2015

> " The poet's fruitful freedom knows no bounds and takes no oath to tell it as it happened.
>
> —*Amores 12.41–42*

- Ovid's full name was Publius Ovidius Naso and was also nicknamed, "The Nose"
- Married three times and had a daughter with his last wife
- Was exiled, ostensibly for his controversial writings in *The Art of Love*
- Transformed the elegiac system into a more humorous and educational verse in his own works, influencing later writers to do the same
- Called himself the professor of love in *Ars Armatora*, more commonly known as *The Art of Love*
- Emphasized psychology, rather than transformation or love, in *Metamorphoses*

Key Works

Metamorphoses, c. 1–6 AD

Ars Armatora (The Art of Love), c 2 AD

Biography

Ovid, a brilliant and witty poet, broadened the genre of epic poetry. Born into an old and respectable Roman family, he scorned the traditional path of public service in favor of poetry. A love poet, his first success, *Amores*, was followed an instruction manual in love, aptly titled *The Art of Love*. However, his most famous work, *Metamorphoses*, does not carry the theme of love at the forefront like his other poetry; instead, it traces transformation. His poetry made him instantly famous in Rome, with all except Augustus. Banished by Augustus under the pretense of the corrupting nature of the licentious *Art of Love*, Ovid died in exile in 17 AD.

Metamorphoses

Metamorphoses is Ovid's most famous work, both increasing his popularity as a poet and proffering an extremely detailed account of Greek mythology. Just as the title indicates, *Metamorphoses* centers around change. The poem describes three clear demonstrations of change: first, an encyclopedic account of the gods; second, a thorough account of ancient heroes; and third, a recounting of history from the fall of Troy to the rise of Rome. Not only does the story tell of transformations, but it also is a transformation in itself: "in many ways the poem, in content and style, mirrors the metamorphoses with which it deals" ("The Style"). Ovid strings the reader from episode to episode (about 250 different stories) so as to maintain continuity while at the same time transforming the entire epic—everything is subject to change, from creation to character. However, there are two notable exceptions to the iron rule of change: first, in the final book Ovid claims that souls cannot change and second, at the end of the work, he states that this work, this masterpiece, will also remain unchanged. His last line of poem concludes:

> " And now the work is done, that Jupiter's anger, fire or sword cannot erase, nor the gnawing tooth of time. Let that day, that only has power over my body, end, when it will, my uncertain span of years: yet the best part of me will be borne, immortal, beyond the distant stars. Wherever Rome's influence extends, over the lands it has civilized, I will be spoken, on people's lips: and, famous through all the ages, if there is truth in poet's prophecies,—*vivam*—I shall live.

Described as "an epic that breaks all of the norms," *Metamorphoses* stays true to Ovid's penchant for parody and remains a very atypical epic. Although written in the form of an epic, dactylic hexameter, Ovid mocks the traditional epic through untraditional content. While most epics are serious, Ovid transformed his tale into high comedy, dosed with the painful love that echoes through his past writings. Clearly, the epic is not simply a recitation of Greek history from creation to the present. Rather, it stands as an extended psychological observation on the nature of change; it is "world history as written by a love poet." Ovid portrays a wide variety of human behavior throughout the poem, turning it into a work of psychology. In doing so, he transforms "what ought to be a profoundly depressing vision of existence into a cosmic comedy of manners" (Kenney xix). Through the diverse behavior of his characters, Ovid exposes a variety of themes, whether it is the power of speech or the justice of the gods, and handles each theme in a different style, utilizing such rhetorical devices as anaphora and chiasmus. Ovid orchestrates the history of Greek mythology so that it not only records the myths in full, but also makes them entertaining and revealing.

Samantha Sherwood, 2015
Lauren Wade, 2015

THE FRONTIERS OF ROME

Warfare continued to carve new boundaries of civilization.

Notable Battle

The Battle of Teutoburg Forest, 9 AD

In time the Roman Empire would come to dominate the southern half of Europe, the southern half of the British Isles, the western half of the Middle East, and the northern tip of Africa, yet never did they push far into the Teutonic North. In 9 AD, a number of Germanic tribes under the leadership of former Roman citizen Arminius ambushed and crushed several Roman legions operating in the area, destroying much of the enthusiasm the Romans had for conquering anything east of the Rhine River. Although the Roman's never totally gave up on the idea, they would never again make significant inroads into the Germanic territories.

JESUS OF NAZARATH ◊ 4 BC–30 AD, *The Way, the Truth and the Life*

In the spirit of *Tiptoeing through the Classics* we have extracted **Ideas 2–5** from *Ideas that Matter* to summarize the essence of the incarnate "Who Am."

Idea #2—Essence of Jesus

Jesus is our North Star and Foundation; he maintains the same as the Key Attributes of God, plus:

- A human person (a man)
- A spiritual person (the only Son of God)
- The most influential person in history
- The most unifying and most divisive person in history
- The greatest leader and the greatest servant ever to live

His Mission:

- The Way, the Truth and the Life
- The Good News to set the captives free
- To save the world
- To forgive and heal

His Desire for Us:

- Eternal Life with Him (relationship, union, bonding, fellowship, attachment)
- Earthly fulfillment now (Fruit of the Spirit, an abundant life)

His Methods:

- Teachings, principles of good living (morals, commandments)
- Forgiveness of sins: grace, the Cross and Resurrection
- Tangible proofs (miracles, fulfilled prophecies)
- Commitment to truth, compassion, goodness, work and creativity

His Message Delivery:

- He was of low social station: a near nobody, low-born in a barn, blue collar, from a remote village, no title, no army, no political office, no money, no beauty, despised, rejected, betrayed, framed a felon, tortured, executed in a horrible way. He rose from the dead and became the most influential person in the history of the World.
- He chose simplicity: clarity, resolve, truth (bread, water, thirst, washing, lambs, flesh, blood, gates, light, darkness, life, vine, branches, sowing, reaping) not big words.
- He was often counter-intuitiveness: seemingly upside down teachings, (turn other cheek, save life will lose it, give the beggar your sweater, go the other way, serve others, first will be last, anti-religious people)

Idea #3—Essence of Christianity, The Bible

The Four First Truths of Christianity from which all other truths follow:

1. There is a Supreme Power of the Universe, God the Father, and He cares immensely for you, so much so that He created you in His image. In common with Him you share all these things: spiritual existence, eternal life, knowledge, rational thought, freedom to choose, emotions and feelings, the abilities to communicate, conjecture, imagine and the ability create.

But, more importantly, you also share with God the ability to: possess truth, be rational, imitate His love, extend goodness, work to improve things and to create beautiful things. You are a magnificent creation.

2. Jesus is the way, the truth, and the life for all people in all nations. Jesus stands alone as the only way to God (not through Mohammed, Confucius, Joseph Smith, Karma, Jihad, good works, or any other man, prophet, imagined deity or human effort). Jesus is God's only begotten Son; He was with God in the beginning. Nothing has been made without Him. He came as a servant leader and He calls us to be just like Him. To know Jesus is to know God.

3. You have two distinct natures in one being: your lower human nature and your higher spiritual nature. You are free to choose which nature leads (dominates) you, free to choose your own long-term destiny, free to follow your higher spiritual nature or your lower human nature. Tragically, you may use your freedom (free will) to detach from God, create evil, be lazy and destroy things. You are being influenced by both your human desires and an external enemy who does not want you to discover these realities of truth. Human nature includes both an evil inclination and a good inclination at war within you.

4. The Bible is one of God's greatest gifts to us. Jesus is the first. The Bible is our instruction manual. It tells us the truth about our spiritual nature and ourselves. It tells us who God is, how He interacts with history and it provides us with the wisdom to be joyful and fulfilled.

Idea #4—Veracity and Teachings of the Bible

The Bible is true and reliable. The Bible coaches us on how to live joyfully through its major teachings:

- The Greatest/Simplest Commandment—Love God with all your heart and with all your soul (personality) and with all your mind, and love your neighbor as yourself (Mt 22:37).
- Be Born Again (Jn 3:3)—Into your Spiritual Life and start growing closer to the Mind of Jesus (Heb 8:10, 1 Cor 2:16).
- Receive and Grant Forgiveness—The Cross, Grace and the Resurrection (salvation, redemption). Forgiveness from God redeems one spiritually and eternally. Forgiveness between men saves and redeems them mentally, emotionally and socially.
- Imitate God's Virtues—Truth, compassion, goodness, work, and creativity.
- Be Like Little Children—Unless you become like little children, you will never enter the kingdom of heaven (Mt 18:3).
- Feed the poor—Clothe the naked, visit the sick and imprisoned (Mt 25:42)
- The Golden Rule (Mt 7:12)
- Men will disappoint you; even the finest of men (religious men) remain sinners, and worst of all, outright hypocrites (see Mt 7:15).
- The Second Coming of Jesus—One of every 13 verses in the New Testament refers to the second coming of Jesus.
- Prayer is our conduit to Jesus and God.
- We believe the Bible is true and reliable. Some will argue over every date, every age, every statistic, every parable, every allegory, every metaphor, every simile and every Hebrew, Latin or Greek word meaning. We believe that arguing over these details is a distraction from our faith. We believe in the veracity of the Bible as expressed in the above major teachings.

The debate about the inerrancy of the biblical text should be put to rest so we can focus on the important messages of the Bible to mankind. We can affirm with intellectual integrity that all Scripture is inspired by God without needing to prove the inerrancy of the written text. The real issue is the power of its content.

Jesus is so simple, yet it can take a lifetime to understand Him.

66 | Unity in the essentials; liberty in the non-essentials; charity in all things.

—*Augustine of Hippo*

Idea #5—The Greatest Product Ever

Jesus and the Gospels represent the "greatest product" the world has ever known—nothing else even comes close. Please forgive the crude analogy metaphor, describing Jesus as a "product." But consider this: it is fitting in the sense that products offer benefits to the buyers of those products—why else would anybody buy or believe anything?

Many products available in the world compete for our attention and the attention of young people around the world. They are advertised by celebrities and promise great benefits. Some are useful and some never live up to the advertising. However, no product can offer the benefits that Jesus offers.

We are fully convinced that if our students choose to "buy into Jesus," they will receive the greatest set of benefits ever offered to any human being: peace of mind, selfless purpose, and meaning in to life, fulfillment, contentment and life everlasting! Isn't that what everybody should be searching for?

The more complete list of these benefits is known as the Fruit of the Spirit, which, in addition to the above, consists of: love, joy, peace, patience, kindness, goodness faithfulness, gentleness and self-control. We also add other virtues, such as compassion, justice, forgiveness, knowledge, perseverance, humility, cheerfulness, resilience, selflessness, generosity, appropriate self-esteem, a nature of awe, and freedom from guilt, greed or fear. These are the most meaningful things in life. If you met someone with these characteristics, you would want this person for your best friend.

But there is more good news. These benefits are a free gift—all you need to do is ask Jesus and follow His instruction manual (the Gospels), and you will receive all these benefits. Some of these benefits may arrive immediately in your life, and others will appear over time if you continue to follow the instruction manual. That's what Jesus is mostly about—helping you live the Good Life in relationship with Him. Most importantly, the icing on the cake—you will live forever in heaven.

NEW TESTAMENT, 40–95, *The Messiah Arrives*

66 | "Which commandment is the most important of all?"

Jesus answered, "The most important is, 'Hear, O Israel: The Lord our God, the Lord is one. And you shall love the Lord your God with all your heart and with all your soul and with all your mind and with all your strength.' The second is this: 'You shall love your neighbor as yourself.'"

—Mark 12:28–31 ESV

- Jesus often spoke in parables, short stories told to make a point.
- The Bible is the most widely sold book in the history of the world.
- The word "Testament" also means "covenant." The New Testament, therefore, got its name because Christians believe that it is the revelation of the New Covenant anticipated in Jeremiah 31:31.

- Most of the New Testament is written in Koine Greek, which was the lingua franca of its day. This shows the authors' desires to reach the common person with the Gospel of Jesus.
- Jesus's name in Hebrew is Yeshua, which means, "God will save."
- At least 10 authors contributed to the making of the New Testament.
- The core of the message of the New Testament is that someone can be saved only by faith in Jesus Christ.
- Most Christians believe that, along with the Hebrew Bible, the New Testament is the complete and authoritative word of God.

Structure of the New Testament

Much like the Old Testament, the New Testament is a collection of books written by various authors. However, the New Testament covers a more focused period of time, less than 100 years. Christians believe that the Old and New Testaments together comprise the complete and authoritative teachings of God: "the Bible not only explains God, it explains the world in which we live; it explains not only things that are right, but things that are wrong" (Chambers 27). The first four books of the New Testament are gospels, narratives that include the life and teachings of Jesus Christ. The book of Acts tells the history of the first Christians and the Church. With the exception of the book of Revelation, the rest of the New Testament is made up of letters, or epistles. The Epistles were written by Christian leaders to their churches intended to correct belief and encourage believers. The final book of the New Testament, Revelation, fits generally in the genre of prophecy. Revelation depicts what will happen in the future and encourages people to maintain their belief in Jesus.

Jesus

Harkening back to the opening of the Hebrew Bible, John 1:1–3 states of Jesus, "in the beginning was the Word, and the Word was with God, and the Word was God. He was in the beginning with God. All things were made through him, and without him was not any thing made that was made." Thus, John shows a great number of New Testament themes in the very first section of his book. As Craig Blomberg points out, "the first 18 verses [Of John] reflect theologically on Jesus's pre-existence with God as the logos ("Word") who becomes incarnate, and thus this text functions as a prologue to the entire Gospel."

The New Testament centers itself around the belief that Jesus was God in the flesh. He was both fully God and fully man. Christians claim Jesus lived a sinless life and died in perfect obedience to God (Phil 2:6–7); Wayne Grudem expresses this critical paradox, suggesting that, "though the New Testament clearly affirms that Jesus was fully human just as we are, it also affirms that Jesus was different in one important respect: he was without sin, and he never committed sin during his lifetime." As John 1:1 states, Jesus created the universe. Jesus has always been God and always will be God.

The Messiah

When Jesus came and walked among the Jewish people, expectations of the Messiah coming were high: "the prophetic tradition and royal psalms, foresee a scope and majesty in the rule of the messiah that no anointed leader of Israel ever obtained" (Hastings 425). Jews of Jesus's time period believed that someone in the bloodline of King David would come to rescue them from their persecutors (2 Sm 7). In Jesus's age the persecutors were the Roman Empire, but the Jewish people suffered through hundreds of years of foreign oppression before the Romans rose to power. The New Testament often portrays Jesus as fulfilling the prophecies that speak of The Messiah (Mt 1, Mt 2:16–18, Lk 2:4). When Jesus starts his teachings, it is clear that many Jews hoped he was The Messiah. Followers of John asked Jesus, "are you the one who is to come (The Messiah), or shall we look for another?" (Mt 11:3). The New Testament teaches that Jesus was The Messiah, but not in the ways the Jews expected.

Jesus upset common expectations of The Messiah. The Jews expected The Messiah to save them from their enemies; Jesus ultimately came to save them from their sins: "for God so loved the world that he gave his only Son, that whoever believes in him should not perish but have eternal life" (Jn 3:16). As each of the Gospels progresses, it becomes increasingly clear that Jesus came to die for the sins of humanity. "Jesus was able to bear all the wrath of God against our sin and to bear it to the end. No mere man could ever have done this, but by virtue of the union of divine and human natures in himself, Jesus was able to bear all the wrath of God against sin and bear it to the end" (Grudem 578).

In the Hebrew Bible, believers would place their hands on an animal and sacrifice that animal to atone for their sins. Jesus became that sacrifice for all of mankind. When he died, he paid for all the sins of humanity. On the cross, Jesus cried out, "it is finished" (Jn 19:30), which meant that nothing further was required to pay for the debt of sin. As John 3:16 states, all that was expected of someone to be saved was for that person to believe that Jesus died for his or her sins and to follow His commandments. Jesus showed that he conquered death by being raised from the dead three days after his crucifixion (Mt 28, Mk 16, Lk 24, Jn 20). Jesus's conquest of death proved to his believers that he had the power to fulfill all that he had promised.

The Holy Spirit and the Early Church

Jesus foretold his death and said that it would be advantageous to his followers, the disciples, because the Holy Spirit would come after him (Jn 16:5–15). When someone believes in Jesus as savior, the Holy Spirit is said to dwell in him or her (Rom 8:12). The role of the Holy Spirit is to continue the saving work that Jesus began by dying on the cross. The Holy Spirit led and taught the early believers who, as they started a community, the church, which continued to grow. Of these believers, Peter was the most prominent member. Peter preached to the masses in Jerusalem and oversaw the conversions of thousands of people on a holiday called Pentecost (Acts 2). Pentecost completes the sequence of events that began with Christ's death, including his resurrection and ascension, and now provides the opportunity for God to bestow his Spirit upon all his people. After Pentecost, a great persecution hit the church of Jerusalem, and the first Christian martyr Stephen was stoned to death (Acts 7). His persecution led many Christians to leave Jerusalem, which spread the faith to new regions of the Roman Empire. Paul of Tarsus, who instigated and oversaw the persecution of Christians, miraculously came to believe in Jesus as The Messiah (Acts 9). Paul would become the greatest missionary in church history and be the reason why the church spread to the ends of the Roman Empire. He would also go on to write the majority of the New Testament as he led the church into the future.

Death and the Afterlife

The New Testament teaches that after death those who believe in Jesus will go to be with him in paradise, but those who do not believe will go to be punished. This is most clearly seen in the story of the rich man and Lazarus (Lk 16:19–30). "A great chasm" is said to separate believers from non-believers in this story. While in either punishment or paradise, those who have died await the day of the return of Jesus to earth. When Jesus returns, every person will be resurrected from the dead, culminating the Hebrew Bible's notion of judgment and afterlife. It is important to clarify that the New

Testament teaches that the resurrection is not merely spiritual, but physical as well. In the resurrection, every human being will regain a human body. When Jesus comes back, and every person is resurrected, all people will receive their final judgment (Rv 20). Those who do not believe will be thrown into a lake of fire, while those who are believers will continue to live with Jesus. When Jesus returns, he will create a new heaven and a new earth (Rv 21). God ultimately fixes and makes new everything that was destroyed by man's disobedience.

MARCUS FABIUS QUINTILIANUS, 40–96, *Father of Children's Education*

> " The mind is exercised by the variety and multiplicity of the subject matter, while the character is moulded by the contemplation of virtue and vice.
>
> —*Institutio Oratoria Book II*

- Was the first professional rhetorician to be employed by the state
- Said that the goal of education was to make civilized men with high principles
- Believed that one must talk about morally justifiable topics to be a good speaker
- Leaves the *Institutio Oratoria* as his only remaining work
- Believed that knowledge is acquired over time through proper training and learning
- Strongly encouraged all young boys to receive education before the age of seven
- Was a literary critic who disapproved of the artificiality of writing, suggesting that writing and speaking should sound natural
- Believed it was possible to attain moral perfection

Key Works
Institutio Oratoria, c. 94

Biography
Born in Calagurris, Spain in 40 AD, Marcus Fabius Quintilianus, the son of a rhetorician, moved to Rome where he received his education studying under the orator Domitius. After receiving an education, he practiced as a legal advocate and defended the Jewish Queen Berenice. Quintilian returned to Spain in 57 AD, and then left again for Rome where he became the first professional teacher of rhetoric to be employed by the state. Among his students were the historian Tacitus, Senator Pliny the Younger, and various heirs of the emperor Domitian. After marrying in his forties and losing both children with his young wife not much is known of Quintilian's personal life. After teaching the Roman elite for more than 20 years, he wrote a series of volumes—the *Instituio Oratorio*—that are responsible for his fame to the present.

Theory of Learning
Quintilian's *Institutio Oratoria* outlines the proper upbringing and education for a child. He firmly believed that everyone in contact with the child impacts its development. Quintilian elaborates on the importance of having educated slaves and nurses who influence the child. In Book I of *Institutio Oratoria*, he says that a child should start learning before the age of 7 because "the elements of reading and writing are entirely a matter of memory," and the memory is "its most retentive" during childhood. Quintilian claims that enjoyment is one of the most important aspects of young education: if the child is congratulated, praised and rewarded, he will be more willing to engage in the subject matter and offer

answers. In addition, Quintilian was opposed to the corporal punishment used by many Roman teachers because he believed that it was disgraceful and that "if a boy has a disposition so intractable that he cannot be corrected by scolding, he will become hardened even to your blows." Rather than flogging a child, in Book II Quintilian suggests that the teacher should "should talk a great deal about what is good and honorable; the more often he has admonished his pupils, the more rarely will he need to punish them." An honorable teacher does not give in to his anger, but rather is straightforward with his students and persistent in his work. When a child has reached the age where he is reading and writing, he should begin lessons in Grammaticus. However, Grammaticus must be paired with lessons in Greek or Latin, music, astronomy, and philosophy, so that the children have a better understanding of the poems that they are interpreting. In Book I of *Institutio Oratoria*, Quintilian explains that "unless the foundations for the future orator have been carefully laid by the Grammaticus, the whole superstructure will collapse." Quintilian was adamant in reiterating the importance of educating young children with proper teachers to create civilized young men with high principles.

Human Nature and the Theory of Knowledge

Quintilian taught that man was made up of two parts: the soul and the mind. The gods crafted the soul for the purpose of living in heaven, and created the mind for learning and reason. In book I of *Institutio Oratoria*, Quintilian states that reason is "natural to man: as birds are born for flying, horses for speed, beasts of prey for ferocity, so are we for mental activity and resourcefulness." He believed that knowledge existed, but could only be attained through proper studies. In Book II of *Institutio Oratoria*, Quintilian compares an orator to an artist, saying that knowledge is to an orator as a paintbrush is to a painter. In fact, he believed that if enough knowledge was attained, one could become perfect by moral standards and in all ways. His belief that man is inherently good allowed him to have a positive outlook on humanity and a perennially optimistic view in his educational efforts. In Book I, Quintilian metaphorically used climbing a hill to represent discovering new ideas: "But even if we fail, those who make an effort to get to the top will climb higher than those who from the start despair of emerging where they want to be, and stop right at the foot of the hill." He believed that scholars should use the works and findings of others to discover ideas of their own. His theory that knowledge is acquired through study inspired him to write *Institutio Oratoria*, where he outlined the importance of education.

Makayla Dahl, 2016

PLUTARCH, 46–120, *The Philosophical Biographer*

" For though all persons are equally subject to the caprice of fortune, yet all good men have one advantage she cannot deny, which is this, to act reasonably under misfortunes.
—*Parallel Lives*

- Highly influential in the city of Delphi both politically and religiously
- Was a priest of Apollo at the Oracle of Delphi (interpreting the god's intentions) for more than 20 years
- Taught by the Egyptian Platonist Ammonius who was the head of the Academy in Athens
- Established a philosophical school in Chaeronea

- Historian and biographer of the Greco-Roman world; his *Lives of the Noble Greeks and Romans* (commonly called "Plutarch's Lives" or "Parallel Lives") is the source of much of our biographical knowledge of famous Greek and Roman men
- Major source of historical subjects for early modern literature and drama, including Shakespeare
- His non-historical writings dealt with moral questions, religion, cosmology, politics, Platonism, Stoicism, and Epicureanism
- Advocated for a partnership between Rome, which he called "the power," and Greece, which he called "the educator"

Key Works

Moralia, c. 118–120
Parallel Lives, c. 90–100

Biography

Though a biographer himself, Plutarch's life, ironically, can only be pieced together through casual references within his works. It is believed that Plutarch was born around 46 AD in the city of Chaeronea near Thebes. He was supposedly born to a wealthy family who offered him a "liberal education at Athens, where he studied physics, rhetoric, mathematics, medicine, natural science, philosophy, Greek, and Latin literature." In this time, it is said that Ammonius of Lamptrae, who may have been his primary influence in Platonic philosophy, personally tutored Plutarch. After finishing his education in Greece, Asia Minor, and briefly in Alexandria, Plutarch returned to Chaeronea where he married Timoxena around 68 AD. About this time, Plutarch established a philosophical school, where he taught while also representing his people before the Roman governor and Rome. Plutarch traveled much during this time period and spent a majority of his life in Italy, mainly between 75 and 90 AD, lecturing on philosophy and ethics. The last years of his life were mostly spent in Delphi, where he enjoyed the years of the Pax Romana and held the rank of head priest for 20 years. The exact location of his death is unknown, but it is believed that he died around 120 AD somewhere around Delphi. In his lifetime, Plutarch achieved notability as one of the greatest writers of his time through his works on morality, philosophy, and ethics as well as biographical and historical accounts in his *Parallel Lives*.

Morality and Virtue

Although most known for his biographies, Plutarch's philosophies on morality and virtue are also extremely valuable, as they help to better explain his approach to the documentation of people's lives. Because Plutarch was greatly influenced by Plato, he primarily investigates the virtue of the human individual. Plutarch agrees with Plato and his belief that the human soul consists of different parts—the higher property an intelligent form of reason, and the lower property concerned with the appetites of the material world and body. So Plutarch concludes that human virtue is derived within the balance of these two parts of the human soul.

Plutarch also believed that man could never separate reason from passion, stating that "while by reason [man] still continues to oppose passion, he continues in the passion, and again, while mastered by passion he plainly sees his error by the light of reason: and neither through passion has he done away with reason, nor through reason is he rid of passion, but being back and forth from one or the other he lies between them both." In this Plutarch reveals his belief that a sort of balance is necessary between the two parts of the soul, as one can never drive the individual soul to act without the other. This exemplifies Plutarch's belief that a man of moderation, having both reason and passion in balance, is morally virtuous. Plutarch used this moral code as a framework for analyzing the Greek and Roman lives he documented. And so, it is his perception of what is unjust, unworthy, ignoble, or immoral that has distinguished his work as a historian.

Parallel Lives

Plutarch's goal in *Parallel Lives* is to offer moral edification to the reader through the summary and comparative analysis of historical Greek and Roman figures. What separates his biographical account from others is its emphasis on the moral development and influence of famous men and how this impacts their historical legacy. Although the primary purpose of the text is its ethical presentation of individuals and the moral lessons to be learned from their lives, Plutarch places emphasis on the historical value to be found in precisely and meticulously detailing their acts and works.

Plutarch was also motivated to illustrate the parallels between Greek and Roman cultures in order to emphasize and cultivate a sense of mutual respect between the two civilizations and highlight examples of ethical goodness in both. Plutarch's work had a profound impact during his time and was universally praised. It was considered an essential schoolbook in many Greek speaking regions, and the Roman emperor Marcus Aurelius even rode into battle with a copy of it next to him. The influence and fame of *Parallel Lives* was not limited to Plutarch's time period alone. He set a standard of excellence in the examination of historical characters according to their moral principles and their exemplifications. The work is considered a key historical and moral doctrine of the ancient world; it was Shakespeare's primary source for his Roman history plays and praised by Francis Bacon for its portrayal of characters and their inner virtues or vices. Although the direct influence of *Parallel Lives* has diminished since the 16th and 17th centuries, it is still considered an authoritative historical account of famous Greek and Roman figures and has immense value to be found in its moral teachings.

Nathaniel Whatmore, 2015
Nate Kosirog, faculty
Daren Jonescu, advisor

EPICTETUS, 55–135, *The Monotheistic Stoic*

> " What is the first business of one who practices philosophy? To get rid of self conceit. For it is impossible for anyone to begin to learn that which he thinks he already knows.
>
> —*Discourses*

- Was a slave during his early life; his owner allowed him to study Stoic philosophy (named for the Stoa in the Athenian marketplace, where the movement's founder, Zeno, liked to teach), but this owner allegedly also broke his leg, crippling Epictetus for the remainder of his days
- After he gained his freedom, he taught in Rome until all philosophers were banished in 89 AD
- There are no known writings of Epictetus; his pupil, Arrian, transcribed and compiled the *Discourses* and the *Enchiridion* ("The Manual") from Epictetus's lectures and discussions
- Marcus Aurelius quotes Epictetus's teachings often in his *Meditations*
- As he refused, on principle, to be controlled by earthly desires, he lived in poverty, saying he owned only the earth, the sky, and a cloak

- Epictetus's teachings often echo the teachings of Socrates, Diogenes the Cynic, and Zeno of Citium: manage your own soul, do not give credence to the alleged power of others to control or harm you
- Defined freedom as the disciplined separation of one's mind and will from all external influence or concern for the body
- Said of life under tyranny, "You may fetter my leg, but my will not even Zeus himself can overpower."
- Insisted (like Socrates) that there is no contradiction between being moral and pursuing one's own genuine well-being; proper self-regard is care for one's own soul, which is good both for the agent and for those who benefit from interaction with the free soul

Key Works

Discourses (Composition date unknown)
Enchiridion (Manual) (Composition date unknown)

Biography

Epictetus, a renowned ancient Roman philosopher, was born in 55 AD in Hierapolis, Rome. He became a slave to Epaphroditus, secretary to Nero. After being freed by his master, Epictetus began studying with Musonius Rufus, one of the great philosophers of the Roman Empire. After spending much time with Rufus, Epictetus began teaching in Rome until Domitian exiled all philosophers in 89 AD. He traveled to Nicopolis of Epirus (western Greece) to establish a school and continue his teaching, where he remained for the rest of his life. He was an acclaimed teacher, but, like Socrates, documented nothing. However, one of his students, Arrian, composed a record of his oral teachings. Eight of these *Discourses* were created, yet only four have survived the passage of time. These four records, combined with a summary of his central points, form what is known as *The Manual*. These works demonstrate Epictetus's style of teaching and his careful study of Stoic doctrine. Epictetus taught students how to lead better lives using the "three topics," which are three areas in which one must train in order to become "good." These topics include the study of desires, action, and assent. Successful training in these areas eliminated desire, which allowed one to be free from making defective moral judgments. Epictetus taught until his death in 135 AD in Nicopolis.

Stoicism and Happiness

As a Stoic philosopher, Epictetus believed that the main goal of philosophy was to find happiness through the renunciation of free will. What prevents people from achieving happiness is that "people in general are not free. That is, they fail to achieve what they desire or to avoid what they wish to avoid." Epictetus believed that freedom was gained when one understood what was truly under his control and became unconcerned about the things that are beyond control. For Epictetus, the only things under human control are thoughts and emotions. Everything external to thoughts and emotions should be treated with indifference. Even the human body is considered external to oneself because humans ultimately have no control over the health of the body. Epictetus clarifies in *Discourses* book 4, "must I, then, not desire health? By no means, nor anything else that belongs to another: for what is not in your power to acquire or to keep when you please, this belongs to another."

For Epictetus, what we cannot control does not belong to us; our striving to change those circumstances equates to ingratitude. He clarifies this point with an analogy of a great banquet where the gods hosts humans: "External things are like dishes set before us by the gods. We should therefore use them gratefully and with enjoyment. However, we should never think of asking our hosts for dishes other than the ones they see as appropriate to set before us." In his belief, every external thing that a person receives is a test to help control the passions. A person should receive things with gratitude but should not desire more than what is given. To desire more would be to base happiness on things beyond control, which will ultimately bring misery.

Ethics

For Epictetus, destruction of desire can produce positive moral results. One example of this is in the area of greed. When someone no longer desires money, he will no longer fight with people over, say, wealth or power. In fact he will submit to others in this area. Since inappropriate desire generally motivates immoral decisions, removing desire from the moral equation immediately decreases the motivation for corrupt acts. Despite this change in motivation, it could be argued that without any form of passion a person might not partake in positive ethical actions, such as feeding the poor or being a good father. Both these actions seem to require a desire to do good. Epictetus responds to this with an appeal to maintain natural human relations.

Doing everything according to reason is natural for a human and everything good is in accordance with reason, he argues. Therefore, doing good is the most rational and natural thing for a human to do. If humans fail to do what is natural to them in their relational roles, they lose their humanity. Thus if a man is brutal he is losing his position as a man who has no natural faculty of brutality, and adopts the position of, say, a wolf (who has). Therefore, a father or mother should act in a loving manner towards his or her child because this is the natural role toward a child. In the *Discourses* book 3 Epictetus says, "your father has a certain duty, and if he shall not fulfill it, he loses the character of a father, of a man of natural affection, of gentleness." However, while a parent should act in a kind manner towards a child, Epictetus believes that if someone's child dies, this should not bother the parent because the child's death is ultimately beyond a parent's control. Ultimately, the Stoicism of Epictetus cultivated dispassionate human responses to any circumstance that they might face.

God in Rational Acceptance of All Things

Epictetus's view of God differed from that of many Stoics. While still encompassing stoic influences, he viewed the divine in a manner that was more personal than most other Stoics. The traditional Stoic view thought of humans as tiny manifestations of God, each human an extension of God himself. This view is similar to pantheism, the belief that everything in the universe is God.

In contrast, Epictetus thought of God as omnipotent and separate from humanity, and therefore the goal of the human life was to be submissive to this divine authority. Epictetus followed his God very closely and submissively, because he acknowledged him as the creator of the universe, his own thoughts submitting to the natural course of the universe. He actively yearned to bring God's desires into fruition. In the *Discourses* book 3, he describes God as a righteous, omniscient general because he always acted perfectly rational. A general is allowed to command his troops in the way that he wills. Epictetus uses this analogy to explain all of life, even death. When someone dies, Epictetus simply views this as God, the good general, sounding an order of retreat. Ultimately, the deceased person's service is no longer required. With this understanding of the cycle of life, Epictetus was able to maintain a dispassionate view towards death. In submitting his will to God, Epictetus secured himself a happy life because his desires were aligned to, or supplanted with, the desires of God.

John Reid, II
Daren Jonescu, advisor

TACITUS, *55–120, Rome's Political Historian*

> My purpose is to relate the facts about Augustus—more particularly his last acts, then the reign of Tiberius, and all which follows, without either bitterness or partiality, from any motives to which I am far removed.
>
> —*The Annals*

- Was born into a highly influential political family
- Served as senator and, later, as consul in 97 AD
- Wrote with a unique style attributed to education in rhetoric and language precision
- Interpreted battles through a lens that lacked military knowledge
- Wrote accurate and diverse histories because of access to documents and letters from the imperial archives
- Claimed that his writing's purpose was to represent the period of history "without either bitterness or partiality"
- Believed that the future could be shaped through the examination of the lessons of the past

Key Works

Agricola, c. 96
Germania, c. 98
The Histories, c. 105
The Annals, c. 116

Biography

While there have been many historians of Rome, Tacitus is regarded as the greatest. He was born into a wealthy family around the year 55 AD. His family's wealth made many things possible, especially an excellent education and marriage to the only daughter of Agricola, a general and governor of Britain. Still, his family's wealth was from the business realm, not the political, which probably limited Tacitus's ability to involve himself in politics. However, the Roman Empire eventually provided Tacitus the opportunity to succeed politically with the blessing of Emperor Vespasian.

Tacitus served under Vespasian's sons Titus and Domitian, eventually rising to the esteemed position of governor of Asia. The years under Domitian seem to have been the hardest for Tacitus. Many examples throughout his writings illustrate the shame and guilt he felt from his participation in the atrocities of Domitian. While his political career was significant, it was Tacitus's writings that left the largest imprint on history. Tacitus provided the basis for most of what we know about the emperors from the first century. His factual representation of what happened, as well as his emphasis on sticking to an unbiased representation, have set him apart and made him the most reliable historical source we have on that period of Roman history.

Style

Tacitus's legacy emanates not only from what he wrote, but also in how he wrote it. Tacitus is known for writing from extensive research, and, in turn, documenting the emotional impact of events on the individuals he observed. Tacitus had the "ability to sum up the salient characteristics of an individual in a few sharp, epigrammatic phrases," enabling him to record the existence of an individual and the essence of what made the individual significant and unique. Even with these considerations, Tacitus emphasized the descriptions "without either bitterness or partiality"—he simply recorded what happened around him in as unbiased a way as possible. Detailing the brutality of some emperors, for example, shows Tacitus's bold focus on clarity. Through his descriptions, he achieved his goal of shaping the future through the examination of the past. He influenced many famous leaders throughout history by conceptualizing the modern concept of "tyranny, of political freedom, and of martyrdom for a great political cause." Tacitus's legacy as a historian is due in large part to his ability to document factual events in a condensed style and to describe the inner character of individual leaders in an incisive fashion.

Nate Kosirog, faculty
Nathaniel Whatmore, 2015

NICOMACHUS OF GERASA, 60–120, *A Mystic Mathematician*

> " You calculate like Nicomachus!
>
> —Character from Lucian's *Philopatris*

- Believed strongly in the philosophy of Pythagoras
- Viewed reality as mathematical in nature
- Associated numbers with different gods and states of being
- Studied perfect, abundant, and deficient numbers
- Supported his theories with numerical examples instead of proofs
- Believed that music and mathematics were closely related
- Held considerable influence, despite a philosophical approach to the study of mathematics
- Had his works read by schoolchildren even into the Middle Ages
- Has only two complete surviving works: *Introduction to Arithmetic* and *Manual on Harmonies*

Key Works

Introduction to Arithmetic, 80–110
Manual on Harmonics, 80–110
Art of Arithmetic, (lost)
Life of Pythagoras, (lost)

Biography

Nicomachus of Gerasa enjoyed the highest reputation as a mathematician. Even after his death, his works continued to be studied by generations and generations of schoolchildren. However, there is very little written knowledge of the man himself. Historians have been left with little choice but to make educated inferences about his life through clues found scattered in his writings and those of contemporaries. What is clear is that he was a follower of Neopythagoreanism, a group of thinkers who viewed Pythagoras as the central and original figure in the whole Greek philosophical tradition, whom he likely encountered in Alexandria. Nicomachus even attributes the ideas of Plato and Aristotle to Pythagoras. Nicomachus imbibed Pythagoras's mystical view of things, particularly math and numbers. This belief in the divinity of numbers was central to both the philosophy of Nicomachus and his persona. Nothing else is known about the circumstances of his life and death.

Number Theory

Like all Pythagoreans, Nicomachus believed that numbers were more than mathematical symbols used for counting. In his philosophy, different numbers were associated with different gods and states of being. The monad (the primary element of the number one), for example, "was identified with the primordial chaos, which existed before the gods, but … was also identified with the sun and with Apollo." Additionally, Nicomachus believed that numbers formed the essence of all things. Understanding life and the world, therefore, meant understanding numerical integers. This is what Nicomachus sought to do in his study of arithmetic.

Nicomachus took a particular interest in perfect numbers, those whose factors add up to that original number. Six, for example, is a perfect number because $1 + 2 + 3 = 6$. He postulated that the nth perfect number has n digits, and that all perfect numbers end in 6 or 8 alternately. However, he never attempted to prove this theory or any of his other ideas. He simply gave numerical examples. While this perfect number concept worked well for the known perfect numbers at the time—6, 28, 496, and 8128—it could not be considered true for all values known today.

Nicomachus's "rather strange approach to numbers" can further be seen in his ideas on abundant and deficient integers. An abundant number is one whose factors added up to a value greater than the original number; 12 is the first of these $(1+2+3+4+6)$. A deficient number is one whose factors add to a value less than the original. For example, 8 $(1+2+4)$ and 10 $(1+2+5)$ and all prime numbers are deficient. Nicomachus described the essence of these numbers when compared to a perfect value:

> In the case of the too much, is produced excess, superfluity, exaggerations and abuse; in the case of too little, is produced wanting, defaults, privations and insufficiencies. And in the case of those that are found between the too much and the too little, that is in equality, is produced virtue, just measure, propriety, beauty and things of that sort—of which the most exemplary form is that type of number which is called perfect.

This is a good example of how Nicomachus contributed abstract ideas such as morality to numerical values. Clearly, his writings were not focused only on pure mathematics but on the mystical side of arithmetic as well. Yet his works did contribute to modern mathematics in that they included the first Greek times tables and separated the study of arithmetic from that of geometry.

Music and Math

In his *Manual on Harmonics*, Nicomachus continued to explore mystic philosophy, except this time focusing on music instead of numerical numbers. He assigned each planet a musical note, except for Earth because he believed it to be standing still. Therefore, when the planets circled the Earth in their spheres, they would produce the inaudible harmony of a world working in perfect order.

In this work, Nicomachus tells the story of how Pythagoras was walking by some blacksmiths when he heard how the hammers beating iron on the anvil [gave] out sounds fully concordant in combination with another. Nicomachus tells how Pythagoras discovered that the different chords were produced by varying hammer weights and how "the interval of an octave was produced in a 2:1 ratio, that of a fifth by weights in a 3:2 ratio, [and] that of a fourth by weights in a 4:3 ratio." In other words, Pythagoras discovered that numbers and musical harmony are related. This discovery fit in well with Nicomachus's philosophy that the natural world revolves around arithmetic and integers.

Tatjana Scherschel, 2015

PTOLEMY, 100–170, *Earth-Centric Astronomer*

> " I know that I am mortal by nature, and ephemeral; but when I trace at my pleasure the windings to and fro of the heavenly bodies I no longer touch the earth with my feet: I stand in the presence of Zeus himself and take my fill of ambrosia, food of the gods.
> —*The Almagest*

- Earned the title "The Father of Geography" for his atlas of the ancient world
- Had his personal life obscured by history; from his writings, we know he made his astronomical observations from the Egyptian city of Alexandria from 127–141 and was a Roman citizen of Greek descent
- Was educated and knowledgeable of the work of his predecessors: he summarized and built upon the ideas of those before him, and we owe much of our current knowledge on the ancient astronomers and geographers to his efforts
- Is known for his two most influential works, *The Almagest*, which described his theories on astronomy, and *Geography*, "a formidable synthesis of the geographical knowledge of the classical world"
- Described, in *The Almagest*, his Ptolemaic system, which detailed the movement of the planets and other heavenly bodies in a earth-centered universe—a flawed model that seemed so accurate that people accepted it until the 16th century, well over 1,000 years later
- Developed what would be the standard atlas for 1,300 years with his *Geography*, equally influential with *The Almagest*, and which so underestimated the world's size it made Columbus believe he could easily reach Asia by sailing west
- Was also heavily interested in astrology, and his work *Tetrabiblos* became a defining authority on the subject; in addition, he excelled at mathematics and relied heavily on geometry to explain his theories

Key Works

The Almagest, c. 145–150
Geography, c. 150
Tetrabiblos, c. 150–170

Biography

Little is known of Claudius Ptolemaeus's (Ptolemy's) personal life. Even the exact dates of his birth and death evade historians. However, we do know from *The Almagest* that he made astronomical observations from the city of Alexandria during the years 127–141. Like many thinkers, he dedicated his entire life to learning and discovery. "The heavens" particularly captivated him, and throughout his life, he mapped over 1,000 stars, 300 of which had never been charted before. A man highly dedicated to the ideas of reason and logic, he sought to consolidate Aristotle's geocentric theory that earth is at the center of the universe with the fact that the planets and stars do not always travel in a straight line or even at a constant speed. His resulting Ptolemaic system, described in *The Almagest*, is surprisingly accurate, and scientists rarely questioned it for hundreds of years. Interested in the earth as well as the heavens, Ptolemy left his mark on the field of geography by mapping out the world in his famous *Geography*. He also refused to let his belief in reason restrain his love for the stars, and he attempted to reconcile logic with astrology.

The Heavens Above

Ptolemy did not start from scratch in his ideas about the heavens. He was an educated man who understood the theories of those who came before him, and wrote extensively about the ideas of others. Many historians even acclaim his work as being a complete summary of eight centuries of Greek geocentric thought about the nature of the cosmos. Ptolemy, however, was not satisfied in merely expressing the viewpoints of others; he felt compelled to explain them according to the laws of reason, logic, and math.

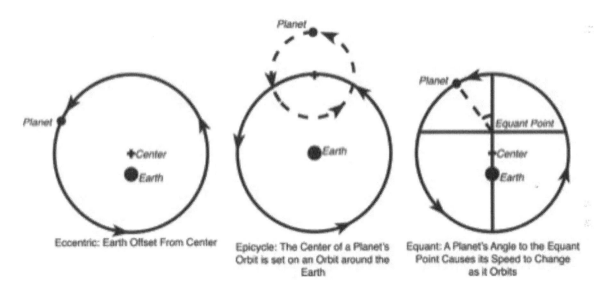

Ptolemy's System—Eccentric, Epicycle, Equant

From the beginning of his studies, Ptolemy accepted the Aristotelian belief that the earth lay in the center of the universe, surrounded by quintessence, a perfect fifth element. This quintessence, or *aether*, was divided into distinct spherical shells, each of which carried either one of the five known planets (Mercury, Venus, Mars, Jupiter, or Saturn), the moon, the sun, or the stars. According to Aristotle, the movement of these spheres explained the movement of the planets. Yet Ptolemy and many others observed that "heavenly bodies did, in fact, not move with perfect circular motions: they sped up, slowed down, and in the cases of the planets even stopped and reversed their motions." Yet despite these incidents concerning the movements of the planets, Ptolemy stubbornly refused to abandon the ancient belief that the universe was one of perfect circular motion, and that all this motion revolved around Earth.

To explain the movement of heavenly bodies, Ptolemy devised three basic models: the eccentric, the epicycle, and the equant. The first and most simple, the eccentric, simply placed Earth slightly away from the center of the planet's orbit. Although this notion went against the idea of Earth as the center of the universe, the displacement was minimal and was considered a slight bending of the rule rather than a violation. The epicycle model was a bit more complicated: here the planet traveled in a circle, but the center of this circle also traveled in a circle around the earth. This movement accounted for the retrograde motion of the planets.

Ptolemy created the equant model, the most difficult construction to visualize, in an attempt to explain how the planets only "appear" to undergo changes in speed. In this model, the center of motion (the "equant point") was separate from the center of the planet's orbit. According to Ptolemy, the planet always revolved around this equant point at a uniform speed, and in order for the body to retain this constant rate when the equant was not equidistant from all points of the planet's path, the planet had to speed up or slow down at certain points on its circular path. Slightly confused? Alfonso X of Castile, after learning about the Ptolemaic system stated, "If the Lord Almighty had consulted me before embarking upon his creation, I should have recommended something simpler."

Mapping the Earth

Even though his first love was for the heavens above, Ptolemy also made significant contributions to the study of geography. His influential *Geography* was both a complete atlas of the ancient world and a guide on how to create accurate maps.

Ptolemy's World Map

In writing down various scientific methods to mapmaking, Ptolemy hoped to remove religion and myths from the art of mapmaking and make cartography an exact science. Ever the astronomer, he believed in using the stars as well as math to calculate what the world looked like. Therefore, he heavily endorsed the use of latitude and longitude, and went as far as recording the locations of over 8,000 places in the ancient world. He also spent a great deal of time devising ways of representing the spherical Earth on a two-dimensional surface. Yet his work was a far cry from accurate, and it showed the world as much smaller than it actually is and failed, of course, to illustrate the Americas.

Ptolemy and Astrology: The Logic in Stars

It may seem surprising at first that Ptolemy, a man who put so much emphasis on rationality, spent much of his time studying astrology, but his intention was to reconcile the study with logic and science. As Ptolemy himself stated in *Tetrabiblos*, "As for the nonsense on which many waste their labour and of which not even a plausible account can be given, this we shall dismiss in favour of the primary natural causes." Ptolemy's quest, therefore, was to explain logically and scientifically how movements in the stars and planets affected human life on Earth.

Most of his ideas rested on the scientific concept (at the time) that different planets had different characteristics depending on their relationship with the sun and with the Earth. Ancient thinkers viewed the former as a source of heat and light and saw the latter as a source of moisture. Saturn, therefore, was thought of as a "cold and dry" planet because it was located far from both the sun and Earth. Even today cold and dry places are associated with sickness and death. Ptolemy extended this idea, believing that "the constant movement of the planets creates an ever-changing atmosphere to which all the Earth's creatures are sensitive." Ptolemy blurred the lines between Earth and heaven, believing that the celestial atmosphere into which a child was born would affect him greatly. A newborn's spirit, for example, would suffer from being born into the harsh environment of Saturn, just as his body would suffer if it had been born in a freezing desert.

An Influential Man

Ptolemy, despite his brilliance, was essentially wrong about many of the topics he thought about. He believed that the universe was centered on the Earth, and conjuured an entire complicated system to explain it. We know now that the solar system revolves around the sun, and gravity is the force behind the planet's movements—not epicycles and equants. Ptolemy envisioned a world with one large ocean and with Europe, Africa, and Asia as the only continents. We know now the Earth is significantly larger and has seven total continental landmasses.

So why is the study of Ptolemy so important? The answer is that his work was so influential. His geocentric universe and the laws explaining it were incredibly accurate, and allowed scientists to make precise predictions on where the stars and other heavenly bodies would be at a certain time. Because of this accuracy and complexity, it should be of little surprise that even when Copernicus pointed out the fatal flaw—that the Earth moves—astronomers were reluctant to abandon it. His *Geography* was the only surviving work of its kind, and when it resurfaced around 1410, it corrected major flaws in medieval thinking, such as the notion that Earth is flat. It was also *Geography*, with its misjudgment of Earth's size, which influenced Columbus to sail west to Asia. As for his study of astronomy, Ptolemy's *Tetrabiblos* was considered then and remains a defining authority on the subject.

Tatjana Scherschel, 2015

> " What is thy vocation? To be a good man.
>
> —*Meditations*

- Roman Emperor at the end of the Golden Age of Rome
- Desired peace but was forced into conflict for the majority of his rule
- Considered to be one of the few Roman Emperors concerned with the good of the people
- Writings tended to be reflective in nature, not likely meant for wide readership
- Heavily influenced by the Socratic element of Stoic thought (see Socrates and Epictetus), seeing it as the motivation for right rule, void of material self-interest and focused on the duties, rather than the personal advantages, of power
- Emphasized the Stoic ideal of moderation and the self-sufficiency of reason: "The rational principle which rules has this nature, that it is content with itself when it does what is just, and so secures tranquility."

Key Work

Meditations, 167 AD

Biography

Born to a wealthy Iberian family in 121 AD, Marcus Aurelius was later adopted into the family of Emperor Antonius Pius at the insistence of Emperor Hadrian, Aurelius's first adoptive father. Adoption by Pius assured Aurelius eventual rule of the Roman Empire. As a student, Aurelius was influenced by the teachings of Epictetus, and as a result he is said to have lived a life of moderation and self-denial. The death of Antonius Pius in 161 AD thrust Marcus Aurelius into power along with his brother Lucius. Though he desired peace, rebellion and invasion dominated his time as emperor. Still, like Antonius Pius, Marcus Aurelius's reign included social reforms and a general emphasis on what was good for all classes of individuals. This emphasis on social reform exemplifies his application of Stoic thought to political ideology. While his actions as emperor suggest a Stoic influence, his writings explicitly confirm it. His significance lies mostly in his exemplification of how Stoic thought had influenced the thinking of the day as well as its influence on leadership.

The *Meditations*

Marcus Aurelius contemplated his life and decisions in what is now referred to as his *Meditations.* These writings are unique in that they contain "random memoranda meant for himself alone, jotted down while on military expeditions, and reflecting his doubts and indecisions as well as his faith and his philosophy." As a result, the text resembles a journal more than a traditional philosophical discourse—an effort to question his life's actions. *Meditations* is famous for its depiction of the Stoic worldview in a personal context, illustrating the significant influence that Stoic thought had on Roman life.

In *Meditations*, Aurelius focuses primarily on the three areas of thought he found most important: morality, value for human nature and human life, and the political application of these concerns. Aurelius begins *Meditations* by detailing the lessons he acquired in life from the people around him. For example, he praises his adopted father for his "compassion" (I:16) and spends significant time describing how he aspires to "not display anger or other emotions," but rather "to be free of passion yet full of love" (I:9). These reflections underscore the importance of service to others, rather than bowing to one's self-serving passions. Another theme that surfaces in *Meditations* is Aurelius's concern with making the right choices rather than needing correction; for instance, he emphasizes "*staying* on the path rather than being *kept* on it" (I:15), or being "straight, not straightened" (VII:12). In a sense, he depicts life to be of greatest value when it is led by the self, rather than dictated by those who surround. These reflections on character led Aurelius to develop an ethic of personal responsibility.

Human Behavior

Aurelius believed that "people are our proper occupation," a belief that provides the impetus for his instructive writings. Aurelius also felt that man's contentment in life rested in companionship, that "joy for humans lies in human actions" towards other humans, i.e., any act of kindness, justice, or love. While Aurelius's reign often necessitated his being at war, he desired peace and despised the idea of corrupt human interaction: "to obstruct each other is unnatural … to feel anger at someone, to turn your back on him: these are obstructions." Aurelius believed that life was valuable and that man was responsible for benefitting, and not obstructing or fighting with, his fellow man.

Political Application

Aurelius attempted to apply the ideals he sets forth in *Meditations* both politically and personally. He learned "to recognize the malice, cunning, and hypocrisy that power produces" (I.11). As such, Aurelius acknowledged the corrupting nature of his own position of power and worked to uphold humility. He was also concerned about fairness; he recalls that his first teacher taught him "not to support this side or that in chariot-racing, [or] this fighter or that in the games" (I.5). Furthermore, Aurelius's perspective towards leadership recognized the importance of his subject's welfare: "what injures the hive injures the bee" (VI.54), a metaphor that highlights the connection between a leader's well being and that of his people; and "to do harm is to do yourself harm, [and] to do injustice is to do yourself injustice—it degrades you" (IX.4). Through his writing of *Meditations*, Aurelius arrives at an ethic that every act a person commits ultimately affects him personally.

Nate Kosirog, faculty
Nathaniel Whatmore, 2015
Daren Jonescu, advisor

LUCIAN OF SAMOSATA, 125–180, *Satirist of Philosophy*

> " I now make the only true statement you are to expect—that I am a liar. This confession is, I consider, a full defense against all imputations. My subject is, then, what I have neither seen, experienced, nor been told, what neither exists nor could conceivably do so. I humbly solicit my readers' incredulity.
>
> —*A True Story*

- Was a Syrian satirist who enjoyed mocking philosophical and religious movements
- Wrote his own ideology in some of his works, despite being a satirist
- Learned Greek at a young age and wrote only in Greek, even though he was Syrian
- Wrote enough about himself that most known information about him is from his various books
- Believed that those who rejected the Greek gods were ignorant, and attacked them through his satires
- Traveled through the ancient world until late in his life when he was in need of money

- Wrote the first science fiction story: his *True Fictions*, a parody of unreliable historical sources, describes a war to rule the Morning Star by the (non-human) people of the Sun and Moon

Key Works

Dialogues of the Dead, c. 150–180
Dialogues of the Gods, c. 150–180
Herodotus, c. 150–180
A True Story (also called *True History*), c. 150–180

Biography

Lucian of Samosata was a Greek satirical writer and philosopher who is believed to have been born in 125 AD in Syria. Not much information has survived the passage of time; in fact, most of the information known about Lucian comes from his own works. His native language was Aramaic, but he mastered Greek. He is best known as a "sophistic rhetorician in Greece, Italy, and Gaul," but he traveled throughout the ancient world for most of his life. Lucian completed approximately 80 written works, and though all are in dialogue form, they span the rhetorical, philosophical, and satirical. While still appreciated for his other collections, Lucian's most famous works are his satirical writings. Through these parodies, Lucian attacks the philosophers of the time, the most notable attacks being on various religious movements. Finally, in need of money, Lucian settled down in Roman Egypt, where he accepted a government position. Lucian eventually died around 180 AD in Athens, Greece.

Philosophy through Parody

Much like his modern counterpart Voltaire, Lucian incorporated his philosophy into satire. He enjoyed ridiculing philosophers and other epic poems, which are observed in his series of *Dialogues*, which include *Dialogues of the Gods*, *Dialogues of the Sea Gods*, and *Dialogues of the Dead*. In *Dialogues of the Dead*, Hermes and Menippus are talking, and Menippus wishes to see Helen. Hermes points out a skull in the corner, to which Menippus is shocked and replies, "And for this a thousand ships carried warriors from every part of Greece." Hermes tells Menippus that she is beautiful, to which Menippus says that Helen's beauty was "short-lived, quick to fade." Through this short dialogue between Menippus and Hermes, Lucian exposes human folly in Homer's epic, making fun of the soldiers who fought for Helen. Lucian's form of philosophy is more thoroughly expressed through satire, earning him a place with notables such as Erasmus, Aristophanes, and George Orwell.

Stylistic Choices in *Herodotus*

Using techniques before applied only by rhetoricians, Lucian's innovative style combined forms of narrative, formal description, comparison, and praise into one unique whole. This literary form is best seen in his work *Herodotus*. The story illustrates the details of how the Greek writer by the same name gained fame and fortune "reading his stories aloud at the Olympic games." Lucian used great detail in his works, even describing how the audience was enraptured by Herodotus's stories due to "the elegance of his diction, the harmony of his periods, the familiar aptness of his native Ionick, and his richness of expression." In addition to his lilting syntax, Lucian added illustrations to his work to add more detail. In *Herodotus*, Lucian adds the caption for his graphic, "It represents a very fine chamber containing a nuptial bed" and goes on to further explain the significance of the picture of the bed in relation to his story. *Herodotus* was one of Lucian's shorter works, written "to establish a relaxed relationship with the audience." Lucian's incorporation of comedy and solemnity in combination with his unique style formed an attention-grabbing mechanism to convey his philosophical views. In *Herodotus* the subject matter, much like many of his other works, included ridicule of the idea of organized religion. Through humor and mockery, Lucian was able to prepare his audience for one of his longer and more significant works, while still providing ample entertainment for the reader.

Father of Science Fiction

Despite primarily being a satirist, Lucian is also considered the true father of the science fiction genre. His book *A True Story* is a parody of other works at the time that claimed to use mythology as reliable sources. The story tells the tale of a Greek ship that is whisked away in a whirlwind to another world. There, the king tells the dwellers of the ship that "the inhabitants of the sun" and "the inhabitants of the moon has [sic] been at war with us for a long time now." and he implores the protagonist to help them. At this time, the idea of occupying places in space was unheard of, considering that most people of the time perceived the moon and sun to be gods. He also suggested the existence of aliens. Lucian describes creatures on the moon as being different in anatomy, as the women "carry their children in the calf of their leg" while the men's "noses run of honey" and they "sweat milk … of such quality that cheese can actually be made of it." Despite the original intention of his story as parody, Lucian managed to develop a new genre that has influenced much modern fiction.

Legacy

Lucian's 80 works are still considered incisive critiques. While his satires were primarily disguised in a dialogue format, they were still considered and read as satires. Despite being one of the most notable writers of parody, Lucian's philosophical books are also admired. Even though Lucian could also be considered a philosopher, he mocked much of the ideologies of the time, expressing his mockery through his satires. His most notable satire is his *Dialogues of the Gods*, a caricature of the religious movements, in which he parodies other forms of faith, particularly Christianity. Overall, Lucian's ability to both philosophize and mock landed him a spot as one of the most distinguished authors of his time.

Nikki Brandon, 2015
Julianne Swayze, 2016
Daren Jonescu, advisor

GALEN, 129–216, *The Physician*

> The chief merit of language is clearness.
>
> —*On the Natural Faculties*

- Wrote hundreds of different treatises on medicine, physiology, philosophy, and rhetoric
- Formed the foundation of the world's knowledge about medical practice until the 16th century, with his teachings and findings
- Advocated for the union of medicine and philosophy, which influenced Eastern scientists throughout the Medieval Ages

Key Works

Three Commentaries on the Syllogistic Works of Chrysippus

On the Passions and Errors of the Soul
On the Movements of the Heart and Lung, c. 150
On Demonstration
On the Usefulness of the Parts of the Body, c. 175
On the Natural Faculties, c. 174
The Method of Cure, c. 179
On the Equality of Sin and Punishment
The Slight Significance of Popular Honor and Glory
The Refusal to Divulge Knowledge
Introduction to Dialectics

Biography

Born in 129 AD in the heart of Asia Minor, Pergamon, Galen enjoyed a childhood of wealth, influence, and education. Inspired by a dream of the Greek god of healing, Galen's father encouraged his son to study medicine. After his father's death, Galen continued his studies by traveling across Crete, Cyprus, Phoenicia, Palestine, and finally Alexandria. After studying in the immense library of medical works in Alexandria, Galen returned to Pergamon to practice as a physician. Though human dissection was illegal in his day, Galen relentlessly sought to increase his understanding of the human body by operating on wounded gladiators and dissecting apes, dogs, pigs, and other animals.

Seeking to continue his studies, Galen later traveled to Rome but was "disappointed … by the ignorance and laziness of many of the Roman doctors he met." Unsatisfied with relying on traditional medical lore, Galen sought to further his medical knowledge through performing experiments and collecting empirical data. In 169, Roman emperor Marcus Aurelius called upon Galen to document and treat the plague that was sweeping across the war-torn Germanic region. After returning to Rome, Galen served as a physician to both the emperor Marcus Aurelius and his son Commodus. In this time, Galen published vast amounts of research before his death in 216 AD.

Medicine

As a researcher and physician, Galen was a pioneer in anatomy. Today, he is credited with being the first to understand the differences between veins and arteries. Through his experiments and dissections of animals, Galen also discovered the importance of the nervous system and "recognized that the brain directed bodily movements and was also the center of thought and reasoning." Galen was the first to practice the "pulse check," a method that is still used to help determine heart arrhythmia in patients. Finally, Galen discovered that he could more accurately determine the ailments of his patients by analyzing the coloration of urine. In addition to making his own contributions to the field of medicine, Galen also played a key role in documenting and preserving ancient medical practices. Some argue that without Galen's preservation, the vital medical practice founded by Hippocrates in the fifth century BC would have become extinct.

Philosophy

Galen firmly felt that "philosophy was essential to the proper practice of medicine: the best doctor was also a philosopher, whether or not he realized it." A strong proponent of logical reasoning, Galen believed that rationalistic thinking would allow a doctor to quickly and accurately diagnose problems. Galen also advocated for clarity and simplicity in medical rhetoric. As he wrote in *On the Natural Faculties*, "The chief merit of language is clearness, and we know that nothing detracts so much from this as do unfamiliar terms; accordingly we employ those terms which the bulk of people are accustomed to use."

Galen also understood medicine within a teleological framework. According to Galen's theory, "Each part of the body had been designed teleologically, for a particular purpose, and any alteration or imbalance in its basic elements, qualities, or humors resulted in illness." In other words, Galen believed that all parts of the body served a unique purpose, and that illnesses were caused by parts of the body failing to perform their exact function within bodily systems. Based on his animal research, Galen also theorized about the connection of the bodily systems with the soul. According to his view, animals and humans each contained three bodily systems that corresponded to the three parts of Plato's soul: the appetites, the spirited, and the mind. Though science in the Western world no longer emphasizes the importance of philosophy in medicine, many of Galen's ideas were translated into Arabic, and traces of his philosophies are still found in Eastern medical thought.

Ryan Russell, 2015
Jackson Howell, 2015

PLOTINUS, 205–270, *The Founder of Neoplatonism*

> " Thus the act of production is seen to be in Nature an act of contemplation, for creation is the outcome of a contemplation which never becomes anything else, which never does anything else, but creates by simply being a contemplation.
>
> —*The Enneads*

- Was considered the founder of "Neoplatonism," a systematized, mystical interpretation of Plato's thought
- Had his writings edited and organized as *The Enneads* by his most famous student, Porphyry
- Rejected Christianity, but his views about the cosmic order, the soul, and the nature of evil influenced Augustine, leading to the melding of Christianity with Greek thought in the Middle Ages
- Died in a friend's estate in Campania, after the assassination of Emperor Gallienus, who admired him
- Proposed a cosmic hierarchy of three elements—the One, the Intelligence, and the Soul—plus Matter
- The One: Similar to Plato's "One" or "Good," an indefinable source of all being, knowable only by a "vision" of the Intelligence, which desires unity with its source
- The Intelligence: the pure mind, separate from matter or change, thinks only the eternal Forms or Ideas (see Plato) and the One Itself; knowable only by the higher Soul which loves and contemplates it
- The Soul is one being with two aspects: the higher Soul (World Soul) seeks unity with the Intelligence by contemplating the Ideas; the lower Soul produces representations of the Ideas in Matter, i.e., the natural world of individuated objects that we experience around us
- Matter is pure potential, receptive to Ideas imposed on it by the soul's productive activity
- In producing our earthly world, the lower, individuated soul *forgets* its relation to the Intelligence; it must learn, via love (Greek *Eros*) to return to the pure Ideas it has forgotten (see Plato's theory of recollection)

- The soul obsessed with external reality loses contact with the Good by admiring what is *inferior to itself*, rather than the Intelligence (its superior); thus, Plotinus' answer to "the problem of evil" which became central to Christian philosophy—i.e., How is evil possible in a world emanating from a purely good source?—is that it arises from the forgetful soul's confused infatuation with its own material products

Key Work

The Enneads, 250

Biography

Plotinus is thought to have been born in Egypt in 205 AD. He later moved to Alexandria (his first documented location) in search of a teacher. While there, he attended the lectures of many philosophers, not finding any of them satisfactory until he discovered the teacher Ammonius Saccas. Plotinus studied under Ammonius for 11 years until 242 AD, when he decided to join the Emperor Gordian on an expedition to Persia. Although the Emperor's desires were military, Plotinus supposedly expected to engage with the famed Persian philosophers in his pursuit of wisdom. The expedition never achieved its military or philosophical goals, however; the Emperor was assassinated in Mesopotamia, causing Plotinus to flee to Rome. When in Rome, Plotinus opened an academy to teach his interpretation of Plato. He taught there for 20 years, after which his most famed student Porphyry arrived and urged Plotinus to turn his treatises into systematic form. Thus, Plotinus, through his pupil Porphyry, began to compose the *Enneads*, an assimilation of "refutations and corrections of the positions of Peripatetics, Stoics, Epicureans, Gnostics, and Astrologers," and an interpretation of Plato, whom he considered to be the highest authority on all things philosophical. With its interpretation of Plato's the One, the Intelligence, and the Soul, as well as his view on the human individual, the *Enneads* solidified the significance of Plotinus as philosopher.

Introduction to Plotinus's Philosophy

Plotinus's philosophical writings are some of the most complex of the classical world. Initially, it is helpful to see his ideas as forming a "downward path of being." This is because in Plotinus's philosophy there is a downward movement from the One to the Intelligence (Nous), which is made of two levels, best understood as the result of God's thinking. From there, the downward movement continues on to the Soul, which is made up of the Cosmic Soul (three parts) and the Individual Soul. Each of these levels is connected in some way to the One. Through this, Plotinus also describes a salvation narrative that includes the upward climb of the Soul, as it "tries to free itself from the domination of the body and find its way back to its natural domain, the realm of God and eternal truth."

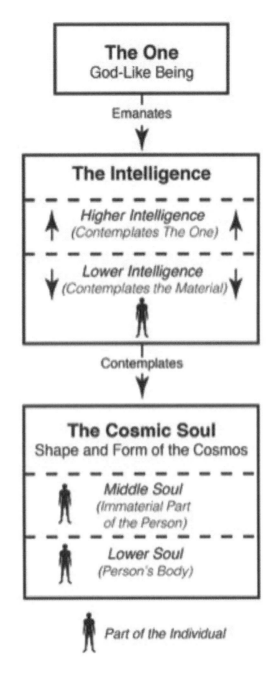

Plotinus's Triumvirate

The One

The simplest way to understand the One is to consider it to be similar to God. While central to Plotinus's philosophy and interpretation of Plato, Plotinus never explicitly defined "the One," believing that it simply couldn't be put into words. This should illustrate that, according to Plotinus, the One is ineffable and its name is appropriately vague. Still, Plotinus spends a significant amount of time in the *Enneads* elaborating on what the One is and is not. Plotinus describes the One as the singular, quality-less, self-contained, center of the framework of the cosmos. He also states that everything emanates from the One, the One transcends all beings, but the One is not a being. Though not a being, the One still "begets all beings." The One is also explained as being "cognizant of nothing, yet still ignorant of nothing, and through this, a distinction is created between our knowing and the One's knowing." We also see in the One's begetting of all beings that the One reveals a sense of its power, and, according to Plotinus, can be contemplated only through the Intelligence.

The Intelligence (Nous)

The Intelligence is an entity that is derived from the One. Still, the One does not consciously generate the Intelligence, but rather emanates it. Plotinus defines the Intelligence as an entity having a dual purpose: "to contemplate the 'power' (*dunamis*) of the One, which the Intelligence recognizes as its source, and to meditate upon the thoughts that are eternally present to it, and which constitute its very being." In this way, the aim of Intelligence is to think and contemplate the power of its superior, the One, and also reason through thoughts and ideas that exist around it in the material world. One way to look at this dual purpose of the Intelligence is to consider the mind to be made up of two levels: a higher level, which is parallel to the mind of God yet still distinctly different as it is meant to try and understand this God, and the lower, which is used in completing an everyday task, reasoning through reality, or dealing with human interaction.

Through the dual purpose of Intelligence, Plotinus explains the connection between the Intelligence and Being, writing that "the being of the Intelligence is its thought, and the thought of the Intelligence is Being … for none of the Beings is outside the Intellectual-Principle or in space; they remain for ever in themselves, accepting no change, no decay, and by that are the authentically existent." Plotinus elaborates on this relationship by describing the Intelligence as the governor of the cosmos, which "persists in governing, without flaw," while Being governs as Intelligence sorts through the Ideas (*eide*)—the objects of contemplation which compose the Intelligence. The Being acts as a "productive capacity of Difference," conducting discernment between the Ideas that compose the Intelligence that then become immortal essences of the Soul—a catalyst of "independence of self-sameness of all existents proceeding from the Intelligence." Through this, Plotinus explains that the Intelligence, a transcendent, unbiased source, enables the Soul to contemplate. Through this contemplation, the Soul is then able to utilize Intelligence through reason, and within this reason, to eternally contemplate the "power" of the One (never the One itself) and rationally meditate on thoughts and events that are present to it. According to Plotinus, the Intelligence connects the Soul to the cosmos and the One in the spiritual realm. Through this, Plotinus justifies his understanding of how we know there is a God, or the One. He resolves one of Plato's greatest questions: "How can human minds know the eternal Forms?" Plotinus answers that this is possible because the human minds are extensions of the cosmic mind, which is the "natural home of the Forms."

The Soul

The Soul is the lowest part of Plotinus's Triumvirate. It is the place where Plotinus believed the cosmos took "objective shape and physical form." The Soul as described by Plotinus is not to be simplified into something that exists in the individual. He makes it clear that there is a Cosmic Soul and multiple souls within that. The Cosmic Soul can be split into three parts: the upper level, which explains "motion and change in the world," the middle level, which is the "source of life," and the lower, giving "rise to specific bodies." The multiple Souls existing within the Cosmic Soul can be found in the middle level and can be subcategorized as immortal pieces of all types of beings: humans, animals, and plants. This is exemplified when Plotinus states, "If any one of them contains this engrained life, that one is the soul." Different types of beings have different souls; plants and animals have vegetative and sensitive souls while humans possess those plus a rational soul.

In the Soul, Plotinus also distinguishes between two parts: the Contemplative (higher) piece that connects with the Intelligence, and the Active (lower) piece that descends into the physical realm, shaping the cosmos. This is significant because it draws a clear connection between the Soul and the Intelligence (higher), illustrating how Plotinus thought the Soul had specific influence on the physical world (lower). These different roles of the Soul explicate its being tasked with applying the ideas of the Intelligence through life and then returning them to divine status in the Intelligence. It is in this lower part of the Soul that suffering and falling to vice occur, leading to the falling away of the Soul from the Intelligence and the One. Plotinus thus claims that the Soul must take three steps to return to that desired unity: first, pursue the cultivation of virtue, reminding the Soul of divine virtue; second, attempt investigation, seeking to understand the One and the Intelligence; and finally, exercise contemplation through which one asks what the proper act and mode of the Soul is. This pursuit of the Intelligence by the Soul and the responsibility of the Soul to pursue its divine status was how Plotinus viewed the interaction of the physical world and the spiritual.

Ethics of the Individual and the Personality

Within the division of the Soul, Plotinus begins to describe the physical world of what he calls the living being, or the human being. The living being is categorized within the lower being of the Soul—the individual souls that unite in the Cosmic Soul. Plotinus describes the Cosmic Soul as being a source of light that illuminates "the formerly dark 'prism' of matter." Within this illumination, the rays of the Cosmic Soul then begin to become differed in their fragmentation. These fragmented rays of the Cosmic light then attain a passive character in which they are given "the ability to be affected by the turbulence of matter as it groans and labors under the vivifying power of the Soul."

With this turbulence of matter, Plotinus describes the beginning of a soul's personality. The interaction between the physical world (matter) and the individual soul thus begins to shape the human race, even down to the individuality of a person. Plotinus defines personality as "something accrued, an addition of alien elements that come to be attached to the pure soul through its assimilative contact with matter." This personality is the lower Soul's reaction to the physical realm as it animates the matter around it. Plotinus makes it clear that the Soul, although surrounded by the material, is an immortal and transcendent being; however, he suggests that "the spoiled souls of the great mass [find it] difficult to recognize their divinity and immortality." Here, Plotinus admits that the lower Soul can become affected by the material world and become forgetful of its divinity within the Cosmic Soul. Continuing this thought, Plotinus touches on ethics by explaining the individual's return to divinity and unity with the Cosmic Soul. Plotinus agreed with Plato that the individual soul's greatest purpose is to achieve as much likeness as possible to God. Plotinus even describes the soul as having a "most God-like phase." This God-like aspiration shapes Plotinus's core ethical belief. Plotinus believed that the only purpose of the soul was to use Intelligence to contemplate the power of his superior, so an individual should automatically assume this superior power is an imitable figure whose ethics should be replicated.

Influence on Christian Thought

Behind Plato and Aristotle, Plotinus has been considered the third most important philosopher of the ancient world, partially because of the impact of his philosophy on Christianity. He is described as the philosopher that draws the connecting line between the Greeks and "the beginnings of Christian philosophy." One example of how Plotinus achieves this is by demonstrating an apparent lack of divide between religion and philosophy. We also see his significant impact on Christianity through his eventual influence on the first Christian philosopher and theologian Augustine. Still, it is important to note that while Plotinus impacted Augustine significantly, Augustine's philosophy yields to scripture where the ideas of Plotinus and scripture disagree.

Nate Kosirog, faculty
Nathaniel Whatmore, 2015
Daren Jonescu, advisor

CONSTANTINE THE GREAT ◊ 272-337, *The First Christian Emperor*

> " To all who entertain just and sound sentiments respecting the character of the Supreme Being, it has long been most clearly evident, and beyond the possibility of doubt, how vast a difference there has ever been between those who maintain a careful observance of the hallowed duties of the Christian religion, and those who treat this religion with hostility or contempt.

—to the inhabitants of the province of Palestine

- Was the son of army officer Favius Valerius Constantius and his concubine
- Encountered Christianity within the imperial court during a period of the persecution of Christians
- Fought with his father as a military tribune
- Was a brilliant military strategist
- Was declared emperor by the army upon his father's death
- Triumphed in civil wars against Maxentius and Licinius in the Battle of the Milvian Bridge
- Reportedly had a dream telling him to paint the Christian monogram on the shields of his army
- Became the ruler of the Roman empire, ending the Tetrarchy, and beginning the rule of dynastic succession
- Authorized new gold coins and a new tax for trade
- Gave God the glory for his victories, converted to Christianity, and promoted religious tolerance through the Edict of Milan
- Ordered the First Council of Nicaea which created the Nicene Creed
- Suppressed pagan practices
- Built a new imperial home at Byzantium, "New Rome," which the Romans renamed "Constantinople" to honor him
- Set aside the place of Jesus's tomb in Jerusalem for construction of The Church of the Holy Sepulchre and built many other churches
- Maintained a deep personal commitment to Christianity, which included a responsibility to spread Christianity; considered himself the 13th Apostle
- Created the example of a Christian imperial governing class that brought about a Christian, biblical culture in the Roman Empire

Key Works
"Edict of Toleration"
"Opening Address at Nicaea"
"Fourth letter to Eusebius about the Restoration of the Divine Books"
"Letter to Empress Helen"

Biography

Constantine I, Flavius Valerius Constantinus, is the first Christian Roman emperor as well as the creator of a Christian culture in his new empire. He was born to a military leader, Constantius, who was a deputy emperor under Emperor August Maximian. Constantine was raised in the Eastern Emperor in the court of Diocletian. He composed in Latin and learned of Christianity during a time of the great persecution of Christians begun under Diocletian.

When Constantius died as he fought with a campaign in Britain, the army chose Constantine for their emperor. Constantine began a number of complicated wars in a victorious effort to take over the Eastern Empire from Maximinus. Then he conquered Licinius and became the single emperor of both the East and the West. Throughout his military successes, Constantine gave credit to his conversion to Christianity and God's support. He believed himself to be God's chosen instrument of peace and prosperity.

The Christian monograms Constantine had painted on his men's shields characterized the remarkable Battle of the Milvian Bridge against Licinius. He maintained that he had received these instructions from God.

Soon after his victory Constantine created the Edict of Milan. The document gave respect to Christians and returned any property that had been taken from them. He also began the Basilica Constantiniana (San Geiovanni in Laterno) as well as several other churches. He made laws that gave the church and the clergy privileges so that they might give "Supreme service to the Divinity."

Constantine took his faith to his troops, and promoted Christian practices while suppressing pagan ones, believing his duties as a Christian to be requisite to his office. He is remembered for Constantinople founded as separation from Rome. His remarkable military success showed him to be a master of political strategy even as he conquered the Franks, Sarmatians, and the Goths. However, his reputation of brutality toward his enemies is notable. His three surviving sons brought about the dynastic succession pattern, part of his lasting legacy elevating the new importance of Christianity and its followers. The new biblical culture took its place alongside established Greek culture.

THE COUNCIL OF NICAEA, 325

Constantine, troubled by controversy in the church, brought about The Council of Nicaea and delivered the opening address. Constantine felt that Arius of Alexandria was arguing over trivial differences, and Arius should work toward peace within the church. While the conflicts weren't resolved at that meeting, the council, comprising bishops from Egypt and Libya, was unified as a body representative of the Christian church, who agreed on several important things. Coming out of the gathering, *The Nicene Creed* states that Christ is "the substance of the Father." It affirms the belief that God is the maker of all things and that through Jesus saved us with his life, death, and ascension. The creed confirms a belief in the Holy Ghost with the stipulation that God created him. The council also resolved the universal date for celebrating Easter. In addition, the *Acts of the Council*, approximately 20 canons, delineates the treatment and behavior of the clergy.

The First Bibles

As part of the persecution of Christians, the Roman Emperor Diocletian ordered all Scripture to be burned in 305 AD. Newly converted to Christianity, trying to preserve the written records for all eternity, Roman Emperor Constantine authorized Eusebius of Caesarea in 312 to produce 50 copies of what would become "The first complete Bibles." An estimate of the modern day cost to hand copy each of the 50 books is $125,000 each. About 75 years later, Bishop Jerome of Dalmatia repeated the process.

JEROME ◊ 324–420, *The Vulgate Bible*

> " The Scriptures are shallow enough for a babe to come and drink without fear of drowning and deep enough for theologians to swim in without ever reaching the bottom.

- Joined a group of ascetics who introduced him to Monasticism
- Made a lifelong study of the Bible
- Studied Hebrew as a hermit in the desert of Chalcis
- Became ordained as a priest
- Served as Secretary to Pope Damascus
- Founded a monastery of men and women in Bethlehem
- Wrote in four categories: translations of the Bible, polemical treatises, historical works, and letters
- Began in Old Latin and Greek
- Concluded using what he called "Hebrew truth"
- Is known for his translation of the Bible (from Greek, Hebrew, Amaric) into the Vulgate Latin language

Biography

Eusebius Hieronymus Sophronius—Jerome—working alone, spent 23 years translating the Bible into the common Latin of the people. His father, Eusebius of Caesarea, had copied 50 complete Bibles years earlier. Jerome was a scholar who studied Scripture and learned Hebrew, working for Pope Damasus in 382. At this point the Old Testament was written in Greek. Because not everyone knew Greek, the first translations were in Latin, Syriac, and Coptic, resulting in a number of poor Latin manuscripts that differed from one another. With the blessing of Pope Damasus, Jerome thought it wise to glean the truth by going to the original Greek, making sure to correct prior work. Jerome carefully provided a new Latin translation from the Hebrew that was entirely verified. He even went to Jewish rabbis for verification.

Jerome's "Divine Library," what he called the Bible, became known as the Vulgate or common language Bible. Martin Luther and scholars for a thousand years regarded this translation as the foundation for all translations.

AUGUSTINE OF HIPPO, 354–430, *Doctor of the Church*

> " You [God] stir man to take pleasure in praising you, because you have made us for yourself, and our heart is restless until it rests in you.
>
> —*Confessions*

- Was sexually promiscuous before converting to Christianity
- Studied both Manichaean and Neo-Platonic philosophy
- Refuted heresies, such as Manichaeism, Donatism, and Pelagianism
- Often interpreted the Bible allegorically, claiming that one's allegorical interpretations are accurate if they support the perfect power, eternality, and goodness of the Trinity
- Considered sin not an entity in itself but merely the product of a disordered, human will
- Originated numerous perspectives on the scriptures that are debated to this day:

  Original Sin
  The Fall
  The Holy Trinity
  Just war theory
  Predestination

Key Works

On the Free Choice of the Will, 387–395
On Genesis, 388–416
Confessions, 397–398
On Christian Doctrine, 397–426
City of God, 413–426

Biography

Augustine was born on November 13, 354, in Thagaste, North Africa. His father, Patricius, was a pagan influence in Augustine's upbringing, in contrast to his mother, Monica, the voice of God in his early life. The young Augustine studied rhetoric at Madura where he fell in love with it, disappointing his father by rejecting a career in law. Shortly after arriving in Carthage for further study, Augustine began a 10-year relationship with a woman who bore him his only child, his son, Adeodatus. During this time Augustine also joined the religious group known as the Manichaeans, who believed in the cosmic struggle between a good spiritual world and an evil material world, an involvement which later inspired many of his literary projects. After working as a rhetorician in Carthage and Rome, Augustine moved to Milan where he became captivated by the sermons of Ambrose. It was in Milan that Augustine abandoned his Manichaeism for Neo-Platonism, and, in 386, his Neo-Platonism for Christianity.

Upon converting to Christianity, Augustine spent over a year studying Christian doctrine and practice until his return to Thagaste in 388. Once there he established a conclave wherein he and some friends engaged in a life of meditation and study. Augustine's monastic period ended with the sudden death of his son in 389 and his own election to the priesthood in 391. During his time as priest, and later as a bishop of Hippo, Augustine produced many exegetical texts concerning Christian doctrine. He was bishop for 35 years until his death in 430.

Manichaeism

Augustine's personal history greatly impacted the content and style of his writing. In the earliest years of his life, he became disillusioned with the apparent contradictions of Christian thought. As a result, he joined the Manichaeans, a rival religious group that ridiculed much of the Bible. Manichaeism was a dualist religion whose members believed in two all-powerful and eternal forces that meshed to form the material world. One of these forces was spiritual and good, the other material and evil. After rejecting Manichaean thought, Augustine became an outspoken critic of the belief system.

On Genesis and Scriptural Interpretation

On Genesis marks the beginning of Augustine's texts on Scriptural interpretation. Because of the great differences between Manichean and Christian creation accounts, the book of Genesis became highly contested ground for the two religions. Augustine's own fascination with the book of beginnings is apparent throughout his career. The Manicheans considered all matter evil, and any attempt to associate goodness and/or God with matter was unthinkable. Consequently, the Manicheans would not allow for a non-literal interpretation to defend the Christian worldview. For this reason, many of the verses in Genesis, such as Genesis 3:8, which discusses God "walking in the garden," were considered ridiculous because God could not possibly walk in a material world with a material body.

By providing sufficient allegorical alternatives to the literal interpretations of the Manichaeans, Augustine not only provided rational grounds for trusting Scripture, but also highlighted the inconsistencies of Manichean philosophy. In the first book of *On Genesis*, Augustine addressed many of the flawed interpretations of Genesis offered by the Manicheans, beginning with the question, "If God made heaven and earth in some beginning of time, what was he doing before he made heaven and earth?" According to Augustine, this question places God and creation in a point of time, which is improper because God stands outside of time. Time only began with the creation of the universe, and God existed prior to this creation because he always existed. For "before the beginning of time there was no time. ... We cannot therefore say that there was any time when God had not yet made anything."

He continued his critique of the Manicheans and study of Scripture in both his *Unfinished Literal Commentary* and *The Literal Meaning of Genesis* wherein he established his *regula fidei*, or rule of faith. Augustine claimed that proper Scriptural interpretations have their origin within the Church, whose collective faith allows for accurate interpretation of the Bible. This *regula fidei* demands interpretation that is consistent with God's omniscience, omnipresence, and omnipotence, as well as the existence of the Holy Trinity. Thus, Augustine developed a rule of faith that allowed one to interpret the Bible from a non-literal perspective.

Confessions

Augustine's autobiography, *Confessions*, is his most famous piece. In it, he explores his journey from sin to God, showing the relationship between the human soul and the divine. Many modern readers are attracted to the confessional nature of the work, but Augustine's aim was not merely to recount personal sin but to praise God for His mercy and grace.

Confessions comprises 13 books. The first nine concern Augustine's biography, while the final four are a study of Genesis 1 to 3. Again we see Augustine's fascination with that period. Besides being a battleground between Manichaeans and Christians, the text also highlights three pivotal themes for

Augustine: creation, fall, and redemption. Therefore what might seem like a weird detour away from the central content of *Confessions* is actually vastly important to Augustine.

In *Confessions* Augustine takes up more issues central to his belief system. One is man's deep need for God. In examining his progression from sin to faith, he delivers his famous quote, "You [God] stir man to take pleasure in praising you, because you have made us for yourself, and our heart is restless until it rests in you." Augustine believed that humanity was characterized by a constant, inward battle. Every individual struggles between the desire to do good and a desire to do evil. In order to find peace in the midst of this battle, one must undergo "conversion," an inward turning of the will, which ultimately means loving God for God's sake and not for the sake of the self. In the process of conversion, individuals seek God through free will. However, since humanity is flawed, this free will is an imperfect means of attaining conversion. While humanity must willingly seek God, it is ultimately God who seeks and saves humanity. This idea is captured in the Latin phrase, *"Do ut des"*—"I give so that you'll give."

Human Freedom and the Privation Theory of Evil

Augustine addresses the problem of evil in multiple texts, including *Confessions* and *City of God*. He was staunchly opposed to Manichaean dualism and would not allow the existence of a God who is not simultaneously good and all-powerful. This can put the believer into a bit of a conundrum, though. If evil is a created thing, it would have its origin in God, but this cannot be, since God is perfectly good. However, if a created thing arose apart from God's will, that would mean there is another source of being outside God, thus challenging His omnipotence.

In order to settle this conflict, Augustine contended that sin is not a real thing in itself, but, rather, a privation of the good: "Evil has no existence except as a privation of the good, down to that level which is altogether without being." All goodness finds root in God; therefore, anything straying from God falls into evil.

For Augustine, "evil exists in our inordinate love of a lesser good." Humanity wrongly perceives the pleasure of sin to be the good, "but it is a lesser good, and it becomes evil because it is a substitute for God." Thus, sin is real insofar as it is a product of human choice. Because humanity has free will, we have the ability to choose an existence apart from God and use the gifts of God for autonomy. Adam was as free to take the fruit in the garden as he was free to obey God. In making this choice to sin, however, humanity cuts off its life source—which is God—and so becomes less and less human until it ceases to be.

The City of God and the City of Man

Augustine's Privation Theory greatly impacted his view of history and the world. In his text, *City of God*, Augustine provides a theological interpretation of history, dividing the world into two cities: the City of God and the City of Man. This text came in response to the sack of Rome in 410. The sack of the "city on a hill" led many people to question the strength and validity of the Christian God. In response to these doubts, Augustine explained that the fall of Rome, and the cause of all wrongdoing, was not God but man.

Humanity brought pain and sin due to its disordered love, causing a schism in a world once made perfect. When human nature fell, it became dominated by itself, falling prey to passions of the flesh. As a result, humanity desired domination over all other things, leading to pride, which is the willingness to dominate, and be dominated by, things other than God.

The fall of man led to the creation of the two cities. The City of Man is "based on self-love and transitory goods," and is "destined to perish." The City of God is "based upon worship of God" and "is eternal." There is no external cause of evil besides an evil will "for when the will abandons what is above itself, and turns to what is lower, it becomes evil—not because that is evil to which it turns, but because *the turning itself* is evil." Thus, humanity's disordered loves built the City of Man, and it is only by returning to God that one approaches the City of God, which will not have full existence till the "consummation of history." Until this time, those who seek God gather together in the City of Man as a "society of pilgrims of all languages, not scrupling about diversities in manners, laws, and institutions whereby earthly peace is secured and maintained, but recognizing that … they all tend to one and the same end of earthly peace." This society is called the church.

"Uti" and "Frui"

Augustine often discussed the proper "use" (*uti*) and "enjoyment" (*frui*) of riches. He insisted that all things come from God and are thereby made good through God. For Augustine, "To enjoy anything means to cling to it with affection for its own sake. To use a thing is to employ what we have received for our use to obtain what we want, provided that it is right for us to want it."

Because human nature is flawed, people often times seek joy in the creations of God and attempt to use God as a means of attaining them. In so doing, they twist the proper order of things. Because all wealth is of "instrumental value" and not "intrinsic value," humanity removes the good of wealth when it uses it apart from God. More importantly, if one does not use all wealth, ultimately, to enjoy God (for he is the only intrinsic good), this wealth "becomes an idol in place of God." In order for people to find peace and joy, Augustine says they must become dependent upon God. By seeking God for their own sakes, individuals will come to see God's ceaseless pursuit of them, which can lead to an internal transformation of the self. Whereas the individual once sought God for his own sake, he learns to love God for God's sake. Complete acceptance of the divine will allow for the fullest form of human existence, whereby humanity learns to love and enjoy all things through and for God.

David Eschrich, researcher

THE FALL OF ROME, 476

Once Constantine came to power in 313, he stopped the persecution of Christians, and Christianity became the religion of the state. Many historians consider this the start of Rome's fall. Constantine split the Roman Empire in half, placing control of the Western section in Rome and the Eastern part in Constantinople. This action weakened Rome even more by splitting its people, military, and resources. The eastern part of the empire thrived while the Western fell under heavy attack.

In 410 AD the Visigoths arrived at Rome to find it undefended and vulnerable. They looted and burned the city and left. This invasion was the first of many that would leave Rome in smolders. Throughout the next few years more attacks occurred, leaving the Roman military weak. For the next 60 years Rome was constantly attacked and pillaged.

The Battle of Chalons, 451 AD

Beleaguered on all sides by barbarian hordes, the battle of Chalons in Gaul (modern day France) marked the last Imperial Roman victory before its ensuing collapse. Struggling alongside the Visigoths to hold back forces of Attila the Hun, the Romans managed to repel the Huns at the cost of leaving much of Gaul looted and pillaged, their own military forces exhausted from the fight. The Roman Empire itself had already been split in two by this point over various socio-political turmoils. Soon the Western half would fade, leaving only the Byzantines to the East.

Finally, in 476, the Germanic tribe led by Odoacer took over Rome and forced the last Emperor Romulus to leave. For hundreds of years after the fall of Rome, the Eastern Empire grew and thrived, becoming known as the Byzantine Empire. Since technically this part was no longer part of the Roman Empire and Rome itself was overrun with Goths, the great Empire that was Rome disappeared in its most meaningful and influential form.

Chapter 3
The Middle Ages
476–1300

*There is within every soul a search
for happiness and meaning.*

—Thomas Aquinas

THE FALL OF THE ROMAN EMPIRE marks the transition from the Roman period to the middle ages. Rome had managed to keep Europe in one piece, tying it together with road systems, trading routes, water systems, and a central government. When Rome fell the unity of Europe vanished with it. The only stability to be found was in the Roman Catholic Church. Europe thus fell under what is called Christendom, a type of religious government spearheaded by the church in Rome. The Pope had absolute power, similar in many ways to an emperor. The Pope regularly interfered with government affairs, leading to a power struggle between the Church and the State. Many religious sects had their own military, making them practically a nation of their own. Since power was so easily obtainable, warmongering was commonplace. The Church and State warred with one another openly, pushing many nations further away from a unified empire. Many tiny nations arose, each with its own army and castle. The lord in charge of the castle gave land to men who fought with and for him, and those who worked the land were given protection from attack.

In the 12th century, things began to calm down immensely; agriculture, traveling, and trading improved, allowing every class to have a steady diet and safety. Populations increased steadily throughout Europe, and with it ideas began expanding throughout the land. Gothic-style art and culture became popular, due to the new stability. Arts and rhetoric became a focus for many people, and this shift towards the arts is the first signs of the renaissance, which began in the 14th century.

The 13th century was marked with social and artistic advancement. Gothic style hit its peak and many new groups were rising up to take small portions of political power. Education improved as well; the church no longer controlled the majority's way of thinking, and Europe moved into the era of Scholasticism, which is the pursuit of philosophical questions using reason and Christian theology. Over time, Scholasticism and the return of the classics helped pave the way for the Renaissance era.

THE SONG OF THE NIBELUNGS, 400, 500, *German Epic Poem*

The *Nibelungenlied*, translated as *The Song of the Nibelungs*, is an epic poem written in Middle High German. Although the author is unknown, the poem is praiseworthy because of its literary style as well as the masterful combining of the themes of love and violence. The story tells of Siegfried from the Netherlands who is praised in the court of Worms for conquering the Nibelungs and for slaying a dragon. Kriemhild, daughter of the king of Worms, is renowned for her beauty, but she has vowed to remain unmarried because of a bad dream she had about the death of her husband. Her brother Gunther, however, schemes to give her in marriage to Siegfried if Siegfried will help him win the desirable Brunhild, Queen of Iceland. Siegfried uses an invisibility cloak to help Gunther win the suspicious Brunhild and to fool her on their wedding night. However, when she recognizes the deception, Brunhild seeks vengeance on Siegfried for his scheming and enlists Gunther to carry it out. Kriemhild, too, is understandably upset and seeks revenge against Brunhild. After an extended battle, Gunther, Hagan (his accomplice), and even Kriemhild herself are each killed.

The *Nibelungensas* was written from oral stories of the fifth and sixth centuries. Chief among the national traditions preserved by the monks recalls the Huns and their queen Brunhilda, who conquered the

Burgundians. This particular legend is recreated in the Nordic tradition as well in the *Volsunga Saga, the Prose Edda, the Poetic Edda, the Legend of Norma-Gest*, and others.

In its origin a pre-Christian story, the *Song of the Nibelungs* was probably transcribed after 1200. We know the story today from 37 documents written from the 13th–17th century, Codex A, kept in the Bavarian State Library. The poem's influence on art and music includes Richard Wagner's creation for the operatic stage, *Der Ring des Nibelungen*, made up of four musical dramas including *Siegfried*. The first complete cycle of *The Ring* premiered in 1876.

Natalie Hathcote, 2017
Cole Watson, 2018

MOHAMMED ◊ 570–632, *The Founder of Islam*

" Evil always puts on lipstick. Why else would anyone be attracted to evil?

—*Author Unknown*

The Five Pillars of Islam

1. Submission to Allah—the Muslim profession of faith—Shahadah
2. Prayer five times each day—Salat
3. Charity for the poor, alms giving—Zakat
4. Fasting during the month of Ramadan—Sawm
5. The lifetime pilgrimage to Mecca—the Hajj

The Unspoken Pillars of Islam (the pig)

- Jihad—slaughter of the infidels
- Leadership through totalitarianism and fear; intimidation is the norm
- Ownership of women; they are chattel, personal property with few rights
- Execution of homosexuals
- Honor killings of children
- Slavery, even in modern times
- A culture of hatred and death
- Coercion, oppression, and power trump freedom and liberty
- Rampant illiteracy

The Life of Mohammed

Pre-Hijra (The migration from Mecca to Medina, 622)

- He was born in Mecca, Arabia.
- Orphaned at an early age, he was raised by his uncle, and worked as a merchant.
- He was described as a sweet man who seldom laughed: dignified, delicate, nervous, impressionable, given to melancholy, pensive, and illiterate, but with a distinguished ancestry.
- At 25, he married Khadija, a 40-year-old wealthy widow with several children.

- He was a "seeker" searching after God.
- He studied Judaism, Christianity, and the pagan religions of Arabia.
- He occasionally retreated to a cave for several days for seclusion and prayer.
- Monogamous, Mohammed's wife Khadija bore him daughters but no sons.
- At 40, he reported that he was visited by the Archangel Gabriel and received his first revelation from God; many more visions followed.
- Khadija believed in and encouraged him.
- Three years later Muhammad started preaching these revelations publicly.
- He proclaimed that "God is One," that complete "surrender" to Him (*Islam*) is the only way acceptable to God, and that he was a prophet and messenger of God.
- He gained a few followers early on, and met hostility from some Meccans.
- Khadija died in 619.
- After 12 years of struggle and persecution in Mecca, Mohammad and his approximately 70 followers moved 200 miles north to the town of Yathrib, later to be named Medina.
- This migration is known as the "Hijra" and marks the beginning of the Islamic calendar as 622.

> By their fruit you will know them.
>
> —Matthew 7:16

Post-Hijra (The last 10 years)

- The last 10 years of Mohammed's life were brutal and telling.
- He had trouble feeding his followers.
- He authorized the raiding of caravans, approving violence, murder and theft.
- He defined rules for dividing up the spoils of war: 80% for the raiders, 20% for Mohammed.
- He authorized the destruction of three Jewish villages.
- He planned 65 military campaigns (i.e., caravan raids and battles) and personally led 27 of them.
- He took on 10 wives (one was 8 years old) and two concubines.
- He was said to have two big indulgences—women and power.
- He condoned the assassination of three poets who had mocked him.
- He condoned the practice of vendetta and revenge, practices already in the Arab culture.
- He approved of the killing of anyone, including sons and daughters, who rejected Islam.
- He broke a treaty with his main enemy, the Quraish tribe.
- He rebuilt the Kaaba, which was originally a pagan idol.
- He died at the age of 62.

Compare and contrast Mohammad with Jesus. That should answer your questions about Islam.

> No stronger retrograde force exists in the world.
>
> —Sir Winston Churchill, *The River War*, 1899

THE EARLY ISLAMIC CONQUESTS, 622–750

The seventh century brought with it the rise of a new religion in what would come to be known as the Middle East: Islam. Established by the Prophet Muhammad in 610 AD, Islam grew rapidly throughout the region both by choice and by the sword, ultimately filtering through most of Asia Minor, North

Africa, India, China, and even Spain. The results, historically speaking, have been mixed. The Islamic societies left behind by these conquests produced their fair share of advancements in the fields of math, science, medicine, art, and architecture, but they would also become the source of many conflicts throughout history, including a staggering amount of modern ones.

Notable Battle

The Battle of Tours, 732

Also known as the Battle of Poitiers. Although the march of Islam saw countless battles of varying import, for our purposes the most crucial is their defeat at the city of Tours, France, where Charlemagne and his troops fought to keep Islam out of Europe having already lost much of Spain. Charlemagne's victory ensured the preservation of Christianity and the distinction of Europe as outside Muslim authority.

BEDE ◊ 672–735, *Beloved Historian, Monk, and Linguist*

" Holy Scripture is above all other books not only by its authority because it is Divine, or by its utility because it leads to eternal life, but also by its antiquity and its literary form.
—"De Schematibus"

- Was born at Jarrow in Northumberland
- Was given over to the monastery at Wearmouth for his education, starting at age 7.
- Spent his entire life within the monastery
- Became a priest at 30
- Was given the title "Venerable Bede"
- Was named Doctor of the Church by Leo XIII
- Was known for his piety, simplicity, moderation, gentleness, and breadth of view
- Was considered to be an extraordinary historian and linguist
- Was the first historian to date events *Anno Domini*—AD

Key Works

Ecclesiastical History of the English People, 731

Biography

Bede's chronology is recorded in the last chapter of his own remarkable *Ecclesiastical History of the English People*. He was born in Northumberland, and at age 7 he was given into the care of Benedict Biscop for his education at Wearmouth monastery. He spent his entire life in the monastery, living with monastic discipline and daily study of the Scriptures. He sang daily, finding joy in learning, teaching, and writing. Ordained as a priest at 30, Bede spent the remainder of his life making notes on the Scriptures, based on readings of others as well as his own interpretation. He was beloved by his community, who called him *Venerabilis*, just one of their respectful terms. He was declared Doctor of the Church or "Doctor Ecclesiae," as well, and is celebrated in the Catholic Church year on May 27th.

Probably the most learned man of the time, Bede valued literary property, always being careful to note what others had written. Bede's writing is so extensive that no collection of complete works has ever been printed. He was scrupulous in collecting and recording history in an effort to separate facts from hearsay. His remarkable skill is demonstrated in his *Historia Ecclesiastic Gentis Anglorum*, which provides a foundation for everything we know of the history of Christianity in England from the beginning. Bede also wrote chronological treatises that summarize the general history of the world, starting with Creation. However, Bede's writings on the Scriptures are the most important of his works. He was the first to translate the *Gospel of John* in Old English and wrote many commentaries, including one on the Pentateuch. Also a witness on the tradition of the Gregorian chant in England, Bede wrote hymns and poems as well. A matchless linguist, Bede's translations from Latin and Greek to Anglo Saxon gave the British people a much more accessible Christianity.

BEOWULF ◊ 700–1000, *English Heroic Poem*

Scholars speculate that *Beowulf* was composed in sixth-century Scandinavia, probably repeated orally for years, and transcribed in Anglo-Saxon England. It is the longest epic poem in Old English, at 3,182 lines. Just one copy of the epic poem exists as part of a manuscript, *The Nowell Codex*, kept in the British Library in London. By analyzing the scribes' handwriting, scholars have determined that the copy was made in the 10th or 11th century. The manuscript contains some other writings too, including a homily on St. Christopher, "The Marvels of the East," and "Letter of Alexander to Aristotle."

The story takes place in Scandinavia, where the hero Beowulf comes to the aid of the neighboring Danish King. In this effort, he slays the dragon Grendel by cutting off his arm. Grendel's mother seeks revenge by attacking the king's hall, but Beowulf prevails, and kills her. Crowned King of the Geats— his Scandinavian home—Beowulf lives well for 50 years until the appearance of another dragon. As he fights and slays that dragon, Beowulf is himself killed. The story ends with Beowulf's funeral and a heartfelt lament.

While the importance of *Beowulf* wasn't recognized until the end of the 18th century, it is now widely lauded as a classic story of the triumph of good over evil. Beowulf has been translated in many languages and provided inspiration for modern stories portrayed in a variety of art forms. J.R.R. Tolkien, most widely known for his fantasy series *The Lord of the Rings*, was by day a philologist who worked widely in Old English texts and even provided a popular translation of *Beowulf*.

Toby Coffman, faculty

SONG OF ROLAND, c. 1000, *Classic French Epic*

The origin of the *Song of Roland* (*Chanson de Roland* is its original French title) is uncertain; however, almost undoubtedly only one person wrote it. It is the first documented piece of French Literature—an epic poem spanning about 4,000 lines of verse. *Song of Roland* is structured as 291 paragraphs, known as laisses. There are 10 syllables in each line, with the final syllable in the line repeating in assonance rhyme with the last syllable in the line before and after any given line. Here is an example of the structure of a laisse and of individual lines within. From laisse 87:

66 Roland is fierce and Oliver is wise

> And both for valour may bear away the prize.
> [...]
> Here is our place we'll stand here abide:
> Buffets and blows be ours to take and strike!

This French epic is based on a real battle in 778, known as the Battle of Roncevaux, which occurred during the rule of Charlemagne, King of the Franks. The battle pits the Franks, Charlemagne's army, against the Saracens of Spain, Marsilion's army. The battle reaches its fevered pitch when Charlemagne demands of the Saracens: "you must receive the faith of Christ Our Lord." They refuse.

The epic poem highlights the virtuousness of the French in comparison to the Saracens, making the battle between good (the Christians) and evil (the Muslims) a central theme: Charlemagne is "the portrait of the ideal earthly sovereign—just, prudent, magnanimous, and devout," and Marsilion is portrayed as "the king who hates God's name." *Song of Roland* comprises four sections, and the divisions spur from the key topics in the epic. The first section tells of Ganelon's betrayal against his stepson, Roland, and against Charlemagne, the King. The second section tells of Roland's martyrized death. In the third section, Charlemagne laments and avenges Roland's death. Finally, in section four, Ganelon receives punishment for his betrayal, and although short and simple in its style, the *Song of Roland* achieves epic stature. It is not a romantic anecdote, but a great poem on a great theme.

Briauna Schultz, 2013

WILLIAM THE CONQUEROR ◊ 1028–1087, *The Norman Conquest*

William was initially called the Bastard, as his father, Robert I, Duke of Normandy and a descendent of Viking raiders, never married his mistress Herleva, William's mother. Although never well educated in the cultural standard of the time, William learned all of the skills of a strong rider, swordsman, and archer, leading to his knighthood in 1043. In Normandy France at this time, the monarchy ruled powerful dukes who controlled the land, their communities, and the produce. As William managed the lands his father had given him, he had "a belief that a ruler must rule as thoroughly and authoritatively as possible." By the time King Henry I of France died, William was the most important lord in the land.

As a boy, Edward visited his relatives in Normandy. Later, because Edward was an ancestor of Alfred the Great, the English governing body known as the Witan selected him King in 1042. He would come to be known as King Edward the Confessor of England. He married Harold Godwinson's daughter, from an influential family. Because they had no children, the ambitious Harold desired to become the king himself someday. Meanwhile, Edward's distant cousin William the Bastard thought he should eventually inherit England's throne. He had, after all, known him in Normandy, and he was the closet relative to Edward.

Harold Godwinson and Edward argued in the early 1060s, prompting William to curry favor with Edward. He visited Edward, later reporting that King Edward named him successor during their meeting.

The argument continued when Harold, on a diplomatic mission to France, shipwrecked off the Norman coast and was captured by a Norman vassal. Harold and William mended their relationship, although William insisted that he would release Harold if he promised to help him attain the throne upon King Edward's death. Just two years later, the Witan named Harold Godwinson as king, and he accepted. William was furiousm and set out to take revenge in England.

Harold readied for battle, but unfortunately had to go directly to defend English land in Northumbia, because the King of Norway had invaded. Harold defeated those armies, yet didn't prepare properly to meet William's. Consequently, William's men were able to defeat England, killing Harold and thus eliminating William's rival. William triumphantly took over London and all of England, to be crowned king in 1066 by the Witan.

William changed England forever by creating a feudal system with a plan that gave him ownership of all English land. By this bold move, he took over a standing army as well as vast tax revenues. The creation of the Domesday Book, a record of every vassal's resources, has given historians a great deal of information about 11th-century England.

THE GREAT SCHISM OF 1054

The Schism of 1054, sometimes called *The Great Schism* or *The East-West Schism* was a division within the Catholic Church between the Latin West and the Greek East that produced the modern Roman Catholic and Greek Orthodox Churches.

The differences between the Eastern and Western branches of Catholicism began as subtle ones, like language and location, but as Western missionaries bringing Roman Catholicism east began to meet with Eastern Missionaries bringing Byzantine Catholicism west in central Europe, differences between the groups came to light. Aside from a language barrier—the Romans spoke Latin while the Byzantines spoke Greek—they also had different practices regarding fasting and the Eucharist. Eastern Christians accepted married priests while Western Christians required priests to remain celibate. Perhaps the most dramatic difference between the two was their respective understandings of papal leadership. The Western Church accepted the Pope as the supreme voice of the Church, but the Eastern Church saw the Pope as merely having received the honor of primacy among the bishops. He was simply the leader of a group of *Patriarchs* who were in charge of leading the Church as a group. Finally, there was a difference in the profession of the Nicene Creed: The West added the words *"and the son"* after the profession of belief in The Holy Spirit "which proceeds from the Father" in an effort to prevent heretics from professing the Creed. The East argued that the wording of this was a confusion of the trinity as well as an insult to the Eastern Church, which was not consulted by the West regarding this change.

The official split was also influenced by political changes. In the 11th century, The Pope was given freedom from the government. This new level of political control meant that the Pope could potentially depose and reinstate bishops, elevating him above any other earthly judge. The Eastern Christians, who believed that the Church was meant to be lead by a group rather than an individual, rejected this belief outright. Michael Keroularious's direct rejection of Pope Leo IX's demand for submission to the papacy led to the development of the official Schism between the churches. In 1054, Pope Leo IX decided to respond to differences arising between the Roman Church and Byzantine Church by excommunicating Michael Keroularious (sometimes styled *Cerularius*), Patriarch of Constantinople. In response, Michael Keroularious decided to excommunicate Pope Leo IX, thus starting his own church, which would come to be known as the Greek Orthodox Church.

A Millennium of cultural differences between the East and the West made the Schism permanent. Though Pope Paul VI and Patriarch Athenagoras met in 1964 and simultaneously lifted the excommunications in 1965, the Schism has remained socially permanent. People are set in their ways, and the two religions, while no longer officially upholding their previous hostilities, have grown into separate entities.

THE FIVE RELIGIOUS INTELLECTUALS, 1058–1225

Isn't it fascinating that in a brief spurt of history, the world produced five highly influential religious intellectuals: al-Ghazali from Mesopotamia, Averroes from Spain, Maimonides from Spain and Egypt, Anselm from England, and Thomas Aquinas from Italy (two Muslims, a Jew, and two Christians)?

While they differed in their homelands, backgrounds, and beliefs, they all had in common a search for the nature of God and man and their relationship to one another. Islam was at the height of its glory, leading the world in science, medicine, mathematics, poetry, architecture, commerce, transportation and military affairs. All of these men were deeply involved in philosophy and theology. And all of them responded to Aristotle's foundation of reason.

ANSELM ◊ 1033–1109, *A Rational Philosopher and Theologian*

> Behold, one night during Matins, the grace of God shone in his heart and the matter (the definition of God) became clear to his understanding, filling his whole being with immense joy and jubilation.
>
> —Anselm's biographer, Eadmer

- Was a philosophic theologian
- Entered the monastery of Bec in Normandy in 1060
- Rose to the position of prior and head of the monastic school in Caen 3 years later
- Wrote *Monologion*, a discussion of the nature and existence of God
- Believed that God is the highest good and that everything depends on God (based on Augustine's work)
- Developed the Doctrine of Atonement, as the result of study and writing
- Consecrated the Archbishop of Canterbury in 1093
- Conflicted with the King over church reform
- Fled England to Italy for several years
- Returned to England and continued his work on the Sacraments until his death

Key Works

Monologian (Monologue), 1077
Proslogion (Discourse on the Existence of God), 1078
Cur Deus Homo (Why God Became Human), 1098

Biography

Anselm of Canterbury, also called Anselm of Aosta and Anselm of Bec, was born in the Italian Alps. He left Italy forever and moved to Burgundy after the death of his mother and conflicts with his father. He traveled to Normandy to study with Lanfranc, the prior at the monastery of Bec, and after just three years of the monastic life, he was appointed prior of Bec and head of the school. There Anselm began his study on the existence and nature of God. He argued that in order for man to make judgments on anything, the best of that thing must exist for making comparative judgments. Therefore, he reasoned, the best is God. Furthermore, using the argument of contingency (everything comes from something), one must also assume that existence of a thing depends on or came from something. Therefore, the origin of everything, the first cause, must be God. Because his students asked him to record his teachings, Anselm began to write them down. In his first book, *Monologion* Anselm relied on the work of Augustine, in particular, and was committed to writing a reasonable argument that would persuade the non-Christian of the existence of God. Anselm's second work, *Proslogion,* influenced the philosophical thought of the time. The treatise argues his unique definition of God. Again, paralleling an idea of Augustine's, Anselm asserts that nothing can be imagined that is greater than God. He develops the definition further, explaining that man's mind can conceive of God, and God actually exists in reality.

Anselm found himself faced with two controversies that propelled him to respond with two letters that were published in *Cur Deus Homo.* Anselm spelled out his beliefs on The Incarnation of Christ (a person who embodies in the flesh a deity, spirit, or abstract quality). and the doctrine of the Atonement (separation for a wrong or injury). Because of his careful explanation of Christ's incarnation, Anselm's work is a foundational document in the history of theology.

When the archbishop of Canterbury died, King William Rufus initially left the position vacant in his effort to avoid strong opposition from the Church, as he planned to take control of the English Church. Finally the king, fearing criticism, appointed Anselm to take the position of Archbishop of Canterbury in 1093. In his new position, Anselm defended the church, approved of church reform, and recognized Urban II as the pope; all of these actions created conflict with the King. Finally Anselm felt the pressure to flee England in 1097. He went to southern Italy, continuing a close relationship with the Church. When William II Rufus died in 1100, his brother, the new monarch, wanted Anselm back in England. Before he would return Anselm forged a compromise with Henry on issues surrounding lay investiture and feudal homage to the crown. In 1106 Anselm returned to England as archbishop. He died in 1109, leaving the legacy of his work to his students and the future.

AL-GHAZALI ◊ 1058–1111, *A Sufi Mystic*

> " Declare your jihad on thirteen enemies you cannot see—Egoism, Arrogance, Conceit, Selfishness, Greed, Lust, Intolerance, Anger, Lying, Cheating, Gossiping and Slandering. If you can master and destroy them, then you will be ready to fight the enemy you can see.

- Was a religious philosopher and unquenchable skeptic
- Learned Sufism from a friend of his father's

- Sought for certainty in knowledge by looking carefully into all he learned
- Doubted reason as a way to truth; he reasoned through a quest for truth
- Launched a two-pronged written attack on philosophers
- Believed that matters of faith can neither be proved or disproved
- Pronounced that everything is a result of God's will
- Believed that God knows the world as a whole without having knowledge of individuals and the particulars of creation
- Held the doctrine that the human soul is part of God
- Endured challenges by many, including the Spanish Muslim Ibn Rushd (Averroes)

Key Works

The Incoherence of the Philosophers, 1095
The Alchemy of Happiness (Revival of the Religious Scientists), 1096
Revival of the Religious Sciences: Selections including "The Remembrance of Death and the Afterlife," 1096
The Deliverer from Erros, 1108

Biography

Ḥāmid Abū Muḥammad ibn Muḥammad al-Ghazālī was trained as a Sufi by a friend of his father's. He learned the beliefs and laws of Sufism, a strict and legalistic type of Islam whose followers believe it to be the original, purist form of Islam. As a young man al-Gazali joined the Nizamiyyah Academy of Nishapur where he was eventually appointed at 34 to the position of the chair of theology. Widely recognized as a skilled debater, al-Gazali questioned the practices of Sufism while seeking enlightenment. The backdrop of philosophical differences between the Shi'ites and the Sunnites troubled him. As a result he became critical of the unimportant debates with the very strict canons of Islam. These matters went against all that he believed about the worthlessness of the senses and reason.

He gave up his position to pursue a monastic life of travel, meditation, and writing to search for truth. His conclusion was a theory of knowledge that allowed him to accept the beliefs of the Quran. In 1105 al-Gazali wrote an autobiography, *The Deliverer from Error*, which attacks every form of knowledge as well as all of the current philosophical methods. The same year al-Gazali founded a seminary in Tus, where he died in 1111.

Attack on Philosophers

First, in *Intentions of the Philosophers*, al-Gazali details carefully the beliefs of philosophers from the time of Aristotle to reveal their efforts to influence Muslim ideology with Hellenic beliefs. He classifies all of the philosophers into the categories of materialists, naturalists, and theists. Materialists believe in the material world without God. Naturalists deny that man's soul is immortal even as God's world reveals a divine order. The theists (al-Ghazali includes Plato, Aristotle, Al-Farabi, and Ibu Sina) he felt were his most significant opponents, as they were able to refute the beliefs of the materialist and the naturalist. However, they believed that religious tenets could be proven, which conflicts with al-Ghazali's firm position that there was no need to argue any position that couldn't be brought about through reason.

Al-Ghazali went on to battle against "causality." He unequivocally supported the Quran by asserting that everything flows from God's will (such as the orderliness of nature) rather than from his characteristics. And in opposition to Aristotle and Ibn Sina, al-Ghazali confirmed (as shown in the Quran) that God knows each person and every part of the cosmos, and directs everything by his will. Al-Ghazali collected these ideas in *Revival of the Religious Sciences*, which even now influences Sunnite believers. He returned to his first beliefs through the very reason that he denied.

Belief System

Al-Ghazali's belief system bordered on pantheism, yet he provided believers with a knowledge of God and all that is possible with God. He believed that God is all-powerful, "transcendent and immanent," and that God's beauty is apparent in his creation. Furthermore, al-Ghazali recognized the power of man's soul to communicate with God. When al-Ghazali viewed the soul as like God, critics claimed that he was mistaken for not clarifying what is divine and what is human. Probably because al-Gazali himself declared his own mystical encounters with God, he wrote about how we can, after study, arrive at an "otherness" which reveals God.

Effects

By the time al-Ghazali died in 1111, scientific investigation and philosophical and religious toleration were all experiences of the past. Schools limited their teaching to theology. Scientific progress came to a halt.

THE BATTLE OF HASTINGS, 1066

The Battle of Hastings is perhaps one of the single most well-known battles in human history for many reasons. On a surface level it marked the success of the Norman invasion of England and the rise of William the Conqueror to the throne as King William I, whose policies would come to profoundly influence English society, language, religion, and culture up into the modern day. On a more conceptual level, however, it demonstrated the supremacy of the combined armed attack, a strategy by which several different types of military units worked in tandem to support one another on the field of battle. William's use of cavalry, infantry, and archers in this manner would change European warfare forever.

THE CRUSADES, 1096–1487

When Pope Urban II declared a holy war in response to the Byzantine Empire's call for aid against the Seljuk Turks, could he have imagined the bloodshed that would follow for centuries to come? Initially enamored with the prospect of relieving Jerusalem from Muslim control, the Crusades would become a sprawling series of military conflicts, prolonged sieges, and back-and-forth attempts at expansion. Although arguably launched with high-minded intentions, the legacy of the Crusades is largely one of excess and loss on both sides. Darker still, it provided an early sense of legitimization for the conquest of "Heathen" lands to come in the Age of Discovery.

AVERROES, 1126–1198, *A Muslim Polymath*

" All that is wanted in an enquiry into philosophical reasoning has already been perfectly examined by the Ancients. All that is required of us is that we should go back to their

> books and see what they have said in this connection. If all that they say be true, we should accept it and if there be something wrong, we should be warned by it.
>
> —*On the Harmony of Religions and Philosophy*

- Was well-educated in Islamic faith, the Quran, law, and all areas of science
- Wrote widely, becoming notable for his detailed *Commentaries on the Works of Aristotle*
- Strongly promoted Aristotle, and soundly criticized those who had misinterpreted him
- Saw no disparity between philosophy and religion; both are ways to truth
- Believed in the two parts of man, the human and the divine
- Criticized al-Ghazali, whom he felt had the faith all wrong
- Inspired Averroism, a philosophical movement of the 13th century, founded on his beliefs
- Inspired the growth of Scholasticism in Western Europe

Key Works

Commentaries on the Works of Aristotle, 1169–1178
Kulliyat (Generalities), 1169–1178
Tahafut al-tahafut (The Incoherence of the Incoherence), 1179

Biography

Abū l-Walīd Muḥammad bin Aḥmad bin Rušd, known as Ibn Rushd or Averroes, was born in Cordob, Al Andalus, in modern-day Spain. His family of important jurists provided him with training in the Islamic faith, the Quran, and natural sciences. As a young man, Rushd assisted the Moroccan ruler to found colleges, and was appointed Qadi of Seville and later of Cordoba. A qadi is a judge who reviews civil, judicial and religious matters according to Islamic law. Almost always a favorite of the ruler Yaqub al-Mansur, Averroes traveled throughout the country and began writing. His commentaries on Aristotle were so well received that he became known as "The Commentator" to the medieval West. He combined a devotion to Aristotle's ideas with vast knowledge of sciences, igniting the future of critical discussions of science and religion.

The short and middle Aristotle commentaries were written between 1174 and 1180. He wrote extensively on law, philosophy, medicine, physics, astronomy, and psychology. Averroes died in Marrakesh, Morocco, in 1198, but his influence lived on.

Philosophy

Averroes wrote from his background in jurisprudence and philosophers, including Aristotle. While he admired the work of his mentor Ib Sina, Averroes couldn't agree with Ib Sina's mystic version of knowledge. He followed the Quran in his presentation of philosophy: Through reason man can see creation, which will lead him to an understanding of the creator. Therefore, philosophy leads to truth, which can also found in holy writings. Averroes maintained that we receive God's word through dialectical, rhetorical, and demonstrative syllogism. He defends the value of combining research findings with texts to enable a scholar's reinterpretation, and draws support for his idea by citing the Quran, which delineates the verses with literal meanings and those with several implied meanings. He believed that only scholars have the ability and the right for this kind of interpretation, an opinion that differed from al-Ghazali. Averroes used *The Incoherence of the incoherence* to attack al-Ghazali and all other philosophers who had misrepresented Aristotle's work. He attacks al-Ghazali's *Incoherence of the Philosophers* by asserting that God knows each of his creations. He explains that God is part of the universe and creates the order of the world, just as a human's ability to conceptualize God keeps him separate from divinity.

Influence

In addition to his reputation as Commentator of Aristotelian philosophy, Averroes was recognized by Dante in the *Inferno* as one of the greatest philosophers of all time. Although controversial, Averroism, the13th century philosophical movement, gained popularity in universities throughout Europe. Latin translations of Averroes's work encouraged renewed study of Aristotle and the growth of Scholasticism.

MAIMONIDES, 1135–1204, *The Sephardic Simplifier*

> We each decide whether to make ourselves learned or ignorant, compassionate or cruel, generous or miserly. No one forces us. No one decides for us, no one drags us along one path or the other. We are responsible for what we are.
>
> —*Mishneh Torah*, Hilkhot Teshuvah 5:2

- Was a Jewish philosopher, scholar, and physician from Spain
- Wrote an important code of Jewish laws based on oral laws
- Was forced to leave with his family when the Almohads (a fanatical sect of Islam) took over
- Turned to practicing medicine out of economic need
- Wrote extensively about Jewish law from the earliest times
- Created the "Thirteen Articles of Faith," required for all Jews, in *The Torah Reviewed*
- Clarified a rational approach to Judaism in *The Guide for the Perplexed*
- Has influenced Jewish and non-Jewish scholars

Key Works

Letter on Apostasy, 1165
Commentary on the Mishnah, 1168
The Torah Reviewed, 1178
Mishna Torah, 1180
The Guide for the Perplexed, 1191

Biography

Born in Egypt, Maimonides of Egypt was also called Moses Maimonides and "Our Rabbi/Teacher Moses Son of Maimon." Maimonides was born into a prominent family in Cordoba, Spain, where he demonstrated a remarkable capacity for learning to his father, an accomplished man, and his other teacher. The family enjoyed full religious freedom until extreme Islamists, the Almahads or "Unitarians" took over in 1148 and forced everyone to commit to Islam. The Maimons had no choice but to keep silent about their Jewish faith and to pretend adherence to Islam or flee. They lived there for 11 years while Moses studied Judaism and the sciences. Then the family left for Fez, Morocco, where they hoped to be anonymous as Moses continued studying rabbinics and Greek philosophy. When one of Moses's teachers, Rabbi Judah ibn Shoshan, was killed for his Judaism, the Maimons fled to Egypt. Hence, Moses is a Sephardic because he was a descendant of Jews who left Spain or Portugal after the 1492 expulsion.

Moses was faced with his father's death just after they arrived. His brother died in a shipwreck while trying to redeem some of the family's inheritance, and as a result the family lost all they had. So Moses used what he had learned of the medical science to begin practicing as a doctor, and was so skilled that he became the physician to the Saladin and his son. He worked with the Jewish community as a teacher and a counselor of sorts.

Commentary on the Mishna Torah—Talmudic law derived from the Jewish oral tradition. In this important commentary written over 10 years, Moses summarizes and explains Jewish law from the beginnings to the third century. Notable in this work is an essay listing the "Thirteen Articles of Faith," required beliefs of Judaism:

1. The existence of God.
2. God's unity and indivisibility into elements.
3. God's spirituality and incorporeality.
4. God's eternity.
5. God alone should be the object of worship.
6. Revelation through God's prophets.
7. The preeminence of Moses among the prophets.
8. The Torah that we have today is the one dictated to Moses by God.
9. The Torah will not be replaced and nothing may be added or removed.
10. God's awareness of human actions.
11. Reward of good and punishment of evil.
12. The coming of the Jewish Messiah.
13. The resurrection of the dead.

Moses worked for the next 10 years on *The Torah Reviewed*, written in Hebrew, going through Jewish law and doctrine. Chapter 10, "Laws about Giving to Poor People," is well known, particularly where Maimonides spells out the Eight Levels of Giving, moving from the best to the least kind of generosity:

1. Giving an interest-free loan to a person in need; forming a partnership with a person in need; giving a grant to a person in need; finding a job for a person in need; so long as that loan, grant, partnership, or job results in the person no longer living by relying upon others.
2. Giving *tzedakah* (charitable giving) anonymously to an unknown recipient via a person or public fund, which is trustworthy, wise, and can perform acts of tzedakah with your money in a most impeccable fashion.
3. Giving tzedakah anonymously to a known recipient.
4. Giving tzedakah publicly to an unknown recipient.
5. Giving tzedakah before being asked.
6. Giving adequately after being asked.
7. Giving willingly, but inadequately.
8. Giving "in sadness" (giving out of pity): It is thought that Maimonides was referring to giving because of the sad feelings one might have in seeing people in need, as opposed to giving because it is a religious obligation. Other translations say, "Giving unwillingly."

During the next 15 years Moses produced in Arabic *The Guide for the Perplexed* and sent it to his favorite disciple Joseph ibn Aknin. The religious philosophy he explains gives the case for a more reasonable Jewish philosophy, one which pulls together science, philosophy, and religion. He supports teaching logic in the tradition of Plato and Aristotle to aid in developing a deep understanding of God. He believes that anyone, even a Gentile, can become a prophet (the purpose of the human race) if he studies, meditates, works hard toward and reaches the perfection of thinking, of physical refinement, and flawless spirituality. In other words, God does not need to intervene for man to attain the level of prophet. Later this remarkable letter was translated into Latin and other European languages as it gained importance. Maimonides continued writing about the problems within the community as well as medical and health rules. He died in 1204.

Importance

Maimonides is regarded as one of the most important Jewish scholars and philosophers in history. The 14-volume *Mishneh Torah* is still an authority on law and ethics, and is taught in Jewish academies. Maimonides had an immediate influence in his lifetime, too, with his beliefs that combined Aristotle's precepts with his own biblical faith. As a result, even Thomas Aquinas mentioned Maimonides in his own journey of faith.

Jeff Culver, faculty
Matt Guillod, 2012

THE MONGOL CONQUESTS, 1206–1294

The Mongol Empire was unusual in many ways. Initiated by a nation of steppe nomads with little in the way of infrastructure or an agricultural tradition, it nonetheless would come to form the largest contiguous land empire in recorded history. Under the banner of Genghis Khan, a capable and shrewd military commander prone to both honor and cruelty, the Mongols conquered the majority of Asia and the Middle East, all the way up to the periphery of Europe where they encountered heavy resistance from the Slavic peoples of what would one day become Russia.

An interesting tale, but what does this have to do with Europe you may ask? First, the Mongol advancement temporarily unified much of the territory it passed through, allowing for easier trade across the Silk Road between Europe and China. Second, the Mongols brought with them the Bubonic Plague, which would in time decimate Europe in the 14th century. Third, Mongol aggression caused Russia as we know it to form in response, and to eventually push back the Mongols hordes, claiming much of their land in the process.

Finally, on a somewhat darkly humorous note, Genghis Khan's conquests killed enough people to measurably lower the entire planet's carbon emissions for several years, a global "cooling" which yielded a number of environmental changes.

> " Three things are necessary for the salvation of man: to know what he ought to believe; to know what he ought to desire; and to know what he ought to do.
>
> —*Two Precepts of Charity*

- Was the most influential Catholic philosopher, and the most profound interpreter of Aristotle's works, although he could not read Greek
- Wished to synthesize Aristotelian philosophy with traditional Christian theology, supporting faith with reason and observation to explain the *telos*, or purpose, of natural life, and of nature as a whole
- Attempted to develop a systematic teaching about all aspects of the divine and human worlds
- Arrived at five rational proofs for the existence of God, from five different elements of human experience (e.g., motion, design) that would be logically impossible without an unchanging *first cause* (i.e., God)
- Said that all things have a knowable essence which is combined with being to make them real; God is the only being whose essence is *Being itself*, so there is no real distinction between His essence and existence (i.e., between *what* He is and *that* He is); hence God *is* eternal Being, from which all other beings derive
- Believed, following Aristotle, that happiness is a life of active virtue, i.e., of living according to good habits
- Accepted Aristotle's moral and intellectual virtues, but added Christian theological virtues (faith, hope, charity) as the sources of the *highest* happiness; both natural and theological virtues give joy, but only theological virtues bring true happiness
- Considered law the ordering of reason for the common good, and distinguished four types: eternal, divine, natural, and human, the greatest of these being the eternal
- Laid the foundations for modern theories of limited government and natural rights with his accounts of natural and human law; believed human law must not legislate virtue, but limit itself to forbidding only the vices which must be forbidden for society to survive (murder, theft, etc.); government must protect individual free will and private moral education as the means to self-determination and personal salvation

Key Works

On Being and Essence, 1252–1256
Summa Contra Gentes, 1264
Summa Theologica, 1274

Biography

Italian priest and scholastic theologian, Thomas Aquinas is one of the most influential medieval minds. He was born to a noble family in early 1225 at his father's castle in Roccasecca, and found his life transformed by his encounter with the new academic movement known as Scholasticism, an Aristotelian revival. Aquinas was thus introduced to Aristotle at the Benedictine Abbey of Monte Casino, where he studied until age 14. Aristotle's work proved a major influence on Aquinas, whose commentaries on the philosopher are cited to this day. Due to a disagreement in the church, Aquinas was sent to study at the University of Naples, where he would secretly join a group of Dominican monks called the Order of Friar Preachers.

When his parents discovered this in 1244, they sent two of Aquinas's older brothers to kidnap him and hold him captive in their castle. For the next year, Aquinas's family pushed him to leave the Dominican order, even sending a prostitute to tempt him. During his yearlong imprisonment Aquinas developed his passion for and knowledge of the Bible. After his release in 1245, he was summoned to Paris where he would finally escape the control of his parents. While there, he studied under Albertus Magnus, a famous philosopher from whom he would receive his scholastic inspiration. When he returned to the University of Paris in 1252, he obtained his master's degree in theology and was asked to join the university as a teacher. However, he was called away by papal courts and would, instead, tour Italy teaching for the next 10 years. During this time he wrote his most influential work, the *Summa Theologica*. Before his death on March 7, 1274, Aquinas was given permission by the Order of Friars Preachers to open a new school, which became the Thomistic School of Theology.

Rebirth of Aristotle

In the 12th and 13th centuries, there was a rediscovery and rebirth of Aristotelian philosophy. This revival of ancient philosophy brought about a new academic movement known as Scholasticism. In monastic schools across Europe, educators taught all manner of subjects using Aristotelian logic. This method of determining truth through human observation and deduction caused many medieval theologians to fear the incompatibility of theology and philosophy. Theological truth appeared unrelated to philosophical reasoning, as theology was a product of Divine Revelation, not human rationale.

Aquinas was greatly inspired by Aristotle's works, and did not consider them incompatible with Christian theology. Like Aristotle, Aquinas placed great importance on the ultimate purpose, or *telos*, of all objects and beings. By examining the nature of a thing or person, one could determine its *telos* and so achieve its fruition. So Aquinas promoted what he called "natural theology," a means of determining truth via "principles known by the natural light of the intellect." While Aristotle was a proponent of natural reason, he would not have supported natural "theology" as Aquinas did.

Aquinas encouraged the use of human observation and deduction, and believed that all natural reason, if employed and guided correctly, ought to culminate in theology, the study of the divine. For Aquinas, if one properly integrates philosophy and theology, he is a "wise" person because he "gives things an appropriate order and direction and governs them well." More specifically, his attention is "turned toward the universal goal, which is also the universal source," or God. Thus, Aquinas wished to synthesize traditional Christian theology with Aristotelian logic. In so doing, he not only showed the compatibility of philosophy and theology, but also made Christian theology more approachable.

Happiness

Happiness (*eudaimonia* to Aristotle) had a much deeper meaning to the ancient Greeks that it does to we moderns. It described the goal of life—that which we seek *for itself alone*. We seek happiness so that we may be happy. Happiness is joy or contentment or a state of well spiritual being or the Fruit of the Spirit, encompassing love, joy, peace, patience, kindness—the Good Life. Aristotle argues that every organism has its purpose in the universe, and the purpose (the goal) of human life is happiness. We humans desire happiness for its own sake.

Many confuse the words happiness and pleasure. But happiness is an end in and of itself, while pleasure is a means to the end of happiness. The pleasures in life are of limited duration: sex, food, sports, music, wealth, fame, power, beauty, good grades, amd more can be good, but they are fleeting. They do not last and, in themselves, are not sufficient or necessary for long-term happiness. Many people have achieved such pleasures in great abundance and yet are not genuinely happy.

To some extent happiness arises out of genetics, life circumstances, and good fortune. But much more often genuine happiness arises out of how we act, how we liv,e and how good we are. Since we cannot control how lucky we are, we must focus on living the Good Life, with the intrinsic goal of attaining life's happiness.

Natural and Theological Virtues

Aquinas believed that all conscious actions are directed toward happiness, regardless of the actual result of these actions, and a happy life is a virtuous life. A virtuous life consists in "good" habits—habits being "dispositions of the will." By continually repeating certain actions and disciplines, one disposes his will in a particular direction. For instance, if a man takes a glass of wine at 3:30 pm every day, his body will begin to crave that glass at that time every day. He has been habituated to drink wine at that time. The same could be said of more abstract states, like courage. If one regularly exhibits resilience in the face of fear, he will become more courageous.

Aristotle also believed a virtuous life was a happy life, but he promoted what Aquinas would call the "natural virtues." Natural virtues are habits one can discover and develop regardless of his religion, and they are discernable via the intellect. Among these Aquinas includes justice, temperance, fortitude, and prudence. Justice is the ability to rightly construct and order one's relationships. Temperance is the ability control the passions which act contrary to reason. Fortitude is a resilience to fear and danger, and prudence is wisdom, the "principle whereby the will is ordered by reason." Among these "cardinal virtues," prudence is the most important, as it underlies them all.

Aquinas considered these four virtues cardinal (fundamental) because all the virtues of the philosophers such as Aristotle fall under them. As well, any of these virtues could be practiced by one who is not Christian. While Aquinas certainly believed such actions contribute to happiness, he did not believe they allowed for the fullest happiness. This is because they are not focused upon the greatest of goods, or God, who is the source of all good. Consequently, Aquinas asserted the existence of "theological" virtues, which can only be acquired by the direct revelation and grace of God, "because such happiness surpasses the power of human nature, man's natural principles, which enable him to act well according to his power, do not suffice to direct man to this same happiness. Hence it is necessary for man to receive from God some additional principles, by which he may be directed to supernatural happiness." These principles are the theological virtues of faith, hope, and love. The theological virtues are "infused in us by God," and they enable people to achieve the supernatural goal of bringing them together with God.

Eternal, Natural, Human, and Divine Law

Aquinas often discussed "law," which he considered "nothing other than an ordering of reason for the common good from one who has care of the community." Law concerns reason, rather than the will, since law is a "measure of acts." As such, law is primarily concerned with the *telos*, since reason, not will, guides things to their respective ends.

Turning his focus once more to *telos*, Aquinas determined that there are several types of law: those that achieve merely human or natural ends, and those which achieve supernatural ends. The highest law is eternal law, which is the very "mind or reason of God" Himself ; eternal law is the "exemplar of divine wisdom … moving all things to their due end." Though man may strive for eternal law, it remains out of his grasp because it is part of God's very being. However, people are capable of enacting *natural law*, which is the effect of God's eternal law, as captured in Creation. Like the natural virtues, natural law is universal, perceivable to anyone, whether or not he is Christian.

When man applies natural laws to the specific "circumstances of earthly life," he thereby enacts human law. However, because of man's sinful state, God intercedes to correct the human distortion of natural law. This direct revelation and correction of God is called divine law. An example of divine law includes God's presentation of the Ten Commandments to the Jews. By setting up his series of four law types, Aquinas allows for universal agreement on moral law. He does not establish a model of morality that is dependent upon being Christian. But, his model, while universal, reveals the need for Divine intervention, as well as a "basis for criticism" when human law comes into conflict with natural law.

The Five Proofs

In the initial chapters of his *Summa Theologica*, a work intended to educate young Christians on the elementary principles of Christian faith, Aquinas provides five proofs for the existence of God. Though his chapter on the Five Proofs is small, comprising only a minuscule portion of the *Summa*, it is one of the most debated and discussed segments of Aquinas's work.

Though distinct, each of Aquinas's proofs relies on the same, basic principle: there cannot be an infinite regression of causes. Consider the first of his ways. In his first proof, entitled "The Way from Motion," Aquinas tells that some things move, and their movement is caused by things outside themselves. Each of these things, which he calls "movers," is moved independently of its own force. This said, there cannot be an infinite chain of movers causing one another to move. Imagine a chain of upright dominoes. After flicking the first domino, each domino falls due to the force of the one falling into it. These dominoes were ultimately caused by the hand of someone who pushed the first domino; they were not caused by the movement of a limitless chain of falling dominoes. There must be some sort of outside, unmoved caused that started the chain of falling dominoes. Aquinas's other ways are "The Way from Motion," "The Way from Efficient Causation," "The Way from Possibility and Necessity," and "The Way from Gradation."

Toby Coffman, faculty
David Eschrich, researcher
Daren Jonescu, advisor

DANTE, 1265–1321, *The Supreme Poet*

> " Midway in our life's journey I went astray from the straight road and woke to find myself alone in a dark wood.
>
> —*Inferno*

- Suffered exile from his native Florence for political reasons from 1302 to his death in 1321, despite being an ardent patriot of the city
- Fell madly in love with Beatrice Portinari at the age of nine; after her death, he remained loyal to her memory and she featured heavily in his poetry
- Was not formally educated, but was an insatiable reader and a natural poet
- Served as one of six priors (counselors) of Florence before his exile
- Wrote *The New Life*, his first major work, as a combination of poems and a narrative about the poems
- Began his unfinished *Convivio* and wrote his best-known work, *The Divine Comedy*, after his exile
- Showed the justice of God as it related to the afterlife in the *Comedy*
- Is widely recognized as having written one of the greatest poems ever composed—*The Divine Comedy*, comprising Hell, Purgatory, and Heaven
- Sought to save his readers's souls in *The Divine Comedy*; its evangelistic message was not merely to excite with his gruesome imagery of hell

Key Works

The New Life, 1295
Convivio, c. 1305–1308 (unfinished)
The Divine Comedy, c. 1313–1321

Biography

Like a great artist or a Brazilian soccer player, Durante Degli Alighieri is known to history simply as Dante. Born in Florence in 1265 as a member of the lesser nobility, Dante was embroiled throughout his life in the political controversies that were a perpetual fixture in his native city. Dante received little in the way of formal education, relying instead on his keen mind, unflinching memory, and voracious appetite for literature and philosophy for his education.

At age 9 a momentous event occurred that in many ways charted out the poet's future path: he saw for the first time and immediately fell deeply in love with Beatrice Portinari. Though Dante's intense affection for Beatrice, who died at age 24, was never reciprocated, Beatrice's presence invades the rest of Dante's life, and her influence is palpable in each of his major works. Most famously, in Dante's magnificent *The Divine Comedy*, Beatrice is the woman who sends Virgil to guide Dante through the afterlife, eventually meeting him in paradise.

His first major work, *The New Life*, was finished by 1295 and has been called the "first autobiographical work in modern literature." Dante found himself on the losing side of a civil conflict in Florence and was exiled from his beloved city in 1302. In his exile, Dante found refuge in Verona before traveling throughout Italy. He spent time in Paris, and settled in Ravenna from 1317 until his death. With significant irony, the poet most associated with Florence wrote his most famous poem, *The Divine Comedy*, while in exile. He also wrote but did not complete a work of philosophy called *Convivio*, which was to look at different topics by explicating a canzone (song) about the topic. After traveling to Venice in 1321, Dante contracted malaria and died. As a fitting postscript to his involuntary exile, the city of Florence attempted on at least six occasions to have Dante's remains removed from Ravenna and restored to Florence. The rulers of Ravenna resisted—some enterprising Franciscan monks even hid his bones after a papal declaration that his remains be returned to Florence—and to this day Dante remains entombed in Ravenna, the city of his exile.

Justice

Dante was a firm believer in justice, both cosmic (God's) and worldly. In his work *The Monarchy*, written about the same time as *The Divine Comedy*, he declares, "the world is ordered in the best possible way when justice is at its most potent." Though the *Convivio* was uncompleted, scholars speculate that the subject of the final canzone was to be based on the concept of justice. Dante's yearning for justice was no doubt magnified by his years in exile. Like Aquinas, the Aristotelian concept of justice was united with the Christian concept of charity in Dante's worldview.

When Dante and Virgil enter hell, the inscription over the gate includes the famous line "Abandon hope, all ye who enter here," but above that haunting inscription is one more directly theological: "Justice impelled my mighty architect." God created hell as an expression of divine justice. An interesting feature of *Inferno* in particular, and one responsible for so many of the gruesome images contained therein, is the balance between the punishment and the crime. The suicides of the seventh circle are trapped inside branches, unable to escape the prison of the self, reflecting the selfishness that, for Dante, was at the heart of suicide. The lifelong angry in Circle 5 gnaw on one another continually. On the same level, the perpetually sad, who never offered a kind word to another, constantly gurgle on mud just under the surface of a pond as they try to speak. The punishment, so to speak, seems to match the crime. In Canto 19 of *Paradiso*, an eagle tells the character Dante that justice is God's will and that a human's finite understanding can never fully comprehend the depths of God's justice. Given justice's role in *Paradiso*, it should be noted that Dante's idea of justice was not restricted to punishment for crimes. He believed that those in heaven were there due to justice fulfilled just as much as the sinners in hell were justly placed into that horror. Those in paradise have met requirements of divine justice either in their lifetime or in their struggle through purgatory.

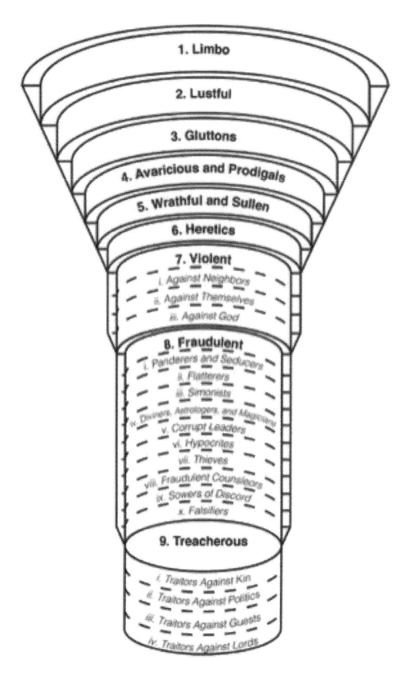

Dante's Nine Levels of Hell

Crime and Punishment

The idea of *sin*, humanity's crimes, and *hell*, our punishment for those crimes, is the defining feature of the *Inferno*. Dante composed the *Inferno* as the first part of his *Divine Comedy*. With Virgil sent by Beatrice to be his guide, Dante descends through the numerous circles and sublevels of hell, describing each one in brutal detail. Dante's hell comprises nine concentric levels and is almost entirely his own invention.

The uppermost is the largest and contains the least severe offenders, virtuous pagans and unborn children. Descending through the levels, the crimes become more severe until they reach their most heinous in the ninth circle. There Satan is frozen into the ice at the very bottom of hell, where with his three heads he chews on Dante's worst offenders: Judas, Brutus, and Cassius, those who were traitorous toward their masters. One of the more confounding features of hell to a modern reader is the fact that some levels appear out of order. For example, Dante places murderers in the seventh circle, above flatterers, who reside in the second pouch of the eighth. The implication is that flattery is worse than murder. Scholar Joan Ferrante clarifies the possible reason for such an ordering: "deception [is] worse because it betrays the natural trust between people and this undermines the social structure."

In general, the sins primarily against the body are punished less painfully (and exotically) than the sins against the mind or even nature. The upper levels are populated with people given over to lust: gluttons, hoarders, and debtors. In Dante's schema, it is one thing to kill a man, but it is something altogether different to betray your father. For the most part within the text, there is little discussion about the particular order or place of each category of sinner. All were evil and offended the divine justice of God. None, it appears, are particularly repentant of their crimes. Satan's place of primacy in hell can be thought of as twofold: as the first traitor against his master, God, he has pride of place at the bottom of hell; and as the chief deceiver of everyone else within hell, he is the ultimate fraud and thus the ultimate destroyer of the social structures human society relies upon.

Love

Given the enormous popularity of the *Inferno* section of *The Divine Comedy*, the temptation to view Dante as a poet of damnation and death can be dominant. But it is important to remember, even if one reads only *The Inferno*, that love was central to Dante's life in a way that the horrors of hell were not. Dante's undying love for Beatrice provided the moral clarity of the entire *Divine Comedy* and enlivened his earlier poetic and artistic achievements. In the prose section of his first major work, *The New Life*, Dante promises to "speak no more of Beatrice until he shall be able to say of her what was never said of any woman."

Love, too, is at the center of heaven, as expressed in *Paradiso*. Lamenting the short shrift often given to *Paradiso*, Robert Baird writes, "For the same reasons that he looked to heaven for justice rather than therapy, Dante rejected this comforting view of literature [the one expressed in modern writing on heaven]. He wanted his poem to save your soul, not to salve it." Wherever one aligns theologically with Dante, what ought never to be in dispute is that Dante was not trying to titillate his readers with bloody gruesomeness in hell, but to move them to repentance. In his letter to Can Grande, his benefactor and protector in Verona, which forms the dedication to *The Divine Comedy*, Dante makes the aim of the work explicit. This is a comedy, after all, something that starts off badly and ends well. It would be a tragedy if it ended in hell. Dante writes, "But if the work is considered according to its allegorical meaning, the subject is man, liable to the reward or punishment of justice, according as through the freedom of the will he is deserving or undeserving. ... The aim of the work is to remove those living in this life from a state of misery and to guide them to a state of happiness."

Toby Coffman, faculty
Ryan Russell, 2015

The Icelandic sagas are historical tales focused on the adventures of warriors and royalty throughout the 10th century. Authored anonymously, the Icelandic sagas, including *The Story of Burnt Njal*, likely came from traditional oral stories passed from generation to generation. *The Story of Burnt Njal* first follows the story of a monarch named Hrutr. Readers question matters of justice and legacy as the events of Hrutr's life unfold. Soon more characters are introduced: Gunnar and Njal are two friends whose story emphasizes the cost of revenge as well as the standards of masculinity. With Gunnar's warrior status and Njal's wise insight the two manage to override the inevitable consequences of revenge and pride for a time, until Njal's prophecy is proved true and Gunnar is exiled. After remarking at the beauty of his homeland, Gunnar decides to live as an outlaw instead of submitting to his punishment of exile. This leads to Njal being burned to death along with his sons. The tale questions the effectiveness of revenge as well as whether revenge is a just explanation for violence. And while revenge is a main part of the storyline for the Icelandic sagas, it can be of comfort to find that respect is one value that remains throughout the battles and trials between characters.

The Story of Burnt Njal has been studied for centuries, and its lessons have transformed both literature and concepts of morality, but it has been constant in its portrayal of man. In the end, man is seen as human and capable of forgiveness: despite feelings of hatred and vengeance, the characters are eventually able to reconcile and show readers that peace is a very real possibility.

Sagas as Historical Texts

The Story of Burnt Njal is an example of a saga that serves as a reliable reference to Icelandic history. It was told by men who experienced the events themselves and knew the characters on a personal level. Many sagas, including *The Story of Burnt Njal*, survived only orally until being transcribed 100 years after the events of the story had occurred. The written versions of these stories came along with the introduction of Christianity and the Roman alphabet. These sagas all support each other by providing similar facts and names of the people and events that took place.

Sagas were not just stories to the people of their time; they were part of tradition and, as a result, part of the culture. By applying knowledge of events in *The Story of Burnt Njal*, it is evident that labor was a respected practice in ancient Iceland. No matter their rank or ancestry, warriors and farmers alike worked with their livestock and their land. Their skills as smiths and welders accompanied their tactics as warriors and leaders. These features of man during Njal and Gunnar's time are seen in the saga's capable characters. This is just one of the many examples of how readers are able to use *The Story of Burnt Njal* as a reference for learning about the daily life in ancient Icelandic times.

Natalie Hathcote, 2017
Cole Watson, 2018

THE VÖLSUNGA SAGA ◊ c. 1270

The Völsunga Saga is the 40-volume mythological story of the origins, life, and descendents of the great Norse king Völsung taken from Viking poems. Written in Icelandic prose, it tells the rise and fall of the Volsung clan, which includes the story of Sigurd. Sharing the same source material, The Song of the Nibelungs was written in Middle High German as an epic poem in the 13th century. While similar, the two pieces differ in their emotion, style, and implications.

The Story of Volsung

After inheriting his father's kingdom, Völsung has twins: his daughter Signy, whom he promises in marriage to Siggeir, another king, and his son Sigmund, to whom Odin, king of the gods, gives a sword of great power upon Signy's betrothal. Siggeir betrays Völsung, murdering him and all his sons aside from Sigmund. After killing two of her weak sons by Siggeir, Signy sleeps with her twin brother, Sigmund, and gives birth to a stronger child named Sinfjotli. Sinfjotli proves to be stronger than his slain predecessors and is trained by his father Sigmund, who lusts for revenge against Siggeir. Sinfjotli and Sigmund set fire to Siggeir's hall, killing him and his wife Signy. The famous child of Sigmund and his new wife, Borghild, is named Helgi. While raiding, Helgi meets Sigrun, a beautiful woman who he determines to marry, though she is already betrothed to a king named Hodbrodd, whom Helgi kills. After Sinfjotli duels and kills a brother of his stepmother Borghild, she poisons and kills him in retaliation, thus prompting her husband Sigmund to expel her from his home. Sigmund later falls in love with a woman named Hjordis, for whose hand he battles King Lyngvi. His magic sword breaks in half during combat and he is killed. Sigmund gives the shards of his sword to Hjordis, who is pregnant with his child, and instructs her to flee. She entrusts her son Sigurd to a man named Regin, who seeks vengeance against his brother Fafnir, a dragon, for killing his father. Sigurd reforges his father's blade and executes Lyngvi, his father's killer. He then slays the dragon, taking control of its treasure, which includes the magical ring Andvaranaut, which brings misery to all those who possess it. Killing the deceitful Regin after hearing birds discuss his plans to betray Sigurd, he eats Fafnir's heart and grows strong and powerful. Sigurd then falls in love with a warrior maiden he awakens named Brynhild, promising to marry her. After being given a forgetfulness potion, he marries Gudrun despite his betrothal to Brynhild. Sigurd then aids his stepbrother Gunnar in persuading Brynhild to marry him. When Brynhild discovers that she was tricked into the betrothal, she murders Sigurd and then commits suicide. Gudrun, Sigurd's widow, then marries King Atli. Failing to persuade them to turn over Fafnir's fabled treasure, Atli has Gudrun's brothers murdered. In retaliation, Gudrun kills her children by Attila and feeds them to him, later concluding the saga by killing him in his drunken stupor.

Christian Appropriations

The Völsunga Saga became a keystone of the Norse Christian tradition from the 11th through roughly the 13th century. Satan, depicted as a dragon in Christian tradition, was traditionally shown being slain by the Archangel Michael. Michael, however, was traditionally the patron saint of the Norwegian people's longstanding enemies. Thus, the Norwegians chose Sigurd, slayer of the dragon Fafnir, as their patron defender against Satan.

In addition, the Völsunga Saga has influenced several fictional writers of both the 19th and 20th centuries, such as Richard Wagner in his *Ring of the Nibelung* and J.R.R. Tolkien's *Lord of the Rings* trilogy. Wagner's *Ring* was an allegory for the controversial industrial and social revolutions occurring in the 19th century. It drew heavily from the *Völsunga Saga*, using many of the characters assuming different names, events, and deities found in the saga with some deviations from the original Saga.

The Saga influenced Tolkien's work as well. The ring Andvaranaut, coveted by many within this mythological world, also has incredible power to corrupt and cause misery. This inspired Tolkien's invention of the One Ring in his *Lord of the Rings* series. The One Ring, which has the power to corrupt and even kill its possessor, is widely desired for its magical powers. In addition, many of the species found in *Lord of the Rings* were originally found in Norse mythology, particularly in the Saga.

The Comparison with *The Song of the Nibelungs*

The *Song of the Nibelungs* is a later version of the story. It has been described as "less powerful" because of its inclusion of the details of courtly love, such as weeping and wailing, preparations for journeys, and unimportant speeches. *The Song of the Volsungs*, on the other hand, get its impact from the brutal, emotional story without frills. In search of temporal pleasures, the people of the *Volsung Saga* kill to get what they want. Women have no importance except to urge men to action. *The Song of the Nibelungs* contains chivalry and courtly love, which characterize a heroic narrative, as well as some of the values of the courtly tradition. However, even that story tells of heroes who stab one another. Women are depicted behaving willfully against God. Like Eve, the woman is the villain.

Tyler King, 2016
Cole Watson, 2018

Chapter 4
The Renaissance and Reformation
1350–1600

*In questions of science, the authority of
a thousand is not worth the humble
reasoning of a single individual.*

—Galileo Galilei

FRANCESCO PETRARCA ◊ 1304–1374, *Father of the Renaissance*

> ❝ True love—or rather, the truest—is always obsessive and unrequited. No one has better dramatized how it scorches the heart and fires the imagination than Petrarch did, centuries ago. He dipped his pen in tears and wrote the poems that have shaped our sense of love—its extremes of longing and loss—ever since.
>
> —J.D. McClatchy

- Was a scholar of the Greek and Roman classics
- Became a cleric who traveled with the church and searched for ancient texts
- Discovered Cicero's letters
- Was called "Father of Humanism," a philosopher of the Renaissance
- Wrote poems, letters, and histories
- Popularized the sonnet in a form named after him—Petrarchan
- Was named Poet Laureate of Rome in 1341
- Developed Italian as a language distinct from Latin, along with Dante and Boccaccio

Key Works

Epistolae metricae
Africa
De viris illustribus
Secretum meum
De vita solitaria
Trionfi
De sui ipsius et multorum ignorantia

Biography

Born in 1304 in Arezzo, Italy, Francesco Petrarca (known to the English-speaking world as Petrarch), inspired renewed interest in the classics as well as poetry. His family moved to Avignon, France when he was a child, and he eventually embarked on legal studies to please his father. He switched to literature after his father's death. He became a cleric, which made him eligible for ecclesiastical postings, and these supported him as he pursued his passion for classic literature. Traveling extensively as an emissary of the Catholic Church, he consulted educated men and searched for classical works. He was smitten with a woman named Laura (whose true identity has never been verified) upon seeing her in the Church of St. Clare at Avignon, and she inspired his most famous poems, the cycle of sonnets known as *Rime*. Petrarch survived an outbreak of the Black Death by promising to bequeath his extensive library to the city of Venice in return for a house that protected him. The plague, however, killed many of his friends and his beloved Laura. He alternated between periods of "sensual pleasures" and intense study and research, and gained a reputation as the foremost scholar of his time. His later life was largely composed of diplomatic missions, study, and immense literary activity, including the writing of hundreds of letters to friends. He died just short of his 70th birthday.

Classical Recovery & Christian Appropriation

Petrarch became the link between classical culture and the Christian message, underscoring the claim that Petrarch was a founder of humanism. He valued the moral world of the classics and retreated from what he felt was "corrupt life." Petrarch continually revised his work, including the poems inspired by Laura and a series of biographies of heroic men through whom he showed the continuity of the ancient work, the classical world, and Christianity. When he was named Poet Laureate of Rome, Petrarch put his laurel wreath on the tomb of the Apostle in St. Peter's Basilica as a sign of his growing faith.

Laura's Poems and the Sonnets

Petrarch's spiritual shift inspired him to write more secular history, and *De vita solitaria* embraces the solitary life of man in nature, study, and prayer. Upon his discovery of the letters of Cicero, he wrote letters to his cherished ancient authors and collected his own letters. Later he revised *Rime*, a new version of Laura's poems, which included those written during her life and those written after her death; both sections show his spiritual growth from falling in love and thinking of "worldly pleasure" alone to a pure and more meaningful love of God and an appreciation of the world. These poems, known as *Canzoniere*, reveal a new standard for lyric poetry, a poetry of man's feelings as well as a new appreciation for form and language. *Canzoniere* consists of 317 sonnets, which follow the form of Guittone of Arezzo. Petrarch developed the sonnet form and popularized what came to be known as the Petrarchan sonnet. Petrarch is revered for his revival of the past and his belief in the possibilities of man's ability to grow in understanding with the guidance of Providence.

THE HUNDRED YEARS WAR, 1337–1453

Hundreds of years following the death of William the Conqueror, his descendants claimed rights to the throne of France. The result was a series of wars that have come to be thought of as a single, all-encompassing conflict: the Hundred Years War, one of the longest military engagements yet held between two nations.

The Hundred Years War would see the rise of professional troops over the use of conscripted peasant soldiers, alongside a number of other refinements to the art of waging war, as well as the sprouting of the early kernels of nationalism that would come to define England and France for much of the rest of their respective histories. England would eventually withdraw from the war to become embroiled in its own civil war, while France would sink into less than ideal post-war living conditions.

Notable Battles

The Battle of Agincourt, 1415

Perhaps the most well-known skirmish of the Hundred Years War, and one of England's greatest victories, the Battle of Agincourt saw the infamous employment of the English longbow, which dominated many of the conflicts to follow. This battle has since been immortalized by the two-fingered salute, or "V" sign, derived from the motion one makes while pulling back a longbow.

The Battle of Orleans, 1428

Facing stark odds following their defeat at Agincourt, the French at the Battle of Orleans won an important turnaround victory. Led by the fabled Joan of Arc, this battle saw the liberation of Orleans and a new wave of nationalistic fervor among the French people. The victory at Orleans opened the way to crown the new French king, and spared the French the fate of the Irish under English rule.

GEOFFREY CHAUCER, 1342–1400, *The Father of English Literature*

" Yet do not miss the moral, my good men. For Saint Paul says that all that's written well is written down some useful truth to tell. Then take the wheat and let the chaff lie still.

—*The Canterbury Tales*

- Wrote *The Canterbury Tales* in vernacular English, which is why he is known as the father of English literature
- Served in the English army during the Hundred Years War
- Became a member of the royal court as King Edward III's valet
- Wrote during the late middle ages, and was motivated by the works of Dante, Boccaccio, and Petrarch
- Lived in Kent and was a member of Parliament
- Was the first poet buried in the Poet's Corner of Westminster's Abbey

Key Works

The Book of the Duchess, c. 1368
The Legend of Good Women, c. 1386
Troilus and Criseyde, c. 1380
The Canterbury Tales, 1388–1398

Biography

Geoffrey Chaucer is one of the most celebrated authors in the English Language, and he is "considered a cultural touchstone, if not the very wellspring of literature in the English language." The exact year of Chaucer's birth is unknown; however, he was born in London sometime between 1340 and 1345. He came from a well-off middle class family—his father John was a vintner—and was educated at St. Paul's. Chaucer learned French, Latin, and Italian before joining the army and serving in the Hundred Years War. He was captured but was ransomed by King Edward III, eventually marrying Phillipa Pan, one of the Queen's ladies, and serving in Edward's court. Under the largesse of the king, the Chaucers travelled to Italy twice, putting Chaucer in touch with the works of Dante Alighieri, Giovanni Boccaccio, and Francesco Petrarch, works that would influence his own writing career. Chaucer began writing in earnest, producing famous works such as *The Parliament of Fowls* and *Troilus and Criseyde* before turning his attention to his unfinished *Canterbury Tales*. He served as both justice of the peace and a member of parliament later in his life, dying in 1400. He was buried in Westminster Abbey in what today has become famous as Poet's Corner.

The Canterbury Tales

The Canterbury Tales is a collection of fictitious stories narrated by pilgrims on a journey to the Shrine of Saint Thomas Becket at the Canterbury Cathedral. The collection is organized into 10 fragments that each contain multiple tales, inspired by Boccaccio's *Decameron*. According to "The General Prologue," Chaucer intended to include 120 tales in the collection, two for each pilgrim on the way to Canterbury and two for each pilgrim on the way back to Southwark. However, Chaucer died before he was able to complete *The Canterbury Tales*, finishing just 22 tales.

The narrator's prologue takes place at the Tabard Inn in Southwark before the pilgrimage to Canterbury. The narrator had "spoken with them, every one, / That [he] was of their fellowship [at once]," and the prologue goes on to tell about "the state of every one / Of all of these, as it appeared to me, / And who they were, and what was their degree." The narrator describes each of the pilgrims in order based on their social status from highest to lowest. The military (which includes the nobility) comes first, followed by the clergy, and the laity. Thus, the knight is described first, and is portrayed as one who "loved chivalry, / Truth, honour, freedom and all courtesy. / Full worthy was he in his liege-lord's war."

The narrator then paints a picture of the clergy, including pilgrims such as the prioress, the monk, and the friar. The laity encompasses everyone else, such as the merchant, the farmer, the lawyer, the cook, and the shipman. For both the military and clergy level, each pilgrim is described in great detail. However, some pilgrims in the laity level are clumped together rather than individualized like the other pilgrims: "A haberdasher and a carpenter, / An arras-maker, dyer, and weaver / Were with us, clothed in similar livery, / All of one sober, great fraternity." Throughout *The Canterbury Tales*, Chaucer uses "estate satire to expose and pillory typical examples of corruption at all levels of society," according to Steven Greenblatt in *The Norton Anthology of Literature*. This satire peeks through descriptions of the pilgrims' facial features, the clothes they wear, the foods they like to eat, the things they say, and the work they do. All these are clues not only to their social rank but to their moral and spiritual condition.

John Foley, in his Introduction to a BBC version of the *Tales*, says, "Chaucer's tale is both traditional and unprecedented," because unlike Boccaccio's collections of tales from a group of people within the same social class, Chaucer's collection "combines a wealth of diverse tale types." The pilgrimage to Canterbury in Chaucer's collection allows for an assortment of characters with different vocations and social statuses to come together to tell their tales, which creates a diverse representation of English life during the late medieval period. Though written in a dialect we now call Middle English and therefore at some remove from our own way of speaking, Chaucer's work remains accessible to the careful reader.

Brandon Martinez, researcher
Remington Swingle, 2016

THE BLACK DEATH, 1346–1353

The Black Death originated in central Asia, wiping out roughly 25 million people in India, China, and other nearby lands. Traders from Asia brought the disease to Constantinople in 1347, which allowed it to quickly spread to Genoa, Naples, Venice, Marseille, and other Mediterranean ports. At about the same time, ships carrying Crusaders from the Middle East helped the disease to spread around Europe. By the time it reached Paris in June 1348, the Plague had already killed thousands of people in Southern France, Italy, and Spain. It reached London several months later, and by 1350 all of Europe, including The Netherlands, Germany, Scandinavia, and Russia, had been hit by the mysterious disease. Scholars estimate that by 1353, the plague had taken the lives of 25 million Europeans, killing 50% of Londoners, 66% of Oxford University students, 80% of the population of Marseille, and 30% of Italians, which had been heavily populated prior to the outbreak.

There are three forms of the disease: bubonic, septicemic, and pneumonic. Though the Bubonic variety is the most well known, the pneumonic variety was the most common because it was easier to spread. The bubonic plague involves painful swelling of the lymph glands in the armpits, groin, and neck. Left untreated, these enlargements become *buboes*, painful, pus-filled skin infections that pop and spread the disease via contact, whether that contact is with clothes, furniture or other household objects, a pet, or a person. These buboes, also called *plague boils*, would eventually turn black—as would other skin at the time of death—because of blood clots, hence the term Black Death.

Those with the bubonic form of the disease were capable of spreading the pneumonic form as well. When an infected person coughed, little droplets of fluid that carried the disease were released into the air for others to inhale. The pneumonic variety of the plague caused the sufferer to cough uncontrollably, which was incredibly painful. Eventually, the sufferer coughed so much that the lining of his or her lungs would become irritated, and long-term patients would cough up blood. Though the pneumonic form wasn't as painful as the bubonic or the septicemic forms, it was still deadly.

The septicemic form was probably the most painful and dramatic of the three. Large numbers of bacteria in the body caused disseminated intravascular coagulation, a condition in which large amounts of debris in the bloodstream cause hemorrhages under the skin. The hemorrhaging turned the infected person's skin black. These victims died almost immediately, within one to three days of showing symptoms of the disease. People died so fast that the idea of a "Christian burial" was abandoned almost completely. People became so desperate to get rid of the rotting corpses that they turned to digging huge mass graves, dumping bodies in the river, and throwing a bunch of bodies onto boats to be sent someplace far, far away from Europe.

As the plague moved from community to community, decimating populations along the way, physicians tried to figure out what was causing it. Hypotheses ranged from air or water contaminants, lack of purifying sunshine, eating too much fruit, and being near too many dead bodies, to the planets being aligned in a specific way or God simply hating Medieval Europe and all of its depravity. In fact, The Black Death is caused by a bacterium called *yersinia pestis*, which was present in burrowing rats at the time, but which did not wreak havoc until the black rat spread to Europe with a specific kind of flea. These rats thrived in heavily populated cities, especially those near ports, where there was readily available water. The rats' fleas bit them in an effort to eat blood. Instead of receiving a satisfying blood meal, the fleas' digestive tract became plugged with plague bacteria, which eventually created an uncontrollable voracity in the fleas. The hungry fleas tried to eat whatever they could find, including humans. Upon biting a human, the flea spread the disease. When symptoms manifested in the humans, the disease spread to other humans.

Though the European Black Death was arguably the most devastating and thus the most memorable case of the plague, there have been other historical instances. The first outbreak was probably around

540 BC in Egypt, and is often called the Plague of Justinian. Another outbreak occurred in 19th-century China, which allowed scientists to finally isolate the cause of the illness.

THOMAS Á KEMPIS, 1380–1471, *The Contemplative Theologian*

> " The kingdom of God is within you, says Christ, our Savior. Turn yourself, therefore, with all your heart to God, and forsake this wretched world, and you will soon find great inward rest. Learn to despise outward things, and give yourself to the inward things, and you will see the kingdom of God will come into your soul.
>
> —*On the Imitation of Christ*

- Wrote *On the Imitation of Christ*, with 6000 editions, the most widely read spiritual work besides the Bible
- Followed Gerard Groote's spiritual order, "The Brothers of the Common Life"
- Believed the individual should empty himself and take on the life of Christ, through Scriptural study
- Was regarded for his ability as a copyist and a counselor
- Transcribed at least four copies of the Bible

Key Works

On the Imitation of Christ, 1420–1427

Biography

Thomas á Kempis, or Thomas Haemerken ("little hammer"), was a scholar and priest from the town of Kempen, Germany. Kempis was the son of a blacksmith and a schoolteacher and was known as a boy intent on study and quiet reflection. After initial years of education, he entered the school of Deventer in 1395, where he became a skilled copyist. The school at Deventer was run by Florentius Radewyn, a follower and contemporary of Gerard Groote, famed founder of the Brothers of the Common Life. Kempis was profoundly influenced by his time with the Brothers, who took no vows, but lived a life of poverty, chastity, and obedience. After his stay at Deventer, he entered the Augustinian convent at Mount Saint Agnes, where his older brother, John, served. He was ordained in 1413, and in 1429 he became sub prior, an official of the convent. Though there was mild tension when the Pope rejected the local bishop of Utrecht, Kempis's life was a quiet one. His fellow priests recognized his predilection for meditation and removed many of his administrative duties. Among his accomplishments, Kempis translated the Bible at least four times, a feat which clearly influenced the nature of his personal writings. His most famous work, *On the Imitation of Christ*, contains many references to Scripture and, next to the Bible, remains the most popular spiritual text of all time. Kempis lived approximately 60 years in the priesthood, 20 of which were spent in the quiet life of a student, counselor, copyist, and writer.

On the Imitation of Christ

Though Kempis was highly regarded as a copyist and counselor during his lifetime, his legacy has been preserved through his work *On the Imitation of Christ*. This piece, whose full title includes the subtitle, "to the contempt of worldly goods," focuses on the reshaping of the individual for and toward Christ.

During the 15th century, the notion of "imitation" meant far more than mere mimicry. To "imitate," in a spiritual context, entailed a self-emptying and a subsequent filling.

For Kempis, the individual must rid himself of all *vanities*, or worldly pleasures and securities. Worldly pleasures—whether knowledge, sex, physique, or comfort—should not define and ground the individual. Following in the tradition of Aristotle and Thomas Aquinas, Kempis believed that self-knowledge, discovering the purpose of humanity, was the surest route to personal fruition. Kempis believed that self-knowledge led the individual to God, and dependency on God allowed for the truest and most joyful self.

Kempis believed that imitation occurred through active self-denial, which took place through the proper study of Scripture. During the Middle Ages, many ascetics, such as the flagellants, used self-imposed physical punishments to empty the self. Kempis did not ascribe to physical asceticism of this sort; rather, he believed the individual ought to both empty and fill himself through intense study of Scripture. In all the *Imitations*, Kempis presents the Life of Christ as the highest study possible to a mortal. By presenting and approaching the Scriptures as essentially about the "life" of Christ, one avoids Biblical study as a purely "intellectual" project, according to Kempis. Rather, by reading the Bible as a literary embodiment of Christ, one gradually takes on the body of Christ Himself and, so, puts into practice the characteristics of the Divine life. This approach was common to the order that schooled Kempis at Derwent, the Brothers of the Common Life. The order's founder, Gerard Groote, promoted the lifestyle of the early Christian communities in Antioch, wherein individuals would gather in homes to read and discuss the words of Christ. Members of this order led strict, ascetical lives. However, they were forbidden from begging and were required to provide for themselves. Kempis was a devoted follower of the Brothers' ways of life.

In the centuries after its publishing, the *Imitation* was translated into four languages. It quickly became one of the most popular spiritual guides available. Many, however, found Kempis's book of a "selfish monkish type." Kempis promoted a transfer of agency from the self to Christ, via Scriptural study. Though few people rejected the authority and influence of Scripture, many did not elevate Scriptural study in the manner Kempis did. His emphasis on personal meditation seemed an insular approach to spiritual development, as many individuals were not inclined, or even capable, of close textual study.

David Eschrich, researcher

JOHANN GUTENBERG ◊ 1395–1468, *The Printing Press*

> " Yes, it is a press, certainly, but a press from which shall flow in inexhaustible streams, the most abundant and most marvelous liquor that has ever flowed to relieve the thirst of men! Through it, God will spread His Word. A spring of truth shall flow from it: like a new star it shall scatter the darkness of ignorance, and cause a light heretofore unknown to shine amongst men.

- Invented the printing press with moveable wood or metal letters
- Printed the world's first book in volume, *The Gutenberg Bible*, or 42-line Bible
- Relied on the investment of Johann Fust to produce the massive bible

- Is credited with the writing of *Catholicon*, an encyclopedia

Biography

Johannes Gensfleisch zur Laden zum Gutenberg was a blacksmith and a goldsmith, and most importantly, an inventor. He was born in 1395 in Mainz, Germany, the son of a patrician. Little is known of his early life. He was exiled from Mainz during a bitter struggle between the guilds and the patricians and moved to Strassburg (now Strasbourg, France) around 1428. He took the technology of the wine press and added to it movable, raised letters made of metal which could be covered with oil-based ink on a large printing press. The letters were placed on a type bed where they were inked and pressed on paper with a screw press. Paper was added after the type was re-inked to reproduce the page. The type could be moved to create new pages which were arranged and bound into a book. By 1450, he was able to interest a wealthy financier, Johann Fust, in his invention, and received a large sum from him. Fust later sued Gutenberg who lost control of his printing establishment. Records indicate he received a pension from the Bishop of Mainz starting in 1465 and although scholars debate his financial situation at his death, he was probably not destitute.

Before Gutenberg's improvement, books were produced in handwritten manuscripts and with woodblock printing. Gutenberg's first printings, probably around 1450, were of a Latin grammar and a German book of prophecies called the "Sibyllenbuch." They were printed with a crude "DK" type of Gutenberg's invention that was put together with inconsistent line lengths. These first 30-page pamphlets were the first steps in the production of the two-volume Gutenberg Bible of 1300 pages, measuring 16" by 12". Johann Fust, a wealthy investor, helped not only with hiring the four compositors who put together the type and brought their own type cases, but also with the purchase of excellent paper and vellum for the job.

Gutenberg invented a new and improved, smaller font type for the Bible. Probably produced in two years, Gutenberg made180 copies, 40 of which were on vellum. Then he hired a rubricator to provide titles, heading, chapter initials and numbers in blue or red. Finally, some of the first purchasers from Germany and throughout Europe hired an illuminator to paint beautiful, ornate borders, giving each Bible its own unique style. Gutenberg had planned that the size and precision of the Bible would facilitate public reading or monastery reading from a lectern.

Gutenberg changed the world with his printing press by making possible mass-produced books, which turned out to be not only economical but accessible. The publication and circulation of information, specifically with the Gutenberg Bible, broke the clerical and elite control of knowledge and stimulated learning for all people. As a result, the middle class grew, and vernacular languages replaced Latin as the language of the people. Mass communication gave rise to many changes in politics and religion and a climate of questioning. The spread of knowledge because of the printing press accelerated the Renaissance, Reformation, The Age of Enlightenment, and the Industrial or Machine Age. It wasn't until the 19th century that the steam-powered rotary press improved upon Gutenberg's hand-operated press.

LEONARDO DA VINCI, 1452–1519, *The Renaissance Man*

> " Those who are in love with practice without knowledge are like the sailor who gets into a ship without rudder or compass and who never can be certain whether he is going. Practice must always be founded on sound theory, and to this Perspective is the guide and the gateway; and without this nothing can be done well in the matter of drawing.
>
> —"Of the Mistakes Made by Those who Practice Without Knowledge"

- Wrote and sketched on a regular basis on single sheets of paper in an assortment of sizes
- Accepted an invitation from King Francis I to live in the French chateau Clos Luce
- Had 17 half-brothers and half-sisters
- Loved animals and lived as a vegetarian
- Had an IQ of 190, one of the highest ever recorded
- Wrote and sketched in over 13,000 pages in his journals
- Wrote backwards and flipped his characters in his journals; to decode the message, he used a mirror's reflection
- Drew early prototypes of flight machines, such as helicopters and hang gliders
- Studied anatomy and physiology by using cadavers in morgues
- Left his paintings unsigned, so scholars sometimes struggle to distinguish which paintings are his; *Mona Lisa* and *The Last Supper* are his most recognized works
- Lived with the Duke of Milan From 1482–1489, creating war machines such as tanks, trebuchets, and guns
- Produced sketches of human muscles that were incredibly precise, considering the lack of resources and knowledge of his time
- Started to design a canal that connected two rivers with the Mediterranean Sea and the Atlantic Ocean in his later years, but it remained unfinished
- Wrote on this deathbed: "As a day well spent makes it sweet to sleep, so a life well used makes it sweet to die"

Key Works
Paintings
Virgin on the Rocks, 1486
Vitruvian Man, 1490
The Last Supper, 1498
Mona Lisa, 1503–1517
Manuscripts
Drawings of Water Lifting Devices, 1481
Flying Machine, 1485
Vitruvian Man, 1490

Biography

Leonardo Da Vinci once claimed that "time stays long enough for anyone who will use it." Da Vinci certainly used his allotted time on earth, working as a painter, a scientist, an architect, a botanist, a mathematician, a musician, an engineer, a sculptor, an inventor, an anatomist, and a writer. The archetypal "Renaissance Man" of the Renaissance humanist era, Da Vinci was born in 1452 as an illegitimate son to a notary and a peasant woman in the Vinci region of Florence. At 14, he became an apprentice to Andrea di Cione, a famous artist of the time, under whom he studied the humanities. He then became certified in the Guild of St. Luke for artists and doctors of medicine. Florentine monasteries commissioned him to paint *Virgin on the Rocks* and *Last Supper*. In 1499, he became a military engineer and architect. Da Vinci returned to Florence from 1500 through 1506 where he painted *The Battle of Anghiari* and the iconic *Mona Lisa*. He also lived at the Vatican in Rome, where he studied anatomy and physiology by using cadavers in morgues. In the last years of his life, his right hand became paralyzed, but he continued to write and draw in his journals. In 1519, he died while at the French chateau Clos Luce; legend holds that his good friend King Francis I held Da Vinci in his arms as he passed.

Paintings

Da Vinci is best known as a painter. Two of his teachers, Andrea del Verrocchio and Hugo van der Goes, significantly influenced his early style. He completed his first painting, *The Baptism of Christ*, in 1475. Da Vinci experimented with different types of paint and texturing. Rather than mixing colors on a palette, as his contemporaries did, he applied paint directly to the canvas, using thin layers to build texture. He completed *The Last Supper* after three years of work in 1498. Unfortunately, a few years later the painting started to fall apart. *The Last Supper* has been restored several times throughout history, altering the look of the original piece.

Da Vinci worked on his next major masterpiece, the *Mona Lisa*, for 16 years, with periodic breaks. *Mona Lisa* is one of the most recognizable and controversial faces in the world. Possible subjects of the painting include Lisa del Biocondo or perhaps Da Vinci's mother. This question is one of the art world's most enduring mysteries. Famed for her intriguing smile, *Mona Lisa* now hangs in the Louvre museum in Paris. Da Vinci made many sketches capturing facial expressions; one theory that has surfaced about her smile comes from these studies. The theory is that Da Vinci created *Mona Lisa* with the intention of capturing her using the two muscles which make a reflexive smile: "the zygomatic major which resides in the cheek, tugs the lip upward, and the orbicularis oculi, which encircles the eye socket, [squeezing] the outside corners into the shape of a crow's foot." Upon seeing a smile using the two muscles mentioned above, one often reflexively smiles back, which may have been the reaction Da Vinci wanted to elicit from viewers of his master work.

Technique

Da Vinci used human models for his paintings, even for the religious figures, such as Jesus. Each of his paintings took years to finish, partly because he worked intermittently, but also because he applied different approaches to improve his techniques. He studied the geometry of shadows and effects of light, attempting to incorporate precise shading in his work. Writing in his journal, Da Vinci processed his findings on light and shadow:

> The eye in an illuminated atmosphere sees darkness behind the windows of houses which are light. All colours when placed in the shade appear of an equal degree of darkness, among themselves. But all colours when placed in a full light, never vary from their true and essential hue.

Da Vinci used other realistic elements in his paintings. His perfection of aerial perspective makes his realism unique. While painting, he observed that a bluish haze increases as the object moves further away, and that blurring facial features create a more natural look. He employed these techniques on both *The Last Supper* and *Mona Lisa*.

Journals

Da Vinci wrote and sketched in over 13,000 pages in his journals. He wrote the majority of his journal reversed and flipped into a mirror image for privacy, and in order to keep all these disparate sketches organized, he grouped his pages by unifying theme. Subjects included human anatomy and physiology, parachutes, helicopters, flying machines, war vehicles and weapons, animal body parts (such as monkeys, bats, cows, bears), and countless others. His entries demonstrated unprecedented genius in his field and anticipated many modern inventions. The remarkable accuracy of his sketches can be attributed to his use of human cadavers obtained from the morgue. He drew many sketches of human faces, and fastidiously studied the way people expressed emotions and the progression from youth into old age. In his journal, he wrote, "the noblest pleasure is the joy of understanding" and in those thousands of pages, he worked to understand the world better than anyone else during his time. Scholars during the Renaissance emphasized the separation between arts and sciences, but Da Vinci, not formally educated in mathematics or Latin, joyfully spanned the intellectual boundaries of his day. The scientific community did not take Da Vinci seriously until many years after his death, finally publishing his entries featuring human anatomy and physiology in 1680.

Natural Philosophy

Baldassare Castiglione, in *The Book of the Courtier,* wrote of his friend, Da Vinci: "One of the greatest painters in the world despises the very art in which he is unique; instead of it, he takes up the study of a philosophy in which he discovers wondrous ideas and novel chimera of a kind that he could never depict despite all his painterly abilities." As Castiglione sums up, Da Vinci, though an extraordinary painter, enjoyed the study of natural philosophy much more. He once read William of Ockham, a forefather of empiricism, who said, "The order of the world is entirely contingent on the divine choice, [so] it is … impossible to deduce it *a priori.* If we want to know what it is, one must examine what it is in fact." Da Vinci appreciated observations and experiences and practiced the following method: "close observation, repeated testing of the observation, precise illustrations of the subject, object, or phenomenon with brief explanatory notes."

Perhaps because of his close observation of the natural world, Da Vinci practiced vegetarianism and cared for all living animals. He was "always treating them with infinite kindness and patience. As a proof of this, it is related that when he passed places where birds were sold, he would frequently take them from their cages, and having paid the price demanded for them by the vendors, would let them fly off into the air, restoring them to their lost liberty." His theological philosophy remains unclear; however he wrote, "without the organic instruments of that body, it [the 'spirit'] can neither act nor feel anything."

Briauna Schultz, 2013

THE OTTOMAN INVASIONS, 1453–1683

The conclusion of the Hundred Years War saw the end of one conflict but the start of another with a series of ultimately failed invasions launched by the Ottoman Empire. Initiated by Suleiman the Magnificent in a bid to expand into central Europe, his efforts and those of his successors were repeatedly dashed by European cooperation, leading ultimately towards the (temporary) cessation of the Islamic Middle East as a serious threat to Christian Europe with the defeat of the Ottomans at Vienna by the Holy Roman Empire.

THE BORGIA POPES, 1455–1503, *Corruption within the Papacy*

The aristocratic Borgia family (from the Crown of Aragon) originated in Valencia, Spain, and moved to Italy when Alfons de Borja was appointed Cardinal in 1444. Eleven years later he was made Pope Callixtus III. Always outsiders in Italy, the Borgia family was well known for avarice and love of power. They would stop at nothing—not even murder—to achieve ever more influence and power. Callixtus III helped along the career of his nephew, Rodrigo Borgia, who also became a pope, Alexander VI. His reign, particularly, was characterized by crime: theft, bribery, and murder. Machiavelli lauded him as a man who knew what it meant to seize power.

Pope Alexander VI fathered several children with his mistresses; he loved them all deeply yet manipulated them for his own purposes. For example, Pope Alexander VI appointed his son Cesare cardinal. Then when Cesare realized he wasn't suited for the role, he was appointed military commander, and in that position tried to bring the city-states under his control. Likewise, Rodrigo gave his illegitimate daughter Lucrezia into marriage three times in order to attain his country's advantage with other countries. Her first marriage was annulled, the second ended when her husband was murdered by Cesare's servants, but the third marriage was happy. After Pope Alexander's death, Lucrezia became known as a patron of the arts.

The Borgia family name suggests evil and treachery because their actions were motivated by selfish desires and resulted in moral atrocities and the ruination of others.

DESIDERIUS ERASMUS, 1466–1536, *Prince of the Humanists*

> Do not be guilty of possessing a library of learned books while lacking learning yourself.
> —*The Correspondence of Erasmus: Letters* (1484–1500)

- Is considered the foremost northern Renaissance humanist author and scholar
- Felt inspired on his path to humanism by Thomas More, Thomas Fisher, and John Colet
- Sympathized with elements of the Protestant Reformation, but ultimately did not participate
- Debated with Martin Luther over the issue of the freedom of the will in salvation
- Believed that salvation was a synergistic combination of man's free will and God's grace
- Published the first text of the Greek New Testament
- Established his reputation for sharp wit and intellectual satire with his humorous tract, *In Praise of Folly*

Key Works

In Praise of Folly, 1511
Greek Text of the New Testament (*Novum Instrumentum omne*), 1516
Education of a Christian Prince, 1516
On the Freedom of the Will, 1523

Biography

Desiderius Erasmus was a scholar and writer who played a significant role in the development of Renaissance humanism in northern Europe. Born around 1466 in Rotterdam, he was the second illegitimate son of a priest and a physician's daughter. After his parents died, Erasmus and his brother were sent to a school run by the Brothers of Common Life, who preached simple devotion to Christ. He was greatly influenced by his contact with them and trained as an Augustinian monk and then as a priest. Erasmus pursued his doctorate of theology at the University of Paris. In the course of his studies, he came to despise scholastic theology because of its excessive subtlety and its curiosity about things that were far removed from the common man. Erasmus made it his ambition to employ the tools of humanist scholarship in the service of religion. He spent six years in England, teaching at Cambridge and writing, and was later, upon his return to his homeland, an honorary councilor to the 16-year-old archduke who would become Charles V. Erasmus produced a number of influential works during the first few decades of the 1500s, including *Handbook of the Christian Soldier* (1504), *Adages* (1508), *The Praise of Folly* (1511), and *Education of a Christian Prince* (1516). In addition to these writings, Erasmus published the New Testament in Greek for the very first time in 1516.

When Martin Luther burst onto the theological scene in the second decade of the 1500s, Erasmus was initially very sympathetic to the German monk's ideas. He shared many of Luther's concerns about the moral condition of the church, but ultimately he believed that Luther's solutions were too extreme. He viewed the early years of the Protestant Reformation as the "Lutheran Tragedy" and attempted to be a moderating voice in the conflict. For his efforts, Erasmus earned the distrust and ill will of both sides. He is most commonly viewed as a thinker whose ideas and writings helped to create the proper intellectual environment for the Protestant Reformation. He died in Basel, Switzerland in 1536.

Philosophy of Christ

Erasmus introduced his belief in the philosophy of Christ in the pages of *Handbook of the Christian Soldier*, a work that gained wide circulation by 1515. The heart of this philosophy was that the reform so badly needed in the church could be achieved by returning to writings of the early church and Scripture. Erasmus believed that it was the laity who would lead the way in this reform movement. His *Handbook* was designed as a layperson's guide to the Bible, which helped to unfold the "law of Christ," a pattern of practical morality based on the example of Jesus. It called for an inner religion that was stirred by the transformation that came from reading Scripture. Erasmus's philosophy of Christ emphasized the inward state of an individual's heart as the focal point of religious life. In response to Erasmus's message, lay people began to express a greater interest in reading the Bible and early church writers, such as Augustine. This, in turn, helped to pave the way for many of Martin Luther's reform efforts that depended heavily on the Bible's authority and the thinking of Augustine.

In Praise of Folly

Published in 1511, Erasmus's most popular and widely read work is the satirical *In Praise of Folly*. In the short story, the personification of folly stands in front of a crowd and presents a dramatic monologue detailing the role of folly in the development and sustainment of civil society. Folly makes the ironical claim that the happiest life is the life of a fool; in a society of fools, only those who delude themselves into a false sense of happiness and meaning are able to enjoy their lives.

The harmony and propagation of the human race necessarily depends on foolish misapprehensions of the world, since the harsh truths of reality only strip away the disguise and reveal a world full of disillusionment and futility. In other words, "self-love and flattery oil the wheels of society and keep it running smoothly … the comedy of life is a play that can be entertaining only so long as its basic illusion is kept up." Folly then turns her focus on the vain attempts of philosophers and theologians to explain the world and how they constantly go in circles on preposterous and absurd ideas. While philosophers love to proclaim their insight into how the world works, all they offer are wild conjectures; they cannot give guidance since "their total lack of certainty is obvious enough from the endless contention amongst themselves on every single point."

In a similar manner, theologians focus themselves on seemingly surreal and bizarre questions like whether or not Christ could have been a woman, animal, or vegetable, and how Christ might have preached and been nailed to the cross if he had taken the form of a vegetable. Although the work is satirical, similar questions like these can be found in many writings by the scholastic theologians during Erasmus's time. He tried to highlight the ridiculous nature of certain theological assertions. Folly concludes her speech by emphasizing Christ's folly in dying for the salvation of a sinful humanity and the folly of a Christian life in its attempt to find value in the spirit and not in earthly goods.

Debate with Martin Luther over Freedom of the Will

At the beginning of the Protestant Reformation, Erasmus encouraged the efforts of Martin Luther as he took his stand against the corrupt practices of the church. In 1519, Luther squared off against Johann Eck in the Leipzig Disputation. He and Eck debated the issues of grace, freedom of the will, and papal authority. When Luther criticized the church's emphasis on the importance of the will in salvation as a means of cooperating with the grace of God, Erasmus publicly voiced his disagreement with Luther's ideas in *On the Freedom of the Will*. He opposed Luther's idea that individuals are incapable of cooperating with God to secure their salvation, arguing:

> We can placate those who cannot bear that man can achieve any good work which he does not owe to God, when we say that it is nevertheless true that the whole work is due to God, without whom we do nothing; that the contribution of free choice is extremely small, and that this itself is part of the divine gift, that we can turn our souls to those things pertaining to salvation, or work together (*synergein*) with grace.

Luther responded in 1525 by writing *On the Bondage of the Will*. He praised Erasmus for identifying the role of the will in salvation as a critical issue in the debate over justification by faith, but Luther warned Erasmus that he might "perhaps rightly attribute some measure of choice to man, but to attribute free choice to him in relation to divine things is too much." The rift between Erasmus and Luther over freedom of the will placed Erasmus outside of the Protestant camp. Luther was grateful for Erasmus's production of a Greek New Testament text and his critique of the church, but lamented that these things had not led him to the same conclusions as Luther and his followers.

Brian Davis, faculty

NICCOLÒ MACHIAVELLI, 1469–1527, *Prince of Political Philosophy*

> When it is absolutely a question of the safety of one's country, there must be no consideration of what is just or unjust, of merciful or cruel, of praiseworthy or disgraceful.
>
> —*Discourses on Livy*

- Operated in the delicate and dangerous politics of Renaissance, pre-unified Italy

- Received an intensely humanist education, which informed his interest in republican government, political philosophy, and old-fashioned notions of "Fortune"
- Saw humankind as inherently and unavoidably greedy, fickle, and self-interested
- Believed that a good ruler should take whatever actions necessary to preserve political order and maintain the integrity of the state, regardless of how "good" or "bad" those actions are
- Laid out detailed, practical advice to rulers of both monarchies and republics in *The Prince* and *Discourses on Livy*
- Perceived humankind to be largely at the mercy of Fortune, which constantly shifts his circumstances, especially where and when he least expects it
- Remained deeply skeptical of the Church, which he saw as corrupt and responsible for weakening man's ability to take "evil" but necessary political action
- Was ambiguous about how he viewed monarchies; seems to have generally favored popular republican government over tyranny
- Has not been treated kindly by history; the term "Machiavellian" refers to behavior characterized by underhanded opportunism

Key Works

The Art of War, 1521
Discourses on the First Decade of Titus Livy, 1531
The Prince, 1532

Biography

The name Niccolò Machiavelli conjures many negative associations. A Renaissance Florentine statesman, his contributions to modern political thought have inspired, disillusioned, and confounded students, scholars, and politicians for nearly 500 years. Born of a middle-class family in Florence, Italy, and steeped in the classical humanities by his father, Machiavelli was elected to the Florentine government at the remarkably young age of 29, and in short order rose through the ranks to become a Chancellor and a primary ambassador for his beloved city-state. A master diplomat, a popular playwright, and a man of letters, Machiavelli was a spectacular orator, and applied the skills he learned through his humanist education—particularly of Cicero—to wield influence at home and abroad and to study the ways in which political power could be seized and maintained in the treacherous political environment of Renaissance Italy. Though he was eventually removed from office amid great political and personal scandal, tortured, jailed, and banned from political life, Machiavelli was an unwavering supporter of Florentine republicanism and a unified Italy through the end of his life. The political treatises he wrote during his unfortunate "retirement"—particularly *The Prince* and *Discourses on Livy*—were geared toward achieving these things for himself and for his fellow Florentines. He died in a small town outside Florence, and his tomb is in the church of Santa Croce which, ironically, he had been banned from entering in his final years.

The Ends, The Means, and Human Nature

These texts detail the management and preservation of a well-functioning state, whether one headed by a monarch (discussed in *The Prince*) or one founded along popular, republican lines (dealt with in *Discourses*). While the particular philosophical, political, and historical points differ between the texts, a consistent theme unifying all of Machiavelli's works is an emphasis on results, or ends, over and above methods, or means. While it is a gross oversimplification to define Machiavelli's political philosophy as "the ends justify the means," Machiavelli did adhere to the philosophy that, when faced with a choice between the preservation of political rule and the collapse of the state, all actions should be taken to achieve the former and prevent the latter, regardless of how "wicked" those actions may be in the eyes of traditional morality. Sometimes, Machiavelli insists, it is better to be "not good" than "good," depending on the particular circumstances of the day and the potential losses that may result from hewing to the typical Christian ethics of humility, honesty, and loyalty.

Machiavelli's outcome-driven political philosophy springs in large part from his conception of human nature. For the Florentine statesman, men and women are fundamentally "ungrateful, changeable, pretenders and dissemblers, avoiders of dangers, and desirous of gain." This anthropological perspective, while highly cynical, is likely a result of Machiavelli's political environment, which was filled with warlords (some of them Catholic popes) dedicated to viciously conquering various regions of what is now called Italy. As a Florentine ambassador, Machiavelli played an intensely active role in the regional politics of his era, and was a firsthand witness of the extent to which politics and power are influenced by what he perceived to be the innate greed and fickleness of humankind. Given this understanding of human nature, it is no surprise that Machiavelli advocated for political rulers to "learn to be able to be not good ... according to necessity," since "a man who would wish to make a career of being good in every detail must come to ruin among so many who are not good."

"Bad for the Sake of the Greater Good"

Practically speaking, the Machiavellian ruler—whether a single individual, or a ruling body such as a council or legislature—must deploy compassion and cruelty as needed to cultivate the love, fear, and respect of the population over which it rules. This might mean assassinating or exiling enemies; crushing unruly segments of the populace; lying and breaking oaths for political expedience; publicly supporting others while covertly working against them; or otherwise violating traditional Christian ethics, all for the paramount goal of preserving political order and consolidating it for those who seek to rule. Of course, the effective ruler, the one who is willing and able to be "bad" for the sake of some greater "good," must be capable of adapting his actions to the wildly changing circumstances of the political arena: "The man who conforms his way of proceeding to the quality of the times is happy, and similarly ... he whose proceedings the times disagree with is unhappy."

Machiavelli's Cosmology—Fortune Meets Virtue

For the student of political theory, it is worth noting some peculiarities in Machiavelli's terminology. Machiavelli frequently references the concepts of "virtú" and "Fortune." The first of these terms roughly translates to "virtue," but not in the moral sense familiar to modern readers. For Machiavelli, "virtue" referred to "a person's or a thing's intrinsic and essential strength, regardless of whether this is morally good or bad." "Fortune," on the other hand, was a vague cosmological force—perhaps even divine—that controlled the constantly shifting sands of man's circumstances, despite, and often conflicting with, his efforts to the contrary. For Machiavelli, the "virtuous" ruler—that is, the truly effective one—was the one who could manipulate his particular circumstances to his best advantage, minimizing losses and maximizing gains, adapting his behavior to best achieve his desired outcome, and potentially even turning the tide of Fortune to work with him rather than against him. It is unclear to what extent Machiavelli believed humankind to be in control of its destiny. In Chapter 17 of *The Prince*, he suggests that "fortune is the arbiter of half of our actions, but that she indeed allows us to govern the other half of them, or almost that much." But the potentially catastrophic influence of Fortune cannot always be avoided: like a river, Fortune "shows her power where virtue is not prepared to resist her; and she turns her rushing current here where she knows that embankments and dikes have not been made to hold her."

The Machiavellian Guide to Religion and the Church

All this talk of virtue and Fortune raises important questions regarding Machiavelli's religious or theological views, which were, unsurprisingly, unorthodox. The Florentine politician consulted astrologers and believed in the influence of the cosmos on human affairs, a belief much in vogue in Renaissance Florence. Machiavelli was also certainly skeptical of the Church, which he saw as a politically motivated organization whose corrupted message of moral goodness had "caused many of the problems in contemporary society." For Machiavelli, Christianity "glorified humble and contemplative men more than active ones," a development that has "rendered the world weak, and given it in prey to wicked men, who are able to manipulate it safely, since mankind, in order to go to Heaven, thinks how to endure the beatings it receives, rather than how to avenge them." For this reason, as Machiavelli saw it, it is critical for the successful, effective, "virtuous" ruler to break from traditional Christian morals, and even use Christianity as a tool in achieving the paramount goal of political order and stability.

Defender of Tyranny, or Republican at Heart

To many readers, Machiavelli's philosophy of power presents an uncomfortable recipe for tyranny. Certainly his suggestions for eliminating political opposition and bribing loyalty from others stray far from what is traditionally believed to be "good," democratic government. But scholars widely believe that Machiavelli was fundamentally a believer in popular government, particularly republicanism, and that he was no fan of monarchy or dictatorial regimes. Even in *The Prince*, particularly Chapter Five, Machiavelli criticizes monarchies as cultivating far too much revolutionary passion amongst their people. Still, there remains significant ambiguity as to how Machiavelli truly felt about republics and principalities; it is possible that he generally favored the former but accepted the necessity of the latter for the sake of "simple political survival in … unpredictable and violent times."

Legacy

History has not been kind to Machiavelli. In various places at various times, he has been called everything from an "embodiment of evil" to a "spokesman for political liberty." His philosophy has been adopted by some of the most ruthlessly amoral figures in global history. Even his name has become a term for underhanded opportunism. Nonetheless, in many ways, Machiavelli launched the modern "science" of politics, particularly relating to theories of governance, political liberty, and classical republicanism.

Brandon Martinez, researcher
Colman R. McVaney, 2016

NICOLAUS COPERNICUS, 1473–1543, *Astronomer Who Moved the Earth*

" In opposition to the general opinion of mathematicians and almost in opposition common sense I should dare to imagine some movement of the Earth.

—On the Revolutions of Heavenly Spheres

- Was a Prussian astronomer and mathematician who saw the planetary movement in a geocentric, or earth-centered, universe as being too complex and irrational
- Held to the old Greek idea that all the planets, including Earth, revolve around the sun in circular orbits
- Proposed a heliocentric solar system that was revolutionary and interpreted as an affront to the church—it challenged the idea of a heavenly realm, suggested a universe of staggering size, and questioned established religious beliefs
- Detailed his life's work in *On the Revolutions of Heavenly Spheres*, which he was reluctant to publish since he feared public outcry
- Made the list of the church's forbidden books with *On the Revolutions of Heavenly Spheres*, despite dedicating it to Pope Paul III
- Inspired both the Scientific Revolution and the Enlightenment with his principle of challenging established "truths"

Key Works

"Commentariolus," 1510–1514
Narratio Prima (written by Rheticus), 1540
On the Revolutions of Heavenly Spheres, 1543

Biography

Nicolaus Copernicus was born into a well-to-do merchant family in Poland during the European Renaissance. He had the financial means to attend four different universities as a young man, and he educated himself in astronomy, canonical law, classical languages, mathematics, geography, philosophy, and medicine. While attending the University of Bologna in Italy, Copernicus became acquainted with the distinguished astronomer Domenico Maria de Novara, who inspired Copernicus's love for the stars. Despite this newfound passion for astronomy, Copernicus did not pursue stargazing until after he completed his doctorate in canon law. The years spent studying theology earned the young scholar a prestigious position as the canon of a cathedral in Frauenburg, a post that allowed him free time to speculate about the world above. Before long, Copernicus's thoughts and ideas about the universe heralded the Scientific Revolution and brought the once-unquestionable authority of traditional thought crashing down. He died of a stroke in 1543.

A Simpler Universe

Copernicus was a simple man who sought to understand the complexity of the universe around him. He saw God as a perfect being and believed that the universe of his creation should also be perfect and blissfully simple. Thus, Copernicus naturally opposed Ptolemy, the ancient astronomer who was idolized in Renaissance Europe. Ptolemy's complex system for planetary movement was based on the idea that the earth was the center of the universe. Like any attempt to describe how a square peg fits into a round hole, Ptolemy's efforts to describe how the universe could revolve around the earth were convoluted and riddled with inaccuracies.

Refusing to believe that God would create such a cumbersome system, Copernicus dared to believe that an alternate explanation for the universe was possible. He soon stumbled onto "an old Greek idea being discussed in Renaissance Italy: that the sun, rather than the earth, was at the center of the universe." Copernicus instantly set out to prove this heliocentric theory of the heavens. He postulated that the sun stood unmoving at the center and that the six known planets, including Earth, revolved around the sun.

By removing the earth from its privileged position in the center of the universe, Copernicus could explain some of the apparent irregularities in planetary movement. For example, the fact that planets appear to move forward then backward had puzzled astronomers for centuries, but Copernicus's system demonstrated how this "retrograde motion [was] simply due to the changing view of the planets from the earth." This combination of two radical ideas (that the sun was in the center of the world and that the earth actually moved) made the universe infinitely simpler. According to Copernicus, all apparent irrational movement could be "verified of the mobility of the Earth," meaning that if a star appears to be moving strangely, the issue is not with the star but with the fact that the observer is on a spinning sphere that is revolving through space around a larger sphere; in short, the earth is not exactly an ideal viewing platform. Yet, even Copernicus's reworking of the Ptolemaic system was imperfect—he never guessed that orbits were not circular or that the sun was not the only or even the central sphere that influenced planetary orbits.

Publishing *On Revolutions*

Copernicus understood that his ideas would infuriate the scientific and Christian communities alike. Consequently, he was extremely reluctant to publish his heliocentric theory. Sometime between 1510 and 1514, Copernicus did outline his ideas in the essay "Commentariolus," which was privately circulated but never published. He then fell silent for many years while he continued to perfect and refine his work. Eventually, a friend named Rheticus realized the full revolutionary impact of the work and urged Copernicus to publish immediately." Copernicus finally agreed to discreetly publish a summary of his ideas under the title *Narratio Prima*, but Rheticus remained unsatisfied. When Copernicus was on his deathbed, Rheticus finally convinced the aged scientist to let him prepare his life's work, titled *On the Revolutions of Heavenly Spheres*, for publishing. *On Revolutions* still did not exactly cause the uproar that Copernicus dreaded and Rheticus desired: "the plain fact is that few people took much notice at first." Soon, though, scientist such as Tycho Brahe, Johann Kepler, and Galileo Galilei began expanding Copernicus's theory, and the resulting outcry was every bit as loud and as damaging as Copernicus had feared.

The Scandal

To many in the modern world, it is hard to grasp why people were outraged by Copernicus's theory. Copernicus's ideas threatened to change much more than just the earth's location on the cosmic map; he challenged long-held assumptions about God, humankind, and the world itself. By removing the earth from the center of the universe, Copernicus suggested that it was simply one planet among many others.

Yet since the time of the ancients, religious authorities around the world firmly taught that the earth was completely separate from the planets, stars, and other bodies in the heavenly realm. The earth was different because it was a fallen world that had been corrupted by sin. The skies above, however, were supposedly divine and perfect, where God himself dwelled. By suggesting that the earth was just another heavenly body and no different than any other planet, Copernicus effectively called into question heaven and the realm of God. As the German poet Johann Wolfgang von Goethe asked: "What became of Eden, our world of innocence, piety and poetry; the testimony of the sense; the conviction of a poetic-religious faith?" Copernicus dared to challenge the authority of religious leaders who taught that geocentricity was essential to Christianity. The very notion that Aristotle, Ptolemy, and even the church could be wrong about something as significant as the universe itself implied that they could be wrong about other concepts as well. Those in power in the church were not willing to surrender their claim on absolute truth so easily; yet, Copernicus and scientists after him succeeded in proving the heliocentric theory, leaving a lasting blemish on the "unquestionable" authority of religious leaders.

Tatjana Scherschel, 2015

MICHAELANGELO ◊ 1475–1564, *The Greatest Sculptor*

> " If we have been pleased with life, we should not be displeased with death, since it comes from the hand of the same master.

- Was a painter, sculptor, architect, and poet
- Was bound as an apprentice to Domenico Ghilandaio at 13
- Studied classical sculpture in the Medici gardens of the Medici family, and anatomy with the Augustinian friars
- Was given the commission for "Pieta" by Cardinal Jean Bilheres de Lagrualas
- Completed the immense 14' statue of David for the Cathedral of Florence
- Began the decades-long work for the tomb of Pope Julius II
- Painted the ceiling of the Sistine Chapel when asked by Julius II
- Was appointed architect of St. Peter's Basilica at Vatican City
- Worked on a number of reflective Pietas in his old age

Biography

Michelangelo di Lodovico Buonarroti Simoni was an Italian sculptor, painter, architect, poet, and engineer of the Renaissance. Considered to be the greatest living artist while he was alive, he lived at the same time as Leonardo da Vinci and Raphael. He was born in Caprese, Italy, to a banking family of moderate means. His teachers recognized his remarkable abilities at an early age and offered him opportunities for education in the arts and anatomy. He learned panel painting and fresco painting from Domenico Ghirlandaio, to whom his father (having recognized that his son had no head for business) apprenticed him at the age of 13. Then he studied under the sculptor Bertoldo di Giovanni, Donatello's pupil. He also studied anatomy at the Hospital of Sto Spirito, having obtained special permission from the Catholic church to work with cadavers.

At just 21, Michelangelo sculpted "Sleeping Cupid," which he or his agent "aged" (by processes unknown) and sold to a cardinal as an antique. Despite being outraged when he discovered the fraud, the cardinal was so impressed by the young sculptor's skill that he invited him to work for him in Rome. With this patron, Michelangelo traveled to Rome where he spent the rest of his life. The Pope, the Medici family, and other wealthy dignitaries commissioned a variety of projects. Pope Julius II commissioned him to build a tomb, but interrupted Michelangelo's work on that to have him paint the ceiling of the Sistine Chapel, perhaps his most monumental and famous work. His masterpiece is a transcendent example of High Renaissance art, incorporating Christian symbology, prophecy, and humanist principles that he had absorbed in his youth.

Although he painted and sculpted throughout his life, working on the Sistine chapel had damaged his health, and he turned his efforts to architecture. Michelangelo remodeled buildings in Rome, as well as the Palazzo del Conservation. He designed the Laurentian Chapel and the Medici library before being named chief architect of St. Peter's Basilica in 1546. His architectural work at St. Peter's became the grandest gift to Christendom, with the primary purpose of honoring God. He died on February 18, 1564, weeks short of his 89th birthday. Unlike many artists, Michelangelo achieved fame and fortune during his life, although he also had his share of detractors, including Leonardo Da Vinci. He was so famous that two biographies were written about him during his lifetime. Art lovers through the centuries continue to revere his creations, and his name is synonymous with the best of the Italian Renaissance.

THE SPANISH INQUISITION, 1478–1834

The period known as the Spanish Inquisition was a time of intense persecution against the Jewish people in Spain from 1478 to 1834. The Inquisition began when King Ferdinand V of Spain married Isabella I. The two were devout Catholics, and they believed that the Jewish residents of Spain were a detriment to the unification of the nation and the strengthening of the national Christian faith. While traditional historical accounts hold that the Inquisition was instituted largely as a way to remove the "negative" influence of true Jews from the true *conversos*, Revisionist historians contend that the Inquisition was an attempt by the Spanish monarchy to sabotage the growing economic and political power of Jews. In either case, Pope Sixtus IV issued a proclamation in 1478 authorizing Ferdinand and Isabella to institute an Inquisition into the problem of the Jews in Spain. However, with the passing of the Alhambra Decree in 1492, the Inquisition took a disastrous turn; this "Edict of Expulsion" gave Jewish inhabitants of Spain four months to leave Spain or face a death sentence.

At this point the Pope tried to restrain the power of the Inquisition, but he was too late. Ferdinand and Isabella, capitalizing on their newfound church support, had already enacted plans for the handling of the Inquisition, and its foundations of hatred, mistrust, and prejudice were laid too deep to be uprooted by the Pope's recantation. Many scholars believe that as many as 400,000 Jews were forced to exit the country, while others contend that the number was between 30,000 and 40,000. This mass exodus saw Jews emigrate to Turkey and Portugal, among other nations. Tensions in Portugal—already aggravated by conflict between native Jews and Christians—were further inflamed by the addition of nearly 20,000 Jews. This led to King Manuel of Portugal's decision to expel the Jews from Portugal, offering them 10 months to exit the country or face death. Both Inquisitions caused mass numbers of Jews to convert to Christianity due to their reluctance to leave their respective homelands. The *conversos*, converts to Christianity in response to the Inquisition, were widely mistrusted and persecuted due to widespread suspicion that they were practicing Judaism in secret.

After the expulsion of the Jews and many of the *conversos*, the Inquisition's focus shifted to the persecution of those perceived as "heretics" by the Catholic church. These so-called heretics were often those who had had conflict with the church, and at the turn of the 17th century, these heretics were often reformists. Those suspected to be heretical were apprehended and then tortured into false confessions by Inquisitory officials working as officers of the Catholic church. After torture elicited confessions, the victims were sentenced to prayer and fasting as a method of "purification." The church, unwilling to act as an executioner, would turn those they wanted terminated over to civilian compatriots, who burned the accused at the stake. The decline of the Inquisition was instigated by Joseph Bonaparte, eldest living brother of Napoleon Bonaparte, who officially excised the power of the Inquisition in 1808. After a string of monarchs variously resurrected and disallowed the Inquisition, it finally ceased in Spain for good in 1834.

SIR THOMAS MORE, 1478–1535, *"A Man for All Seasons"*

> " But to find citizens ruled by good and wholesome laws, that is an exceeding rare and hard thing.
>
> —*Utopia*

- Was born in London to a well-off family
- Matriculated at Oxford after serving as a page in the Archbishop of Canterbury/Lord Chancellor's home
- Considered himself a staunch Catholic
- Enjoyed the liberal arts, but pursued a law career
- Had a high regard for law and order
- Established a good friendship with Desiderius Erasmus
- Became a member of Parliament and ultimately joined the royal service of King Henry VIII
- Wrote his famous *Utopia* in 1516 while on a diplomatic trip in Flanders
- Became Lord Chancellor of England in 1529
- Emphasized classically educating his children, including daughters
- Persecuted Protestant "heretics," wrote against Luther, and ordered public burnings of Protestant literature
- Lost his head in 1535 for refusing to recognize the new Church of England and Henry VIII as its head
- Was canonized by the Roman Catholic Church and made the patron saint of politicians
- Coined the word *utopia*, meaning "no place" in Greek

Key Works

The History of King Richard III, c. 1513
Utopia, 1516
A Dialogue Concerning Heresies, 1529
A Dialogue of Comfort Against Tribulation, 1534

Biography

Often heralded as "England's greatest humanist," Sir Thomas More distinguished himself as a witty, law-loving, devout Catholic, known for his service to King Henry VIII and his celebrated *Utopia*, which scholars have analyzed and debated for centuries. Born in 1478 to a wealthy, middle-class London family, More grew up just as the Renaissance was arriving in England. He attended the prestigious

Saint Anthony's school as a boy and worked as a page for a few years for Cardinal John Morton, the archbishop of Canterbury and Lord Chancellor of England. Morton, impressed with More's sharp mind and engaging personality, sponsored More to go to Oxford, where he thrived as a student of the liberal arts and classical languages. However, More left Oxford to study law, like his father, for he valued order and obedience above all and thus appreciated legal studies. In 1499, More met Erasmus of Rotterdam, the illustrious Christian humanist, and the two became lifelong friends, sharing a love for Greek satirists and other classics. Erasmus, whose writing More had encouraged, later hailed More as "a man for all hours" in his preface to his *Praise of Folly*. While a law student, More lived in a Carthusian monastery, which fostered his pious lifestyle, and he debated joining the priesthood. He ultimately chose to practice law, but religious life always held strong attractions for him.

His legal occupation ushered him into politics and royal service when he was elected to Parliament in 1504. More's Parliamentary work soon attracted the attention of the king, beginning a long career in Henry VIII's court in various appointments. As a trusted counselor and diplomat, More developed an intimate friendship with Henry VIII, and the peak of his royal service came in 1529 when he was appointed Lord Chancellor of England. Proving to be a devoted family man, More was a faithful husband to both his first and second wives and strove to educate his children, including his daughters, in the classics.

The Reformation, however, revealed another side of his otherwise witty and agreeable disposition as he did everything in his power to fight it—from outlawing Protestant literature to prosecuting heretics. However, when Henry VIII broke from the Catholic church to divorce Catherine of Aragon, More resigned due to his divided allegiance between Catholicism and his king. Shortly after, Henry VIII required English citizens to take an oath recognizing Anne Boleyn as queen, her children as legitimate heirs, and Henry as the head of the new Church of England. More, though not troubled by the new queen, was deeply troubled with rejecting the Pope. When More refused to accept or comment on these terms, Henry VIII sent him to the Tower of London for a year to "reconsider." More "did not seek martyrdom and defended himself by every legal means," but in July 1535, he was tried and convicted of high treason. More was beheaded July 6, and in 1935 the Roman Catholic Church canonized him and "declared him the patron saint of politicians."

Utopia

Thomas More's most famous work, *Utopia*, is a celebrated work of humanist and political scholarship whose original intent has perplexed contemporary scholars. More began writing *Utopia* in 1515 on a diplomatic trip to Flanders. He wrote what would be the Second Book while abroad, adding an antecedent book in 1516 upon his return. This First Book depicts a conversation between the characterizations of Thomas More and his friend and fellow humanist, Peter Giles, and a fictional New World traveler named Raphael Hythloday. According to Wayne A. Rebhorn, the First Book focuses on "one simple question: Should a learned humanist … remain a kind of unattached intellectual, or should he enter the service of a monarch in order to better the state he lives in?" Rebhorn suggests that More wrote the First Book of *Utopia* out of hesitation concerning entering public life. As the three characters' debate shifts from public life to communal societies, Raphael mentions an "island [off the coast of the New World] where an ideal, cooperative society flourish[es]," telling his skeptic companions, "But if you had been with me in Utopia … then doubtless you would grant that you never saw people well ordered, but only there." The discourse in the First Book creates a framework to describe Utopia in the Second Book, which serves as More's record of Raphael's oral account of his five years in Utopia. The Second Book illustrates Utopia's government, economic and social structures, and religious outlook. On the island, which King Utopus reportedly settled and founded in ancient times, there exists what many scholars have considered a proto-communist system, for the Utopians reject private property, shun profit, and work for the common good while practicing religious tolerance.

Government and Politics

As Raphael Hythloday's account of Utopia unfolds, a distinct, governmental structure arises. Utopia is a "federation of 54 largely independent, though remarkably uniform, city-states," equally distanced apart and well protected. Every 30 Utopian households elect their own leader called a syphogrant, every 10 of which adhere to a leader called a tranibore. All of these elected officials then make nominations and appoint a prince to serve for life. The tranibores and a couple of syphogrants accompany their prince to the council house in the capital city and comprise the Utopian legislature. They address any issues "concerning the commonwealth," never discussing any "matter the same day it is first proposed" to prevent any "hasty or rash" action. In addition, a general council meets annually with three representatives from each city-state present. A prince bears no distinction "by a crown or diadem royal," and the people "willingly exhibit … due honor without any compulsion" to the other officials. The Utopians condemn lawyers (ironic, since More was one), believing in clear and simple law crafted so that "every man should be put in remembrance of his duty." In the absence of excessive laws, the council determines punishments, which can include slavery, "according to the heinousness of the offense." It is difficult to label More's Utopian government, for while it does have representative government—both with the democratic syphogrant elections and the republican election of the princes—it aristocratically only allows "the learned" men to hold office, the princes serve for life, and the rest of the people live highly regimented lives in what appears to be a communist structure.

Economy and War

Perhaps the most salient feature indicating a communist system in Utopia is the economic construct, which shapes the daily lives of the Utopians, yields a continual surplus, and provides economic alternatives to war. Utopia's key economic characteristics include the nonexistence of private property and profit and the obligation of all to labor. All things are communal in Utopia, exhibited by the fact that none of the houses have locks: "Whoso will, may go in, for there is nothing within the houses that is private, or any man's own." Agriculture, or "husbandry," comprises the backbone of the Utopian economy, and all citizens work as farmers in their city-states, alternating with a more specialized, urban trade. Hythloday notes that the syphogrants are to "take heed that no man sit idle, but that every one apply his own craft with earnest diligence." Each citizen works a six-hour day, and Hythloday asserts: "That small time is not only enough but also too much for the store and abundance of all things that be requisite either for the necessity or commodity of life."

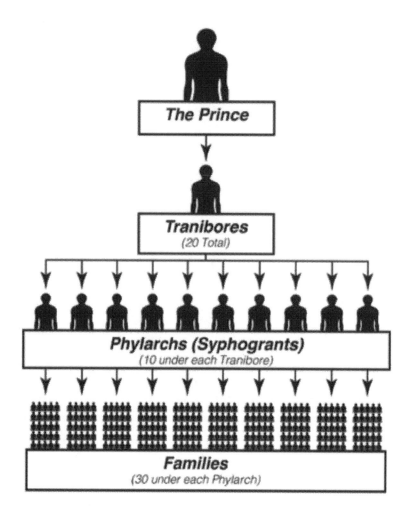

Thomas More's Utopia

Noting the strong work ethic and practical array of occupations in Utopia, More seems to tacitly criticize the "idle" work ethic and petty jobs of his day. Because Utopia experiences a constant surplus, it conducts a booming international trade with neighboring countries, giving some to their poor and selling the rest, which brings an influx of gold and silver to Utopia. With its regimented and proactive workforce, a resulting surplus, and a stockpile of what the rest of the world deems valuable, Utopia holds an advantageous position when faced with potential war. Though they strive to avoid war, only going to battle "either in the defense of their own country, or to drive out of their friends' land the enemies that have invaded it," they do train their own men and women for war in the event they cannot hire sufficient mercenaries. The Utopians' main use for their gold and silver is to pay off potential enemies, but if this proves ineffective, it is used to hire mercenaries, "for they had rather put strangers in jeopardy than their own, knowing that for money enough their enemies themselves ... may be bought or sold." In his depiction of the Utopian economy, Hythloday emphasizes that prosperity is not the same as wealth; defending and providing for the commonwealth in the long-term, Utopia's economic equality directly relates to its social structure and how its citizens live.

Society and Lifestyle

The Utopians live with all things common. Hythloday notes that the cities are practically identical, claiming, "Whoso knoweth one of them, knoweth them all." With common provisions, all the houses the same—and unlocked—and the people all dressed in similar, neutral clothing, the Utopians live with no social division. The only class that exists in Utopia is a scholarly class, which More commonly refers to as "the learned." The work requirements do not apply to "the learned," for they have "a perpetual license from labor to learning" if they show academic promise as children. From this group the Utopians select their officials. In humanist fashion, all citizens are encouraged to study and enrich their minds. Just as they have regimented hours of the day for work, there are also hours in their day for personal pursuits, meals, and play. They spend their free time doing or studying what they please and many attend daily lectures. Hythloday recounts that "the wits ... of the Utopians, inured and exercised in learning be marvelous quick" and tells that he was able to quickly teach them Greek, bringing with him stores of classical literature.

Hythloday's account highlights the Utopians' driving desire for "felicity," which comes from pursuing pleasure, which he defines as "every motion and state of the body or mind where in man hath naturally delectation ... whatsoever is naturally pleasant, so that it may be gotten without wrong or injury." A preoccupation with good health and "liberty of the mind" distinguishes Utopian life. Living under this guiding philosophy of pleasure and ultimate felicity, however, leaves room for selfishness, and according to Sanford Kessler:

> Although the Utopians grounded their morality on enlightened self-interest, they knew that reasoning about morals was insufficient to make pleasure-oriented people virtuous. Intelligent people, in their view, tend to maximize pleasure "by fair means or foul," seek to avoid death at all costs, and are only restrained by fear of punishment. ... Such views led the Utopians always to add religious principles to their repertoire of rational arguments when discussing moral philosophy.

Unrestrained pursuit of pleasure raises a need to limit self-interest and thus corruption in the workforce and government. Consequently, the basic moral code needed to guide the Utopians manifests itself in religion.

Religion

Freedom and tolerance distinguish Utopian religion. Hythloday states, "For this is one of the ancientest laws among them: that no man shall be blamed for reasoning in the maintenance of his own religion." However, this religious freedom exists within a set of undisputed beliefs enforced by highly respected priests. Such a system disqualifies any doctrine deemed harmful or dangerous to the commonwealth. All Utopians believe in an afterlife in which "vices be extremely punished and virtues bountifully rewarded," and where their ancestors are "present among them." All of Utopia believes in "one chief and principal god" they call Mythra, but all are free to worship however they please and according to their view of Mythra; some sanctify the sun, moon, noble ancestors, and more. What most Utopians naturally believe in, though, is an invisible, omnipotent deity beyond human understanding, making them highly receptive to Christianity. According to Hythloday, Christianity appeals to the Utopians especially because "Christ instituted among His all things common," in harmony with their own society. Utopians are free to share their beliefs and civilly try to persuade others of their faith but cannot do so violently or with "displeasant and seditious words." Utopia's religious tolerance prevents the communist society from falling to human selfishness and pride, which Hythloday calls "the princess and mother of all mischief." This raises some of the most difficult questions concerning the relationship between *Utopia* and More's own convictions.

The Ambiguity and Legacy of *Utopia*

More's intentions in writing *Utopia* remain unknown and still spark scholarly debate. Ian Adams and R.W. Dyson, of the University of Durham, assert that *Utopia*, while "discussing issues in a light and literary yet serious way," is "difficult to gauge" with respect to More's driving motives, and C.S. Lewis writes in *The Oxford History of English*, "All seem to be agreed that [*Utopia*] is a great book, but hardly any two agree as to its real significance; we approach it through a cloud of contradictory eulogies." Disconnects between the text and More's life are at the heart of the debate. More's Utopia is a communistic world laced with representative government that avoided war, yet More was the leading counselor to an absolutist monarch who viewed war as a way to consolidate power. Another area of debate concerns the religious tolerance in *Utopia* in light of More's vigorous persecution of Protestants. Kessler suggests that More might have supported religious tolerance in non-Christian societies, but that "it is not clear … that More ever considered anything like Utopian religious freedom desirable for Europe." As Russel K. Osgood maintains, "The wonder of More's Utopia is that … the utopian author can still be critiquing his own society and legal order."

While More may not have left the world with definitive answers from *Utopia*, he did leave the world with a new word, and a new literary genre, which would generate its inversion as well—dystopia. According to Adams and Dyson:

> " While More's *Utopia* is not the first picture of an ideal society … he did coin the word "utopia" and began a self-conscious tradition of utopian writing that continues to this day. In keeping with More's own character, it is a complicated and ambiguous tradition. The nature and purpose of utopian literature is an open and contested question that continues to be debated.

Elizabeth Palms, 2014

THE PROTESTANT REFORMATION

The Reformation was a religious upheaval that took place in the early 16th century. Whereas earlier reformers of the Catholic church—figures such as John Wycliffe and Jan Hus notable among them—had sought to reform aspects of Catholic practice, Martin Luther and the reformers that followed in his wake sought to fundamentally rethink Catholic theology on matters such as salvation, the Eucharist, and the role of Scripture in the church. Particularly incensing to the early reformers were various medieval Catholic practices, notably the sale of indulgences (forgiveness of sins at a price), that they believed diluted the true gospel message of simple faith in Christ. The start date of the Reformation is traditionally ascribed to October 31, 1517, when Martin Luther, still a pious monk, nailed 95 theses for discussion to the door of the Cathedral at Wittenburg. Luther's theological emphases revolved around what have become known as the *solas* of the reformation: *sola scriptura* (the Bible as the sole authority in matters of doctrine), *sola fide* (justification by faith alone, not works), *sola gratia* (faith itself as a gift of grace alone). In 1521 Pope Leo X excommunicated Luther. He was asked to explain his beliefs at the Diet of Worms before Holy Roman Emperor Charles V. Because he was defiant and refused to take back what he had written, Charles V called him "an outlaw and a heretic."

The ripples from Luther's actions and writings spanned the continent. Ulrich Zwingli of Switzerland wedded the state to a reformed church in Zurich. John Calvin, the other enduring figure from the time, set up his reforms in Geneva, emphasizing doctrine (including predestination) that would come to be associated with an extant theological school named for him, Calvinism. Even Henry VIII, initially so hostile to Luther and his efforts, came around and oversaw modest reforms to the English church that would one day develop the Anglican branch of Protestantism. Just north of England in Scotland, John Knox put a Scottish spin on Calvinism and created what is still known as the Presbyterian wing of the Reformation. Radical reformations sprung up as well throughout Europe, with splinter sects denying everything from the Trinity to the virgin birth. Even in countries with a strong Catholic church, such as Spain and Italy, what has been called the Counter-Reformation worked to undo many of the excesses that drew the ire of the early reformers. But the damage had been done, and since that momentous day 500 years ago the "holy catholic church" of the ancient creeds has been anything but universal.

MARTIN LUTHER, 1483–1546, *The Father of the Protestant Reformation*

" He deserves to be called a theologian, however, who comprehends the visible and manifest things of God seen through suffering and the cross.

—*Heidelberg Disputation*

- Was a German Augustinian monk
- Catalyzed the the Protestant Reformation with his writings
- Advocated the doctrine of justification by faith alone
- Believed the teaching of Scripture took priority over the edicts and pronouncements of popes and church councils
- Translated the Bible from Latin into German
- Argued with Erasmus over the issue of the freedom of the will in salvation
- Disagreed with Ulrich Zwingli over the presence of Christ in the Lord's Supper at the Colloquy of Marburg
- Married Katherina von Bora, a former nu, in opposition to the idea that priests cannot marry and must remain celibate
- Promoted the idea that every believer is a priest

Key Works

The Ninety-Five Theses, 1517
To the Christian Nobility of the German Nation, 1520
The Babylonian Captivity of the Church, 1520
The Freedom of a Christian, 1520
The Bondage of the Will, 1525
Small Catechism, 1529
Large Catechism, 1529
Smalcald Articles, 1537

Biography

Martin Luther lived a life defined by theological controversy. In 1505, shortly after embarking on his studies to become a lawyer, Luther was caught in a violent thunderstorm. In a moment of panic, he vowed to Saint Anne that he would become a monk if he survived the storm. By 1507, Luther had joined the Augustinian Order and become a priest. As he advanced in his theological studies, Luther began to question the nature of the pope's authority and the validity of the church's message of salvation. This led to his *Tumerlebnis* (tower experience) where his understanding of justification by faith developed. During his early years as a theology professor at the University of Wittenberg, Luther first garnered attention in 1517 when he wrote his *Ninety-Five Theses* in response to Johann Tetzel's peddling of indulgences in Wittenberg. In this work, Luther attacked the corrupt practices of the church with regard to the forgiveness of sins. This ignited a firestorm of controversy that ultimately led to Luther's excommunication in 1520 and his famous speech at the Diet of Worms in 1521 where, when asked to renounce his ideas and his writings, he refused, claiming that his conscience was "captive to the Word of God."

After his decisive break with the Roman church, Luther devoted himself to preaching and writing. He authored numerous biblical commentaries, theological treatises, and a German translation of the Bible. As a leader in the growing Protestant Reformation, Luther continued to find himself in the middle of controversies for the rest of his life. These controversies included his dialogue with Erasmus over the role of the human will in salvation, his criticisms of both sides of the Peasants' War in 1525, and his debate with Ulrich Zwingli over the presence of Christ in the Lord's supper in 1529. By the time of his death in 1546, Luther had paved the way for a host of Protestant reformers in the generations to follow.

Sola Scriptura (Scripture Alone)

Two pillars of authority in Martin Luther's time determined the practices and message of the church: Scripture and ecclesiastical tradition. When Luther first began to voice his concerns about the practice of selling indulgences and other church practices that concerned him, the debate quickly focused on which of these two pillars was more authoritative. At the Leipzig Disputation in 1519, Luther caused a stir when he contended that Scripture must be held higher than church tradition and the teachings of popes and councils. He reasoned that since popes and church councils are capable of error, the Bible has to be the standard for determining the shape and practice of the Christian faith. The next year, in *To the Christian Nobility of the German Nation*, Luther reinforced this idea when he claimed, "Scripture alone is our vineyard in which we must all labor and toil." When opponents argued for the tradition of the church over Scripture by appealing to the authority of the early church fathers, Luther countered that he "must be defeated with Scripture, not with the uncertain teachings and lives of men, no matter how holy they may be." Armed with this principle of Scripture alone as the final authority in the church, Luther spent the rest of his life trying to help the church return to its Biblical foundations in terms of its gospel message and practices.

Justification by Faith Alone

Luther's most significant dispute with the church of his day revolved around the question of how an individual can be made right with God. Coming out of the Middle Ages, the church viewed man's spiritual condition before God as one of extreme infirmity due to original and ongoing sin. To be right or justified before God, individuals needed a constant infusion of God's grace through the sacraments of the church. This infusion of grace could not be earned on the part of the individual, but the church had gradually come to teach that God pledged Himself to grant grace to those who did the best that they could (*facere quod in se est*). In this way, it became possible for the sinner to expect grace from God based on the sinner's own natural abilities and good works. As Luther began to lecture his way through the Bible at Wittenberg during the second decade of the 1500s, he soon arrived at a radically different conception of justification. He saw the sinner's position before God not as someone ill needing a constant infusion of medicine, but as a guilty and condemned criminal awaiting a certain and just execution. Luther saw sinners as totally helpless and without any resources of their own with which to barter for mercy.

Drawing from his understanding of the New Testament, he unfolded God's gracious solution to this dilemma: a double switch. Jesus Christ takes the place of the accused sinner before God, exchanging His perfect righteousness for the sinner's condemnation. When God looks at the sinner, He now sees the perfect obedience of His own Son and legally declares the sinner to be righteous. At the same time, the just punishment for the sinner's crimes is completely satisfied by Christ's death on the cross so that no present or future condemnation remains. This exchange comes not as a result of any good works that the sinner has done, but entirely as a gift of God's grace through faith placed in Jesus Christ alone. As Luther put it, "Through faith in Christ, therefore, Christ's righteousness becomes our righteousness and all the he has becomes ours; rather he himself becomes ours." Despite the claims of his critics, Luther still valued good works, but he emphasized that they were the fruit of a Christian's life, not what earned this life in the first place.

Clerical Marriage

In the 16th century the church taught that in order to be a monk, nun, or priest one had to be celibate. As a result, Luther spent the early years of his ministry as a celibate monk. Once he made his break with the church over the issue of justification by faith, Luther continued to examine other church practices in light of what the Bible taught. When he turned his attention to the issue of clerical celibacy, Luther could not find any biblical support for it as an essential requirement to be a man or woman of God. This led him to claim in the *Smalcald Articles* that "The papists had neither authority nor right to prohibit marriage and burden the divine estate of priests with perpetual celibacy. On the contrary, they acted like antichristian, tyrannical, and wicked scoundrels, and thereby gave occasion for all sorts of horrible, abominable, and countless sins, in which they are still involved." In 1527, Luther married Katherina von Bora, a nun he had aided in a daring escape from her convent in 1523. Their household became a living testimony to the developing Protestant conviction that ministers could marry and have children.

The Priesthood of All Believers

Luther believed that the church of his day had become a twisted distortion of the church prescribed by the New Testament. In particular, he was troubled by how the priests and the laity were being viewed as two distinct classes of Christians. On the basis of biblical passages such as 1 Peter 2:9 and Revelation 1:6, Luther argued that all Christians are priests in the sense that they are able to minister to each other and intercede for one another before God. He drew attention to how Christians are united and stand on equal ground by virtue of their shared faith in Christ. Luther did recognize the need for a formal priestly office within the church, but he warned, "there is no true, basic difference between laymen and priests, princes and bishops, between religious and secular, except for the sake of office and work, but not for the sake of status." This biblical reorientation of the relationship between the clergy and laity helped to give rise to more congregational forms of church government in other branches of Protestantism in the generations that followed.

Brian Davis, faculty

Rachel Jeffries, 2015
Brady Weisner, 2016

HENRY VIII ◊ 1491–1547, *Notorious King of England*

" I like her not!

—to Cromwell, regarding Anne of Cleves

- Was a learned, skilled, attractive man, the second son of Henry VII
- Married six times in an effort to fulfill his earnest desire for a male heir
- Was headstrong and opinionated, with the single purpose of his own power
- Became disillusioned with his first wife, Catherine of Aragon (Spain)
- Divorced and married again, against the will of the Roman Catholic Church
- Executed subordinates to solidify power
- Wase excommunicated from the Roman Church
- Created and led the Church of England
- Confiscated extensive monasterial properties
- Conducted wars with Scotland and France
- Died of complications to his ulcerated leg

Biography

Henry, the second son of Henry VII, was a learned, skilled, attractive man who succeeded his father as king at age 18. He married six times in an effort to provide a male heir to ensure domination over the British Isles and France. Headstrong and opinionated, with the single purpose of preserving and strengthening his own power, Henry wasn't suited for marriage. He was disappointed and disillusioned with his first wife Catherine, his brother's widow, when she failed to give birth to an heir, so he tried to nullify the marriage by appealing to the Catholic church. Pope Clement VII's refusal to annul Henry's marriage to Catherine not only angered Henry but also fueled the fire of the coming Reformation. Subsequently, Henry married Anne Boleyn, who also failed to produce an heir. This time he tried using *The Act of Succession* to claim his marriage to Anne was illegitimate. (Had he succeeded, this would also have made their daughter Elizabeth—who became Elizabeth I of England—illegitimate and ineligible for the throne.) When that failed, he had Anne executed for treason and adultery.

In another move to assert himself, Henry attempted to be affirmed in the role of head of the church by *The Act of Supremacy*. However, he was thwarted by Bishop John Fisher and Thomas More, among others, who refused to approve him. In retaliation Henry executed them and, as a result, was excommunicated himself by papal order. The next day Henry married Jane Seymour, who soon gave birth to an heir at last—Edward. Unfortunately, Jane lived only 12 days after Edward's birth, and Henry, who perhaps genuinely loved Jane, remained unmarried for three years.

Henry's new chief minister, Thomas Cromwell urged him to break with Rome and establish himself as the head of the Church of England. Cromwell, acting on Henry's behalf, then dissolved 800+ monastic communities and scooped up their considerable wealth for the royal coffers. As Henry continued to seize what power he could for England, he decided to marry again, and Cromwell suggested he make a political alliance with the Protestant princess Anne of Cleves. Henry and Cromwell hoped the new union would provide increased opportunity to join forces with the Continental Protestant powers in order to avoid an attack by Charles V of France. Henry hated Anne on sight and found her ugly, however, and blamed Cromwell for the marriage. Cromwell began to lose favor and eventually endured the fate of those who displeased the despotic monarch—he had his head chopped off.

Henry's next political and personal decision was to annul his marriage to Anne to make an alliance with the teenaged Catherine, part of the powerful Howard family. Catherine, like Anne Boleyn before her, was accused of adultery and treasons and ended her life on the chopping block at the Tower of London. Henry married one last time to Catherine Parr, who outlived him.

Without the advice of his longtime advisor Thomas Cromwell, Henry worked alone on improving his country's political position with bold moves that brought enormous changes to England and the continent. While at war with Scotland, he committed England to fruitless and expensive war with France. In the process of gaining military strength, he expanded the navy as he had planned, affirmed the union with Wales with the *Statute of Wales,* and made Ireland a kingdom. Within England itself Henry instituted *The Reformation Statutes* which included the *Act in Restraint of Appeals* to make England an empire and appointed himself head of the Anglican Church with the *Act of Supremacy.*

Henry died of complications to his ulcerated leg, which had been infected for years, and was laid to rest beside the one wife he truly loved, Jane Seymour, in St. George's Chapel at Windsor Castle. He was succeeded by their son, Edward VI.

FRANCOIS RABELAIS, 1494–1553, *The Religious, Raucous, and Risqué*

> " Do what thou wilt.
>
> —*Gargantua and Pantagruel*

- Grew up in Chinon, France, where his father practiced law
- Became a Franciscan monk, but switched to the Benedictine order after his monastery took his Greek texts away from him
- Left monastic life and studied medicine
- Read and edited ancient medical texts by Hippocrates and Galen in the original Greek
- Published his magnum opus, *Gargantua and Pantagruel*, under the name Alconfribas Nasier, an anagram of Francois Rabelais
- Donated his limited wealth to the poor upon his death
- Was known for extremely crude and often dark humor
- Believed that laughter was therapeutic and signified good health
- Reconciled with the church, having left the monastery via papal bull
- Advocated for church reform, but opposed a complete split with the Catholic church
- Crafted a "utopian" model of a monastery in *Gargaunta and Pantagruel* called the Abbey of Thélème, where both men and women are free to study and live as they see fit
- Was a humanist of the northern Renaissance

Key Works
Pantagruel, 1532

Gargantua, 1535

Le Tiers Livre ("The Third Book"), 1546

Le Quart Livre ("The Fourth Book"), 1552

Biography

Embodying humanist passion for reviving the classics in scholarship and in examining Renaissance-era Christianity, François Rabelais was a French monk and, eventually, a physician. He established himself as an eccentric humanist known for his vulgar but tacitly philosophical writings. Though various details of Rabelais's life remain unknown, scholars generally accept his birth year to be 1494. Born the son of a lawyer at Chinon, he supposedly went to the "convent of Seuilly to be made a monk" at age 9. Ordained at a Franciscan monastery, Rabelais grew to appreciate recently resurrected studies in ancient Greek. Such Greek texts held some of the earliest known versions of the New Testament, but when the French Catholic authorities at the Sorbonne denounced them for their frequent contradiction of the Latin Vulgate, Rabelais's monastery confiscated his Greek book collection, prompting him to leave the Franciscan order for the more accommodating Benedictine order. In 1530, he left his new monastery to travel and to pursue medical studies, and he was able to read the ancient but esteemed medical writings of Hippocrates and Galen in Greek. Upon taking a position as town physician at Lyons, a humanist center, Rabelais continued to edit classic medical works by Hippocrates and other Greeks and wrote his famous pieces, *Gargantua and Pantagruel*.

Rabelais showed himself to be a "religious moderate" who advocated reforming the Catholic church and opposed the complete split with the church promoted by Protestants such as John Calvin, who criticized Rabelais for "not going far enough." Eventually, he appealed to the papacy for an "absolution from violation of monastic vows" to be reconciled with the church after leaving his monastery and was allowed to return as a priest and practice medicine without pay. Scholars believe that Rabelais died in Paris in April 1553.

Gargantua and Pantagruel

Rabelais's magnum opus is a somewhat unorthodox collection of satire. *Gargantua and Pantagruel* relays the story of the giant, Gargantua, and his son, Pantagruel. These two giants are highlighted as well-educated, pleasure-seeking, self-satisfying, witty creatures that come to discover what it means to choose "virtuous lives." The giants' world allows complete freedom for sensual and intellectual experience where "excessive discipline is considered evil". Some of the giants' escapades are frivolous and gross, such as young Gargantua climbing to the top of Notre Dame to drown Parisians below in a "piss-flood." Other episodes are more profound, like Gargantua's forgiveness and blessing to an invading army he defeats.

Through both the silly and the serious, Rabelais deals with self-indulgence, education and the value of knowledge, church doctrine, and mercy. First completing *Pantagruel* in 1532 and later adding *Gargantua*, Rabelais originally wrote under the name Alconfribas Nasier, a narrative alter ego and anagram of François Rabelais. With countless crude references and inappropriate shenanigans, the books had "something to entertain—and to offend—nearly everyone" and were "popular with both the scholarly elite and the middle class." Despite the Sorbonne's continual banning and censuring of the books, to which Rabelais eventually added a third and fourth book, *Gargantua and Pantagruel* have carried Rabelais's legacy both as a writer and as a patron of the northern Renaissance.

Style: Vulgarity, Vernacular, and Characterization

If any one word can describe Rabelais as a writer it is *vulgar*. Extensive bodily references, potty humor, and detailed accounts of physical punishment clutter the pages of *Gargantua and Pantagruel*. According to Carl Rollyson of Baruch College, "Rabelais maintained the medieval spirit of the farces and fabliaux in his violent imagery, his vulgarity and his preoccupation with sexual matters," but nonetheless embodied a "Renaissance spirit … in his style, an overflowing of verbal exuberance, a rich compound of slang, odd words, jargon of the various professions, interminable lists, and other heterogeneous elements." Not only was Rabelais liberal with his crude humor and obscene descriptions, but he wrote them in the vernacular and was one of the first French writers to do so, contributing to his work's accessibility and thus popularity.

The elaborate characters in Rabelais's work also distinguish his writing style. Rollyson describes Rabelais's characters as "unforgettable," for both Gargantua and Pantagruel undergo distinct characterization as they mature from bawdy, but "curious, witty, garrulous, and loving" young giants into "kind lords" whose "earlier wit changes to wisdom." The two giants are surrounded by other witty companions and other characters remain less developed as comic victims. Rabelais's vulgar comedy, often mediated through his characters, provided marketable entertainment to a newly expanded audience of his day.

Philosophy of Humor and Medicinal Laughter

During a time when "man's unique capacity for laughter was the subject of intense debate," Rabelais asserted that laughter was therapeutic, and he capitalized on his medical knowledge to create comedy through coarse details about the body and brutal punishments, such as mutilation. Alison Williams of the University of Wales-Swansea claims that "the learned language of the anatomist allows Rabelais to use dissection as a type of palliative for the reader" as his "focus on minutiae of the body's internal structures" fosters "indifference toward the target of humor." Readers are too distracted by the detailed anatomy references to feel emotional attachment and sympathy for the victim, thus making him a comedic victim. In addition, by creating transient characters introduced only to be beat up or killed for the reader's entertainment, along with thoroughly developing the characters of Gargantua and Pantagruel, Rabelais crafts a form of comedy Williams likens to watching a slapstick cartoon such as *Tom and Jerry*.

Rabelais's medical experience also manifested itself in his "twin persona of author-doctor who cares for the reader-patient." From the opening of *Gargantua*, Rabelais cast himself in the role of a doctor, beginning with a few lines of reassuring verse:

> Good friends, my readers, who peruse this book,
> Be not offended, whilst on it you look:
> Denude yourselves of all deprav'd affection,
> For it contains no badness nor infection:
> 'Tis true that it brings forth to you no birth
> Of any value, but in point and of mirth;
> Thinking therefore how sorrow might your mind
> Consume, I could no apter subject find;
> One inch of joy surmounts of grief a span;
> Because to laugh is proper to the man.

Establishing his readers as patients of the human experience in this way, Rabelais created credibility as a satirist and "encouraged his readers to look on the inevitabilities of human life with a sense of humour which may be ironic, self-deprecating, even sick, but which is also ultimately healthy."

Attacks on the Church

Though not a separatist, Rabelais did desire church reform and was displeased with the Sorbonne's rules and regulations, such as denouncing the Greek New Testament in favor of the Latin Vulgate. "Amid all the ribaldry in *Pantagruel and Gargantua* … lurk[s] hostility toward the church" as "Rabelais invokes the patron saint of cuckolds" and other subtle gibes at the church. One of Rabelais's most salient protests against the church is his Abbey of Thélème in *Gargantua*. In the story, Gargantua commissions this abbey to be what many scholars have called a utopian monastery where both men and women can live according to one governing rule: "Do what thou wilt." Rabelais described how honorable the people at the Abbey are, adorns them with colorful and gold-embroidered velvet clothing, and noted "all their life was spent not in laws, statutes, or rules, but according to their own free will and pleasure." The Abbey of Thélème represents a departure from the monastic life Rabelais had known and reflects his Christian humanism, a call to reform striving to justify modern education with religious doctrine.

Humanism

In all areas—writing style, humor, and distaste for doctrinal regulations on education—Rabelais demonstrated Christian humanist qualities. Though his writing contains some tenets of medievalism, "Rabelais introduced the spirit of the Renaissance with his rejection against Scholasticism, his confidence in antiquity, his faith in science, and his belief in human progress" along with his stylistic energy and details. Rabelais's writings often include catalogues of ancient—especially Greek—thinkers, further reflecting a northern Renaissance style. In addition, Rabelais's views on therapeutic laughter and the way in which he cast himself as the "author-doctor" in *Gargantua and Pantagruel* display humanism by highlighting "the role played by the mind in the treatment of the body and the duty of the doctor to balance" these two. With an emphasis on "treating patients" mentally, Rabelais thus exhibited humanism in his approach to humor. Perhaps Rabelais's greatest Christian humanist display was in his creation of the Abbey of Thélème in *Gargantua and Pantagruel*. Through the Abbey, Rabelais conveyed his distaste for medieval ritual and restrictions on education, such as he experienced in his own Franciscan monetary. From his imagery of the beautiful garments worn by the members of the Abbey to the abounding free thought and study that these people exercise, he subtly criticized the medieval educational system. In such ways, Rabelais wove his Christian humanism into his works.

Elizabeth Palms, 2014

JOHN CALVIN, 1509–1564, *The Great Systematizer of the Reformation*

> " It is certain that man never achieves a clear knowledge of himself unless he has first looked upon God's face, and then descends from contemplating him to scrutinize himself.
>
> —*Institutes of the Christian Religion*

- Was a talented organizer and refiner of Reformation theology

- Leaned heavily on the writings of Augustine
- Articulated a strong doctrine of Predestination wherein God decides people's eternal fate
- Organized the Reformed church in Geneva
- Shaped the government in Geneva through his consistory
- Played a role in the burning of Michael Servetus for heresy
- Condoned the beheading of Jacques Gruet
- Influenced Protestantism through his sermons, commentaries, and Institutes of the Christian Religion

Key Works

Institutes of the Christian Religion, 1559 (final edition)
Calvin's Bible Commentaries, 1540–1565
Calvin's Sermons, 1541–1565

Biography

Although he is most commonly associated with his reforming work in Geneva, John Calvin was born in Noyon, France, in 1509 to middle class parents. He began his schooling at the University of Paris to become a priest, but he was influenced by his father to pursue a civil law degree instead. During the early 1530s, Calvin began to sympathize with Protestant ideas that were making their way into France. In 1533, he was involved with a speech given by Nicholas Cop promoting Martin Luther's doctrine of justification by faith, and was forced to flee Paris for Switzerland. He settled in Basel and began to work on the first edition of his *Institutes of the Christian Religion*, a detailed handbook on the main points of Christian doctrine.

In 1536, Calvin decided to move to Strasbourg so that he could continue his writing. On his way there, he had to detour through Geneva where the local Protestant leaders implored him to stay and help with their work establishing a church. Calvin, however, was forced to leave the city in 1538 when his attempts to reform church discipline and doctrine met with strong resistance from the Genevan citizens. Calvin found refuge in Strasbourg, where he developed an influential friendship with fellow reformer Martin Buber. By 1541, religious and political conditions in Geneva had worsened and the citizens appealed to Calvin to return in order to stabilize church and city life.

When Calvin returned to Geneva for a second time, he held a position of respected authority, and resistance to his plans to reform religious life in the city eventually died out. Calvin established the Genevan Consistory to enforce church discipline and founded the Genevan Academy to train future pastors. For the rest of his life, Calvin exerted a strong influence on Protestants throughout Europe through his preaching and his writing. He wrote biblical commentaries and a large number of devotional, doctrinal, and polemical pamphlets. Most significantly, Calvin published his final edition of his *Institutes* in 1559. This expanded fifth edition of his most famous work remains influential in Reformed theology today. Worn out by his responsibilities, he died in 1564; his burial place is unknown.

Systemization of Reformation Theology

By the time Calvin became established as an important leader in Geneva, some of the early theological battles of the Protestant Reformation had already been fought. Fueled by the desire to be faithful to the original teachings of the Bible, thinkers like Martin Luther and Ulrich Zwingli had engaged the church in Rome on a number of important issues. What was lacking was a systematic presentation of the core biblical doctrines of the Protestant position. It was Calvin, with his training both as a lawyer and a theologian, who provided a coherent framework for understanding and teaching Reformed theology when he wrote *Institutes of the Christian Religion* in the 1530s.

Originally, Calvin envisioned the *Institutes* as a small guide to help people understand the Bible and basic Christian doctrines. As he preached and taught in Geneva, Calvin continued to revise and expand the content of the *Institutes* until it reached its full 80-chapter length in the final 1559 edition. He shaped its contents around the basic structure of the Apostles' Creed. Book I begins with God the Father and His creation of and care for the world. Book II addresses the fall of mankind into sin and God's provision of Jesus Christ as the redeemer. Book III turns to the work of the Holy Spirit as the giver of faith and applier of redemption to God's people. Book IV closes out the *Institutes* with Calvin's understanding of the church and its role in the world. Writing without the constant demands of theological and social controversy that dogged earlier reformers like Luther and Zwingli, Calvin was able to provide a work that organized and refined the thinking of the Protestant Reformation and presented it in a comprehensive and concise fashion.

Providence and Predestination

In *Institutes of the Christian Religion*, Calvin expressed the idea that nothing in life happens by chance. He argued that "anyone who has been taught by Christ's lips that all the hairs of his head are numbered will look farther afield for a cause and will consider that all events are governed by God's secret plan." This led Calvin to affirm a strong doctrine of providence in which God assumes a caring, effective, and active role in governing and preserving his creation. Calvin's idea that nothing happens without God's order or permission was a source of great comfort for those living in the uncertain and tumultuous times of the 16th century, but it also raised the issue of God's role in salvation.

Calvin advocated a strong view of human sinfulness, claiming that man is "so depraved in his nature that he can be moved or impelled only to evil." This meant that salvation was impossible if it depended upon the will and actions of man. Calvin's answer to this problem was his doctrine of predestination, which he defined as "God's eternal decree, by which he compacted with himself what he willed to become of each man. For all are not created in equal condition; rather, eternal life is foreordained for some, eternal damnation for others." Thus, for Calvin, if someone is saved, it is because God has chosen to be merciful to this person and has worked in such a way that that he or she will most assuredly come to faith in Christ. This choice is founded on God's "freely given mercy, without regard to human worth," and his choice to give other people over to damnation is made according to "His just and irreprehensible but incomprehensible judgment." Calvin offered this doctrine of predestination not as a means of satisfying human curiosity about God's sovereignty, but as a means of comforting Christians with the reality that if God had chosen them for salvation, their salvation was secure because it did not depend on them in any way. Only God could take people who were so hopelessly wicked and regenerate them into people who were righteous before him.

Church and State in Geneva

The idea of the church was an important part of Calvin's theology. He devoted a significant portion of the *Institutes* to outlining what he believed to be the biblical model for church structure and government. When Calvin returned to Geneva for a second time in 1541, he worked diligently to establish a working version of this model. He used his training as a lawyer and his expertise as a theologian to develop the consistory and the Geneva Academy to function alongside the church.

The Genevan Consistory was a council of elders tasked with the enforcement of church discipline. Calvin believed that this discipline was necessary if religious life in Geneva was to conform to the biblical ideals of the reformers. Often the government of the city and the consistory came into conflict as Calvin sought to regulate the lives of Genevan citizens through church discipline in a manner that was much stricter than the local laws. This conflict stemmed from Calvin's view that "civil government has as its appointed end, so long as we live among men, to cherish and protect the outward worship of God, to defend sound doctrine of piety and the position of the church, to adjust our life to the society of men, to form our social behavior to civil righteousness, to reconcile us with one another, and to promote general peace and tranquility." Alongside the consistory, Calvin founded the Genevan Academy to serve as a training ground for future pastors in reformed churches. During the last decades of Calvin's life, Geneva became a haven for persecuted Protestants from all over Europe. Some refugees from England ultimately returned to their native country during the reign of Elizabeth I and became the catalysts for the Puritan movement.

Brian Davis, faculty
Rachel Jeffries, 2015
Brady Weisner, 2016

THE BATTLE OF CAJAMARCA, 1532

With the discovery of the Americas by Christopher Columbus in 1492 came the Age of Discovery, and with it the European military dominance of the New World. In the name of God, glory, and gold, a number of expeditions were launched with the aim of sometimes subjugating, sometimes civilizing the American peoples to European standards. The Battle of Cajamarca, a surprise attack led by Francisco Pizarro against the Incan king, marked the end of the Pre-Columbian era of American history. Key to the battle was Pizarro's use of cavalry and cannons, which the Incan military had no response to.

MICHEL DE MONTAIGNE, 1533–1592, *Essayist*

" [Display virtue] according to the opinion of Plato, who says that steadfastness, faith, and sincerity are real philosophy, and the other sciences which aim at other things are only powder and rouge.
—"Of the Education of Children"

- Learned Latin, and read the classics independently
- Spent nearly a decade composing his famous Essays, a term which he invented
- Traveled extensively while being elected as mayor of Bordeaux
- Remained Catholic in the war between Catholics and Protestants, though was deeply suspicious of the absolutist claims of any sect
- Was respected as a negotiator in religious conflicts and by Catherine de Medici to work with Henry of Navarre

Key Works

Essays, 1580, 1588, 1595

Biography

Michel Eyquem de Montaigne, a philosopher of the French Renaissance, wrote *Essays* ("attempts"), popularizing the essay form as a literary genre. In his own lifetime, Montaigne was admired more as a statesman than as an author. He was born on an estate near Bordeaux, France, to a well-to-do family. The family fortune derived from commerce, and his father was mayor of Bordeaux. Young Michel was tutored at home, exclusively in Latin; he didn't learn French until he was 6. His education continued at the College of Guyenne and then at the University of Toulouse where he studied law. He then embarked on a life of public service in the family tradition, becoming a magistrate, a member of the Board of Excise, and a member of the Parliament of Bordeaux. He married the daughter of one of his parliamentary colleagues and they had six daughters, five of whom died as infants. He retired from public life in 1570 to devote himself to writing. In 1580, he embarked on more than a year of traveling, returning only when he heard he had been elected to his father's old job—mayor of Bordeaux. He accepted the position reluctantly, but served for two terms. He spent the last years of his life at his chateau, beset by various illnesses, and died of an inflammation of the tonsils (which deprived him of speech) while hearing mass in his room.

What Does Montaigne Know?

The tendency in Montaigne's essays to digress into anecdotes and personal ruminations was seen as detrimental to proper style rather than as an innovation, and his declaration that, "I am myself the matter of my book," was viewed by his contemporaries as self-indulgent. In time, however, Montaigne would come to be recognized as embodying, perhaps better than any other author of his time, the spirit of freely entertaining doubt which began to emerge at that time. His most famous remark, "*Que sçay-je?*" ("What do I know?") is repeated even now: *Que sais-je?* Remarkably modern even to readers today, Montaigne's attempt to examine the world through the lens of the only thing he can depend on implicitly—his own judgment—makes him more accessible to modern readers than any other author of the Renaissance. Much of modern literary non-fiction has found inspiration in Montaigne, and writers of all kinds continue to read him for his masterful balance of intellectual knowledge and personal storytelling.

Montaigne was responding to a pessimistic world after the Renaissance. He witnessed the Calvinistic Reformation and the Wars of Religion, which were characterized by fanaticism and cruelty. So Montaigne wrote books about himself, attempting to uncover the truth of man's existence. The title "Essays" reflects Montaigne's spirit of exploration and assessment. Constantly revising the three books of *Essays*, Montaigne summarized an enormous amount of learning in a variety of fields, while demanded the process of thinking and inquiry. These are important tenets of his belief system:

- The philosophy of free judgment goes against the scholastic's way of thinking; instead of finding reasons for our inherited belief, we should question how we got to that place.
- Philosophy is morality itself; each person should determine his own path.
- Experience, action, and thinking are the best paths to knowledge.
- We should take all opinions into account, taking nothing as absolute truth, i.e., "natural judgment."
- What is accustomed can clouds us and overpower us—we are affected by our culture.

- True reason and judgment are known by God and are available to man.

Jeff Culver, faculty
Natalie Hathcote, 2017
Michelle Stalnaker, faculty
Cole Watson, 2018

WILLIAM GILBERT, 1544–1603, *Father of Electricity*

" Stronger reasons are obtained from sure experiments and demonstrated arguments than from probable conjectures and the opinions of philosophical speculators.

—*De Magnete*

- Became a leading force in the scientific revolution by developing an early stage of the scientific method
- Thought it was foolish to rely solely on one's thoughts for developing a theory because the mind is very biased and full of mistakes
- Used experimentation to develop all of his theories; this was not necessarily a new concept, but he carried it further by noting all of his procedures and materials used in his experiments
- Spent close to 15 years writing his most important work: *De Magnete* or *On the Magnet*
- Broke his *De Magnete* into six books divided into chapters and focused all of his theories and studies on magnetism
- Used experimentation to form theories, which was an innovative step in science (even though many of his theories didn't hold up)
- Was the first to recognize electricity and distinguish magnetism and electricity as two distinct subjects
- Found the Earth had magnetic properties and theorized that the Earth was a big lodestone—a piece of iron oxide that is completely magnetic

Key Works
De Magnete, 1600

Biography
A gifted doctor and a leading figure in the scientific revolution, William Gilbert was a Cambridge graduate who joined the Royal College of Physicians—a regulating body—yet spent most of his time studying magnetism. Born into a family of some wealth in Colchester, England, Gilbert entered St. John's college, Cambridge, as a 14-year-old in 1558. He received a B.A., an M.A., and finally an M.D., after which he became a senior fellow at the univerisy. In the 1570s, he set up a medical practice in London. Over the course of 16 years he wrote his opus, *On the Magnet*, carefully chronicling his experiments and discoveries. Gilbert was the first scientist to "discover" electricity, even though many of his theories on it and its separation from magnetism ended up disproved. *De Magnete* was published in 1600 and gained a lot of praise from educated Europeans, and in that same year he was elected president of the College of Physicians. In 1601 Gilbert was appointed the Royal Physician, serving Queen Elizabeth I and King James I. Gilbert died on December 10, 1603, at the age of 59. He never

married. A collection of essays, *De Mundo Nostro Sublunari Philosophia Nova* (*New Philosophy about our Sublunary World*), was published by his brother after his death.

De Magnete

William Gilbert's *On the Magnet* made a major contribution to science. He was a spark in the Scientific Revolution, using experimentation and quantifiable data to support his scientific and philosophical ideas. Gilbert was not the first to use experiments in order to confirm or deny a theory, but he was the first scientist to write down the procedures and materials he used in his experiments. Gilbert's experiments for this work mainly took place in a blacksmith workshop. Through testing and experimenting with lodestones (magnetic pieces of iron oxide), he made many discoveries in the field of magnetism. For example, he showed how magnets lose their attractive force when under intense heat. In many ways his methods are present today in the scientific method of discovery.

Terrestrial Magnetism and Electricity

William Gilbert drew two revolutionary concepts from his work in *De Magnete*—the idea of terrestrial magnetism and the discovery of electricity. Gilbert's conclusion for his theory of terrestrial magnetism was actually confused with that of gravity, but the idea that the earth had magnetic properties and was like a lodestone was true. Gilbert reasoned that magnetism is how all the entities of the earth are kept together. He drew this conclusion by taking flakes of iron and putting them close to a lodestone and then farther from the stone. When they were close to the stone they joined together, but when taken further from the stone, they separated: "Thus it is that the foundations of the earth are conjoined, connected, held together, magnetically." Gilbert's second great finding within *De Magnete* was that of electricity. Through observing the "amber effect," the attraction of clothing to amber stones, he found that this was a different kind of attraction than magnetism. He named this *electricity*; today we call this *static electricity*. Although many of the conclusions he drew regarding the relationship between electricity and magnetism were disproved—like the two being completely separate and that electricity only attracts—he set the stage for future scientists by making the first observation of pure magnetism and electricity.

Brady Weisner, 2016

MIGUEL DE CERVANTES, 1547–1616, *The First Novelist*

> " Finally, from so little sleeping and so much reading, his brain dried up and he went completely out of his mind.
>
> —*Don Quixote*

- Wrote *Don Quixote*, debatably the first novel in the western world
- Was captured by pirates and lived in slavery for five years
- Created a complex story of a man more comfortable in his fantasies than his realities in *Don Quixote*
- Made Don Quixote a distinctive character by writing his dialog in Old Castilian Spanish, whereas the rest of the novel was written in a a modern Spanish dialect

Key Works

Don Quixote, 1605

Biography

Miguel de Cervantes Saavedra was an author, a poet, and a playwright. The fourth of seven children, he was born in Spain on September 29, 1547, to a poor apothecary. Little is known about his life before 1569, but records indicate that, likely because of his father's job, his family frequently moved. It is also almost certain that he did not attend university. In 1569 humanist Juan Lopez de Hoyos wrote a volume to commemorate the death of Queen Isabel de Valois. Cervantes contributed three poems to this work; these are among his first published writings. In 1570, he joined the Spanish forces. In September 1575 pirates captured his ship. He was forced into slavery until his rescue in 1580. In 1584, he married Catalina de Salazar y Palacios, who was 18 years his junior. He began to write plays in the late 16th century. He published *Don Quixote* in 1605. Following *Don Quixote*, he published several short stories and poems. He died in 1616.

Don Quixote—Brief Synopsis

The book, often called the first novel, chronicles the adventures of the eponymous character and his companion, Sancho Panza. Perhaps the greatest Spanish literary work of all time, the work had a palpable influence on the development of the modern novel and its influence has been broadly perceived throughout Western literature. At the outset of the story, Don Quixote is introduced as a simple man, nameless and idealistic, who seeks to live out the fabulous escapades detailed in his treasured collection of tales of chivalry, knights, and romance. Fancying himself a knight, he eventually takes on Sancho as his page, and, throughout the course of the first part of the book, seeks out quests and noble affairs to indulge his whimsical longings. Though comical in its enactment, the story of Quixote has tragic aspects, as the regal aspirations of this anachronistic man begin to corrupt and overtake his mind, driving him from masquerades to madness.

Though Part One of the story is heavily steeped in wit and humor, the plot becomes more serious with the second entry, which, though now published as an integrated addition to the book, was originally its own distinct sequel, released 10 years after the initial publication of *Don Quixote*. During this subsequent act, Sancho is portrayed as manipulative, and he often takes advantage of Don Quixote's madness. Another man who has taken up a similar guise in order to attempt to "cure" Quixote eventually defeats Quixote. This leads Quixote, now reclaiming his given name, Alfonso Quixano, to retire from his quests. Cured of his insanity, he returns home and eventually dies, his legend concluded.

Satire and Chivalry

As Don Quixote attempts to uphold the chivalric codes of yore, a rift develops between him and the powerful people of his age. Those around him have given up the code of honor from medieval times, and, because he decides that he's going to bring it back, fewer and fewer people understand him. His behavior seems ridiculous to those he meets. Though he is trying to capture the exciting practices of a bygone era, his behavior makes him a laughing stock. His relationships with those outside of his enchanted world are deadlocked, as he can't wrap his head around the rationalism of others. Quixote looks just as silly to others as they look to him, and this is no accident. Cervantes deliberately satirizes thoughtless chivalry by juxtaposing it with the rationalism and objectivity of the day. He contrasts the old with the new, showing readers that, while the olden ways might seem admirable, trying to capture the past with little thought is ultimately foolish.

EDMUND SPENSER, 1552–1599, *The Poets' Poet*

" For whatsoever from one place doth fall,
Is with the tide unto an other brought:
For there is nothing lost, that may be found, if sought.

—*The Faerie Queene*

- Was an English poet inspired by Homer and Virgil to write a great epic
- Wanted to show that the English language could be as beautiful as Greek and Latin
- Wrote the epic *The Faerie Queene*, which is his best-known work
- Began his writing career by translating poems for anti-Catholic propaganda; The Catholic Church is also one of the allegorical villains in *The Faerie Queene*
- Created the "Spenserian Stanza" for *The Faerie Queene*, which consists of nine lines: eight lines of iambic pentameter and one line of hexameter
- Lived richly in Ireland for 19 years until his castle was burned down; he died a year later, penniless in London
- Is often called "the poets' poet" because of his influence on later writers such as Milton, Keats, Shelley, Lord Byron, Wordsworth, and T.S. Eliot

Key Works

The Shepheardes Calender, 1579
Amoretti, 1595
Epithalamion, 1595
Prothalamion, 1596
The Faerie Queene, 1596

Biography

The son of a cloth-maker, Edmund Spenser came from a family with limited means, but his natural writing ability and quick intellect earned him a scholarship to Cambridge University. There, he completed both his bachelor's and master's degrees before being appointed the secretary of Arthur Grey, the Lord Deputy of Ireland. Though Lord Grey moved back to England two years later, Spenser lived in Ireland for the next 19 years. He began writing poetry by translating selected poems to publish in anti-Catholic propaganda literature. He soon began writing his own sonnets and collections, but Spenser's greatest undertaking was *The Faerie Queene*, which he envisioned as a 12-book epic poem about virtuous knights. His poetry often contained praises of Queen Elizabeth I, who rewarded Spenser with great wealth. Spenser married Elizabeth Boyle in 1594, and his works *Amoretti* and *Epithalamion* celebrate their love. During an Irish rebellion in 1598, Spenser's castle was burned down, and he fled to England in financial ruin. He died just a year later of unknown causes; some say he died of starvation, others claim he was ruined by grief. Although Spenser completed only the first six books of *The Faerie Queene* before he died, he is still considered one of the greatest epic poets of all time.

The Shepheardes Calender

In 1579, Edmund Spenser published his first major work, *The Shepheardes Calender*. The *Calender* was a collection of 12 short, pastoral poems. Always drawn to experimentation, Spenser's 12 poems contained 13 different metrical schemes, including three types of couplet, three types of four-line stanzas, and a sestina. He initially received a great deal of criticism for his use of archaic, old-fashioned wording as he wrote from the point of view of pastoral shepherds. However, critics later realized that Spenser's simplistic language and lamentable spelling were intentionally meant to achieve a rustic effect, and were likely even a subtle homage to medieval writer Geoffrey Chaucer. Unlike many poets of the day, Spenser did not pride himself on lofty verbiage, but preferred using realistic and accessible language. In *Julye* in the *Calender*, Spenser writes, "And he that strives to touch the starres, / oft stombles at a strawe." In other words, if one cannot understand everyday life, his grander aspirations would be futile. The publication of the *Calender* indicated that Spenser already had plans to write an epic. Since the time of Virgil, pastoral poetry has often been viewed as a stepping stone to ambitious poetic endeavors.

The Faerie Queene—Innovative Form and Unfinished Allegory

Inspired by the epics of Homer and Virgil, Spenser always dreamt of writing an English epic as grand and as beautiful as those in Greek and Latin. He once wrote a letter to his friend about this dream, saying, "Why a God's name may not we, as else the Greeks, have the kingdom of our own language?" True to this vision, Spenser's writing in *The Faerie Queene* explores new depths of sensuousness and musicality in the English language. The entire epic is written in nine-line "Spenserian stanzas," which consist of eight lines of iambic pentameter (five stressed syllables), and a final hexameter (six stressed) line at the end. His multi-layered poetry is at once fantastical, political, moral, and deeply artistic, but his greatest goal was that his readers would grow in virtue merely by reading *The Faerie Queene*. He once explained this intention to a friend, saying, "The generall end of all the booke ... is to fashion a gentleman or noble person in virtuous and gentle discipline."

The six completed books of *The Faerie Queene* each feature a knight meant to represent a different virtue. The virtuous knights each face the lures and frights of villainous temptations, including Pride, Lust, Lechery, and Despair. One such monster appears in the first canto of Book One; the beast of Errour attacks the Protestant Knight Redcrosse by vomiting "bookes and papers" that are meant to represent the propaganda spread by the Catholic church during the Reformation. However, the Catholic monster is ultimately defeated by Redcrosse, who represents the virtue of Holiness. The other knights of Temperance, Chastity, Friendship, Justice, and Courtesy also face wicked allegorical monsters, but the moral aspect of *The Faerie Queene* is just one layer of Spenser's complex work.

On a political level, Gloriana, the queen of Faerieland, represents Queen Elizabeth I. Like Elizabeth, Gloriana rules over a fractured kingdom that threatens to slip into chaos. Spenser, who was deeply affected by the Irish rebellions against England, affirmed his allegiance to Queen Elizabeth by writing of Gloriana's perfection and power, referring to the allegorical Gloriana as "that greatest Glorious Queene of Faerie lond." Spenser's allegiance was richly rewarded by the queen, who presented Spenser with a personal estate as well as a yearly pension.

Gloriana was not Spenser's only strong female character; *The Faerie Queene* features a number of other powerful heroines. One example is the Knight Britomart in Book III; this female knight represents the virtue of chastity, and she often shows more mental and combat skill than her male counterparts.

When her companions desert her in pursuit of a beautiful woman, Britomart courageously continues on alone:

> The whiles faire *Britomart*, whose constant mind,
> Would not so lightly follow beauties chace,
> Ne reckt of Ladies Loue, did stay behind,
> And them awayted there a certaine space,
> To weet if they would turne backe to that place:
> But when she saw them gone, she forward went,
> As lay her iourney, through that perlous Pace,
> With stedfast courage and stout hardiment;
> Ne euill thing she fear'd, ne euill thing she ment.

Spenser's powerful portrayal of females in *The Faerie Queene* points to his progressive attitude concerning women. This attitude reflects the societal changes in a time when male subjects were becoming accustomed to bowing before a ruling queen.

Although *The Faerie Queene* is a fantastical story of lion-hearted knights, vile monsters, and cunning sorcery, Spenser also interweaves common truths into his tale. In his allegory, Spenser's knights face tensions that represent the struggles of everyday life. His heroes embody both outstanding bravery and unshakeable sinfulness. Instead of resolving this paradox of the human experience, Spenser seems to revel in the tension between heroism and human weakness. He remarks in Canto 8 of Book I, "Ay me, how many perils doe enfold / The righteous man, to make him daily fall!" Spenser never completed his epic work, so the tale lacks resolution; the story is suspended before good fully triumphs against the threat of evil. His unfinished work is a symbol for every "knight" who struggles in the unending conflict between virtue and depravity within himself.

Annalisa Galgano, 2013
Ryan Summers, former faculty

FRANCIS BACON, 1561–1626, *Father of the Modern Scientific Method*

> If a man will begin with certainties, he shall end in doubts; but if he will be content to begin with doubts, he shall end in certainties.
>
> —*The Advancement of Learning*

- Worked as Lord Chancellor and held significant political influence, but is best known for his expansion in scientific inquiry
- Focused on empiricism—testable data—rather than rationalism
- Created a formulaic system for expanding theories and ideas, known as the scientific method
- Advocated for civil rights and the scientific process through his writing on utopian society
- Reformed law by giving it structure and a strong foundation in the use of evidence
- Influenced philosophy by replacing moral philosophy with natural philosophy

Key Works

The Advancement of Learning, 1605

Novum Organum Scientiarum, 1620
New Atlantis, 1624

Biography

Francis Bacon was born on January 22, 1561, in York House, London. At the young age of 12 he enrolled in Trinity College, where he spent his next three years. Later, he traveled to Paris as a secretary to the English Ambassador, so that he could receive his political education. While studying in Paris he came to enjoy experimental observation, a method of testing ideas repeatedly with different variables to obtain truth. After his father died in 1579, Bacon returned to England where he studied law. Queen Elizabeth's opposition to his advancement initially cut short his political aspirations. In spite of the Queen's opinion, however, Bacon gained a seat in Parliament with the help of his uncle. In Parliament he came into conflict with the Earl of Essex. Because of this, he decided to work for King James against Parliament. Eventually rising to the rank of Lord Chancellor in 1621, Bacon was attacked by Parliament on charges of accepting bribes and was banned from public office. He dedicated the rest of his life to writing. He died in 1626 from bronchitis caused by one of his scientific experiments.

Scientific Inquiry

The core fundamentals of Francis Bacon's work on scientific inquiry are based on empiricism rather than rationalism. Empiricism is the belief that knowledge is gained through sense experience. Rationalism has its roots in Aristotelian philosophy—the belief that reason should be the primary, if not the only, source of knowledge. Bacon described knowledge as being found through "the discovery and demonstration of sciences and arts" that "must analyze nature by proper rejections and exclusions; and then, after a sufficient number of negatives, come to a conclusion on the affirmative instances." Through the lens of empiricism, Bacon formed the basis for modern scientific theory: begin with a theory to be tested, form a prediction, experiment, collect observations, and create new theories based on your findings, in a continuous cycle of refinement. The format he created is still used today in experimentation and has led to countless developments in science. Bacon thought that rationalism, which did not start with experimentation of the natural world, hindered scientific inquiry. Bacon argued that drawing a general conclusion from a small pool of evidence is not likely to hold true. He instead theorized that a more accurate conclusion could be found through his scientific method, illustrated below.

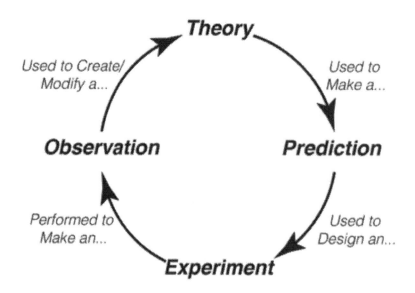

Sir Francis Bacon's Scientific Method

The Four Idols

Bacon's belief in the scientific method of induction (arriving at a conclusion by combining a series of things that are true) led to his theory of the four idols. The four idols were essentially what Bacon considered to be the four major problems with scientific inquiry at the time.

Idols	Problem
Idols of the Tribe	Human perception distorts reality and hinders scientific actuality
Idols of the Cave	Human experiences and biases can hinder scientific inquiry
Idols of the Marketplace	The misinterpretation of words and concepts
Idols of the Theater	The stubbornness of philosophers in believing false theories or building theories on top of widely accepted philosophy without proving or questioning it first

Bacon thought that science depended too much on generalizations rather than observation, emphasizing his empiricist views. He believed that science could be more accurate if it was not hindered by the four idols but rather focused on what could be found tangibly.

New Atlantis

Bacon's scientific beliefs carried into the way he viewed sociological structures. An island without slavery or debtor's prisons, that believed in the separation of church and state and religious freedom, and which was centered around scientific inquiry and high morality—this was Bacon's utopia. He created the fictional island of Bensalem, in *New Atlantis,* and gave it a government and population that allowed all of his key ideas on rights, laws, and freedom to flourish. The island is where "the end of [their] foundation is the knowledge of causes, and secret motions of things; and the enlarging of the bounds of human empire, to the effecting of all things possible." Through *New Atlantis* Bacon attempts to describe what he believed to be the apex of culture and society in perfection. While not revolutionary, his ideal of religious freedom and the tolerance of others had a long-lasting legacy in the English colonies in the Americas.

Law and Philosophy

Bacon sought to reform law and philosophy, and his "ultimate aim was to transform natural processes for the common good." In reforming the law, he wanted to have records of legal cases, make the law system more productive, and provide a "firm foundation for legal practice." Next, he wished to have formal procedures of law so that one could identify the source of authority in every situation. Lastly, he desired to demonstrate how to compose and defend arguments. He was concerned not only with the structure of law, but also with the rhetoric of it. According to Bacon, rhetoric "should help to focus the mental powers, to organize one's thoughts in the most economical fashion, and even to provide vivid images or representations of situations that enabled one to convince oneself of a case." While most of his reforms were not adopted until after his death, Bacon influenced jurisprudence (philosophy of law) by seeking to bring England under one theory of law.

As Bacon sought to change law, he also changed philosophy, replacing moral philosophy with natural philosophy. Being an empiricist, Bacon used senses and observations to formulate his ideas about nature; however, unlike his Aristotelian counterparts, he rejected the idea that deductive arguments using metaphysical premises would result in true scientific knowledge. Additionally, he scolded scholastic thinkers because their reliance on scripture and Aristotle prevented new scientific discoveries. Although he himself did not make experimental discoveries, his writings cultivated the now-standard belief that science must root truth in observable facts of the natural world, not myths of tradition. By instituting natural philosophy, Bacon laid the foundation for natural sciences as well as physics.

Savannah Cressman, 2011
Trisha Rouleau, 2015

WILLIAM SHAKESPEARE, 1564–1616, *The Bard of Avon*

> " All the world's a stage, / And all the men and women merely players. / They have their exits and their entrances, / And one man in his time plays many parts.
> —Jaques in *As You Like It*

- Is arguably the most influential writer in all of history
- Grew up in Stratford-on-Avon in relative affluence, and then moved to London, probably to pursue acting and writing
- Wrote 37 full plays, 154 sonnets, and coined 1,700 new English words
- Avoided the rampant copying of plays due to the lack of a copyright law, by delivering an actor's lines of to him moments before the scene in which he went on; for this reason, his plays weren't published until after his death (*The First Folio*)
- Acted in his company, the King's Company
- Married Anne Hathaway who was pregnant with their first child—the two had three children together

- Composed sonnets and started to gain a name for himself through them when the theaters across London closed because of civil unrest and the plague
- Was part owner of the Globe Theatre, which featured many of his plays; it burned to the ground during a performance of *Henry VIII* and was rebuilt the next year in June 1614

Key Works

Henry VI, Part One, 1590
The Taming of the Shrew, c. 1592
"Venus and Adonis", 1593
Romeo and Juliet, 1594–1595
The Merchant of Venice, 1596–1598
Much Ado About Nothing, 1598–1599
A MidSummer-Night's Dream, 1600
Hamlet, c. 1600
Macbeth, 1606
King Lear, 1608
Sonnets, 1609
The Tempest, 1610–1611

Biography

William Shakespeare's plays, though almost 500 years old, still influence every aspect of modern life. His unique life provided him with fodder for writing; he knew well the heart of human relations and struggles. From the 1,700 English words he coined, including "lonely," "swagger," and "eyeball," to his 37 plays that have inspired innumerable productions and adaptations—including *West Side Story* (*Romeo and Juliet*), *She's The Man* (*Twelfth Night*)—to his sonnets, Shakespeare's legacy extends to an almost indescribable fame.

Shakespeare was baptized on April 26, 1564, in Stratford-on-Avon in Warwickshire, and was born a few days before this. He was third-born of at least eight children, yet he was the first to survive past infancy, making him the eldest son to John Shakespeare and Mary Arden. Although records were lost, scholars believe Shakespeare attended the free grammar school, the King's New School. During his childhood, his family was wealthy and influential due to his father's position as high bailiff. But when Shakespeare turned 13, his father's fortunes took a turn for the worse, and the young man was forced to learn a trade. Some believe that he worked killing calves at this time and would give grand speeches and performances before a slaughter. In November 1582, when Shakespeare was 18, he married the farmer's daughter, Anne Hathaway, who was eight years his senior and already pregnant with their first child, Susanna Shakespeare. She subsequently bore him twins—Hamnet (who died when he was 11) and Judith.

The years between 1585 and 1592 are often referred to as "the lost years" because there is no record of Shakespeare's affairs or careers. In 1592 his name appeared in a London pamphlet. At this point, his "life was divided between his work in London and his family in Stratford," and he was working in the theater as a playwright and actor with Lord Chamberlain's company. Although actors had low social status, his company's backing by Lord Chamberlain, and later by King James I, allowed him to enjoy security against total destitution. From 1592–1594, when the theaters closed because of the plague and civil unrest, Shakespeare's reputation as both a poet and a playwright began to flourish. During his time with the company, he wrote on average two plays a year, developed interest in the Globe theater, and performed for Queen Elizabeth I multiple times. In 1611, he retired from his life in London and died of a fever in Stratford on April 23, 1616. He was buried in Holy Trinity church in Stratford. In 1623, the first collection of his edited works were published, entitled the *First Folio*.

Many rumors surround the life of William Shakespeare. In *Putnam's Monthly* in 1856, Delia Bacon published, for the first time, the rumor that Shakespeare did not write the majority of the plays attributed to him, which likely stemmed from the popular idea that an uneducated man such as William Shakespeare could not have penned the plays. Mark Twain, Charlie Chaplin, and Sigmund Freud, along with many other intelligent men and women throughout history, have questioned Shakespearean authorship. Other rumors and conspiracies of Shakespeare include his sexuality (many scholars will argue that he harbored homosexual tendencies), that he was Catholic (he was generally thought to be strongly Anglican), and his appearance (the common picture of Shakespeare was simply a copy made after his death). Despite the arguments and controversies concerning his life, Shakespeare's work lives on.

Governing Themes
Because Shakespeare wrote in three different genres of theatre—tragedy, comedy, and history—and wrote sonnets covering a wide variety of subjects, the themes and topics addressed in his works are numerous and varied. A few, however, he addresses more regularly.

Love
The topic of love appears in nearly every Shakespeare play. His "star-cross'd lovers," Romeo and Juliet, have become household names synonymous with romance. Love is found not only in his lightest comedies, between Benedick and Beatrice in *Much Ado About Nothing* or Miranda and Ferdinand in *The Tempest*, but also in his darkest tragedies, between Othello and Desdemona in *Othello*, and Cordelia and the King of France in *King Lear*. Love permeates every story, for better or worse.

The love that Shakespeare portrays in his work goes beyond physical appearances. In one of his most famous sonnets, Sonnet 130, he describes his mistress as a rather ugly creature, saying her hair is like wires and her breath is malodorous and her voice is grating, but he loves her all the same. He writes, "and yet, by heaven, I think my love as rare / As any she belied with false compare." In *King Lear*, the King of France falls in love with Lear's daughter Cordelia not for her looks but for her honesty, integrity, and courage in dealing with her father. Although many of his romances happen at first sight—such as Romeo and Juliet or Ferdinand and Miranda in *The Tempest*—there appears to be some deeper level of romance between his characters, something that transcends the outward appearance and goes straight to the soul.

Love usually triumphs when it appears in a Shakespearean play. The confusions, misunderstandings, and betrayals that would keep couples apart often resolve. In *Much Ado About Nothing*, the wicked Don John's attempts to keep Claudio and Hero apart do not succeed. Not only do Claudio and Hero have a happy ending, but Benedick and Beatrice—a man and a woman who could not stand each other early in the play—end up engaged, as well. In *A Midsummer Night's Dream*, some mischief by the sprite Puck and the Fairy King Oberon brings Helena the husband she wanted, Demetrius, who tried to marry Hermia. But in the end, Demetrius says, "the object and pleasure of mine eye, / Is only Helena." And even though Othello murders his wife, as the play closes he realizes his wife was innocent and kills himself, saying, "I kiss'd thee ere I kill'd thee. No way but this, / Killing myself, to die upon a kiss." This love may be tragic, twisted, and disturbing, but it is love all the same.

Nature of Evil

On the subject of things tragic, twisted, and disturbing, Shakespeare's villains are some of the darkest ever to appear onstage. Their motivations almost always boil down to two things: revenge or power— or some combination of both. In Hamlet, the thirst for power sets off a chain of suffering. The ghost of Hamlet's father wants revenge on his brother for killing him, so Hamlet puts an elaborate plan into motion that ends up killing nearly everyone, including himself. Even in *Much Ado About Nothing*, a comedy, a desire for vengeance motivates the villainous Don John to spoil any love and happiness near his brother or his brother's friends' lives. Iago in *Othello* works his malicious machinations for both revenge and power: Othello gives another officer in the army a promotion Iago wanted, and he's a little bitter. To avenge this slight, Iago "follow[s] [Othello] to serve [his] turn upon him," masterfully manipulating Roderigo, Cassio, and Othello himself to send Othello, his wife Desdemona, and many others to the grave. The lust for power and revenge is even stronger in Shakespeare's historical plays, which John Gassner in his book *Masters of the Drama* calls "analys[es] of crime-stained greatness." In part three of Henry VI, Richard Plantagenet exclaims, "My ashes, as the phoenix, may bring forth / A bird that will revenge upon you all: / And in that hope I / throw mine eyes to heaven, / Scorning whate'er you can afflict me with." Power and revenge drive most evils in the works of Shakespeare.

Justice and the Prevailing Good

Although many of his writings are rife with darkness and tragedy—the entire cast dying, witches orchestrating the slaughter of kings and armies, two young lovers tragically murdered over a ridiculous family feud—Shakespeare's work often promotes the eventual triumph of good. Throughout his plays, Shakespeare depicts many villains brought to justice. At the end of *Macbeth*, the rightful king, Macduff, slays Macbeth and is restored to the throne, announcing, "By the grace of Grace, / We will perform in measure, time, and place," before he is crowned king. God is reinstated as the supreme ruler, and the allusion to music suggests that all in the kingdom of Scotland has been restored to harmony as the play ends.

As *Hamlet* concludes, Laertes attempts to kill Hamlet with a sword laced with poison during a duel, but, when he himself is injured by the same sword, he admits that he is "justly kill'd with [his] own treachery" and shouts out, "the King, the King's to blame." Laertes dies, Hamlet kills the King, and Fortinbras of Norway claims the throne, restoring yet another kingdom to order by doing away with the villain. In *Much Ado About Nothing*, Don John's plot to break apart Hero and Claudio is foiled when they eventually get married, and at the end of the play, he is "brought with armed men back to Messina" for his trickery. Finally, in his tragedy *King Lear*, Shakespeare emphasizes the inevitable fate of those who misrule a kingdom and plot dark intrigues: both malevolent daughters die, Regan having been poisoned by her sister, and Goneril committing suicide because the majority of her family is dead. Whether it is be comedy, tragedy, or history, villains eventually pay for their evil ways.

While the inescapability of Fate would seem to lead to more suffering than good, in Shakespeare's works Fate also provides justice, righting cosmic wrongs. In his tragedy *Romeo and Juliet*, although the star-crossed lovers both perish, they do "with their death bury their parents' strife." At the expense of the two youths, their families abandon their feud, showing that good may prevail, even in a dark situation. In *The Tempest*, Prospero, the exiled Duke of Milan, is eventually restored to the throne that his conspiring brother stole from him. Shakespeare's *Comedy of Errors* ends after two sets of identical twins, separated at birth, who have been confused and confusing all the people of Ephesus, realize what has happened and announce, "We came into the world like brother and brother; / And now let's go hand in hand, not one before another." In the end, good triumphs over the events that have unjustly splintered the lives of some of Shakespeare's characters.

Mortality of the Material World

The ephemeral nature of life haunts Shakespeare's writings. In his 15th sonnet, when he writes that all living things can hold "in perfection but a little moment," he depicts the evanescence of the mortal. Macbeth's famous monologue captures the belief that life is a "brief candle" and then goes on to pronounce:

> Life's but a walking shadow, a poor player
> That struts and frets his hour upon the stage
> And then is heard no more. It is a tale
> Told by an idiot, full of sound and fury,
> Signifying nothing.

Shakespeare often depicts life as fleeting, and death, inevitable. There seems to even be a depressing trend of hopelessness; the striving and struggles of man, along with his youth and his best times, are a brief, temporary flash. In all of his tragedies, death awaits the evil, the vain, and even the innocent. Unquenchable death prowls throughout his plays and sonnets, devouring everyone, leaving no one untouched.

However, Shakespeare does proffer hope, a break from a depressing view of life and death. In his sonnets, he presents his idea that people may live on in their youth through the written word. When talking to a love in Sonnet 19, he announces that his "love shall in [his] verse ever live young." A common theme at the time, the woman essentially becomes immortal and incorruptible through his published works. Shakespeare reinforces this idea in his famous Sonnet 15 when he, once again, refers to his love and tells her, "all in ware with Time for love of you, / As he takes from you, I engraft you new." His written word allows her to live on in the hearts and minds of every generation after she dies. Shakespeare combats the idea of the short and meaningless life with his idea of immortality through writing—thus the quintessential artist sees his ultimate hope through art itself.

Caroline Fuschino, 2015

THE PURITANS, 1564, *The Mayflower: 1620*

The term "Puritan" was first used to insult reformist Protestants. Protestants were brutally persecuted in order to punish them for heresy during the reign of the devout Catholic Mary I (1516–1558). Hundreds of Protestants fled England for the continent. There they encountered the stringent Protestantism of John Calvin.

Many of these exiles later returned to England, hopeful that when Mary died and Elizabeth I took over, they would have more freedom to worship as they chose. In fact, Elizabeth had created an

Elizabethan Religious Settlement that allowed for a broad version of Protestantism. Yet she gave herself the role "Elizabeth Supreme Governor of the Church of England." The Protestants, introducing Calvinism to England, desired reform, which Elizabeth found too extreme. When James I came into power in 1566, they hoped that he might accept some of their suggestions. The only idea that met with his approval was having the Bible translated into English, resulting in the *King James Bible*. The Puritans gained importance through the reign of Charles by growing their influence in Parliament. Yet, when they came up against the crown on a tax issue, the bloody English civil war of 1542 ensued and brought about Charles's execution.

The Puritans were a subset of the Protestants in England who wanted to "purify" Protestantism. They wanted to focus Christianity on morality and the New Testament rather than the politics of human beings, believing that neither a pope nor a reigning monarch held religious authority over them. They believed that everyone had the right to read and interpret the Bible. To accomplish the goal of helping everyone to read and to hold church services in something other than Latin, they encouraged education. In short, the Puritans valued simplicity without ceremony and without the ostentatiousness of the Catholic Church. They disdained frivolity and believed that only things done specifically to serve the Lord had value. The Puritans believed in "divine providence" wherein God inflicted appropriate justice on the impure.

The Puritans consisted of two groups—Conforming Puritans, Dissenters who continued in the Church of England even though they didn't support it; and Nonconforming Puritans, Separatists, who believed that the English church couldn't be reformed. The Dissenters mostly stayed in England at first as part of the Church of England. The Separatists migrated to North America because they felt their only course was to leave a hopeless church and begin again. One such group of Separatists came across the Atlantic on the *Mayflower* to land in Plymouth. Twenty years later, a group of Dissenters bought the stock of the Massachusetts Bay Company in order to migrate to Massachusetts for a "religious experiment." They settled in Salem and relocated near the Charles River to found Boston. Thousand of Puritans followed them to New England in the next decade.

GALILEO GALILEI, 1564–1642, *The Father of Modern Science*

> " I do not feel obliged to believe that the same God who has endowed us with sense, reason, and intellect has intended us to forgo their use.
>
> —*Letter to the Grand Duchess Christina*

- Possessed a rebellious personality and the mind of a genius
- Believed in the powers of experimentation and observation to prove new ideas or to verify the old
- Had little patience for those who supported Aristotelian ideas when experimentation clearly proved the ancient philosopher wrong
- Discovered the isochronism of the pendulum, uniform acceleration, the law of inertia, and the concept that falling bodies (regardless of weight) have the same acceleration
- Used the telescope to study the night sky—discoveries included four of Jupiter's moons, sunspots, and our own moon's craters

- Began to heavily support Copernicus and his vision of a sun-centered universe when his astronomic observations proved that Aristotle's belief in a perfect, earth-centered universe was incorrect
- Ran into trouble with the church for his endorsement of a heliocentric universe and was placed under house arrest when he was about 70
- Is called "the father of modern science" for his endorsement of the experimental method and for shifting the focus of the study away from blind acceptance of ancient ideas
- Believed strongly that religious authorities should not meddle in the scientific realm and often quoted Cardinal Baronis, saying that the "Holy Spirit intended to teach us in the Bible how to go to heaven, not how the heavens go."

Key Works

The Starry Messenger, 1610
On the Sun Spots, 1613
Letter to the Grand Duchess Christina, 1615
The Assayer, 1623
Dialogue on the Two Chief Systems of the World, 1632
Dialogue of the Two New Sciences, 1638

Biography

Galileo Galilei was born in Pisa, Italy, to a noble but impoverished family in 1564. His father, Vincenzo, had "a highly independent, combative turn of mind, which the flame-haired Galileo inherited." Galileo possessed not only his father's rebellious streak, but also his genius in mathematics. Vincenzo, however, was determined that his son would not follow his path and become either a mathematician or musician—two professions that he knew from experience did not pay well. That is why young Galileo ended up going to school in a monastery. To his father's horror, Galileo seemed to take all too well to the monastic life, and Vincenzo absolutely did not want him taking up the life of a poor man of the cloth.

So, at 14, Galileo was sent to study medicine at Pisa University. There, he began to openly challenge his teachers. He would stand up during a lecture and question his professors and their Aristotelian ideas, an action that seemed to border on blasphemy, seeing as Aristotle was held in impossibly high esteem at the time. Realizing that Galileo would never have the calm, comforting demeanor of a doctor, Vincenzo relented and allowed his son to be tutored in mathematics. Galileo fell in love with the subject and was brilliant with numbers. It did not take long for the young genius to discover the Greek geometer Euclid, a man who firmly believed that as long as an idea could be proven through demonstration, it could be considered true.

This concept would guide Galileo throughout most of his life. When he was older, Galileo embarked on a teaching career, first at the University of Pisa, which he soon left because of the low pay and because he was tired of being denounced for his "criticism and disrespect," and then at the University of Padua where he thrived for 18 years. On campus, he "was a distinctive figure who strode around the precincts in disheveled clothes and without the regulation academic gown." Fitting into the genius stereotype, he was a man who cared more about abstract theories and numbers than his appearance. Throughout his entire life, he was constantly inventing and experimenting with new ideas, the latter of which would bring him into conflict with religious authorities. Galileo died in Arcetri, near Florence, of fever and heart palpitations in 1642.

Experimenting with Motion

A man with limitless curiosity, Galileo did not rest until he had all the answers. He was fascinated by motion and wondered about the laws and theories guiding it. The story goes that when he was a teenager, he was bored in church and watched a chandelier swinging above him. In doing so, he noted "the amount of time it took the lamp to complete a single swing remained constant, even as the [amplitude or height] of the swing steadily decreased." This principle, called the isochronism of a pendulum, had important applications in timekeeping and was used to make the first pendulum clock.

Perhaps one of Galileo's most famous experiments with motion was his study on the behavior of falling bodies, which reportedly was performed on the Leaning Tower of Pisa. Standing on top of the tower, the scientist repeatedly dropped two objects of different weights side-by-side and noted how they always hit the ground at the same time. He summed up these observations in *The Two New Sciences*: "Aristotle says that 'an iron ball of one hundred pounds falling from a height of one hundred cubits reaches the ground before a one-pound ball has fallen a single cubit.' I say that they arrive at the same time." This principle not only went against Aristotle but also against common sense. However, Galileo had proven it through experimentation, a practice that he found indispensable.

In fact, many claim that Galileo's "greatest achievement was the elaboration and consolidation of the experimental method." One of Galileo's more famous experiments concerning motion had to do with acceleration. As he describes in *Two New Sciences*:

> A piece of wooden moulding ... was taken; on its edge was cut a channel a little more than one finger in breadth. ... We rolled along it a hard, smooth and very round bronze ball ... noting ... the time required to make the descent.... We now rolled the ball only one-quarter of the length of the channel; and having measured the time of its descent, we found it precisely one-half the former. ... In such experiments [over many distances], repeated a full hundred times, we always found that the spaces traversed were to each other as the squares of the times, and that this was true for all inclinations of the plane.

In this experiment, Galileo discovered two key facts concerning mechanics and physics. First, a uniform force (gravity, in this case) produces a uniform acceleration. Second, being at rest is not the natural state of objects. Instead, an object in motion stays in motion unless stopped by some outside force. These two ideas would form part of the bedrock of modern physics and the study of mechanics.

Observing the Stars

Many students remember Galileo for his observations of the heavens and for his work in astronomy. While he did not invent the telescope lens (that credit goes to named Hans Lippershey, a Dutch spectacle-maker), he was the one who had the genius to use it at night to look at the stars and planets. What he saw would forever change humanity's perceptions of the world above, and leave Aristotelian ideas in shambles. As Galileo wrote in *The Starry Messenger*, "the moon is not perfectly smooth, free from inequalities, and exactly spherical, as a large school of philosophers considers with regard to the moon and other heavenly bodies. On the contrary, it is full of inequalities, uneven, full of hollows ... just like the surface of the earth itself." This revelation that the moon was not a perfect, glowing sphere defied the Aristotelian belief that every heavenly body was perfect and part of a divine realm above.

Galileo also observed that Jupiter had four moons orbiting—clearly it was not alone in its own crystalline sphere. Yet the most disturbing fact about the moons of Jupiter to Galileo's contemporaries was that they were orbiting Jupiter, not Earth. Suddenly, the whole idea of a geocentric universe was in question. Galileo was challenging Aristotle not only in physics but in astronomy as well, and he found himself supporting Copernicus's heliocentric theory, or at least some version of it. And with each new discovery, he became more and more convinced of his position. He discovered that Venus has phases like the moon and for the same reasons: "Venus did not make its own light but was in fact illuminated by the sun." He stared at the sun with his telescope and learned that it had various dark spots (therefore it was also not perfect) and that it rotated on its axis. And by observing the Milky Way, he finally concluded that "the galaxy is nothing else but a mass of innumerable stars planted together in clusters."

Conflict with the Church

Galileo's observations clearly indicated that Aristotle's perfect heavenly world that revolved around a fixed Earth was nothing but a myth. Yet the authorities of the day still dogmatically defended this picturesque universe because it fitted neatly with the Bible, leaving the realm of the heavens purely in God's control. Galileo's belief in a heliocentric universe could easily be seen as heretical, and the 17th century was no time to be branded a heretic.

Well aware of the dangers of defying the church, Galileo traveled to Rome in 1616 to defend himself, but the only statement he received was "a stern warning not to 'hold or defend' the Copernican ideas." Frustrated and still as rebellious as he had been as a youth, Galileo seethed until 1624, when the more sympathetic Urban VII became pope, at which time he tried again. Urban allowed Galileo to write about the different theories for the universe as long as he did not to presume to judge which one actually existed. Yet in his resulting work, *Dialogue on the Two Chief Systems of the World*, he clearly defended Copernican ideas while lampooning those of Aristotle and Ptolemy. As a result, he was dragged back to Rome on trial for heresy. At almost 70 years old, Galileo was unwilling to face the harsh punishments of disobeying papal authorities, so when he was ordered to recant and to deny that the Earth moves around the Sun, he did. Yet when he was being led away for imprisonment in his own home, legend has it that he muttered "eppir si muove" (yet it does move). Galileo spent the rest of his days under house arrest where he continued his observations and research even after going completely blind in 1637. The church admitted its mistakes concerning Galileo 350 years later.

Tatjana Scherschel, 2015
Jessica Goeser, researcher

JOHANNES KEPLER, 1571–1630, *Pioneer in Astronomy*

> " The diversity of the phenomena of nature is so great, and the treasures hidden in the heavens so rich, precisely in order that the human mind shall never be lacking in fresh nourishment.

- Received much criticism from the Catholic Church due to his belief in a heliocentric solar system as opposed to a geocentric system
- Had a castle, Uraniborg, and a lavish observatory funded by King Frederick II
- Collected the most accurate astronomical data in the history of the world in his time
- Assisted Brahe, an astronomer and a Danish aristocrat; Kepler compiled Brahe's data into a paper, *Astronomia Nova*
- Included the first two laws of planetary motion and a new model for the solar system in *Astronomia Nova*
- Hypothesized ellipses for planetary orbit, which accounted for the difficult-to-chart path of Mars

Key Works

Astronomia Nova, 1609
Harmonices Mundi, 1619
Somnium, 1634

Biography

Johannes Kepler played a key role in the development of astronomical theories and mathematics during the 16th and 17th centuries. Born in Germany in 1571, Kepler was raised by his mother before being educated at the University of Tübingen, where he became a magister (teacher) and started his studies in theology. Once done, Kepler married and moved to Austria, where he was able to publish his first highly successful work, *Mysterium Cosmographicum*. He then went to Prague in order to work with the astronomer Tycho Brahe. After Brahe died in 1601, Kepler took over as Imperial Mathematician. During this period, Kepler wrote multiple works on optics, astrology, and astronomy, including a paper containing his first two laws of planetary motion and what is possibly the first science-fiction novel in the world, *Somnium*. Eventually, he moved to Linz to become a professor and mathematician at Landschaftsschule. Around the peak of the witch trials in Europe, Kepler's mother was accused of being a witch; however, Kepler was able to successfully defend her against prosecution. During his time in Linz, he wrote one of his most famous works on philosophy, *Harmonice Mundi*. In 1630, Kepler died in Regensburg, but not before making a lasting impact on the astronomical, mathematical, and philosophical communities.

Tycho Brahe

Tycho Brahe was a Danish aristocrat born in 1546. He was primarily interested in observational astronomy and was so successful that King Frederick II of Denmark gave him the island of Hven, 10 kilometers out from the coast, and paid for a functional observatory there. The aptly named Castle of Heavens, Uraniborg, would grow into the best observatory the world had yet seen. When King Frederick died, however, Brahe moved to Prague, where Emperor Rudolph II appointed him Imperial Mathematician and set up a new observatory in Benatsky Castle. He was given a new assistant,

Johannes Kepler, a gifted mathematician and theorist. While Brahe was only amassing data at the time, Kepler would later use it in a new solar theory.

Heliocentric Model

Kepler spent nearly eight years compiling Brahe's data into a new solar model, one that proved Copernicus's heliocentric view (the Earth as the center of the universe). He did, however, make several changes to Copernicus's idea, including disproving the ancient belief that planets orbited in circles. Instead, he argued, they travel in near-perfect ellipses. He also proved that they move at varying speeds, not constant ones, and that the sun wasn't at the center of the orbits but rather slightly offset, at a focal point of the ellipse. This new model took up nine hundred folio pages. It was simpler and more elegant than any previous ideas, but the Catholic Church allowed it only for use in calculations, and not as a reflection of reality. The Church's two main objections to *Astronomia Nova*, Kepler's book documenting his astronomical research, were related to heliocentrism and Kepler's insistence on ellipses. The clergy at the time believed the earth had to be the center of the universe because they had no other way to explain the way objects always fell toward the center of the earth. Kepler wasn't able to provide any explanation for this phenomenon. The Church also disliked his idea of ellipses, which they thought removed all uniformity and flew in the face of the ancient belief in the perfection of circles. Kepler's findings were correct, however, and Galileo Galilei would later prove them using the newly invented telescope.

Jack Beebe, 2012
Jeff Culver, faculty
McCarthy Nolan, 2016

WILLIAM HARVEY, 1578–1657, *Father of Modern Physiology*

> " The heart of animals is the foundation of their life, the sovereign of everything within them, the sun of their microcosm, that upon which all growth depends, from which all power proceeds.
>
> —"Dedication to King Charles"

- Recognized the heart as a pump for the body's blood (the first to do so)
- Described blood flow in the human body—pushed through arteries and veins by the heart in one direction
- Graduated from University of Padua as Physician at age 24
- Gave lectures throughout England on human anatomy
- Believed in experimentation to prove or disprove theories
- Served as physician to two kings, King James I and King Charles I
- Laid the foundation for embryology (the study of embryos) and supported the theory of epigenesis (development of growth of embryos)

Key Works

"On the Motion of the Heart and Blood" ("De Motu Cordis"), 1628
"On the Generation of Animals" ("De Generatione Animalium"), 1651

Biography

The eldest of seven sons, Harvey was born on April 1, 1578, to a family of merchants in Folkestone, Kent. Entering college at 16, he went on to complete his medical studies at the University of Padua, which was a premier medical school at the time, keenly interested in the introduction of experimental methods to test ideas and theories. There, he studied under famed anatomist Hieronymus Fabricius, who greatly impacted the direction of Harvey's studies. After graduating with honors, Harvey joined the College of Physicians in London and married Elizabeth Browne in 1604. He served both King James I and King Charles I while maintaining a position as Lumleian Lecturer at the College of Physicians, which allowed him to pursue his research. Although his discovery of the circulation of the blood is considered his greatest achievement, his publication of "De Generatione Animalium" in 1651 laid the foundation for embryology, claiming that embryos develop through a building up of parts. Harvey died of a stroke on June 3, 1657. One scholar wrote of Harvey's discovery of circulation, saying, "it remains to this day the greatest of the discoveries of physiology, and its whole honor belongs to Harvey."

Circulation of Blood in Human Body

From the time of Galen, a Greek physician working 1,000 years earlier, the medical world accepted the theory that the liver somehow caused blood travel through the body. For more than 10 centuries, physicians listened to the heartbeat without guessing that it was a pump; most thought it was merely a filter of sorts.

At University of Padua Harvey became puzzled by the many one-way valves in the body. Harvey and his advisor were the first to theorize that these valves and the pumping of the heart were responsible for the circulation of the blood in the body. In order to contradict 1,000 years of accepted medical theories of circulation, Harvey need empirical evidence of his own theories, which he accumulated through experimentation.

Harvey gave demonstrations using a live dog strapped to a table and silenced. He would expose the beating heart and coronary artery, then sever the artery and note the prodigious quantity of blood pumped uselessly out by the heart. When the heart stopped, the blood stopped. He would remove the lifeless animal and make his conclusions in Latin, then the language of science, to the somewhat horrified group of doctors.

It is interesting to note that Galen's liver theory had the backing of the Catholic church. Before Harvey, a Spanish scientist named Servedo challenged Galen's theory and was ultimately burned at the stake as a heretic in 1616. Conveniently enough, Harvey presented his theory in England, a country not so stringently governed by the Catholic faith at the time.

Embryology

Although Harvey did not propose entirely accurate theories of fertilization, his work did lay the foundation for modern embryology, focusing on such issues as conception, embryogenesis (the branch of biology and medicine concerned with the study of embryos and their development), and spontaneous generation (the supposed production of living organisms from nonliving matter). Exploring the generation of animals, a study most likely influenced by his mentor Fabricius, Harvey eventually accumulated his work into the book *On the Generation of Animals*, which his friend published for him. In this book, Harvey denounced spontaneous generation and supported the theory of epigenesis: an embryo develops from the successive differentiation of an originally undifferentiated structure. He also established the theory that all life originates in the egg. Ultimately, he moved science away from antiquated theories of generation through this seminal work.

Brady Weisner, 2016

CARDINAL RICHELIEU ◊ 1585–1642, *Clergyman, Nobleman, Statesman*

" Carry on any enterprise as if all future success depended on it.

- Was the son of the lord of Richelieu, provost of the King
- Did not intend to become a priest; after studying at a Parisian militry academy, accepted a bishopric at a young age when neither of his older brothers was able to do so
- Fought to establish royal absolutism in France and end Spanish-Hapsburg hegemony in Europe
- Served as chaplain to the queen of France (Anne of Austria), as secretary of state, and then "first minister," making him one of Louis XIII's primary councilors
- Survived an assassination plot from the King's brother Gaston, Queen Anne, and the Comte de Scissons; the conspirators were beheaded
- Founded the Academie Francaise, which monitored the development of the French language
- Was the acknowledged architect of France's greatness in the 17th century, and a contributor to the secularization of politics during the Thirty Years War
- Was portrayed Richelieu in Alexander Dumas' *The Three Musketeers*

Armand Jean du Plessis, Cardinal-Duke of Richelieu, commonly referred to as Cardinal Richelieu, was the son of the lord of Richelieu, provost of the King. Armand studied in Paris and at a military academy. When his brothers were unable to accept the nomination to be the bishop of Luçon, Armand was designated. Because he was too young for the usual canonical sanction, he went to Rome for dispensation and consecration. In Paris he worked on a degree in theology. There, he came to the attention of the Queen Mother and regent for Louis XIII, Maria de Medici, who tapped Richelieu to negotiate with the Prince of Conde and then to act as Secretary of State for Foreign Affairs and War.

Years of intricate palace negotiations and intrigues ensued, during which Richelieu served first Louis XIII's queen, Anne of Austria, and then the out-of-favor Queen Mother whose regency was overthrown. He spent time in exile in Avignon before being recalled to the palace to serve the re-ascendant Marie de Medici. The Queen Mother had two desires: to sit in the King's council, and to make sure Richelieu would be nominated as cardinal. These goals would allow her to control royal policy with Richelieu's influence. After some resistance by the King, she was, in fact, invited to the council and the Pope appointed Richelieu a cardinal. Richelieu was eventually part of the King's council and then chief councilor.

As the King's principal minister, Richelieu gathered a group of followers as he followed the King absolutely. Richelieu's actions pleased the queen mother for a time, but she gave him up when he advised the King to fight Spain at France's northern border. Subsequently, Richelieu faced more discontent from the noblemen who, together with the King's brother Gaston, Queen Anne, and the

Comte de Scissons, plotted to have him killed. Three of the perpetrators of the failed plots were beheaded.

Richelieu was motivated by his belief in an unavoidable war with Spain. After attempting to enlist support from Germany, Richelieu continued to negotiate with Spanish emissaries in the ongoing fighting on the northern and eastern borders of France. Richelieu died as the war continued.

Among Richelieu's achievements is founding the Academie Francaise, a distinguished society that has carefully monitored development of the French language.

Alexander Dumas portrayed Richelieu in *The Three Musketeers*.

THE DEFEAT OF THE SPANISH ARMADA, 1588

Spain had long been in conflict with Britain over power and religious differences when Mary Queen of Scots was executed in 1587, and England's church became the Protestant Church. In an attempt to overthrow Queen Elizabeth of England—fueled in part by England's harassment of Spain's New World operations, but also by England's adherence to Protestantism rather than Catholicism—the "Invincible" Spanish Armada was dispatched to bring the British Isles to heel.

King Philip I of Spain sent a fleet of 130–150 ships to conquer England and reinstate the Catholic Church. His attack on Britain's navy was, in part, an attempt to defend Spain against recent attacks on his northern territories (the Spanish Netherlands), and an attempt to secure more trade with other countries. He hoped also to lessen Britain's competitive power in commerce and in the New World of the Americas.

Philip planned to sail his "invincible" Spanish Armada ("la felicissima armada"—the most fortunate fleet) along the English Channel to bolster the forces of the Spanish Netherlands led by the Duke of Parma. Philip hoped that the size of his fleet and the resulting confusion of the British would be enough to defeat them, despite the superior ships of the British. Philip and his commander, the Duke of Media Sidonia, knew the British ships to be longer, lighter, and more agile than their Spanish counterparts, with the capacity for more guns. They planned to approach in a crescent formation.

Spain's first mishap occurred when the British, led by Sir Francis Drake, captured a ship and another blew up. The fleets were well-matched as they fought one another up the English Channel. The Armada anchored at Calais, waiting for communication from the Duke of Parma. Meanwhile, the British sent eight fire ships at midnight toward the Spanish ships, who rallied by cutting their moorings to allow them to move out and defend themselves. The darkness caused collisions and confusion. The next morning, despite the wind, the fleets fought hard in the Battle of Gravelines until they both ran out of ammunition. At that point, with a change of the wind to the north, the Spanish ships were blown off the sandbanks. Because the Duke of Parma failed to join in the attack (he had been blockaded in the harbor), Medina Sidonia wanted only to return home, so he set out in a northern direction.

Defeated but with minimal losses, the armada, trying to outrun English ships, was caught in a freak storm that decimated half its remaining forces along the rocky coasts along Scotland and Ireland. A mere 65 ships returned to Spain, This victory emboldened the Protestant cause, lending credence to the belief that God was on their side.

In a second effort, Philip returned with a smaller fleet the following year, but stormy weather caused the Spanish ships to turn back. England attempted to stop these incursions by undertaking the Drake-Norris Expedition, also known as "Counter Armada of 1589." They were defeated with heavy losses.

RENÉ DESCARTES, 1596–1650, *Father of Modern Philosophy*

❝ God can never cause me to be nothing so long as I think that I am something.

—*Meditations*

- Was the father of analytical geometry and a leading mathematician
- Was born with tuberculosis and had little chance for survival, but a midwife brought him back to health—his name, "René," comes from the Latin word *renatas*, meaning "reborn"
- Was a seminal figure in modern philosophy, challenging the teleological (purpose-based) theories of nature found in Medieval and Ancient physics and metaphysics
- Did not trust the senses; believed understanding of the world and our minds must be grounded in reflection and reason alone, without preconceptions based on sense experience
- Began his philosophizing with "radical doubt": imagine away all you think you know, including the existence of a rational world and even certainty about whether you are awake or dreaming right now, and then discover whether you can be certain of anything at all through thinking alone
- Granted that an "evil demon" *could* be deceiving us about things we think we are certain of
- Arrived through radical doubt at his famous "*Cogito, ergo sum*"—"I think, therefore I am"—meaning that one thing my mind cannot doubt is that it *is* thinking, and that if I am *thinking* (conscious), then I must *exist*
- Said that while we are certain we exist as minds, we can doubt whether we have bodies; hence thought is a necessary attribute of humans (thinking substances), but extension (body) is not; leads to development of "Cartesian Dualism" of mind and body
- Propouned dualism: that the world has thought (mind, rational subject) and extension (matter, spatial properties), and these two are fundamentally (not just conceptually) separate

Key Works

Discourse on the Method of Rightly Conducting the Reason and Seeking for Truth in the Sciences, 1637
Meditations on First Philosophy, 1641

Biography

René Descartes was born on March 31, 1596, in La Haye, France. One year after his birth, his mother, Jeanne Brochard Descartes, died. Although his father, Joachim, remarried, Descartes and his siblings were raised by their grandmother. In 1606 he entered La Flèche, a Jesuit college where he remained for eight years. By the time he finished his schooling, he believed that most subjects were impractical, and he "came to feel that languages, literature, and history relate only to fables which incline man to imaginative exaggerations."

At 18 he was a young noble who went to serve in the army of Prince Maurice of Nassau. While traveling, he sought out scientists, philosophers, and mathematicians, such as Isaac Beeckman, who inspired Descartes to include math and science in his writing. In 1619, Descartes had three dreams in which he "interpreted their symbols as a divine sign that all science is one and that its mastery is universal wisdom." He then worked to prove that "if one could generalize man's correct method of knowing, then one would be able to know everything." He moved to Paris and then to Holland, where he lived for the next 20 years. Although he was not married, he had a daughter, Francine, who died at the age of 5.

Descartes spent the rest of his career writing and defending his controversial positions. As he continued his studies, he developed views counter to the accepted Aristotelian and church views. At the time, the church condemned the idea that the earth moves while the sun remains still, because it supposedly contradicted scripture. Galileo Galilei wrote a book on this topic, for which he was condemned and put on house arrest. Descartes learned of Galileo's fate while he was finishing his own book in the same vein as Galileo, called *The World*. Because of this tempestuous religious climate, Descartes did not publish the book and exercised caution in his writings for the rest of his career. Eventually, he was persuaded "that he had to go to war with the Jesuits." One way to circumvent critique was to write in an autobiographical style, wherein he could speak of truths as he deduced them, thus avoiding a flagrant attack on the church. However, because his works seemed to conflict with the church, many of his books were condemned or prohibited. As his career as a philosopher faded, Descartes became a teacher for Queen Christina of Sweden, but he soon lost his health due to the northern climate. He became ill and died in Stockholm in the year 1650, at the age of 53.

The Method

Descartes' Method was of one of doubt. He effectively pushes the "reset" button on everything he knows and starts over. He resolves to go slowly, to achieve circumspection in all things, and to reject as false anything he can doubt. In abandoning all former truths, Descartes then provides four principles by which he conducts his search for truth: (1) Not to accept anything as true unless it is evident, (2) to divide difficulties into parts and to work on the parts individually, (3) to conduct his thoughts from simplest to most complex matters, and (4) to omit nothing from his explanation. These principles guided Descartes to his most famous maxim: *Cogito ergo sum* (I think, therefore I am).

First Principle of Philosophy

Relying upon his first-person account to guide the reader through his own revelation, Descartes discards the senses as a source of truth "because our senses deceive us"; furthermore, even if he were not a body, he would still exist, which means that the body is not necessary to him and is, in fact, distinct from him. Then it occurs to Descartes that even if he judges that he cannot trust the senses, there is still an "I" that doubts. Even if he is deceived, he must first exist in order to be deceived; from this he concludes that "I think, therefore I am" should be received "without scruple as the first principle of Philosophy." He further concludes that from "I think, therefore I am," he knows he is "a substance the whole essence or nature of which is to think." This inaugurates what is called "Cartesian dualism." Descartes is a thinking thing in a world of physical stuff.

God and Truth

Using the First Principle to direct his continued search for truth, Descartes creates a general rule that can govern his inquiries; he suggests that "the things we conceive very clearly and distinctly are true." In this way, he is able to keep doubt from creeping into the precepts or principles that he rationally discovered; he goes about proving the existence of God in the same way. His thought of God demonstrates that God exists, for if his imperfect and finite nature was all there is, then he would not be able to think of a more perfect being. From this, Descartes concludes that the thought of God necessitates the idea's existence, since something could not have come from nothing (or, something more perfect could not have come from something less perfect); he could not possibly be the cause of the idea of God, since the idea is foreign to Descartes' nature. He describes his thought process in the Meditations:

> And when I consider that I doubt, that is to say, that I am an incomplete and dependent being, the idea of a being that is complete and independent, that is of God, presents itself to my mind with so much distinctness and clearness—and from the fact alone that this idea is found in me, or that I who possess this idea exist, I conclude so certainly that God exists, and that my existence depends entirely on Him in every moment of my life—that I do not think that the human mind is capable of knowing anything with more evidence and certitude.

For Descartes, our fallibility is proof positive of God's existence. As regards the nature of God, he again surmises from our deficiencies that God is a "substance that is infinite [eternal, immutable], independent, all-knowing, all-powerful, and by which I myself and everything else, if anything else does exists, have been created." The argument can be reiterated, perhaps too simply: I exist; I exist with the idea of God, which could not have come from me; therefore, God exists.

Now, given that there is no hope of gaining knowledge if God deceives us as to the true nature of the world, Descartes must prove that God provides a trustworthy epistemological foundation. By nature God is perfect; deception is an imperfection. To conceive of God deceiving us is to conceive of a perfect being with an imperfection—an impossibility. Thus, God is not a deceiver (and would not create a malicious evil demon to deceive either), and so all errors in judgment and perception come from us.

Jeff Culver, faculty
Jessica Goeser, researcher
Daren Jonescu, advisor

PIERRE CORNEILLE, 1606–1684, *Modern French Playwright of Tragedy*

> True, I am young, but for souls nobly born valor doesn't await the passing of years.
> —*Le Cid*

- Wrote about the tension of heroic love and devotion to duty and is considered the father of French tragedy
- Was criticized for failing to adhere to the classical standards of the principle of the three unities
- Achieved great success with *Le Cid* which immortalized "gloire," a combination of noblesse oblige, virtue, force of will, and self-esteem
- Gave up the theater temporarily when the French Academy repeatedly decided against him

Key Works

Melite, 1629
Le Cid, 1637

Cinna, 1643
Polyeucte, 1642

Biography

Pierre Corneille was born in Rouen, Normandy. He studied law and initially became a lawyer. After four years, he took a different path and acted on his love of literature to write his first play, the comedy *Melite*. Supported by Cardinal Richelieu, he experienced early success with the dramatic comedy, yet critics took issue with Corneille's very popular tragicomedy, *Le Cid*. They attacked Corneille's modern approach because he didn't adhere to the classical standards of the "principle of three unities, believability, and good taste." They took issue with the break in the unity of time (one day), the unity of place (a single palace or city), and the unity of action (no shock to the audience). Corneille had also made the "error" of combining tragedy and comedy, a combination unacceptable to a pure classicist. Finally, Corneille deviated from the normal pagan stories set in Greece or Rome by positioning *Le Cid* in Medieval Spain within a Christian context. Consequently, Corneille aligned his next play, *Horace*, with classical tradition. Subsequently, Corneille created *Horace*, *Cinna*, and *Polyeucte*, which gave Corneille masterpieces that were produced for audiences throughout the next three centuries.

After his marriage to Marie de Lampenere and the birth of six children, Corneille continued to write prolifically although without as much success. He published an edition of his complete plays which contained three "Discourses on Dramatic Poetry" explaining contemporary stage theory. Considered France's major modern playwright, Corneille has been compared to the great 17th-century dramatists Jean Racine and Moliere. His characters are praiseworthy, choosing reason and honor, and allegedly give the theater, "heroes the public could admire rather than pity."

JOHN MILTON ◊ 1608–1674, *The Devil's Advocate*

> ❝ I cannot praise a fugitive and cloister'd vertue, unexercis'd and unbreath'd, that never sallies out and sees her adversary, but slinks out of the race, where that immortal garland is to be run for, not without dust and heat.
>
> —*Areopagitica*

- Served as chief propagandist for the Commonwealth government and Oliver Cromwell
- Published *Paradise Lost*, *Paradise Regained*, and *Samson Agonistes*
- Mixed classical learning with Christian theology, most notably in the elegy *Lycidas*
- Wrote mostly in Latin for works commissioned by the Commonwealth to justify the actions of Cromwell's regime and alleviate the horror felt on the continent by the execution of Charles I
- Focused almost exclusively on theological topics in his later poetry—the fall of man, Christ's temptation in the desert, and Samson in the throes of blindness; *Paradise Lost* is widely considered one of the great all-time works in the English language
- Was an expert linguist, proficient in all contemporary European tongues as well as Hebrew
- Went blind and relied on his daughters acting as amanuenses (secretaries); composed sections of *Paradise Lost* at night and then recited blank verse to his daughters in the morning

Key Works

Lycidas, 1637

Areopagitica, 1644
Paradise Lost, 1667
Paradise Regained, 1671
Samson Agonistes, 1671

Biography

John Milton was born December 9, 1608, to an affluent family in London. His father was a scrivener and a musician who generously supported his precocious son's learning endeavors. Milton attended St. Paul's Cathedral school and then Cambridge University, where he dedicated six years to what he called "studious retirement," focusing on reading, linguistics, and discerning his vocation. Rather than entering the ministry, as might have been expected for someone as highly educated and theologically minded as Milton, he sensed his calling as a poet.

He left his retreat at Hammersmith to travel on the continent, impressing European intellectuals in the literary salons of cities from France to Italy. He even met Galileo in Florence. Hearing news of the impending civil war, Milton rushed back to England to serve in the capacity to which he was most suited: author. He became a translator and diplomat for the rebel contingent under Oliver Cromwell, writing numerous tracts defending the actions of the Cromwell regime, most notably the execution of Charles I in 1649, of which he was one of the most ardent supporters.

During the time of the Commonwealth, Milton's diminishing eyesight failed him completely, and by 1652 he was totally blind. Milton's blindness became a key motif for him in his later poetic works, most significantly in the sonnet "When I consider how my light is spent" and his final major poem, *Samson Agonistes*. After the death of Cromwell in 1658 and the restoration of the crown to Charles II in 1660, Milton barely escaped with his life. Embittered by the turn taken by his nation, he lived out his life in relative seclusion. However, it was during this 14-year period that Milton's vocation as a poet became most fully realized, with the publication of *Paradise Lost*, a less ambitious sequel, *Paradise Regained*, and his final major work, *Samson Agonistes*. Milton died due to complications arising from gout shortly after editing the second and authoritative edition of *Paradise Lost* in 1674.

Liberty and Liberality

Perhaps the principal animating theme of Milton's work and theology is the idea of liberty. Milton's emphasis on our moral freedom often led him into controversy. Works like *The Doctrine and Discipline of Divorce*, in which Milton argues for legal divorce on the basis of lack of compatibility employing "a boldly antiliteral reading of the Gospels," were widely denounced and shocked his Puritan audience. Milton was unflappable, though, holding that the whole weight of Scripture tended toward freedom and love.

Milton's emphasis on liberty was brought into further clarity during the English Civil War and the Commonwealth period. With the execution of Charles I, Milton was forced to double down on his belief that individual liberty superseded the supposedly divine right of kings. His tactic was to draw a distinction between a king and a tyrant. A king must be served, but a tyrant need not be afforded the same deference. In the words of his prose tract *The Tenure of Kings and Magistrates*, "It is lawful, and hath been held so through all ages, for any, who have the power, to call to account a tyrant, or wicked king, and after due conviction, to depose, and put him to death."

Even in *Paradise Lost*, Milton goes out of his way to convey to the reader Adam and Eve's complete freedom to choose not to sin in the garden, via conversations between God the Father and God the Son, and in warnings Adam receives by the angel Raphael in the Garden of Eden. Even after the fall, Benjamin Myers argues that given the explicit language of prevenient grace in Book XI, in opposition to the prevailing Calvinism of the time which Milton rejected, "God has elected all people to participate in the grace of salvation. But God has also predestined the freedom of all human beings, leaving them free to reject their own election." Rather than damning all souls, God gives the ultimate freedom—the freedom to choose grace—to all people. This liberality is the centerpiece of Milton's theology and enlivened his political thinking and fervent republicanism.

Truth Smashes Falsehood

Milton was a stalwart believer in the power of truth to triumph over falsehood. It is this conviction that bolstered his more controversial beliefs and opinions, confident as he was that his views would prove true. In the preface to the highly controversial *Doctrine and Discipline of Divorce*, Milton compares the rejection of his heterodox views on terminating matrimony to that of the Jews rejecting Christ (really): "In such a posture Christ found the *Jews*, who were neither won with the austerity of *John the Baptist*, and thought it too much licence to follow freely the charming pipe of him who sounded and proclaim'd liberty and relief to all distresses: yet Truth in some age or other will find her witnes, and shall be justify'd at last by her own children." Milton, clearly, sees himself as an emissary of truth in his own age.

After the censorship of the *Divorce* tracts by the state publishing office, Milton roused himself to defend truth in his most vehement language in the *Areopagitica*, his defense of freedom of the press. Catherine Belsey has called the document, originally intended to be read in front of parliament, "one of the founding and canonical texts of modern liberalism." Indeed, many American founders, especially Jefferson and Adams, were inspired by Milton. "Let [Truth] and Falsehood grapple," he writes, "who ever knew truth put to the worse in a free and open encounter?" The danger in suppressing the struggle for truth is that wisdom will be suppressed as well and truth obscured for generations. Moreover, the struggle to discern truth is a by-product of an individual who loves wisdom. Milton writes, "Where there is much desire to learn, here of necessity will be much arguing, much writing, many opinions; for opinion in good men is but knowledge in the making." Truth, by defeating falsehood, shows herself to be true and compels men toward knowledge.

Milton's Ardent Patriotism

When a young John Milton declared his vocation to be Epic Poet in *The Reason of Church Government*, the subject of his epic as first envisioned was a history of the British people—"[I resolve] to fix all the industry and art I could unite to the adorning of my native tongue"—most likely an Arthurian legend put into epic verse. He would do for England what Virgil had done for Rome. While eventually the subject of the epic shifted to the fall of Adam and Eve in the garden, Milton's pride as an Englishman remained undeterred.

It is important to note that despite similar efforts by Spenser, Shakespeare, and the translators of the *King James* Bible, the English language was viewed as inferior to the continental languages, especially French and Italian, and the English populace was widely viewed as barbaric and uncultured. Milton's desire to see England supreme above other nations as a Christian republic motivated his unrelenting efforts in the cause of the Commonwealth. In *The Doctrine and Discipline of Divorce*, he exhorts his nation to "not forget her precedence of teaching nations how to live." Not only ought England to be equal to other nations, but it ought to lead other nations. Wordsworth recognized this spirit when he praised Milton as the man whose return would be capable of "giv[ing] us manners, virtue, freedom, power." The freedom of the English people, freedom from the constraints of political and religious tyranny, consumed Milton in the period 1640–1660. His political tracts of the period were engraved on the front with his name in Latin and the appellation *Angli*, or Englishman, in large print right underneath. He wanted to remind his readers of his native origin.

Paradise Lost

Paradise Lost is almost solely responsible for Milton's continued clout within both the academic community and popular culture. In the poem, Milton seeks to "justify the ways of God to men" by poetically explaining the fall of Adam and Eve in the garden. The poem is epic in scope, ranging from a war in heaven with the rebel angel Lucifer and his armies battling the angels who remained loyal to God, to the creation of the world and Adam and Eve, the temptation of Eve by Satan, Adam and Eve's sin and removal from the garden, and the future course of the world. It culminates in the sacrificial death of the Son of God on the cross. *Paradise Lost* begins *in medias res*, midway through the action, with the defeated armies of Satan languishing in the newly created hell. It ends with Adam and Eve, fallen in sin, leaving the Garden of Eden and making their way in the wild.

Paradise Lost is a rich and comprehensive work of art, but two perennial issues still receive scholarly attention: the question of the hero of the epic and the freedom of Adam and Eve to reject temptation.

Satan and the Hero of *Paradise Lost*

The question of the hero of *Paradise Lost* has kept writers busy since William Blake famously declared in *The Marriage of Heaven and Hell* that Milton was "of the Devil's party without knowing it." Since then, a number of schools of thought have formed around the question of the hero and the role of Satan. The intention here is not to put the question to rest, but to frame it for the first-time reader of the poem. For a time after Blake, it was a foregone conclusion that Satan was the hero. He had all the best speeches and the great rebel spirit to never "repent or change / Though chang'd in outward lustre." The terms of the debate have since shifted to a more nuanced approach.

In the novel approach of Stanley Fish, "Milton writes Satan as an easily sympathized and alluring character because the very nature of Satan is parallel to the very nature of sin." In other words, because sin is attractive to the reader, Satan is attractive to the reader. Commenting on Fish's thesis, Edward T. Oakes notes that "the reader is supposed to feel drawn to Satan, for from Adam and Eve we have all inherited an inclination to find Satan's sin attractive." Satan thus appears to be the hero to the degree that we as readers are sinners. Fish argues that showing his readers their own sin was precisely Milton's intention. C.S. Lewis takes the straightforward approach of remembering that Satan is Satan and, therefore, the Father of Lies and the greatest enemy to a fervent Christian like Milton. For Lewis, Satan is a liar wrapped up in a deluded fight against the very power that created him and still allows him to exist. In *A Preface to Paradise Lost*, Lewis writes "But I do not know whether we can distinguish [Satan's] conscious lies from the blindness which he has almost willingly imposed on himself." Satan is not a hero, then, but a liar trying to convince other fallen angels to soldier on with him in a pursuit even he does not believe will be successful: eternal war with God. Whatever we decide about this issue—and it is always fun to play devil's advocate, so to speak, and argue for Satan as the hero—we must be sure to pay careful attention to the comments the narrator of *Paradise Lost* makes after Satan's famous speeches and during Satan's journey to earth. And, as Lewis suggests, though it may seem elementary, don't forget that he *is* Satan.

Freedom in the Garden

Another vexing issue for readers of both *Paradise Lost* and the biblical sources is the freedom of Adam and Eve. If the fall was preordained, then what choice did they really have but to eat the apple? Book III is a counsel scene in heaven between God the Father and God the Son. God the Father sees Satan making his way to earth and is certain that he will be successful in tempting man to "transgress the sole Command" given to Adam and Eve: the prohibition against eating the fruit from the tree of the knowledge of good and evil. God here seeks to remove personal blame for the fall, arguing "I have made him just and right / Sufficient to have stood, though free to fall." He continues, arguing that predestination did not overrule their own wills and that even if he has foreknowledge of the fall, that "foreknowledge had no influence on their fault."

Adam and Eve, from the perspective of God, are free to resist temptation. In Book V the angel Raphael, sent to visit Adam and Eve and warn them of the possibility of encountering Satan, responds to a question about obedience. He tells Adam, "That thou art happie, owe to God / That thou continu'st such, owe to thy self." Obedience to God is not compulsory or extorted by "fate," but voluntary and rooted in love. According to the most authoritative figures in the poem, God and the loyal angels, Adam and Eve were free to reject Satan's temptation and remain in a committed and intimate relationship with God. They chose not to, in the terms of the poem, out of their own free will.

Cole Baker, 2012
Toby Coffman, faculty
Ryan Russell, 2015

THE THIRTY YEARS WAR, 1618–1648

It goes without saying that the years following the Protestant Reformation were tumultuous in many ways, dividing cities and nations and states against themselves. When the Holy Roman Empire sought to enforce religious unity across its length and breadth, the northern Protestants banded together to oppose it. Soon this civil war drew in aid and attention from other countries, shifting to a conflict regarding the balance of power over Europe itself. After 30 years of devastations, the Peace of Westphalia established the French and the Swedish as the preeminent political powers on the continent. The Holy Roman Empire, meanwhile, splintered ever closer to dissolution, the religious rights of its people secured, but their populations significantly diminished.

MOLIÈRE, 1622–1673, *The King of Comedy*

66 Beauty without intelligence is like a hook without bait.

—*Tartuffe*

- Was a French playwright who wrote 32 comedies
- Renounced his inheritance to start a theater troupe, which exists to this day as the *Comédie Français*

- Scandalized theatergoers with *Tartuffe*, his most famous play, when it was first staged
- Created the word *"moron"* through a character in his play *La Princesse d'Elide*; it was later added to the English lexicon
- Redefined comedy by mixing farce, comedy of manner, simple irony, and depth to create comedic masterpieces
- Worked as the leading actor, manager, director, and playwright of his troupe
- Is remembered for his dramatic death: he collapsed in the middle of a performance and then died a few hours later

Key Works

L'École des femmes (The School for Wives), 1663
Le Misanthrope (The Misanthrope), 1666
Tartuffe (The Hypocrite), 1669
L'Avare (The Miser), 1669
Le Bourgeois Gentilhomme (The Bourgeois Gentleman), 1670
Le Malade Imaginaire (The Imaginary Invalid), 1674

Biography

Jean-Baptiste Poqelin (Molière) was born in Paris as the son of a prosperous merchant. His father was the furniture dealer and upholsterer to the court, so he had the means to provide his son with an excellent education at one of the best schools in France. Poqelin was 15 when his father died, and he inherited his father's business and court position. After achieving his law degree at age 21, Poqelin was overcome with a passion for theater. He gave up his inheritance, adopted the stage name Molière, and started a theater troupe with 11 other actors. They were unsuccessful at first, experiencing severe financial troubles, and Molière was imprisoned twice for debt. The troupe was forced to move into the provinces, where they toured before returning to Paris in 1658.

Molière experienced his first success with the performance of *Les Précieuses Ridicules* in front of the king. Not only did this performance put his troupe in good favor with the king, but it also began his journey to become the greatest actor of his time. His second play, *The School for Wives*, was not as popular; it was considered scandalous and was banned because it encouraged women to become freethinkers. After the performance of his most famous work, *Tartuffe*, Molière was charged as a criminal and the play was outlawed because it was perceived as an attack on the church. Molière wrote 32 comedies and created many enemies by comedically mocking the follies of others. Despite provoking many enemies, Molière's plays became very successful. In 1665, after great fame and many successful shows, his troupe was renamed "The King's Troupe." He was married at 40 to a 20-year-old actress named Armande Béjart with whom he had three children. Unfortunately, two of his children died, and Molière's marriage was famously unstable. For the last seven years of his life, Molière was often sick due to a pulmonary illness. During the first performance of his final play, *The Imaginary Invalid*, Molière collapsed onstage and died only a few hours later.

Distinctive Comedic Style

Molière relied heavily on farce, which he combined with comedies of manners to create an entirely new style of comedy. His writing contained three distinguishing qualities: comic inventiveness, richness of fabric, and social insight. Molière was an actor-manager-director-playwright, which gave him a deeper insight into the world of theater and expanded his imagination. He drew much of his inspiration from commedia dell'arte. Molière created incredibly rich characters that combined seriousness with absurdity; their various follies served as a social satire that would delight and shock audiences. Molière's incisive satire and social criticism earned him a reputation as a moralist: "By drawing self-incriminating précieuses, prudes, zealots, philosophers, doctors, lawyers, and self-obsessed bourgeois, Molière attacks what they represent." For example, Molière often contrasted the foolishness of high-society women with intelligent, assertive, and more likable female characters who were unimpressed by shallow fashion. This inventive style is credited with developing the genre of comedies of manners and making comedic plays just as deep and complex as the sophisticated tragedies of his day.

Samantha Sherwood, 2015

BLAISE PASCAL, 1623–1662, *God's Gambler*

" Reason's last step is the recognition that there are an infinite number of things which are beyond it.

—*Pensées*

- Lost his mother when he was 3 years old, so he was raised exclusively by his father, a tax collector
- Received the bulk of his education from his father, who excluded math in his teaching until discovering Pascal's natural ability
- Developed Pascal's Theorem, a proof about the properties of circles, at 16
- Invented the first calculating machines, created to aid his father in his tax work
- Is credited with inventing the syringe and hydraulic press, based on a principle of the effects of external pressure upon liquid known today as Pascal's Law
- Used aphorism and humor to make philosophical arguments; this idiosyncratic, personal style would later influence the thinking and writing styles of Voltaire, Rousseau, Nietzsche, and many others
- Left his final two works unpublished; they were released after his death
- Thought the problem of humanity was its inability to find truth and happiness with rational certainty
- Underwent dramatic personal conversion to Christ on the night of November 23, 1654, an experience about which he wrote a private account (discovered after his death) titled "Fire" and ending with these words (in French and Latin): "Total submission to Jesus Christ and to my director. Eternally in joy for a day's trial on earth. I shall not forget thy word. Amen."
- Believed reason alone cannot prove that the Christian God exists, but rational men may choose whether to believe based on a calculation of the benefits of belief or disbelief
- Combined his pioneering work in probability theory with his study of Christianity to produce the famous "Pascal's Wager" regarding whether or not to believe in God, as follows:
  - If we *believe* in God and He exists, we gain Paradise; if he does not exist, we lose very little
  - If we *disbelieve* and He exists, we suffer eternal punishment in Hell; if He does not exist, we gain very little

o   A rational man, faced with the choice between two sets of options—great gain or little loss vs. great loss or little gain—will always choose the option of great gain or little loss;

o   Therefore, reason forces us to "wager" on belief in the Christian God, out of self-interest

Key Works

The *Provincial Letters*, 1656
The *Pensées*, 1670

Biography

Blaise Pascal was a distinguished 17th-century French mathematician, physicist, inventor, philosopher, and theologian. He was born in Clermont-Ferrand, France in 1623. His father was a minor government official, and his mother died when Pascal was only 3. Left widowed, his father moved Pascal and his two sisters to Paris in 1631; seven years later, they moved to Rouen so their father could accept the job of royal tax commissioner. Pascal's father taught him from a young age, and though his father was a brilliant mathematician, he disregarded the subject for several years to ensure his son received a well-rounded education. However, at age 12 Pascal began to study math and discovered key principles of geometry.

Pascal published his first work, *Essai pour les coniques*, in 1640 after joining a scientific discussion group at age 16. He continued to make mathematical discoveries in number theory, geometry, and probability theory, including his experiments with vacuums. When his father was bedridden after breaking a hip in 1646, the Pascal family was exposed to the Catholic reform movement of Jansenism. Pascal's religious conversion came after a near-death experience crossing the Pont Neuf. Combined with his previous study of probability and his recent religious transformation, he went on to propose one of his greatest theories—this time pertaining to the existence or nonexistence of God—known as Pascal's Wager. During the coming years, Pascal drafted many works, including what is still considered one of the greatest French literary masterpieces, *Lettres provinciales*, a series of letters in which he defended Antoine Arnauld by satirizing his Jesuit opponents and their theological and moral views. He then began two of his greatest philosophical works, *Pensées* and *De l'espirit géométrique*. Both were left unpublished when he died, but were eventually printed in the 18th century by various editors. He died in 1662 in Paris from a malignant tumor that spread to his brain. Today, his influential discoveries bear his name and are still used in classrooms around the world: Pascal's Triangle, Pascal's Law, Pascal's Theorem, and Pascal's Wager.

The Wager

After his religious conversion in 1655, Pascal came up with one of his greatest propositions, The Wager. Pascal laments in *Pensées 233*, "reason can decide nothing here." Pascal acknowledged that there is no way to prove, beyond doubt, whether or not God exists by rational argument. Instead, he says we must look at it as if we are placing an obligatory bet. If one chooses to believe in God and there is a God, the reward is eternal gratification. If there is no God, however, nothing has been lost. On the other hand, if one chooses not to believe in God and God exists, one endures eternal distress. If God doesn't exist, the unbeliever gambled correctly but wins nothing except "the time [one] would be spending in worship." All must choose one way or another; all will end up either gaining much and losing little, or winning little and losing much.

	God Exists	**God Does Not Exist**	**Risk**

Belief =	Eternal Pleasure (Huge Payoff)	**OR**	Loss of Some Worldly Pleasure (Small Loss)	=	Low
Unbelief =	Eternal Torment (Huge Loss)	**OR**	Gain of Some Worldly Pleasure (Small Payoff)	=	High

Based on this logic, Pascal says that there is no rational decision other than to believe in God. Pascal used the idea of "belief as a safe wager" to create a logical argument for all to see the truth of Christianity.

The Anthropic Argument

Pascal in the *Pensées* created what modern scholars call the anthropological argument, meant to persuade people toward following the Christian faith, based on observations from "the point of the human condition." Pascal proposes that Christianity explains what humans observe about themselves better than any other philosophical system. There are two seemingly contradictory aspects to human nature that must be explained: humans are both great and wretched at the same time. Illustrating this contradiction in *Pensées 434*, Pascal exclaims, "What a chimera, then is man! What a novelty! What a monster, what a chaos, what a contradiction, what a prodigy! Judge of all things, imbecile worm of the earth; depositary of truth, a sink of uncertainty and error; the pride and refuse of the universe."

In comparing other philosophies, Pascal found that they failed because "they either exalt [human] greatness at the expense of wretchedness or they exalt wretchedness at the expense of greatness." Pascal comments on the philosophies of Epictetus and Montaigne to illustrate his point. For Pascal, Epictetus fails because the standards of living that he expounded upon are beyond a human being's capacity. Thus, Epictetus exalts humanity's greatness, but fails to take into account its wretchedness. Montaigne makes the opposite error, in Pascal's mind, focusing too heavily on human ignorance and assumes its inability to find truth. So he maintains human wretchedness at the expense of human greatness. Pascal believes the Christian notion of human nature reflects this ontological paradox fully. Created in the image of God, humanity rejoices and exhibits greatness; corrupted by the Fall from Eden, humanity cowers in wretchedness and sin. This style of argument is called an abductive argument, which is to argue that one's belief is the best explanation for what is observed.

John Reid II, researcher
Daren Jonescu, advisor

ROBERT BOYLE, 1627–1691, *The Father of Chemistry*

    " I confess, that after I began ... to discern how useful mathematicks may be made to physicks, I have often wished that I had employed the speculative part of geometry, and the cultivation of the specious Algebra I had been taught very young.

—*The Usefulness of Mathematicks to Natural Philosophy*

- Wrote some 40 books on both theology and science
- Had a rigorous technique of experimentation and observation that drew him into the study of chemistry
- Provided the foundation for the Scientific Method as we know it today

- Discovered Boyle's Law, which states the volume and pressure of a gas are inversely proportional if the temperature remains constant, $PV = nRT$
- Persisted, along with Robert Hook, in the experiment that established Boyle's Law, even though it was quite controversial among scientists of the day
- Talked of "our invisible college," referring to the society that agreed to acquire scientific knowledge through rigorous experimental investigation; it became *The Royal Society*
- Refused the presidency of *The Royal Society*
- Was a corpuscularian—someone who believes that everything is composed of minute particles

Key Works

The Sceptical Chymist, 1661

Hydrostatical Paradoxes, 1666

Essays of the Strange Subtilty, Great Efficacy, Determinate Nature of Effluviums, 1673

Biography

Born at Lismore Castle in Munster, Ireland, Boyle was the youngest of 14 brothers and sisters. Due to his father's wealth, Boyle had the privilege of a private tutor for most of his childhood. During the time of the English Civil War, Boyle and his classmates conducted many scientific experiments at Oxford University. This group, called the Invisible College because they had no set meeting place or time, was very committed to scientific discovery through empirical means rather than pure logic; it eventually became the Royal Society of London, whose purpose was "to recognize, promote, and support excellence in science and to encourage the development and use of science for the benefit of humanity." After he left Oxford, Boyle moved in with his sister Katherine, Viscountess Ranelagh, who had a house in London's fashionable Pall Mall district. There, Boyle built his own laboratory, and, with the help of a master engineer, Robert Hooke, and various assistants, was able to carry out the experiments he desired, publishing a book per year. In 1608, Boyle refused the presidency of the Royal Society because he did not wish to swear an oath. He wrote in confirmation that there was no conflict between faith and science, that "for him a God who could create a mechanical universe—who could create matter in motion, obeying certain laws out of which the universe as we know it could come into being in an orderly fashion—was far more to be admired and worshipped than a God who created a universe without scientific law." He was sickly throughout his life and died at age 64, perhaps partly due to his grief over his sister's death a week before.

Boyle's Law

Boyle rejected the Aristotelian views and embraced corpuscularian thought—a physical theory that supposes all matter to be composed of minute particles. His experiments led him to believe in a vacuum, and he recorded his results so that others could reproduce his findings. Additionally, Boyle was the first to think of chemical elements as "certain primitive and simple, or perfectly unmingled bodies." Around 1650, Boyle studied the relationship between the pressure and the volume of a confined gas held at a constant temperature. He observed that the product of the pressure and volume are observed to be nearly constant. The product of pressure and volume is exactly a constant for an ideal gas. This concept of Boyle's Law is still important today in science and engineering, from steam motors to rocket engines.

Theology

Boyle was Anglican and clung to his religion throughout his entire career, unlike many scientists who believe science is superior to religion. He worked in his community to support his religion by funding educational and missionary work while penning many theological essays. His writing on religion focused on revelation, reason, and nature; in fact, he found that being a scientist perhaps placed him in a more advantageous spot from which to praise God, writing in *The Excellency of Theology, compared with Natural Philosophy* that "he is the fittest to commend divinity, whose profession it is not." Through his many works on religion and theology, Boyle meant to combat the rise of atheism in the scientific profession. Wanting to make scientific discoveries in the name of God, Boyle hoped to glorify God through his discoveries, finding what God had created for humans to find. This unique devotion to religion, one that broadened his search for truth rather than limited it, resulted in a significant contribution to a modern conception of the relationship between God and the natural world.

Scientific Method

Prior to Boyle, science revolved around theoretical debate rather than experimentation. Scientific arguments were settled by means of logical analysis; whatever was argued best was accepted as truth. Combating this method of confirming scientific truth, Boyle practiced the method of scientific discovery, rooted in the observation of controlled and replicable experiments. Similar to Harvey, Gilbert, Bacon, and Galileo, Boyle joined the long line of scientists who conducted experiments and published their findings based on observation. His legacy cannot be disputed, contributing in many ways to science: "(1) An emphasis on experiment instead of reason. (2) Publication of experimental results. (3) Popularization of scientific discoveries. (4) Collaboration of scientists in professional societies. (5) Mathematical formulations of laws. (6) Putting all claims about nature, no matter the reputation of the authority, to the test of experiment." Much of the scientific method scientists use today derives from his experiments and processes.

Brady Weisner, 2016

JOHN BUNYAN ◊ 1628–1688, *Pilgrim's Progress*

" So I saw in my dream, that just as Christian came up with the cross, his burden loosed from off his shoulders, and fell from off his back. ... Then was Christian glad and lightsome, and said, with a merry heart, "He hath given me rest by his sorrow, and life by his death."

—Christian in *Pilgrim's Progress*

- Was an English writer and Baptist preacher
- Served in the Parliamentary army for three years during the English Civil War
- Followed his father's career as a tinker (tinsmith)
- Joined the Bedford Group of nonconformists, or Puritans, as their preacher
- Went to jail for 12 years for refusing to give up preaching
- Began the religious allegory *Pilgrim's Progress* during his imprisonment
- Wrote nearly 60 books, primarily based on his sermons

Key Works

Grace Abounding to the Chief of Sinners, 1668
The Pilgrim's Progress, 1667–1672

Biography

John Bunyan was born in Elstow near Bedford, England. At 16, he joined the Parliamentary army and saw the beginnings of the English Civil War. After three years, he left the army to take up his father's work as a tinker (a tinsmith primarily repairing household utensils). Bunyan married and then became interested in the church. He was a freethinker who joined the nonconformists of the Bedford Group as their preacher. The restoration of the monarchy, wherein Charles II returned to power, prompted many changes in the government. One was less tolerance by the Anglican Church for religious nonconformists (Puritans) such as John Bunyan. Because the new laws restricted non-Anglican religious gatherings, he was told to give up preaching; when he refused, he was arrested. During the 12 years he spent in jail, Bunyan wrote a spiritual autobiography, *Grace Abounding to the Chief of Sinners*, and began *The Pilgrim's Progress*. Later he went briefly to jail again, but continued as the pastor of the Bedford Meeting until he died. The Church of England still honors him with an annual celebration day, while the Episcopal Church in the United States acknowledges his death on their liturgical calendar.

The Pilgrim's Progress

Bunyan's most famous work, *The Pilgrim's Progress*, has been read through the centuries. One biographer described it as "the book which has probably passed through more editions, had a greater number of readers, and been translated into more languages than any other book in the English tongue." In the book, Bunyan writes of a man on a journey symbolic of the journey a penitent Christian might make to true righteousness. The narrative appealed to the uneducated masses in part because Bunyan wrote in a common style without using high-flown literary language. Christian, the main character and traveler, reflects the struggle Bunyan himself had with his desire for holiness. (He criticized himself severely in his autobiography, documenting his tortuous path riddled with deprecation and despair.) Christian encounters danger and temptation with others in challenging places—Evangelist, Obstinate and Pliable in the City of Destruction and the Slough of Despond. Christian's trip does not end with his conversion, although he does change in an amazing way early in the story. On a hill Christian sees a cross—the sight caused the burden on his shoulders to be released. Through Christian's encounter, Bunyan reveals his belief in "sanctification," a release from the old life to one that is Christ-like, accepting Jesus' teachings. Christian continues on, changing his life goals. Similar to Christian, Bunyan realized that his own righteousness was from heaven, not his own heart. His autobiography reveals that he shed the self-hatred that had shackled him. Because he feared that his fictional story might depart too far from the accepted norms for writing about Christian beliefs, he began his book with an apology. Inspired and convicted by the volume, the first colonists of the New World carried *The Pilgrim's Progress* with them. They identified with the hero in his search for the future God had designed as they were doing by setting out for the New World. *The Pilgrim's Progress* has been read by generations for the excitement of the story as well as the deep religious metaphors within.

CHRISTIAAN HUYGENS, 1629–1693, *The Scientist Fueled by Innovation*

" I believe that we do not know anything for certain, but everything probably.

—*Oeuvres Completes*

- Was born into a prominent family during the 17th century
- Earned a degree in law, but never put it into practice
- Made significant astronomical discoveries with a new telescope of his own design
- Analyzed Galileo's studies of pendulums to create the first pendulum clock
- Is recognized as a founder of dynamics
- Promoted Descartes' "mechanical explanation"
- Believed that light was a wave
- Suffered from illness most of his life

Key Works

De Circuli Magnitudine Inventa, 1654
Horologium, 1658
Horologium Oscillatorium, 1673
Discours de la cause de la pesanteur, 1690
Traité de la Lumière, 1690

Biography

Christiaan Huygens was born in a time when the greatest minds in Europe were caught up in the fervour of scientific discovery. Galileo was fighting the Catholic church, Hooke and Leeuwenhoek were discovering microscopic life, and Newton was inventing calculus. Christiaan's family was one of the most eminent in both the political and literary worlds of the Netherlands. His father, Constantijn, was a dignified and well-known Dutch diplomat, and household visitors included the poet John Donne and the philosopher René Descartes.

Although he graduated from the College of Breda with a degree in law, Huygens was chiefly interested in mechanics and mathematics. He quickly established himself in the field, exploring conic sections and calculating the area of a circle with more accuracy than anyone else in his time. With his brother, he studied the night sky with a modified telescope of their own design. Making several important discoveries such as the Orion nebula (thousands of stars forming in Orion's sword), Huygens soon realized that he needed "an exact measure of time" if he were to continue to study astronomy and report his findings accurately. Thus, he made one of his greatest contributions to science: the pendulum clock. For this work he gained international fame and was granted a position in the French Royal Academy of Sciences located in Paris, France.

Uninterested in the lavish Parisian social scene, Huygens spent the majority of his time conducting scientific research. He wrote several treatises on physics that were noted not only for their intellectual value but also for his elegant style. Newton once claimed that "among modern writers [Huygens] had most closely approximated the style of the ancients." Plagued by poor health, Huygens returned to his native Holland, studying what would become an early form of projectors before dying in 1695.

Astronomy

After his time at the University of Breda, Huygens turned his attention to the stars. He felt drawn to Saturn and wished to study it further. However, he was limited by the technology of his time. Huygens was not the type of man to give up due to lack of resources, however; he simply decided to design and build a telescope that would allow him to see sharper and more detailed images. Focusing on the lens, he developed better ways of grinding and polishing lenses for telescopes and it was not long before he was building some of the most powerful lens telescopes of the day.

Using his advanced telescope, "Huygens' first observations yielded the discovery of the Orion nebula and of a new satellite to Saturn as well as a truer description of the rings about that planet." He even began to consider the possibility of extraterrestrial life: "We shall be less apt to admire what this world calls great … when we know that there are a multitude of such Earths inhabited and adorned as well as our own." He strayed from astronomy after the need for an accurate timekeeping mechanism arose, but he returned to the production of more advanced telescopes toward the end of his life.

Pendulum Clock

Excited by his discoveries in astronomy, Huygens realized that future work in the field would require a precise time-keeping device. Clocks of his day were highly inaccurate, most of them off by at least 15 minutes or more per day. Determined to invent a more precise clock, Huygens realized that his first step would be to find a device that would keep a constant, regular motion to which a clock could be geared. This led him to research the unfinished studies of Galileo who was forced off his own work on pendulums when he went blind.

Huygens learned from Galileo that the period of a pendulum's swing remains approximately the same even for different sized swings. This meant that a pendulum, with its constant and regular motion, would be the perfect device around which to build a clock. On the verge of a breakthrough, he studied pendulums intensively, eventually learning that perfect "tautochronism" (*exactly* equal time of each swing) can be obtained if the path of the pendulum's end follows a cycloid curve. To obtain this cycloid shape, Huygens placed a metal ball at the base of the pendulum to guide its movement. He then devised a system of falling weights that kept the pendulum itself in motion. By 1656, Huygens had created the first working pendulum clock. It was accurate to within a minute per day, far more precise than the antiquated models. He patented the clock in 1657, making it "the preferred timepiece in the Western world and it would remain so for three hundred years." This led him to his work on producing a working marine clock to correctly determine longitude at sea.

Light and Mechanics

From a young age, Huygens looked up to and admired the philosopher René Descartes. He even read *Principles of Philosophy* at age of 16. For good or ill, he became a steadfast believer in the mechanical explanation of the phenomena of nature along the lines proposed by Descartes, In this philosophy, matter fills all space and is infinitely divisible, making it impossible for atoms to exist. Like Descartes, Huygens believed that all forces on earth resulted from the motion of matter. He did not believe in invisible forces, including Newton's force of gravity. This was not the only dispute between Newton and Huygens. Huygens steadfastly believed that light was a wave, while Newton was convinced that light was particle.

Determined to prove Newton incorrect, Huygens explained how light's ability to refract, reflect, and diffract could be explained from his wave theory of light. Diffraction (change in the directions and intensities of a group of waves after passing by an obstacle or through an aperture), for example, was simply caused by two or more wave trains crossing each other, causing an interference of wave fronts. While neither Newton nor Huygens ever converted the other, Huygens continued to extrapolate his theory on light. He proposed that light was a longitudinal wave, a wave in which the displacement of the medium is parallel to the direction in which the wave is traveling. Furthermore, he postulated that light waves travel through an invisible substance called "aether." Light was the subject matter of his most famous work, *Traité de la Lumière*.

Huygens also explored mechanical physics, a subject closely related to his studies in light. He lived in Paris, conducting work under Gottfried Wilhelm Leibniz, the man credited with inventing calculus along with Newton. With his help, Huygens derived a formula useful in discovering the time it takes a pendulum to swing, explored the laws of centrifugal forces, and advanced the theory that an object's center of gravity could never rise of its own accord above its initial position. As a result of his research, Huygens has since been regarded as one of the founders of the science of dynamics.

Brady Weisner, 2016

BENEDICT DE SPINOZA, 1632–1677, *The Saintly Rebel*

> Of all the things that are beyond my power, I value nothing more highly than to be allowed the honor of entering into bonds of friendship with people who sincerely love truth. For, of things beyond our power, I believe there is nothing in the world which we can love with tranquility except such men.
>
> —*Letters*

- A rebel spirit
- Of Sephard-Portuguese origin
- Expelled from the Amsterdam Jewish community
- Gave his family inheritance to his sister
- The founder of modern biblical criticism
- Had his writings banned by the Catholic Church
- Denied the immortality of the soul
- Rejected the notion of a providential God
- Lived a saintly life and had many friends; kept his needs to a minimum and was very frugal
- Was buried in a Christian graveyard
- Became the first secular Jew of modern Europe
- Was a rationalist, influenced by the great medieval Jewish philosopher, Maimonides
- Became an expert in polishing optical glass to make a living; was visited by scholars Huygens and Leibniz
- Suffered from tuberculosis
- Practiced Judaism until he was excommunicated for questioning orthodoxy, especially regarding the divinity of the Bible; saw the Bible as a historical, natural document
- Accepted Cartesian language of substances having "attributes" (essences) according to which we identify them (e.g., extension is the attribute of bodies), but rejected Descartes's distinction

between infinite and created (divine and material) substances; all attributes are essences of the one infinite substance, God

- Identified God with Nature, and all other (supposed) substances as mere "modes" or emanations of God
- Humans experience God (Nature) only under the attributes of thought and extension (mind and matter), but God, being infinite, must actually have *infinite* attributes, beyond the limits of human experience
- If humans are not really individual substances, but only modes of God/Nature, then we are governed by Nature's laws; hence no free will; belief in freedom is caused by ignorance of Nature's causal relations
- Denying free will, Spinoza saw little value in the moral foundation of Christianity, e.g., personal choice
- Man can act morally only if he can free himself from his passions through knowledge (overcome ignorance)
- Practically, the improvement of man towards knowledge of God/Nature demands freedom and toleration
- An honest, sincere, mistaken human being

Key Works

Ethics, 1677
A Treatise on Religious and Political Philosophy, 1670
Hebrew Grammar, 1677
Letters, 1677
Opera Posthuma, 1677
On the Improvement of Understanding, 1677

Biography

Baruch Spinoza, born into a Jewish family who had fled religious persecution in Portugal, attended a synagogue school where he studied Talmudic and biblical texts. Skilled at language studies, Baruch became fluent in Spanish, Portuguese, Dutch, Hebrew, Latin, Greek, and German. He began to question many precepts of the Jewish church, including the reality of Providence, the immortality of the soul, and the Law given by Moses and Abraham. He committed a "monstrous deed" by rejecting Jewish authorities, and was punished by being served with a *cherem* (a ban). He changed his name to Benedict when his congregation charged him with atheism and warned everyone to reject him because he was cursed by God.

Spinoza turned to teaching at a private academy in Amsterdam where he became interested in mathematics, physics, and politics. Under the leadership of the former Jesuit and freethinker, Francisus van den Enden, he learned ancient literature and philosophy. From Maimonides's *Guide for the Perplexed*, Spinoza observed that religion could be a product of reason. Then he joined a free religious sect, the Collegiants, and began writing his philosophies of Cartesianism (study of René Descartes), God and his relationship to man, and *Ethics*.

Later, Spinoza worked as a lens grinder in a suburb of The Hague, the seat of the Dutch government, and at the same time published personal philosophies and corresponded extensively with many scientists and philosophers. He made Christian friends in an exploration of Christianity and the concept of destiny. Fascinated with the philosophies of René Descartes and Leibniz, he believed that to use mathematical reasoning would bring about certainty for all knowledge. He concluded that God is a supreme rationalist, and man's mind is a free power separate from the physical world. This is mind-body dualism. Spinoza articulated his ideas by writing *Rene Descartes' Principles of Philosophy* (1663), which pointed out what he saw as Descartes' errors. He died at 44 of a lung disease, possibly caused by inhaling glass while grinding optical lenses.

Ethics and Other Writings

Spinoza is well known for his five-volume treatise *Ethics*. The first book is about God, whom Spinoza defines interchangeably with "nature" and "substance." He maintains that a single being (God) is self-caused, "causa sui," the first cause, an "absolutely infinite being." Everything else is an effect and produces all that it is from the cause. He argues that logically God exists by definition; no reasonable argument exists denying God. To Spinoza, reason is identical to cause, logically separating that which causes from that which is caused.

The second book defines "psychophysical parallelism," which is the belief that man can perceive only two of God's infinite attributes—thought and extension. Man must go past his opinion and past his scientific understanding to intuition about the whole of reality. Each individual can see only his own unique perspective; his body is the result of the idea. Spinoza explains morality of conduct through the understanding that each person can act according to his own mind, while passion can cause part of the action. We show virtue when we know how to act in step with nature, and we suffer when we have unworthy ideas. Our struggle to reduce our passions and use self-control is life's struggle. Conquering one's passions with self-control takes us from "human bondage" to Spinoza's idea of freedom, "blessedness." Therefore when we work toward knowledge of God, we can experience true freedom.

Spinoza's personal resolutions are spelled out in *On the Improvement of the Understanding*. He had been dissatisfied with what he saw as men's search for "riches, fame, and the pleasure of sense," which results in a pathetic existence. He realized that, in order to change this, man must think about what he loves, moving from perishable things to an understanding of his part in a larger system. *More Geometrics*, the subtitle of *Ethics*, reflects using geometric methods with deductive reasoning to prove his arguments.

In Jerusalem at the Jewish and National Library, librarians put Spinoza's writing in the general reading room rather than the Judaic reading room in order to show his reputation as a thinker in the general history of philosophy. Roger Scruton, religious philosopher, has said about Spinoza that he, "wrote the last indisputable Latin masterpiece, and one in which the refined conceptions of medieval philosophy are finally turned against themselves and destroyed entirely." And Hegel wrote, "You are either a Spinozist or not a philosopher at all."

Matt Guillod, 2012
Daren Jonescu, advisor

> " It is no longer a passion hidden in my heart: It is Venus herself fastened to her prey.
>
> —*Phèdre*

- Was a French playwright best known for his classical Greek style and use of alexandrine meter
- Left the church despite being raised in the Catholic sect Jansenism; he returned later in life
- Wrote about the carnal corruptions of man
- Was reputed to have had affairs with several of his leading ladies
- Poisoned (allegedly) one of Racine's mistresses, Thérèse Du Parc
- Worked as King Louis XIV's personal biographer

Key Works

Alexandre, 1665
Andromaque, 1668
Britannicus, 1669
Phèdre, 1677

Biography

Jean Baptiste Racine was a man divided between a strict religious tradition and a love for the Greek classics. In his youth, he endured tragedy when both of his parents died and he moved in with his grandparents. Under their watch, he went through a rigorous education at Port Royal, considered one of the best schools of its time, where he received a Jansenist education. Jansenism is the French-Catholic sect that blends concepts such as Calvin's predestination and Augustine's original sin and depravity. This religion, specifically its view on human depravity, would influence his work throughout the rest of his life. Racine also encountered Greek literature while at school, and the Greek writing style would later become entwined with Racine's own distinctive style. After considering a priestly vocation, he moved to Paris in 1663 to become a writer. Success followed immediately with the performances of Racine's most famous plays, including *Alexandre*, *Andromaque*, and *Britannicus*. With these plays, he began to gain a reputation as a writer of scrupulous form and political depth.

While his characters suffered through tragedies onstage, Racine's personal life took a dark turn. He gradually deserted his religious beliefs for a licentious lifestyle. His reputation suffered when he deceived acting companies by ditching them at whim, and seduced actresses and dropped them when another leading lady came along. After the immense success of *Phèdre* in 1677, he went to work for Louis XIV as his official historiographer. He wrote two final plays at the queen's behest, which returned to the religious themes of his youth. Despite his contentious early life, when he died in 1699, he had earned the respect of the people and is remembered for his contribution to the arts in France.

Greek Influence

Racine's writing took place during the neoclassical period, and his body of work reflects both his cultural influence and his studies of Greek literature. His plots and characters were similar to Greek tragedies, and he strictly adhered to the classical Aristotelian unities—action, place, and time—in his plays; all of his stories took place during one day in one location around one action. Racine's religious upbringing (and the lingering ideology that influenced him throughout his life) might seem to have been at "constant warfare" with his neoclassical culture, but in reality the stripped-down aesthetics of the Greek tragedy fit perfectly with his ideas of corruption and carnality.

Alexandrine Style

Alexandrine meter contains 12 syllables, with two stressed syllables appearing at the end of each hemistich (half of the line of verse). Thus the first hemistich of a line of alexandrine meter has five unstressed syllables followed by a sixth stressed syllable, a caesura or pause, then another five syllables followed by a stressed sixth syllable. Just as iambic pentameter hopes to mirror the natural rhythms of the English language, alexandrine meter mirrors the natural rhythm of the French language; it is, in fact, tailored to the French language, limiting its use to French verse and making it difficult for non-French speakers to fully appreciate. Racine uses the alexandrine style to showcase his classical Greek subject matter and style of playwriting. The uninterrupted alexandrine syllables allow him to write long, epic speeches in long, epic rhythms. Mary Lewis Shaw calls Racine's work the "supreme realization of the alexandrine." While Racine didn't adhere strictly to the form's pattern of stressed and unstressed syllables, Shaw offers him this praise because he did master the form's principle of maintaining balance and symmetry while creating a natural, fluid movement. Essentially, Racine is to alexandrine what Shakespeare is to iambic pentameter.

Lust and Love in *Phèdre*

Phèdre displays the problems caused by corrupt lust parading as love. Racine exhibits this depravity through Phèdre and the lust she feels for Hippolytus, her stepson. When faced with the news of the king's death, Phèdre's corrupt nature sees the opportunity to explore her lust; however, Hippolytus denies her. Following Hippolytus's rejection, another messenger comes along and tells everyone that the first messenger was wrong: Theseus is still alive and will arrive soon. Terrified of Hippolytus speaking to his father, Phèdre formulates a plan to exonerate herself, hiding her shameful actions by telling King Theseus that his son attempted to rape her. King Theseus believes the lie and is understandably infuriated with his son, screaming, "Traitor, how dare you show yourself before me / Monster, whom Heaven's bolts have spared too long!" Hippolytus leaves the scene in a hurry, but in his haste he crashes his chariot and dies. After the messenger reports Hippolytus's death to the king, Phèdre's guilt overwhelms her, and she realizes she cannot carry on the lie. In the final scene, a grief-stricken Phèdre drinks poison and, with her final breaths, confesses her revolting secret. Phèdre is "undone by [her] passions, driven to ruin by ungovernable impulses." Through this plot and others like it, Racine examined the Jansenist view of the completely hopeless depravity of mankind.

Cole Baker, 2012
Jackson Howell, 2015
Susan Isaac, researcher

THE ENGLISH CIVIL WAR, 1642–1651

No single cause sparked the English Civil War; rather, a series of events culminated in the Royalists of the British monarchy fighting against its own Parliament. Parliament, which denounced Catholicism, objected to the marriage of King Charles I to a French Catholic princess, and to his tolerance—even promotion—of Catholicism. Additionally, the monarchy and Parliament wrangled about financial issues, especially war costs. This disagreements resulted in a general feeling of mistrust and frustration between Parliament and the monarch. In 1642, war broke out between the Parliamentarians and the Royalists.

Three crucial battles determined the course of the English Civil War.

The Battle of Marston Moor, July 2, 1644

At Marston Moor the Royalists lost not only the northern region of England, but also their dominant military reputation. Oliver Cromwell, a Parliamentarian leader, gained renown for his military actions. This was a huge blow to the Royalists' confidence and reputation.

The Battle of Naseby, July 14, 1645

They compounded their losses at the Battle of Naseby, where Parliamentarian forces met the Royalists outside of the village of Naseby. The Royalist forces were trying to relieve Oxford from a siege. The Royalists, at a disadvantage in troop numbers and position, lost the Battle of Naseby, forcing King Charles I to retreat.

The Battle of Worcester, September 3, 1651

Finally, the Battle of Worcester, the ultimate battle of the English Civil War, served as the monarchy's last stand. Cromwell led the Parliamentarian forces to victory against Charles II and the Scots, forcing Charles to flee and the Royalists to disband.

A Parliamentary victory brought with it many changes to England, including the execution of its standing king, Charles I—an unprecedented act.

Following the victory, England became a commonwealth under the rule of Oliver Cromwell, who, as Lord Protector, attempted to bring Protestantism to Ireland and helped establish the responsibility of the crown to rule with parliament's consent. Cromwell's success at eliminating the monarchy was cancelled out by his death when Charles II regained power and was crowned King of England.

OLIVER CROMWELL ◊ 1599–1658, *Lord Protector*

> " His character does not appear more extraordinary and unusual by the mixture of so much absurdity with so much penetration, than by his tempering such violent ambition, and such enraged fanaticism with so much regard to justice and humanity.
>
> —David Hume

- Descended from Henry VIII's minister, Thomas Cromwell
- Was devoted to God and the Puritans
- Tolerated the divergent Protestant ideologies of the time
- Fought on the side of the "Roundheads" (Parliamentarians) in the English Civil War and helped defeat the Royalists after he was appointed principal commander
- Signed King Charles's death warrant
- Defeated the Irish forces, occupied Ireland, and ended the Irish Confederate Wars
- Passed penal laws against Irish Catholics and confiscated their land
- Accepted the appointment as Lord Protector of England, Ireland, Scotland, and Wales
- Was known for his assertive approach to foreign politics
- Died of natural causes, but was then exhumed from Westminster Abbey, hung, and beheaded by the conquering Royalists

- Sparked controversy because of his treatment of the Catholics and harsh treatment of Ireland

Biography

Born in Huntingdon, England in 1599, Oliver Cromwell was a member of one of the wealthiest and most influential families in East Anglia. He received a good grammar-school education and then went to Cambridge, attending a college with a strong Puritan ethic. When his father died, Cromwell returned to the family home to take care of his mother and seven unwed sisters. In 1620, he wed Elizabeth Bourchier, the daughter of a London leather merchant; they had nine children. His political career began when he became a member of Parliament in 1628, where he reportedly made little impact. When King Charles called the next Parliament, 11 years later, Cromwell was again a participant. When the English Civil War broke out in 1642, he became an officer with the "Roundheads," or Parliamentary army, despite scant experience with the local militia. He was a born leader and his success with his regiment, the Ironsides, propelled him to become a commander of the New Model Army fighting against Charles I and the Royalists. In 1647, he did his best to reconcile the King, Parliament, and the army, but when this failed he remained loyal to the army. Cromwell became a powerful figure in Parliament, working for the dissolution of the monarchy and the House of Lords. He was one of the signers of King Charles I's death warrant.

The Royalists regrouped in Ireland, and Cromwell commanded the army which defeated them and occupied the country. Catholic-owned lands were confiscated and given to English settlers. With the implementation of the *Instrument of Government*, Cromwell received the title "Lord Protector" in 1653. He shared political power with Parliament and a council of state. He headed a tolerant, inclusive and mostly civilian government that sought to restore stability after the Civil War, and refused the crown when offered it. He sought to reform the worst parts of the legal, judicial, and social systems, and clamped down on what he perceived to be immorality, including drunkenness and theaters.

He died on September 3, 1658, and received a state funeral. When the Royalists returned to power fewer than three years later, they dug up his body, "executed" it, and re-buried it at Tyburn, where criminals traditionally were hanged.

SIR ISAAC NEWTON, 1642–1727, *A Genius with an Attitude*

" Sir Halley, I have studied the matter, you have not!

—to astronomer Edmond Halley

- Formulated the law of inertia, $F=ma$, and discovered that every action has an equal and opposite reaction (Newton's three laws of mechanics)
- Discovered the law of universal gravitation
- Coinvented calculus, the mathematics of natural growth and decay (see Leibniz)
- Proved white light to consist of a spectrum of colors with his famous prism experiment
- Invented the first reflecting telescope
- Viewed the earth and the heavens as part of a single universal system governed by rational laws
- Believed in using the processes of experimentation and observation to uncover truth
- Accepted both the Bible and creation as being God's Word
- Viewed the science vs. theology debate as pointless and detrimental to the pursuit of knowledge

- Had a short temper and large ego; could not stand criticism and experienced more than one nervous breakdown
- Earned substantial fame and recognition in his life but never made any close friends; he was socially awkward and insecure at heart
- Revolutionized physics, math, and science itself

Key Works

Philosophia Naturalis Principia Mathematica (Principia), 1678
Opticks, 1704
De Analysi, 1711

Biography

Isaac Newton, possessor of one of the greatest scientific minds ever, was not supposed to survive a single day. Born prematurely on Christmas Day in 1642, he was so small that his mother claimed he could easily fit into a quart pot. His eventual survival gave him a deep conviction that he had a special purpose in life. After his mother abandoned him to remarry—Newton's father died before he was born—unsympathetic grandparents raised the toddler. The young Newton was understandably embittered. An introvert, he was a round peg in square hole in a formal schooling environment. He was reunited with his mother when he was 12, following her second husband's death. She attempted to turn Newton into a farmer, but failed because he found farming boring. His uncle intervened and arranged for Newton to enter Trinity College at Cambridge where he was a mediocre student and received a degree without distinction.

During a closure of Cambridge due to the plague, Newton returned to the farm and came up with the fundamental thinking for his subsequent work on gravitation and optics, and developed his system of calculus for his own use. During this time, the idea of gravity came to him by way of a falling apple, a seemingly legendary story that is actually true according to Newton himself. He was sitting alone under an apple tree on the farm when an apple hit him in the head, giving him both a headache and the idea of gravity. He began to write and publish and his theory on light being composed of particles, which prompted criticism from some members of the Royal Society and international scientists. After forming an intense rivalry with another member of the Royal Society, Newton went into a rage—he never handled criticism well—and suffered a nervous breakdown. When his mother died soon after, he absented himself from the scientific community for six years. During his self-imposed exile, he began working on his theory of gravitation and planetary orbits. He published his *Principia* as a result of these studies. Newton's fame rose as *Principia* became better known, and he found himself in elite intellectual circles and the political arena.

After a second nervous breakdown in 1693, during which friends claimed he became deranged and paranoid, Newton lost his interest in science and decided to pursue a political career. He became the Warden of Mint and reformed the British currency by moving it from the silver to the gold standard. Newton never understood the notion of science as a cooperative venture, and he became quite tyrannical in his role as president of the Royal Society. He never married and never made many friends, despite his ever-growing fame. Those few who did befriend him began to worry about his mental stability, and for good reason. However, the line between genius and insanity is often blurred, and Newton was most likely dancing the fine line between them. He died in 1727 at the age of 84.

Optics

One of the first subjects to hook Newton's attention was optics, a branch of physics dealing with the behavior and properties of light. From an early age, he was adamant that light was composed of particles, not waves, as René Descartes, Christiaan Huygens, and others proposed. He believed that the ability of light to refract (to change direction after passing through a medium) and reflect could be explained only if light were made of particles, because waves did not tend to travel in straight lines. From his experiences with telescopes and day-to-day observations, Newton also thought that white light was more complex than what Aristotle and previous philosophers believed.

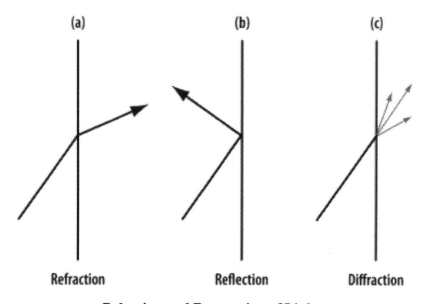

Behavior and Properties of Light

Deciding to kill two birds with one stone, Newton set up a demonstration to prove both of his beliefs. This was his famous prism experiment. Using two glass prisms, Newton illustrated how white light splits into a spectrum when it hits a prism at just the right angle. By placing a second prism in the line of the colored light, Newton proceeded to demonstrate how the spectrum condenses back into white light after passing through the second prism. This proved that the colors composed the white light itself and did not come from corruption within the glass, as many people had believed when the experiment was done with only one prism. Furthermore, the experiment illustrated how light can travel in a straight-line as was characteristic of particles, not waves.

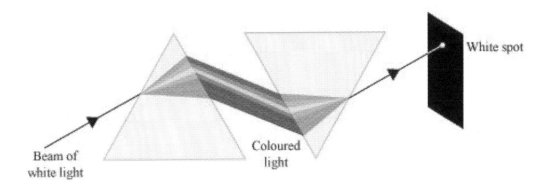

Newton's Prism Experiment

Newton's work with prisms illustrated how rainbows form from light passing through water droplets and seemed to settle the debate on the complexity about white light, but not everyone was convinced about light being composed of particles. Robert Hooke pointed out the ability of light to diffract (meaning to pass through a small opening and then to spread out over a large area) and claimed that only waves could behave in that manner. Newton argued that diffraction was simply another form of refraction. The debate on the nature of light would not be resolved until over a century later, when Einstein would prove both theories wrong. The truth is that light is both wave and particle, not one or the other.

Mechanics and Gravitation

Newton is most well known for his work with mechanics and gravity. However, Newton did not come up with the laws of motion solely by his own genius. Rather, he synthesized the theories of those who came before him into three concise statements. They are as follows:

1. An object in a state of uniform motion tends to remain in that state of motion unless an external force is applied to it. This is the Law of Inertia.
2. The relationship between an object's mass, m, its acceleration, a, and the applied force, F, is $F=ma$.
3. For every action there is an equal and opposite reaction.

Newton took this idea of natural laws and applied it to the age-old conundrum of planetary motion. Surely there was some rule that governed the movement of the heavenly bodies but also applied to objects here on earth. Inspired by a falling apple, Newton took the astronomy of Copernicus, as corrected by Kepler's laws, with the physics of Galileo, and formulated the law of universal gravitation. According to this law, every body in the universe attracts every other body, and the force of this attraction is proportional to the mass of the objects and inversely proportional to the square of the distance between them: $Fnet = m \cdot a$. Suddenly, the "whole universe—from Kepler's elliptical orbits to Galileo's rolling balls—was unified in one majestic system." Gravity explained why planets orbited the sun in the way that they did and also why fruit falls from a tree branch. This one law paved the way for countless other discoveries and showed the world to be an organized system, one Newton believed nevertheless to have been created by God.

Mathematics

The debate over who invented calculus, Newton or Gottfried Leibniz, developed into a contentious feud, thanks to the egos and attitudes of both men. However, history illustrates that both came up with the technique independently, with Newton having done so just slightly before Leibniz. Newton's reason for developing calculus was to have "a practical tool by which to attack problems regarding the effects of gravity and as an accurate calculator of planetary motion." He emphasized analysis and attempted to describe the effects of forces on motion with respect to time. Velocity, for example, is the primary derivative of position, while acceleration is the secondary derivative of position. Both Newton and Leibniz worked with differentiation and integration and both recognized how the two were inverse processes. Their practical genius pioneered modern mathematics and gave scientists a powerful tool moving forward.

Worldview

Although Newton's laws and observations paved the way for deism and the belief of God being a distant "clockmaker," Newton himself did not adhere to such a worldview. He was deeply religious and spent more time on theology than on science. Newton believed God to be active in the world and saw both God's Word and the work of His hands as being sacred and true. However, he was not interested in getting involved with the science versus religion debate, which he saw as pointless and detrimental to gaining knowledge of any kind. He wrote that "we are not to introduce divine revelations into philosophy [science], nor philosophical [scientific] opinions into religion." As for science, Newton believed that truth could be discovered through experimentation and observation. He is known as the "Father of Modern Science" for his support of and tireless adherence to the scientific method. He conducted experiments, took careful notes, formulated a theory, performed verifying experiments, and carefully wrote it all down so that another might repeat the process. This method governs how all of science is conducted today.

Tatjana Scherschel, 2015

GOTTFRIED W. LEIBNIZ ◊ 1646–1716, *Metaphysics, Human Understanding*

> " Leibnitz saw in his binary arithmetic the image of creation. He imagined that Unity represented God, and Zero the void; and that the Supreme Being drew all beings from the void, just as unity and zero express all numbers in this system of numeration.
> —*Pierre-Simon Laplace*

- One of the three great figures (with Descartes and Spinoza) of 17th-century *rationalism*, the belief that reality obeys mathematical principles, and hence that knowledge may be attained (only) through reason operating on the basis of these principles, as opposed to *empiricism*, which relies on sense experience
- Had the long-term goal to unify the Christian churches , himself a Lutheran
- Built the first calculator that could add, subtract, divide, and multiply
- A major mathematician: at the same time as Isaac Newton, explained infinitesimal calculus, assuming that the derivative is not a limit; worked on determinants as he practiced systems for solving linear equations

- Was a polymath whose thinking influenced later developments in physics, technology, biology, medicine, geology, psychology, linguistics, and many other areas; corresponded with a vast range of scholars
- Proposed the famous "Principle of the Identity of Indiscernibles": no two distinct things can be perfectly similar in all ways, i.e., there is only one existent of any "kind," since no two things are truly alike
- All qualities of a substance, including spatial and relational properties, are part of the complete definition of that substance, which means time and space do not exist independently of objects; time and space exist *because* objects with particular temporal and spatial properties exist
- All substances are unique ("discernible") and indivisible *monads*; every monad is defined fully by its position in direct or indirect relation to all other things, stretching without limit into the past and future
- Hence, each monad has a definite, eternal relation to the entire universe, which means two important things: (a) cause-effect is illusory, since all relational properties preexist time and space; and (b) instead of causality, monads exist in a web of definite, eternal relations Leibniz calls a "pre-established harmony"
- There are infinite possible worlds (imaginable harmonies), but our real one is "the best of all possible worlds" because God, who is perfectly good, would necessarily choose the best world according to reason
- Leibniz's answer to "the problem of evil": since reason establishes that this is the best possible world, God, who has perfect reason, must have determined that some evil was *necessary for the world's goodness* (for example, we need evil to challenge us in order to develop virtue, which is the human mode of goodness)

Key Works

Meditations on Knowledge, Truth, and Ideas, 1684
Discourse on Metaphysics, 1686
Primary Truths, 1689
New System, 1695
Specimen Dynamicum, 1695
On the Ultimate Origination of Things, 1697
On Nature Itself, 1698
New Essays on Human Understanding, 1704
Theodicy, 1710
Monadology, 1714

Biography

Gottfried Wilhelm Leibniz, a child prodigy, is recognized as a "universal genius." He was born into a Lutheran family of well-educated philosophers and into a world recovering from the Thirty Years War. Educated in the Scholastic tradition and ancient and medieval philosophy, Leibniz taught himself Latin and Greek. He went to the University of Leipzig at 15, earning his doctorate in law at the University of Altdorf at age 20. Rather than accepting a professorship, he chose public service. Working for a pious Catholic diplomat, Johann Christian von Boineburg, Leibniz was encouraged to help develop a metaphysical harmony between the Catholic and Lutheran doctrines.

Leibniz's dream to develop a universal scientific language that used the methods of calculus provided a foundation for his all his work. His first writings expound his theories of "logical calculus." On a diplomatic mission to Paris, he met with many great thinkers, including Christiaan Huygens, who gave his mathematics new impetus. While reading Pascal, Leibniz began work on differential calculus and the infinite series and invented a calculating machine that did all four arithmetic operations. In the last years of his life he was accused of taking Newton's ideas on calculus; historians now realize that the scientists formulated their ideas separately.

After the death of his employer, Leibniz moved from Paris to Hanover to begin working for the court as a librarian and a historian. On his journey, he stopped in Amsterdam to talk with Spinoza, the famous Jewish philosopher. He corresponded with philosophical leaders as he continued to write prolifically. Leibniz died in 1716 with most of his writings unpublished in a state of disorganization. Many have since been published, but even now have never been compiled into a single body of work.

Leibniz's Philosophy

Leibniz's first published political philosophy began with a letter that he wrote as an introduction to another's work. In his deep belief in the harmony of all knowledge, he attempted to fuse Aristotle's idea of form with the mechanical ideas of physics. Following the teachings of Plato, Leibniz believed in the Supreme Being of God who created the world, continues to care for the world, and cannot be denied. He maintained that everything depends on God while God depends on nothing. Also in the Platonic tradition, Leibniz subscribed to the theory of plentitude, which is the belief that God has created a diverse world where, in sympathy with all of nature, He desires as much unity as possible. He believed that the Perfect God gave all human beings a little of His divine attributes; therefore, each unique person is an imperfect picture of some of God's characteristics. Leibniz reinforced the principle of harmony throughout his writings with the definition of harmony—"diversity through identity."

His entire philosophy, in the absence of a single compilation, has been pieced together by scholars. Leibniz refined and developed in his thinking, as well, which has made the task difficult. His reckoning of Aristotelianism, Platonism, Christianity, and 17th-century philosophy prompted this statement:

> " I flatter myself to have penetrated into the harmony of these different realms and to have seen that both sides are right provided that they do not clash with each other; that everything in nature happens mechanically and at the same time metaphysically but that the source of mechanics is metaphysics.

He responded to the two modern schools of thought—Descartes versus Hobbes and Spinoza. He came to believe these principles and employed them in his metaphysical and philosophic proofs:

1. The Principle of the Best—God always acts for the best. *Discourse on Metaphysics* argues that, "God is an absolutely perfect being." Therefore, in infinite wisdom, he behaves in the most perfect way. He has created the best of all possible worlds.
2. Predicate-in-Notion Principle—The predicate is contained either explicitly or implicitly in that of the object. In *Primary Truths and the Discourse on Metaphysics*, Leibniz describes truth as a proposition that contains an implication of what is going on. The word "bachelor" contains the understanding "single man," for example.
3. Principle of Contradiction— "A proposition cannot be true and false at the same time, and that therefore *A* is *A* and cannot be *not A.*"

4. Principle of Sufficient Reason—There is no effect without a cause. Everything that happens has a reason we can see when enough information is known. He admits that we cannot understand many reasons.

5. Principle of the Identity of Indiscernible—"If two things share all properties, they are identical. Yet, two identical things that exist in different locations are different because of time and place."

6. Principle of Continuity—"Nature never makes leaps." Any change passes through some intermediate change. In *New Essays* he explains that motion cannot come from complete rest, only from minute details that can't be seen.

Truths of Reason and Truths of Fact

The two principles of contradiction and sufficient reason defend his definition of the two truths, also described as necessary truths and contingent truths. The truths of reason are explicit statements of identity, or reducible to explicit identities by substitution of the definitions of their terms. A truth of fact can't be arrived at by a similar analysis. Truths of fact are explicit statements of identity, the grounds for whose truth may not be known to us. Leibniz states that all ideas cannot come from experience, yet experience gives us the thoughts that we can extract the ideas within us.

On this subject, Leibniz uses a distinctive metaphor: "A piece of marble has veins that indicate or are disposed to indicate shapes that a skillful sculptor can discover and exploit. Similarly, there is a 'disposition, an aptitude, a preformation, which determines our soul and brings it about that [necessary truths] are derivable from it.'"

Mathematics and the Sciences

In 1675 Leibniz developed his own ideas of calculus, and worked on notation, developing $\int f(x)\, dx$ and the product rule for differentiation. Other achievements include the binary system of arithmetic—the foundation of digital computers—and determinants. Leibniz developed the first mass-produced mechanical calculator, which he called the arithometer. He also made significant contributions in the fields of physics, probability, biology, medicine, geology, psychology, linguistics, politics, law, ethics, theology, history, and philology.

Matt Guillod, 2012
Daren Jonescu, advisor

DANIEL DEFOE, 1660–1731, *The Father of Journalism*

" It is never too late to be wise.

—*Robinson Crusoe*

- Changed his surname from Foe to Defoe to sound more like a gentleman
- Was imprisoned several times for his political views, debt, and accusations of libel
- Wrote *Robinson Crusoe*, a novel about a sailor marooned on an island for 30 years
- Worked as a spy for the British for over 20 years before gaining popularity as a writer
- Is credited with inventing the literary style of formal realism

Key Works

The Farther [Further] Adventures of Robinson Crusoe, 1719
The Fortunes and Misfortunes of the Famous Moll Flanders, 1722
Everybody's Business is Nobody's Business, 1724–7

Biography

Though much of his personal life is shrouded in mystery, it is known that Daniel Defoe lived an exciting life as a novelist, journalist, and spy. He was born into a butcher's family in 1660, and although his family was not poor, the young Daniel Foe changed his last name to Defoe in an effort to appear more sophisticated. The eldest of three siblings, Defoe graduated from Newington Green School in 1683. He decided to become a businessman, but soon became caught in an inescapable web of debt. After being incarcerated in debtors' prisons, he claimed bankruptcy in 1692. By 1703, Defoe renounced the business world and aspired to be a political writer. However, his inflammatory words angered his political rivals, and Defoe was imprisoned multiple times for slander. Once, while he was in jail, Defoe was hired as a government spy and writer. After working as a British spy for over 20 years, Defoe began writing fiction. Influenced by Jonathan Swift, Defoe's best-known novels, *Robinson Crusoe* and *Moll Flanders,* are satirical and heavy with irony. Defoe died of a stroke in 1731, and though he did not experience notable fame during his lifetime, *Robinson Crusoe* has become a literary classic.

Formal Realism

Many credit Defoe with inventing the literary style of formal realism in his novel *Robinson Crusoe.* In the tradition of formal realism, authors attempt to make their fictional stories so realistic that they appear to be the accounts of actual events. Although he is not the first author to attempt to realistically portray the human experience through narrative, Defoe's style was unmatched in his time. He avoided flowery language and idealized characters, focusing instead on commonplace details that made the story realistic and more accessible to readers. Defoe placed an enormous emphasis on details in an effort to give a full and thorough report of the human experience.

Robinson Crusoe

Robinson Crusoe is the story of a young man absconds to London and embarks on a series of adventures, until he is shipwrecked on a remote island. Crusoe, the protagonist, struggles to survive on the island using only the resources he has available. Defoe's narrative is so detailed that many readers insisted that the story had to be true. Crusoe eventually discovers a stranger's footprint sand; he befriends the stranger and lives on the island for 28 years before returning to England a changed man.

There are three major themes in *Robinson Crusoe*. First, Crusoe must confront and overcome his fear in order to survive. Initially he is terrified even of his own shadow, but he comes to conquer his fear and master the art of survival. Crusoe must also confront the reality of the human condition; he concludes that man will always exploit nature to survive; in fact, the book suggests that's why we are here on earth. Lastly, Crusoe comes to understand the proper place of wealth. In the beginning of the novel, Crusoe is careful and miserly with his money. Once he is stranded, however, he realizes that an item's value cannot be measured in money but in utility. Defoe's realistic writing style guides readers in experiencing the same struggles and lessons as Crusoe himself.

Samantha Sherwood, 2015
Lauren Wade, 2015

> " We have just enough religion to make us hate, but not enough to make us love one another.
>
> —*Thoughts on Various Subjects*

- Gained fame as one of the most effective satirists in history
- Wrote numerous satirical pieces that harshly critiqued the English upper-class
- Considered satire an effective way to reveal false perceptions of life in the 18th century
- Outsold all other prose pieces in the 18th century with the original publication of *Gulliver's Travels*
- Gave much of his wealth to the poor and posthumously donated his entire estate to build the first mental hospital in Ireland

Key Works

Tale of a Tub, 1704
Gulliver's Travels, 1726
A Modest Proposal, 1729

Biography

An acclaimed satirist and clergyman, Jonathan Swift was born in November 1667. Though English by heritage, Swift moved to Ireland during the time of the Restoration in England. After his father's death, Swift's mother left the young boy in the care of his uncle, who enrolled him in Kilkenny College. Swift graduated from there at 14, entering Trinity College Dublin in 1682. He had an extremely poor academic record and received a degree only by special dispensation. The closing years of his education were accompanied by the threat of war, and his college advised students to flee the city until the quarrel between Prince William of Orange and King James II was complete.

Swift was ordained a priest in 1695 and soon began publishing anonymous pamphlets on popular political controversies. In 1704, he launched his literary career with *A Tale of a Tub*, followed by many other well-known works, such as *Journal to Stella* and *Gulliver's Travels*. Swift's satirical writings on social injustice, the poor, and the Irish made him a bestselling, albeit highly controversial, author in the 18th century. After his death in 1745, Swift was buried in St. Patrick's Cathedral with this epitaph above his grave: "Here lies the body of Jonathan Swift, Doctor of Divinity and Dean of this Cathedral Church, where savage indignation can no more lacerate his heart."

Satire

Jonathan Swift is often misunderstood because of his predilection for satire. In addition to his explicit, political essays, he wrote many satirical works in which he employed parody, mockery, and wordplay. Because Swift relied so heavily on satire, many scholars still debate his underlying messages. Swift believed there were "Two Ends that Men propose in writing Satyr": "private satisfaction" and "Publick Spirit." Swift found satire a personal delight as well as a vehicle for civic responsibility; he also thought of it as a prime method for educating. In "An Epistle to a Lady," Swift writes that satire can "Make you able upon sight / To decide of wrong and right / Talk with sense whate'er you please on / Learn to relish truth and reason." Swift believed satire was a powerful pedagogical tool because it "lead[s] to the painful knowledge of the world's falsity and of our own shortcomings."

This revelation of "painful knowledge" is arguably Swift's chief reason for writing at all. Though misanthropic, Swift truly was a champion of the downtrodden. As a parish priest, he experienced first-hand the suffering of Irish peasantry at the hands of English aristocrats and landlords. In "A Modest Proposal," Swift's most famous indictment of social injustice, he suggests that Irish families use infants as a source of food. This idea is an over-literal adaptation of the common economic motto, "people are the wealth of the nation." Swift's essay takes this literally, and also takes a "cannibalism charge—directed historically at the native Irish—and turns [it] back on the English colonial rulers and absentee landlords … who are already consuming Ireland and her people, and doing so out of mean self-interest disguised as rational economic policy."

Gulliver's Travels

Gulliver's Travels sold more copies than any other novel in the 18th century and remains to this day an intriguing and debated text. Like the rest of Swift's writings, it focuses on the seminal question, "What is man?" Is he good or evil, monstrous or divine?

The story is a compilation of four nautical journeys led by the protagonist, Lemuel Gulliver. He is a moderately intelligent, resourceful, and patriotic person, meant to portray a "reasonably decent example of humanity, with whom a reader can easily identify." Gulliver gets shipwrecked on four different islands, each containing a non-human species, each a reflection and critique of the nature of humankind and the state of Gulliver's society. On the first island, Gulliver encounters a race of miniature people called the "Lilliputians." Though physically endearing, this civilization is industrious, cunning, and deceitful. On several occasions, they subject Gulliver to all manner of ingenious tortures in order to use him as a military weapon. As the reader comes to know the Lilliputians, he begins to see humanity's "likeness to them, especially in the disproportion between [its] natural pettiness and [its] boundless and destructive passions."

The next place Gulliver visits is the island of Brobdingnag, inhabited by giants. As with the Lilliputians, Swift shows a disparity between the appearance of these creatures and the reality of their nature. The Brobdingnagians are brutish in appearance but noble in nature. They maintain a utopic society, governed by a philosopher king. In his talks with Brobdingnagian king, Gulliver encourages the use of industrial, military technology that is popular in England, yet unheard of in Brobdingnag. The philosopher king quickly silences Gulliver's military discourse, effectively "[revealing] the difference between what England is and what it ought to be."

On his third voyage Gulliver visits the island of Laputa, where he encounters a race steeped in theoretical and speculative reasoning, with whom he finds himself in constant debate. This voyage is likely an extended allegory of political life under the administration of the Whig minister, Sir Robert Walpole. The last place Gulliver visits is the island of the Hoyhnhnms, an intelligent race of horses who live by pure and unadulterated reason. The Hoyhnhnms are a narcissistic and cruel race with beliefs compatible with Social Darwinism. They enslave an ape species known as the Yahoos, which are "obscene caricatures of the human body," have "no glimmer of reason," and are "mere creatures of appetite and passion." After leaving the island of the Hoyhnhnms, on which he is treated as a mindless Yahoo, Gulliver returns to England and lives a confused, reclusive life with domesticated horses as his only companions. His final state of confusion and hopelessness forces the reader, like Gulliver, to question the true nature of humanity.

David Eschrich, researcher

WILLIAM CONGREVE, 1670–1729, *A Master of Comedy*

❝ I find we are growing serious, and then we are in great danger of being dull.

—*The Old Bachelor*

- Was an English playwright and poet best known for his comedy, *The Way of the World*
- Wrote only five plays—four comedies and one tragedy
- Counted authors Pope, Swift, Addison, and Gay among his close friends
- Wrote comedies of manners about the Restoration
- Fathered Lady Mary Godolphin, who married William Orange-Nassau, the man who would eventually overthrow King James II

Key Works

The Way of the World, 1700

Biography

William Congreve led a short career of both great success and great disappointment. Born in England but raised in Ireland, Congreve attended Kilkenny School, where he found a lifelong friend in Jonathan Swift; the two attended Trinity College in Dublin together. Although formally studying law, Congreve was far more attracted to the wit and drama of the theater, and spent much of his time at Will's Coffeehouse conversing with poets and playwrights. There he became a friend and student of the playwright John Dryden. Congreve's first comedy, *The Old Bachelor*, was an instant success. His teacher Dryden commented, "It was the best first play I have ever read." Encouraged by his quick success, Congreve wrote another play titled *The Double Dealer*. Though it was more sophisticated, *The Double Dealer* was slightly less successful than his first work. The only tragedy Congreve ever wrote, *The Mourning Bride*, became one of the most famous tragedies of the century. Despite his growing fame, his next comedy, *The Way of the World*, initially met with little success, though it would later become his best-known play. Disheartened, Congreve gave up writing plays and took up wine commissioning in 1705. Though he never married, he had a child with his longtime lover and leading lady Duchess Bracegirdle of Marlborough. Their daughter, Lady Mary Godolphin, would eventually marry William Orange-Nassau, the man who would overthrow King James II in the Glorious Revolution. In the last years of his life, Congreve suffered from poor health and gout. He died in 1729 after sustaining internal injuries when his carriage collapsed.

Comedy of Manners

The majority of Congreve's plays were comedies of manners about the Restoration. During the Restoration, the English monarchy was restored, and a new system of government was established. Comedies of manners are typically satirical, realistic, and humorous, concerned with the manners of an artificial, highly sophisticated society. Congreve's plots usually centered around the scandalous love affairs of one or more couples. Although intriguing and often hilarious, the most important aspect of the plays is not found in the plot, but rather in the witty dialogue and commentary on human failings. This style of comedy accomplishes its criticism by making light of the foolishness of the upper class.

The Way of the World

Despite its initial unpopularity, *The Way of the World* eventually became Congreve's most famous play and is considered a perfect comedy of manners. It is a comedy about the uninspiring reality of life, as opposed to the idealizations and dreams of the characters. The plot centers on a ladies' man who cleverly convinces a conceited and wealthy widow to give him her niece in marriage. The witty eventually triumph over the foolish in this story of deception, disguise, intrigue, and love. Like many comedies of manners, *The Way of the World* mirrors society during the time of the Enlightenment and the Glorious Revolution. In his tale, Congreve's characters begin to question authority and take the matter of marriage into their own hands rather than simply obeying the demands of their elders. The story also reflects common personalities and social customs of the time; the main character, Mirabell, reflects a contemporary narcissist, seeking only his personal satisfaction. Ultimately, twisted schemes are overcome by virtue and love. While clever and entertaining, *The Way of the World* poignantly reflects the changes that were occurring in English society.

Samantha Sherwood, 2015
Lauren Wade, 2015

GEORGE BERKELEY, 1685–1753, *The Real Idealist*

> " It is indeed an opinion strangely prevailing amongst men, that houses, mountains, rivers, and in a word all sensible objects, have an existence, natural real, distinct from their being perceived by the understanding.
> —*A Treatise Concerning the Principles of Human Knowledge*

- One of the major figures (with Locke and Hume) in 17th–18th century *empiricism*, the belief that all knowledge must begin from sense experience, as opposed to *rationalism*, which relies on pure reason
- A priest of the Church of Ireland; attempted to found a college in Bermuda; later named Bishop of Cloyne
- Important theorist about the nature of vision and distance perception
- Greatly influenced the philosophies of Hume and Kant
- Famous for defending two positions: *idealism* (all that really exist are minds and mental events) and *immaterialism* (matter is an abstract hypothesis without real existence)
- Berkeley's central ideas are crystallized in the phrase *esse est percipi*, "to be is to be perceived"; the so-called material world is made up only of ideas in the mind
- Contended that there's no sound reason to believe that anything can exist outside of our direct experience
- We never experience the "matter" of an apple—all we experience are sensations like redness, sweetness, roundness, firmness, etc.—which is to say matter cannot be perceived, so it should not be presupposed
- If to be is to be perceived, why don't objects disappear when we close our eyes?—because God (the infinite mental substance) sustains the sensible world's uninterrupted existence by *perceiving it continuously*

Key Works

An Essay towards a New Theory of Vision, 1709
A Treatise Concerning the Principles of Human Knowledge, Part I, 1710
Three Dialogues between Hylas and Philonous, 1713

Siris, 1744

Biography

Considered one of the three greatest British empiricists behind Locke and Hume, George Berkeley challenged the standard view on distance vision and wrote on metaphysics; his major achievement was the advancement of his theory of "immaterialism." Berkeley was born March 12, 1685, in Kilkenny, Ireland, and grew up in Dysert castle. When he was 11, he attended the Duke of Osmonde's school in Kilkenny, where he was placed in the second class. At 15, he attended Trinity College. The curriculum at Trinity was "notably modern" and young Berkeley was exposed to new science and philosophy that was hostile to widely accepted Aristotelian ideas. He obtained his master's degree from Trinity in 1707 and went on to become a senior fellow 10 years later, also becoming ordained as an Anglican minister.

After publishing *A Treatise Concerning the Principles of Human Knowledge* and *Three Dialogues between Hylas and Philonous* in his mid-20s, he traveled the Continent, spending time in London, France, and Italy. His charm and wit won him many friends, and he became acquainted with Jonathan Swift, Joseph Addison, Sir Richard Steele, and Alexander Pope. Concluding his trip, Berkeley returned to England in the midst of a social crisis; he began to believe that "Europe was in spiritual decay and that the New World offered hope for a new golden age." He traveled to Rhode Island to await funding for a college he hoped to start in Bermuda to teach natives the principles of Christianity, but after several years there he was forced to return to Ireland when Parliament withdrew its support. Berkeley divided his library between Harvard and Yale before sailing for Ireland. He was appointed Bishop of Cloyne in 1734, and published his best-selling book in his lifetime, *Siris*. When his eldest son died, his own failing health began to worsen, and Berkeley retired to Oxford where his youngest surviving son attended school. He died January 4, 1753, while his wife read him a sermon. He was interred at Christ Church.

Against Abstraction

In the introduction to *The Principles of Human Knowledge* Berkeley sets out to discover the principles of "doubtfulness and uncertainty, those absurdities and contradictions" that have crept into philosophy, commencing with abstractionism. He summarizes his argument against abstraction in a two-pronged attack:

> To be plain, I own myself able to abstract in one sense, as when I consider some particular parts or qualities separated from others, with which, though they are united in some object, yet it is possible they may really exist without them. But I deny that I can abstract from one another, or conceive separately, those qualities which it is impossible should exist so separated; or that I can frame a general notion, by abstracting from particulars in the manner aforementioned—which are the two proper acceptations of abstraction.

Here Berkeley concedes that it is possible to "imagine a man with two heads"; in that sense, he can abstract a body part and imagine it existing elsewhere. However, the other two forms of abstraction Berkeley finds inconceivable. First, he contends that it is impossible to abstract singular qualities from concurrent ones; for example, he cannot think of "color" or "motion" without also conceiving of an extension simultaneously. "Color" cannot exist in the mind without some*thing* being colored, having dimension, taking shape. Second, he is able to "consider the hand, the eye, the nose, each by itself abstracted or separated from the rest of the body. But then whatever eye or hand I imagine, it must have some particular shape or colour." In this way, even from countless experiences of hands, he cannot conceive of a general, purely abstracted, notion of "hand." The moment he frames "hand" in his mind, the hand cannot be general but becomes particular, receiving qualities such as size, shape, and color. Consequently, he concludes, "I cannot by any effort of thought conceive of the abstract idea." If, then, there are no purely abstracted general notions of things, Berkeley is poised to give an ontological account less susceptible to the skeptical attacks of his day.

Berkeley's Ontology

Two key components govern Berkeley's ontology—his view of what really exists: the object and the subject. For Berkeley, "*esse* is *percipi*," which is to say that "to be" for an object means "to be perceived." A thing does not exist if a subject is not perceiving it. It follows that objects are dependent on the mind for existence. In other words, if a tree falls in the woods and no one is there to hear it, for Berkeley, there's no tree! In *Principles*, he repeatedly encourages his readers to test his theories in their own minds. He considers objects around him, saying that they cannot have an existence distinct from being perceived. Consider a fire. The heat, the light, and the color are all ideas unified around the idea signified as "fire." Nothing about our experience of fire indicates that there is something else, a thing-ness of fire that exists outside of our experience, because if we cannot perceive it, it does not exist for us. Berkeley determines objects are, therefore, ideas. *Esse* is *percipi*.

Even though objects are ideas, or collections of ideas, Berkeley does not deny the real existence of things. Objects of knowledge are ideas imprinted on the senses. In saying that objects are ideas, Berkeley illuminates the mind-dependent nature of things; however, he does not argue that ideas are dependent on a man's will for existence because "they are not generated from within the mind itself." Berkeley uses the example of an apple. An apple is a collection of ideas that are observed by the senses and are accounted as one distinct thing, which we signify by the name "apple." Although the apple is dependent upon one's mind in order to be perceived, the sensory appreciation of an apple is not voluntary, which means that objects, even under his immaterialist theories, remain objective and real. Thus, ideas are "real things," even if they are not material things.

Without matter, Berkeley sidesteps the "idea of" things; for him, there is only the idea that the mind perceives, no hidden thing-ness that we cannot access through the senses. In fact, Berkeley holds that only an immaterialist account of such objects can avoid skepticism about their existence and nature. Since we cannot conceive of mind-independent objects (for we could not think of that which we cannot think without thinking on it), they must not exist. The troubling pursuit of thing-ness, or of the essence of things inaccessible to us by the senses, utterly dissolves under Berkeley's ontological theory. Only that which is perceptible to the subject is knowable, and only that which is knowable for the subject is perceptible.

The Subject and God

In presenting the second component of his ontology, the spirit, Berkeley commences with an argument he considers self-evident from experience. While objects are ideas, subjects are spirits, which is what is meant by the term "I." He admits that we consider ourselves ignorant of the nature of spirit only because we do not have "an *idea* of it" because it "is neither an idea nor like an idea." Spirits and ideas are so disparate in nature that nothing is common to both natures. Consequently, spirit is the only substance that is not known through perception, as it is the perceiver; its existence consists only in perceiving and thinking. In this way, we can learn of the spirit not through sensory experience of it, but through experience of its effects. He writes:

> A spirit is one simple, undivided, active being: as it perceives ideas, it is called the *understanding*, and as it produces or otherwise operates about them, it is called the *will*. Hence there can be no idea formed of a soul or spirit: for all ideas whatever, being passive and inert, *vide Sect.* 25, they cannot represent unto us, by way of image or likeness, that which acts. A little attention will make it plain to anyone, that to have an idea which shall be like that active principle of motion and change of ideas, is absolutely impossible. Such is the nature of *spirit* or that which acts, that it cannot be of itself perceived, but only by the effects which it produceth.

Although this thinking seems contradictory to his previously asserted *esse* is *percipi* doctrine, the notion of spirit is known to us and signifies a real thing; otherwise, Berkeley suggests we would not be able to "affirm or deny anything of it."

Berkeley's conception of God grounds his philosophy. God is the cause of our objective reality. Obviously, our ideas perceived through the senses must have a cause. However, unlike ideas of imagination, our ideas of sense do not depend upon our will (i.e., a chair will not appear and disappear at our will), so our minds cannot be the cause. In Berkeley's ontology, neither could material objects cause ideas since matter does not exist. Finally, ideas cannot be caused by other ideas since ideas have no will or agency. Therefore, ideas must be caused by some other mind—for Berkeley, that mind is God. He argues that God alone has the scientific consistency and the immense power required to be the mind that causes all ideas of sense. Accordingly, God holds our world in place by continually perceiving it.

Jeff Culver, faculty
Jessica Goeser, researcher
Daren Jonescu, advisor

ALEXANDER POPE, 1688–1744, *A Master of Satire*

> To err is human, to forgive, divine.
> —*An Essay on Criticism*

- English neoclassic poet and essayist, famous for satire
- Suffered from a disease that caused him to grow to only four and a half feet tall; many of his poems are full of malice and targeted at those who mocked him.
- Became very wealthy translating Homer's *Iliad* and *Odyssey*
- Crafted a profound satirical plea for social reform with his most famous work, *The Rape of the Lock*
- Perfected the heroic couplet
- Defended himself and his works while also attacking authors who had criticized him in his mock-epic, *The Dunciad*

Key Works

An Essay on Criticism, 1711
The Rape of the Lock, 1712–14
The Dunciad, 1728
An Essay on Man, 1733–34

Biography

Alexander Pope was born with two inescapable handicaps: his Catholic upbringing and a spinal deformity. His Catholicism meant that he was distrusted by many and barred from most educational opportunities. His disease of tubercle bacillus caused him to have a weakened spine, so he never grew taller than four and a half feet; he could not sit upright without the assistance of a heavy bodice. He was mocked incessantly for both his deformity and his Catholic faith, but "he was always a master of making the best of what he had." Regardless of these handicaps, Pope taught himself to write by copying from published books. By doing so, he learned French, Italian, and Latin. To say he was a prodigy would be an understatement; Pope was a poetic genius. After nine years of study, Pope began writing. His first major piece, *An Essay on Criticism*, was a satire mocking John Dennis, his enemy in a years-long feud. Pope also took on the great challenge of translating the writings of Homer, which took him 12 years. This undertaking made Pope wealthy enough to afford a private estate in London. After living independently for a time, he moved to Chiswick with his parents. There, he secretly used the tunnel that led from his garden to the lawn on the Thames where he met with his friends in the "Scriblerus Club," who amused themselves by parodying and ridiculing bad writers. He was eventually overcome by his poor health and died in 1744. Fans and scholars exhibit amazed gratitude for his unlikely life: "That he lived at all is remarkable; that he became one of the greatest poets in the English language is almost a miracle."

The Satire

Most of Alexander Pope's works are famous for their satirical, dark, and vengeful themes, which served the dual purpose of evoking laughter and provoking enemies. *The Rape of the Lock* is a mock epic of an outrageous inter-family feud and continues to be Pope's most famous work. Ian Mackean, a literary critic of Pope's work, writes about Pope's satirical stance on the frivolous feud by saying, "Throughout the poem Pope continues to make this point through his use of the mock-epic style, which itself takes a trivial incident too seriously, and uses disproportionately grand language to describe an unworthy subject." For example, after the woman's hair is cut in *The Rape of the Lock*, Pope writes, "The meeting points the sacred hair dissever from the fair head, forever and forever! Then flashed the living lightening from her eyes, and screams of horror rend the affrighted skies." By writing that the cutting of a lock of hair has eternal and divine consequences, Pope implicitly emphasizes the absurdity of the woman's vanity.

Pope's other famous satirical piece, *The Dunciad*, is a deliberate work of revenge against his various critics. All the "heroes" of Pope's satirical epic are subjected to his mocking vendetta. For example, a goddess named Dulness summons all authors, booksellers, and critics to participate in heroic games. Pope blatantly names a number of the participating characters after his various enemies, including James Moore Smythe, John Oldmixen, Leonard Welsted, and Richard Blackmore. These characters compete to win favors through bribery, plagiarism, and even sewer-diving.

An Essay on Criticism

Modeled after Horace's criticism and style, the *Essay on Criticism* is primarily addressed to fellow poets and critics. It is meant as both an encouragement and criticism toward writers and their critics. Pope offers constructive criticism primarily using the keywords of neoclassicism criticism: wit, nature, ancients, rules, and genius. He splits his essay into three parts. First, he discusses the compromise of these terms through learning, creativity, and humility. Second, he explores the causes of poor criticism. Finally, he describes good criticism and lauds great critics of the past. Taking a more conciliatory approach toward critics than in his earlier satire, Pope encourages critics to be gentle. He states that his aim in this work is to present "what oft was thought but ne'er so well expressed." Exhibiting a sharpness contrary to the gentleness that he seeks, Pope criticizes the arrogant: "Trust not yourself; but your defects to know." He also reprimands the poet who simply copies the classical works instead of inventing something unique, and he censures the poet who writes solely for the music of the verse, disregarding content and meaning. To soften the sting of his own criticisms, Pope scribes his famous line, "Good nature and good sense must ever join; to err is human, to forgive divine."

An Essay on Man

Pope's *Essay on Man* discusses the problem of justifying the ways of God to man, and Pope proposes that "man must submit to his ordained place in the Universe because 'whatever is, is right.'" He suggests the acceptance of man's lowly position is the solution to reconcile God and man. Man is not the apex of all things, he warns, and he urges men to accept their place in the Great Chain of Being. He begins by unpacking the principle of the Great Chain of Being; this illustration places God as one extreme and the lowliest atom at the other, with man acting as a link in the middle. Instead of realizing and accepting his earthbound nature, man, being overcome with pride, attempts to reach upward when really "the bliss of Man is not to act or think beyond mankind." Illuminating the confusion man experiences by "hanging in between" atoms and the divine, Pope imagines that man swings between the two, which is why he struggles to accept his rightful place.

Critics claim that Pope's didactic poem is overly aggressive, but it fits with his style of parodying the genres, symbols, situations, and rhetorical schemes of other great writers throughout the work. Additionally, Pope appeals to his readers' common sense; in one of the most notable examples of his plain reasoning, Pope describes what life would be like if man had overdeveloped senses. He illustrates how pointless it would be for men to have heightened eyesight since that would only be useful to regard insects, and how painful it would be to have increased hearing, for every roar would be deafening. In this way, Pope justifies man's perfect biology and criticizes man's grasping nature. The purpose of *Essay on Man* is to teach readers to "laugh where we must, be candid where we can; but vindicate the ways of God to man." In addressing some of the most popular anthropological questions, Pope provides several rational justifications for the world as it is, relying on God's infinite wisdom and goodness as the ultimate reason for why this world is the best of all possible worlds.

Legacy

Pope addressed many contemporary issues in the hopes that his provocative satire would spur societal change. He also made a major contribution with his translation of the *Iliad*, though its accuracy is still debated. Pope perfected the heroic couplet by taking the plain form of verse and giving it life. He was greatly admired by Lord Byron and imitated by T.S. Elliot in drafts of *The Waste Land*. Pope is also one of the most quoted authors in history, praised for both his message and his wit. In *An Essay on Man*, he describes man as "created half to rise, and half to fall; Great lord of all things, yet a prey to all," clearly never sacrificing beauty or substance in his work.

Samantha Sherwood, 2015
Lauren Wade, 2015

THE GLORIOUS REVOLUTION, 1688

A mere 37 years after the English Civil War came the final chapter in the Catholic/Protestant power struggle for control of England. In league with English Parliamentarians, William of Orange, the Dutch stead holder, invaded England and overthrew King James II. The decisive battle of the Glorious Revolution was fought in 1690 on the Boyne River in Ireland. William of Orange's army decisively defeated James II and the Catholics, thus initiating Ireland's 200 years of oppression under the English. William's successful invasion of England with a Dutch fleet and army led to his ascending the English throne with his wife Mary (Mary II of England, James's daughter)—ergo William and Mary.

In the Parliamentary Bill of Rights Act of 1689, William and Mary's authority was confirmed, along with a Bill of Rights affirming:

- Limits on the powers of the English monarchy
- The rights of Parliament
- The prohibition of cruel and unusual punishment
- The right to bear arms for defense
- The consent of the people, as represented in Parliament.

These ideas reflected those of the John Locke, and they quickly became popular in England.

This Bill of Rights supports the Magna Carta in further defining the uncodified British Constitution. It is one of the inspirations for the US Bill of Rights.

HENRY FIELDING, 1707–1754, *The Original English Novelist*

> " Reader, I think proper, before we proceed any further together, to acquaint thee that I intend to digress, through this whole history, as often as I see occasion, of which I am myself a better judge than any pitiful critic whatever; and here I must desire all those critics to mind their own business, and not to intermeddle with affairs or works which no ways concern them; for till they produce the authority by which they are constituted judges, I shall not plead to their jurisdiction.
>
> —*The History of Tom Jones, a Foundling*

- Caused great controversy with his satirical plays, inspiring legislation against them
- Is widely considered to be the first great English novelist
- Parodied *Pamela*, another of the early novels of the time
- Wrote in a mock style of Cervantes, with many episodic entries and tangential plot lines ultimately leading to an apparently meaningless conclusion
- Served as London's Chief Magistrate; credited with creating the original London police force

Key Works

An Apology for the Life of Mrs. Shamela Andrews, 1741
Joseph Andrews, 1742
Miscellanies including The Life of Mr. Jonathan Wild the Great, 1743
The History of Tom Jones, a Foundling, 1749

Biography

Henry Fielding was born on April 22, 1707, in Somerset, England. He attended Eton College, where he received a substantive education and made invaluable acquaintances. After graduating from Eton, Fielding began to forge his own place in the world, but following an escapade involving the courtship of a wealthy and distant cousin, he found himself in legal trouble and returned to his studies, this time at the University of Leiden in Holland. This educational endeavor was short lived, however, and due to financial shortcomings, he left the college and took up playwriting. His plays were primarily satirical, often scathing analyses of the corruption of society and politics. In 1734, Fielding married his first wife, Charlotte Cradock. He also continued with his plays, but this soon came to an end, as Sir Robert Walpole passed an act (in response to a particularly biting theatrical piece of Fielding's) mandating that all new plays had to be approved and licensed by the lord chamberlain before production.

His career as a playwright drawing to a close, Fielding tried his hand at journalism, editing and writing a newspaper. In 1744, his wife succumbed to illness and died. In 1745, the Jacobite Revolution swept across the nation, stirring him to write a political pamphlet. During this time of strife, he also helmed a weekly political publication and a similar weekly periodical the following year. He remarried in 1747, to Mary Daniel, the pregnant mother of his child, despite controversy regarding the circumstances of the marriage, and would father four more children. Public opinion of Fielding's marriage to Daniel remained negative, but in spite of this Fielding achieved the position of London's Chief Magistrate. He used this newfound power to revolutionize the justice system and clean up the streets. Fielding's health began deteriorating, and he travelled to Lisbon, Portugal, in 1754. During the journey, he chronicled the voyage, which would be printed as one of his last works. Shortly after his arrival, he died.

Novels

In the early 1740s, he published his novel *An Apology for the Life of Mrs. Shamela Andrews*, a direct mockery of *Pamela*, a popular novel at the time, and its sequel *Joseph Andrews*, a parody that starts as simple wittiness, but evolves into a substantial and revealing look at the human psyche. He then published *Miscellanies*, containing many of his works, including the incredibly successful, *The Life of Mr. Jonathan Wild the Great*, another satirical story, which spins the tale of an infamous criminal and his life. In 1749, he published the wildly popular novel, *Tom Jones*, or *The History of Tom Jones, a Foundling*, which became his most successful work. It details the life of Tom Jones, a boy abandoned at birth and raised by a wealthy landowner. Throughout the course of the novel's self-contained 18 books, smaller story arcs are introduced and characters develop numerous complexities, adding many layers of depth. The plot leans heavily on sexuality and promiscuity, issues that, at the time, made the book a controversial read. Though not the first English novels ever written, Fielding's books were the first to achieve such a level of success and recognition. In many ways, his novels were analogous to Cervantes's *Don Quixote*, a book that Fielding both emulates and mocks. He acknowledges the fact outright on the original title page of *Joseph Andrews*, stating "The History of the Adventures of Joseph Andrews, and his Friend Mr. Abraham Adams. Written in Imitation of the Manner of Cervantes, Author of *Don Quixote*."

Political Career

Fielding's political views could be easily observed in his plays, with his burlesques focusing their sights on imperfections present in society, culture, government, and more. Sir Robert Walpole, the prime minister at the time, took a particular disliking to the biting commentary of Fielding's plays. In fact, many of the plays were directed at Walpole in particular. His attacks from the stage were only the beginning; Fielding began studying law and was admitted to the bar in 1740, thereafter taking a direct role in improving the society he had satirized. While he was no longer able to convey his satire through plays, his writings on politics were prolific. In 1748, he was named the Chief Magistrate of London. From this position, he was able to effectively combat crime and corruption in London. "With his half brother and fellow magistrate Sir John Fielding (son of Edmund Fielding and Anne Rapha), Fielding attempted to establish new standards of honesty and competence on the bench," Moreover, Fielding established the "Bow Street Runners," a group that is often looked to as the first police organization of London. The work of the Fielding brothers led to a dramatic decrease in criminal activity.

Donovan Bassett, 2017

SAMUEL JOHNSON, 1709–1784, *Lexicographer of the English Language*

" I hate mankind, for I think myself one of the best of them, and I know how bad I am.
—from Boswell's *Life of Johnson*

- Compiled the first comprehensive dictionary of the English language and became known as "Dictionary" Johnson
- Was known for his great wit
- Traveled the Highlands and Hebrides with James Boswell, who later wrote a book on their adventures and conversations titled *Life of Samuel Johnson*
- Worked his way up from poverty, becoming quite wealthy after he published his *Dictionary*
- Published a periodical called the *Rambler* that discussed his opinions on morality, literature, society, and politics
- Was a proud man who did not accept charity; he even refused to accept or wear a pair of shoes given to him when he was destitute
- Was immortalized in Boswell's *Life of Samuel Johnson* in 1791, a book often called the best biography in the English language

Key Works

The Rambler, 1750–1752
Dictionary of the English Language, 1755
The History of Rasselas, Prince of Abissinia, 1759
The Idler, 1758–1760

Biography

Samuel Johnson wrote poetry, novels, plays, essays, and articles, but his greatest achievement was his *Dictionary of the English Language*, the first standard dictionary of the English language. He was born in 1709 in Lichfield, England, to a destitute bookseller whose financial state continued to decline throughout Johnson's childhood. When he was a baby, Johnson contracted a tubercular infection, scrofula, which left him deaf in one ear, blind in one eye, and with a face disfigured from scar tissue. Throughout his life, he also combated melancholia, a depressive mental disease that left him on the brink of insanity. After attending the Lichfield Grammar School, he went to Oxford, but had to drop out after a year due to lack of funds. While at Oxford he met and married a wealthy widow, Elizabeth "Tetty" Porter, who was more than 20 years his senior, and together they opened a school. When the school failed in 1737, he moved to London to become a writer. He wrote for the *Gentleman's Magazine* for 10 years. In 1747, he published the *Plan* to his magnum opus, the *Dictionary of the English Language*, which "established the practice of elucidating definition of words by quotations from leading authors." Even though it had taken 40 French academics 40 years to compile their French dictionary, it took Johnson only seven years with six part-time assistants to finish his, and he wrote many other poems and essays during the same time. He wrote very little for the last 20 years of his life, and died in 1784 after a siege of dropsy. He was buried in Westminster Abbey. His *Dictionary* revolutionized the future of definitions, and its successors have become a household staple. Many scholars claim that the biography of his life, written by his friend James Boswell is the greatest biography in the English language.

Dictionary

Johnson is most famous for producing the world's first comprehensive English dictionary, which he published in 1755. He had a high view of language in general, once declaring that language "must have come by inspiration." Inspiration wasn't the source for rhetoric or the beauty of language, but for the fact of language at all. Inspiration was needed to "inform [man] that he may have speech; to inform him that he may have speech; which I think he could no more find out without inspiration, than cows or hogs would think of such a faculty." The *Dictionary of the English Language* included 40,000 words and took him only seven years to compile.. The majority of his definitions include quotations from famous authors using the word being defined, and this dictionary has been the basis for the majority of newer English dictionaries.

Although some scholars believed his work would impede the alteration and growth of the English language, Johnson knew his dictionary could not retard its evolution. The reasons language changes, he asserts in his *Preface* of the dictionary, are because of those in commerce who have "frequent intercourse with strangers to whom they endeavor to accommodate themselves," the new and combined words that scholars frequently invent, the expanding scientific universe that has need for new words to describe new phenomena, colloquial and improperly used words that illiterate writers use and the public loves, translation, and the mixture of two languages that produces a third.

Johnson was often humorous in his definitions. His definition of "oats" for example is, "A grain, which in England is generally given to horses, but in Scotland appears to support the people." His definition of "dull": "Not exhilarating; not delightful; as, *to make dictionaries is* dull *work*." Dull or not, the dictionary made Johnson's reputation and displays the diligence and wit for which he ultimately became famous.

Morality, Fiction, & Biography

Johnson recognized that literature has the power to greatly affect the mind and morality of the reader. In his *Rambler* No. 4 concerning fiction, Johnson warned against the emerging fiction of his day, which "exhibit[ed] life in its true state … and [was] influenced by passions and qualities which are really to be found in conversing with mankind." Fiction was getting too realistic and losing its ability to instruct. Like Plato, Johnson was concerned about the effects of fiction on the minds of youth. Contemporary fiction was dangerous because youth are "easily susceptible of impressions … and consequently open to every false suggestion and partial account." With older fiction, the events and people were so radically different from life that no one would attribute the character's virtues and vices to reality and be tempted to emulate them in his own life. However, with the new, more relatable and realistic fiction, a man could realistically copy the actions of the characters of which he reads. To deter this deterioration of man due to literature, Johnson states that "the best examples only should be exhibited" in fiction.

Johnson thought that readers only really connected to a book if the author could "give [them] an interest in happiness or misery" that they could recognize and relate to by past experience. Shakespeare, he ascertained, did an amazing job with this as his characters "act and speak as the reader thinks that he should himself have spoken or acted on the same occasion." On the other hand, one of the minor defects of *Paradise Lost*, which Johnson otherwise highly praised, is that the characters of Adam and Eve "act and suffer in a state which no other man or woman can ever know." Because of their uniqueness, as well as the familiarity the reader would have with the biblical story of the fall, their actions can "raise no unaccustomed emotion in the mind."

Both because of his moral commitments to fiction and his preference for a personal interest in the protagonist of the story, Johnson especially maintained in his *Rambler* No. 60, that "no species of writing seems more worthy of cultivation than biography, since none can be more delightful or more useful." He claimed that properly written biographies could comfort or advise readers in similar situations. Because of the universality of human nature and the fact that there "is scarce any possibility of good or ill but is common to humankind," biographies instruct people facing any problem. Notably inconsistent for Johnson is that while disparaging immoral characters in fiction for corrupting readers, he was rigidly factual in his biographical writing. But the subjects of biography are often immoral, or have immoral episodes. This makes one wonder just who ought to have biographies written about them.

Happiness & Hope

Samuel Johnson does not immediately strike the average reader as a happy person. In reply to a question about whether or not man is ever happy, Johnson replied with his trademark wit, "never, but when he is drunk." Johnson's most famous poem, "The Vanity of Human Wishes," gives a catalogue of the different traditional avenues to happiness—money, power, religion, patriotism—and how ultimately all end in, well, vanity. The only hope in the world is to trust in the providence of God, and even that doesn't necessarily guarantee one a happy life in the conventional sense. Trusting in God's providence means resting in his decisions, believing that "whate'er he gives, he gives the best" even if that "best" is not easily or immediately observable. God will give the one who trusts in him "love," "patience," and "faith," the "goods for man the laws of Heaven ordain." And with love, patience, and faith "celestial Wisdom calms the mind / And makes the happiness she does not find." Said another way, humans simply cannot find happiness on their own terms and can find happiness only in the virtues given by faith.

Happiness is approached on similar terms in *Rasselas*, a fable in the mold of the *Arabian Nights*, where the hero, though granted every desire, finds that this does not lead to happiness. Rather, he finds: "'I know not,' said the prince, 'what can be the reason that I am more unhappy than any of our friends. … I am unsatisfied with those pleasures which I seem most to court; I live in the crowds of jollity, not so much to enjoy company as to shun myself, and am only loud and merry to conceal my sadness.'" There is more to happiness than the mere fulfillment of desire. Like in "The Vanity of Human Wishes," the path to happiness is to turn one's eyes toward the eternal and away from the ephemeral.

Princess Nekayah, at the end of the story declares: "To me … the choice of life is become less important; I hope hereafter to think only on the choice of eternity." Samuel Joeckel observes that both works at the end "terminate their dreary, pessimistic surveys of the human condition by reorienting readers from considerations of the present to expectations of the future, for hope."

Hope is central to Johnson; in *Rambler* No. 203, he calls hope "the chief blessing of man." Joeckel goes on to spell out the differences between the classical definition of "happiness" and the 18th-century variation of Johnson's world. For Aristotle, happiness was inextricably linked to virtue, and was therefore difficult to achieve but theoretically achievable by all, if only each person persevered in virtue. However, in the 18th century the definition shifted away from the objective meaning of Aristotle and the ancients and took on a more subjective connotation. Joeckel notes, "According to the definition of psychological happiness, any person, regardless of moral character, can quite properly experience happiness as long as he or she can at some moment declare, 'I am experiencing happiness.'" What qualifies as happiness is not meeting some objective moral standard, but personal preference. It becomes clear, then, that Johnson was arguing against the contemporary, subjective meaning of happiness that located happiness in a frame of mind, however fleeting, and wished to revert back to the older objective and virtuous meaning of the term. Ultimately, Johnson wanted to direct his readers to true happiness, which was only to be found in faith in and service to God.

Toby Coffman, faculty
Caroline Fuschino, 2015

LAURENCE STERNE, 1713–1768, *A Clergyman's Mastery of Innuendo*

   "   Digressions, incontestably, are the sunshine;—they are the life, the soul of reading;— take them out of this book for instance,—you might as well take the book along with them.

—*The Life and Opinions of Tristram Shandy, Gentleman*

- Suffered from incurable tuberculosis for all of his life
- Had his body stolen shortly after burial, it ended up in a lecture room at Cambridge
- Worked as a priest throughout his life, and was known for his generosity toward his parish
- Foreshadowed the stream-of-consciousness style, popularized hundreds of years later
- Inspired 20th-century Virginia Woolf, James Joyce, Samuel Beckett and Monty Python (even though it took hundreds of years for his sense of humor to become popular)

Key Works
The Life and Opinions of Tristram Shandy, Gentleman, 1759
A Sentimental Journey, 1768

Biography
Although he was born into a poor Irish military family in 1713, Sterne received an upper class education. He studied at Jesus College, Cambridge and became an ordained priest in 1738. A moderately successful clergyman and a moderately unfaithful husband to the ill and plain Elizabeth Lumley, Sterne didn't begin seriously writing until 1759. In the interest of winning an argument, he

wrote *A Political Romance*, which satirized the clergy system. Surprisingly, his peers didn't appreciate the pointed humor and the book was banned on their recommendation. Sterne responded just as any stubborn artist would and began work on a longer, more satirical, and more sexually scandalous comedy—*The Life and Opinions of Tristram Shandy, Gentleman*. He continued to write comedy despite being plagued with tragedy throughout the next few years: the death of his mother and uncle in addition to the mental breakdown of his wife due to their estrangement. The witty and satirical *Tristram Shandy* was initially published anonymously due to its sexual nature, but was very well received and gained even more popularity when it came to light that a man of the church was the author. Laurence Sterne became a household name; quickly he came into wealth and the company of King George III, among other important figures. As his tuberculosis worsened, he and his family were forced to move to France—inspiring his less shocking *A Sentimental Journey*. Sterne engaged in an open affair with the very much younger and the very much married Eliza Draper until his death in 1768. Days after his burial, the body was stolen and mysteriously ended up in an anatomy lecture in Cambridge. Sterne's writings are cited as ancestor to the stream-of-consciousness writing style and his humor is still popular today—plainly influencing the works of Samuel Beckett, Virginia Woolf, and James Joyce as well as the sharp wit of Monty Python and Benny Hill.

Less Life, More Opinions of *Tristram Shandy*

Sterne's comedy, *Tristram Shandy*, published in nine volumes between 1759 and 1767, was known for its humor, its scandalous content, and its odd style. His unique style and obscene commentary shocked the literary world. However, Sterne avoided major trouble despite the book's obvious sexual overtones; it seemed the clergyman had mastered the art of innuendo and, ergo, had an innocent explanation for every seemingly foul scene or joke. The story very loosely follows the amusing family surrounding Tristram. Over the course of the nine volumes the narrator gives many more opinions about others' lives than he does information about his own. By the end, Shandy has told of his conception, birth, baptism, and accidental circumcision—not necessarily in that order. He even ends the book before he started it, paying no attention to linear progression. The actual plot of *Tristram Shandy* took backseat to style and ideology. The story of Shandy's birth devolves into a tangent about the maid's pockets which leads to a story about another man in town and then, a few chapters down, Shandy lazily finds his way back to the original story—somehow lacing philosophical views on life between subtle literary and political references and ill-placed sexual puns. He seems to recognize that his love of a good digression will result in his inability to keep up with time as it's moving now—he will never catch himself, and therefore the story of his life will never be completed when it takes longer to write than live.

His unique comedic style came as a shock to readers in his time, and fell out of favor before being resurrected in the 20th century. The Romantics and Victorians still admired his work, but held up *A Sentimental Journey* as his primary (certainly more dignified) work. The novel itself, although long and arguably pointless, was well received for its dark and sexual humor.

Clockwork Orange: Shandy Edition

The unconventional time scheme of *Tristram Shandy* is noteworthy. The narrator is supposedly born under a stopped clock. Scholars suggest the clock is linked to order and conventionality, both of which are rejected by the narrator as evidenced by the way he chooses to write his story. Sterne does not tell the story of Tristram's life in chronological order, but rather by pulling at a string of loosely related stories from many different times and from multiple perspectives. The narrator stops often to defend his right to do so: "For in writing what I have set about, I shall confine myself neither to his rules, nor to any man's rules that ever lived." The narrator also points out his inability to keep up with time, as it has taken him a whole year to write only of the first day of his life. This recognition spotlights how pointless it is to write the novel. In fact, the entire book is arguably pointless. Perhaps the best evidence of this is in the last chapter of the last volume where the whole cast gathers to discuss the story of a sterile bull. Mrs. Sterne asks what the story is about and is answered with "'a cock and a bull' says Yorick, 'and one of the best of its kind, I ever heard.'" This is both an example of Sterne's clever use of double meanings and a telling ending to his story. Yorick is obviously referring to the bull's penis and not a chicken, a popular Sternian sexual spin, but a cock and a bull story is also a phrase referring to a long, implausible, and meaningless story. this one, however, is apparently one of the best. Sterne therefore tips his hat to himself as he closes his meandering work.

Trisha Rouleau, 2015

DENIS DIDEROT ◊ 1713–1784, *Encyclopedist Extraordinaire*

> " This is a work that cannot be completed except by a society of men of letters and skilled workmen, each working separately on his own part, but all bound together solely by their zeal for the best interests of the human race and a feeling of mutual good will.
> —clarifying the definition of his Encyclopedia

- Was abandoned by his father for not studying law; he had to write sermons and other works for 10 years to afford living in Paris
- Got arrested and imprisoned for his views against the traditional interpretation of scripture and for challenging the political authority of his day
- Believed that a proper encyclopedia has the power to change the way people think and bring about intellectual revolutions
- Wanted industries and crafts to share their methods of production in order to advance mankind's mechanical knowledge
- Believed that science is capable of benefiting one's life and moral intuitions and wanted scientific advancements to be assimilated into the wider culture
- Challenged the church as an ultimate source of knowledge and argued against any divine authority of rulers
- Befriended many influential enlightenment philosophers, including Rousseau and Voltaire, and was a part of their social circle

Key Works

Pensees Philosophiques, 1746
Lettre Sur Les Aveugles, 1749
Encyclopédie, ou Dictionnaire raisonné des sciences, des arts, et des métiers, 1772
Le neveu de Rameau, 1805
Jacques le fataliste, 1796
Estil bon, Estil méchant, 1834

Biography

Denis Diderot was born in 1713 in Langres, France, the eldest of seven children. He was well educated at a young age by the Jesuits, and was sent to Paris in the winter of 1728 to further pursue his studies. Although his father, a master cutler, assumed that he was entering into law, Diderot received a masters in philosophy in 1732 and began a career as a writer. Enraged by his son's refusal to enter into legal studies, his father disowned him, and Diderot spent the next 10 years doing odd jobs in order to continue living in Paris. During the period between 1734 and 1744, not much is known about his life and pursuits. However, he met and befriended the philosopher Jean-Jacques Rousseau around 1741 and, although it became a source of unhappiness for him, married Anne-Toinette in 1743. Diderot began to build connections with like-minded writers of his time, including Voltaire, and set about making his name known. In 1745, he was approached by a publisher to head a French translation of the English encyclopedia after other translators had withdrawn from the project. Diderot accepted the offer and decided to alter the original intent of the project in order to broaden its scope and present revolutionary political, scientific, and philosophical ideas.

Diderot's works were highly controversial for his time; his *Pensees Philosophiques* (*Philosophical Thoughts*) was burned by order of the Parliament of Paris for its attacks on Christianity, and his *Lettre Sur Les Aveugles* (*Letter on the Blind*) led to his imprisonment due to its challenge against the idea of a providential God and the deist morality of his time. After spending three months in prison at Vincennes, Diderot was released and immediately resumed his editorial work on the encyclopedia. In 1751, the first volume was released. It was immediately opposed and suspended in 1752 based on objections to the rebellious nature of the entries regarding political theory and religion. After being detained and searched for incriminating evidence by the French government, Diderot continued editing additional entries for the encyclopedia and was subsequently involved in further controversies up until all 28 volumes were released in 1772.

After Diderot complete the encyclopedia, Catherine the Great of Russia purchased his library and appointed him the librarian, giving him a source of income for the remainder of his life.

His works testify to the radical changes he experienced in his personal philosophy. He went through a religious crisis at a young age, gradually transitioned from Roman Catholicism to deism, and ultimately ended as an atheistic materialist. Despite the opposition he faced during his time, Diderot had a fiercely self-motivating spirit and a desire to the assimilate science into the culture of his time. He was a much more effective speaker than writer and is better known as a passionate force for change than as a well-reasoned philosopher. He valued the pursuit of knowledge above all else and believed that only through mutual cooperation and uncensored accesses to radical ideas can mankind properly advance. On his deathbed in 1784, his last words were "Le premier pas vers la philosophie, c'est l'incré" (The first step toward philosophy is incredulity).

Encyclopédie

The *Encyclopédie, ou Dictionnaire raisonné des sciences, des arts, et des métiers* (*A Systematic Dictionary of the Sciences, Arts, and Crafts*) was an ode to the power of human rationality. The underlying foundation of the work was a strong belief in the progressive power of human reason unhindered by religious or political influences. In this manner, Diderot did not want it to be simply a reference tool; his goal was to challenge ordinary ways of thinking and advance the idea that science and rational philosophy are essential aspects of society that humankind should seek. The encyclopedia is structured into three main sections: memory (history), reason (philosophy), and imagination (poetry). Under each section are multiple entries from a variety of authors who present a summary and analysis on differing topics.

The encyclopedia was revolutionary because of entries that challenged the belief that the church should be the ultimate source of knowledge, and those that opposed the divine authority of political rulers. Additionally, multiple entries described the arts and trades of the time and presented elaborate illustrations (called plates) of the techniques artisans used. Diderot believed that a thorough and descriptive account of industry and trade allowed the reader to appreciate the complexity of different crafts and to understand the role of an artisan in society as a whole. He believed that the liberal arts had inadvertently discredited the value of studying the mechanical arts, or industry, instead of properly praising and recognizing the value found in craftsmanship. He wanted scholars and academics to leave the comfort of their universities and spend time at artisans' workshops in order to gain practical knowledge and further their understanding of the world in general. Diderot challenged the notion that craftsmen's methods should remain secret, and sought to publicize the different methods used in industries to help all producers advance their understanding of the mechanical world and bring about the "easing of labor, its liberation from routine, and the summons to pride in its enlightenment."

Materialism and the Primacy of Reason

The majority of Diderot's personal views are found in the essays he released before the encyclopedia and in his posthumously published works. In the manuscripts issued after his death, Diderot advances his materialist philosophy and speculates on the origin and development of life without divine intervention. He found life to be profoundly ambiguous and human nature to have paradoxes and contradictions that could be resolved only through reason apart from theological influences. Four works of prose fiction released posthumously contain Diderot's views on the freedom of human sexuality and value found in societal tolerance.

He believed that the only way to make science appealing to the masses was to emphasis its capability to improve the character and moral fiber of the individual. He argued against the notion that there are certain truths too deep for ordinary understanding; only philosophy derived from everyday experiences and genuine intuition allow the common man to unveil the intimate connection between humanity and the natural sciences. Diderot did not want unnecessarily complicated or impenetrable mathematical abstractions to get in the way of understanding the role of science in human nature and the value in enlightened reason. Thus, the encyclopedia does not focus on the divisions between the natural sciences, but rather establishes their continuity and presents a holistic account of human knowledge grounded on reason alone.

Matt Guillod, 2012

IMMANUEL KANT, 1724–1804, *A Copernican Revolution for the Mind*

> " Two things fill the mind with ever-increasing wonder and awe the more often and the more intensely the mind of thought is drawn to them: the starry heavens above me and the moral law within me.
>
> —*Critique of Practical Reason*

- Is often regarded as the most influential thinker of the past 200-plus years; *both* major movements in 20th-century academic philosophy (linguistic analysis and postmodernism) are traceable to Kant's theories
- Was deeply self-disciplined and so devoted to his strict daily routine that his neighbors in Königsberg set their clocks by his afternoon walk
- Was inspired to revolutionize philosophy in response to empiricists devaluing human reason
- Was driven by the problem of reconciling the mechanistic laws of modern physics with the possibility of free will and moral choice
- Thought he had inaugurated a "Copernican Revolution" in epistemology: In the same way that Copernicus reversed men's understanding of the relationship of sun to earth, Kant sought to reverse how we see the relationship of mind to world
- Proposed that the world we perceive—the "phenomenal" world governed by Newtonian laws—is a *product of the mind's own categories of understanding* restructuring sense data received from outside; hence the real external world *in itself* (the "noumenal" world) is permanently beyond reach of human reason
- Believed that philosophy, i.e., pure theoretical reason, falls into illusion when it tries to theorize about the world as it is in itself (beyond our possible experience)—we cannot have knowledge of that realm
- Theoretical reasoning must refocus on critical analysis of the mind's own processes, in order to understand the meaning and limits of our own mental activities (Kant's systematic extension of Hume's philosophy)
- Modern physics gives us knowledge of the world of sense experience; the permanent and inescapable human questions about things lying beyond experience—God, freedom, immortality—cannot be answered by theoretical reason
- *Practical* reason holds the key to saving human dignity from the degradations of mechanistic science
- The classical moral emphasis on virtue as a means to satisfying the desire for happiness has, according to Kant, been contradicted by the truths of physics; desire and happiness are merely our delusional ways of describing our participation in the deterministic cause-effect mechanism of nature
- If we are controlled by nature's laws when we act on desire (self-interest), then moral freedom demands rejecting our interest as a motive, and acting only according to rationally determined duty; we must feel that we have legislated our own actions with practical reason in order to feel free
- We legislate our actions with reason by applying a logical test to each maxim on which we consider acting; the test is called the categorical imperative: "Act only according to that maxim which you can without contradiction will to be a universal law," for example:
  - If you consider telling a lie, ask yourself, "What would happen if all men told lies?"
  - Reasoning tells us lies are only effective if people believe them; if everyone lied, no one would believe anyone anymore, and lying would no longer be effective

- o Hence lying cannot be universalized without contradiction, so we must not do it
        - o Therefore, the rational moral agent (self-legislated, i.e., free) must obey the duty to always tell the truth, *regardless of practical consequences*
- Rational moral agents comprise a "kingdom of ends" in which everyone recognizes everyone else as an end in himself, and not a means to others' purposes; hence, practical liberty is the only just social arrangement

Key Works

Critique of Pure Reason, 1781
Groundwork of the Metaphysic of Morals, 1785
Critique of Practical Reason, 1788
Critique of Judgement, 1790
Religion within the Limits of Reason Alone, 1793

Biography

Immanuel Kant was born into a working class family on April 22, 1724, the fourth of nine children. His parents were saddle makers, and his mother was an eager convert to Pietism, a sect in Protestantism that emphasized feelings and religious faith over doctrines and reason. Kant was the first great modern philosopher to also be a professor; he spent his life at the local university, where he lectured on topics ranging from philosophy to geography and even cosmology. At 31, he published a work on the origin of the universe that contained the initial formulations of the currently accepted view—the nebular hypothesis. Kant produced his greatest works in middle to old age: he started his revolutionary books about knowledge and ethics when he was 57 years old.

Kant was known for his wit, grace, and wisdom. He was also a popular professor: to find a spot at his early-morning lectures, one had to arrive an hour early. He never married, and though he loved solitude, he also loved to converse for hours every day with friends. He lived in Konigsberg, East Prussia (now Kaliningrad, Russia), all of his life, and was so disciplined in his studies that citizens would literally set their watches by him as he walked past their houses. According to the poet Heinrich Heine:

> I do not believe that the great clock of the cathedral there did its daily work more dispassionately and regularly than its compatriot Immanuel Kant. Rising, coffee drinking, writing, reading college lectures, eating, walking, all had their fixed time, and the neighbors knew that it was exactly half past three when Immanuel Kant in his grey coat, with his bamboo cane in his hand, left his house door and went to the Lime tree avenue, which is still called, in memory of him, the Philosopher's Walk.

When Kant gave his last lecture in 1796, he was losing his clarity of mind and was eventually unable to recognize old friends and complete simple sentences. After his death on February 12, 1804, the entire town of Konigsberg, as well as people from all over Germany, attended his funeral.

Kantian Epistemology: A Philosophy of What We "Kant" Know

Kant proposed a new account of metaphysics and epistemology that has had tremendous impact on the shape and development of modern philosophy. At the time, Kant was faced with a growing problem in philosophy. The increasing acceptance and success of scientific discoveries were progressively shaping the world according to deterministic scientific principles. Newton's gravitational laws were considered the pinnacle of scientific advancement during Kant's time, and they demonstrated that the motion of matter is governed entirely by physical laws. Presented with this mechanistic picture of the world, can humans—who are part of the material world—actually have free will? Kant's goal was to reconcile the advancements in scientific knowledge with the highly intuitive belief that we act freely.

He begins by proposing that the world we perceive is not all that exists; there is a categorical difference between what appears to us, called objects of phenomena, and how things exist "in themselves," objects of noumena. Everything in the universe is necessarily interpreted by humans according to our perceptive capabilities, but this does not imply that our perception of the universe is the only method of viewing things or even a correct method of interpretation.

Think of it this way: upon birth, all humans are born with an innate pair of "human tinted" lenses that they look through in order to perceive and understand the world. It is our very nature as humans to perceive the world according to human lenses; they can never come off. These lenses include things such as our perception of three-dimensional space, our conception of time, and our belief in cause and effect. Thus, we know that before we ever perceive something, we will perceive it as in space, in time, and subject to the laws of cause and effect.

Since we are unable to remove the lenses through which we view the universe, we are unable to conceptualize anything outside of our human perception of the world. The world that is presented to us is shaped by the laws and principles that humanity gives it. In this manner, space and time are "inescapable modes of experience for us." However, this does not imply that space and time are distinct from us and are the proper way to look at the world; the mind creates the idea of space and time as a means of understanding the universe according to the lenses we are given at birth. Some creatures perceive in infra-red, some in ultraviolet; human brains are wired to perceive in their own distinctive way. So while things exist in themselves away from human lenses as noumena, it is impossible for us to ever experience them and we can see only the phenomena. In a similar fashion to how Copernicus had changed the way science looked at the universe, Kant believed he had changed how philosophy understood the mind and had achieved his own philosophical "Copernican Revolution." Kant broke the illusionary chains of perceptive knowledge and allowed us to properly view our metaphysical place in the universe through pure reason alone: "All our knowledge begins with the sense, proceeds thence to understanding, and ends with reason, beyond which nothing higher can be discovered."

A Priori Knowledge: How Far Can Reason Take Us?

After proposing that we necessarily interpret the world according to our perception of it, Kant sought out what could be known about the world prior to any perceptual experience. This is called *a priori* knowledge (Latin for "from the earlier") that is accessible before experiencing the world. In other words, these are truths that can be reached through pure reason alone and are "entirely independent of the human mind." Kant proposed that mathematics and rules of logic are a priori forms of knowledge that are accessible from reason alone without any exposure to the world. Having established what he viewed as unassailable bodies of knowledge, Kant asked the next crucial question: What, if any, a priori truths can be established about the foundations of metaphysics and theology?

In the *Critique of Pure Reason*, Kant argues that we can have a foundation only for objects of possible experience, or objects found in the phenomenal world. Since objects like God and the reality of the universe "as they exist in themselves" are part of the noumenal world, they are inaccessible to us, and any speculation on their nature is ungrounded. This has tremendous implications for the limits of human knowledge. Only the aspects of the universe that can be perceptually experienced and fall under the human frame of reference are accessible to us. As the philosopher Bryan Magee explains, "If you try to raise questions about how the cosmos should be characterized quite independently of the limits of any possible experience, or if you try to talk about God and the soul, then your enterprise must collapse and be in principle vacuous."

Moral Philosophy: Should You Lie to a Murderer?

Kant accounts for moral philosophy alongside a mechanistic view of the world by considering humans members of both the phenomenal and noumenal worlds. As phenomenal objects, or in the world of appearances, we operate according to the universal laws, and through observation of our material processes it may be concluded that we are strictly determined. As noumenal objects, we possess a free will that is expressed through moral deliberation; it is in this regard that we are "transcendentally free." Remember that noumenal objects are outside our intellectual grasp, so while our free will is apparent, it is impossible for us to fully explain its existence.

While the moral law establishes our free will (Kant says that "ought implies can"), the exact nature of morality has yet to be determined. Kant begins his ethics with the common moral intuition of a good will. Someone with a good will does not expect any reward for their actions. The good will is always good independent from its effects, and operates according to moral duty alone. Even if negative consequences result from one's actions, as long as one acted with good intentions derived from a genuinely good will, then the consequences do not matter (morally speaking). In Kant's words, "a good will is good not because of what it performs or effects, not by its aptness for the attainment of some proposed end, but simply by virtue of the volition; that is, it is good in itself … its usefulness or fruitfulness can neither add nor take away anything from this value." Thus, the moral worth of an action does not rest in its consequences but in the action itself, insofar as it was aligned with a good will.

For example, imagine a child is drowning in the ocean and I swim out to rescue her on the basis of my duty to be a moral person and help others. Now imagine the same situation, but I swim out to rescue the child because I see that she has wealthy parents and I expect to be rewarded for my actions. In both scenarios the consequence is the same—a child is saved from drowning. Clearly, however, my actions in the first case have significantly more moral worth than the second.

In the same way, the moral law operates irrespective of the consequences of actions; we must be dutiful to the moral law for its own sake and not for any perceived benefit or compensation. Kant formulates this principle with the categorical imperative, an absolute and unconditional requirement that must be obeyed under any and all circumstances. If a potential murderer knocks on your door asking if you've seen his victim, you must not tell a lie. It is called categorical because it applies to us on the condition that we belong to the category of humanity; it is a binding moral requirement on every person. Kant offers at least two different formulations of the categorical imperative: act in such a way that you never treat humanity merely as a means to an end, but always as an end in itself. Additionally, he argues that we should be able to universalize our actions without contradiction.

Jessica Goeser, researcher
Daren Jonescu, advisor

Chapter 5
The Enlightenment and Whispers of Revolution

*The deterioration of every government
begins with decay of the principles
on which it was founded.*

—Montesquieu

T HE ENLIGHTENMENT or "Age of Reason" started around the end of the English Civil War in 1651 with the publication of Thomas Hobbes' *Leviathan*. Hobbes opened the discussion of what government "ought to be," and brilliant minds engaged in the discussion. Far-reaching changes ensued. With new discoveries came questions about ancient and traditional views of the world. People began questioning and challenging old systems of government, scientific thinking, and religion. The driving factor behind challenging these systems was the idea that "human reason and goodness could create a peaceful, prosperous society and perfect people." Basically, people wanted to explore the world, their options, and indulge in new ideas without the preconceptions of tradition. "Reason" was the new buzzword. Philosophers, scholars, and thinkers alike used reason to delve into their new focuses: politics, religion, philosophy, and humanitarian affairs. People challenged established theories and practices in these areas to bring about new governmental forms, scientific theories, and ethics. For instance, the Enlightenment paved the way for the creation of the United States and its unique form of democracy. Notable theorists and philosophers of the era include Rousseau, Voltaire, Montesquieu, Locke, Bentham, Kant, Hume, and Adam Smith, as well as the American founding fathers. These thinkers challenged the way government was run and brought about massive reforms that stretched across the globe; their ideas and practices were not limited to a small area.

Some scholars believe that the Enlightenment concluded in 1789 with the beginning of the French Revolution, while others extend it through the revolutionary and Napoleonic periods to 1815. Regardless of when it ended, the Enlightenment propelled human thinking and creation to new heights in its short period. It revolutionized the world and the way in which humankind interacted with one another and with nature.

HUGO GROTIUS, 1583–1645, *The Father of International Law*

" A man cannot govern a nation if he cannot govern a city; he cannot govern a city if he cannot govern a family; he cannot govern a family unless he can govern himself; and he cannot govern himself unless his passions are subject to reason."

—*On the Law of War and Peace*

- Spoke of "the laws of Nature and Nature's God," which feeds into the first paragraph of The Declaration of Independence; he was the first since Thomas Aquinas to do so
- Escaped prison in a book trunk; was a high-risk, wanted-dead politician; also survived a shipwreck
- Was a prodigy of the Baroque Era
- Authored *On the Law of War and Peace* (his most famous work)
- Was hailed by Lord Byron as "one of the greatest men in Europe," while Voltaire found him "boring"
- Inspired Woodrow Wilson, who used Grotius's ideas to help shape the League of Nations, the precursor of the United Nations
- Wrote in a difficult to read style because of his refusal to separate ethics, politics, and law
- Believed that natural law was above all other laws and was derived rationally

Key Works

Adamus exul (The Exile of Adam), 1601
Christus patiens (The Passion of Christ), 1608
De jure belli ac pacis (On the Law of War and Peace), 1625
De veritate religionis Christianae (On the Truth of the Christian Religion), 1627

Biography

Hugo Grotius, a jurist, a politician, and a writer in Europe during the mid-17th century, was born in the Netherlands in 1583 to a middle-class and well-educated family. Impressively, Grotius, with the guidance of his ambitious mother and father, started to write poetic elegies in Latin at the age of 8, and was a student of Faculty of Letters at University of Leiden at 11, defending his doctoral thesis in 1597. At 15, he traveled to France on an embassy mission with the leading politician Johan van Oldenbarnevelt; while there, he earned his law degree in 1598. When he returned to his home country, Grotius opened his law practice. His clients included Oldvenbarnevelt, the Dutch East India Company, and Prince Maurice, who, impressed by Grotius, hired him as the Attorney General of Holland, Zeeland, and West Friesland. Grotius married Maria van Reigersbergen with whom he had three daughters and four sons. In 1613, he was appointed as the Pensionary (the equivalent to a governor) and in that context found himself on the wrong side of religious disputes, which were settled at the Synod of Dordrecht in 1618. Grotius and his moderate cohorts (followers of Arminius) received life sentences. However, Grotius regularly had trunks of books delivered to him and was smuggled out of prison in one of the trunks. He escaped to Paris where the French government allotted him a small pension. He began his famous work, *De Iure Belli Ac Pacis,* or *The Law of War and Peace.* After finishing this work, he spent a brief time back in the Netherlands, but the government put a high price on his head, so he emigrated to Hamburg, Germany. Eventually, Grotius became Sweden's Ambassador to France in 1634 and helped write the treaty ending the Thirty Years War. Ten years later, Queen Christina ordered him to assume a new position in Stockholm. He left France for Stockholm in March of 1645, but was shipwrecked off the coast of Pomerania. Returning from Sweden to Germany some months later, he again suffered a harsh journey and died of exhaustion on August 28, 1645.

Style

Most readers of Grotius grapple with his bland and complicated prose and his reliance upon classical and biblical allusions. His writing can lose readers not familiar with ancient culture. In his Prolegomena to *On the Law of War and Peace,* he writes, "the testimony of philosophers, historians, poets, finally also orators will be used to prove the existence of this law of nature." He was a conservative writer who sought to take the best knowledge of the past and to make it relevant to the conditions of the modern world. Grotius is also known for his refusal to separate politics, ethics and law. He believed that his principles were a "basis of normativity, [and] not just a portion"; his philosophies governed all of life and so he felt it unnatural to organize his ideas by limiting subjects. Not only does this web of thoughts make him difficult to read, but his penchant for using multiple phrases to express one concept did as well. For example, he had multiple names for natural law and international law.

Theory of Natural Law

Philosophers remember Grotius today as "the father of natural law." He is often mistakenly credited with the creation of secular natural law because in laying the foundation for his natural law theory, he wrote, "what we have been saying would have a degree of validity even if we should concede [*etiamsi daremus*] that which cannot be conceded without the utmost wickedness, that there is no God, or that the affairs of men are of no concern to him." Although he does not break from the divine, Grotius suggests that natural law is not dependent upon the existence of God. The law of nature grounds itself in us. Many of his writings discuss natural law, specifically its locus in human nature. Grotius proposed that the intrinsic rational and social aspects of human nature governed natural law; he wrote in the Prolegomena to *On the Law of War and Peace*, "the mother of right—that is, of natural law—is human nature." Nature has instilled in us a barometer of moral law, and as such our very nature, our rationality, allows us to judge if an action is in conformity to the laws of nature. One scholar explains, "for him, natural law obliges us to perform actions which conduce to our rationality, sociability and need for self-preservation." Partly motivated by the moral double standards of his time, Grotius suggested that natural law created a universal moral demand; all rational, social beings fall under its scope. In the 17th century, many Europeans believed they did not need to treat indigenous people in the Americas and elsewhere with the same moral courtesy because they were not Christians. The idea that natural law is present in all rational beings permeates Grotius's writings because he firmly believed that the indigenous were subject to natural law and should therefore be treated morally. He believed that the rights of human beings lay in their duty to uphold the natural laws.

Political Theory

Grotius's chief contribution to political theory is the commoditization of rights. He explains:

> To every man it is permitted to enslave himself to any one he pleases for private ownership, as is evident both from the Hebraic and from the Roman Law. Why, then, would it there not be as lawful for a People who are at their own disposal to deliver up themselves to some one person, or to several persons, and transfer the right of governing them upon him or them, retaining no vestige of that right for themselves?

The rights, which he defines through his normative theory of natural law, he then commodifies; rights can be traded, just like a possession. From this conception of the possibility of the transference of rights Grotius addresses the idea of sovereignty. He defines sovereignty as the "that power … whose actions are not subject to the legal control of another," because a sovereign is subject to no superior power and has the right to establish executive power. If a sovereign comes to power through legitimate means, then the people have transferred their rights to that head, and the "people," as Grotius explains, when making itself subject to a king, "retains its sovereignty over itself, although this must now be exercised not by the body, but by the head." In this way, the people do not exercise sovereignty by any other means than by entrusting their rights to a government or ruler of some kind. Although not in line with liberal political theories, there is, in Grotius's eyes, no inherent power on the part of the people to re-take sovereignty that was given to another." However, Grotius did state exceptions to this rule. Sovereigns should be subject to three limitations on their power: they must follow natural law, divine law, and international law before they can exercise sovereignty. Grotius provides a unique blend of liberal and non-liberal political theories that propounds the rights of the individual and yet subsumes them into an executive government.

International Law

Grotius is known as the father of modern international law because he was among the first to set up a clear premise for it. He established that international law has two parts: the law of nations and *"isu gentium* proper." The law of nations is a mutual agreement between states to achieve a common advantage while *"isu gentium* proper" is when states make separate enactments that are in agreement. While both of these are universal, they are distinct from natural law in that they have a basis in human will rather than in reason. His largest contribution to international legal thought was his belief that while there is a division between the law of nature and the law of nations, the law of nations is rooted in the law of nature. And although the law of nations is subject to change and is constantly changed, the law of nature remains unchanging. One scholar summarized his theory, writing that "the Grotian tradition views international politics as taking place within an international society in which states are bound not only by rules of prudence or expediency but also by imperatives of morality and law." Thus, Grotius aimed to use his conception of natural law to provide the groundwork for a "normative framework for the newly emerging states system—a framework that accommodated statist tendencies and filled the void created by the collapse of the unity and authority provided by the Church of Rome."

Legacy

Grotius influenced 17th-century Europe through his contributions to European international law, which shaped their international system as we know it. Additionally, he influenced writers such as Byron, Leibniz, Reid, Hutcheson, and Hume, each declaring Grotius as "one of the greatest men in Europe," even if Voltaire did call him "boring." It was even rumored that King Gustav Aldoph slept with one of Grotius's works under his pillow next to his Bible. As a prison escapee, a politician, and a shipwreck survivor, Hugo Grotius may be the most interesting diplomat-jurist-author of his time.

Colman R. McVaney, 2016
Samantha Sherwood, 2015
Lauren Wade, 2015

THOMAS HOBBES, 1588–1679, *Founder of Modern Political Philosophy*

> " During the time men live without a common Power to keep them all in awe, they are in that condition which is called Warre; ... And the life of man, solitary, poore, nasty, brutish, and short.
>
> —*Leviathan*

- Was an Oxford-educated philosopher deeply connected to the English monarchy and aristocracy
- Saw natural phenomena as the result of predictable, scientific, physical, and chemical processes, including the human body and mind, making him a mechanistic materialist
- Viewed man as inherently and unavoidably self-interested (in contrast to Locke), a result of the innate demands of human physiology, while also capable of discerning long-term benefit
- Rejected any notion of metaphysically defined "good" and "evil," positing that the terms merely describe human "desires and aversions"
- Hypothesized that the state of nature is a state of war, in which conflicts between individuals are unavoidable and destruction of life and property rampant
- Theorized that the social "covenant," or an agreement amongst a community to submit to a mutually selected political authority, provides the solution to the insecurities of the state of nature

- Argued that the covenant gives rise to the sovereign, whose political authority is absolute and must be employed for the security of all in the commonwealth, even at the cost of civil liberties
- Posited that the sovereign's government, once established, may not be revoked or altered by the people (again in opposition to Locke)
- Questioned the validity and reliability of Scripture and viewed religion as a political phenomenon rather than a matter of truth

Key Works

Leviathan, 1651

Biography

In the world of modern political philosophy, Thomas Hobbes is a veritable institution. Born in Malmesbury, England and abandoned by his father as a child, Hobbes attended Oxford University at 14 (sent by his uncle). During his five years as an undergraduate, he developed an impressive mastery of logic but was bored by the Aristotelian education offered by his tutors. After leaving Oxford, he became tutor to the son of a prominent aristocrat, a position that provided him access to a large library, opportunities for travel abroad, and the chance to interact with the English nobility, whose patronage reinforced his already conservative, royalist ideology.

After a period of travel in Europe, during which he interacted with the rising anti-Aristotelian thinkers of the day, including Francis Bacon and Galileo Galilei, Hobbes devoted himself to the study of the classics and "natural philosophy," especially geometry, physics, and psychology. The English Civil War and the establishment of the Commonwealth led to a self-imposed exile in France, where he began to publish unorthodox works on the sciences, politics, and religion. Against this backdrop, Hobbes prepared his greatest and most well-known work, *Leviathan*, in which he laid out a rationalist explanation for political organization and monarchical authority. Hobbes returned to England before the end of the Commonwealth, but continued to be embroiled in political controversy due to the ambiguously atheistic leanings of his published works. Charges of atheism continued to plague him until his death at the age of 91.

Thomas Hobbes, Mechanistic Materialist Extraordinaire

Primarily, Hobbes was a materialist, or one who abandons superstitious, spiritual, or mystical interpretations of natural phenomena in favor of physical, chemical, or historical explanations for them. Furthermore, he was a believer in mechanism, the idea that human beings and other living things operate like machines, with disparate parts interacting to determine the motion of the body and the mind. As a result, he believed that human thoughts and behavior could be studied scientifically and broken down into causes and processes to better understand the fundamental rules of human conduct, both individual and social. For his contributions in that vein, Hobbes has been credited as the founder of analytic philosophy and modern "political science."

The Human Machine: The Nature of Man as the Basis for Political Organization

In his magnum opus *Leviathan*, Hobbes eschews traditional, religious explanations for political authority and lays down a scientific, anthropological basis for it. Where much prior political philosophy sought to justify the existence of monarchy by citing Scripture and theories of "divine right," Hobbes sought to develop a rationalist approach to issues of political organization and government by employing the same deductive, mechanistic principles he had adopted in his metaphysical, mathematical, and experimental work. This required a theory of human nature, which Hobbes saw as inherently self-interested. Ruled by the physiological passions of the body in which he is trapped, man, according to Hobbes, is necessarily drawn to seek that which is beneficial for him and to avoid that which is detrimental. This biological fact makes men "essentially individual, nonsocial, competitive, and aggressive," captives to the demands of their physiology and predisposed to move towards the short-term satisfaction of bodily desire, often in contradiction of the efforts by reason or rationality to steer the ship of the body towards long-term benefit.

A Matter of Rational Choice: The Hobbesian Sense of Right and Wrong

As his materialist inclinations would suggest, Hobbes rejected any notion of metaphysically defined "good" and "evil," instead assuming that the terms describe merely human "desires and aversions." Nonetheless, he believed that mankind possessed a "rational part" allowing for the reasoned analysis of desire and the distinction between short-term and long-term benefit. Man is capable of making choices that contradict his immediate impulses, in particular the choice to give up his liberties and submit to political authority for the sake of long-term security.

The materialism of Hobbes's worldview required him to describe morality in terms of rational choice—that is, in terms of benefit and loss. "Right" and "wrong," then, refer in the Hobbesian sense to "rules of conduct ... necessary for human beings to live at peace with one another and to enjoy the benefits of civilization, because if people do not abide by those rules they will fall into a miserable condition of insecurity and violence." Since self-interest may drive an individual to hold others accountable to the rules of morality but not himself, it is necessary to formulate a system of social and political governance "by means of which men can preserve themselves in safety and security within a durable community."

The Hobbesian State of Nature

As John Locke would do 40 years later in the *Second Treatise of Government*, Hobbes in *Leviathan* invites his reader to explore the nature of effective government by imagining man in the hypothetical "state of nature," without government or any meaningful socio-political community. Unlike Locke, however, who presented the state of nature as a state of relative peace in which individuals generally respect one another's lives and property, Hobbes argues that the state of nature is really the "state of war," in which conflicts between individuals are persistent and unavoidable, and destruction of both life and property is rampant. The relative equality of men in the state of nature—in terms of physical strength and mental cunning—means that the fight over limited resources is never able to be settled. This presents tremendous inconveniences to both life and property, for "if any two men desire the same thing, which nevertheless they cannot both enjoy, they become enemies; and ... endeavor to destroy or subdue one another."

These types of conflicts can be avoided, Hobbes argues, by universal adherence to the "laws of nature." While such laws are traditionally posited by many other theorists, including Locke, as having originated in divine commandment, Hobbes instead considers them to be mere "axioms of prudence," to be obeyed by any agent "who is both rational and afraid of death." Among them are the principles against murder, theft, and assault, all of which are acts with potential short-term benefits in the state of nature but substantial long-term costs.

Unfortunately, the laws of nature are hardly observable in the state of nature, where unlimited self-interest and the lack of governmental authority make adherence to any rules of conduct highly dangerous. In the state of nature, "notions of Right and Wrong, Justice and Injustice have … no place," and no individual will rationally adhere to moral rules that can only handicap his ability to defend himself and his property. Universal adherence to the laws of nature can be ensured only, Hobbes argues, by the creation of a socio-political system that incentivizes obedience and punishes transgressions.

The Social Contract as the Grandest of Political Bargains

This system comes in the form of the "social contract," or an agreement among the individuals of a community to submit to the commands of a mutually selected political authority—in essence, a government. The function of the social contract is straightforward. By consenting to the contract—or as Hobbes referred to it, this "covenant,"—an individual gives up his liberty under the "right of nature" in exchange for the protection and provision of a "sovereign." The sovereign may be a representative body or a monarch, but no matter its form, its decrees are absolute, and the individual who consents to its rule must submit or risk punishment.

Like all political agreements, the Hobbesian contract is well thought of as a bargain between self-interested but rational agents. The coercive authority vested in the sovereign is a form of "mutual guarantee," an enforcement mechanism whereby each individual party to the social contract is incentivized to obey its terms—that is, to "forbear from harming one another." Becoming a party to the social contract is, therefore, the only rational choice for individuals who fear for their own security in the long-term; their consent, while at first glance against their self-interest, is really their safest bet against the inconveniences of the state of nature.

The Sovereign

The unison of the people into a single political community, what Hobbes calls the "commonwealth," for the sake of mutual security gives rise to the "sovereign," the collective power responsible for ensuring adherence to the laws of nature by all parties to the contract. For Hobbes, the only viable form for the sovereign to take is that of a single monarch. This monarch is charged with laying down laws for the prosperity and security of the commonwealth, and all members of the political community are subject to his will, which, by virtue of the social covenant, is equivalent to the aggregate will of the "multitude." Unlike Locke, Hobbes argues for the absolute, unchecked, lifelong power for the ruling monarch. This absolute submission required by Hobbes's social contract leaves little room for disobedience to the sovereign.

Cole Baker, 2012
Joshua E Fernalld, 2016
Jackson Howell, 2015
Brandon Martinez, researcher
Ryan Russell, 2015

> " The end of government is the good of mankind; and which is best for mankind, that the people should be always exposed to the boundless will of tyranny, or that the rulers should be sometimes liable to be opposed, when they grow exorbitant in the use of their power, and employ it for the destruction, and not the preservation of the properties of the people?
>
> *—Second Treatise of Government*

- Was educated at Oxford—a philosopher and physician active in English politics
- Published *Two Treatises of Government*, in favor of constitutional, limited government, after the Glorious Revolution of 1689
- Held that all knowledge arises from experience, not innate or "native" knowledge
- Believed in the strict separation of church and state, but not for atheism
- Argued that man organizes into political society in order to avoid the inconveniences and dangers of living in the state of nature
- Formulated a theory of the social contract as the basis of political society
- Believed that the laws of nature, which give each individual an equal measure of liberty, apply universally and are discoverable by reason
- Argued that when government abuses its authority by violating the natural rights of individuals without their consent, the people may alter or remove it, possibly by force
- Is hailed as the "Father of Classical Liberalism" and frequently credited with laying the philosophical foundation for the American Revolution

Key Works

A Letter Concerning Toleration, 1689
An Essay Concerning Human Understanding, 1689
Two Treatises of Government, 1689

Biography

John Locke was an Oxford-educated philosopher and physician whose Enlightenment-era works on human rationality and classical liberalism have become classics in the world of political theory. A talented writer and political strategist, Locke befriended the first Earl of Shaftesbury, and through his friend's influence began delving into the complex politics of 17th-century England. Locke went so far as to participate in a plot against Charles II, whose Catholic sympathies had aroused great opposition among the English gentry. The plot failed and, with his abettor Shaftesbury imprisoned, Locke suffered a brief, self-imposed exile in Holland before returning to England after the Glorious Revolution of 1689. From then until his death in 1704, Locke became active once again in national politics, becoming a member of the Board of Trade responsible for English economic policy. He also published work in philosophy, on Christianity and religion, and on metaphysics, in particular *An Essay Concerning Human Understanding*. His most famous work, the second of his *Two Treatises of Government*, was likely written during his participation in the plot against Charles II, but was published with slight modification as a justification of the English Whig movement after the 1689 revolution.

Locke's Enlightened Epistemology

Before considering his political philosophy, it is necessary to understand Locke's epistemic background, which grew from the Enlightenment's obsession with "Reason" and rationality. To Locke and his fellow Enlightenment "philosophes," the resolution of the fundamental problems plaguing humankind's political life was to be sought through careful, rational analysis and by appeal to the mental faculties, which were often latent but could be cultivated through practice and application.

In his foundational *An Essay Concerning Human Understanding*, Locke lays out a detailed framework for the mental processes necessary to the rigorous pursuit of philosophical truth, which he believed was absolute but not innately known by the individual. He held that all knowledge arises from experience, famously arguing that the mind was a "tabula rasa"—a blank slate prior to experience. Further, his distinction between "primary" and "secondary" qualities has been influential. Primary qualities are properties actually possessed by the objects we perceive—things like mass or solidity. Secondary qualities, however, aren't actually in the object, but are in our minds. For example, Locke holds that objects aren't really colored, nor do they "smell," but instead, those traits are simply in our minds and produced by the object.

Separation of the Church and State

Consistent with his liberal political philosophy, Locke was a staunch supporter of religious toleration. In *A Letter Concerning Toleration*, he argues that "The only business of the Church is the salvation of souls, and it in no way concerns the commonwealth, or any member of it, that this or the other ceremony be made use of." Similarly, he asserts that the state should avoid wading into the thicket of religious doctrine, not only for the sake of the individual caught between the strictures of his government and the demands of his faith, but also for the government itself, which, he says, loses credibility in the earthly realm when it attempts to regulate the affairs of the heavenly.

The State of Nature: The Hypothetical Basis for Locke's Political Philosophy

The primary elements of Locke's political philosophy are to be found in his *Second Treatise of Government*, which begins with a compelling but hypothetical image of human community before the development of civil society and modern political institutions. This supposedly pre-historic lack of government Locke refers to as "the state of nature," wherein individuals adjudicate disputes between themselves and protect their own lives and property via the enforcement of certain universal "laws of nature," which can be discovered by the exercise of the mental faculties. Whereas the Hobbesian state of nature is essentially anarchistic, where individuals enjoy the right to take any action they please, Locke presumes a much more ordered state of nature, where individuals are forbidden by the universal law of nature from harming others or their possessions. He insists that the state of nature is a *state of liberty*, yet *it is not a state of license*," for "being all *equal and independent*, no one ought to harm another in his life, health, liberty, or possessions." Thus, in the Lockean state of nature, man has a natural right—equal to that of all others—to the preservation of his life, liberty, and property. With individuals prone to violate that law, however, those possessions are never entirely secure.

Locke's Social Contract and the Birth of Political Society

The security hazards posed by the state of nature, says Locke, lead humanity to organize itself into civil and political society, to avoid war and mutually protect life, liberty, and property. To limit conflict between individuals, or at least to provide a mechanism for such conflicts to be fairly and conveniently resolved, individuals "quit the state of nature" and consent to be mutually governed by popularly decided laws, whose purpose is "not to abolish or restrain, but *to preserve and enlarge freedom.*" While Locke himself hardly uses the term, political philosophers frequently refer to this type of agreement as the "social contract." The "reparation and restraint" of trespasses against the law of nature become the responsibility of the community as a whole. The social contract can be thought of as a transaction, in which people give up a significant amount of liberty in exchange for the substantial conveniences of fair, consistently enforced safety and security. Without consent, Locke asserts, the compact between the individual and his fellows to be bound by the laws of society cannot be valid.

The Constitutive Power and the Establishment of Government

Locke's social contract does not in itself give rise to modern government. Rather, it organizes individuals into a common society, bound together by mutual consent to the terms of the agreement to leave the state of nature. This society, according to Locke, then promulgates the institutions of government, vesting the powers to make laws into a legislative body—probably a parliament—and the power to enforce the laws into an executive body, such as a prime minister. The civil society formed by the social contract possesses the "constitutive power." That is, the power to institute governments and, should they become tyrannical, tear them down.

The distinction between the institutions of government and the constitutive authority provides normative justification for the revolutionary removal of bad government. According to Locke, since humankind leaves the state of nature and enters into civil society for the sake of preserving life, liberty, and property, "the power of the society, or *legislative* [institutions] constituted by them, can *never be supposed to extend farther, than the common good.*" The only end of a government created by the constitutive power is "to secure every one's property, by providing against those … defects … that made the state of nature so unsafe and uneasy."

Any government action in contradiction of this end, according to Locke, violates the fundamental principles underlying the social contract, and is an abuse of the trust placed in the institutions of government by civil society. Particularly odious abuses of governmental authority include the violation of the "rule of law," which provides for the equality of all members of civil society under the law, and the exercise of arbitrary power in violation of the right of the people to possess and control their lives and property. Any government that does just that places itself in a state of war with the individual whose rights have been offended, for it has broken the trust placed in it by the constitutive power, defeating the ends for which humankind leaves the state of nature and enters civil society in the first place.

The Constitutive Power and the Dissolution of Government

Perhaps Locke's greatest contribution to political philosophy, particularly the classical liberalism of the American revolutionaries, is his notion of the alteration and dissolution of government, which he argues may be carried out by the constitutive power—made up of the members of a civil society—when government becomes tyrannical. Despite the prior formation of a government whose laws are said to regulate all parties to the social contract, Locke argues that "there remains still *in the people a supreme power to remove or alter the legislative [power],*" and by extension the executive, "when they find the [members of the] *legislative* act contrary to the trust reposed in them."

While Locke takes pains to note that his political doctrine is not "revolutionary" in nature—people, he says, revolt only after a "long train of abuses"—he does make clear his belief that sufficiently tyrannical government may be justly toppled by violence: "Using force upon the people without authority, and contrary to the trust put in him that does so, is a state of war with the people … and wherein the safety and preservation of the people consists, the people have a right to remove [government] by force." Nonetheless, this right may be justly exercised only sparingly, strictly against the use of unjust and unlawful *force*" by the government, where no petition for peaceful remedy may be made to the law.

Cole Baker, 2012
Jackson Howell, 2015
Brandon Martinez, researcher
Colman R. McVaney, 2016
Benjamin Rocklin, 2017
Ryan Russell, 2015

MONTESQUIEU, 1689–1755, *Philosopher of Liberty*

    The tyranny of a prince in an oligarchy is not so dangerous to the public welfare as the apathy of a citizen in a democracy.
—*Reflections on the causes of the rise and fall of the Roman Empire*

- Influenced the formation of the US Constitution
- Was known for his wit and sharp satirical criticisms of wealthy French culture
- Spent four years on *The Spirit of Laws* and employed as many as six secretaries to help him organize his research before he felt it was ready for publication
- Proposed that all forms of government function according to a fundamental and animating principle associated with the cultural traditions and heritage of the people
- Boosted wine sales from his family's estate when *The Spirit of Laws* was so highly praised in England
- Defined "Liberty" as a peaceful state of mind away from danger; believed that the government must be separated into different divisions of power in order to protect the citizens
- Proposed that there be checks and balances between the legislative, executive, and judicial branches of the state in order to guard against arbitrary abuses of power

Key Works
Persian Letters, 1721
The Spirit of the Laws, 1748

Biography
Born at his family's estate, La Brède, in 1689, Charles-Louis de Secondat, Baron de La Brède et de Montesquieu (his parents couldn't settle on a name) was the son of a wealthy French family. As an infant, his parents gave him into the care of a poor man's wife in order to teach him to relate to the less fortunate, yet he received an excellent formal education. He earned a law degree from the University of Bordeaux in 1708 and inherited the family estate after the death of his uncle in 1713. In addition to the estate, Montesquieu was given his uncle's office in the Parliament of Bordeaux and was socially and financially secure at 27.

Though anonymously published, he became famous for the satirical *Persian Letters* that took aim at the Roman Catholic Church. Motivated by his success, he sold his office in Bordeaux and embarked on a tour around Europe, spending two years traveling. After his time abroad, he returned to France in 1734 and began work on his magnum opus, *The Spirit of Laws*. The work generated a multitude of reactions after its publication in 1748; it was universally praised in England, rebuked in France, and placed on the Index of Forbidden Books by the Roman Catholic Church in 1751. Eventually, the work was accepted as a masterpiece throughout Europe and America. Montesquieu achieved worldwide fame with the release of *The Spirit of Laws* and felt that he would be unable to produce anything else that matched its quality; it would have an essential influence on the Constitution of the United States.

The Spirit of Laws

While Montesquieu was familiar with all previous schools of thought, he was never a partisan of any one idea. He saw different governmental systems as being appropriate to certain conditions or certain peoples, and did not seek to establish any one best system. He believed that governments are separated in form by their animating principle, and distinguished between three main structures: republics, monarchies, and despotisms. He described the animating principle of a government as a set of "human passions which set it in motion" and which can be corrupted or destroyed unless properly maintained. Montesquieu then illustrates each of the three forms according to their principle, explains the role of education pertaining to each form, and describes how corruption can occur and the preventative measures to be taken against it.

A republic, where the people are the sovereign, is animated by the principle of political virtue and must educate its people to love their country and have "a constant preference of public to private interest." Monarchies, wherein one person governs "by fixed and established laws," are animated by the principle of honor and must educate the people to have a heightened sense of honorable ambitions and self worth. Despotic governments, where "a single person directs everything by his own will and caprice," are founded on the principle of fear and should use education to delude the minds of the citizens and break their spirit of rebellion.

Creating a functioning and continually stable republic or monarchy is difficult; Montesquieu considered them "masterpiece(s) of legislation, rarely produced by hazard, and seldom attained by prudence," that will devolve to despotism if they fall under corruption. In contrast, creating and maintaining a despotic government is not nearly as because it does not require any balance of power and relies only on the despot terrifying the people into submission. Montesquieu argues that to carry out proper political reform, lawmakers must understand the relation between a country's laws and the fundamental principle guiding the country's government.

Liberty and Separation of Power

The second, and arguably the most influential, section of *The Spirit of Laws* details Montesquieu's conception of liberty and the protective measures that must be in place to continually uphold liberty. He defines political liberty as "a tranquility of mind arising from the opinion each person has of his safety. In order to have this liberty, it is requisite the government be so constituted as one man need not be afraid of another." According to this definition, liberty does not give one the right to do as he or she likes and thus slip into relativism. If it did, then people would have the right to harm each other (since they can do whatever they want), and this would destroy individuals' confidence in their own safety. Laws that secure the safety of the people while simultaneously granting each citizen as much freedom as possible uphold liberty. Accordingly, the people must feel the greatest possible confidence that the state will not abuse its power against people who abide by the law.

To ensure the state does not abuse its authority, Montesquieu proposed his landmark theory of the separation of governmental powers. He argues that the state should be separated into legislative, executive, and judicial branches with checks and balances in place to offset any misuse of power. The legislative branch is a collective of representatives who speak on behalf of the people, and it alone has the power to tax, thus preventing executive branch overreach. Additionally, the legislative branch must be separated into two groups, with each having the power to stop the other from enacting laws, thus preventing an unequal balance of power. The executive branch ought to be in the hands of one individual who controls the army and has the power to veto acts proposed by the legislative branch. The judiciary branch is independent of the other two powers and must restrict itself to applying and judging laws on particular cases in a consistent and fixed manner. Its judgments must conform to the law passed by the legislative branch; it is the mouth that pronounces the law but does not enact it.

Influence on America's Constitution

Montesquieu's doctrine of the separation of powers had tremendous impact on the formation of the United States' government. The majority of modern US historians accept the thesis that Montesquieu was the most influential philosopher during the formation of the Federal Constitution; one even asserts that *The Spirit of Laws* was Jefferson's political bible in 1776. In his analysis of US governmental structure, President Woodrow Wilson stated, "The admirable expositions of the *Federalist* read like thoughtful applications of Montesquieu to the political needs and circumstances of America. … Our statesmen of the earlier generations quoted no one so often as Montesquieu, and they quoted him always as a scientific standard in the field of politics." In fact, James Madison, considered the philosopher of the Constitution, frequently quoted Montesquieu's works and wanted the separation of powers in the United States to remain faithful to what was proposed by the "illustrious Montesquieu."

This does not imply that certain aspects of Montesquieu's political philosophy were not contested; by 1806, Jefferson had come to disagree with the idea of an animating principle of political virtue guiding the state and instead argued that the principles of the rights of man were necessary for the foundation of a republic. Despite this disagreement, and others of the same ilk, the founders of the Constitution saw the state's power as a threat to liberty and followed Montesquieu's proposal that a nation must focus on the method and effect of power in order to uphold liberty and protect against arbitrary abuses of the state's authority.

Brian Davis, faculty
Colman R. McVaney, 2016
Benjamin Rocklin, 2017
Tatjana Scherschel, 2015

VOLTAIRE, 1694–1778, *The Apostle of Infidelity to Everything*

> " Those who can make you believe absurdities can make you commit atrocities.
>
> —*Questions sur les miracles*

- Was a French author, playwright, and satirist whose ideas still induce controversy
- Was immensely popular and resolutely persecuted by various audiences
- Published pamphlets criticizing the church under 108 different pen names, but each contained his signature phrase, *"Escrasez l'Infâme!"* which means "Wipe out the infamy!"
- Penned his most famous work, *Candide*, as a scathing satire on the theory of optimism, or the idea that humankind lives in "the best of all possible worlds"
- Considered mankind evil by nature and was a skeptic, yet dedicated many years to helping the condition of peasants in his town of Ferney
- Was buried in secret, against church orders, by friends who smuggled his body out of Paris

Key Works

Candide, 1759

Biography

François Marie Arouet was born in 1694 to a bourgeois family in Paris. Educated at the Jesuit college Louis-le-Grand, Arouet left school at 17. His clever poetry made him a favorite among French aristocrats, but his keen satire was not universally appreciated. Arouet was imprisoned in the Bastille for 11 months in 1717 after writing critically of the French government. During this time, Arouet adopted the pen name "Voltaire." Despite being denied paper, Voltaire spent his imprisonment writing his tragic play *Oedipe* between the lines of his allowed books.

This was not to be Voltaire's last sentence; he was exiled to England from 1726–1729, where he made the acquaintance of authors such as Jonathan Swift, Alexander Pope, John Gay, and George Berkeley. In 1734, he fled Paris again after publishing his subversive *Philosophical Letters*. After this, Voltaire was invited to live in the court of Frederick of Prussia. However, Voltaire's opposition to Frederick's aggressive military practices earned him a treason charge. Unable to return to Paris, Voltaire found sanctuary in Geneva until he clashed with the Swiss authorities over permission to perform his theater pieces. Voltaire finally settled in the French town of Ferney, where he established an estate and became a strong advocate for the poor. He built a number of personal businesses that employed and brought income to the lower class in his town, later renamed Ferney-Voltaire in his honor.

Throughout his life, Voltaire was ardent in his criticism of French government and the Catholic church. Though he considered himself a deist and saw the usefulness of religion as a tool for political power, Voltaire had deep skepticism about the problem of suffering, especially after a 1755 earthquake that destroyed most of Lisbon. His scathing writings on religion made him a lifelong enemy of the clergy. To dodge persecution, Voltaire used an estimated 108 pseudonyms for his critical publications and pamphlets. Scholars can trace his works back to him because each contains his catch-phrase, *"Escrasez l'Infâme!"* or "Wipe out the infamy!" Voltaire's most famous work, *Candide*, is a satirical novel that explores different theories of human nature and criticizes the popular theory of "optimism," or the idea that the world is as perfect as it could possibly be.

Voltaire died in 1778 while visiting Paris, the city of his birth and his most beloved subject of scorn. His ambivalent feelings toward the city were reciprocated, and his death was met with mixed reactions of sorrow and sighs of relief. The philosopher's death is subject to a number of legends; many have claimed he made a deathbed conversion with a priest by his bedside. Others insist that when the priest urged Voltaire to renounce Satan, Voltaire replied, "Now is not the time for making new enemies." Because Parisian clerics refused to allow Voltaire a proper burial, his body was smuggled out of Paris by friends and buried in the abbey at Champagne. In 1791, Voltaire's remains were moved and enshrined in the Pantheon.

A Passionate Opponent of Optimism

Optimism, a popular philosophy at the time, was first introduced by Gottfried Leibniz and endorsed by the philosopher Jean Jacques Rousseau, who argued that the present world is "the best of all possible worlds." According to this theory, even disasters like the Lisbon earthquake that so disturbed Voltaire were considered the best things that might have happened to the human race. Indeed, the earthquake sparked Voltaire's resistance to the theory. He wrote to a friend, "One would have great difficulty in divining how the laws of movement operate such frightful disasters in the best of all possible worlds." Shortly after, Voltaire penned "Poème sur le désastre de Lisbonne," or "Poem on the Lisbon Disaster," which revealed his contempt not only for optimism, but also for a God that would allow such a tragedy. He wrote "What! Would the entire universe have been worse without this hellish abyss, without swallowing up Lisbon? Are you sure that the eternal cause that makes all, knows all, created all, could not plunge us into this wretched world without placing flaming volcanoes beneath our feet? Would you forbid it to show mercy?"

In 1759, Voltaire published *Candide*, the searing satire of optimism that would become his most legendary work. Voltaire's protagonist, Candide, describes optimism as, "a mania for insisting that everything is all right when everything is going wrong." For instance, Candide's teacher Pangloss stubbornly insists that he is glad to have contracted syphilis, saying, "It was a thing unavoidable, a necessary ingredient in the best of worlds; for if Columbus had not in an island of America caught this disease … we should have neither chocolate nor cochineal." The teacher concludes, "Private misfortunes make for the public good, so that the more private misfortunes there are, the more everything is well."

A firm believer in free will, Voltaire emphasizes that the sinfulness of humankind is proof against optimism. In the novel, Candide asks, "Do you believe that men have always slaughtered each other as they do today? Have they always been liars, cheats, traitors, brigands, weak, flighty, cowardly, envious, gluttonous, drunken, grasping, and vicious, bloody, backbiting, debauched, fanatical, hypocritical, and silly?" Voltaire argues that because all men make evil decisions to the detriment of the earth and one another, the belief in optimism and the belief in free will are incompatible. However, *Candide* ends with a practical and literally down-to-earth response to the dissonance of life: we should abandon philosophical speculation altogether and simply "cultivate our garden." Since Voltaire did not believe that ultimate truth could be known with certainty, he suggests that the best way to live is to replace the pursuit of broader metaphysical questions with a humble focus on everyday needs and simple pleasures.

Rejection of Religion

Though Voltaire remained a deist throughout his life, he is well known for his scathing dismissal of the world's major religions. He penned a play in 1741—*Le Fanatisme ou Mahomet le Prophète*—that condemned the founder of Islam as an "imposter," a "false prophet," a "fanatic," and a "hypocrite." He was no kinder to Christianity, calling it "the most ridiculous, the most absurd, and the most bloody religion which has ever infected this world." This loathing of religion was partly a response to the abuses of power Voltaire observed in the clergy of his day, but also to the horrible suffering in the Lisbon earthquake. Voltaire could not reconcile the injustice of such a tragedy with the concept of a just God.

Despite his firm rejection of the church and its leadership, Voltaire recognized that religion could be a valuable political tool in creating social order. In *Epître à l'auteur du livre des Trois imposteurs* he famously wrote, "If God did not exist, it would be necessary to invent him." However, he drew much ire from the clergy by pointing out how often the church had misused its influence over the people. "Those who can make you believe absurdities," he wrote in *Questions sur les miracles*, "can make you commit atrocities."

Joshua E. Fernalld, 2016
Annalisa Galgano, 2013

THE WAR OF SPANISH SUCCESSION, 1701–1714

The turn of the 18th century saw with it the death of the last Habsburg King of Spain, which raised the question of who would succeed him. The dying king named one of the grandsons of Louis XIV (of France) as his heir, but much of the rest of Europe would not accept a coronation that would leave France—already the focal point of continental politics—with even more power than it had before. England, the Dutch Republic, Austria, and fragments within the Holy Roman Empire all banded together to put the son of Austria's Leopold I in command of Spain instead.

The war itself was a complicated mess, whose results were equally complicated. The Spanish empire was divvied up between various powers, the Spanish themselves reduced to their home peninsula and American holdings. Louis XIV's grandson was permitted to rule, but required to renounce any claim to the French throne to keep the two countries from becoming one. He did so, and reigned over Spain as King Philip V.

Notable Battles

The Battle of Blenheim, 1704

The turning point of the Spanish succession, in which France's ally Bavaria was knocked out of the war and the Grand Alliance supporting Leopold I's son was kept intact. Failure here dashed French hopes of a quick victory, and turned the tide in favor of its enemies. Had Louis XIV's forces triumphed here, it would have signaled the start of a new age of French dominion over the continent.

The Battle of Poltava, 1709

As the War of Spanish Succession ravaged the continent proper, another war was held in the north between Russia and Sweden. Peter the Great, Czar of Russia, sought to assert his country's place at the table of political power. By defeating the Swedish decisively at Poltava, he began the death spiral of Swedish control over the north, and the rise of Russia to take its place. Sweden would never fully recover from this blow.

JOHNATHAN EDWARDS ◊ 1703–1758, *The Great Awakener*

> So God communicates to his people of his own happiness. They are partakers of that infinite fountain of joy and blessedness by which he himself is happy. God is infinitely happy in himself, and he gives his people to be happy in him also.
>
> —*Unpublished Sermon*

- Was a Scottish empiricist philosopher, teacher, and Presbyterian pastor
- Became a key figure in the Great Awakening before the Revolutionary War, and perhaps the foremost American theologian of all time
- Was best known for his oft-anthologized sermon "Sinners in the Hands of an Angry God," which was used to propagate belief in the sour Puritanism, and hellfire and damnation emphasized by early American religion
- Provided intellectual validity to the phenomenon of the Great Awakening with his essay *The Religious Affections*
- Inspired the modern missions movement through his book *The Life of David Brainerd*, a biography of a young missionary to Native Americans
- Focused on God's beauty as a central theme of his work, eliding the usual charge of joyless drudgery
- Wrote prolifically: his *Yale Complete Works* series is 26 volumes long, including published works, miscellany, sermons, and Biblical notations

Key Works

"Sinners in the Hands of an Angry God," 1741
The Religious Affections, 1746
The Freedom of the Will, 1754

Biography

Jonathan Edwards, perhaps America's greatest theologian and a key figure in the Great Awakening, was born in 1703 in Connecticut. His father was a tutor and, along with his older sisters, helped prepare Edwards for college. He entered Yale before his 13th birthday and, after graduating, was called into ministry, working in New York City with a brief stint tutoring at Yale, before taking the role of pastor in Northampton, Massachusetts. In Northampton he married Sarah Pierpont, the daughter of a prominent New England family. They went on to have 11 children.

The revival that became the Great Awakening had one of its first big victories in Northampton, when 300 young people were admitted to the church in a six-month period. Edwards became an apologist for the Awakening, defending it in his work *The Religious Affections* from those who found emotion contrary to true faith. Edwards was dismissed from Northampton in 1751 and, clearly hurt by the episode, began to focus his attention on missionary work to the native populations. Edwards accepted a pastorate in Stockbridge, Massachusetts and worked with the local Housatonic Indians until accepting the presidency of Princeton College in 1757. He arrived in New Jersey in January of 1758, and died of complications from a smallpox inoculation in March.

"Sinners in the Hands of an Angry God" Revisited

Edwards sermon, "Sinners in the Hands of an Angry God," is perhaps his best known work, still taught in high schools today. He actually gave the sermon twice, once at his home church in Northampton, and once in Enfield, Connecticut. The sermon is read as a quintessential example of the Puritanical focus on hellfire and brimstone preaching. The degree to which Edwards is so tied to this one sermon is unfortunate, because, as Dane Ortlund argues, "Edwards is famous for scaring people out of hell with divine wrath, but he labored far more to woo people into heaven with divine love." In their book *Theology of Jonathan Edwards*, Michael McClymond and Gerald McDermott show that Edwards dropped these hellfire sermons in his midlife, probably reflecting "a maturing of his convictions about what the sermon is meant to do." Indeed, Edwards himself reflected in his later years that his earlier hellfire sermons had been largely ineffective. Yet this is how history knows the man. It is as if a contemporary scholar and professor's life's work was reduced to an intemperate tweet.

However, it is worth giving some attention to the sermon itself, if only because of its prominence in American literature and culture. In it, Edwards argues that people are at all times in God's hands so that "there is nothing that keeps wicked men at any one moment out of hell, but the mere pleasure of God." God's sovereignty is key for Edwards. He expounds upon the fact that since all humanity is worthy of hell because of its fallen nature and chosen depravity, it is only by God's "power and mere pleasure" that people are not already damned. Edwards goes on to compare human beings to spiders or "some loathsome insect." After establishing humanity's damnable condition apart from grace, Edwards then expatiates upon that grace. He ultimately calls his entire audience to leave their present "miserable condition" and enter upon a "happy state." Edwards believed this doctrine applied to himself as much as to an unrepentant individual in his congregation.

The Beauty of God

In the end, Edwards was more interested in God's beauty and love than his wrath. Edwards wrote in *The Religious Affections*: "God is God, and distinguished from all other beings, and exalted above 'em, chiefly by his divine beauty." Ortlund points out that for Edwards, God's beauty is inextricably linked to his holiness, so that the goal for the Christian is to "understand that supreme loveliness is found only in supreme holiness." This link between God's holiness and his beauty makes Edwards' position in a sermon like "Sinners in the Hand" all the more intelligible. Ortlund sums up Edwards's vision of the Christian life as follows: "By nature, we are sinners in the hands of an angry God. But by grace, we are saints in the hands of a beautiful God. This is the pulsating core of Edwards's vision of the Christian life." He quotes Edwards scholar John Bombaro who claims, "Edwards was not obsessed by the wrath of God but by his beauty." That Edwards's legacy in the popular imagination has been reduced to one sermon is unfortunate. He keyed in to a cyclical tenet of the Christian faith: that as we grow in understanding of our own sinfulness our estimation of God's beauty grows; and, as our estimation of God's beauty grows, we grow in understanding of our own sinfulness.

BENJAMIN FRANKLIN ◊ 1706–1790, *An American Polymath*

> " We are all born ignorant, but one must work hard to remain stupid.

- Was a polymath: author, printer, political theorist, politician, postmaster, scientist, inventor, and diplomat
- Helped establish the US as a Founding Father
- Served as Ambassador to France prior to Thomas Jefferson

Key Works

Poor Richard's Almanack, 1732
Experiments and Observation of Electricity, 1751
Autobiography of Benjamin Franklin, 1771

Biography

Ben was born in 1706 to a soap and candle maker in Boston. He had 27 siblings and was the last boy and the 15th of them all. He went to school until age 10, when his dad took him out to help make candles. At 12 years old, Benjamin got a story published in the *The New England Courant* under the pen name Mrs. Silence Dogood. In 1723 he moved to New York to work on his trade as a printer. He was soon fired, but he made the best of it as he realized he had so much spare time and wrote the pamphlet *"A Dissertation upon Liberty and Necessity, Pleasure and Pain."* Soon he returned to Philadelphia to discover that his childhood sweetheart had married someone else. He worked as a bookkeeper and held other various jobs. He also fathered a child out of wedlock. In 1727 Franklin formed a group called "Junto" that was a self-improvement and social event and opened his own print shop with a partner. After publishing another pamphlet, "The Nature and Necessity of a Paper Currency," he bought the *Pennsylvania Gazette* from one of his old bosses. In 1730 he married and had another child. When his publications started to get noticed in 1732, he was elected Grand Master of the Pennsylvania Masons, Clerk of the State Assembly, and Postmaster of Philadelphia. In 1740 he invented the Franklin stove and joined the Militia. He testified against the Stamp Act, helping lead to its repeal. In 1775 he was elected into the Second Continental Congress as the postmaster, and he mapped out all the postal routes for the colonies. He was also one of the five people to draft the Constitution, and was involved in the making of the Articles of Confederation as well. He became the first Ambassador to France, but before leaving for the post his wife died. While there, he proposed to and was rejected by a 74-year-old widow. Franklin was respected by everyone, including King Louis XVI. After a decade he returned to America and became the ambassador for Pennsylvania at the Constitutional Convention, where the Constitution was created. He also was a participant in Pennsylvania Society for Promoting the Abolition of Slavery.

Inventions

Bifocals, Electricity (explored it), Lightning Rod, Franklin Stove, Mapping the Gulf Stream, Swim Fins, Glass Armonica, Flexible Urinary Catheter, Odometer and "Long Arm"

Franklin's Aphorisms

"Without continual growth and progress, such words as improvement, achievement, and success have no meaning."

"It takes many good deeds to build a good reputation, and only one bad one to lose it."

"Tell me and I forget. Teach me and I remember. Involve me and I learn."

"Well done is better than well said."

"In this world nothing can be said to be certain, except death and taxes."

"Do not fear mistakes. You will know failure. Continue to reach out."

"Money has never made man happy, nor will it, there is nothing in its nature to produce happiness. The more of it one has the more one wants."

"The Constitution only gives people the right to pursue happiness. You have to catch it yourself."

"Honesty is the best policy."

"Time is money."

"Words may show a man's wit but actions his meaning."

"A penny saved is a penny earned."

"Three can keep a secret, if two of them are dead."

"There are three faithful friends—an old wife, an old dog, and ready money."

"As we must account for every idle word, so must we account for every idle silence."

"Genius without education is like silver in the mine."

"There are three things extremely hard: steel, a diamond, and to know one's self."

"I didn't fail the test, I just found 100 ways to do it wrong."

"Hunger is the best pickle."

"Don't throw stones at your neighbors if your own windows are glass."

"Who is wise? He that learns from everyone. Who is powerful? He that governs his passions. Who is rich? He that is content. Who is that? Nobody."

"Half a truth is often a great lie."

"I guess I don't so much mind being old, as I mind being fat and old."

"It is easier to prevent bad habits than to break them."

Where liberty is, there is my country."

"Never take a wife till thou hast a house (and a fire) to put her in."

Colman R. McVaney, 2016

THOMAS REID ◊ 1710–1796, *Founder of the Common Sense School*

> " And, if we have any evidence that the wisdom which formed the plan is in the man, we have the very same evidence, that the power which executed it is in him also.
> —*Essays on the Powers of the Human Mind on the Principles of Common Sense*

- Was a Scottish empiricist philosopher, teacher, and Presbyterian pastor
- Organized the Aberdeen Philosophical Society (called "The Wise Club") at King's College
- Followed Adam Smith as regent at the College of Glasgow
- Founded the Scottish School of Common Sense, a philosophical movement within the broader Scottish Enlightenment
- Influenced philosophical thinking in Great Britain and the United States
- Argued against the skeptical empiricism of Locke and Hume; believed previous thinkers created skepticism by falsely assuming that ideas and images are the mind's *representations* of objects, which naturally leads to doubt about the correctness of the representations

- Believed, by contrast, that common sense preconceptions about perception are valid, e.g., that what we perceive is real, and basically what it seems to be; our "ideas" are not mind-produced representations, but direct apprehensions of properties existing in external objects; hence, no need to doubt their validity
- Denied that psychological motives or influences determine our choices; believed that the very fact that we deliberate and agonize over the best decision establishes, by common sense, that man intuits that he has ultimate power over his own choices and actions, i.e., moral liberty

Key Works

An Inquiry into the Human Mind on the Principles of Common Sense, 1764
Essays on the Intellectual Powers of Man, 1785
Essays on the Active Powers of Man, 1788

Biography

Thomas Reid was born in Kincardineshire, Scotland, to a Presbyterian minister from a family of clergy. Following his family's direction, he studied general arts and divinity, ultimately gaining admittance to the ministry of the Church of Scotland. Reid explored moral questions as he worked first as a presbytery clerk, a librarian, and then minister of New Machar. Responding to Francis Hutcheson's *Inquiry into the Original of Our Ideas of Beauty and Virtue*, Reid published *An Essay on Quantity: Occasioned by Reading a Treatise in which Simple and Compound Ratios are Applied to Virtue and Merit*. When Reid was appointed regent at King's College in 1751, he taught the whole of the arts curriculum except Greek, and began a notable teaching path. At that time he joined others in philosophical inquiry by founding the Aberdeen Philosophical Society, known as the "Wise Club," and published the beginnings of *An Inquiry into the Human Mind, on the Principles of Common Sense* in 1764. His next educational challenge was to follow Adam Smith as the Chair of Moral Philosophy at Glasgow College where he became involved with the university government, the Glasgow College Literary Society, and the General Assembly of the Church of Scotland. Reid continued to detail his own common sense ideas that debated science, politics, and economics. After retiring from teaching in 1780 Reid published *Essays on the Intellectual Powers of Man* and *Essays on the Active Powers of Man*. These works showed the creation of Reid's moral sense in relation to the ideas of other philosophers such as Hutcheson (aesthetics), Lord Kames (divine goodness and human freedom), George Turnbull (providential naturalism), and David Hume (sentiment).

Even after his death in 1796, Reid's influence in France, Germany, Great Britain and the US grew; the 1970s brought about a resurging interest in Reid.

School of Common Sense

Reid's study of David Hume inspired his writing *An Inquiry into the Human Mind on the Principles of Common Sense*, which took issue with Hume's "theory of ideas." Reid, himself following the thoughts of Descartes, Locke, and Berkeley, objected to Hume's theory asserting that when the mind senses something it creates an idea which replaces the object itself. Reid believed that our perceptions are *direct* objects of the mind. He believed that he was extending previous philosophical thinking. "All knowledge and all science," he wrote, "must be built upon principles that are self-evident; and of such principles every man who has a common sense is a competent judge." Reid argued that using common sense will diminish the skeptical ideas that what we know is only known through our own experiences;

he believes that we can observe the outside world and make our own decisions using that information (agent-causal theory of free will).

Reid didn't view philosophy as an end in itself but as a scientific method that considered how human psychology determines outcomes in science and faith, a new approach to philosophy. When Hume read Reid's first manuscript, Hume commented, "I wish that the Parsons would confine themselves to their old occupation of worrying one another, and leave Philosophers to argue with temper, moderation, and good manners." Reid dissented with Locke's doctrine of ideas (Hume's as well) which influenced Reid's view of man's relationship with God. Locke assumed that our perception and experience can produce what we know. Believing this to be too limiting, Reid said that even if we can't *prove* the real world or the work of the mind, both are facts just *because* we perceive them; they need no proof, and they form the basis of all proof. Reid postulated that our moral sense and our conscience emanate from our intuition, and because these characteristics are original qualities of the mind, we can determine our own will. And added to that, we have, according to Reid, "the power of the agent to do well or ill" as a "gift of God."

Colman R. McVaney, 2016
Daren Jonescu, advisor

DAVID HUME, 1711–1776, *The Antagonist Skeptic*

> " Reason is, and ought only to be the slave of the passions.
>
> —*A Treatise of Human Nature*

- Belonged to the school of British empiricists, believing that legitimate human thinking must be rooted in sense-perception; but was a more extreme skeptic about reason and certainty than all other empiricists
- A philosophical prodigy; entered University of Edinburgh at age 11; began writing his greatest work, *A Treatise of Human Nature*, at 16
- Befriended Jean-Jacques Rousseau while staying in France, but when Hume brought his new friend back to England, Rousseau became frightened that Hume was planning a conspiracy against him and fled
- Was eulogized by Adam Smith: "Upon the whole, I have always considered him, both in his life-time, and since his death, as approaching as nearly to the idea of a perfectly wise and virtuous man, as perhaps the nature of human frailty will admit"
- Basis of his skepticism about reason: Cause-effect relations cannot be known with certainty, because…
  - A cause is a particular thing with a particular effect (e.g., this aloe soothes this burned skin)
  - There is no rational certainty that another object similar to the first will cause a similar effect (i.e., nothing about the appearance of another aloe leaf shows us *self-evidently* that it will soothe a burn)
  - Hence, a causal inference (aloe soothes burns) is not a pure rational judgment based on the definitions of ideas, but a mere claim about matters of fact, based on experience

- Experience shows us only the sequential relation that has been observed in the past, but there is no valid reasoning from past events to future events ("X^1 followed Y^1 yesterday" cannot be used to prove with certainty that "X^2 will follow Y^2 tomorrow")
    - Therefore, causal inference is based on *habit* or *custom*, not reason (we have frequently seen aloe soothe burns, so we *assume* each new aloe leaf will have the same effect)
- Our practical beliefs follow the unprovable but natural assumption that the future will resemble the past
- Passion, not logic, moves us to action; hence, morality is governed not by rational argument but by *sentiment* based on *sympathy*; this suggests we have a natural moral sense, analogous to our natural (non-rational) assumption about cause and effect (i.e., that the future will resemble the past)
- Deeply influenced Rousseau and Kant with his profound critique of our faith in reason, the latter of whom said reading Hume awakened him from his "dogmatic slumbers"

Key Works

Treatise of Human Nature, 1739
An Enquiry Concerning Human Understanding, 1748
An Enquiry Concerning the Principles of Morals, 1751
Dialogues Concerning Natural Religion, 1779

Biography

David Hume, a skeptical philosopher and British empiricist, wrote in *A Treatise of Human Nature*, "To hate, to love, to think, to feel, to see; all this is nothing but to perceive." He is considered one of the most influential Western philosophers to date because he rejected the idea that reason controls man and embraced the philosophy that all that we could ever know comes from the experiences that we have had.

Hume was born into a Presbyterian family in Ninewells, Scotland, on May 7, 1711. By the time he was 2, his father had passed away, leaving only his mother to raise him and his two older siblings. At 12, he attended the University of Edinburgh, studying law, but after three years he left the university without a degree. Hume published his first book, *Treatise of Human Nature*, in 1739; he later revised it several times in order to make it more accessible to the populace. In the years 1744 and 1751, Hume applied twice for the chair of moral philosophy at Edinburgh, but he was declined both times. Instead, he pursued work outside traditional academia, becoming a tutor to the Marquis of Annandale. He then worked as an undersecretary of state in London in 1767. In 1769 he moved back to Edinburgh, built a house, and continued to revise his philosophical theories until his death in 1776.

Causation

Some have suggested that David Hume debunked the traditional conception of causation with a game of pool. In his *Treatise* he asks us to consider "the shock of two billiard-balls" as they knock into each other; if asked why ball B shot down the table, we would respond that ball A caused ball B to move. Here, Hume would stop us and question our grasp of causation with the problem of induction. We assume that ball A will move ball B because in our past experience that has been the case; however, just because we've experienced something before does not give us certitude that it will happen again. And that is the problem with induction—experience can never exclude the possibility that we might experience something contrary to our previous experiences. If all we can know comes from experience, then we can never truly know that one thing necessarily causes something else.

Consequently, for Hume, causation is a philosophical relation that does not provide us with certainty, despite being essential to our daily lives. Hume argued that cause and effect are connections, not certainties; they are relations, not logical absolutes. Experience provides us with "constant conjunction," from which our minds have the impression that necessity exists. So while Hume said that we are not reasonably able to make causal inferences about the world, he did allow for causation as a psychological, though not logical, necessity. He concluded, "Thus though causation be a philosophical relation, as implying contiguity, succession, and constant conjunction, yet it is only so far as it is a natural relation, and produces an union among our ideas, that we are able to reason upon it, or draw any inference from it."

Ethics

In Hume's day, two major ethical theories competed to establish how good and evil are discovered: rationalism and sentimentalism. Rationalism proposes that a good person relies on reason to govern his actions while sentimentalism suggests that the feelings of approval or disapproval which an action elicits enable a man to cultivate a moral sense. Hume provided four key arguments against rationalism, using his naturalist epistemology, thus supporting sentimentalism. The two most well-known arguments are briefly summarized as follows.

The argument from motivation avers that reason alone does not motivate an action of the will. Hume wrote, "Utility is only a tendency to a certain end; and were the end totally indifferent to us, we should feel the same indifference towards the means." So reason is "not alone sufficient to produce moral blame or approbation"; reason instructs us and allows us to make use of *sentiment*, the feelings that virtuous or pernicious activity elicits. For example, just knowing the connection between exercise and losing weight will not move you to exercise, unless you want to lose weight. Because reason fails to be the motivator of action, moral judgments must not be rational.

The argument from truth and falsehood contends that since reason deals with truth, and actions cannot be true or false, but rather are good or bad, reason cannot inform moral choices—whereas sentiment can. Hume contended that our moral evaluations stem from sentiment, which means that "virtues and vices are those traits the disinterested contemplation of which produces approval and disapproval, respectively, in whoever contemplates the trait, whether the trait's possessor or another." Sympathy operates in us to produce moral evaluations by allowing us to feel the emotions of pleasure or pain associated with certain actions and then to generalize those feelings to produce a moral approval or disapproval.

It should be noted that sympathy itself is not a feeling but a mechanism by which we can experience the feelings of others. The moral action is a mere sign of the motive, of which we either approve or disapprove. Consequently, Hume propounded this maxim: "That no action can be virtuous, or morally good, unless there be in human nature some motive to produce it, distinct from the sense of its morality." This is readily seen when we consider the isolated act of pushing someone; before making moral evaluations of the act, we would first sympathize with the actors involved, and consider the relationship and contingencies of the situation. Was it an accident? Was it malicious? Was it to prevent a horrible calamity? The sentiments aroused by the actions would direct our evaluation of it. This is an oversimplified example of Hume's ethical theory, but the conclusion remains: virtuous actions are those actions which general observation of our sentiments reveals a "pleasing sentiment of approbation."

Philosophy of Religion

Hume's empirical epistemology (that all knowledge comes through the senses) is foundational to understanding the arguments he presents against religion. Being a skeptic, Hume cannot be considered an atheist or theist; he is merely taking up the mantle of the skeptic and shaking the foundations upon which religious belief exists. In the *Dialogues of Natural Religion*, Section IX, Hume has his characters work through the problems of the first cause argument, centering around the fact that having a first cause is not a logical necessity.

Based on the principle of sufficient reason, he concludes:

> It is conceivable or logically possible that there exists a causal series that came into existence uncreated or has always existed without any further cause or ground for its existence. This is not to say that the world is created or produced by nothing; nor is it to say that the world was produced by itself—as both these claims would be absurd. All that is claimed is that it is conceivable that the world is not created or produced or the effect of anything.

Additionally, Hume dissects the argument of intelligent design in several of his works, including *The Natural History of Religion*. Using the analogy of a house, he concedes that when we look at a house, we immediately and naturally conclude that the house had "an architect or builder"; the argument from design applies the same reasoning to the existence of God, from the order of creation to the existence of a creator. However, he argues that the analogy fails; there is no logical comparison of the universe, which is vast and in which we are but a small part, to a house, which is finite and common to our experience. Once again, for Hume, our ability to know only that which we've gleaned through experience limits, and perhaps prohibits, knowledge of an infinite being. In *A Treatise of Human Nature*, he reveals the vital nature of his skeptical concerns against religion: "Generally speaking, the errors in religion are dangerous; those in philosophy only ridiculous."

Cole Baker, 2012
Jessica Goeser, researcher
Briauna Schultz, 2013
Daren Jonescu, advisor

JEAN-JACQUES ROUSSEAU, 1712–1778, *Champion of Freedom and Equality*

> Man is born free; and everywhere he is in chains. One thinks himself the master of others, and still remains a greater slave than they. How did this change come about? I do not know. What can make it legitimate? That question I think I can answer.
> —*The Social Contract*

- Responded to the ideas of Thomas Hobbes and John Locke in many of his works

- Saw society as the origin of inequality among people due to human interaction causing pride and jealousy
- Explored why people should submit to the chains of government
- Believed laws are for the good of all people, and that laws, not anarchy, provide true freedom
- Suggested that mankind is unable to be "healed" back to its basic state of solitary freedom and natural liberty; instead, society should implement ways to cope with these "vices"
- Thought that the "general will" was what was best for the state as a whole, but the "general will" is not just the sum of the wills of the individual citizens
- Posited that sacrificing one's freedom for the state gives one more freedom and a better life through what the state can provide
- Cautioned that it's very difficult to determine the general will because people want what is selfishly best for themselves, not what is best for the state
- Thought that the goal of education was to cultivate the student's natural abilities and compassion for others
- Influenced the French Revolution, Immanuel Kant, Karl Marx, and John Rawls

Key Works

A Discourse on the Origin of Inequality, 1754
Émile, or On Education, 1762
The Social Contract, 1762
The Confessions, 1782

Biography

A classical opera composer and a widely-known author of philosophy, Jean-Jacques Rousseau was a man characterized by tensions. Born in Geneva, Rousseau fled to France when he was 16, where he remained for 14 years and converted to Catholicism. He then traveled to Paris to become a composer. While in Paris, Rousseau was intrigued by the writings of his new friends, Denis Diderot and Étienne Bonnot de Condillac, who helped develop his interest in philosophy. He published his first major work, *Discourse on the Arts and Sciences*, in 1750. Although it won a competition held by the Academy of Dijon, many scorned it due to its controversial opinions on the effects of the Reformation.

In 1755, his second discourse, *A Discourse on Inequality*, was published. Also widely discussed, it was successful, yet its bold philosophical claims continued to anger many. Rousseau followed this work with *The Social Contract* and *Émile*. Both of these, however, were deemed unacceptable in France because of their claims about religion, and the French authorities forced Rousseau to flee to Switzerland. During exile, Rousseau wrote his autobiography, *Confessions*. This story outlined his entire life. In many cases it was apologetic regarding the events in his life that caused so much controversy. Eventually Rousseau made his way back to France, where he died in 1778. Even in death, Rousseau continues to intrigue modern philosophers and spark debate regarding science, education, and society.

Discourse on Inequality

Contrary to the beliefs of thinkers such as John Locke and Thomas Hobbes, Rousseau believed that "the first humans were not social beings, but entirely solitary." Rousseau posited that humankind was free from negative attitudes in its early years. In the first part of his *Discourse on Inequality*, he describes this near-perfect, solitary state of man. Unlike Thomas Hobbes, who wrote that before society people lived "poor, nasty, brutish and short" lives, Rousseau described solitary humankind as peaceful and free. In the second part of his discourse, he attested to the idea that the origin of human vices came from the original formation of society, that jealousy and hate stemmed from human relationship. The concept of society often involves comparing possessions with one's neighbor. This comparison is what brought about envy and pride. Rousseau introduced the idea of "two kinds of inequality, natural and artificial." Natural inequality pertains to attributes such as strength and intelligence, while artificial or moral inequality comes from ideas of men. The societal vices—jealousy, pride, greed, etc.—are what lead to moral inequality. Due to the material-oriented focus of the vices, those who have more possessions than their neighbors receive higher status.

General Will

In his essays, especially *Social Contract*, Rousseau often discussed the concept of the general will and how it relates to the proper form and role of government. To him, a state functions best and provides the most good for its people when the general will, or the will of the sovereign, guides it. As Nigel Warburton explains, this "sovereign" is an abstract moral concept, not a monarch as modern readers think of it, that represents the wishes of the people, not in a way that individually benefits themselves, but in a way that advances the society. This idea is easiest to understand, says Warburton, "when it is compared to the will of all. It may be that all the individuals who together make up the state … desire a reduction in taxation. … However, if the whole state stands to gain by keeping taxes high, then that is the general will, even though the individuals with their personal interest do not wish to pursue this policy." While people must, by the nature of this system of government, sacrifice their personal freedom for the improvement of the state, Rousseau argued that they will gain more for their investment than otherwise.

A basic flaw in this idealistic scenario, however, is the matter of determining what the general will is; since all people in society naturally want what is individually best, they will rarely act towards the sovereign ideal. Rousseau thought of this problem and it "troubled [him] greatly. 'How', he asks, 'can a blind multitude, which often does not know what it wills because it rarely knows what is good for it, carry out for itself so great and difficult an enterprise as a system of legislation?'" Rousseau solved this problem through the added position of the legislator, a god-like figure whose only purpose would be to produce laws, who can think in terms of the furtherment of the general will. This proposition is almost directly opposed to his other views, specifically, his belief in the natural goodness of mankind, as it would appear that he believed humans needs a guide, one above them in knowledge and power.

Philosophy of Education

Rousseau's *Émile* describes the education—from birth to adulthood—of the pupil Emile. Rousseau believed that humans are good by nature, and this is the basis for his child-centered philosophy of education. He thought the goal of education was to cultivate each child's natural abilities; the teacher protects and cultivates the natural goodness of the child. This differs from a view of education in which the teacher is an authority figure who lectures according to a set curriculum.

Rousseau distinguished two types of self-love: *amour-propre* and *amour de soi*. *Amour de soi* is a natural feeling of love that we have towards ourselves: we almost can't help but be interested in self-preservation and "looking out for Number One." In contrast, *amour-propre* is our self-worth based on comparisons with others. It forms in relationship with others, but can often result in humans basing their self-worth on feeling superior to other people. Rousseau thought that when *amour-propre* becomes corrupt, it results in misery and bad behavior, so an important part of education is trying to keep the student from developing this corrupted self-love. While many human relationships involve domination or subordination, Rousseau wanted the educated child to show compassion for others.

Legacy

Rousseau widely influenced Western philosophy and political thought. His works were important in the French Revolution since they defended the rule of the people and attacked hereditary monarchy. His concept of the general will influenced Immanuel Kant's view that morality is separate from one's individual happiness. He was an important thinker on freedom and human relationships since he articulated a vision of humanity in which all people are happy, fulfilled, and free.

Jack Beebe, 2012
Jeff Culver, faculty
McCarthy Nolan, 2016
Joshua E. Fernalld, 2016

ADAM SMITH, 1723–1790, *Father of Modern Economics*

> " It is not from the benevolence of the butcher, the brewer, or the baker that we expect our dinner, but from their regard to their own self-interest. We address ourselves not to their humanity but to their self-love, and never talk to them of our own necessities, but of their advantages.
>
> —*An Inquiry into the Nature and Causes of the Wealth of Nations*

- Was a Scottish philosopher and a key figure in the Scottish Enlightenment
- Wrote two influential books on the nature of man and the study of why some nations remain rich while others seem destined for poverty
- Explained the behavior of man through self-interest, as well as the role of government in justice and the influence of the "man of system" in *The Theory of Moral Sentiment*
- Delineated the inherent power of "free-markets" and the work of the "invisible hand" within economic systems in *The Wealth of Nations*
- Opposed government intrusion into economics, and saw the power in trading with others who had a comparative advantage in producing items at a lower cost
- Wrote of the advantages in specialization, where an individual or country concentrates its efforts in producing only items it can make very well and uses that comparative advantage in trade

Key Works

The Theory of Moral Sentiments, 1759
An Inquiry into the Nature and Causes of the Wealth of Nations, 1776

Biography

It can be argued that Adam Smith is the most influential man of modern history. His works are still studied and referenced in ongoing debates about economics, politics, and policy. Not much is known about Smith's early life except that his father, who was a judge advocate, died shortly after Smith's birth in 1723. It is rumored that Smith was briefly kidnapped by gypsies in his childhood but was soon rescued. After completing his studies at the University of Glasgow and Oxford, Smith became a professor of rhetoric at the University of Edinburgh, where he formed his theories on natural liberty and economics. After his publication of *The Theory of Moral Sentiments*, he became popular and began to devote most of his lectures to economics and political issues. In 1776, Smith published *An Inquiry into the Nature and Causes of the Wealth of Nations*, which also became an immediate success. Much of his personal life remains a mystery because he requested that all of his personal correspondence be destroyed after his death in 1790.

The "Invisible Hand"

The "Invisible Hand" is a metaphor that Smith used to explain the self-regulated marketplace. Later described as "market equilibrium," the term refers to how markets react between consumer and firms. Consumer demands are met by a firm's ability to charge a price that both can agree upon. If another firm can offer a better item, or an item at a lower cost, consumers will tend toward that firm. There is little room for government to interfere, as private transactions between two parties have no need for government interference. A practical application of the invisible hand is that of supermarket lines for a cashier. If there are two lanes open, people, without direction, will even out the lines, thus allowing for the most efficient, and quickest, way to pay for the goods offered by the firm. The invisible hand, though it cannot be seen or regulated, governs all economic activity. Smith argued that governments that try to control the invisible hand will only harm their own citizenry.

Self-Interest

Smith's best known, most controversial, and most misunderstood principle is the idea of self-interest. Many conflate this idea with selfishness, but Smith distinguishes between selfish and self-interested in the opening of *The Theory of Moral Sentiments*:

> How selfish soever man may be supposed, there are evidently some principles in his nature, which interest him in the fortunes of others, and render their happiness necessary to him, though he derives nothing from it, except the pleasure of seeing it. Of this kind is pity or compassion, the emotion we feel for the misery of others, when we either see it, or are made to conceive it in a very lively manner. That we often derive sorrow from the sorrows of others, is a matter of fact too obvious to require any instances to prove it; for this sentiment, like all the other original passions of human nature, is by no means confined to the virtuous or the humane, though they perhaps may feel it with the most exquisite sensibility. The greatest ruffian, the most hardened violator of the laws of society, is not altogether without it.

Simply stated, a self-interested man usually benefits others. For example, if one looks to make as much money as she can, she would have to offer a product that others desire, thus benefiting society. Self-interest is mutually beneficial, and self-interest (rather than pure selfishness) drives the market. In *Wealth of Nations*, Smith writes, "It is not from the benevolence of the butcher, the brewer, or the baker that we expect our dinner, but from their regard to their own self-interest. We address ourselves not to their humanity but to their self-love, and never talk to them of our own necessities, but of their advantages." Self-interest, working in concert with the invisible hand, provides those goods and services that a society seeks. Self-interest causes people to act, produce, and provide. Society functions because the market coordinates all actions in spontaneous order.

Division of Labor

Maybe the greatest insight of *Wealth of Nations* is Smith's promotion of the division of labor and specialization. He uses a very simple example of labor at a pin factory. He explains that if a pin factory did not use the division of labor by educating workmen or acquiring the proper machinery, it "could scarce, perhaps, with his utmost industry, make one pin in a day, and certainly could not make twenty." The workers cannot specialize in a specific part of the manufacturing in which they are the most skilled in an assembly-line process; instead, they must work on each part of the pin-making process for each pin. Smith summarizes the benefits of the division of labor: "First ... the increase of dexterity in every particular workman; secondly ... the saving of the time which is commonly lost in passing from one species of work to another; and lastly ... the invention of a great number of machines which facilitate and abridge labour, and enable one man to do the work of many." Thus, everyone works more efficiently and productively.

The specialization and division of labor are not only beneficial for single factories or nations but also for international trade. In *Wealth of Nations*, Smith writes, "If a foreign country can supply us with a commodity cheaper than we ourselves can make it, better buy it of them with some part of the produce of our own industry, employed in a way in which we have some advantage."

The Role of Government

Smith addresses the role of government in both *The Theory of Moral Sentiments* and *Wealth of Nations*. In *The Theory of Moral Sentiments*, Smith wrote that governments must establish only those rules that protect citizens from foreign aggression. Most famously, Smith advocated for governments to protect the natural rights of every citizen to life, liberty, and property. He also believed that the government should produce money, facilitate commerce, provide youth education, and maintain infrastructure. A proponent of limited government, Smith warned against "the man of the system," or a despot who made unilateral decisions.

Kurt Gutschick, faculty

WILLIAM BLACKSTONE, 1723–1780, *Father of English Common Law*

" The law, which restrains a man from doing mischief to his fellow citizens, though it diminishes the natural, increases the civil liberty of mankind.

—*Commentaries on the Laws of England*

- Is credited with taking a large step to formalizing common law, although his work was often critiqued for its wide generalizations on political terminology
- Publicized his works before their publication by giving multiple lectures
- Was known for succinct and concise speeches which he formalized in writing

Key Works

An Analysis of the Laws of England, 1756
A Discourse on the Study of the Law, 1758
Commentaries on the Laws of England, 1765–1769

Biography

William Blackstone was instrumental in the formation of concise, common law. Born in Cheapside, London, he received his Bachelor of Civil Law degree from Oxford University before working as a barrister, a type of English lawyer, for seven years. He became involved in Oxford's administration and financial management before leaving his barrister career to focus on teaching and lecturing on English law. His lectures were renowned for their exposition of English law in plain language suitable for the common person, and he eventually compiled and published them in four volumes, entitled *Commentaries on the Laws of England*. The tremendous success of the work across England and its colonies made Blackstone wealthy and popular, and with his growing influence he became a member of Parliament, eventually joining the Court of the King's Bench, where he remained until his death in 1780.

Commentaries on the Laws of England

Commentaries on the Laws of England, Blackstone's magnum opus, provided the first condensed and reliable statement of English law available to, and readable by, the general public. The commentary's four volumes were designed for both law students and laymen alike. The work was instrumental in the development of common-law judicial systems in England and throughout the world, including the United States, and for many decades was required reading for first-year law students in English-speaking countries. The *Commentaries'* popularity and reliability made it usable by courts across the world as an accurate statement of fundamental legal principles, and it continues to be cited by the US Supreme Court about a dozen times a year. Blackstone's most famous contribution, that it is "better that ten guilty persons escape, than that one innocent party suffer," has entered the public consciousness in America and Europe since his first utterance of it in the 1760s, and while scholars continue to debate the concept, it—along with countless other Blackstonian principles—continues to be studied by legal students to this day.

Joshua E. Fernalld, 2016
Jackson Howell, 2015
Brandon Martinez, researcher

EDMUND BURKE ◊ 1729–1797, *Sympathy for the American Revolution*

" The only thing necessary for the triumph of evil is for good men to do nothing.

- Was a free-thinker, a 16th-century liberal
- Entered college when he was 15
- Served for a long time as a Member of Parliament
- Sympathized with the American colonists embarking on revolution, but opposed the French Revolution
- Founded modern conservatism
- Represented classical liberalism

Key Works

"American Taxation"

"Conciliation with America"
"Reflections on the Revolution in France"
"Second Speech on Conciliation"
"Speech on Declaratory Resolutions"
"Thoughts on the Cause of the Present Discontents"
"Tracts relating to Popery Laws"

Biography

Edmund Burke as born in 1729 in Dublin to an Irish family. At 15 he attended Trinity College there and, after graduating, published his major works, *Vindication of Natural Society* and *A Philosophical Inquiry into the Origin of Our Ideas of the Sublime and Beautiful*, in 1756 and 1757 respectively. Also in 1757, he married Jane Nugent. In 1765 his political career began when he landed the job of secretary to a Whig leader in Parliament. In 1770 he published the pamphlet *Thoughts on the Cause of the Present Discontents*, which was controversial for opposing King Henry III and taking the side of the American Colonists.

Work

What set Burke apart from everyone else was that he truly supported the American Revolution; for a member of parliament this was highly unusual. He believed that the British government was being unwise and inconsistent: "claims of circumstance, utility, and moral principle should be considered, as well as precedent." In other words, he was saying that the British were being too hard-headed with their legalism, and that they should listen and understand the American point of view. He gave two speeches on it: *On American Taxation* (1774) and *On Moving His Resolutions for Conciliation With America* (1775). However, the British imperial policy continued to ignore him.

Colman R. McVaney, 2016

GEORGE WASHINGTON ◊ 1732–1799, *The Father of America*

> " But lest some unlucky event should happen unfavorable to my reputation, I beg it may be remembered by every gentleman in the room that I this day declare with the utmost sincerity, I do not think myself equal to the command I am honored with.
>
> —Upon accepting his role as Commander in Chief, 1775

- Served as the first president of the United States of America (1789–1797, two terms)
- Was a wealthy planter who owned tobacco plantations and slaves
- Worked as a surveyor and soldier
- Served as a senior officer in the colonial forces during the French and Indian War
- Was the Commander-in-Chief of the Continental Army
- Presided over the Constitutional Convention
- Freed all his slaves by his final will
- Was bled to death due to his doctors' desperate and antiquated treatments in 1799
- Denied he was the king or the dictator of America and, as a result, engendered the respect of the people as a great and humble leader

Biography

George Washington was born in Pope's Creek in Westmoreland, Virginia, the eldest child of Augustine Washington and Mary Bell. Only 11 when his father died, young George became the responsibility of his half-brother. Washington was home schooled, and studied with the local church to become very well educated. He became a surveyor in Virginia's Western Territories and inherited a great amount of land when his half-brother died. In addition, he was given the role of adjutant of the colony, making him the major general in charge of training the militia in the area. Then, as a senior Army officer, he led the colonies in the early stages of the French and Indian War.

Washington married Martha Dandridge Custis and began life at his estate, Mt. Vernon. From the House of Burgesses, he led Virginia in their denial of British colonial power. A delegate to the Continental Congress, Washington moved from statesman to commander.

Washington took command of a pathetic militia of poorly unorganized and insubordinate men. Nevertheless, he was able to take back Boston from the British and then overcome them in New Jersey. After a defeat in Philadelphia, Washington wintered his troops at Valley Forge. The years 1777–1778 have been described as a period of "want and misery." Yet Washington turned it all around when Congress increased his powers and bolstered his military training and morale-building efforts. Washington's forces finally met General Cornwallis and the French military on Oct. 19, 1781.

Subsequently, Washington helped reorganize what he felt was a weak government. He presided over the Constitutional Convention and lobbied for acceptance of the Constitution. He was unanimously chosen the first President. He worked for one-party unity but failed when two parties emerged. Re-elected in 1793, Washington fought battles with his own government. Trouble with the Whiskey Rebellion, the Native Americans, British, and Spanish challenged him and played a part in his refusal to serve a third term. His "Farewell Address" warned against "permanent alliances" with foreign powers. He died in 1799.

Joshua E. Fernalld, 2016

JOHN ADAMS ◊ 1735–1826, *An American Noble Man*

> " I must study politics and war that my sons may have liberty to study mathematics and philosophy.
>
> —In a letter to his wife, 1780

- Served as the second President of the United States and was the first President to occupy the White House
- Fathered John Quincy Adams, the sixth president
- Practiced law and defended the British soldiers after the Boston Massacre
- Promoted a republic (not democratic) form of government
- Promoted strong central government (anti-Republican)
- Opposed slavery
- Played a leading role in creating the Declaration of Independence
- Helped negotiate the Treaty of Paris with Thomas Jefferson and Benjamin Franklin

- Traveled to Europe to help other countries negotiate commerce treaties
- Drafted the Massachusetts Constitution in 1780
- Died on July 4, 1826, the 50th anniversary of the signing of the Declaration of Independence, the same day that Thomas Jefferson died

Key Works

Dissertation on the Canon and Feudal Law
Defense of the Constitutions of Government of the United States of America

Biography

John Adams was born in 1735 in Quincy, Massachusetts. He studied at Harvard and earned his undergraduate and master's degrees. He considered entering ministry until he faced the bitterness of the Great Awakening, so he decided to become a lawyer instead. He began his political life with writing anti-Stamp Act resolutions and defending John Hancock against smuggling charges. In 1770 he represented the officer in charge of British troops in the Boston Massacre, where he defended them wholeheartedly because of his commitment to each person's right to a fair trial. The immediate reaction to this was critical, but later his actions gained him respect and the reputation of a fair and just man who could represent Massachusetts in their legislature. In 1773 Adams supported the Boston Tea Party and went on to serve as Massachusetts' delegate to the First Continental Congress.

After the first battles of the Revolutionary War, Adams was encouraged in his hopes for American independence when the General Court directed him to establish American liberties that we would not allow Britain to erode. A year later, when Congress created the first army, Adams named George Washington the Commander-in-Chief. In 1776 Congress approved his proposal of states having their own governments. Later that year he helped create the Declaration of Independence. Within months Adams was serving on around 90 committees, the most of any other congressman. His first foray into diplomacy was, after securing recognition by European governors, to borrow money from the Dutch.

Diplomatic Career

In 1779, Adams was one of the American diplomats sent to Paris to negotiate a treaty to end the Revolutionary War and craft a commercial treaty with Great Britain. He and two other American diplomats ignored the warning from Comte de Vergennes (the French foreign minister) to consult him before any agreement with Great Britain, and they finalized the peace settlement. After that, Adams stayed in Europe from 1784 to 1785 to help arrange treaties of commerce with many European nations. In 1785 he became the original US minister to the United Kingdom. By 1788, Adams had accomplished peace terms and secured Dutch loans, but he never came to terms with the British on some diplomatic issues that had resulted from the war. He returned home to America after a decade in Europe.

The Presidency

When George Washington became President, Adams was elected Vice President for the eight years. He disliked and grew frustrated with the position because he had little sway with the President or politics in general. In 1796, he won the Presidential election, defeating Thomas Jefferson, the Federalist candidate, who became Vice President.

Adams was caught in the middle of his own Cabinet as the war between the French revolutionaries and the counterrevolutionaries of several European nations raged. The United States wanted to take a neutral position, especially in the war between England and France. However, the parties were divided in their loyalties—the Jeffersonians sympathetic with France and the Federalists with England. Although Adams prepared for war, he worked toward a peace with France that would stem the strong conflicts within the United States. These actions caused the break between Adams and the Hamiltonian wing of the Federalist Party. While the peace has been described as both "enlightened statesmanship and good politics," Adams's position was weakened, and he lost his reelection to Thomas Jefferson.

Despite his disappointment that the American people failed to support him, Adams continued to be involved in public affairs. He was proud of his son John Quincy Adams and continued thoughtful correspondence with his friends and associates. He died in 1826 at 91, just a few hours after Thomas Jefferson died.

Colman R. McVaney, 2016

THOMAS PAINE ◊ 1737–1809, *American Political Theorist*

" I love the man that can smile in trouble, that can gather strength from distress, and grow brave by reflection. 'Tis the business of little minds to shrink, but he whose heart is firm, and whose conscience approves his conduct, will pursue his principles unto death.
—*The American Crisis*

- Immigrated to America in 1774, just before the Revolution
- Authored *Common Sense* and the *Rights of Men*
- Involved in the French Revolution, 1789–1799
- Attacked Edmund Burke, resulting in his trial and conviction *in absentia* in 1792
- Was elected to the French National Convention, despite his inability to speak French
- Was arrested and imprisoned in Paris during 1793–1794
- Proposed a guaranteed minimum wage and was arguably the first Socialist
- Was shunned by George Washington
- Returned to America in 1802, where he was ostracized for his ridicule of Christianity

Key Works

Common Sense, 1776
American Crisis, 1776
Public Good, 1780
The Crisis, 1776–83
Rights of Men, 1791
The Age of Reason, 1794
Letter to George Washington, 1796

Biography

Thomas Paine was born in 1737 in Thetford, England. Paine dropped out of school by age 12 to help his father. Unhappy in all of his jobs at age 19, Paine was searching for purpose. He sailed the seas and finally ended up as a tax officer in England where he managed to get discharged twice in four years. At the same time he was complaining about low wages, Paine met Benjamin Franklin, who helped him immigrate to Philadelphia. Paine soon became a journalist, beginning with a criticism of slavery and the slave trade. *Common Sense*, a 79-page pamphlet demanding the independence of the colonies, drew attention to his passion as well as his extraordinary writing skill. *Common Sense* was reprinted in the newspapers of other colonies, translated into German, and reprinted in England, Scotland, Holland, and France. George Washington called the direction of the piece a "powerful change" as Paine focused blame on George III and monarchies in general. Joining the Continental Army, Paine was not a good soldier. On the other hand, his army experiences prompted his writing of *The Crisis* papers where his personal discouragement resonated with his countrymen: "These are the times that try men's souls. The summer soldier and the sunshine patriot will … shrink from the service of his country; but he that stands it now, deserves the love and thanks of man and woman." In 1793, after two years of serving on Congress's Committee on Foreign Affairs, Paine wrote his final tract of *The Crisis* series. He concluded his "trying men's souls" with this hopeful thought: "'The times that tried men's souls' are over—and the greatest and completest revolution the world ever knew, gloriously and happily accomplished."

On a trip to Europe, Paine met Edmund Burke. Although the two were friendly at first, Paine was incensed with Burke's public renouncement of the French Revolution and support of the monarchy. In his rebuttal, The *Rights of Man*, Paine championed republican views and urged the English to overthrow the king. While the pamphlet became popular, the English government sought to arrest Paine. He fled to France and assisted in the writing of a new French Constitution. The French radicals of the time disliked Paine's unwillingness to support the execution of Louis XVI, so he was imprisoned for 11 months. Paine wrote an angry Letter to George Washington when Washington didn't see to his immediate release.

In 1794, Paine took up a new subject, a defense of deism. He believed in the Creator but renounced "revealed religion." England's criticism that the book was atheistic didn't quell the circulation of what has been called a clear description of the "rationalist theism of the Enlightenment." America didn't embrace Paine when he returned in 1802 either. Friends shut him out for criticizing Washington and traditional Christianity. He was buried on his farm in 1809.

Looking back on Paine's amazing impact, we recognize Paine's commitment to take away the chains of "tyrannical and false systems." He fought for peace and justice with every pen stroke.

Joshua E. Fernalld, 2016

THOMAS JEFFERSON ◊ 1743–1826, *The Author of The Declaration*

> " … that all men are created equal …
>
> —*The Declaration of Independence*

- Was elected third President of the United States, serving from 1801–1809

- Owned slaves and spoke against slavery
- Died bankrupt
- Was principal author of the *Declaration of Independence* where he boldly wrote "… that all men are created equal"
- Initiated the Louisiana Purchase
- Designed and built Monticello
- Founded the University of Virginia
- Negotiated the peace treaty that ended the Revolutionary War; joined Benjamin Franklin and John Adams in France for this effort in 1783
- Became estranged from John Adams over the issue of Federal powers but reconciled with him late in life
- Died on July 4, 1826, the 50th anniversary of the signing of the *Declaration of Independence*, the same day that John Adams died

Key Works

A Summary View of the Rights of British America, 1774
Declaration of Independence, 1776
Statute of Virginia for Religious Freedom, 1779
Notes on the State of Virginia, 1781

Biography

Thomas Jefferson was born on April 13, 1743, at Shadwell plantation outside of Charlottesville, Virginia. The third of ten siblings, he was born into a well-to-do family. As a young man, he loved playing in the woods, practicing the violin, and reading. Jefferson began his education at age 9 by studying Latin and Greek at a local private school. At 15 he decided to take on other classical languages, literature, and math. He then studied at the College of William and Mary to become one of the most educated lawyers of the Virginia bar. Jefferson wanted to use the law to shape society. Furthermore, he believed in the value of education, particularly to elevate all people, including laborers and farmers, and in the importance of all people being given the opportunity to govern themselves.

In college, Jefferson had eclectic interests in languages, mathematics, and natural sciences and encountered the philosophy of William Small who introduced him to the ideas of the Enlightenment. Small reinforced a belief that man's reason could solve every problem.

After joining the Virginia House of Burgesses in 1768, Jefferson spoke against Britain's control over the colonies. Although his position was considered a little extreme, Jefferson's writing impressed his readers. Subsequently, as a member of the Second Continental Congress, he was appointed to a committee to write the Declaration of Independence. Writing by himself, he finished the job in 18 days.

He was elected a Virginia governor who is known for initiatives to secure religious freedom and to protect the people against unfairness in inheritance issues. Later, as a Continental Congress delegate, Jefferson crafted the original document behind the Northwest Ordinance of 1787, which banned slavery for the Northwest Territory and any new states. His world expanded with his new role as minister to France at the start of the French Revolution.

When Jefferson returned to the US, President Washington appointed him Secretary of State. He clashed with th Secretary of the Treasury, Alexander Hamilton, on the role of government, which resulted in two opposing parties—the Federalists (with Hamilton) and the Republicans or Democratic Republicans (Jefferson's group). While Hamilton desired a strong central government under the direction of the wealthy, Jefferson supported a central government that merely oversaw foreign affairs. He continued to believe in the farmers and workers making up state and local governments to handle local matters. Disappointed when Washington's administration followed Hamilton's ideology, Jefferson resigned his cabinet post. Three years later, he opposed John Adams (a Hamiltonian) in a bid for the presidency. When Jefferson lost, he became Vice President. Working closely, the men clashed, particularly on the passing of the Alien and Sedition Acts. Restricting the voting rights of immigrants and interfering with the critical press rankled Jefferson, who defended freedom and the Constitution. Many believed in Jefferson and he defeated Adams in his bid for a second term. During Jefferson's two terms, he worked hard to simplify government and curtail spending. He is lauded for the Louisiana Purchase in 1803, which gave Americans twice the land area for expansion.

Jefferson spent his last years at Monticello, the home he built. The University of Virginia is a product of his design, down to the original faculty and curriculum. Jefferson finally restored his relationship with John Adams; both died on July 4, 1826, 50 years after signing the Declaration of Independence.

Joshua E. Fernalld, 2016

JOHN JAY ◊ 1745–1829, *Founding Father and first Chief Justice*

" No power on earth has a right to take our property from us without our consent.
—Address to the People of Great Britain, at the First Continental Congress, 1774

- Led the opposition to slavery
- Was born into a wealthy New York family
- Served as ambassador to Spain and France with Ben Franklin
- Signed the Treaty of Paris in 1783
- Argued for strong, centralized government
- Collaborated with James Madison and Alexander Hamilton to produce The *Federalist Papers*, intellectual defenses of the proposed Constitution
- Wanted a prohibition against Catholics holding office
- Was appointed as the first Chief Justice of the United States

Key Works

Federalist Papers (with others), 1787–1788
Address to the People of the State of New-York, on the subject of the Federal Constitution

Biography

John Jay was born in 1745 in New York City into a wealthy merchant family with eight children. He was educated as a lawyer at King's (Columbia) College. As Robert R. Livingston's law partner, he negotiated a boundary disagreement between New York and an adjacent state. Meanwhile, he continued to be conservative in the movement against England. As part of the effort, it is speculated that with the New York Committee of Fifty-One, he wrote a draft of a manifesto that preceded the First Continental Congress; the document encouraged deputies from each colony to aid Boston. However, when the first Congress convened, Jay wanted to try every possible unification effort with England before boycotting. However, the Second Continental Congress saw the Revolution begin at Lexington-Concord. Jay went from hoping for a peaceful solution to supporting resistance to England. In 1777 he helped write the New York constitution and became President of the Continental Congress.

Negotiator

Early in the Revolutionary War, Jay traveled to Spain to persuade Charles III to give Americans access to navigation on the Mississippi and to secure a loan. Although he failed in getting help for the diplomatic cause, he joined Benjamin Franklin in Paris for the peace negotiations that ended the Revolutionary War. Jay served as foreign secretary to the Continental Congress and then acting Secretary of State. George Washington appointed him Chief Justice of the Supreme Court, where he officiated some foundational decisions, including Chisholm v. Georgia, a precursor to the Eleventh Amendment. He made an important contribution as the drafter of Jay's Treaty, which quelled an impending war with Great Britain. When elected governor of New York, he sacrificed his court appointment. After two terms, he returned home to a life of domestic leisure. He died in 1829, honored by having several schools named after him. The John Jay College of Criminal Justice in New York is just one institution that remembers him as "conservative and consolidating."

Colman R. McVaney, 2016

JAMES MADISON ◊ 1751–1836, *Federalist Papers*

> " The essence of government is power; and power, lodged as it must be in human hands, will ever be liable to abuse.
> —Speech in the Virginia constitutional convention, 1829

- Owned slaves
- Was Father of the Constitution and an intellectual
- Served as fourth President of the United States of America
- Sponsored the *Bill of Rights*
- Collaborated with Alexander Hamilton and John Jay to produce The *Federalist Papers*, intellectual defenses of the proposed Constitution
- Led the nation into the War of 1812
- Started his political life as a Federalist, but upon reconsideration became Anti-Federalist

Key Works

Constitution of the United States, 1787
The Federalist Papers (with others), 1787–1788
The Bill of Rights (with others)

Biography

Born in 1751 in Orange County, Virginia, James Madison attended The College of New Jersey, later named Princeton University, to study history, law, and government. Madison acted on his preparation when the American Revolution began. He championed independence after observing England's response to the Boston Tea party, and became a delegate to Virginia's Provincial Convention where his colleagues' admiration earned him the opportunity to participate in the Continental Congress in 1779. Madison earnestly sought individual liberty, which initially manifested itself against Virginia's persecution of the Baptists in 1774 and later against taxes that supported Christian education. He felt the taxes would "blur the distinction between church and state." He spoke for equality for all citizens.

A devotee of theorists like John Locke, Madison worked to pass an Act for Establishing Religious Freedom. He was disappointed that slavery continued in Virginia despite the state's progress in other human rights. At this time he also helped write the Constitution. The Articles of Confederation had lost their effectiveness in that they granted states control without any central authority. Because a central authority would be able to put the economy in order, mint currency, and regulate the army, the delegates needed to create a federal union. Madison was instrumental in crafting a document that reflected, in part, the Virginia Plan. He also agreed that checks and balances were essential, so the House, Senate, President, Supreme Court and state governments all had authority. After weighing his fears for a federal union that had too much power with his desire for protecting individuals, Madison agreed to help write the Bill of Rights. Free exercise of religion, speech, assembly, and the press would be exempt from government control. Madison, Alexander Hamilton and John Jay wrote the *The Federalist*, 85 essays to promote the necessary ratification. Later, he wrote to protest The Alien and Sedition Acts, denouncing them as unconstitutional. The Alien Act gave the president license to remove aliens considered a threat to national security, while the Sedition Act allowed persecution for anyone who spoke out against an individual in the federal government.

President Thomas Jefferson appointed Madison Secretary of State. America's conflicts with Britain and France were resulting in trade issues and "impressment" of American sailors. At Madison's urging, Jefferson enacted the Embargo Act to cut off American trade with those countries. It was ineffective and was repealed just as Madison came into office as President. Although he had resisted war, Madison asked Congress to declare war on Britain. The War of 1812 lasted two years, and was won with Andrew Jackson's triumph at New Orleans. In peacetime, Madison was able to work on improving the country by building canals and roads. He also established a national university and bank. Following his Presidency, Madison was head of the American Colonization Society to end slavery, yet he never freed his own slaves. He could see ahead to a Civil War brought about by forcing the south to abolition. James Madison was a thoughtful man of peace and liberty.

Joshua E. Fernalld, 2016

ALEXANDER HAMILTON, 1755–1804, *Little Lion*

" And it is long since I have learned to hold popular opinion of no value.
—Letter to Washington, 1794

- Was an economist, politician, and soldier who fought in the Revolutionary War

- Started life as an illegitimate child in the West Indies, with a father who abandoned him and a mother who died
- Attended prep school in New Jersey and King's College
- Served as General Washington's aide-de-camp during the Revolutionary War and led important missions
- Was selected, along with James Madison, as the first US Presidential speechwriter
- Co-authored *The Federalist Papers* with John Jay and James Madison and helped author the Constitution
- Served as a leader for the Federalist Party
- Was appointed first Secretary of the Treasury in the United States
- Accepted a duel with rival Aaron Burr and died at Burr's hand

Key Works

The Federalist Papers (with others), 1787–1788

Biography

Alexander Hamilton made great contributions to America through his role in setting up the national government and its economy. Born into humble beginnings as an illegitimate child in the West Indies, Hamilton suffered his father's abandonment at 10 and his mothers death when he was about 13. He moved in with relatives, who helped him raise enough money to be educated at a prep school in New Jersey. Later, Hamilton graduated from King's College, now known as Columbia University. He quickly aligned himself with the patriotic cause in the American Revolutionary War and caught George Washington's attention with his patriotic pamphlets. Washington chose Hamilton as his aide-de-camp and sent him on several important missions. Hamilton married Elizabeth Schuyler and involved himself in national politics. He later attended the Constitutional Convention, arguing for a strong national government after observing the various weaknesses of the Articles of Confederation. He wrote 52 out of 85 of the *Federalist Papers*, and was soon named the first Secretary of the Treasury by George Washington. Hamilton is credited with launching America's economy by establishing a national bank and several different types of tariffs and taxes. He later purportedly insulted rival Aaron Burr, who challenged the unapologetic Hamilton to a duel; Hamilton died at Burr's hand in 1804.

Federalist

After it became clear that a new document needed to replace the Articles of Confederation, a fierce debate arose between the Federalists and the Antifederalists. Hamilton, a key figure at the Constitutional Convention, strongly advocated for the Federalists. He believed in a strong central government and an economy based on manufacturing and industry instead of agriculture. Other key figures aligned with the Federalist cause were George Washington, John Jay, John Marshall, and James Madison. Under the pseudonym "Publius," or "of the public," Hamilton, Madison, and Jay authored *The Federalist Papers*. The influence of the *Papers* is reflected in many aspects of the Constitution of the United States.

Soon after he was elected president, George Washington appointed Hamilton as his Secretary of the Treasury. The financial system Hamilton launched was decidedly Federalist. One of the most controversial aspects of his program was the formation of a central Bank of the United States. Jefferson, the greatest rival of Hamilton, argued that the Constitution gave the federal government no explicit power to make such a bank. Hamilton then invoked the "necessary and proper" clause in the

Constitution, determining that the federal government may pass laws that prove to be necessary to the governance of the country. Since the government was given explicit allowance to collect taxes and regulate trade, Hamilton argued that a federal bank was necessary to carry out these duties. This debate resulted in the theory of "loose construction," which stipulates that the government may interpret which powers are implicitly given by the Constitution.

A Trident Government

One of the most remarkable features of the government set up by the Constitution was a three-pronged government with a division of powers. The legislative branch was to make and produce laws, the executive branch was to carry them out, and the judiciary branch was to judge in manners of dispute and appeals to the government. Hamilton was quick to point out in Federalist Paper No. 78 that "the judiciary is beyond comparison the weakest of the three departments of power" as it could "never attack with success either of the two." Therefore, he saw it as necessary "that all possible care is requisite to enable it to defend itself against their attacks." However, the judicial branch was given the power of "judicial review," which allowed it to void laws that the judiciary decided were in conflict with the Constitution. The result was a three-branch government in which each branch was held accountable by the others.

Power to the People

One of the Founding Fathers' most important concerns was that a corrupt dictator would unjustly use his power to oppress the people. Hamilton wrote that the design of the US government precluded this scenario. Not only did its three branches check each other's power, but the state governments also gave power to the people in opposing the federal government when necessary. Additionally, the distances that separated each state government safeguarded against any efforts by the federal government to seize complete control. Should one state fall, Hamilton wrote, "distant States would have it in their power to make head with fresh forces."

Kurt Gutschick, faculty
Colman R. McVaney, 2016
Benjamin Rocklin, 2017

THE SEVEN YEARS WAR, 1755–1764

In 1754 the British began attacking disputed French positions in North America, while Prussia, rising from the ashes of the Holy Roman Empire, was busy competing with Austria for power. Aiming to curtail Britain's rise to prominence, France allied with Austria. Prussia, sensing a war, preemptively struck Saxony and started a war that would embroil most of Europe and her colonies beyond—a grim foreshadowing of what was to come in the 20th century.

The war was brutal, but ended well for Britain and Prussia. Britain laid claim to a number of France's colonial territories, including the bulk of its claims in North America, and Prussia rose from relative obscurity to become the a new great power in its own right. France, meanwhile, lost much of its foreign territory and became saddled with war debts that would grind its people down.

THE AMERICAN REVOLUTION, 1775–1781

The American Revolution, otherwise known as the Revolutionary War, fought between Britain and its 13 American colonies, was the formative period of the United States.

Nearly 200 years after the founding of the first English colony at Roanoke, the 13 Colonies sought to rebel against what they deemed unfair treatment by their mother country, and revolted against British rule. The ensuing war gave birth to the United States of America, which would come in time to stand as the great superpower of the West and the world in general.

The war between the colonies and the British did not arise overnight. Rather, there were many causes, none of which would have resulted in war on its own, but which all culminated in the eventual conflict. First, the Seven Years War (French and Indian War) between the French and British colonists and involving the American Indians, drained the British treasury. Attempting to pay off its debt, Britain levied taxes on colonial goods including sugar, tea, paper products, and stamps. Outraged over these taxes, the colonists gradually united, believing that Britain had no right to tax them when they lacked representation in Parliament. Tensions between the colonies and the British became increasingly agitated when colonists found themselves having to house the occupying British soldiers. Events such as the Boston Tea Party, during which the colonists dumped a shipment of tea from the British East India Company into Boston Harbor, were used as propaganda to further inflame the colonists and the British.

The American Revolutionary War was also important for the colonists' use of guerilla warfare to even the odds and overtake the well-trained British troops, as well as the employment of nationalism to rally the general public behind a cause that was seen as their own (rather than just that of the government or aristocracy). What lingers in our memory is a war of empowered individuals fighting for freedom and the republic values of the classical Greeks and Romans.

Notable Battles

The Battles of Lexington and Concord, 1775

Origin of the fabled "Shot heard round the world," and the start of open hostilities between the British and the American colonists. Conflict peaked when, on April 19, 1775, 700 British troops were deployed to Lexington and Concord to seize rebel supplies and munitions and capture revolutionaries Samuel Adams and John Hancock.

However, the American minutemen learned of their plans beforehand, allowing the militia stationed there to resist effectively. The affair turned violent, forcing the British retreat to Boston. Many consider this the official beginning of the war.

Out of the Second Continental Congress came the Articles of Confederation, which would govern the new United States, and the appointment of George Washington as commander of the Continental Army. The Revolution's first major battle centered around the British-held city of Boston. As news of the war's outbreak circulated, the British began to fortify Boston as a stronghold. After multiple months of siege, the colonists finally liberated the city from British control.

Congress then sent an early draft of the Declaration of Independence to London and officially adopted a final draft of the Declaration on July 4, 1776. Though some had initially viewed the war as a conflict to reconcile the colonies with the mother country, it was now clear that autonomy from Britain was the uncertain, but desired end goal. From late 1776 to 1777, the colonists suffered a string of defeats, losing control of New Jersey, New York, and the capital of Philadelphia. Between 1777 and 1778, the Continental Army wintered at Valley Forge, but poor planning and lack of supplies led to the deaths of 3,000 soldiers and the defection of roughly 1,000 more.

Notable Battles

The Battle of Saratoga, 1777

Prior to this battle, the idea of an American victory would have seemed laughable too much of Europe, and a British victory inevitable. However, General George Washington's desperate fight and hard-won victory against the British here was enough to garner the more serious interest of the European nations, many of whom would come to support America's efforts in order to shake loose Britain's dominance of the Western sphere. Notably, The Battle of Saratoga dispelled French reservations about allying with the colonists. France officially declared war on Britain, and the Netherlands and Spain followed suit.

The Battle of Yorktown, 1781

The climax of the Revolutionary War, after which the United States was at last recognized as a distinct country by Britain. External support from the French lent America the funds and men it needed to defeat General Lord Cornwallis's army at Yorktown as they attempted to board ships to New York in October 1781, and it brought the British to the negotiating table.

The French would come to be deeply affected by the American victory, and would channel many of the same emotions into their own revolution to follow.

Sporadic conflicts continued throughout the course of the peace talks until the Treaty of Paris was signed on September 3, 1783. Severing all ties from Britain, this newborn country began its journey to become one of the superpowers of the modern era.

EDWARD GIBBON, 1737–1794, *Historian of the Fall of Rome*

> " The various modes of worship which prevailed in the Roman world were all considered by the people as equally true; by the philosophers as equally false; and by the magistrate as equally useful.
>
> —*The History of the Decline and Fall of the Roman Empire*

- Received little formal education, but read his way to Oxford at age 15 and became a historian
- Was forced to leave Oxford after only one year as a result of his decision to convert to Roman Catholicism; his family sent him to Switzerland to study under a Calvinist minister
- Served as a captain in the Hampshire militia during the Seven Years War before beginning his most famous work

- Traveled to Paris, Lausanne, and Rome after leaving the militia and decided to study the fall of the Roman Empire
- Stirred up violence in 1776 with the 15th and 16th chapters of his first volume, which offered a controversial take on the problems with early Christianity and its role in the fall of the Roman Empire
- Published *The Decline and Fall of the Roman Empire* in six volumes from 1776–1788; the work was notable for disregarding many conventions of historical work and for an ironic detachment

Key Work

The Decline and Fall of the Roman Empire (6 vols), 1776–1788

Biography

Edward Gibbon, author of *The Decline and Fall of the Roman Empire* (hereafter *Decline and Fall*), one of the most popular historical works of modern times, came to prominence in England in the late 18th century. He was born in 1737 in Putney, Surrey, into a wealthy English family. His father was a member of parliament. Edward was a sickly child and did not receive much schooling other than from the books he read and from a series of tutors throughout his childhood. When he was 15, his father sent him to Oxford to receive a standard aristocratic education. However, Edward was expelled after only one year for making the shocking decision to convert to Roman Catholicism. His father immediately responded by sending Edward to Lausanne, Switzerland, to be mentored by Daniel Pavillard, a prominent Calvinist minister. This paid off for the elder Gibbon when Edward Gibbon returned to Protestantism.

Edward then spent four years in active service in the Hampshire militia during the Seven Years War, eventually earning the rank of captain, but he left the service at the conclusion of the war in 1762. After this, Gibbon made a grand continental tour, traveling to Paris, Lausanne, and Rome where he discovered his interest in the Roman Empire. It was here that he had his first inclination to specifically study the history of the rise and fall of Rome. He returned to London in 1765, where he was elected to Samuel Johnson's literary club, in addition to later receiving a seat in parliament.

In the midst of this, Gibbon began to work in earnest on *Decline and Fall*, his best known work. He published the first volume in 1776, and he completed his work in 1787. The 15th and 16th chapters in the first volume were the most controversial at the time and continue to be so today. In these chapters, Gibbon offered the controversial thesis that the spread of Christianity contributed to the fall of Rome. While still regarded as a masterpiece, those chapters caused violent controversy in 1776 when first published. Gibbon was appointed a lord of trade in 1779 and was an active member in parliament until 1784 when a ministry abolished the Board of Trade. He returned to Lausanne in 1783 to complete volumes five and six. He returned to England to see his final volumes through press, and died there on January 16, 1794, from complications due to edema and gout. While certainly controversial and containing factual errors, Gibbon's epic work is still engaging. The two chapters on Christianity are a must-read for those who wish to understand the Enlightenment critique of the subject.

The Fall of Rome

Gibbon was not the first historian or philosopher to hypothesize the causes of the fall of Rome. J.G.A. Pocock, in his multivolume *Barbarism and Religion*, traced the historical view of the fall of Rome. He summarized it as follows: "Rome itself perished by her conquests, which being made by great Armies, occasioned such power and insolence in their commanders, and set some citizens so high above the rest … that she was enslaved by ingrates whom she had employed to defend her." Speaking to this current of thought, W. Clark Gilpin noted that for the Italian thinkers in the Renaissance, the "idea of decline included the distinctive theme that greatness contained the seeds of its own decay." He elaborated: "the exercise of liberty had won an empire, but empire, in turn, had subverted the civic virtue on which republic depends."

Gibbon seemed to have some sympathy for these views. He argued that under Emperor Justinian, the empire was so weakened economically and politically that even if "all the Barbarian conquerors had been annihilated in the same hour, their total destruction would not have restored the empire of the West." But the source of that weakness for Gibbon was not liberty run amok or greedy generals, but rather the growing sect of Christianity that undermined the foundation of the Roman Empire and precipitated its fall. Gibbon, though by no means hypercritical of Christianity, found it his duty as a historian to record what he saw as the cause of the fall. At the beginning of his controversial chapters on religion, he delineated the differences between a theologian and a historian: "The theologian may indulge the pleasing task of describing Religion as she descended from heaven, arrayed in her native purity. A more melancholy duty is imposed on the historian. He must discover the inevitable mixture of error and corruption which she contracted in a long residence upon earth, among a weak and degenerate race of beings."

Barbarism and Religion

Decline and Fall is most famous for the way it treated the triumph of the Christian religion in the pagan Roman culture as contributing to the fall of Rome and the descent into the darkness of the Middle Ages. Gibbon saw the fall of Rome as representing "the triumph of barbarism and religion." Many events led to this claim. One is the sacking of the Alexandrian library in 389 AD by Archbishop Theophilus, who destroyed more than 200,000 volumes of Greek and Roman literature. Gibbon called Theophilus a "bold, bad man whose hands were alternately polluted with gold, and with blood." In 529 AD, the Emperor Justinian, perhaps the last Roman emperor, closed down the remaining schools that taught in the Greek tradition. Gibbon commented, "the Gothic [the Germanic armies that had sacked Rome] arms were less fatal to the schools of Athens than the establishment of a new religion, whose ministers superseded the exercise of reason, resolved every question by an article of faith, and condemned the infidel or skeptic to eternal flames."

Apart from historical events engineered in the name of Christianity, Gibbon further argued that it was the *substance* of early Christianity that caused the fall of Rome. For Gibbon, there is a "dark cloud that hangs over the first age of the church." First among these problems is the rigid exclusivity of the early church, which Gibbon argues Christians adapted as a feature of their inherited Jewish faith. For Gibbon, the ancient world was in "harmony" and with "facility" respected each other's superstitions. The one faith that refused to be tolerant was ancient Judaism. Christianity maintained this exclusivity as the one true faith, but added a missionary zeal to its proclamation. This allowed for the rapid growth of the sect.

Christianity's emphasis on heaven and the afterlife was also unique at the time. Moreover, the early Christian texts and thinkers encouraged the faithful to believe in the imminent end of the world. Such a belief helped spread the faith, but it also focused the believers' attention away from worldly duties in favor of eternal ones. Gibbon rounded out his view of the spread of Christianity by attributing it to three other historical factors: "the miraculous powers ascribed to the early church"; "the pure and austere morals of the early Christians," which were in many ways exemplary to Gibbon; and, finally, "the union and discipline of the Christian republic, which gradually formed an independent and increasing state in the heart of the Roman empire." This last factor gave rise to the distinction still present in many sects of Christianity between the clergy and the average member of the church.

In the 16th chapter of *Decline and Fall*, Gibbon blamed Christians for the martyrdom they faced at the hands of the Romans. The antagonistic relationship the faith adopted toward Rome, which the church sometimes referred to as Babylon, caused them to distance themselves to such a degree that they were placed outside of the toleration typical of the time. The substance of Gibbon's critique is not a wholesale critique of Christianity, but only of the apocalyptic, intolerant version of the faith that flourished in the late Roman Empire. Keith Windschuttle finds in *Decline and Fall* an "affirmation of the author's Christian faith," though he takes broad license to get there. On the flip side of men like Theophilus, Gibbon praised Pope Gregory the Great, the philosopher Boethius, and the Christian monks who preserved the works of antiquity through the dark ages. Windschuttle goes on to assert that much of the mockery in the book toward the excesses of religion can be explained by Gibbon's Protestantism. In the 19th century, a number of "sanitized and annotated" Christian editions of *Decline and Fall* gained popularity. Furthermore, Gibbon lived roughly a century after the wrenching religious wars of the 17th century, and in line with other Enlightenment thinkers, he blamed the wars on overreaching spiritual authority, "the principal cause of 17th-century anarchy and religious warfare." Given this position, it is only natural that Gibbon would react against religion and religious authority in the manner he did when writing about the fall of Rome.

Enlightenment and Progress

If the barbarism of religion caused a descent from the heights of classical antiquity and the toleration of Roman society, the antidote to this barbarism was the Enlightenment view of progress, of which Gibbon was an ardent believer. Stephen Snobelen calls *Decline and Fall* "a triumph of Enlightenment scholarship." Gibbon was able to harness a huge body of scholarship in order to make his claims about religion, miracles, and the cause of the dark ages.

Part of the requirement for progress was mastery of nature, the birthright of humans according to Christian theology, and that would become possible to a greater degree than had been achievable before. In Gibbon's vision, mastery of nature was a "vital rudimentary precondition for the development and maintenance of human civilization." As the capacity to rule over nature increased, civilization progressed, and liberty could be extended to all. But Gibbon did not take the hard line on religion that other Enlightenment thinkers did. He did not wish to ban religion in this march toward progress. As in Gibbon's harmonious view of the pagan world, various sects and factions must submit to the broader cultural imperatives of toleration and peace. One can speculate that religious leaders might chafe at the notion of submitting their authority to that of the government and culture, but one can also understand what drove Gibbon to relegate religious authority to that position.

Toby Coffman, faculty

JAMES BOSWELL, 1740–1795, *The Great Biographer*

> " He who has provoked the lash of wit, cannot complain that he smarts from it.
>
> —*The Life of Samuel Johnson*

- Recorded Samuel Johnson's life in his acclaimed biography, *The Life of Samuel Johnson*, with the aid of his staggering memory and scrupulous journaling
- Contracted gonorrhea 17 times in 30 years because he was a chronic womanizer; he vowed to change his ways numerous times but never found the strength
- Had a complicated relationship with his home country of Scotland; at one point he took diction classes to get rid of his accent, but another time he cursed the English and wished for another battle of Bannockburn
- Set himself the task of writing a 10-line poem every day while studying in Holland; he wrote one for each of the 100+ days he was there
- Met Samuel Johnson when he was 23 and formed a deep bond that allowed him to produce his great work on Johnson's life
- Had a tortured relationship with his own father and clearly clung to Johnson as a kind of father figure
- Was a charismatic figure and often quite brash: on a tour of Europe, he met and befriended Rousseau and Voltaire
- Took particular interest in Mary Bryant near the end of his life; she was a convict who escaped a penal colony in Australia

Key Works

The Life of Samuel Johnson, 1791
The Private Paper of James Boswell from Malahide Castle, pub. 1928–1934

Biography

James Boswell, lawyer and essayist, secured literary fame when he published his biography, *The Life of Samuel Johnson* (hereafter *The Life*), which he attempted to write "as [Johnson] really was; for I profess to write, not his panegyric, which must be all praise, but his Life; which, great and good as he was, must not be supposed to be entirely perfect." Boswell's contemporary critics and friends of Johnson did not easily accept this engaging and open tone, but his style immortalized him as the innovator of the modern biography.

He was born October 29, 1740, in Edinburgh, Scotland. Throughout his childhood, he was plagued by his mother's suffocating Calvinism and his father's coldness. In 1753, he attended the University of Edinburgh, where he studied the arts and law. At 18 he kept a journal, wrote poetry, and "had already trained himself to listen, to observe, and to remember until he found time to write it all down." By "temperament he was unstable, emotionally and sexually skittish," and Boswell soon earned a reputation as a womanizer after having multiple affairs, including one with Rousseau's mistress. He eventually settled down, at least temporarily, and married his cousin Margaret Montgomerie, with whom he had five children. In 1759, his father sent him to the University of Glasgow to separate him from an actress.

On May 16, 1763, when he was 23 years old, he met Samuel Johnson at Tom Davies's London bookshop, and thus began their 20-year friendship. They took a three-month journey together through the Scottish Highlands and the Hebrides islands; the notes that Boswell took of their journey became the basis of his biography on Johnson. Four years after Johnson's death, Boswell began his work on his magnum opus, which he published May 16, 1791, bringing him fame and recognition. He died May 19, 1795, after weeks of serious illness, and was buried in his family vault in Auchinleck. Frederick A. Pottle later said that he "may in his practical choices have been a very foolish man, but if he gives you a book that breathes magnanimity, it can only have happened first, because he has a mind and heart capable of understanding magnanimity, and secondly, because he had the rare power of expressing magnanimity in words, had literary genius of a high order." It is a fitting epitaph to a mercurial life.

The Life of Samuel Johnson

Boswell's literary fame and longevity is almost entirely bound up with his biography of the great man of letters, Samuel Johnson. Boswell was a longtime friend of Johnson and took pains to record nearly everything he witnessed in personal conversation with Johnson or in interactions between Johnson and others. In *The Life* he writes of their first meeting: "This is to me a memorable year; for in it I had the happiness to obtain the acquaintance of that extraordinary man whose memoirs I am now writing; an acquaintance which I shall ever esteem as one of the most fortunate circumstances of my life."

Johnson and Boswell actually only spent about a year in each other's presence, conducting most of their relationship from a distance through letters. A good deal of their time together was during Johnson and Boswell's adventurous trip to the Scottish Highlands and the islands of the Hebrides, where Alan Klehr notes, "while Johnson observed Scotland, Boswell observed Johnson." This was unique in biography at the time, so much of which was done at a distance. Apart from time spent together, Boswell was deeply intimate with Johnson's life story. Johnson had once advised Boswell that "nobody can write the life of a man, but those who have eat and drunk and lived in social intercourse with him." Indeed, the two men had a deep and intimate relationship, an idealized father/son rapport with one another.

Apart from the deep personal interaction and their numerous letters, Boswell drew extensively on his private journals, other letters of Johnson's that he could acquire, Johnson's vast amount of public writings, and every piece of biographical data he could glean from Johnson's other friends and acquaintances. The result is what many have labeled the best biography in the history of the English language. Even more unique than Boswell's close access to Johnson, his deep personal relationship, and the diligent secondary research is the fact that Boswell was equally diligent to treat his subject with complete honesty. In the introductory section to *The Life* he writes, "Johnson will be seen as he really was; for I profess to write, not his panegryic, which must be all praise, but his Life … in every picture there should be shade as well as light."

In holding to this position, Boswell was being loyal to Johnson's own view of biography, which stressed factual recitation over commendation or condemnation, a practice Johnson adhered to in his own famous biographies of notable British poets. Johnson sensed that much biography either became uncritical praise or lingered on the sordid details of the subject's life; knowing that his friend "Bozzy" planned on writing his biography, Johnson was adamant that his life be told genuinely, warts and all. The reader can see this when Boswell is forthright in recounting Johnson's fear of death, a surprising fear in a committed Anglican. In trying to press Johnson into conversation on the subject one day, Johnson "was thrown into such a state of agitation that he expressed himself in a way that alarmed and distressed me." Johnson was so out of sorts that he warned Boswell to not return the following day.

This unflinching acknowledgement of faults and curiosities is mingled with Boswell's clearly high regard for Johnson.

Boswell's chapter on Johnson's last days is justly lauded. Johnson kept his wit and his harsh sense of judgment. He called the man who stayed up with him on one of his final nights "an idiot," and accepted an offered pillow with, "that will do—all that a pillow can do." Yet despite his fear, he was resilient in the face of death, eschewing medication so that he could "render up my soul to God unclouded." Boswell confessed himself "unable to express all that I felt upon the loss of such a 'Guide, Philosopher, and Friend.'" His book stands as a fitting tribute to both Johnson the man and Johnson the literary theorist and man of letters.

Toby Coffman, faculty

ANTOINE-LAURENT de LAVOISIER, 1743–1794, *Revolutionary Chemist*

" If everything in chemistry is explained in a satisfactory manner without the help of phlogiston, it is by that reason alone infinitely probable that the principle does not exist; that it is a hypothetical body, a gratuitous supposition; indeed, it is in the principles of good logic, not to multiply bodies without necessity.

—*Réflexions sur la Phlogistique*

- Studied the natural sciences on his own, specifically geology and chemistry, after college
- Worked with Jean-Étienne Guettard to collect data and create a geological map of France
- Was elected to the French Academy of Sciences at 24 as an assistant chemist
- Worked as French tax collector in order to fund his experiments
- Married Marie-Anne Paulze in 1771, who became his scientific aide, learning English in order to translate scientific works for her husband and drawing sketches of their experiments
- Identified and named oxygen and hydrogen, and was the first to understand oxygen's role in combustion
- Emphasized knowledge based on facts, observations, and careful measurement rather than vague supposition
- Articulated the law of conservation of mass, which claimed that mass cannot be created or destroyed during a chemical reaction
- Was the first to claimed that water is not an element but rather a compound of oxygen and "inflammable air" (hydrogen)
- Constructed the first list of elements, a prototype for the periodic table
- Was executed by guillotine on May 8, 1794

Key Works
Opuscules Physiques et Chimiques (Essays Physical and Chemical), 1774
Réflexions sur la Phlogistique (Reflections on Phlogiston), 1786
Méthode de Nomenclature Chimique (Method of Chemical Nomenclature), 1787
An Elementary Treatise of Chemistry, 1789
Annales de Chimie (Annals of Chemistry), 1789

Biography

Antoine Lavoisier was born on August 26, 1743, to a reputable landholding family. He was the only son in the Lavoisier family and became the only child after his sister died at 15. He began attending Collége des Quatre-Nations at 11, eventually leaving in 1761 to pursue a law degree at the insistence of his father, who declared that the study of science was a fine hobby but not a profession. After his graduation, Lavoisier independently maintained his study of the natural sciences, focusing on geology and chemistry. On his own, he published a scientific paper that was presented to the French Academy of Sciences, which eventually led to his election as an assistant chemist at the young age of 24.

Trying to maintain his ability to fund his scientific studies, Lavoisier invested in and took a position with a tax collecting firm, the Ferme Générale. This involvement in the Ferme also led Lavoisier to his wife, Marie-Anne Paulze, who would become a great help in his personal experiments; she soon dedicated herself to her husband's experimentation, taking notes, managing, drafting experiments, and translating foreign works that he could not read. While Marie was never able to have a child, their work together produced many significant experiments that would shape the sciences for years to come.

Unfortunately, as the political climate changed in France and revolution became inevitable, the perception of science altered. Attitudes toward the Academy of Sciences grew increasingly negative as the Academy was viewed as elitist. During this time, Lavoisier took up the post of commissioner of the Royal Gunpowder Administration, where he could better respond to the cultural shift. There, he increased the administration's efficiency while also providing himself with the necessary tools and space for his experiments—specifically, very accurate scales. This position and his prior involvement in the building of a tax wall around the city of Paris, however, would place Lavoisier at the center of the Revolution. There would be no way for him to eliminate the perception of his being a part of the ruling elite, passionately hated at this time. This enabled one of Lavoisier's enemies, Marat, to discredit him, claiming publicly that Lavoisier was in charge of creating a prison for the people with the tax wall. While Marat's hatred stemmed from a scientific disagreement having nothing to do with the wall, Marat's comments instilled animosity towards Lavoisier. On November 24, 1793, Robespierre ordered the arrest of all former shareholders of the Ferme Générale. On May 8, 1794, Antoine-Laurent de Lavoisier was sentenced to death by guillotine, forever mourned by the scientific community.

Chemistry

Antoine Lavoisier is sometimes "considered the father of modern chemistry," having revolutionized the scientific world through his discoveries. He lived in a time when chemistry was considered "an ambiguous discipline owing to its tradition of alchemy, useful art, and pharmaceuticals." The time before Lavoisier was dominated by the belief that all things found their existence in four elements—fire, earth, air, and water—which were believed to compose all physical matter.

Lavoisier, influenced by Joseph Priestley, took steps to disprove this system of belief through his many experiments regarding the element phlogiston. Resulting from alchemy, phlogiston was assumed to be the substance that caused matter to be combustible. Lavoisier was eventually able to disprove the idea of phlogiston by burning numerous materials and meticulously measuring their mass and composition before and after burning. He discovered that during the chemical reaction, the material seemed to give off or draw in air. He determined through an experiment with mercury that the air he had discovered was the actual "phlogiston" in combustion. In this, Lavoisier disproved the theory of phlogiston and also determined that there was a separate element, naming it oxygen or "acid former," which allowed for the combustion. Lavoisier then conducted experiments concerning a flammable gas, which Henry Cavendish had discovered, that had been proven to leave water as a residue. From this Lavoisier formed a hypothesis that water was really composed of two elements: oxygen and the air that Cavendish discovered, which Lavoisier named hydrogen, meaning "water-former." In this final hypothesis, Lavoisier was able to completely disprove the phlogiston theory as well as discover and name two new components of matter.

This process of naming these components of matter interested Lavoisier, and he determined that there was a significant need for a unified nomenclature, which he set out to create. In this time, the Alchemists had defined fire, water, air, and earth as the four major elements, yet Lavoisier believed that the term "element" needed to be redefined. He believed the Alchemists had already once been disproven and their process of nomenclature was "purposely complicated and mysterious" in order to keep their work secret. Lavoisier decided to rename the elements not as four objects of matter but as "bodies that could not be decomposed." Using this definition, Lavoisier described and defined the known 55 elements of the time in a journal publication. Lavoisier's publication is still read today and helped make the creation of the periodic table possible. Lavoisier is also known for his contribution to the idea of the Law of the Conservation of Mass, which he discovered through experiments in respiration and heat transfer in chemical reactions. All of these contributions make Lavoisier's significance clear, helping solidify his place in scientific history.

Nate Kosirog, faculty
Nathaniel Whatmore, 2015

JEREMY BENTHAM, 1748–1832, *The Greatest Happiness Utilitarian*

> " Nature has placed mankind under the governance of two sovereign masters, pain and pleasure. It is for them alone to point out what we ought to do, as well as to determine what we shall do.
>
> —*Introduction to the Principles of Morals and Legislation*

- Was a founding father of Utilitarianism, although he published little and had little influence during his lifetime
- Graduated from law school, but never practiced law
- Studied relentlessly for 8–12 hours a day, trying to articulate his ideas on human nature and how government should work
- Obsessed over an idea for a prison called "Panopticon" for almost 20 years—his idea never came to fruition and almost bankrupted him
- Designed the Panopticon, a spiritual precursor to today's closed circuit camera society (particular in Britain), a prison constructed so that all cells would be visible from a single vantage point, thus forcing all prisoners to suspect they are being watched at all times, as a means of controlling their minds
- Espoused a form of hedonism (see Epicurus): human nature and behavior reducible to the twin motives of attaining pleasure and avoiding pain
- Argued, in a utilitarian twist to his hedonism, that if pleasure is the good, it does not matter whose pleasure it is, so we ought to maximize everyone's pleasure without regard for our own

desires for pleasure; this imposes a radical egalitarianism on his political philosophy, as it means the government, and people in general, ought to be calculating the greatest happiness for the greatest number without regard for the happiness of any individual, including oneself
- Held that moral action and obligation are determined by the question of what will be likely to produce the greatest happiness for the greatest number of people (the basic tenet of utilitarianism), recalling that happiness means the presence of pleasure and absence of pain
- Defined liberty in the modern "libertarian" way, i.e., as the lack of external restraint ("negative liberty")
- Regarded liberty as a societal good, but denied the Lockean position that liberty is a natural condition of man to which we have a natural right; it is merely the best social structure for achieving our collective hedonistic goal of maximizing pleasure and minimizing pain
- Supported representative or self-government with minimal laws as a pragmatic means to the pleasure of liberty; no natural law grounding for law-making (just as no natural liberty or natural rights), so in theory even tyrannical laws are legitimate, since there is no supra-governmental standard against which to judge them as unbinding

Key Works

Fragment on Government, 1776
Introduction to the Principles of Morals and Legislation, 1780
Defense of Usury, 1787
Punishments and Rewards, 1811
A Fragment on Government, Or, A Comment on the Commentaries, 1823
Book of Fallacies, 1824
A Treatise on Judicial Evidence, 1825

Biography

Born in England on February 15, 1748, Jeremy Bentham was greatly torn between two conflicting philosophies on life from his mother and father. His mother was strongly superstitious, while his father was a lawyer who depended on rationalism for his morality. Bentham clung to his father's rationalist worldview, which would end up influencing his views on human nature and political philosophy. Turmoil and political change swirled during Bentham's upbringing, giving him the strong desire to alter government in a way that most promoted the happiness of all citizens. He attended Queens College in Oxford and later studied law at Lincoln's Inn. Bentham was expected to follow in his father and grandfather's footsteps in practicing law but, curiously, he did not. Instead, he spent his days studying and writing his philosophies on human nature, the role of government, and the flaws of traditional government. In 1781, he connected with the Earl of Shelborne, who encouraged him to meet and debate the top lawyers and Whigs of the time. After this, Bentham obsessed over an idea he had for a prison, which he wanted the leader of Russia to adopt. He spent so much time on this unsuccessful idea that he almost ran out of money. He was on the brink of bankruptcy when he received a lucky inheritance in 1796. Many of Bentham's works were not published, and he was still relatively obscure at the time of his death in 1832. However, his thought inspired later philosophers such as John Stuart Mill, who would expand and advocate for Bentham's utilitarian ideas.

Pawns of Pain and Pleasure—Bentham's View of Human Nature

Bentham's view of human nature is foundational to his beliefs on how government should run. He addresses human nature at the beginning of his most influential work, *An Introduction to the Principles of Morals and Legislation.* Bentham believed that humans are solely motivated by two things—pain and pleasure: "nature has placed mankind under the governance of two sovereign masters, pain and pleasure. It is for them alone to point out what we ought to do, as well as to determine what we shall do." For Bentham, all pleasures are equal; there is no qualitative hierarchy of pleasures. However, he does acknowledge that there might be quantifiable differences in pleasures that make us value some pleasures higher than others. For example, the expected duration and certainty of a potential pleasure affects its value in human decision-making. Bentham also believed that humans are far more motivated to avoid pain than they are to seek the increase of pleasure. In other words, humans make decisions out of self-interest, or the highest possible utility. There is an important difference between self-interest and selfish-interest. Selfish-interest would imply that people do only what benefits them as an individual regardless of the effect that action has on others. On the contrary, Bentham states that humans naturally pursue that which provides the greatest good for the most people because that benefits themselves just as much as society. This is defined as the Greatest Happiness Principle, which states that whatever brings the most happiness or utility is moral, while actions that do not bring the greatest possible utility are immoral. For example, a serial killer may derive pleasure from killing people, but his pleasure does not outweigh the pain he would be inflicting on others, so utilitarians would not condone the serial killer's act. It is important to note that the principle of utility is not a prescriptive principle; that is, Bentham does not propose it as a guide for making moral decisions. Rather, the principle of utility guides one's reflection upon actions and helps assess their moral value.

Utilitarianism as a Guide for Governance

Bentham's view of human nature was critical as he formed his political philosophy. He wrote in *An Introduction to the Principles of Morals and Legislation,* "It is vain to talk of the interest of the community, without understanding what is the interest of the individual." Bentham felt that recognizing human hedonistic instincts was crucial to forming an effective ethical or political theory. Once he observed the human tendency to maximize pleasure and minimize pain, Bentham reasoned that governments also ought to prioritize the people's utility. As he described, "utility is … that property in any object, whereby it tends to produce benefit, advantage, pleasure, good, or happiness." Utilitarian ethics, relying on man's instinct to promote his self-interest, declares "that virtue is based on utility, and that conduct should be directed toward promoting the greatest happiness of the greatest number of persons."

In order for governments to provide for the people's greatest utility, Bentham believed that representative government was vital. The most effective government would be one composed of legislators chosen by the people to pursue the best interests of the community. Bentham's ideas posed a significant attack on the beliefs of the social elite who assumed they knew what was best for the lower classes. Yet for Bentham, laws and the government which enacts them should only exist to protect the individual and his happiness; as Bentham explained in *An Introduction to the Principles of Morals and Legislation,* liberty means the absence of restraint, and laws should only exist insofar as they promote liberty. Specifying some unjust laws, Bentham stated, "every order, for example, to pay money on the score of taxation, or of debt from individual to individual, or otherwise, is void." This utilitarian defense of democracy and of limited government led to a unique understanding of how best to promote democratic ideals—universal suffrage, educational reform, and prison reform. A critic of the idea of "natural rights," Bentham believed that rights were only given, or withheld, by the laws of a nation. Consequently, the government should enact laws that protect the rights of all people; however, the burden of reform ultimately lies at the people's feet in the form of their vote.

Kenny Bottoms, 2015
Jessica Goeser, researcher
Daren Jonescu, advisor

ROBESPIERRE ◊ 1748–1794, *French Revolution, Reign of Terror and Power*

" Terror is nothing else than justice, prompt, severe, inflexible.
—*Discourse* of February 5, 1794

- Was elected to the National Assembly which became the Constituent Assembly
- Cared passionately about democratic principles
- Served as President of the Jacobin Club, a left-wing Republican group
- Barred the Girondists' participation in the National Convention, being rabidly against them
- Encouraged the execution of Louis XVI
- Created and became spokesperson for the Committee of Public Safety
- Implemented the Reign of Terror, a mass persecution of the enemies of the Jacobins, opponents to the Revolution, and personal enemies
- Took over the Revolutionary Tribunal
- Made the cult of the Supreme Being an official religion
- Was accused by the National Convention of despotism
- Fled, and was captured and guillotined with 21 followers and 80 supporters

Key Works
Mémoire sur les peines infamantes ("Report on Degrading Punishments")

Biography
Maximilien François Marie Isidore de Robespierre was a French lawyer and politician, who even now remains controversial. When his mother died and his father became despondent and erratic, Robespierre was cared for by his sisters and his grandparents. At 11, he attended the most prestigious college in France, Louis-le-Grand. There, Robespierre integrated two very important ideas of the Enlightenment—classical tradition that embraced Roman law, and philosophy, particularly Rousseau. Uniting these two foundational ideologies, Robespierre distinguished himself as an altruist, concerned with the rights of the people, speaking for unrestricted access to the government offices and universal suffrage, and against abuse of power and religious and racial discrimination. While passionate for social reform and democratic principles, he believed more and more in his own strength and determination, arrogantly taking control of the Revolution and executing every opponent.

He began his climb to power with his election to the National Assembly. His self-confidence and oratorical skill made him popular. He aligned himself with the Jacobins, a left-wing republican group, rising to president of the organization. He heartily approved of the *Declaration of the Rights of Man and of the Citizen*, which was to be the preamble to the French Constitution. Article 3 of the Declaration of

1793 states, "All men are equal by nature and before the law. As such, for the authors of this declaration equality is not only before the law but it is also a natural right, that is to say, a fact of nature." Yet in a series of actions that revealed his method of removing opposition to a cause, Robespierre ensured that members of the Constituent Assembly be barred from being part of the Legislative Assembly dominated by Girondists.

As the country suffered defeats against Austria and Prussia, France's lower classes demanded equality and elimination of the monarchy. The monarchy was brought down in 1792; at the same time Robespierre created a Revolutionary Tribunal and National Convention. Because the Legislative Assembly had been disallowed, the Girondists lost their strength. Robespierre was the first deputy to the National Convention. He encouraged the execution of Louis XVI. Taking control of the situation, he helped create the Committee of Public Safety in 1793; the purpose, ostensibly, was to supervise the actions of the executive. Again eliminating his opponents, Robespierre took steps to force the Girondists out of the National Convention.

It wasn't long before the Committee of Public Safety led by Robespierre overshadowed the National Convention to take charge of France. Robespierre began a mass persecution of the Jacobins' enemies from October 1793 to July 1794; he was the author of the Reign of Terror. He declared that his goal was to eradicate those who opposed the Revolution and reduce the possibility of future invasions. All of this fueled Robespierre's attitude of supremacy and his leadership of the Revolutionary Tribunal. In a most telling act of arrogance, he made the cult of the Supreme Being an official religion based on the philosophy of Rousseau. Catholics and atheists alike criticized the move. Similarly, members of the National Convention felt a growing uneasiness with Robespierre's despotic influence, so Fouché, the French statesman and Minister of Police under Napoleon 1, organized a conspiracy against him. In his absence from a single meeting, Robespierre was accused of despotism.

When he learned that he was subject to arrest, Robespierre fled, but was unable to elude the National Guard. He and 21 of his followers were guillotined the next day, and 80 additional supporters met the same fate the day after. Thus, the Reign of Terror ended and a reaction against the Revolution began.

JOHANN WOLFGANG VON GOETHE, 1749–1832, *The Anti-Philosopher*

> " Is this the destiny of man? Is he only happy before he has acquired his reason or after he has lost it?
>
> —*The Sorrows of Young Werther*

- Wrote novels, plays, and poems hailed as "the history of the high-culture in Germany" during his time
- Enjoyed experimenting with alchemy
- Worked on the wave theory of light, but his conclusions were ignored in favor of Newton's particle theory, although quantum physics has proved both of these theories true
- Was presented as one of six men who were "the height of greatness" in Ralph Waldo Emerson's series of lectures, Representative Men

- Inaugurated the *Sturm und Drang* literary movement with his book *The Sorrows of Young Werther*, which, with Jean-Jacques Rousseau's similar critique of the scientific rationalism of the Enlightenment, emphasized emotionalism and extreme freedom of individual expression
- Embodied *Sturm und Drang*; plagued by thoughts of suicide, he "slept with a dagger by his side"
- Was skeptical of Kant's critique of reason, sensing that Kant was throwing out the baby (human experience and the pursuit of knowledge about the external world) with the bath (the problem of moral freedom)
- Was personally acquainted with several major figures in early 19th-century German thought, most notably Hegel, whose philosophy he liked for attempting to define the developmental process of nature, but disliked for working on an abstract logical level, rather than actually explaining the unfolding of the real nature we experience
- Believed, as Nietzsche later did, that natural development is an unfolding of energy rather than of individual substances per se, and that opposition and limiting constraints are necessary conditions for promoting the process of development, growth itself being essentially a struggle to overcome limits

Key Works

The Sorrows of Young Werther, 1774
The Metamorphosis of Plants, 1790
Elective Affinities, 1809
Faust, 1832
From my Life: Poetry and Truth, 1833

Biography

Novelist, playwright, poet, statesman, scientist, and lawyer, Johann Wolfgang von Goethe was decidedly not a philosopher. In fact, he supposed that philosophy had "by the frequent darkness and apparent uselessness of its subject-matter … made itself foreign to the mass, unpalatable, and at last superfluous." His personal aversion was warranted; his contemporaries and modern scholars consider him a philosopher only in the ancient sense, as a man "of great learning and wisdom whose active life serves as the outward expression of his thinking." His works, however, dominated and revolutionized German culture from the late 18th century to the early 19th century.

Goethe was born on August 28, 1749, in Frankfurt-on-Main, which later became part of Germany. His father was the imperial councilor and pushed Goethe to become a lawyer and settle down. In his younger years, he mastered French, German, Italian, and Greek with the help of his father and tutors. At 16, he attended the University of Leipzig and studied to fulfill his father's hope of wealth, although he gained a reputation in theatrical circles. It was there in 1776 that he fell in love with Anne Catherina Schoenkopf and wrote his first collection of 19 poems dedicated to her, *Annette*.

While visiting Strassburg, Goethe met the unofficial leader of the Sturm und Drang movement, Johann Gottfried Herder, who introduced him to poetry by giving him Shakespeare, Homer, and Ossian. Inspired by the great poetry and company, Goethe "inaugurated the literary movement" of Sturm und Drang when he attained worldwide fame with his book *The Sorrows of Young Werther*. In 1775, a year after completing a draft of the first part of *Faust*, 18-year-old Duke Karl August of Weimar invited Goethe to become a court-advisor and special counsel. Although Goethe eventually was granted the title of emperor and president of the chamber, he regretted that he was too busy to write during his ten years spent immersed in court life.

In 1786, Goethe took a 22-month journey in Italy disguised as the merchant Möler to rediscover his art. In Italy he met the artists Kaufmann and Tischbien, along with the housekeeper Christine Vulpius, with whom he had a scandalous love affair and married in 1806. In 1794, Goethe became "intimate friends and collaborators" with Schiller, a fellow German poet and philosopher, even though they had previously met and did not like one another. Goethe died March 22, 1832, in Weimar, one year after finishing both parts of *Faust*. He famously requested that the servants let in more light minutes before he died. He was laid to rest in Fürstengruft next to Schiller and Herder.

Faust

Goethe's magnum opus, a play based on the legend of Doctor Faustus, branches into two parts, one that he completed when he was 23 and the other just before his death. "Faust: the First Part of the Tragedy" opens with God and the Devil, Mephistopheles, arguing whether the scholar Dr. Faust can be led astray. Questions of life and what "comfort can the shallow world bestow?" frustrate Faust, and he contemplates suicide. In his weakest hour, Faust enters into a pact with the Devil: Mephistopheles agrees to be Faust's guide and give him worldly pleasures; however, if Faust ever says, "so fair thou art, remain," then the Devil can take his soul for eternity. Faust once again becomes young and seduces and impregnates a young girl, Margareta, or Gretchen, her German nickname. Faust, at this point wholly selfish and immoral, abandons Gretchen for a year until he has a terrifying vision of her and goes to see her in jail where she passes into the Heavenly realm.

"Faust: the Second Part of the Tragedy" splits into five acts. The first three acts center around Faust's desire to seduce Helen of Troy, manipulating time and space in order to take her as his own. Helen comes to him, declares her love, and they have a son, Eupherion. Mephistopheles still partners with Faust, but Faust's demands are often beyond the scope of Mephistopheles' power, demonstrating the superficiality of Christianity in that it has no power over other gods, specifically the ancient gods of Greek and Rome. In the fourth act, Faust ingratiates himself with a powerful emperor by helping him to victory in battle, gaining land in reward. In the fifth act, Faust is a rich and powerful ruler and, as he considers his kingdom, remarks that in the future he might say "so fair thou art, remain." Because he utters those words, he dies, but when Mephistopheles attempts to collect Faust's soul, angels come instead to carry his soul to heaven.

Faust demonstrates Goethe's feelings about the natural world, which reflect the Romantic tradition of the time. Faust, clinging to Romantic ideals, retreats to nature in a state of despair that has been created by the scientific world. He finds peace and restoration until his spirit is broken by his return to rationalism, and concludes that it is not man's innate sinfulness but his lack of connection to nature's spiritual power that causes the vacuum in man. Faust is not a hero at all, but a man of moral insufficiency who drags Gretchen with him into a tragic result for both of them. The question Goethe raises at the end in Heaven is a question for the Modernists: Why is Faust saved when he never repented, had no virtuous deeds to his credit, and expressed no religious faith?

Striving

Goethe believed salvation came from continual striving, rather than from any moral or faith-based source. He believed that the nature of man was "to never be satisfied but to feel a compulsion to strive on and on." In the opening scene of *Faust*, God remarks that Mephistopheles can have full reign over the Earth because "man must strive, and striving he must err." Goethe maintained the greatest sin was passivity and lack of action, so no matter the temptation or sin of man, he could still be saved; his sin is inevitable, but if he strives so is his salvation. Faust tells Mephistopheles that if he "be quieted with a bed of ease" and becomes "one of pleasure's devotees," then Mephistopheles can take his soul because he has no desire left to live. Faust's immortal soul will go to the Devil if he wishes to languish in one moment forever and forgo the struggling of mankind. To Goethe, the renunciation of striving leads directly to a relinquishing of the nature of man and salvation. At the play's end, Mephistopheles is devastated that the angels carry away Faust's soul and blames his own trickery in the timing of Faust's death. However, the angels themselves later declare Faust was saved "[f]or he whose strivings never cease / Is [theirs] for his redeeming."

Evolution

Goethe believed in evolution. This is notable, as he initially developed his ideas some time before more systematic presentations of evolutionary theory became public and long before Darwin published his theories. In Darwin's third edition of *Origin of Species*, he acknowledged Goethe as a subscriber to evolutionary thought. He is credited with finding the intermaxillary bone in man in rudimentary form, which later became a foundation of evolutionary doctrine. In *Faust*, there is a glass man named Homunculus who represents "the picture of the human soul" and desires to become a real man, not merely having the mind of one. As he searches for advice, he comes across a man named Thales who tells him, "from moisture all organic living came" and advises him to jump into the ocean. Homunculus represents Goethe's belief in large-scale evolution over time derived from baser creatures in the water. Goethe also believed that the soul was once present but gave its essence up in order to evolve, only to have it re-emerge later in the history of the world. The preexistence of a soul suggests Goethe's belief in some sort of greater cosmic world, either a god or a primitive "reincarnation."

The Church

Goethe's *Faust* showed Goethe's with the greed of institutionalized religion. He felt the church was corrupted because it blessed "him who makes her tasks his care," but did not bless those who really needed help. He also saw the church as gluttonous: it could "swallow gold and lands and such, / And never feel that [it] has had too much." He never accepted the doctrines of any one of the established churches. Faust, when asked about his religion, responded that one's "joy, love, heart, [and] God" are personal and individual, and "[n]ames are nothing but noise and smoke, / Obscuring heavenly light." This statement outlines Goethe's beliefs that God cannot be felt through organized systems of belief, but that He must be felt through the working and living universe.

Sturm und Drang

Sturm und Drang, or Storm and Stress, the late-18th-century German movement that Goethe inaugurated with his first popular novel, *The Sorrows of Young Werther*, exalted "nature, feeling, and human individualism." Sturm und Drang captivated the German public and inspired many imitators. Goethe believed rational thought could take a man only so far, and, as he asserts in *The Sorrows of Young Werther*, man only experiences happiness "before he has acquired his reason or after he has lost it." Sturm und Drang values "emotion over reason, disdain for social proprieties and exhortation for action in place of reflection." This trend of intense action and heightened emotions, often through an individual against his society, punctuates Goethe's plays and novels. Although the emotion that ruled the movement countered any self-discipline, causing it to lose favor quickly, the literary work from Sturm und Drang is the backbone of classic German literature.

Caroline Fuschino, 2015
Daren Jonescu, advisor

HENRI DE SAINT-SIMON ◊ 1760–1825, *Aristocrat and Utopian Socialist*

> " The philosopher … is not just an observer, he is an actor; he is an actor of the highest kind in a moral world because it is his opinion of what the world must become that regulates society.
>
> —*Essay on the Science of Man*

- Foresaw the industrialization of the world and believe science and technology would solve humankind's problems
- Was a failed suicide who only managed to put out one eye
- Led the scientific community, inspired by his vision
- Was a utopian socialist whom people have continued to interpret
- Believed industrialists should lead society, especially to help the poor
- Advocated for Christian socialism as one of its chief founders

Key Works

De la réorganisation de la société européenne (On the reorganization of European society), 1814
Nouveau Christianisme, 1825

Biography

Henri de Saint-Simon was born on October 17, 1760, in Paris, France. Saint-Simon was born to an impoverished aristocratic family and, unlike most people in his situation, was educated by private tutors. At 17 he joined the military and was sent to help the Americans in their fight for freedom from England as a captain of artillery. He returned to France during the French Revolution, invested in newly nationalized lands with borrowed money, and was imprisoned for a time. When released from prison, he was hugely rich as a result of currency fluctuations. He led a privileged and highly social life, but turned to the study of science at the École Polytechnique where he was encouraged to become a social theorist. His works on social theory are his legacy.

After sketching out some initial ideas, Saint-Simon collaborated with Augustin Thierry and Auguste Comte. Challenged by the intellectual rigor of these associates who both agreed and disagreed with him, Saint-Simon became for a time a believer in capitalism. He eventually came to believe in the needs for a spiritual regeneration of modern society, the new Christianity.

Nouveau Christianisme

Saint-Simon had an idea for a peaceful organization and a universal religion to improve the plight of the poor. He believed that society was moving toward peacefulness in a society that produces useful things. He wanted to simplify religion by getting rid of the dogma of Catholicism and Protestantism.

Rejecting many doctrines and rituals of those churches, he wanted to concentrate on Jesus' words in the New Testament. Moreover, he wanted to practice the teachings of Jesus and work toward improving the lives of society's least fortunate.

A small group of scientists gathered to collect and publish Saint-Simon's ideas. With the Exposition on the doctrine of Saint-Simon, they were able to "recruit him posthumously to the incipient socialist movement." They established a journal and began to meet throughout France. A school of Saint-Simon was formed to clarify the master's views. By 1830 (five years after his death), Saint-Simon's thoughts were influencing utopian socialism. Even Karl Marx named Saint-Simon (in addition to Charles Fourier and Robert Owen) in *The Communist Manifesto* as a believer in the new socialism. The ideas of the Saint-Simonians had a pervasive influence on the intellectual life of 19th century Europe.

THOMAS MALTHUS, 1766–1834, *The First Eugenicist*

> " The power of population is so superior to the power in the earth to produce subsistence for man, that premature death must in some shape or other visit the human race.
> —*An Essay on the Principles of Population*

- Became an English cleric and political economist
- Worked as a eugenicist
- Conducted experiments on population growth and overpopulation
- Said unchecked population growth will always increase faster than the food supply, leading to the degradation of society; this line of thinking is called Malthusianism.
- Was fascinated by the fact that the human race had not died off
- Argued that demand and capital are connected

Key Works

An Essay on the Principle of Population, 1798
Principles of Political Economy, 1817

Biography

Malthus contributed greatly to the field of economics by "highlight[ing] the relationship between food supply and population. Humans do not overpopulate to the point of starvation," he contended, "only *because* people change their behavior in the face of economic incentives." Thomas Robert Malthus grew up in a wealthy home in Westcott, England. Schooled at home for his early academic studies, he went to Jesus College, Cambridge in 1784 and was later a reverend in the Church of England. In 1804 he married Harriet Eckersall, and a year later became a professor of History and Political Economics at Hertfordshire. Although he rarely traveled, and lived a quiet life, Malthus did meet friend and economist David Ricardo in 1811. He wrote several books and essays about population growth and economic development, establishing himself as an "economic pessimist." Malthus died in December 29, 1834, in Somerset.

Overpopulation

In a time when optimism dominated philosophical thought, Malthus was known as a pessimist. Malthus claimed that the earth could sustain only a certain number of people. Once that limit was reached, food supplies would not be able to keep up with the demand; without adequate food supplies, poverty and degradation would overtake humanity. In addition to the limitations of food supply, famine and disease, he suggested, helped keep the population in check. He saw this as divine intervention. He continued with this theory in *An Essay on the Principle of Population*, writing that "the increase of population is necessarily limited by the means of subsistence, that population does invariably increase when the means of subsistence increase, and, that the superior power of population is repressed, and the actual population kept equal to the means of subsistence, by misery and vice."

Malthus believed that any law that helped the poor would only increase their desire to have children and lead to an increased demand for food. He stated in *An Essay on the Principle of Population*:

> The labouring poor, to use a vulgar expression, seem always to live from hand to mouth. Their present wants employ their whole attention, and they seldom think of the future. Even when they have an opportunity of saving they seldom exercise it, but all that is beyond their present necessities goes, generally speaking, to the ale house.

His conclusion was that helping the poor and thus increasing population in general, would keep everyone poor and lead to starvation and disease. He stated, "Man cannot live in the midst of plenty" for poverty is man's unavoidable lot.

Demand Creates Capital

Later in his life, Malthus went on to dispute the claim of Jean-Baptiste Say that supply creates its own demand, inventing the phrase "effective demand" to explain that consumers actually set the demand, leaving suppliers to meet it at the appropriate levels. Malthus believed that instead of simply buying what suppliers make, consumers can choose not to buy, thus changing demand. In *Principles of Political Economy*, Malthus wrote, "In general it may be said that demand is quite as necessary to the increase of capital as the increase of capital is to demand." Therefore, the true engine that would get the economy out of a recession would be an increase in spending, not saving. He continued to develop that idea in the same book, stating:

> Every exchange which takes place in a country, effects a distribution of its produce better adapted to the wants of society. … If two districts, one of which possessed a rich copper mine, and the other a rich tin mine, had always been separated by an impassable river or mountain, there can be no doubt that an opening of a communication, a greater demand would take place, and a greater price be given for both the tin and the copper; and this greater price of both metals, though it might be only temporary, would alone go a great way towards furnishing the additional capital wanted to supply the additional demand; and the capitals of both districts, and the products of both mines, would be increased both in quantity and value to a degree which could not have taken place without the this new distribution of the produce, or some equivalent to it.

This advanced idea on how wealth and economies grow would not be put into practice for more than 100 years, when Keynes would take it up.

Legacy

During the time of Malthus's life and writings, there was tremendous growth in the economy. Many economists devoted themselves to studying and explaining why that was happening and how other nations could enjoy the same benefits. Malthus warned that that type of economic growth was not sustainable and that it would lead to dire consequences. His writings "acted as a brake on economic optimism, helped to justify a theory of wages based on the wage earner's minimum cost of subsistence, and discouraged traditional forms of charity." Later economists, such as John Maynard Keynes, picked up on Malthus's idea of demand being the engine behind economic growth. Keynes, like Malthus, would argue that it is the spending consumer who will create incentives for producers to produce. Garrett Hardin would use some of Malthus's thoughts in his "Tragedy of the Commons." Malthus's ideas of overpopulation are still being debated today and one can even find the roots of the global warming debate in his writings.

Kurt Gutschick, faculty

JOHN DALTON, 1766–1844, *Originator of the Modern Atomic Theory*

> " Matter, though divisible in an extreme degree, is nevertheless not infinitely divisible. That is, there must be some point beyond which we cannot go in the division of matter. … I have chosen the word "atom" to signify these ultimate particles.
> —Manuscript Notes, Royal Institution Lecture 18, Jan 30, 1810

- Was an English scientist and devout Quaker
- Became known for his discoveries in meteorology and chemistry
- Discovered laws of the relation between temperature and pressure of a gas
- Published his discovery of colorblindness, which was initially known as Daltonism
- Spurred the development of modern atomic theory with his revolutionary Atomic Theory
- Explained that atoms are invisible and indestructible, and that each element is composed of atoms identical in size, relative weight, and other characteristics
- Wrote that chemical compounds are atoms arranged in specific ways and that chemical reactions are just rearranging atoms

Key Works

Meteorological Observations and Essays, 1793
A New System of Chemical Philosophy, 1808

Biography

Forming the basis of modern atomic theory is merely one of John Dalton's many scientific accomplishments. Dalton was born in 1766 to a prosperous family of English Quakers. When he was 14, he and his brother purchased a school and Dalton worked as a teaching assistant. As a teacher, Dalton studied under various mentors who taught him basic science, mathematics, and even meteorology. In 1793, Dalton began teaching in Manchester, where he wrote about meteorology and published one of his first books, *Meteorological Observations and Essays*. This book was just the beginning of Dalton's work to convert the theoretical subject of meteorology into an empirical science. As part of the

Manchester Literary and Philosophical Society, Dalton began researching color-blindness, a condition he observed in both his brother and himself. His most impactful work, though, was a result of his chemical research. Contrary to the then-common belief that atoms of all matter are alike, Dalton theorized that atoms of different elements vary in both size and mass. In addition to this principle, Dalton also developed laws that explained the thermal expansion of gases, performing countless experiments to determine the effect of temperature on the pressure of water vapor. Dalton later published *A New System of Chemical Philosophy*, in which he explained his theory that elements can be distinguished by their weight. Dalton also theorized that atoms cannot be created nor destroyed. Throughout his life, Dalton remained a devout Quaker before dying of a stroke in 1844. Dalton is best known for forming the foundation of modern knowledge about atomic structure, which continues to inspire experimentation and invention in the field of atomic science.

Dalton's Atomic Theory

Dalton's Atomic Theory was a major transformational step in chemistry that eventually was refined into Modern Atomic Theory. He postulated that all elements are actually composed of "atoms," tiny particles, indivisible and indestructible. All atoms of the same substance were alike in every way: size, weight, and all other properties. All chemical compounds, then, are made up of atoms arranged in whole-number ratios, and all chemical reactions are simply the process of rearranging these atoms. This theory revolutionized the entire field of chemistry, and even to this day his atomic theory is accepted worldwide, with a few minor improvements. Now scientists can forcibly split atoms through nuclear reactions, but Dalton was correct that it is impossible to divide atoms through chemical means.

Modern Atomic Theory

Building upon Dalton's original theories, Modern Atomic Theory is the current representation of the atomic structure. Expanding upon Dalton's idea that elements are composed of atoms, modern scientists are now able to describe the atoms' actual shapes. Modern Atomic Theory states that an atom's "nucleus" is composed of protons and neutrons and is surrounded by an electron "cloud." The number of electrons in the cloud can change the shape of the orbits of the electrons. One more major change in Dalton's theory is in his Law of Multiple Proportions. Dalton assumed that compounds formed from two elements were created in small ratios. For example, he believed that since water comprises hydrogen and oxygen, its chemical formula must be HO. Later, this was proved incorrect as Dalton's calculations of the elements' weights were incorrect. Dalton's calculations also did not account for diatomic elements. Dalton's theories said that singular elements did not form compounds, but this is untrue for compounds such as Oxygen (O_2) and Nitrogen (N_2). Dalton's discoveries have greatly benefitted many fields, including organic chemistry, material sciences, and quantum physics. His research on the atomic structure of elements is the cornerstone of modern chemistry.

Jack Beebe, 2012
McCarthy Nolan, 2016

JEAN-BAPTISTE SAY ◊ 1767–1832, *The Supply-side Economist*

> " The property a man has in his own industry, is violated, whenever he is forbidden the free exercise of his faculties or talents, except insomuch as they would interfere with the rights of third parties.
>
> —*A Treatise on Political Economy*

- Was a French economist and classical liberal
- Got expelled from his post in French government due to his criticisms of French economic policy, but was later re-elected after the French Revolution
- Argued in favor of economic competition, natural property rights, free trade, and the power of saving income
- Started the world's first school of business
- Formed and popularized Say's Law, which remains controversial to this day

Key Works

A Treatise on Political Economy, 1803

Biography

Jean-Baptiste Say was born to a wealthy family on January 5, 1767. He attended a private school in Croydon and was later employed as a merchant. It was not until after his marriage that he started to write and publish his economic ideas. Say was a firm believer in Adam Smith's theories of economic reasoning and a "laissez-faire" role of government. He was employed by the French government during the reign of Napoleon, but later was dismissed due to his controversial economic views. He published his most well known work, *A Treatise on Political Economy*, in 1803. In this work, Say introduced the famous "Say's Law," which states that supply creates its own demand. Say also argued that the nature of property rights is self-evident; when the state violates these natural rights, they are essentially holding the people in slavery. Say opened the first business school in the world and after the Second French Revolution broke out in 1830, he was elected to the council-general. He published a number of other books until his death in 1832, but his *Treatise on Political Economy* is his only work that has continued to influence economists over the past two centuries.

Say's Law

Say's Law can be summarized succinctly: "supply creates its own demand." Say wrote in 1804 that "products are paid for with products." Simply stated, savings are used by banks to loan money to firms in order to create products. Those products are created and bought by consumers, and the supply of those products is what creates its own demand. For example, in the 1980s the idea of a phone that could be carried around in your pocket would have been scoffed at as an impossibility. Fast-forward 30 years and about 50% of Americans own only cell phones and do not even have a "landline." Because firms brought this product to market, a demand for the product was created. Through the use of savings, firms can get the capital they need to create these products. Economists take this idea and argue for policy that allows firms to access loans needed to expand capital.

Legacy

The theory of Say's law gave birth to "supply-side economics," which, during the Reagan years, was employed to combat high unemployment and runaway inflation. The policy prescription was to cut taxes on the suppliers of goods in order to allow them to employ more people and expand the capital of those businesses. The goal of these policies was to generate demand and kick-start the market. This put into practice Say's law (supply creating its own demand) by allowing businesses to increase supplies of goods, while also employing workers who were then able to buy those same goods. Still controversial, Say's ability to organize the thoughts of Smith and others around this idea often dictates policies and banking today.

Kurt Gutschick, faculty
Elizabeth Palms, 2014

JEAN-BAPTISTE FOURIER, 1768–1830, *Origin of Engineering Science*

" The deep study of nature is the most fruitful source of mathematical discoveries.
—*Analytical Theory of Heat*

- Was a French mathematician, Egyptologist, and administrator with the French government
- Excelled in mathematics from a young age
- Developed the Fourier Series—a method of representing wave-like functions
- Wrote the *Analytical Theory of Heat*
- Served under Napoleon in his invasion of Egypt

Key Works

Analytical Theory of Heat, 1822

Biography

Jean-Baptiste Joseph Fourier was born to Joseph and Edmie Fourier on March 21, 1786, their ninth child. By age 10, Fourier had already lost both of his parents, and was sent to a local military school run by Benedictine monks. There, he displayed a high intelligence in mathematics, and, after graduating, stayed on as a teacher. After four years of teaching at the military school, he left to pursue an education at the newly established teacher-training school L'École Normale, where he excelled and became a professor of mathematics within a year of graduating. In 1798, a year after receiving the title of the department chair of analysis and mechanics, Fourier was drafted to Napoleon's army for the invasion of Egypt and was put in charge of archaeological and scientific investigations; it was here that he first became captivated with the mathematics of heat transfer. Throughout the French Revolution he supported his local Revolutionary Committee with fervor, but when the Reign of Terror came about, he attempted to resign "in protest" but had become far too involved. Scholars suspect that Fourier developed myxedema (profound hypothyroidism) from his time in Egypt, which caused him to have an intense sensitivity to cold; he died of a heart attack in 1830.

Analytical Theory of Heat

While in Egypt, Fourier developed an interest in heat. In a scientifically original approach, he "analyzed conduction by representing complicated oscillating quantities as sums of simpler components," meaning he broke down the process into its smaller parts, thus better explaining the overall conduction process, the transfer of heat through matter by communication of kinetic energy from particle to particle with no net displacement of the particles. In his *Analytical Theory of Heat*, Fourier portrayed how the conduction of "heat in solid bodies could be analyzed in terms of a series with sines and cosines as terms"; in other words, he used Fourier series (see below) to explain heat. Through experimentation, he discovered that heat does not follow the mechanical theories, like those of the movement of stars, the transmission of light, or the equilibrium and oscillations of the seas.

Fourier Series

Designed as a part of Fourier's *Analytical Theory of Heat*, a Fourier series is a way to represent a wavelike function as a combination of simple sine waves, expressed through the sum of "an infinite mathematical series with sines and cosines as terms." Originally developed to explain heat, Fourier series have been adapted to mathematical uses in algebra and calculus as well. In order to use a Fourier series to approximate any waveform, Fourier developed a set of rules for attaining the coefficients for the equation so "the series would be finite, and thus *converge* to a useful solution." Through a Fourier series, a sound or any other waveform can be analyzed by its constituent harmonics, and scientific data can be handled more efficiently with a Fourier series as a tool.

Father of Modern Engineering

In the *Analytical Theory of Heat*, Fourier pioneered concepts such as the uniformity of equations and the heat transfer coefficient, concepts used by engineers on a daily basis. The concept of dimensional uniformity is self-evident to scientists and students alike now, but when Fourier wrote about it, it was revolutionary. Much of what he wrote can be applied to many areas of science and engineering, making a strong argument that he is the father of modern engineering.

Madison Thompson, 2015

WILLIAM WORDSWORTH, 1770–1850, *Nature's Nostalgic Poet*

> " Five years have past; five summers, with the length
> Of five long winters! And again I hear
> These waters, rolling from their mountain-springs
> —"Lines Composed a Few Miles above Tintern Abbey"

- Was a prominent British Romantic poet
- Collaborated with Samuel Taylor Coleridge to produce the landmark work *Lyrical Ballads*
- Wanted, along with the other romantics, to change the intellectual climate of his age after being inspired by the French Revolution
- Wrote poetry using natural diction and common subject matter
- Focused on nature in his poetry, partly expressing his concerns about the Industrial Revolution
- Defined poetry as "the spontaneous overflow of powerful feeling; … emotions recollected in tranquility"
- Saw children to be closest to the pure, innocent, and imaginative state needed to commune with nature
- Believed that Nature hints at a Supreme Consciousness that is present everywhere; it is externalized in the natural world, but it inhabits "the mind of man"
- Was named Poet Laureate from 1843–1850

Key Works

Lyrical Ballads, 1798, 1800
"Lines Composed a Few Miles above Tintern Abbey"
"She Dwelt Among the Untrodden Ways"
The Prelude, 1805 (initial completion: he added to it throughout his lifetime; published after his death)
Poems, in Two Volumes, 1807
"I Wandered Lonely as a Cloud"
"London, 1802"
"The World is Too Much with Us"
"Ode: Intimations of Immortality from Recollections of Early Childhood"

Biography

Born in 1770 in Cumberland, England, William Wordsworth had a difficult childhood; his parents both died by the time he was 13. His foster family was not affectionate, which taught Wordsworth from a young age to "depend upon nature for [the] solace" typically provided by human relationships. Upon completing a degree at Cambridge in 1790, Wordsworth spent time in Europe where he was introduced to German Romanticism, which he and Coleridge brought back to England. Returning from the continent, Wordsworth moved in with his sister Dorothy in 1795 and was soon introduced to Samuel Taylor Coleridge, another aspiring poet. The result of their friendship resulted in several poetic masterpieces, published in their joint book *Lyrical Ballads*, and they collaborated for nearly ten years. Several other poets rose to prominence at the same time as Wordsworth and Coleridge, among them Percy Shelley, Lord Byron, and John Keats. Recognizing the "pervasive intellectual and imaginative climate" of their time, Percy Shelley called the poets' revolutionary zeal "the spirit of the age," and Coleridge claimed Wordsworth as "the best poet of the age." Wordsworth moved away, and eventually the "duties of ordinary live seemed to change and wear him down." Wordsworth's last years were prosperous and sorrowful at the same time, with wealth and fame as well as several family deaths until, in 1850, he died at the age of 80.

Romantic Poetry and Style

In the preface to his first major work *Lyrical Ballads*, Wordsworth provides a new definition of poetry—one that comes to characterize the project of the Romantic poets. For the Romantics, composing a poem was a highly personal process. While the Enlightenment thinkers and poets of the 18th century prized reason, order, moral instruction, and imitation of the classics, the Romantics of the early 19th century valued spontaneity, imagination, emotion, and original insight. Representing these values, Wordsworth's famous definition states that "poetry is the spontaneous overflow of powerful feeling; it takes its origin from emotions recollected in tranquility."

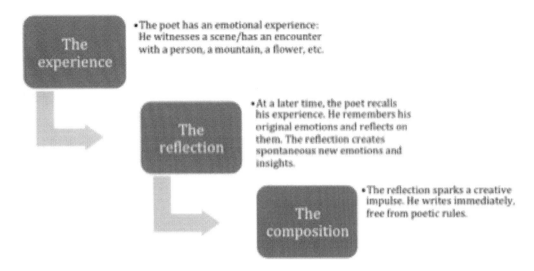

The experience
• The poet has an emotional experience: He witnesses a scene/has an encounter with a person, a mountain, a flower, etc.

The reflection
• At a later time, the poet recalls his experience. He remembers his original emotions and reflects on them. The reflection creates spontaneous new emotions and insights.

The composition
• The reflection sparks a creative impulse. He writes immediately, free from poetic rules.

Wordsworth's Poetic Process

Wordsworth's process demanded a type of writing unrestrained by typical poetic conventions. He aimed to compose in authentic, natural language, using the vocabulary of his inner thoughts. Many of his poems, like "Tintern Abbey," are written in blank verse—unrhymed iambic pentameter.

The Importance of Memory

Much of Wordsworth's poetry centers on the act of recalling a past moment, and the resulting poem demonstrates a back-and-forth negotiation between past and present. In the confrontation with the past, Wordsworth values the "hard-won equilibrium" that emerges with an emotional memory. This process is perhaps best highlighted in his well-known poem, "Lines Composed a Few Miles above Tintern Abbey." In the poem, Wordsworth takes his sister Dorothy to revisit the ruins of Tintern Abbey, a spot where in his youth he "bounded o'er the mountains ... wherever nature led." He mourns that the "aching joys" and "dizzy raptures" of that time "are now no more." However, he finds joy in the perspective of time and age. Instead of experiencing nature as a "thoughtless youth"—all passion, no reflection—he now senses "a presence that disturbs me with the joy / Of elevated thoughts; a sense sublime / Of something far more deeply interfused." Time granted Wordsworth deeper perspective and the gift of reflection. He came to understand that nature had gifted him with memories for the future, memories that would become for Wordsworth a "dwelling place" he revisited for sustenance in times of need.

Wordsworth's longer poetry, such as "Ode: Intimations of Immortality" and *The Prelude*, contain many autobiographical scenes of childhood and early youth. From these works, another Wordsworthian theme emerges: there is a freshness or glory to youth that fades with age. Young eyes see a "celestial light" in nature that becomes dimmer in the sober, more restrained mind of the mature man. Critic Charles Van Doren argues that Wordsworth believed in "the idea that human life is a sad, continuous, and unavoidable falling away from a state of existence that we somehow perceived when we were children but are no longer able to perceive when we grow up."

Nature

Along with his fellow Romantics, Wordsworth idealized nature as "imbued with a significance beyond itself," meaning that, for the Romantics, nature reveals the mind of God or signifies the presence of a sublime, unknowable force. Wordsworth also viewed nature as a retreat from the industrialized and socially corrupted cities. In "The World is Too Much With Us," Wordsworth criticizes the materialistic consequences of the Industrial Revolution in separating people from the natural world: "The world is too much with us; late and soon / Getting and spending, we lay waste our powers;— / Little we see in Nature that is ours." As a retreat from the cities, though, nature not only provides us pleasurable scenery but acts as a teacher, spurring "the growth of [man's] mind to maturity, a process unfolding through the interaction between the inner world of the mind and the shaping force of external Nature." In Wordsworth's view, then, nature is an acting force; it refines raw, emotional thoughts into beautiful reflections that act as a guard against life's ugliness:

> [Nature] can so inform
> The mind that is within us, so impress
> With quietness and beauty, and so feed
> With lofty thoughts, that neither evil tongues,
> Rash judgments, nor the sneers of selfish men …
> Shall e'er prevail against us.

"Tintern Abbey"
Cloie Dobias, 2015
Elizabeth Palms, 2014
Kelly Pippin, researcher

G.W.F. HEGEL, 1770–1831, *Philosopher of History and the Absolute*

> The real is the rational and the rational is the real.
> —*Philosophy of Right*

- The greatest and most influential forefather and intellectual fountainhead of "progressivism"
- Wrote the final definitive works of the German Idealist movement; was a personal colleague, associate, and critic of the other major members of the movement, such as J. G. Fichte and F.W.J. Schelling
- Witnessed Napoleon's march through his conquered town of Jena in 1806; along with Fichte, made the revitalization of the defeated German culture through politics and education a key goal of his system
- Was an early prototype of the "celebrity lecturer," an enormously popular university professor whose multitudes of students believed he would divulge the mysteries of existence in his class
- Believed his insights required new words and concepts, so his texts are extremely obscure to read and often elicit contradictory interpretations
- Claimed that he and his philosophy represented "the end of History," where "end" could be interpreted to mean either the *goal* or the *final step* (virtually interchangeable meanings given the nature of his system)
- Background for understanding Hegel:
    - German philosophy from Kant onward was focused on reconciling rationalism and empiricism, such as by showing that the empirical world of sense experience is partly a construct of pure reason itself (Kant)

- German idealism proper sprang from Kant's argument that human thought cannot know things in themselves but only phenomena (appearances) produced by the mind's own categories of understanding reconstituting the unknowable things in themselves into *human* experience
- The true or absolute idealists took Kant's claim much further, declaring that what he had in effect proved was that the thing in itself is an incoherent notion, since the fact that human minds can posit its existence establishes that it is no more than a projection of the mind's cognitive categories, and thus that the "phenomenal world"—the world of experience as produced by Mind's own operations, which *includes* the confused postulate of a "thing in itself"—is *the only reality*

- Hegel fleshed out the fullest implications of the German idealist position, especially with regard to the temporal aspects of the phenomenal world, with the following reasoning:
  - If all the world, in its formal *and* material elements, is actually the Mind perceived as Object of its own thinking (because there is no "thing in itself" beyond the Mind's operations), then the *development* of life and civilization over time must also be a rational construct produced by Mind
  - This inference transforms history (the past understood as a loosely connected sequence of events depending on contingencies which might have turned out differently) into *History*, a rationally organized progression with its own inherent and necessary logic, similar to the necessary logic of all the other mental constructs that make the phenomenal world a predictable, rational place
  - Mind itself is therefore the subject undergoing progressive development through History, according to a rationally discoverable pattern
- This pattern, in the abstract, is a dialectical process: *thesis* (putting forth a new "certainty"), *antithesis* (introduction of a limiting condition or problem that casts doubt on the complete validity of the thesis), and *synthesis* (a resolution of antithesis into original thesis to produce a richer, more comprehensive idea that overcomes the apparent opposition); the synthesis in turn serves as a thesis for the next stage in logical development / self-discovery
- The reason Mind (also called "Spirit") was not always aware of itself as a universal and developmental substance is that it is only at the conclusion of the process that Mind becomes fully conscious of itself as both the subject and object of a grand *self-revelation*; in other words, Mind only recognizes at the end of its long search that it itself was the object it had been seeking to know all along
- This final stage of self-revelation, when Mind recognizes itself fully as the unity and cohesive meaning of all Historical development, is the stage of Absolute Knowing, and therefore the end of History, in the sense that the development to full self-awareness is complete, and Mind may begin true (non-delusional) philosophizing at last
- Hegel in effect identifies himself with this mature stage of Mind's development, while identifying the mature stage with God as self-revealed collective consciousness
- Since Mind or Spirit is a collective entity, the beginning of its mature stage at the end of History necessitates a new ethico-political philosophy in which freedom is redefined as the voluntary submission of individuals to the collective life of society
- Hence, Hegel's political philosophy (like Fichte's) places heavy emphasis on the state's status as a kind of god, and on state-directed moral and intellectual education as the mechanism of ensuring universal acquiescence to the collective will, i.e., to the Mind as State

Key Works

Phenomenology of Mind, 1807
Science of Logic, 1812–1816
Encyclopedia of the Philosophical Sciences, 1817
Philosophy of Right, 1820
The Philosophy of History, 1837

Biography

Hegel lived in electrifying historical times. When he was 19, the news of the fall of the Bastille rocketed through Europe; many, including Hegel, saw this event as a "glorious dawn." Later, as a professor in 1806, he would admire the Emperor Napoleon marching through the streets of his conquered Jena and see the doors of the University of Jena closed due to the French Occupation. As a result, Hegel briefly became a newspaper editor in Bavaria. He lived during the German Romantic movement, a time when people like Goethe and Schiller were writing, and he became close friends with the poet Hölderlin and the younger philosopher Friedrich Schelling while studying philosophy and theology at the University of Tubingen. Finally, looming large in the philosophical background was the brilliant work of Immanuel Kant, whose *Critique of Pure Reason* was published in 1781. Kant's *Critique* is frequently considered one of the greatest philosophical works of all time, and Hegel's philosophy is a direct response to Kant.

In 1818, the 48-year-old Hegel attained the most prestigious philosophy position in Germany: a professorship at the University of Berlin, succeeding the late German Idealist Johann Gottlieb Fichte. Hegel had been a tutor for a wealthy family, an unsalaried lecturer (and later a professor) at the University of Jena, a principal and high school teacher, a newspaper editor, and a professor of philosophy at the University of Heidelberg. He moved to Berlin with his wife, Marie Helena Susanna von Tucher, and their two boys. He had fathered an illegitimate son, Georg Ludwig Friedrich Fischer, with his landlady in Jena, and Ludwig Friedrich left an orphanage to join Hegel's family when he was 10. In 1831, Hegel, recently decorated for his service to the Prussian state by Frederick William III, fell victim to a cholera epidemic in Berlin. He died on November 14, 1831, allegedly uttering the words, "And he didn't understand me."

History Has a Purpose and a Meaning

Many of Hegel's most important ideas can be understood through examining his conception of history. The ultimate purpose of human nature, for Hegel, is to gain freedom and knowledge, and so he attempted to find a meaning and direction in human history. In Hegel's view, "The history of the world is none other than the progress of the consciousness of freedom." The result of history is the realization of freedom.

Hegel's philosophy is dynamic: it's never still or at rest. There is movement and development at the heart of his thought. The key to this development is Hegel's notion of the "dialectic." Bryan Magee explains that the dialectic means "every complex situation is bound to contain within itself conflicting elements; and these are, of their nature, destabilizing, so the situation can never continue indefinitely." Thus, an initial thesis changes into its opposite—an antithesis—followed by a synthesis of the two opposites, which then becomes its own new thesis. An example may help illuminate Hegel's thought.

Hegel, in an unusual move for a philosopher, uses concrete examples from history to illustrate this dialectical process. For example, in ancient Greece there was harmony between the individual and society until Socrates demanded the use of one's individual conscience. The thesis of Greek harmony led to the antithesis of individual conscience exemplified by the Protestant Reformation, but the instability of individual conscience and radical freedom resulted in the destructive terror of the French Revolution. A synthesis between harmony and individual conscience had to result: a truth found within the two opposites had to emerge. Some other examples that Hegel used are the thesis of being, the antithesis of nothingness, and the synthesis of becoming. He also gave the example of freedom and tyranny synthesizing into law.

This dialectical movement of history leads to a union of freedom and what Hegel calls "absolute knowledge." There is a rational plan and purpose to history, and the dialectic unfolds this plan. The dialectical movement is towards unity because ultimate reality is what Hegel calls "Geist"—mind or spirit. Geist includes both the idea of reality as mental or spiritual—reality as Mind—as well as a religious notion of the "spirit" of the times or the "spirit of the age." History is the story of the development of Mind, but Mind isn't simply the sum of all of our individual minds. Mind is manifested in all things, but it isn't identical with all things. An analogy for Mind might be something like language: language pervades all aspects of our lives, but language isn't identical with the words that someone speaks; there's always much, much more to language.

How Mind Comes to Know Itself: *The Phenomenology of Mind*

Hegel's *Phenomenology of Mind* examines the different forms and development of our consciousness—sensations, understanding, reason, self-consciousness, etc. These are stages of consciousness that move from lower to higher, but one must past through the lower in order to realize the higher. His *Phenomenology* shows how the more limited forms of consciousness, like our basic sensations or awareness of our perceptions, necessarily develop through higher stages like self-consciousness and into what he calls "absolute knowledge."

Another way to conceive of Hegel's task is that he's trying to show that all the branches of philosophy are ultimately unified, and no absolute distinction can be made between them. As he says in his famous preface to the *Phenomenology*, "Truth is the whole." Thus, he believes that the philosophical questions that Kant asked, like "What can I know?" "What ought I do?" "For what can I hope?" and "What is man?" are limited attempts to articulate the Absolute: they're just partial glimpses of the whole. Singer explains that the simpler forms of consciousness will prove themselves inadequate: "This simple form of consciousness will, however, prove itself to be something less than genuine knowledge, and so will develop into another form of consciousness; and this in turn will also prove inadequate and develop into something else, and so the process will continue until we reach true knowledge." This process, as one might have guessed, is dialectical. Thus, the *Phenomenology* is the 750-page project of showing how lower forms of consciousness progress to new forms of consciousness and towards true Philosophy: "actual knowledge of what truly is." Actual knowledge of what "truly is," or what is most fundamentally real for Hegel, is the Absolute.

The Master and Slave Relationship: the Struggle for Recognition

Hegel's famous "Master and Slave" relationship emerges in his analysis of self-consciousness in the *Phenomenology of Mind*. Hegel thinks that we can't achieve self-consciousness alone: it requires recognition of another self-consciousness—another person. We come to know ourselves through what we believe others think about us—similar to the way nations "recognize" a new country through diplomatic relations. This recognition of another doesn't turn out to be peaceful and non-threatening, however. Specifically, as Singer explains, "my self-consciousness is threatened by the existence of another person who fails to acknowledge me as a person." In the quest for a pure self-consciousness—one that rises above life's basic desires and physicality—one person emerges as master and the other as slave.

This relationship between master and slave ends up being unstable and it has an unexpected outcome. Since the master is treating the slave as an object and seeing her as a thing rather than as another self-consciousness, the slave is no longer the true self-consciousness that the master needs. The master can't be satisfied with recognition from a lesser being, so the master isn't getting the recognition she requires to achieve self-consciousness. The slave, of course, isn't receiving recognition either; but by working in the world—creating, fashioning, shaping, and making objects—the slave makes her ideas into something outside of herself: a permanent object. This helps the slave discover that she has a mind of her own. Marx took Hegel's master-slave relationship and applied it to labor: when the worker puts herself into her labors, but someone else owns the fruits of that labor, the worker loses her essence and is oppressed.

Science of Logic: the Study of Purified Ultimate Reality

Hegel's *Science of Logic* applies the dialectical method to our thinking. Many philosophers think that logic doesn't really tell us anything about the world: They see logic as analyzing the form and structure of arguments, but not their content. Hegel disagrees. As an idealist, Hegel believes that when our thinking is examined using logic, reality is revealed. Hegel's goal in the *Science of Logic* is to start with our concepts, and through dialectical analysis, reach the "absolute idea." He describes it like this: "Everything else is error and gloom, opinion, striving, caprice and transitoriness; the absolute idea alone is being, imperishable life, self-knowing truth, and the whole of truth." His goal is to study ultimate reality in its pure form, "without husk in and for itself," generalized from the specific and particular forms that reality takes in the minds of human beings.

Jeff Culver, faculty
Daren Jonescu, advisor

SAMUEL TAYLOR COLERIDGE, 1772–1834, *The Sage of High Gate*

> And what if all of animated nature
> Be but organic harps diversely framed,
> That tremble into thought, as o'er them sweeps
> Plastic and vast, one intellectual breeze,
> At once the Soul of each, and God of all?
>
> —"The Eolian Harp"

- Was a British Romantic poet known for his mystical ballad "The Rime of the Ancient Mariner" and his "conversation poems"
- Had a wide variety of interests, including politics, religion, and literary criticism; in his later years, he became famous for his widely attended living room lectures

- Befriended William Wordsworth; together they published *Lyrical Ballads* in 1798
- Struggled with depression and opium addiction all his life; these elements both fueled and hindered his creative output
- Believed in the "one life" coursing through all natural things
- Became an "unapologetic intellectual elitist" and claimed that intellectuals must be the priests of the national culture
- Committed himself to conservation Christian theology
- Left projects unfinished

Key Works

"The Eolian Harp," 1796
"This Lime-Tree Bower My Prison," 1797
Lyrical Ballads, 1798, 1800
      "The Nightingale"
      "The Rime of the Ancient Mariner"
"Frost at Midnight," 1798
"Christabel," 1798
"Fears in Solitude," 1798
"Dejection: An Ode," 1802
"Kubla Khan," 1816
"To William Wordsworth," 1817
Biographia Literaria, 1817

Biography

Coleridge was born in Devonshire, England, in 1772, the son of a vicar and schoolmaster. He attended college at Cambridge and, though intellectually curious, quickly grew bored with academic life. Never earning his degree, Coleridge, along with fellow poet Robert Southey, socialized with a group of radical religious and political thinkers in the early 1790s. Spurred by the ideals of the French Revolution, Coleridge and his friends planned to start a democratic community in America called "Pantisocracy," but the plan ultimately fell through. Unfortunately, the project had pressured Coleridge to take a wife, Sarah Fricker, whom he did not love. Tension from their marriage would later inform the depressive elements of much of his poetry. In 1795, Coleridge met William Wordsworth, and the two became friends and colleagues, co-publishing *Lyrical Ballads* in 1798, a seminal work for the Romantic movement. However, a deepening depression, fueled by an addiction to laudanum, threatened his creative output and led to a separation with his wife and a falling out with Wordsworth. Amid these troubles, he began lectures on literary criticism, wrote for newspapers, and composed political treatises. In 1816, he moved in with James Gillman, a doctor who helped control, but not eliminate, his opium addiction. He grew more interested in studying religion and politics, ultimately becoming known in literary circles for his conservative social philosophies. As a literary and social critic, "one of his major legacies is the notion that culture, the nation's artistic and spiritual heritage, represents a force with the power to combat the fragmentation of a modern, market-driven society and to restore a common, collective life." Having reconciled with his wife and Wordsworth, Coleridge continued to live with Gillman in London's Highgate neighborhood, where many would come to visit or hear him speak or read aloud in his captivating narrative voice; these home lectures earned him a respected place in the literary world and the epithet "The Sage of Highgate."

The Conversation Poems and Imagination

The term "Conversation Poem" refers to eight poems composed by Coleridge between 1772 and 1834. Early 20th-century literary critic George McLean Harper was the first to use the term as specific to Coleridge, taking it from Coleridge's own subtitle in "The Nightingale: A Conversation Poem." As a general term during the Romantics' day, it meant "a sustained blank-verse lyric of description and meditation, in the mode of conversation addressed to a silent auditor." The Coleridge poems now grouped together under this category are "The Eolian Harp," "This Lime-Tree Bower My Prison," "Frost at Midnight," "Fears in Solitude," "The Nightingale," "Dejection: An Ode," and "To William Wordsworth." For later literary critics, these works specifically came to signify "a new, informal mode of poetry in which Coleridge could use a conversational tone and rhythm to give unity to a poem."

Often, a Conversation Poem opens with Coleridge "speaking," either to another person in the scene of the poem or to himself. For example, "The Eolian Harp" begins with Coleridge addressing his fiancée as they sit in their garden: "My pensive Sara! thy soft cheek reclined / Thus on mine arm, most soothing sweet it is." Similarly, "This Lime-Tree Bower My Prison" opens with Coleridge bemoaning his loneliness as he sits injured in a lime-tree grove, and his friends go walking without him: "Well, they are gone and here must I remain, / This lime-tree bower my prison!" Importantly, Coleridge's conversation poems often follow the same pattern: the poet observes his immediate surroundings, noticing particularities that prompt a flight of mental fancy that then leads to an important realization. The realization is always fueled by the power of imagination; Coleridge's mind travels beyond the confines of his physical surroundings and brings him clarity about the reality to which he returns. In "Frost at Midnight," for instance, Coleridge sits by his sleeping baby on a silent winter's night, watching a piece of soot flutter around the fire. He is suddenly transported back to school and to his "sweet birth place." He realizes that, as a child, he enjoyed his strongest connection to nature and imagination, and he concludes his poem with wishes for his own baby's future imaginative life. According to M.H. Abrams's influential essay on Coleridge, "the [conversation] poem rounds itself to end where it began, at the outer scene, but with an altered mood and deepened understanding which is the result of the intervening meditation."

One Life

Coleridge believed in what he called the "life consciousness" of all individuals, by which he meant man's ability to unify the various aspects of reality through his intellect and imagination. "The Eolian Harp" posits that a divine, creative force flows through all things. In the poem, Coleridge sits in his garden, listening to the sound of the wind as it blows through a harp he has placed in the window. Meditating on the music, he proclaims:

> O! the one Life within us and abroad,
> Which meets all motion and becomes its soul,
> A light in sound, a sound-like power in light,
> Rhythm in all thought, and joyance everywhere—

The harp becomes a metaphor for both the creative intellect of man and the beauty of nature; both man and nature are instruments that channel the music of a greater force:

> And what if all of animated nature
> Be but organic Harps diversely framed,
> That tremble into thought, as o'er them sweeps

> Plastic and vast, one intellectual breeze,
> At once the Soul of each, and God of all?

Coleridge's famous ballad "The Rime of the Ancient Mariner" is also concerned with the link of life between all things. The poem tells the story of a sailor who has committed a crime against the life principle by slaying an albatross. The act of killing the albatross (a symbol of the natural world) temporarily destroys the mariner's "life consciousness," which is Coleridge's theory that man's creative intellect, in harmony with nature, can find unity in the seemingly disparate aspects of reality. With the mariner's "life consciousness" altered, the sun loses its beauty, turning blood red, and the sea swarms with slimy, legged creatures. The mariner, in dejection, hangs the dead albatross around his neck for penance. Without realizing it, the mariner then marvels at and blesses the strange beauty of the sea creatures, and this blessing lifts the curse, reinitiating the creative process. While telling his amazing tale to a wedding guest, the mariner concludes with this moral:

> " He prayeth best, who loveth best
> All things both great and small;
> For the dear God who loveth us,
> He made and loveth all.

This moral reaffirms Coleridge's belief in the divine connectedness of all things. However, unlike the fairly pantheistic message of "The Eolian Harp," the Ancient Mariner evokes a more traditional Christian God. The theology of "Ancient Mariner" reveals concepts that Coleridge processed through much of his work. Christianity had always informed his understanding of the divine, however, after his emergence from opium addiction in the early 1800s, Christianity became his official creed. In writing his *Biographia Literaria,* his meditative work of essays, Coleridge "emerged as the heir to the conservatism of Edmund Burke, an opponent to secularism and a defender of the Anglican Church."

Procrastination and "The Person from Porlock"

Coleridge struggled all his life with motivation and organization, often lacking the drive to complete projects he started. He never finished his degree at Cambridge, for instance, and his utopian project with Robert Southey fell through shortly after. This pattern plagued him, even throughout his most prolific periods. His "drug addiction sapped his strength and will"; his poems were often completed in a "spasm of intense effort" while "writings that required sustained planning and application were left unfinished, or like *Biographia Literaria*, made up of brilliant sections padded out with filler," even with plagiarism. The most famous example of Coleridge's inability to finish his work is his "incomplete" poem "Kubla Khan." In the preface to his poem, Coleridge tells the story of how he fell asleep one night right "at the moment that he was reading the following sentence: 'Here the Khan Kubla commanded a palace to be built.'" Coleridge proceeded to dream a fantastic vision (likely fueled by his opium use), and when he awoke, he immediately sat down to write the poem in his head:

> " In Xanadu did Kubla Khan
> A stately pleasure-dome decree:
> Where Alph, the sacred river, ran
> Through caverns measureless to man,
> Down to a sunless sea.

Coleridge managed to write down 55 lines of poetry before, as he claims in his preface, he was "called out by a person on business from Porlock, and detained by him above an hour." When he returned to his poem, "all the rest had passed away like the images on the surface of a stream." This (perhaps legendary) story not only exemplifies Coleridge's problem with procrastination, but the "Person from Porlock" has become a famous character in his own right, one who symbolizes the frustrations of the writer, namely lack of inspiration, writer's block, and inopportune interruption. In fact, "Kubla Khan," beyond its Romantic language and exotic subject, is now understood as a poem mainly about "the nature of human genius" and the process of committing that genius to page.

Cloie Dobias, 2015
Elizabeth Palms, 2014
Kelly Pippin, researcher

DAVID RICARDO, 1772–1823, *The Investor Economist*

> " Under a system of perfectly free commerce, each country naturally devotes its capital and labour to such employments as are most beneficial to each. This pursuit of individual advantage is admirably connected with the universal good of the whole. By stimulating industry, by rewarding ingenuity, and by using most efficaciously the peculiar powers bestowed by nature, it distributes labour most effectively and most economically: while, by increasing the general mass of productions, it diffuses general benefit, and binds together, by one common tie of interest and intercourse, the universal society of nations throughout the civilized world.
>
> —*The Principles of Economy and Taxation*

- Was a British political economist, known to be part of the classical school of economic thought
- Amassed a personal fortune working as speculator
- Argued in favor of free trade and national specialization
- Is credited with the idea of comparative advantage
- Created the Iron Law of Wages, "which stated that all attempts to improve the real income of workers were futile and that wages perforce remained near the subsistence level"

Key Works

Essay on the Influence of a Low Price of Corn on the Profits of Stock, 1815
The Principles of Economy and Taxation, 1817

Biography

Ricardo was born in the Dutch Republic into a Sephardic Jewish family of Portuguese extract. He received training through his family to become a stockbroker, but was disowned after marrying a Quaker woman. He used his training as a stockbroker to amass a large fortune, earning the bulk of it by speculating on the outcome of the Battle of Waterloo, according to Ricardo's obituary published in *The Sunday Times*. He retired shortly after making his millions and wrote on a number of economic topics, focusing mainly on trade. He was a member of the British Parliament, serving in the House of

Commons; however, illness forced him to retire and he died a year later at 51. When he died, his estate was worth over $100 million in today's money.

Comparative Advantage

Ricardo introduced the idea of comparative advantage, a beneficial effect of specialization. Comparative advantage can exist on a micro and macro scale. Quickly summarized, comparative advantage occurs because a country that trades for products it can get at lower cost from another country is better off than if it had made the products at home. Naturally, individuals and countries will seek to produce that which they can do well. Each entity will specialize, based on a number of different factors such as talent, geography, and availability of resources. Specialization is the key attribute that a country should seek when engaging in trade. Though a country might be able to do something faster and at a greater rate than another country, that country must find what it has a comparative advantage in producing. Ricardo states in his work *Principles of Economy and Taxation*, "two manufacturers may employ the same amount of fixed, and the same amount of circulating capital; but the durability of their fixed capitals may be very unequal." Because of this unequal production, those who are less productive in that market will switch to that in which they are more productive. If left to their own accord, individuals will do this naturally and, if able to trade, will benefit society by producing more goods and services with the least amount of resources. He uses the example of wine and cloth manufacturing in Portugal and England to illustrate his point. Throughout the example, Ricardo states that Portugal can produce more of each in the same amount of time, with the same resources. So why not have Portugal produce both and allow England to just buy what it needs? The first part of the answer is simply, if England can produce nothing that Portugal needs, why would Portugal trade with England in the first place? Also, if Portugal can produce much more wine and just a little bit more cloth, why not have England produce the cloth so that Portugal can produce what it does well, and then each country can trade? This would make both countries wealthier. In light of this example, it is easy to see why countries should focus on that in which they have an advantage, so why does it not happen? In Ricardo's day, most countries were pursuing a policy of mercantilism, which protected that country's industry. Ricardo would point out that oftentimes countries put in place protectionist policies that do not allow for free trade.

David Ricardo simplified Adam Smith's ideas on trade to make them widespread. His notions of comparative and absolute advantage are used to argue for free trade between individuals and countries. The criticism that still exists today is that of job loss in the home country.

Kurt Gutschick, faculty

JANE AUSTEN, 1775–1817, *The Undercover Feminist*

> " There are few people whom I really love, and still fewer of whom I think well. The more I see of the world, the more am I dissatisfied with it; and every day confirms my belief of the inconsistency of all human characters, and of the little dependence that can be placed on the appearance of merit or sense.
>
> —*Pride and Prejudice*

- Was an English novelist who is considered a social satirist, psychologist, and dramatist

- Grew up in an imaginative household that encouraged her to pursue writing and think independently
- Saw marriage as an economic institution, but believed that one should only marry for true love, not for money or power
- Wrote with four main principles of ethics: prudence, amiability, propriety, and dignity
- Sparked modern day authors to imitate her realistic style and romantic themes with her fame and success

Key Works

Sense and Sensibility, 1811
Pride and Prejudice, 1813
Mansfield Park, 1814
Emma, 1815
Northanger Abbey, 1817
Persuasion, 1817

Biography

Jane Austen is considered one of the most brilliant writers of all time. Her novels of romance and wit have entertained and encouraged students, philosophers, and readers worldwide for over 200 years. Born the seventh child and second daughter, Austen grew up in a family that encouraged open education, free speech, imagination, and creativity. The Austen family regularly gathered and wrote productions, inviting friends and family to their home to watch their work. This nurtured and influenced Austen to write more and more on her own; she published her first dark and satirical novel, *Love and Friendship,* in 1789. During her life, she fell in love only once, but the man's family did not approve of the match and tore the relationship apart. Following this heartbreak, a wealthy man proposed to Austen. Austen accepted out of financial concern for her struggling family. However, Austen rethought her decision and later declined the proposal since she was not in love. As she continued to write, age and sickness began to take a toll on her body, and her health quickly declined. She died on July 18, 1817 in Winchester.

Morals and Manners

Jane Austen's novels, though filled with creativity, imagination, humor and lightheartedness, often expressed sharp criticism of society's morality. Each of her works sympathizes with people who struggle to accept moral laws and societal dictates; in her Romantic era, to be good and to be proper were most often one and the same. Austen implemented an ethical foundation that reflected values appropriate for the bourgeoisie, using four guiding ethical principles: prudence, amiability, propriety, and dignity.

These four qualities manifest in her most famous novel, *Pride and Prejudice.* In one scene of *Pride and Prejudice*, the main character Elizabeth exemplifies and is rewarded for her prudence. When Jane, Elizabeth's older sister, falls ill from a downpour of rain and is alone at a distant neighbor's house, Elizabeth, foreseeing that Jane's condition might worsen, hikes through muddy fields to visit and care for Jane. Elizabeth is thus rewarded with more time with Mr. Darcy because of her actions. Amiability, the virtue of friendliness, cloaks Austen's weaker characters with sympathy. Darcy's pride is slowly redeemed through his amiability. Elizabeth begins to favor Darcy when she hears that his pride "has often led him to be liberal and generous,—to give his money freely, to display hospitality, to assist his tenants, and relieve the poor. … He has also brotherly pride, which with some brotherly affection, makes him a very kind and careful guardian of his sister; and you will hear him generally cried up as the most attentive and best of brothers." Austen's third principle, propriety, means to act in accordance with the day's etiquette. At a dance that occurs early in the novel, Darcy's friend asks Elizabeth why she is not dancing, and Elizabeth replies that she is looking for a partner. Darcy, acting with propriety, offers his hand to her. Darcy knows that not to offer his hand in a dance would have been considered rude and against the morality of the time, and readers inwardly praise him for this action. Austen's final principle is dignity, the ability to consider oneself as independent and deserving of respect. Elizabeth exemplifies this by demanding respect from Mr. Darcy. In the midst of moral dilemma, Austen's characters are guided by her four main principles as they explore the world of morality and manners.

Feminism

Austen was certainly a feminist, although she was not as outspoken as more prominent feminists of her era, such as Mary Wollstonecraft. She approaches feminism with a gentle yet satirical tone. As all of her novels focus on romance and marriage, her criticism targets these commonplace practices. Austen perceived that most marriages in her day were economic institutions and business transactions, generally motivated by convenience, status, or need. Contrary to this view, Austen believed that marriage should be built on true love. In *Pride and Prejudice*, she contrasts marriages of convenience, where the woman's natural desire is subordinate to her social survival, with ones of true love. Charlotte marries Mr. Collins because she longs for security, but she has no affection for him, while Elizabeth marries Darcy out of love. Austen's feminism becomes apparent when we see how those women are rewarded for their choice: Charlotte is stuck with a ridiculous husband while Elizabeth enjoys a kind and affectionate partner. Austen's works highlight a woman's ability to reason, rationalize, and think for herself. Austen makes it clear that without independent thought, women are unable to achieve their full potential. One commentator notes that "Austen's heroines navigate through the minefields of their lives by using their heads." Catherine improves her critical thinking skills as she struggles with the complications of a tangled social life in *Northanger Abbey*; Emma learns to censor her thoughts by reflecting on her mistakes; in *Persuasion*, Anne Elliot finds herself after being challenged at Lyme.

Additionally, Austen questioned masculine assumptions about women and their role in society. In the 19th century, men dominated the world of education; women were educated only in order to be marketable for marriage. Through both her own success as a writer and her characters' pursuit of knowledge, she defied the stereotype that women do not need knowledge. "I declare after all there is no enjoyment like reading! How much sooner one tires of anything than of a book! When I have a house of my own, I shall be miserable if I have not an excellent library," announces Elizabeth in *Pride and Prejudice*. By writing compelling heroines who demonstrate independent thought and active minds, Austen subtly confronted prevalent female stereotypes. Although she was not blunt in her declarations of feminism, Austen encouraged her female readers to find feminist ideals exemplified in her stories. In so doing, male readers are also encouraged to welcome the education and intelligence of women.

Realism

Austen is considered a realist because her works accurately reflect believable social situations. Her novels often portray young people searching for a marriage that will maintain or increase their status. She writes of moral dilemmas, social conflicts, and personal worries; the experiences of her characters are often ordinary, from preparing for a dance to enjoying a night by the fire. Her cultural landscape contrasts greatly with other popular novels of the day, which delved into more sensational and provocative plots. Thus, Austen's readers were able to readily identify the world she created. Identifying many of the prominent issues of the time and addressing them with quiet fierceness, "she was willing to state what others only think." Although Austen's works represented reality, some criticize her neat, happy endings. Austen generally ended her stories fairly and merrily for good characters, comically for the absurd, and poorly for the morally bankrupt—endings life does not always provide. Consequently, Austen's realism should be understood as a literary device by which she achieves an empathetic connection with her readers.

Imagination

Benefitting from a childhood full of imagination and creativity, Austen developed a quick wit and an observant eye. In the 18th century, the Austens were a rare family that embraced the imaginative and encouraged children to write and create together with adults. Austen's father nurtured her creativity by allowing her access to his library, which was filled with different genres and topics. All of Austen's novels revolve around a single woman and her journey towards matrimony, a seemingly mundane plot, yet Austen varied this plot so that each novel stands alone as a uniquely meaningful experience. Joseph Epstein states, "Surely this is the definition of genius in a writer: the capacity to make a text that can give and give, a text that is never fully read, a text that goes on multiplying meanings." Each of her novels exemplify the extraordinary power of her imagination, which shaped the classics that readers love today.

Samantha Sherwood, 2015

CARL VON CLAUSEWITZ, 1780–1831, *The Military Strategist*

> " We see, therefore, that War is not merely a political act, but also a real political instrument, a carrying out of the same by other means.
>
> —*On War*

- Rose to the rank of major general in the Prussian army and is best known for his battle against Napoleon in the Waterloo Campaign
- Became the Director of the War College in Berlin
- Made his wife promise not to publish *On War* because he had not finished editing it, but family friends convinced her otherwise after his death
- Didn't benefit from *On War* because it didn't become popular until a time of Prussian military successes 40 years after his death.
- Fought in multiple campaigns and in major battles, but never received any substantial wounds
- Served only a year as a major general before he died of cholera in 1831

Key Work

On War, 1832

Biography

An influential military theorist, Carl von Clausewitz was one of the first strategists to formalize modern military thought in post-Napoleonic Europe. Clausewitz was born in Magdeburg, Prussia, to a family with roots in the military ranks. At 12, he joined the Prussian army and marched into France in 1792, lighting the match of the French Revolution. After Prussia left the war in 1795, Clausewitz focused on furthering his education while being garrisoned for six years. In 1801, Clausewitz entered the War College in Berlin; immediately after graduation, he was appointed as the aide to Prince August of Prussia. During this time period, he witnessed the violent bloodshed of his countrymen during the Prussian defeats of Jena and Auerstädt at the hands of Napoleon Bonaparte in 1806. Clausewitz was taken prisoner only 14 days after the battle. After his release, he returned to reform the Prussian army, but quickly left to join the Russian forces in 1812 after Prussia made an alliance with Napoleon. With the end of the War of German Liberation in 1813, Clausewitz rejoined the Prussian army and pushed out Napoleon during the Waterloo Campaign. In 1818, he was appointed director of the War College in Berlin and wrote his most influential work, *On War*, which focuses on the philosophy and politics of war. This book was not strategically prescriptive, but was intended to shape people's viewpoints on war itself. Finally in 1830, Clausewitz was appointed major general on the Russian frontier, where he contracted cholera and died a year later. He never fully finished *On War*, but his wife published it posthumously after his death in 1832. Clausewitz's work would finally become well known in 1871 after Prussia experienced victory over France.

Philosophy on War

Clausewitz believed that war was a natural occurrence among men and that conflict was inevitable. He understood that peace was the ultimate aim of war, but he also maintained that disputes could not always be solved peacefully. In *On War*, Clausewitz wrote, "philanthropists may easily imagine there is a skillful method of disarming and overcoming an enemy without great bloodshed. ... However plausible this may appear, still it is an error which must be extirpated; for in such dangerous things as War, the errors which proceed from a spirit of benevolence are the worst." If a country refuses to engage in war out of benevolence, then they are susceptible to be taken advantage of. Clausewitz broadly defined war as "an act of violence intended to compel our same opponent to fulfill our will" and "an act of violence pushed to its utmost bounds." During times of war, Clausewitz believed that countries needed to identify and seize advantages wherever their enemy was weakest.

On War mainly focuses on the minds of individuals in wartime. Clausewitz believed "success in war rests on a trinity of forces: the government, the military, and the people." The people are broken into two categories: the soldiers and the citizens. In the mind of the soldier, Clausewitz wrote that there needs to be "initiative, aggressiveness, mental flexibility, and self-reliance at all levels of command." Most of all, though, Clausewitz believed that soldiers ought to be courageous. He wrote:

> " Resolution is an act of courage in single instances, and if it becomes a characteristic trait, it is a habit of the mind. But here we do not mean courage in face of bodily danger, but in face of responsibility, therefore, to a certain extent against moral danger. This has been often called courage *d'esprit*, on the ground that it springs from the understanding; nevertheless, it is no act of the understanding on that account; it is an act of feeling. Mere intelligence is still not courage, for we often see the cleverest of people devoid of resolution. The mind must, therefore, first awaken the feeling of courage, and then be guided and supported by it, because in momentary emergencies the man is swayed more by his feelings than his thoughts.

Interestingly, Clausewitz also emphasized the equal importance of citizens during wartime. The people at home decide the tone of the war; a supportive community is a strength in itself, but a citizenry opposed to war is demoralizing. Clausewitz stressed that an effective government must manage the war front as well as morale back at home.

Politics

In Clausewitz's opinion, war is not a matter of necessity but a matter of desires. War in itself is an extension of man's unquenchable thirst. He wrote that warfare "is not merely a political act, but also a real political instrument, a carrying out of the same by other means." Governments are willing to use the brutalities of war to gain power and authority. Clausewitz also noted that the politics of war involve each part of society; it is something that is "permeated by politics not just in its origins and outcome, but at every level of its conduct." Because of war's tension on each class of society, it acts a unifying force of hegemony. This is why Clausewitz saw war as such a powerful political and cultural tool.

Jackson Howell, 2015

ARTICLES OF CONFEDERATION, 1781–1789

> " I consider the difference between a system founded on the legislatures only, and one founded on the people, to be the true difference between a league or treaty and a constitution.
>
> —James Madison, at the Constitutional Convention

Background

The Second Continental Congress commissioned the Articles of Confederation's drafting in 1776, shortly after independence was claimed. Though not ratified until 1777, the Articles offered the groundwork for the government during the American Revolution. These articles were based on the idea of sovereign states loosely bound by a weak central government. The Articles provided very little in the way of a central government, which was the only way to get all 13 colonies to ratify the plan.

Function

Once America declared independence from Great Britain in 1776, the revolutionaries needed a new system of government to carry out the war and to govern once the war ended. The Articles provided such a government, instituting only one governmental branch, a legislative branch, that needed all 13 states to agree to any changes of in the national government. The Articles gave command of the army, and jurisdiction over some territorial issues, to the central government. The Articles did not contain a means by which to collect revenue or settle issues between states. In addition, once the American Revolution was over, there was no means by which to pay anyone back, either soldiers or those who held debt. This became a major issue within the new nation and almost led to its demise.

Issues

Because there was no way to raise revenue and no way to print money that had value, the new United States almost fell into a civil war. Issues with the Articles culminated in Shays' Rebellion. Daniel Shays was a farmer who had fought in the American Revolution. He was promised pay that never came.

Once the war ended, he returned to his farm, only to find that the bank was repossessing it due to him not paying back his loan. He had no money to do so, as the army still had not paid him for his service, and he had no way of earning any extra money. His situation was not unique as many farmer/soldiers returned to their land to find themselves in the same situation. Because the national government competed with banks in the printing of money, and since the central government owed a large amount and its currency wasn't backed with anything (such as gold), any money the central government printed was worthless; therefore, no one would take it. Shays led a band of former soldiers against a courthouse in his county and attempted to capture an armory. Though the rebellion was quickly put down, this led to the call for a stronger national government.

Significance

Though the Articles ultimately failed, they played a significant role in the early formation of the United States. They helped to set up the Land Ordinance Act of 1785 which shaped the landscape of the United States by specifying how land was surveyed—into one-square-mile pieces. Oftentimes walking around a city, one might find that the city itself is divided into square blocks; this is a holdover from the Articles. In addition, the Northwest Ordinance of 1787 set up how new states were to be admitted into the union, and helped to create a path to abolishing slavery, as newly admitted states could not be admitted as slave states. So, although the Articles were short lived, the legacy they created was long-lasting.

Kurt Gutschick, faculty

THE FEDERALIST PAPERS, 1781–1788

> " If men were angels, no government would be necessary. If angels were to govern men, neither external nor internal controls on government would be necessary.
> —*Federalist 51*

- Was titled "The Federalist" originally
- Were written by Alexander Hamilton, James Madison, and John Jay
- Promoted the ratification of the recently drafted US Constitution

Background

The Articles of Confederation established the first government of the United States of America. These Articles gave almost all governing power to the states and left the federal government very weak. Under the Articles, the federal government had only a legislative branch in which each state had only one vote. In addition, a supermajority was needed to pass any legislation. There was no way to enforce laws passed by the legislative branch, as there was no executive. Starting in the mid-1780s, it became apparent that the United States needed a stronger national government if the states wanted to keep their union. Hamilton, Madison, and Jay wrote the Federalist Papers after the new Constitution was sent to the states for ratification. Their aim was to convince American citizens of the need for a stronger central governing power. In addition, the papers laid out the people's role relative to the government, and the role of the government to the people.

About the Papers

The Federalist Papers were a series of editorial articles, 77 of which were published serially in *The Independent Journal* and *The New York Packet* between October 1787 and August 1788. A compilation of these and eight others, called *The Federalist; or, The New Constitution*, was published in two volumes in 1788. Though the *Federalist Papers* covered a number of topics, they can be broken down into the following categories, A New Order (Papers 1, 2, 11, 85), Compromise of the government and governed (Papers 23, 37, 41–44, 51), a republican form of government (Papers 9, 10, 39, 56–58, 62, 68, 71), how power is balanced between the branches (Papers 28, 45, 46), the need for liberty and the size of government (Papers 17, 33, 47, 69, 84), taxation and representation (12, 32, 36), and the judicial branch (78, 80). Of these, Federalists 10, 51, and 78 tend to be the most studied.

In Federalist 10, Madison speaks of societal factions, which we may see as interest groups today, and their desire to seize and maintain power: "Among the numerous advantages promised by a well-constructed Union, none deserves to be more accurately developed than its tendency to break and control the violence of faction." Madison argues the pluralist view of government, in which some groups win sometimes, but one single group does not win all of the time. This leads to compromise between the factions, and allows a more centrist government. He states that the only form of government that can be effective in doing this is one based upon the Constitution awaiting ratification. "The great security against a gradual concentration of the several powers in the same department consists in giving to those who administer each department the necessary constitutional means and personal motives to resist encroachment of the others." Interesting enough, though many would say that the United States is a democracy, Madison cautions against that form of government. Favoring a republic instead, he says, "[D]emocracies have ever been spectacles of turbulence and contention; have ever been found incompatible with personal security, or the rights of property; and have, in general, been as short in their lives as they have been violent in their deaths." It should be noted that the framers of the Constitution tried to set up a system of representation, not that of rule by the people. One of the main reasons for this is that the framers believed that a majority could vote away the rights of the minority. A careful reading of both the *Federalist Papers* and the Constitution leads to the conclusion that certain provisions were taken to protect the rights of the minority.

Federalist 51 argues for a system of separation of powers, as well as checks and balances of one branch over another. Here is where the true genius of both the *Federalist Papers* and the Constitution resides. Madison feared too much power being in the hands of one person, or even a group of people. The anti-federalists shared this fear, and without their support the Constitution would never have been ratified. Madison had to make clear how government would be forced to restrain itself, saying in Federalist 51, "In framing a government which is to be administered by men over men, the great difficulty lies in this: you must first enable the government to control the governed; and in the next place oblige it to control itself. A dependence on the people is, no doubt, the primary control on the government; but experience has taught mankind the necessity of auxiliary precautions." In other words, a nation must strike a balance between the amount of power given to a government to permit it to govern, and the limits place on it. This was a radical idea. Madison knew men could not be trusted with power, so a system of government that could not be easily changed and which checked its own power needed to be derived. Therefore, a system with three separate but equal branches was created. No branch has supreme power over the others, as was common in other countries at the time in which the executive, most times a sovereign, had power over the legislative element. Though England had tried a separation of two branches, the legislative and executive, Madison saw that a third branch, that of a court system in which people were tried and sentenced in accordance with the laws passed by the legislative and enforced by the executive, was needed. Such a system allowed people even more of a voice in the process since civil suits could be brought to the court by citizens of a state, against that same state. This allowed for citizens to be sentinels over the public rights. As he says in Federalist 51:

> We see it particularly displayed in all the subordinate distributions of power, where the constant aim is to divide and arrange the several offices in such a manner as that each may be a check on the other—that the private interest of every individual may be a sentinel over the public rights. These inventions of prudence cannot be less requisite in the distribution of the supreme powers of the State.

Though each branch has its separate and equal power, the Federalist Papers make it clear that the people are ultimately responsible for guarding and maintaining liberty.

Federalist 78 outlines the need for a Federal Court System. This Paper, written by Hamilton, argues that the judicial branch must be strong and independent. He also argues that justices need lifetime appointments, so as not to be swayed by public opinion and not be in fear of losing their jobs based on who controlled the other branches. In addition, Hamilton wrote in Federalist 78 that the judiciary is the least dangerous branch of government when it comes to eroding the rights of the people.

> The judiciary, from the nature of its functions, will always be the least dangerous to the political rights of the Constitution; because it will be least in a capacity to annoy or injure them. The Executive not only dispenses the honors, but holds the sword of the community. The legislature not only commands the purse, but prescribes the rules by which the duties and rights of every citizen are to be regulated. The judiciary, on the contrary, has no influence over either the sword or the purse; no direction either of the strength or of the wealth of the society; and can take no active resolution whatever. It may truly be said to have neither FORCE nor WILL, but merely judgment; and must ultimately depend upon the aid of the executive arm even for the efficacy of its judgments.

To Hamilton, the judiciary's sole job was to offer judgment as to the laws passed by Congress and enforced by the executive. And what if those rules should violate the Constitution? Hamilton states that it is up to the judiciary to find such a law void. "No legislative act, therefore, contrary to the Constitution, can be valid," he says in Federalist 78. It is up to the judiciary to decide whether or not a law violates the Constitution and if it does, to strike that law down. This is a powerful check on the power of both Congress and the executive branch.

Significance

The *Federalist Papers* were written by a future president (Madison), the first Treasury Secretary (Hamilton), and a Chief Justice of the United States Supreme Court (Jay). A study of the American System of government would be incomplete without delving into them, for without these Papers, the states would not have ratified the Constitution. In addition, many often speculate as to how the Founding Fathers would have thought about a variety of subjects; here is where readers can get an in-depth glimpse into their thinking. These Papers explain the structure of the government the framers of the Constitution hoped to establish. Though they do not carry the weight of law, they should be looked to when deliberating over the power of the government and the Constitutionality of a new law.

STENDHAL, 1783–1842, *On Love*

> Love is like a fever which comes and goes quite independently of the will.

Key Works

The Red and the Black, 1830
The Charterhouse of Parma, 1839

Biography

Marie-Henri Beule is better known by his pen name, Stendhal. A 19th-century French writer, he remains famous for two novels in particular, *The Red and the Black* and *The Charterhouse of Parma*. The main character in the former, Julian Sorel, embodied all that Stendhal had experienced and much he had learned about himself. Stendhal's cousin Daru finagled Stendahl positions in government and the army: a clerical position at the Ministry of War, and an appointment to the remote outpost of Navara. In Italy, he attended opera for the first time and was captivated by the music and Italy itself, especially La Scala Opera House in Milan. His cousin Daru helped him out again by getting him a commission as a second lieutenant and then the job of quartermaster of provisions. Stendhal's fantastic ability to describe a battlefield and the horror of war came from his second stint with the French army invading Bavaria. In his journals he described the Battle of Waterloo with remarkable realism. Two murders reported widely in the news highlighting two working class young men captured Stendhal's imagination, and he had everything he needed to write *The Red and the Black*.

In 1838 Stendhal was moved by the story of the Parmese family and its rise to prominence and with that story as inspiration, he wrote The *Charterhouse of Parma* in six weeks. When contemporary writer Honoré de Balzac was questioned how his writing compared to that of Stendhal, Balzac remarked, "I create a fresco and [he] create[s] statues." He called *Charterhouse* "a great and beautiful book"; Henry James later called it "a masterpiece."

The two heroes of Stendhal's books found an audience in a society that appreciated poor, ambitious, good-looking men who were compelled to become something other than themselves to succeed in the world of the power-hungry.

THE BARBARY PIRATES, 1784–1815

Following the United States' detachment from Britain, they found themselves in a bit of a problem. Now a nation in their own right, they were expected to take responsibility for patrolling their own waters and guarding their own ships. Around this time the Mediterranean was plagued by North African pirates, Ottoman corsairs who proved a constant nuisance to all seafaring countries in the region. America, newly hatched as it was, appeared to be easy pickings. What followed was a period of struggle and refusal in which America sought to assert itself militarily against its transgressors, ultimately succeeding after 30 years of harassment. The ability to defend its people and its interests abroad provided an important milestone for the fledgling nation, and opened the window towards being taken more seriously by its older siblings at the table of diplomacy.

FRANÇOIS GUIZOT, 1787–1874, *A French Politician and Historian*

> " There is mingled good and evil in all the events and governments of this world, and good often arises side by side with or in the wake of evil, but it is never from the evil that the good comes; injustice and tyranny have never produced good fruits.
>
> *—A Popular History of France*

- Was left fatherless when his father was guillotined during the Reign of Terror
- Completed his education in Geneva
- Became Professor of Modern History at the University of Paris in 1812
- Secured a position as Minister of the Interior under Louis XVIII
- Served as Minister of Public Instruction and influenced educational reforms and movements through his post
- Was Influenced by Calvinistic views and politics
- Believed that the sanctified elect, the political elite, were divinely purposed with the mission to govern the masses.
- Supported the constitutional charter of 1814 that emphasized a balance between parliament and the monarchy; he was Liberal politically but only in a limited way and did not support revolutions against the monarchy
- Was Ambassador of London and Minister of Foreign Affairs

Key Works

History of the Origin of Representative Government, 1821–1822
History of the English Revolution from Charles I to Charles II, 1826–1827
General History of Civilization in Europe, 1828
History of Civilization in France, 1830
History of the Republic of England and Cromwell, 1854
History of the Protectorate of Cromwell and the Restoration of the Stuarts, 1856
Memoirs of the History of my Time, 1858–1868
Parliamentary History of France, 1863

Biography

François Pierre Guillaume Guizot was born in 1787 in France a few years before the French Revolution. During the Reign of Terror, Guizot's father, a prominent and influential Protestant lawyer was guillotined for his federalist sympathies. This prompted the family's move to Geneva, Switzerland, where Guizot was educated. During this time, it is believed that Guizot was exposed to the Calvinism that later affected his political outlook and ideals. In 1805, he found himself in Paris where he began to learn from the philosopher and academic Pierre-Paul Royer-Collard. He then became Professor of Modern History at the University of Paris in 1812 until the Bourbon Restoration began. In the First Restoration, Guizot secured a position in the Ministry of the Interior, advocating for the newly established King Louis XVIII. When Napoleon returned during the Hundred Days, Guizot followed

King Louis XVIII into exile. When Napoleon was defeated and Louis returned to the throne, Guizot was rewarded with a ministerial post. In 1820, following the murder of the heir to the throne, Guizot lost his political positions. In his time out of office, Guizot undertook historical research and writing, composing four of his great works within the decade. In 1830, he rose politically again, entering the Chamber as a deputy for Lisieux, then rising to Minister of the Interior in August due to his leading role in the appointment of Louis-Philippe as king. During this time, Guizot is believed to have become more conservative as a series of revolts "instilled in him a fear of anarchy." By 1832, Guizot had become the Minister of Public Instruction, creating one great legislative act in the law of June 28, 1833, where every commune was required to maintain a public school. In 1840, Guizot became Ambassador to London and a few months later, the Minister of Foreign Affairs in a government headed by Marshal Soult until 1848. Guizot was dismissed by Louis-Philippe during the 1848 revolution, and followed the king into exile in England, displaying the devout loyalty that most likely stemmed from his Calvinistic belief that the political elite had a divine mission to govern the masses. During this year of exile, Guizot devoted most of his time to research in the British Archives. He worked on this research until he was able to return to France in 1849 where he retired to his estate in Normandy. In his retirement, Guizot never returned to the political field but focused solely on historical writing and academics, publishing four more historical works before his death on September 12, 1874.

Education Reform

While an advocate for the liberalization of government, Guizot and his protégé Tocqueville saw education as a necessary piece to a successful liberal government. Guizot and Tocqueville emphasized the importance of public education in France to avoid self-destructive anarchy. Guizot wrote in his memoirs, "the grand problem of modern society is the government of minds." To ensure an informed citizenry and thus a stable liberal government, Guizot eventually oversaw the passage of several pieces of legislation regarding education, which was the first time the French government had sought to influence primary schooling. In these reforms, Guizot focused heavily on incorporating the Catholic church in much of his reforms since he believed that competition between secular and religious schools would lead to the best education. As a result, Guizot stands out in French history as an education reformer and as a frontrunner in illustrating the importance that public education would play in the developing of liberal democracies to come.

Legacy

François Guizot significantly contributed to history in two ways: through his promotion of public education and his influence on the development of European liberalism. His influence of European Liberal thought came about primarily through his historical interpretation. Most questions regarding European Liberalism were raised in the years 1800–1820 and Guizot was one of the forerunners of this movement. The political context in which he grew up likely influenced Guizot's thoughts. The Calvinist influence of Geneva, his studies, the Revolutions, and his close relationship with monarchs led him to develop both a respect for the established leadership as well as liberal democracy. As a result, Guizot formed a liberal ideology that differed from the extremes of his day, accepting the limited involvement of a monarchy. This resulted in what some have called the Guizot movement in French politics, which can be defined as the politically liberal movement after the Napoleonic Era that sought to provide stability in France through what Nicholas Toloudis calls, "representative government, constitutional freedom, and properly circumscribed liberties," while incorporating a monarchy for the sake of stability. Still, while Guizot aligned himself at various times with the monarchies, his line of liberal thinking emphasized a minimal state, individualism, and laissez-faire form of government, similar to the political ideology of Locke, Voltaire, Montesquieu, and Benjamin Constant. When individuals with a similar ideology rose to power in 1830, their application of liberalism did not lead to what many thought liberal ideals should; while it led to a diminishing significance of the monarchy, it also resulted in a strengthening of the bourgeoisie class and very little elevation for the poor. These two failures resulted in their eventual overthrow in 1848. While many saw this as proof of weakness in Guizot's application of liberal thought, this strand of liberalism did not completely disappear, returning later in the century under the label of Republican. Guizot's liberal ideals and what resulted from them in the French political sphere shaped his writings about French history, and also influenced individuals such as Marx and Tocqueville.

Nate Kosirog, faculty
Nathaniel Whatmore, 2015

LORD BYRON, 1788–1824, *"Mad, bad and dangerous to be around"*

" And thus the heart will break, yet brokenly live on.

—*Childe Harold's Pilgrimage*

- Was born with a club-foot perhaps caused by his mother wearing tight corsets while pregnant
- Resembled his father, Captain John Byron, a womanizer known as "Mad Jack"
- Became a lord at age 10, inheriting his uncle's title and inheritance
- Gained success as a writer, but was ostracized for his scandalous personal life
- Failed to complete *Don Juan*, which remains the longest English satirical poem
- Is hailed as one of the greatest Romantic poets
- Created a unique Romantic hero, perhaps modeled after himself
- Championed the oppressed, especially in Greece

Key Works

Hours of Idleness, 1807
Childe Harold's Pilgrimage, 1812
Don Juan, 1819–1824; incomplete on Byron's death in 1824
She Walks in Beauty, 1814
The Destruction of Sennacherib, 1815
Epitaph to a Dog, 1808
Heaven and Earth, 1821
The Prophecy of Dante, 1819
English Bards and Scotch Reviewers, 1809

Biography

Born into a failing aristocratic family, George Gordon Byron, better known as Lord Byron, experienced troubles from the beginning: his womanizing father was absent, his passionate mother was emotionally unstable, and his family was in financial ruin. His upbringing lacked any structure or moral instruction, laying a foundation for a lifetime of selfishness and bitterness. When Byron was 10, his uncle passed away, and he inherited the title of Lord Byron and a drastically changed financial situation. Byron was sent to Harrow School in London, then to Trinity College; he was not an exemplary student, but was highly social, and his shame over his clubbed foot made him seek athletic attainment. His lack of discipline led to his wasting of the vast fortune he had inherited, and he was financially limited for the majority of his life. Byron's love life was no less complicated than his financial situation; despite being married, he had numerous affairs, some with men, some with married women, but all damaging his reputation. His short-lived marriage to Annabella Milbanke gave him a daughter, Augusta Ada. His marriage ended when his wife discovered he was having an affair with his half-sister. His wild personal life combined with his openly negative views on his contemporaries resulted in a fairly widespread shunning of Byron among other authors. While his peers didn't favor him, the public loved his work, and he could have made a considerable fortune. Despite his success and his need to get out of debt, Byron refused to collect royalties from his writing in order to, ironically, maintain his reputation as an aristocrat. Although he lived a mostly shallow life, his friendship with John Hobhouse resulted in being drafted into the political crew of the Cambridge Whigs. His political career, however, did not end there. As a young man Byron had developed an affinity for Greece, and in 1823 he helped support the Greek war for independence from Ottoman rule. He was treated as a "Messiah" by the people of Prince Alexander Mavrokordatos in Missolonghi, showering them with money and energy. Because of his actions, he is considered a "champion of oppressed peoples and insurgent nationalities in the modern world." While in Greece, he fell ill and caught an infection when doctors tried to cure him through the popular method of bleeding. Byron died in April 1824; the Greeks mourned the loss of a beloved advocate, the English a popular (and scandalous) writer. Greece declared him a national hero, returning his body to England after removing his heart, which truly belonged to them.

Don Juan

"*Don Juan* is Byron in a nutshell: as he was and as he wished humanity to be; a disillusioned yet continually idealistic portrait of mankind." Byron started to write *Don Juan* in 1818, but never finished his most critically acclaimed poem before his death in 1824, leaving both the 17th canto and Don Juan's journey unfinished. Juan has two radically different parents: a father desirous of passion and love, and a mother devoted to knowledge and reason, mirroring the tension between the Romantic movement's desire for sincere feeling and the neoclassical desire for structure. Juan engages in multiple emotionally charged affairs; even when he rebuffs the advances of one lady, it is not because of the immortality of yet another sexual partner, but because he bursts out in tears over the loss of his previous love. While he does have some victorious moments outside the bedroom, Juan's journey has no real mission and, thus, no real purpose, revealing Byron's view that "although a hero may be admirable and do some impressive things, his deeds cannot lead to any meaningful result." While Juan's journey may mimic Odysseus's long wanderings, it is clear that Byron has no disillusions about the nature of his hero: Juan is emotionally driven, moved by nature, smarter than most, rebellious against social rules, and irresistible to women. "More sinned against than sinning," he gains wisdom in the journey. This, to Byron, is a realistic hero, a character perhaps glorifying Byron's own philandering lifestyle. Whether biographical or not, Byron clarifies that his hero is not the same as other Romantic heroes, even calling Wordsworth out directly, talking about how Juan found a place that would inspire poetry that people would read. Juan shows his defense of the poor and the weak, meeting them with humor and compassion. Juan has been compared to Tom Jones, similar in courage and goodness.

Byronic Hero

In addition to the legacy of promiscuity that Lord Byron left behind, his Byronic hero has survived the test of time and was used by other authors, including Charlotte Brontë, to create antiheroes that readers know and love. Edward E. Bostetter wrote that Byron's "apotheosis of the commonplace is one his greatest contributions to the language of poetry." Harnessing the passion that fueled his adventurous life, Byron's energetic writing style fills his poetry with unique imagery and bold verse. He is hailed as a giant of the Romantic Movement. To the chagrin of scholars and students, Lord Byron's personal memoirs, which he intended for posthumous publishing, were destroyed by his friends who were so shocked by the content of these memoirs that they thought they were protecting his legacy by burning them.

Annalisa Galgano, 2013

ARTHUR SCHOPENHAUER, 1788–1860, *The Philosopher of Pessimism*

" The world is my representation.
—*The World as Will and Representation*

- Admitted to being an atheist, one of the first major Western philosophers, and probably the first major German, to do so openly
- Considered himself the only true heir of Kant, but radically reinterpreted Kant's key concepts
- Was influenced by Eastern philosophy in his belief that the noumenal world (see Kant) is a larger, non-individuated collective essence
- Reclaimed from Kant the term "noumena" in its more proper Greek sense, not meaning "things in themselves" but "objects of knowledge"
- Believed, unlike Kant, that we have some access to the thing in itself, or reality, the underlying essence of all things, since we are both subject and object; hence we can assert certain things about the thing in itself
- Held that the world of direct experience and knowledge—the world of individual existents—is a world of *representations* of the thing in itself, which is not directly apprehended
- Believed that the underlying essence of all things is the *Will*: a blind, endless striving
- Considered morality to be rooted in compassion, rather than rational duties (Kant) or habituated virtue (classical moral theory); compassion arises from the understanding that other people's individual lives are mere phenomenal representations of the collective Will
- Was the ultimate pessimist: as our desires are only manifestations of an aimless and endless Will, one can never be satisfied, he thinks it would have been better never to have existed
- Held that the answer to the problem of the hopelessness of desire cannot be suicide, which only changes the mode of our suffering (since our individual life is only a representation of the eternal Will), but rather to renounce desiring and resign oneself to the state of things
- Had particular influence on Nietzsche (in his depictions of how the world is the product of an impersonal will, and his adherence to a dark aspect of reality as opposed to a more rational philosophical system with some ultimate Good or God at its peak), Freud (especially the notion of the "unconscious" and Wittgenstein (the relation between Will and the world)
- Is also considered the "artist's philosopher" because of the far-reaching impact he had on creative men and inventors of various types, including Richard Wagner, Erwin Schrödinger, Albert Einstein, Otto Rank, Carl Jung, Joseph Campbell, Leo Tolstoy, Thomas Mann, Jorge Luis Borges, and many others

Key Works

On the Fourfold Root of the Principle of Sufficient Reason, 1813, 1847
The World as Will and Representation, 1818, 1844
Parerga and Paralipomena, 1851

Biography

Arthur Schopenhauer was born to a wealthy German family on February 22, 1788, in Danzig, now Poland. Groomed to be a cosmopolitan merchant like his father, Schopenhauer traveled extensively in his youth and was allowed to pursue his scholarly inclinations from a young age. The death of his father, while leaving him rich, also shaped Schopenhauer's future, for his mother, craving the intellectual life, opened a salon which was often frequented by such men as Goethe and the Schlegel brothers. However, tension with his mother grew until it reached a crisis when Arthur was 30 years old, at which time she severed their communication.

Using his private finances to support his studies, Schopenhauer entered the University of Göttingen in 1809 and the University of Berlin 1811, but it wasn't until 1813 that he earned his PhD *in absentia* from the University of Jena. Although not originally intending to study philosophy, Schopenhauer explained in his own words: "Life is an unpleasant business. ... I have resolved to spend mine reflecting on it." After the publication of his chief work, *The World as Will and Representation*, he accepted a lecturer position at the University of Berlin. However, attempting to challenge Hegel, he scheduled his regular lectures at the same time as that most distinguished faculty member of the day, which backfired and left Schopenhauer's lectures nearly empty. He resigned the post and never lectured at a university again.

In 1833, in response to a cholera outbreak in Berlin, Schopenhauer relocated to Frankfurt where he lived alone, except for a succession of poodles. Although his major philosophical works did not garner the praise he expected, in his later years Schopenhauer published a collection of philosophical reflections and aphorisms called *Parerga und Paralipomena*, which did earn him unforeseen popularity. On September 21, 1860, Schopenhauer died peacefully.

The World as Representation

Schopenhauer's philosophy departs from other German idealist philosophers in many respects. He is a transcendental idealist insofar as he denies that the world of experience is the world as it really is. In his major work, *The World as Will and Representation*, Schopenhauer introduces his theory by writing, "no truth is more certain, more independent of all others, and less in need of proof than this, namely that everything that exists for knowledge, and hence the whole of this world, is only object in relation to the subject, perception of the perceiver, in a word, representation." So the world, and everything that exists in it for us to know, is only a representation, not the thing-in-itself. We can sit at a table, but we are limited by our senses in what we can actually know of the table. We define the table by what we sense of it, even though what we see and experience might not be all there is to the table.

Before delving into a discussion of what Schopenhauer means by "representation," we must first unpack his understanding of what it means to be a "subject." Simply put, "that which knows all things and is known by none is the *subject*." The subject is that which thinks, knows, and acts; it is the 'I' by which we experience the world. In this way, everyone is a subject. Yet, everyone is also an object. For Schopenhauer, an object exists independently of the subject and yet is subject to the conditions of being known. An object is an object of experience—it is both transcendentally ideal (conditioned by the subject) *and* empirically real (objectively exists in space, time and causality). Schopenhauer explains that an object "presupposes the subject" and yet is "absolutely what it appears to be"; object and representation are one. What the subject perceives of the object is the representation; there is no fundamental distinction between an object and a representation. In this way, Schopenhauer allows for the plurality of objects in the world (i.e., there are many dogs; they are different dogs; and they are real dogs) and yet he also allows for the unity of representations (i.e., there is a cohesive idea "dog" that is abstracted from our experience with "dogs"). What we encounter through experience is called phenomena, mere representations. Schopenhauer anticipates the immediate response to his theory: "We want to know the significance of those representations; we ask whether this world is nothing more than representation"—is the dog anything more than our experience of it, anything more than shedding and barking?

How Schopenhauer Sees Things

The World as Will

While the world is representation, Schopenhauer additionally posits that the world is will. As human beings, we are uniquely positioned to discover something of the noumenal world (as it really is) because we are simultaneously subject and object; Schopenhauer writes that we are neither a "purely knowing subject" nor a purely phenomenal object. As such, we can learn of things-in-themselves by examining our own relation to ourselves, and the answer for Schopenhauer is Will: "The act of will and the action of the body are not two different states objectively known, connected by the bond of causality; they do not stand in the relation of cause and effect, but are one and the same thing." The thing-in-itself is will.

Schopenhauer expands on the will, showing that it is not an object, but a relation. The will is who we are at the noumenal level; the thing-in-itself is ultimately unknowable except through the will, which manifests itself as action. Will and action are one. Now that we have named the thing-in-itself, phenomena can now be understood as objectifications of the will. The will constitutes representation; it is the relation between the thing-in-itself and a representation. In a way, "all object is the will, in so far as the will has become representation." In a way, the will causes objects; the dog is more than shedding and barking because those things are manifestations of the will. It's almost as if the will were a form of energy essential to all representations; the will is what enables the thing-in-itself to be known by us, even if it's only through representation.

Life, Death and Suffering

At the level of truest reality, we are will. Stripped of ego and individuation, the will is ultimately unknowable and immaterial. He continues to explain, "The will, considered purely in itself, is devoid of knowledge, and is only a blind, irresistible urge"; in other words, while individual acts have some purpose or end, "willing as a whole has no end in view." Essentially, we are driven by a blind "will-to-live," continually striving, never fulfilled because "striving is its sole nature." This explains why "constant suffering is essential to all life" for Schopenhauer—there innately exists a cycle of perpetual dissatisfaction or pain because with desire comes either the attainment or the non-attainment of the want. If we achieve our desire, we are no longer satisfied and must immediately begin striving towards a new desire and remain unsatisfied, and therefore unhappy; or if we do not achieve our desire, we remain unsatisfied, and therefore unhappy.

Additionally, Schopenhauer explains why, if life is so tormenting, death torments us more. He elucidates, "What we fear in death is in fact the extinction and end of the individual, which it openly proclaims itself to be, and as the individual is the will-to-live itself in a particular objectification, its whole nature struggles against death." So while life is suffering and death is the end of suffering, death is also the end of the individual, a fate the will-to-life in us all strives to fight, "struggl[ing] against this flowing away into nothing." Now, should some individuals seek to escape the cycle of perpetual suffering, Schopenhauer suggests that one merely recognize that he is an objectification of the will, which is not fundamentally individual, and divorce oneself from the phenomenal character of self and marry the notion of one will, for there is nothing without the will. He concludes, "we freely acknowledge that what remains after the complete abolition of the will is, for all who are still full of the will, assuredly nothing. But also conversely, to those in whom the will has turned and denied itself, this very real world of ours with all its suns and galaxies, is—nothing." We cannot escape.

Jessica Goeser, researcher
Daren Jonescu, advisor

THE FRENCH REVOLUTION, 1789–1799

The French Revolution erupted a mere seven years after the Treaty of Paris that ended the American Revolution. The fundamental causes of the two revolutions were quite similar: unfair taxation, human rights abuses, class privileges, and oppressive monarchies.

Yet compared to its American counterpart, the French Revolution unfolded to be much more:

- Liberal: Women's Rights, Civil Rights, Slavery abolished (100 years before America)
- Radical: The Reign of Terror, the King and his nobles executed (16,000 to 40,000 deaths)
- Power-Centric: Ending in dictatorship and conquest; Napoleon and his wars of conquest
- Global or International: Inspiring the toppling of many absolute monarchies

It sought to do away with the French monarchy and establish a republic. Instead, it ushered in a period of violence and fear, culminating in the crowning of a Napoleon Bonaparte, a new dictator to replace the old one.

Marking the beginning of the end for the monarchies of Europe, the French Revolution became emblematic of revolutions the world over and inspired several movements toward democracy across the globe. The revolution itself trumpeted the values of liberalism, radicalism, nationalism, socialism, feminism, and secularism, all of which began to sprout more frequently amongst its neighbors.

Chapter 6
The Industrial Revolution and Socialism

Each of us has a natural right, from God,
to defend his person, his liberty,
and his property.

—Frédéric Bastiat

THE INDUSTRIAL REVOLUTION (c. 1760–1850), an era of unsurpassed European technological and economic growth in the 18th and 19th centuries, was one of the most important periods of change in modern history. The Revolution allowed for a massive increase in production, inventiveness and mechanical advances. In the early part of the 1700s, this process began in England: farm tycoons began to purchase small acreages and then enclose their large plots of land with fences. This forced much of the rural populace to migrate into cities to find work. When coke—a type of coal for the smelting of iron—replaced charcoal, industrialists built great ironworks and steel factories, which provided employment for the displaced farm workers. Around this time, the inventions of railways, steam engines, factories, the flying shuttle, and advanced mining techniques overhauled the British market. Desire for increased efficiency drove these changes.

While the Revolution saw great increases in the wealth and productivity of Britain, it also caused unthinkable horrors among the lower class. Because only the most affluent tier of society had any governmental influence, factory conditions were unregulated. The factories were built without any concern for employee safety; they were poorly ventilated, hazardous, and filthy. Disease tore through the cramped workplaces, and worker housing (often provided by the factory owner) was poorly constructed and often unsafe for human occupancy. Children often worked days as long as 16 hours and were given 1/10 the pay that men received for the same work. They were sent into tiny ventilation shafts, where adults did not fit, to perform treacherous maintenance. Outbreaks of diseases such as cholera and typhoid fever became increasingly common, and the barbaric practices of doctors of the day often did more harm than good. Many used leeching and bloodletting, as well as toxins such as mercury and arsenic in their "cures." Life expectancy plummeted. Worse, the lifespan of city dwellers shrunk to half that of their agrarian counterparts. In a case of the cure being, perhaps, worse than the disease, the government established poorhouses for those who could not support themselves. The government designed them to be as much like prisons as possible to discourage the public from using them. Families were separated as punishment.

Despite the ills it brought, the Industrial Revolution began to spread to nations on the European continent in the second decade of the 19th century as the Napoleonic wars wound down. It even spread across the Atlantic to America. Because it had fundamentally changed society, The Industrial Revolution also brought about a new interest in socialism—a belief in the natural peacefulness of people, the social harmony of collectivism, and social justice brought about by equality. The working class had grown in numbers, but not in importance. They experienced social barriers and economic inequalities. New forms of socialism became part of the conversation as activists and legislators tried to improve the lives of everyone through voting and government change. Improvements were incremental. In the 1850s, Parliament began to pass bills regulating factory conditions and wages began to increase. Yet the upper class continued to rule.

Despite the tragedies of the Industrial Revolution, it sparked critical social and economic changes. Nearly every piece of modern technology and accomplishment in recent decades would have been impossible without the inventions and changes brought about by the Revolution. The Industrial Revolution continues to be one of the most important time periods in Western culture.

Socialism is an idea that has been present for a long time, but in the 19th century it had a new appeal. Karl Marx entered the stage with a utopian idea that all people could work as equals and enjoy the same standard of living. Marx saw economic factors in a society as most important in history—that society, in fact, is the history of class struggle. He and Friedrich Engels, fundamental and revolutionary socialists, envisioned in *The Communist Manifesto* a mass uprising of the working class, taking over property in common ownership, with the result of equality. Their vision of an inevitable future of social progress through economic conflict is "scientific determinism."

See the "Socialism" entry in Appendix A: Glossary, for an extended contrast of socialism (including its intellectual brethren—communism, progressivism, collectivism) with free markets and American ideals.

MICHAEL FARADAY, 1791–1867, *An Electric Life*

" There they go! There they go! We have succeeded at last!
—Shouted as Faraday created his first electromagnetic motor

- Worked in the scientific realms of physics and chemistry with a large emphasis on electricity and magnets
- Taught himself nearly everything he knew about science
- Invented the balloon as a toy, at first using pig bladders and animal intestines and filling them with hydrogen
- Turned down an offer to become President of the Royal Society, and also turned down a knighthood and a burial at Westminster Abbey
- Discovered that a changing magnetic field will induce an electric current, and published ahead of an American named Joseph Henry who discovered the same thing at roughly the same time
- Discovered the laws of electrolysis, a technique that uses a direct electric current (DC) to drive an otherwise non-spontaneous chemical reaction
- Invented the Faraday cage, which is now used by cars and airplanes to protect against lightning strikes

Key Works

Chemical Manipulation, 1827
Experimental Researches in Electricity vol. i, 1839
Experimental Researches in Electricity vol. ii, 1844
Experimental Researches in Chemistry and Physics, 1859
The Forces of Matter, 1860
On the Various Forces in Nature, 1873

Biography

Michael Faraday, British chemist and physicist, pioneered electromagnetic induction and created a crude electromagnetic motor. He was born on September 22, 1791, to a blacksmith in the Elephant and Castle section of London, just south of the Thames. His family was not particularly well off, and he received only a basic education. His mother finally pulled from him school after a teacher attempted to correct his speech impediment; he called his brother "Wobert." His family attended the church of a

Protestant sect, Sandemanian, and he was a devout member all his life, although he typically left his religious beliefs out of his scientific research.

At 14, he began a seven-year apprenticeship with a local bookbinder. In his free time, he read the books that came into the shop. In 1810, when binding the *Encyclopedia Britannica*, he came across the 127-page entry on electricity, which fascinated him. Throughout his life he consistently set about to prove the things that he read, and this entry was no exception; he bought two jars and performed basic electrical experiments with them. Wanting to escape his life as a bookbinder and pursue his passion for science, he wrote to the President of the Royal Society, and asked for a scientific position, "however menial," at the society. The President of the Royal Society replied that there was no room for a man like him in the society.

Meanwhile, Humphry Davy was experimenting with chemicals in his lab at the Royal Institution and temporarily blinded himself. In desperate need of an assistant until he regained his eyesight, Davy wrote a letter to Faraday asking him to fill the temporary position because he had been impressed with Faraday's note on the *Encyclopedia Britannica*. Three months later, the institution fired its laboratory assistant and Davy gave Faraday the position permanently.

In a further display of confidence in his protégé, Davy invited Faraday to accompany him and his wife on an extended European tour. Even though tensions between the French and the English were high at the time, Napoleon himself granted Davy and his company special passports to visit French scientists. Upon his return from this trip, Faraday met and fell in love with Sarah Barnard, and they married on June 12, 1821. Shortly thereafter, he began to delve into electromagnetism and worked ceaselessly in this field for the rest of his professional life. His health began to deteriorate, and he experienced age and work related memory loss, so he retired in 1861. He died on August 25, 1867, at Hampton Court on a property given to him by the government as part of a pension.

Electromagnetic Induction

In Faraday's time, scientists widely accepted that an electric current would produce a magnetic field. Many scientists, including Faraday, wondered if the opposite could be true: Would a magnetic field produce a current? Faraday theorized that each current generates a circular magnetic force in the space around the wire—and he was right. A current creates a magnetic field with lines in the form of circles with the wire at their center. Faraday referred to this magnetic field as the "lines of force."

After years of study on magnetic fields and currents, he finally realized that a *changing* magnetic field would produce a current. To prove his theory, he designed a large, non-conducting ring and wrapped two conducting wires around each end so the wires did not touch. Faraday pushed current through one of the wires and used a switch to pulse the current. Because the current varied in strength, so did the magnetic field caused by the wire. Faraday pushed no current through the second wire, but instead hooked it up to a galvanometer, a device that measures current through a wire. Even though Faraday hadn't hooked the second wire up to a battery, the changing magnetic field induced by the first wire caused a current in the second wire. He proved that a changing magnetic field produces a current using electromagnetic induction.

Earlier in his career, Faraday had designed a primitive electromagnetic motor. This motor consisted of a stiff wire suspended in liquid mercury, a good conductor of electricity, and a bar magnet in the middle of the container of mercury. He sent an electric current through the stiff wire, which caused a magnetic field that interacted with the magnet's magnetic field and caused the wire to rotate around the magnet. After his experiment with the electromagnetic ring, Faraday recognized the need for an electromagnetic induction that was able to produce a steady current, instead of the pulses of electricity that his electromagnetic ring created. To remedy this problem, he designed a dynamo, or electric generator that generates direct current. He allowed a copper disk to rotate around a brass axle and placed it between the poles of a strong magnet. When Faraday spun the copper plate, the changing magnetic field produced a weak but steady current. Although his device was not technically a dynamo (it did not include a commutator, which allows the current to flow in only one direction), Faraday is credited with the first electric motor, and one of the first electric generators.

Faraday's Cage

Faraday discovered that a sphere made of conductive materials would carry all of its charge on the surface, leaving a neutral charge in the center of the conductor. This phenomenon occurs because any net charge on a conductor distributes itself on the surface. To demonstrate his finding, Faraday built a cage of conducting material and went inside while he charged the cage heavily with an electrostatic machine. He experienced no ill effects; the inside of his cage was completely neutral. Today, the discovery has many uses, including protecting electronic technology from interference with outside electricity, and protecting passengers in cars and airplanes from lightning strikes.

Chemistry

Although Faraday made scientific leaps in the world of electricity, he originally started as a chemist's assistant. In addition to discovering two new compounds of chlorine and carbon, and the chemical benzene, he also wrote two major laws on electrolysis, which is chemical decomposition produced by an electric current. The first law stated that equal current through the chemical would produce equal decomposition. The second law stated that, for the same amount of current, the amount of decomposition produced depends on the mass of the original chemical. Faraday built a primitive device that Robert Bunsen later used to design the Bunsen burner, commonly used today to heat chemicals in chemistry labs. He also popularized the use of electrochemical terms: electrode, anode, cathode, ion, electrolyte, and electrolysis.

Caroline Fuschino, 2015

NIKOLAI LOBACHEVSKY, 1792–1856, *the Theory of Parallels*

> " There is no branch of mathematics, however abstract, which may not some day be applied to phenomena of the real world.

- Was a Russian mathematician, teacher, and rector at Kazan University
- Advanced mathematical theory by solving a 200-year-old problem
- Discovered non-Euclidian geometry as a basis for physical science
- Failed to achieve full recognition or appreciation in his lifetime

Key Works
"Elements of Geometry," 1826

"Pangeometry," 1855

Biography

Born in Russia, Nizhny Novgord (later Nikolai Lobachevsky), lost his father at an early age and moved to Kazan. He entered the University of Kazan and was educated by two German immigrant professors. Because of his strong mathematical interest and ability, he rose quickly in the university's ranks to the position of instructor. Initially, he taught trigonometry and the number theory of Carl Friedrich Gauss; later he was promoted to associate professor. While there he wrote textbooks on geometry and algebra. Particularly interested the former, he examined Euclid's fifth (parallel) postulate, trying to create proofs for it. He stopped working on the proof when he determined that, contrary to Euclid's assertion, more than one parallel line could be drawn through a point outside a line.

Lobachevsky maintained that his new geometry, "imaginary geometry," included imaginary numbers. He believed Euclid to have created a special case only; more than one geometry can exist. Both systems are consistent and both systems may be used for the expression of space. He shared his new system in a faculty presentation in 1826 and followed up with written explanations, *Geometrical Researches on the Theory of Parallels*. Other mathematicians came to similar conclusions, but Lobachevsky published first. The Hungarian mathematician Bolyai made the same discovery independently at about the same time. Carl Frederick Gauss, having made the same calculations years before, failed to publish because he feared his contemporaries' reactions to such radical thinking. The new theory required an enormous change in the way people perceived the physical world. In fact, William Clifford said that non-Euclidean geometry represents "a revolution in the history of human thought as radical as the revolution begun by Copernicus."

Lobachevsky became rector of Kazan University from 1826–1846. After his death, Carl Friedrich Gauss ensured Lobachevsky's election as an honorary member of the Gottingen Scientific Society. Mathematicians from Italy (Eugenio Beltrami), France (Henri Poincare), and Germany (Felix Klein) thought his ideas should be included in the body of modern mathematics study. Mathematicians have made connections in Lobachevsky's non-Euclidean geometry to the work of Copernicus and Einstein. Scientists celebrate Lobachevsky's influence on modern science, especially modern axiomatics, which proves that propositions arrived at through logical deductions can be the basis of entire sciences.

SIR CHARLES LYELL, 1797–1875, *Father of Geological Evolution*

> When we study history, we obtain a more profound insight into human nature, by instituting a comparison between the present and former states of society.
>
> —*Principles of Geology*

- Was knighted and also made a baronet because of his achievements in the field of geology
- Received the Copley Medal, the highest honor of the Royal Society of London
- Was married to Mary Horner for 41 years
- Formulated the idea that Earth's surface was changing extremely slowly over time
- Traveled throughout eastern America and Canada and supported the Union in the Civil War
- Revised his greatest work *The Principles of Geology* 12 times before he died
- Is buried in Westminster Abbey

Key Works

Principles of Geology (three volumes), 1830, 1831, 1833
Elements of Geology, 1838
Travels in North America, 1845
A Second Visit to the United States, 1849
The Geological Evidence of the Antiquity of Man, 1863

Biography

Born on November 14, 1797, in Kinnordy, United Kingdom, Charles Lyell was the eldest of 10 children. He grew up reading many of the books that his father kept in his study, which sparked his interest in geology and science in general. At a young age, he began to capture butterflies and various aquatic bugs to analyze. Though intelligent, school was not Lyell's forte; he much preferred educational walks through the forest with his father. At 19 he enrolled at Oxford University to study law. Due to his long hours of reading and study, his eyes became weak, so he depended on his outdoor study for a break from the difficult work at college. Although Lyell qualified to practice law, he was much more interested in the science of geology, and his father's financial support enabled him to study it. He traveled to Mt. Etna, where his research provided breakthrough information for his theory of slow geological evolution. In 1848, Queen Victoria knighted Lyell for his accomplishments in the field of geology. His wife died unexpectedly in 1873 and her passing deeply affected him. He wrote, "I endeavor by my daily work at my favorite science, to forget as far as possible the dreadful change which this has made in my existence." He died on February 22, 1875.

Uniformitarianism

Lyell defined geology as "the science which investigates the successive changes that have taken place in the organic and inorganic kingdoms of nature." He disagreed, however, with the normal process of making geological "discoveries." To begin with, Lyell resented how most geologists viewed geology only through the lens of their religion and made assumptions to close the gaps in their "scientific" observations. As Caldwell put it, "Lyell wanted to find a way to make geology a true science of its own, built on observation and not susceptible to wild speculations or dependent on the supernatural." In other words, Lyell wanted to make geology a science of proof and observation rather than speculation. The main tenet of Lyell's works, derived from his observations of well-known geologic features throughout Europe, was that the various landforms on earth had not been created by a supernatural being or through many catastrophic events that quickly changed the surface of the earth, but by very slow natural occurrences over millennia. Lyell said, "Many distinguishing features of the surface may often be ascribed to the operation at a remote era of slow and tranquil causes." Things like the rock cycle (see following figure) can be explained through Lyell's findings because of his theorized small and continuous changes.

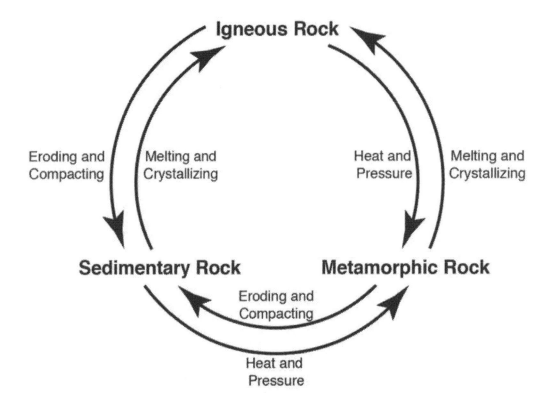

The Rock Cycle

Because Lyell believed that these "ordinary natural processes of today and their products do not differ in kind or magnitude from those of the past ... the Earth must be very ancient." This belief system is referred to as Uniformitarianism; it states that the natural processes that shape the surface of the earth are currently the same as they have been for the duration of earth's existence, providing an explanation for the gradual changes Lyell described. Lyell's discoveries at Mt. Etna, where he proved that the mountain had not been formed by one massive volcanic eruption, but by many very small eruptions over time, greatly supported his alternate theory on the process of geological change. Lyell asserted, "Etna appears to have been in activity from the earliest times of tradition." Although other scientists criticized his new ideas, Lyell remained convinced: "I can only plead that a discovery which seems to contradict the general tenor of previous investigations is naturally received with much hesitation."

Legacy

In addition to his own contributions, Lyell mentored a protégé who would have an even greater impact: Charles Darwin. While Lyell hesitated to accept Darwin's ideas of biological evolution, Darwin was a great believer in Lyell's research: "The very first place which I examined showed me clearly the wonderful superiority of Lyell's manner of treating geology compared with that of any author, whose work I had with me or afterwards read." Without the discoveries and research of Sir Charles Lyell, Charles Darwin might not have had such a legendary effect on the scientific community. Lyell's discoveries apply to Darwin's research because "geology is intimately related to almost all the physical sciences, as history is to the moral." In addition to forwarding Darwin's research, Lyell's writings also changed how most geologists went about their discoveries, moving them from inference and assumption to observation and research.

AUGUSTE COMTE, 1798–1857, *An Exceedingly Difficult Person*

> " Everything is relative, that's the only thing absolute.
>
> —*L'Industrie*

- Is credited with creating both sociology and positivism
- Was an early developer of the ethical and political views now known as secular humanism and progressivism; hoped for a radical reorganization of human societies based on a "scientific view" in which all human concerns are generalized and there are no "non-human" concerns at all
- Had many mental breakdowns over the course of his life
- Was a rebellious child who grew up to be an egocentric adult, but devoted his life to his notion of improving society as a whole, proposing to make the mind the servant of his generalized social conception of "love"
- Had his *Course in Positive Philosophy* banned by the Catholic Church for its anti-theological outlook
- Thought that society progressed through three different stages: the theological, the metaphysical, and the positive
- Believed that knowledge was valid only if proved as scientific fact, and hence that all education must be reformed for the "positive" stage of historical development by removing all moral and "metaphysical" elements of instruction (religion, the soul, etc.) which prevent the formation of a purely fact- and natural law-based mind, which may be utilized for the good of society
- Created his own religion based on of the worship of humanity; a kind of precursor of the modern progressive ideal of sacrificing oneself for the good of others, where "others" should never mean those whom one loves personally (which would not be pure sacrifice, since one has an interest in their well-being), but rather a collectivized humanity as such

Key Works

Course of Positive Philosophy, 1830–42
System of Positive Polity, 1851–54
Positivist Catechism, 1852
A General View of Positivism, 1856
Subjective Synthesis, 1856
Positive Philosophy, 1858

Biography

Auguste Comte, sociologist and founder of positivism, was born into a royalist Roman Catholic family in Montpelier, France, in 1798. The young Comte was quick to demonstrate his natural intellect. He attended École Polytechnique, a Paris school founded in 1794 for the study of advanced sciences. He performed well at the institute, excelling in mathematics, but as a result of his rebellious nature he was denied the opportunity to work there upon graduation. Instead he took up permanent residence in Paris, tutoring in math and reading extensively on history and philosophy. Influenced by the republicanism and skepticism rolling through France, he rejected the ideas of Catholicism, an attitude consistent with his reputation as a rebellious child at school. Comte came to his love of sociology under the guidance of Count Henri de Saint-Simon, who took Comte under his wing as his personal secretary and partner. Saint-Simon was responsible for the idea "that the study of society should be treated as a science" which sparked Comte's interest in sociology. The two men worked together for several years until their views conflicted. They decided to go their separate ways, and it was shortly after this that Comte married Caroline Massin in 1825. The marriage did more harm than good, however, and the two separated in 1842 as a result of violence and unhappiness in the home. Comte later described the relationship as having been "the only error of [his] life."

In 1826, Comte began a series of what should have been 72 lectures to "a subscription list of distinguished intellectuals," but suffered a mental breakdown after the third. For the next 15 years he suffered from mental illness, requiring frequent trips to the mental hospital. Despite this, he continued writing and eventually completed his most famous work, *Course of Positive Philosophy* in 1842. This led to his creation of positivism, which was his greatest accomplishment. Towards the end of his life, he refined his idea of positivism, and believed that the ultimate goal of humanity was to learn to worship itself. Though Comte was a "sombre, ungrateful, self-centred, and egocentric personality" he devoted his life to creating a more prosperous society. He died in 1857 from stomach cancer.

Positivism: Seeing is Believing

In *The Positive Philosophy*, Comte wrote that: "All good intellects have repeated, since Bacon's time, that there can be no real knowledge but that which is based on observed facts." His belief that knowledge comes from observation, and observation alone, was the foundation on which he built his philosophy of positivism, a belief system claiming that all valid knowledge was scientific in nature.

Yet Comte deviated from raw empiricism with his belief that observation and scientific data were worthless if humanity had not already discovered some natural law by which to interpret such data. He wrote, "No real observation of any kind of phenomena is possible, except in as far as it is first directed, and finally interpreted, by some theory." At first glance, this thinking may seem to contradict the idea that science and observation are the basis of all knowledge. However, Comte believed that empirical data must support any explanatory theory or natural law. Like the chicken and the egg, it was a cycle of codependency: there could be no empirical data without theoretical laws and there could be no theoretical laws without data. One proved and explained the existence of the other.

Comte did not have time for the nonsense of religion and imagination. He firmly believed that positivism, which depended on both the scientific method and the circular dependence of theory and observation, needed to replace outdated theological and metaphysical ways of thinking. He went beyond many traditional empiricists by denying the possibility of knowledge of unobservable physical objects. This meant that any question concerning God, creation, or like subjects that could not be answered with scientific facts and observation was beyond the scope of human understanding.

Sociology

Sociology, the study of society, was Comte's passion. He not only named the subject, but also placed it on top of his natural order of sciences, above biology, chemistry, math, and all other classical studies. His approach to sociology was, according to Andrew Wernick in the *Cambridge Dictionary of Sociology*, "comparative and historical, aiming to understand how each type of society was institutionally constituted, and by what logic of development human society passed from one form to another." In other words, he divided it into two branches: one that dealt with the forces keeping society together (family and religion) and one that dealt with how society progressed, or developed, over time.

Comte believed that the ultimate destiny of human society was to arrive at a place where it no longer depended on religion or any other form of "systematic illusion." Science, observable facts, and positivism would reign supreme, and humanity would finally realize that knowledge is limited. However, Comte was not so optimistic as to believe that humanity could reach this point of maturity in an instant. Instead, he believed that society progressed "successively through three different theoretical conditions: the theological, or fictitious; the metaphysical, or abstract; and the scientific, or positive."

Comte defined his theological stage as one in which "the human mind, in its search for the primary and final causes of phenomena, explains the apparent anomalies in the universe as interventions of supernatural agents." Simply stated, man looked to religion and spiritual forces to explain all of his questions. In the metaphysical second stage, best represented by the Enlightenment and pre-revolutionary France, man still had the same questions, but he began to look to abstract, philosophical concepts for the answers. Living in the aftermath of the French Revolution, Comte saw himself witnessing the beginning of humankind transitioning from the metaphysical stage to the third, positive stage, where humankind dropped all questions that could not be explained through science or observation.

Knowing that this change would not be easy, Comte recognized that humanity still required "a philosophy of life that would facilitate the transition and maintain social order." In other words, society needed a few philosophical stitches to hold it together, until humankind realized that looking for answers in both religion and abstract thinking was pointless. To this end, Comte proposed the "development of a secular system of 'common moral ideas,' based on an appreciation of the normative character of all social relations, and the impossibility of social order without a publicly accepted system of values."

Comte exposes this idea of humanity accepting one secular system to new heights of controversy when he began to promote replacing religious faith with the worship of humanity. Known as the Universal Church of the Religion of Humanity, this "religion without metaphysics" had its own catechism, sacraments, priesthood, and rituals. This led author T.H. Huxley to comment that it was "Catholicism minus Christianity." All this proved too much for the Catholic Church, which placed Comte's *The Course of Positive Philosophy* on its Index of forbidden books. In response, Comte compiled a list of only 150 books that were to survive as part of a "Positivist Library." All others were to be destroyed. Clearly, he was a man dedicated to his ideas.

Tatjana Scherschel, 2015
Julianne Swayze, 2016
Daren Jonescu, advisor

HONORÉ DE BALZAC, 1799–1850, *Master of French Realism*

" However gross a man may be, the minute he expresses a strong and genuine affection, some inner secretion alters his features, animates his gestures, and colors his voice. The stupidest man will often, under the stress of passion, achieve heights of eloquence, in thought if not in language, and seem to move in some luminous sphere. ... Are not our finer feelings the poems of the human will?

—Father Goriot

- Mastered realistic and psychological novels, such as *Father Goriot* and *Eugenie Grandet*
- Was a monarchist, a conservative, and a devotee to high society
- Wrote at night, sometime continuously for 15 to 16 hours at a time, while drinking excessive amounts of coffee
- Constructed *The Human Comedy*, his magnum opus, around an interconnected collection of novels and short stories centered on French life post-Napoleon
- Is known as the father of realism in European literature because of his relatable characters
- Created character who, like himself, were obsessed with wealth and social status to their own detriment

Key Works

The Human Comedy, 1831
Father Goriot, 1835
The Lily in the Valley, 1836
Lost Illusions, 1837
Cousin Bette, 1846

Biography

In 1888, the German philosopher Friedrich Engels described Honoré de Balzac like this:

> Politically [Balzac was] a legitimist; his great work is a constant elegy on the irreparable decay of good society; his sympathies are with the class that is doomed to extinction. But for all that, his satire is never keener, his irony never more bitter, than when he sets in motion the very men and women with whom he sympathizes most deeply—the nobles.

Honoré de Balzac was born on May 20, 1799, in Tours, France. For schooling, he attended the religious Order of the Oratory at Vendóme. After the downfall of Napoleon, he moved to Paris with his family. He studied criminal and civil law from 1816 through 1819; however, he had already decided he wanted to pursue writing rather than law.

The first piece he wrote was the historical tragedy, *Cromwell*. By age 30, he had written and published more than 20 novels under various pseudonyms. In 1829, Balzac finally used his own name for the publication of *Les Chouans*. He bought a home in Rue Cassini and commissioned a decorative bust of Napoleon with a base that read, "What he undertook with the sword, I will accomplish with the pen." In the last 20 years of his life, he published 90 novels and novellas, 30 short stories, and five plays. He routinely wrote at night, often becoming so absorbed in his work that he wrote continuously for 15 or 16 hours. This was not Balzac's only quirk; he also insisted on wearing the white robe of the Dominicans and drinking copious amounts of coffee as he wrote. Balzac's most famous work is *The Human Comedy*, an array of interconnected short stories and novels with an emphasis on sociological norms in France.

A monarchist, a conservative, and a devotee of high society, he had an prolific literary career. He also embraced quite a few romantic relationships, most notably with Eveline Hanska, a Polish countess.

Although she was already married to a man from Ukraine, they became very close and corresponded frequently. He first became intimate with her after spending Christmas with her family in 1833 and 1834. Their adulterous relationship continued until her husband died in 1842. The countess would not marry Balzac until he overcame his growing debt. Though she had enough wealth to help, she refused. Over the next few years, the couple traveled together to Russia, Germany, and France. During this time, Balzac wrote, edited journals, raised bananas on a plantation, and revived silver mining in ancient mines in Sardinia. By 1846 he finally paid all his debts, but also caught pneumonia, and his health declined. He married Hanska on March 14, 1850, and died five months later. At the funeral, Victor Hugo eulogized Balzac: "His life was short, but full, more filled with deeds than days."

Wealth and Status—A Toxic Infatuation

Born into a poor family, Balzac longed for the prosperity that aristocrats had enjoyed before the French Revolution. He even changed his last name from "Balssa" to "de Balzac" in an attempt to appear more sophisticated and wealthy. Despite his constant money worries and lifelong debt from a failed business deal, he always aspired to a life of comfort and financial ease. After he announced his intention to become a novelist instead of a lawyer, his parents provided him with a sparse apartment and a meager allowance in order to teach him a lesson about this impractical career choice. This only inflamed his fixation with wealth; in his writing, money is a dominant theme that shapes the values and aspirations of many characters. A majority of Balzac's protagonists attempt to use their intellect to obtain their financial and social goals. Yet this proves to be many characters' downfall. By suggesting that money threatens to eclipse the power of love and virtue, Balzac hoped his readers would discover "that there is far more happiness in another's happiness than in your own."

Exceptional Realism

Literary critics often commend Balzac as the "architect of the modern novel," and he is famous for his innovative realism, skillfully capturing the essence of everyday life in his writing. Balzac based his stories on ordinary people living remarkably ordinary lives; such characters were accessible and beloved by readers. Unlike in most 19th-century French literature, Balzac's characters experienced everyday struggles and circumstances that reflected those of the French people. Additionally, many of Balzac's characters reappeared in his other works; in placing them there, Balzac portrayed a consistent, three-dimensional version of reality that took on different vantage points in each work—something previously unseen in literature. "Reading brings us unknown friends," he wrote; truly, his characters became companions to his readers. Balzac's love for fiction sharpened his understanding of humanity and his circumstances. He wrote, "People exaggerate both happiness and unhappiness; we are never so fortunate nor so unfortunate as people say we are."

Anthropology

Balzac's characters hail from all corners of France. In *The Human Comedy*, he weaves together narratives of nobles and paupers, artists and politicians, thieves and philanthropists, civilians and servicemen, to form a comprehensive and satirical picture of French life. Out of this collection, published over 18 years, three predominant themes emerge: the first, "analytical study," examines the principles that structure society; the second, "philosophical study," explores the motivations behind human actions; and the third, the "study of manners," analyzes how human motivations shape behavior. Author Stefan Zweig once marveled, "Balzac seems to grasp the whole of life in his two hands." The abundance and diversity of the characters within Balzac's fictional France shaped his multifaceted portrayal of French society, and led him to portray wealth and pleasure as man's goal.

Father Goriot asserts Balzac's belief in social Darwinism, or the belief that the most successful people will rise to the top of a hierarchical system. In the story, Rastignac, a student eager for wealth, learns that there is a magic code he must possess to find success in society. When he resolves to "try for success in the great world," he immediately seeks out "the help and protection of women of social standing." Although a silent struggle, social Darwinism enacts itself in the minds of the characters in this novel, motivating murders and mayhem and melodrama. To achieve wealth, which is to climb to the top of the social ladder, Rastignac even schemes with a friend to murder the brother of a girl in whom he's interested—interested in her inheritance, that is, for he is "hungry as a wolf." Balzac observes through Rastignac's accomplice, "Such is life. It is not better than a kitchen full of bad smells. If you have fish to fry, you must soil your hands in frying them; only be sure to wash them when you have done your cookery. That is the moral of the times we live in." The secret of success in society comes from forgetting the cookery and enjoying the meal with newly washed hands.

In *The Wild Ass's Skin*, Balzac again questions the corrupting nature of society and wealth, as a magic animal skin destroys the happiness of a young man, Raphael, who trades a long life for the violent indulgence of his passions. Raphael's thirst for happiness actually destroys his ability to maintain it; he says we are "pleasure-loving" by nature, and yet Balzac clarifies that we are "condemned to a life of pleasure." Throughout this tale, the very desires of the heart keep Raphael from ever enjoying those desires. Balzac presents a conception of man where true happiness is elusive because society dominates the will of man. He cannot find happiness because he cannot be free.

Cloie Dobias, 2015
Briauna Schultz, 2013

FREDERIC BASTIAT ◊ 1801–1850, *Political Philosopher/Economist*

> " Life, liberty, and property do not exist because men have made laws. On the contrary, it was the fact that life, liberty, and property existed beforehand that caused men to make laws in the first place.
>
> —*The Law*

- Was a lucid, superb economic journalist
- Believed in Natural Law theory
- Advocated for unrestricted free markets
- Expressed a just system of laws and how they support a free society in his magnum opus, *The Law*
- Maintained that everyone has a right to protect his person, his liberty, and his property

Key Works

"The Physiology of Plunder," 1848
"Two Systems of Ethics," 1848
The Law, 1850

"What Is Seen and What Is Not Seen," 1850

Biography

Claude-Frederic Bastiat was born on June 29, 1801 in Mugron near Bayonne, France. Orphaned at age 10, he was educated by his grandparents. He attended school until age 17 when he left for a nearby town to help in the family business. Bastiat absorbed the life and the poverty in the town, learning what it meant to participate in the local economy. At 25, when Bastiat's grandfather died, he inherited his land and became a farmer. But his desire to pursue philosophy stirred him to hire a manager to work the farm so he could continue his studies, which he did for the next 20 years. Interested in local politics, Bastiat became the Justice of Peace of Murgon in 1831, and then consul general in 1832. He established the Association of Free Trade and published his ideas through the Association's journal *Free Trade*. A satiric parable he crafted about candle makers seeking the government's protection against the sun got the public's attention. As Bastiat told it, the sun was an unfair competitor because the sun didn't allow candle makers to get as much profit as they wanted. The government, the story suggested, should restrict the sun. This tale of the candle maker's petition was widely repeated as an argument for free trade and an example of the unseen results of "protective government policy." Bastiat wrote more protests against socialism, which he said was protectionism itself. His outspoken effort got him elected to the Constituent Assembly and then the National Legislative Assembly in 1849. Bastiat continuously debated and discussed and wrote about his passion for economic freedom, unrestricted free markets, and the right each man has to protect his person, liberties and property until he contracted tuberculosis and died in 1850, murmuring "the truth, the truth."

Although not appreciated in his time as the noteworthy economist he became, students of his works in succeeding years speculate that he was underappreciated mainly because of his libertarianism. Only recently has he been described as "not only a good political scientist, but also a fine economist."

Bastiat's Economic Ideas

Bastiat was a brilliant synthesizer and organizer of economic ideas. Some of the ideas he wrote about include:

Rights Theory. According to Bastiat, government is necessary only for the protection of life, liberty, and property, "the night watchman state." A government has no duty to help people; this takes the essential purpose of protection too far because it necessitates redistribution of property, which is always unethical. Every citizen is entitled to keep the fruits of his labor. In summary, government should have minimum power and levy minimum taxes while promoting the most liberty possible.

Greed, Two Kinds. Law is perverted when the government takes property from people. People gain property by working for it or seizing it. Men find it less dangerous to take another's wealth by asking the government to do it. They use the law to seize property from one person and give it to someone else. Legalized plunder is a process whereby someone asks the government to do something that would be illegal if he were to do it himself.

False Philanthropy. "Charity" is when an individual gives his own assets to the cause he chooses. When the government forces someone to give his assets, the government is plundering. Although the act may be legal, the government is not ethical.

Utilitarianism. Economists must consider not only the visible effect or a policy or law, but also effects which can't be seen or can't be observed *yet*. A good economist makes decisions based on the effects of all concerned groups in the short and long terms. Many economists just look at zero-sum gain, when one part of the economy gains and another part loses, without taking into account opportunity cost and preference theory.

Physiology of Plunder. There are two ways to acquire the means to improve things: production and plunder. Plunder stops society's improvement because many people seek to live at everyone else's expense. Society would improve if the plunderers would work to create their own wealth and stop expending energy to take the wealth of others. Examples of the four kinds of plunder throughout history are war, slavery, theocracy, and monopoly. When the public is educated about the harmfulness of plunder, change will occur. In other words, moral philosophy points out the evil deed, and political economy demonstrates the negativity of the full effect of the act.

Free Trade. Basing his opinion on utilitarian ethics and rights theory, Bastiat supported unrestricted free trade, being able to trade what one has for what one wants without any interference. When the government takes something from an owner and transfers it to special interests (who haven't provided a service equal to what they are receiving), it is a form of plunder or rent seeking. Tariffs, quotas, and antidumping laws have similar effects: the price of domestic goods rises and producers of domestic good receive monopoly prices. Increased economic efficiency results from free trade.

As Dr. Thomas DiLorenzo of Loyola University sums it up, "Perhaps the main underlying theme of Bastiat's writings was that the free market was inherently a source of 'economic harmony' among individuals as long as government was restricted to the function of protecting the lives, liberties and properties of citizens from theft or aggression." To Bastiat, governmental coercion was legitimate only if it served "to guarantee security of person, liberty and property rights, to cause justice to reign over all."

Joshua E. Fernalld, 2016

RALPH WALDO EMERSON, 1803–1882, *Father of transcendentalism*

> What I must do is all that concerns me, not what people think. … It is easy in the world to live after the world's opinion; it is easy in solitude to live after our own; but the great man is he who in the midst of the crowd keeps with perfect sweetness the independence of solitude.
>
> —"Self-Reliance"

- Championed and defined American romanticism and transcendentalism
- Was a forward thinker—condemning slavery and supporting women's rights
- Disdained society and its homogenizing of intellect, while praising intuition and self-reliance
- Broke all ties with formal religion, although he was ordained in the Unitarian Church
- Championed an optimistic view of man's nature wherein the individual is sacred
- Authored the quote: "Do not go where the path may lead, go instead where there is no path and leave a trail"; it is one of his most widely known (and abused) quotes

- Met William Wordsworth and Samuel Taylor Coleridge While travelling in Europe; their romantic influence can be seen in Emerson's work
- Published his book *Nature* anonymously because the content was so controversial at the time

Key Works

Nature, 1836
The American Scholar, 1837
"The Divinity School Address," 1838
"Self-Reliance," 1841
"Experience," 1844

Biography

Poet, preacher, and philosopher, Emerson is often recognized as the preeminent creator of American thought. James Russell Lowell, one of his contemporaries, described Emerson's influence:

> We were socially and intellectually bound to English thought, until Emerson cut the cable and gave us a chance at the dangers and glories of blue waters.

Emerson was the first American thinker to successfully navigate the dangers and glories of transcendental waters, mapping the philosophy of individualism and intuition within the transcendentalist movement in America. A master of language, Emerson cajoled the masses, criticized the self-righteous, and championed the individual intellect.

Born on May 25, 1803, to William and Ruth Haskins Emerson of Boston, Ralph Waldo Emerson was the second of five surviving sons. When Emerson was eight, his father, a Unitarian minister, died, leaving the family in genteel poverty. In 1821 Emerson, who went by "Waldo," graduated from Harvard but continued his education by entering Harvard Divinity School. Shortly after being ordained as a Unitarian minister, he accepted a position at Boston's prominent Second Church. The death of his first wife, Ellen Tucker, preceded his resignation from the church.

Upon returning from a brief respite in Europe, Emerson took up collegiate lecturing opportunities to share his unorthodox ideas. Although he considered himself a poet, he garnered an illustrious reputation through his essays and lectures. In 1836, his book *Nature* awakened the American public to transcendental themes, themes which he especially developed in the two-volume *Essays*, including in "Self-Reliance," "The Over-Soul," and "Experience." In 1882, Emerson died of pneumonia.

Transcendentalism

Divorcing the sacred and the divine from the religious, Emerson propounds an idealism in which experience is not the final word; instead, intuition supplements what the senses fail to see. In "The Transcendentalist," Emerson asks, "What is the privilege and nobility of our nature, but its persistency, through its power to attach itself to what is permanent?" Man must trust himself to pursue truth; he must cling to the divinity that exists within himself. Consequently, conformity is the chief vice of man. And it is only by practicing self-reliance that one finds true independence. For Emerson, man is action; if he acts for society, he loses himself, but if he acts for himself, he becomes himself. Although "Emerson had no designs to be a philosopher," his transcendentalism joins together Eastern thought and Continental metaphysics; he notes a tension "in the world between good and evil and that it is each person's individual goal to break free from this to heighten their inner self." All that is good and true exists inside man; obligation and tradition often cloak man's innate desire to discover truth, to discover himself. This pursuit and glorification of one's unique self, one's exclusive relation to the world, is transcendental thought.

Transcendental Scholarship

The secret to education, Emerson says, is respect of the pupil. Each student is capable of passion in different areas; each has his own ideas and thoughts. To instill a mutual joy in learning, the educator needs to foster these individual passions. Instructors should teach Latin grammar and arithmetic, but also allow students to relish "the power of beauty, the power of books, of poetry." Educators need to be wary of the monotony of sameness, of the conventional, in favor of allowing the pupils to be themselves and "enjoy life their own way." When the teacher allows the student to bask in his excitement of the subject, teacher and student come together in a symbiotic joy of learning.

According to Emerson, organized education takes the joy and love out of learning. Memorization by rote seeks to educate a man in a career in engineering or accounting, but it sacrifices the "able, earnest, great-hearted man." Emerson criticizes education for focusing on the surface of science and abandoning the "Vast": the "poverty, love, authority, anger, sickness, sorrow, [and] success" that lead to a deepening of the mind and an appreciation for learning. Emerson believes that everyone should be educated; he praises the New England school district for allowing even the poor to study not simply their trade but sciences and arts as well. Emerson thinks that every individual, whether he be "sot or fop, ruffian or pedant," has the capacity to think; thus, reforming education to include every member will lead to a better society.

Ultimately, the learned see nature and realize the measure of all they have learned—knowing oneself and studying nature become one. The sanctity that exists within each man also exists in Nature; here, Emerson's idealism manifests clearly. Man can delight in the nature around him only insofar as he recognizes that the experience of the sun does not stop at merely seeing the sun but rather culminates in seeing the sun shine; the world is not just an experience but a chance to experience what the world represents. In this way, man and nature share some divine nature, eternal and inexplicable, and it is only possible to develop delight in the world by recognizing this shared being. The ability "to produce this delight does not reside in nature, but in man, or in the harmony of both." Only when man truly recognizes nature's duality can man truly know himself.

In "The American Scholar," Emerson argues that while books can provide a mirror of morality and "offer us the influence of the past," they also create the danger of influencing the mind away from the god in ourselves. In order to avoid slanderous gossip and adverse habits, Emerson advocates for three rules when reading: read nothing written in the last year, read only famous books, and read that which brings pleasure. In addition to those books, Emerson recommends that everyone read the great works of Homer, Herodotus, Aeschylus, Plato, and Plutarch because when he shuts the cover, he will be a greater man. In Emerson's mind, the ultimate scholar is one who gleans his own knowledge from the world around him in order to further appreciate himself as an individual.

Transcendental Society

"Self-Reliance," one of Emerson's most esteemed essays, embodies his sociological ideals of independence and intuition. He advocates that we transcend the values of society—regulated religion, government, and education—which pulverize the innate need for original thought and action, for "nothing is at last sacred but the integrity of your own mind." The sacred laws and traditions of society are ultimately meaningless if there is no compulsion in the heart for it to be so, and he pleads, "I hope in these days we have heard the last of conformity and consistency" because those only suffocate the genius's soul. He notes that "imitation is suicide," which illuminates the Emersonian value of authenticity. A man must be himself in order to be a man—the society in which man exists cannot be allowed to dictate his existence. In "Education," he asks, "cannot we let people be themselves, and enjoy life in their own way? You are trying to make that man another you. One's enough."

Despite Emerson's disdain for society, he is not a proponent of total reclusivity. His essay "Friendship" captures the joys and idyllic vision of what true friendship can be. He proclaims that "the essence of friendship is entireness, a total magnanimity and trust." While he treasures friendship, Emerson is hesitant to become too talkative even among his friends, admitting, "I cannot afford to speak much with my friend." Why? Perhaps because he is fearful of losing who he is as an individual; however, his friend Henry David Thoreau says that "friends do not live in harmony merely, as some say, but in melody," which typifies the respectful reciprocity of Emerson's ideal friendship. While society often seems to suggest that friends change for mutual approval, Emerson exhorts individuals to come together in an amiable and cooperative relationship that promotes the individuality of each.

Caroline Fuschino, 2015
Jessica Goeser, researcher
Briauna Schultz, 2013

THE NAPOLEONIC WARS, 1803–1815

Following close behind the French Revolution were the Napoleonic Wars, so named after the French (actually Corsican) general and emperor Napoleon Bonaparte, who sought to establish dominion over the whole of Europe. Although seemingly invincible for a time, Napoleon's armies were ultimately undone by his invasion of Russia, to be finished off later by his myriad opponents.

The Napoleonic Wars saw the official dissolution of the Holy Roman Empire, and fostered the seeds of nationalism among many of France's enemies—notably Germany and Italy, who would later unify as spurred on my nationalist sentiments. The French occupation of Spain left it grasping weakly for its own colonies, which subsequently turned towards revolution. In the face of all this, the British Empire rose from the dust to stand above its peers, the premiere world power in the age of "Pax Britannica."

Notable Battles

The Battle of Trafalgar, 1805

His sights set on conquering Great Britain, Napoleon's naval forces met with those of Admiral Horatio Nelson's off the coast of Cadiz in what was to become the decisive naval battle of the era. Nelson died in the battle, but his brilliant leadership successfully thwarted the invasion and earned him the title "Britain's greatest naval hero."

The Battle of Leipzig, 1813

Also known as the Battle of Nations, this constituted the largest number of deployed troops in a European war at the time. It was Napoleon verses the rest, and the rest won. Napoleon's defeat here, following the conclusion of his disastrous Russian campaign, led to his retreat and defeat in Paris, his subsequent exile, and his last stand at Waterloo.

The Battle of Waterloo, 1815

Napoleon's last stand and final bid for political power, fought in modern day Belgium. Defeated again, Napoleon once again found himself exiled, this time until his death in 1821. France would never again pose an imperial threat to its neighbors, and lost much of its former political preeminence.

NATHANIEL HAWTHORNE, 1804–1864, *The Dark Magician*

> " No man, for any considerable period, can wear one face to himself and another to the multitude, without finally getting bewildered as to which may be the true.
>
> —*The Scarlet Letter*

- Was born to a once-prominent, later-obscure Puritan family in Salem, Massachusetts
- Changed his name from Hathorne by adding a "w" to distinguish himself from his ancestors who took part in the Salem witch trials in the late 1600s
- Received an education at Bowdoin College despite protesting it and insisting on wanting to become an author
- Disliked his Puritan heritage as a result of reflection upon immoral deeds like the Salem witch trials, and exposed the severity of Puritanism
- Scribbled the number 64 obsessively upon scraps of paper in his final years before his death, which happened to be in 1864
- Told his publisher, "Upon my honor, I am not quite sure that I entirely comprehend my own meaning in some of these blasted allegories"
- Had many transcendentalist friends and connections, yet became disillusioned with the movement after a year of working on the transcendentalist Brook Farm
- Emphasized sin and evil in most of his works, especially in *The House of the Seven Gables* and *The Scarlet Letter*
- Did not necessarily practice a religion himself, yet included religious references and beliefs in many, if not all, of his works
- Focused on the religious differences and conflicts between his Puritan past and transcendentalist experiences on Brook Farm in his romances

Key Works

"Young Goodman Brown," 1835
Twice-Told Tales, 1837
The Scarlet Letter, 1850
The House of the Seven Gables, 1851

Biography

Long known to be an epicenter of Puritan activity in the New World, Salem, Massachusetts, became the birthplace of Nathaniel Hathorne on July 4, 1804. The Hathorne family included Puritan magnates, judges, and seamen, and achieved great prosperity and fame. They also participated in the Salem witch trials. This, combined with a decline of fortune, led Nathaniel Hathorne to change his name to Nathaniel Hawthorne to distance himself from relatives involved in the witch trials.

His father died when Nathaniel was four, and his mother moved into her wealthy brothers' house with him and his two sisters. He attended Bowdoin College where he gained an impressive education in English, financed by his uncle, and there made many friends. As a young adult he remained obscure, isolating himself for years in his mother's Salem house and writing anonymous short stories. He joined the transcendentalist experiment at Brook Farm, but became disillusioned within a year and quit. Thereafter, transcendentalist concepts and beliefs influenced his work and clashed with Puritanism in his romances such as *The Scarlet Letter*. After marrying Sophia Peabody in 1842 and finishing his term as surveyor in the Salem Custom House in 1848, he wrote his first bestselling romance, *The Scarlet Letter* and followed up with *The House of the Seven Gables*. (His first novel, *Fanshawe*, had quickly failed and was suppressed by Hawthorne shortly after its publication in 1828.) He was appointed consul at Liverpool, England while his friend Franklin Pierce was in office and wrote several books, such as *Our Old Home*, based on his experiences in England. Unfortunately, Hawthorne lived only a few more months, so these books were the last stories he completed. He died in 1864 of unknown causes, as he refused to allow any medical professional to examine him when his health began to fail.

The Dark Romantic

It may be worth noting that Hawthorne never actually called any of his stories "novels" or "books." Instead, he decided to call each of his works a "romance." He believed that an author, while writing a romance, "has fairly a right to present that truth under circumstances, to a great extent, of the writer's own choosing or creation." The romance, he claimed, was a fictional manifestation of the author's beliefs, yet it still had to "rigidly subject itself to laws," meaning that it could not have imagined beings or figures like those found in works of fantasy. Although he explored some positive themes, such as the importance of the individual, he most often emphasized the innate evil of humanity. Hawthorne's romances quickly led to his reputation as the "Dark Romantic," a testament to his insight into the darker side of human nature and the quality of his contributions to the romantic genre.

The romantic movement originated in the late 18th century, "promoting a heightened interest in nature, emphasizing the individual's expressions of emotion and imagination, and departing from the attitudes and forms of classicism." A submovement called dark romanticism rose in the 19th century, focusing on humanity's innate nature to sin and to do evil. Hawthorne, along with his close friend Herman Melville, became one of the most well known dark romantics, a pioneer in the field who chose to deal with dark and mysterious subjects. His romances depicted the distrust of empirical and scientific knowledge that characterized romanticism. Take for example Chillingworth, a physician in *The Scarlet Letter* who comes to symbolize the blackness of the human heart and the dangers of rationalism. Chillingworth practices science in his darkened laboratory, using his art to ruthlessly torment the fallen priest Dimmesdale and his lover Hester. Likewise, Hawthorne emphasizes the use of intuition and feeling to discover truth and knowledge, a key tenet of romanticism. His stories investigate the human response to sin and evil.

Romantic Individuality

Hawthorne's negative religious experiences, his haunting family connection with the Salem Witch Trials (his paternal great-great-grandfather was party to many death sentences during his tenure as judge), and his failed attempt at the Brook Farm transcendentalist colony left him with negative views of society. *The Scarlet Letter*, in particular, portrays the struggle between the individual and society. The novel begins with "a throng of bearded men, in sad-colored garments" standing outside the town jail, projecting their self-righteous, religious judgment onto the incarcerated protagonist, Hester Prynne. The conflict between the group and the individual continues until the end of the book where Hester, though exonerated, willingly returns to Boston and once again picks up her symbol of punishment, the scarlet letter "A," recasting it to stand for "able" rather than "adulteress." Hester's ability to withstand and even triumph over the pressures of society showcases Hawthorne's faith in the individual.

The Evil of Man

As a dark romantic, Hawthorne deals in the tenebrous and convoluted, yet he addresses nothing quite as chilling as man's innate evil and need to conceal his fallenness. His romances delve into sin, perceived and real, establishing his own belief that everyone sins, even if the severity of the offenses differs. Roger Chillingworth personifies evil in *The Scarlet Letter*, obsessing about his personal grievance. He attempts to "usurp divine rights" because "he made his judgments, prescribed the punishment, and became executor," which Hawthorne finds hypocritical, selfish, and diabolical. Also, Chillingworth tries, by mentally torturing Dimmesdale, "to guide and dominate another existence," a grievous offense that intrudes upon basic human rights and romantic tenets. Through his torture and sinful desires, Chillingworth symbolizes Satan, becoming the very face of evil. In keeping with his philosophy that everyone sins, Hawthorne also saddles his adulterous protagonists with immoral desires and actions, although he mitigates the evils they commit by showing their internal suffering and humble penitence.

The Influence of Sin

The dark romantic continues to stress the impact of sin by showing how one sinful act can swallow generations, leaving the children to pay for the sin of their father. Hawthorne explicitly admits in his Preface to *Seven Gables*, "that the wrong-doing of one generation lives into the successive ones." The curse at the beginning of *Seven Gables* portrays this theme that sin carries over decades, even generations, and does not stop until atoned for. In the opening scene, Maule, a man accused of witchcraft, is being put to death while his house burns. Dying, he curses his persecutors, the Pyncheons, crying out, "God will give him blood to drink!" After Maule is gone, Colonel Pyncheon erects a mansion on the property, revealing his true crime—murder for a mansion. Hawthorne, however, does not allow his characters to sin without sacrifice. Colonel Pyncheon is found mysteriously bloodied and dead in his office. In what seems like more than just bad luck, the Pyncheon family devolves into disrepute, the house and the family members gradually succumbing to the curse of the Colonel—the youngest Pyncheon even murders his own uncle. In this way, Hawthorne suggests that even if the sin is not one's fault, its curse gets passed down generation by generation—and atonement must be made.

Benjamin Rocklin, 2017

ALEXIS DE TOCQUEVILLE, 1805–1859, *An Insightful Reporter*

> " When I refuse to obey an unjust law, I do not contest the right of the majority to command, but I simply appeal from the sovereignty of the people to the sovereignty of mankind.
>
> —*Democracy in America*

- Was born into an aristocratic family in Paris
- Joined the government after completing law school
- Studied prison reform in America, which led to his interest in the study of American democracy
- Explored the successes and failures of American democracy in *Democracy in America*
- Focused specifically on social equality as the heart of American society
- Opposed the July 1830 Revolution, putting him at odds with King Louis-Philippe
- Served as a foreign minister in his last years in government

Key Works

On the Penitentiary System in the United States and Its Application in France, 1832
Democracy in America Vol. 1, 1835
Democracy in America Vol. 2, 1840
The Old Regime and the Revolution, 1856

Biography

The first foreigner to ever write a commentary on American affairs, Alexis de Tocqueville gained great fame with his study of American democracy. Born to an aristocratic family in Paris in 1805, he received education in law and was appointed assistant magistrate at the age of 22. The July 1830 Revolution soon placed King Louis-Philippe on the throne, resulting in a demotion for Tocqueville to a small judgeship without pay. The coronation of Louis-Philippe also put a temporary halt to Tocqueville's political ambitions. Hence, he traveled to America to study the American penitentiary system, and reported his findings to the French government in *On the Penitentiary System in the United States and Its Application in France*. The trip sparked an obsession with both American and democratic culture, resulting in his bestselling, two-volume book *Democracy in America*, which commented on the successes and failures of the American system of democracy. He married Mary Motley in 1835, but they never had children. Tocqueville was appointed to the Chamber of Deputies in 1839, again serving as a deputy after the Revolution of 1848. He served as foreign minister from 1849 until 1851 and then retired. He wrote *The Old Regime and the Revolution* in his last years and died in 1859 of tuberculosis.

The Democratic Revolution

Tocqueville wrote *Democracy in America* as much more than a simple commentary on American government and affairs. He thought that "the spread of democracy was inevitable," necessitating a book that would help "France avoid America's faults and emulate its successes." Tocqueville believed that the spread of democracy was actually God's desire, calling the form of government "a profoundly religious phenomenon." He further suggested that "attempt[ing] to check democracy would be … to resist the will of God."

History, Tocqueville claimed, pointed to democracy becoming the dominant form of government. If one studied history, he or she would "scarcely find a single great event of the last 700 years that has not promoted equality of condition." For this reason, he commented, "[Democracy] is universal, it is lasting, it constantly eludes all human interference, and all events as well as all men contribute to its progress." During his time in government service, he met Francois Guizot. A mentor to Tocqueville and a great influence on his *Democracy in America*, Guizot believed that the downfall of aristocratic government was inevitable, and inspired Tocqueville to write about education in democratic society. Though Tocqueville was inspired by America's new government, he also recognized its flaws. He once compared democracy to "those children who have no parental guidance," causing it to be "acquainted only with the vices and wretchedness of society." Therefore, he wrote a book both to uncover America's errors, so that France wouldn't repeat them, and to pinpoint America's successes, so that France could build upon them.

Equality of Conditions

Tocqueville saw equality of conditions as the core of American democracy, noting that nothing in American society struck him "more forcibly than the general equality of condition among the people." He believed that the principal characteristic American society modeled for the world was providing an equal chance at prosperity to all of its citizens. However, there was one glaring exception.

Tocqueville criticized American slavery as a breach in the nation's development and saw the abolition of slavery as both imperative and inevitable. He saw reflections of French society in the American South; slaves were the equivalents of serfs, and the masters paralleled French nobles and aristocrats. Tocqueville noted that the idleness of the Southern slave masters made them weak and lazy, and compared them to the nobles in feudal societies. He saw northerners, however, as "practical, hardworking, and clever," using their resourcefulness to better improve society: they were thus the embodiment of democratic ideals. As a result, Tocqueville advocated for an end to slavery in America, writing that the institution could not "endure in an age of democratic liberty and enlightenment." Tocqueville saw only two possible options for America's future: "to emancipate the Negroes and to intermingle with them, or, remain isolated from them, to keep them in slavery as long as possible." He prophesied that either resolution would bring woes, a prediction that foreshadowed the Civil War.

Individuality

Tocqueville also criticize American society for the trend of individuality. Individuality, he said, was a feeling that led each member in a community "to sever himself from the mass of his fellows and to draw apart with his family and his friends." He described individuality as a "passionate and exaggerated love of self," that caused an individual to "prefer himself to everything in the world." Although selfishness may "blight the germ of all virtue," individualism was worse, because it, "in the long run … attacks and destroys all other virtues." Additionally, Tocqueville noted that individualism was a phenomenon unique to democratic societies. Due to the interdependent organization of aristocratic and feudal societies, even the most selfish kings, lords, and serfs could not afford to withdraw from society. Tocqueville argued that democracy "breaks that chain [of interdependence] and severs every link in it," creating a situation in which no man owes anything to any other. This lack of dependence allows each man to embrace individualism and withdraw from society. Alone with only his inner circle of family and friends, an individualist seeks only personal gain; cooperation is rendered unnecessary. Additionally, since family names do not decide a man's wealth in a democracy, Tocqueville feared that individualist Americans would forget their ancestors and descendants.

Religion and Democracy

When Tocqueville first entered America, the "religious aspect of the country was the first thing that struck [his] attention." He contrasted religion in France and America, stating that in France "the spirit of religion and the spirit of freedom [marched] in opposite directions," whereas in America "they were intimately united." In interviews with Tocqueville, many priests "attributed the peaceful dominion of religion in their country mainly to the separation of church and state." Tocqueville also noted that men of religious power tended to avoid political power. Paradoxically, he argued that religion in America was attractive to the people precisely because it was not tied to materialism, individuality, or power.

Joshua Fernalld, 2016
Kurt Gutschick, faculty
Benjamin Rocklin, 2017

JOHN STUART MILL, 1806–1873, *The Common Sense Utilitarian*

> If all mankind minus one, were of one opinion, and only one person were of the contrary opinion, mankind would be no more justified in silencing that one person, than he, if he had the power, would be justified in silencing mankind.
>
> —*On Liberty*

- Learned Greek by the age of three and Latin by eight—a prodigy
- Struggled with serious depression and mental lethargy from his early twenties, causing him to doubt the value of his intellectual pursuits; claimed his melancholy began to lift only when he began to read romantic poetry, which also modified his philosophical view in the direction of an increased emphasis on sentimentality, optimism, and a somewhat idealistic belief in unlimited progress as a social goal
- Was a renowned workaholic, dedicated from a very young age to social reform towards increased liberty in the name of general happiness, with happiness defined in the utilitarian manner, i.e., hedonistically
- Started the philosophical radicalism movement with Jeremy Bentham and fought for universal male suffrage and other political reforms, including women's rights
- Amended Bentham's utilitarianism by introducing the idea of higher and lower pleasures into the calculus of "the greatest happiness of the greatest number"
- Defended freedom of speech and association, popularizing the idea of a "marketplace of ideas" in which, when all views are permitted a hearing, truth will out
- Argued that increased uniformity of public opinion is a great threat to freedom, leading to "tyranny of the majority," and therefore that steps should be taken to discourage excessive uniformity of opinion in the name of preserving the open debate that keeps good ideas vigorous, and reminds men of the dangers of bad ideas
- Advocated for the lower classes; argued that safeguarding their rights meant improving their education
- Defined the basis of liberal society by way of a distinction still used among libertarians, between self-regarding and other-regarding actions, the latter alone being legitimately subject to legal restriction

- Presented an object lesson about the dangers of utilitarianism: In his later years, he converted from defending liberty to socialism; utilitarianism's emphasis on the collective good, rather than a principled respect for the value of the individual human being per se, leaves the utilitarian susceptible to the appeal of collectivist political arguments for greater "general welfare," such as 19th-century socialists claimed to offer

Key Works

On Liberty, 1859
Considerations on Representative Government, 1861
Utilitarianism, 1861
The Subjection of Women, 1869

Biography

Enlightened England was the cradle for John Stuart Mill's philosophies. England offered him many different opportunities to develop his core ideals, while he worked with the East India Company, the Anglican Church, and the other philosophers of his time. Early in life, Mill received a painstaking education from his father, an economist and historian. At 3 years old, he was fluent in Greek, and by 8 he was reading classical philosophy, mathematics, physics, and astronomy. He studied Adam Smith and David Ricardo while also reading the classics in their original languages during his free time. He founded a number of intellectual societies and began to contribute to periodicals. In 1823, his father got him a job with the East India Company, and he eventually took his father's place as chief examiner.

In his autobiography, Mill often attributed his success to the work his father set him. His education had a cost, though. At 20, Mill had a mental breakdown and suffered a severe period of depression. This led him to rethink many of his ideas and to form the fundamentals of his philosophy. After he recovered, he married Harriet Taylor, his friend of 21 years. Taylor had a profound impact on Mill's perspective of women's rights and giving women equal footing with civil rights. They had a fruitful relationship for seven years until Taylor died of lung congestion. After her death, Mill finished his work on *Utilitarianism,* which defined many of his key thoughts on political theory and economics. He worked as Lord Rector of the University of St. Andrews and later as a member of parliament with the Liberal Party. Mill's work continued to be influential in social theory, political theory, and political economy even after his death in 1873, when he was buried next to his wife in Avignon, France.

Utilitarianism and the Principle of Utility

Before delving into a discussion of Mill's contribution to utilitarian philosophy, one must be familiar with the principle of utility and its common objections. Bentham first introduced the principle of utility as a consequentialist principle that states that pain and pleasure are innate barometers of ethics. The principle of utility states that actions or behaviors are right in so far as they promote pleasure or happiness, and wrong as they produce pain or unhappiness. However, the principle of utility is not to be used for decision-making; rather, it only assesses the morality of an act.

Mill expands and develops utilitarianism as an extension of common sense, making a few key amendments to Bentham's work. Unlike Bentham, Mill contends that all pleasures are not equal; once a man's basic needs are satisfied, pleasure becomes qualitatively divided. For Mill, man's highest achievements are his highest pleasures; pleasures of intellect, self-development, and imagination reign above the lower pleasures of sex and sleep. This conception of happiness includes man's innate dignity. To say that the principle of utility promotes carnality (as some critics did) is actually a reflection of the objector's low opinion of man. He concludes, "It is better to be a human being dissatisfied than a pig satisfied."

The second objection to which Mill responds is that utilitarianism is too demanding. Here, one objects to utilitarianism because it asks more of moral agents than can be reasonably asked. The fact that agents are supposed to pursue actions that promote the greatest good for the greatest number seems to overestimate the moral fortitude and circumspection of people. Yet Mill clarifies that the principle is not demanding that one act to promote the general interest in all things. This confusion stems from the mistaken belief that in order to make an end goal a reality (promote the greatest good for the greatest number), it must be the motive that impels the action. Mill, however, accepts that smaller, personal motives, such as for oneself or one's family, usually result in a good action that increases the greater good. For Mill, the government alone should deal with the larger picture by promoting the greatest good for the whole society.

Finally, Mill responds to the objection that the principle of utility is really just a principle of expediency; to this, Mill merely concedes. And yet, despite being practical and expedient, the principle of utility does not promulgate immorality, as the word "expedient" seems to indicate. He writes, "Utility is stigmatized as an immoral doctrine by giving it the name of expediency." To be fair, however, Mill does warn against the idea that convenience justifies violating some rule that the principle has already shown to be right. That is, lying cannot be justified solely because it will benefit the perpetrator—this act violates the principle of utility—confirming the truth that ultimate happiness is not always expedient.

Although utilitarianism seems somewhat subjective, Mill argues that our innate desires make the principle of utility a first principle of morality, one that needs no proof, only "self-observation." Every man desires happiness; it only follows that the aggregate goal of man is aggregate happiness. Since "happiness is the sole end of human action," utility grounds morality. What is right is happiness; what is happy is already desirable. In this way, what is moral is innately desirable. Furthermore, Mill propounds that the natural basis for duty to morality lies in the innate desire for unity. One's conscience, which, according to Mill, has been gleaned from society, drives an agent's obligation to unity. To be at one with fellow man compels the agent to act in a certain way. Hence, the principle of utility creates the binding-ness requisite for a moral system through our innate desire for unity and our learned respect for duty.

On Liberty and Democracy

Mill's conception of government cannot be extricated from his philosophical radicalism, which argued for the rationalization of the law and legislation through the application of the principle of unity. Fluctuating between an idealist pursuit of perfect government and a practical harnessing of human nature, Mill's works demonstrate a thoughtful presentation on effective governance. For Mill, the most important aim of government is to "promote the capacities of the people, their 'virtue and intelligence'"—in other words, promote liberty. He writes that studying civil or social liberty is to study "the nature and limits of the power which can be legitimately exercised by society over the individual." The domains of liberty protected by government must include:

> The inward domain of consciousness; demanding liberty of conscience, in the most comprehensive sense; liberty of thought and feeling; absolute freedom of opinion and sentiment on all subjects, practical or speculative, scientific, moral, or theological. ... [and] of framing the plan of our life to suit our character; of doing as we like, so long as what we do does not harm them, even though they should think our conduct foolish, perverse, or wrong. Thirdly, from this liberty of each individual, follows the liberty, within the same limits, of combination among individuals; freedom to unite, for any purpose not involving harm to others: the persons combining being supposed to be full age, and not forced or deceived.

He concludes: "No society in which these liberties are not, on the whole, respected, is free." These capacities, however, "are only secure to the extent that they themselves have the power to protect them." Two key beliefs shaped Mill's optimistic belief in the protection of liberty through democracy: the lower classes are the best protectors of their own liberties, and they could easily become valuable contributors to society through improved education. Thus, the prosperity of a nation relies on the intellectual improvement of its citizens. Progressive in his demands for universal male suffrage and for increased women's rights, Mill points to the "ending of slavery through 'the spread of moral convictions' and the emancipation of the serfs in Russia through 'the growth of a more enlightened opinion respecting the true interest of the State.'" Although Mill approved of a "qualified Socialism," wherein the higher and lower classes subordinate their interests for the sake of the common good, he did not think people had the moral and intellectual strength to make a success of such a government, which left Mill to work with a representative democracy. John Skorupski, in *The Cambridge Companion to Mill*, summarizes Mill's conception of an ideal democracy as "one in which government is ultimately accountable to the people, and in which each group is able, through the franchise, to protect its interests," rising above class issues and considering all things from a rational perspective.

Joshua E. Fernalld, 2016
Jackson Howell, 2015
Brandon Martinez, researcher
Daren Jonescu, advisor

ABRAHAM LINCOLN, 1809–1865, *A Man of Conviction and Compassion*

> Nearly all men can stand adversity, but if you want to test a man's character, give him power.

- Rose from a humble beginning
- Educated himself and became an accomplished lawyer
- Was a gifted orator
- Served as 16th President of the United States
- Opposed the Mexican-American War
- Led America through its greatest crisis—The Civil War—and abolished slavery
- Wrote and delivered the "Gettysburg Address," arguably the finest speech in American history
- Abolished slavery

Key Works

"Gettysburg Address," 1863
Thirteenth Amendment, 1863

Biography

Abraham Lincoln was born February 12, 1809, in Hardin County, Kentucky. His parents were Nancy Hanks and Thomas Lincoln, a farmer and carpenter. He spent his first seven years in Kentucky and then moved with his parents to Indiana, where he primarily educated himself. At Pigeon Creek Farm in Indiana, Lincoln became proficient at wielding the American long ax, which later helped him make a living. Two years after Lincoln's mother died, his father married Sarah Bush Johnston, who reinforced strong values in the family. As a young adult Lincoln held many jobs, including ferrying cargo on the Ohio River and splitting rails for fences. Most significantly, he became known as Honest Abe because of his matchless honesty.

Lincoln went to New Salem to secure a store clerk's position that lasted just a year, and then volunteered in the Black Hawk War. He returned without seeing combat and subsequently ran for a seat in the Illinois state legislature. He lost. He went into business with William Berry with a store; it failed, leaving him with debt. The tide changed when he became postmaster of the village and a county surveyor. Spurred on by John Todd Stuart, Lincoln studied law and passed the state bar in 1836.

After four years of working independently as a lawyer in Springfield, Lincoln married Mary Todd and fathered four children. He won a term in the US House of Representatives in 1846. True to his allegiance to the Whigs, Lincoln opposed the Mexican War. Working at his law practice, Lincoln felt deeply about the Supreme Court's *Dred Scott* decision and decided to campaign for US Senate. After three attempts, he opposed Stephen A. Douglas for the office.

Lincoln even then was honing his thoughts on the union, saying, "A house divided against itself cannot stand … this government cannot endure permanently half slave and half free," just before his famous debates with Douglas. He spoke vehemently against slavery in the debates, but Douglas won reelection. Lincoln's brilliant debating, though, brought him the recognition and support he needed to be considered as a presidential nominee in 1860. Because of divisiveness in both parties, Lincoln received the most electoral votes, but not the majority of the popular votes. As a result, seven southern states seceded when he was elected President. Lincoln wouldn't tolerate the separatist actions and declared war in response to the South's capture of Fort Sumter in 1861. He called for 75,000 volunteers and a naval blockade of the southern coast. The Civil War officially began when four more states seceded.

Lincoln wrote the Emancipation Proclamation, which freed the slaves, and the Gettysburg Address in the midst of the war. He spoke movingly for the union that he was compelled to sustain, and won reelection in 1864 against George B. McClellan. The Confederacy accepted its defeat when General Robert E. Lee surrendered at Appomattox Courthouse in 1865.

Less than one week later, John Wilkes Booth assassinated Lincoln at Ford's Theatre in Washington.

Dignity of All Human Beings

Lincoln praised the "wise statesmanship" of the Founders for affirming the equal dignity of all human beings created in the image of God. From a speech at Lewiston, Illinois, August 17, 1858:

> This was their majestic interpretation of the economy of the Universe. This was their lofty, and wise, and noble understanding of the justice of the Creator to His creatures. Yes, gentlemen, to all His creatures, to the whole great family of man. In their enlightened belief, nothing stamped with the Divine image and likeness was sent into the world to be trodden on, and degraded, and imbruted by its fellows. They grasped not only the whole race of man then living, but they reached forward and seized upon the farthest posterity. They erected a beacon to guide their children and their children's children, and the countless myriads who should inhabit the earth in other ages. Wise statesmen as they were, they knew the tendency of prosperity to breed tyrants, and so they established these great self-evident truths, that when in the distant future some man, some faction, some interest, should set up the doctrine that none but rich men, or none but white men, were entitled to life, liberty and the pursuit of happiness, their posterity might look up again to the Declaration of Independence and take courage to renew the battle which their fathers began—so that truth, and justice, and mercy, and all the humane and Christian virtues might not be extinguished from the land; so that no man would hereafter dare to limit and circumscribe the great principles on which the temple of liberty was being built.

Free Labor

Written more than a decade before the Civil War, an early speech on the tariff, dated December 1, 1847, is exemplary of this theology of labor in combining biblical and republican teachings on free labor and the right to rise:

> In the early days of the world, the Almighty said to the first of our race, "In the sweat of thy face shalt thou eat bread" [Genesis 3:19]; and since then, if we except the light and the air of heaven, no good thing has been, or can be enjoyed by us, without having first cost labour. And, inasmuch [as] most good things are produced by labour, it follows that [all] such things of right belong to those whose labour has produced them. But it has so happened in all ages of the world, that some have laboured, and others have, without labour, enjoyed a large proportion of the fruits. This is wrong, and should not continue. To [secure] to each labourer the whole product of his labour, or as nearly as possible, is a most worthy object of any good government, of democratic government.

Since Lincoln's death, the legend of our 16th President has been burnished by millions of pages of scholarly writings. Many people believe he is the finest leader the United States has ever had. Although he endured much in his time as President, Lincoln continued to be "sensitive, humble, and magnanimous." He is revered, also, for his desire to heal and reconstruct the nation after the war. The Thirteenth Amendment to the Constitution, which abolished slavery, is his most profound legacy; it was passed a few months after his death.

Joshua E. Fernalld, 2016

THE AMERICAN CIVIL WAR, 1861–1865

Following the election of President Abraham Lincoln, the long-brewing tensions between the American north and south burst forth into an open conflict. Although the American Civil War is often (and not incorrectly) attributed to the issue of slavery, it can be better, more broadly understood as being fueled by the issues of states' rights and regional patriotism. "Brother against brother," the American Civil War remains the most costly American war in terms of casualties.

The American Civil War is arguably the single most important event to occur in American history. Many intermeshed factors contributed to causing the war. The economies of the North and South were radically different. While the North had developed a booming industry, the South depended almost entirely on agriculture for its economic stability. Aggressive taxes imposed upon the export of cotton to foreign nations made Northern industrial plants the only market for Southern cotton. This monopoly on the purchase of cotton allowed the North to purchase it at artificially low prices. Slavery complicated the situation as a point of contention between the North and the South. The North had abolished the slave trade years earlier and, while they opposed slavery, few Northerners felt any inclination to fight for the abolition of slavery in the South. However, the massive increase in Union territory in the wake of the Mexican-American War led to a sharp increase in the number of states applying for statehood. While compromises intended to balance the number of free and slave states initially delayed the war, tensions between the North and South began to escalate. These tensions peaked when South Carolina voted to secede as a response to the election of Republican Abraham Lincoln, who vocally opposed the addition of new slave states to the Union. Mississippi, Florida, Alabama, Georgia, Louisiana and Texas seceded soon after to form the Confederate States of America under president Jefferson Davis. On April 12, 1861, Confederate troops opened fire on Fort Sumter, seizing it from the Union and prompting President Lincoln to call up an army to oppose them.

Thus began the bloodiest and most devastating war the American populace ever suffered, with just shy of a million casualties. After both sides engaged in minor offensives under several different commanders, the two most influential commanders on both sides emerged: Robert E. Lee with the Confederates and Ulysses S. Grant commanding the Union. On January 1, 1863, after the battle of Antietam (a Union victory that killed more Americans than any single battle in the nation's history), Abraham Lincoln issued the Emancipation Proclamation, which legally freed all slaves in the South.

Notable Battle

The Battle of Gettysburg, 1863

From July 1–3, Union general George Meade faced off against Robert E. Lee in the battle of Gettysburg. Easily the most well-known battle of the American Civil War, the fighting at Gettysburg lasted three whole days and produced 50,000 corpses. It signaled a turning point in the fortunes of the northern states, however, and inspired Abraham Lincoln's famous Gettysburg Address.

In early 1864, Grant began an invasion of the South. After the capture of Atlanta and several more crushing Confederate defeats, Lee attempted to join with another Confederate army, resulting in his capture, which was followed by the capture of Jefferson Davis, President of the CSA. After the capture of the two most important Confederate leaders, the Confederate resistance collapsed, and on May 10, 1865, the Union declared victory, which ended the war and initiated the Reconstruction Era, despite the assassination of President Lincoln on April 14.

The war's conclusion brought many changes and affirmations. Many watched to see what would become of the great experiment in democracy. Eventually the southern states were brought to heel, and slavery was officially abolished. The effects of the Civil War rippled throughout the rest of American history, down to the Civil Rights movement and beyond, its scars still lingering today in the forms of sectionalism and racism.

CHARLES DARWIN, 1809–1882, *The Father of Evolution*

" The difference in mind between man and the higher animals, great as it is, is certainly one of degree and not of kind.

—*The Descent of Man*

- Was an English naturalist and geologist
- Formulated the theory of evolution and natural selection
- Observed that finches on each of the Galapagos Islands had unique beak shapes that were perfectly adapted to feeding on that island's particular type of food
- Introduced his theories of common ancestry and natural selection in *On the Origin of Species*
- Argued that life began with a single organism, whose offspring mutated and adapted to their environments by "survival of the fittest" over billions of years
- Was controversial in the religious community because his ideas countered traditional understandings of creationism
- Suggested that the earth was billions of years old, that animals were not created in their present form, and that humankind evolved from the same ancestor as all other animals

Key Works

On the Origin of Species, 1859
The Descent of Man, 1871

Biography

Has there ever been a man so divisive, so provocative, or so dangerously misinterpreted? Darwin is not the first scientist in history to have challenged orthodox Christian understandings of the world, but unlike Galileo or Kepler, who have long been exonerated and accepted, Darwin remains hotly controversial more than a century after his death. Born in 1809 as the fifth child of a wealthy doctor, Charles was raised with the expectation that he would follow in his father's footsteps in the practice of medicine. At age 16, his family sent Darwin to Edinburgh to study, but he quit medical school after two years because he found surgical operations nauseating. He transferred to Cambridge to study divinity at Christ's College in the hopes of becoming an Anglican parson. There, he met Reverend Professor John Henslow, who offered Darwin a position as a botanist on the HMS *Beagle*, so Darwin withdrew from Christ's College to sail around the world for five years.

During this journey Darwin recorded observations of different varieties of finches on the Galapagos Islands; these would later serve as the cornerstone of his theory of natural selection. Darwin suffered from poor health after his voyage. Modern physicians suspect that he contracted a tropical infection during his travels, but doctors of the time could not diagnose him. His wife and cousin Emma took care of Darwin's frail health as he began to write a book that would shake the world. After 12 years of refining his ideas, Darwin published *On the Origin of Species by Natural Selection* on November 24, 1859. All

1,250 copies sold out that same day. His second most famous work, *The Descent of Man*, was published in 1871; it, too, received a passionate response from both advocates and opponents. Darwin died of heart failure in 1882, but the controversy Darwin ignited between the scientific and religious communities still has yet to expire.

Darwin's "Tree of Life"—Universal Common Ancestry

"All the organic beings which have ever lived on this earth have descended from some one primordial form," Darwin says in *Origin*. One of his most famous images is a diagram of a tree. At the trunk, there is "one primordial form." Darwin argues that as the first organism reproduced, its offspring dispersed and attuned to their unique environments. As the descendants adapted and reproduced further, the branches in the diagram begin to diverge from the trunk. As millions of years passed, gradual changes accumulated in many different directions, until the organisms on some branches appear wholly dissimilar from organisms on other branches. Darwin was not the first to propose this theory; he built upon Jean-Baptiste Lamarck's theory of an intrinsic "adaptive force" that drives evolution. Instead of an inherent drive within living organisms, though, Darwin attributed adaptation to fortunate genetic mutations that aided organisms in survival. He called this process "natural selection."

Survival of the Fittest—Natural Selection as Nature's Threshing Floor

Darwin formed his theory of natural selection after his famous study of the Galapagos finches. Visiting approximately 20 Galapagos Islands while sailing on the *Beagle*, Darwin observed that each island had its own subspecies of finch with a beak perfectly adapted to its unique way of feeding. He was reminded of the way pigeon breeders used artificial selection to generate the optimal breed of pigeon. In the same way, he supposed that variations in the traits of species arise randomly, and some of these variations might confer advantages in the animal's competition for survival. Over a long period of time, micro-advantages that contribute to increased survival would gradually accumulate into macro-changes. Animals that inherited the stronger traits survived and multiplied until the species itself was distinctly changed. In *Origin*, Darwin described the process like this: "One general law, leading to the advancement of all organic beings, namely, multiply, vary, let the strongest live and the weakest die."

To illustrate the principle of survival of the fittest (a term first coined by Herbert Spencer), Darwin gives the example of wolves and deer. The slimmest, quickest wolves are more likely to succeed while hunting, and therefore are more likely to survive long enough to reproduce and generate more of their kind. Likewise, the slimmest, quickest deer in the forest are less likely to be caught by wolves, while their slow peers will be eaten far more often. The result is that the forest's populations of wolves and deer are both growing slimmer and quicker as the advantaged specimens survive and reproduce while the weaker starve or get devoured.

Humans—Different Merely by Degree

In *Origin*, the applicability of evolutionary theory to humankind was not explicitly stated, most likely for fear of backlash from creationists. The widespread belief in Darwin's time was that humans were inherently set apart from animals, endowed with unique qualities by the creator. Darwin's theory, though, implied that humans are like all other animals: the product of adaptation and chance. Though he did not address this concern in his first work, Darwin wrote his later work, *The Descent of Man*, specifically to elaborate on man's place in a world populated by one common ancestor. Could humankind truly be nothing more special than a well-adapted animal? Was there nothing inherent in humans that set them outside of the inevitable carnal cycle of dying, surviving, and adapting? Darwin argued that while humans were cognitively superior to other animals, the difference between animals and humans was "one of degree and not of kind," which meant that humans were indeed a result of the exact same process as every other animal. He wrote, "Man with all his noble qualities … still bears in his bodily frame the indelible stamp of his lowly origin."

Scientific Criticism

Darwin addressed the criticism he received from his contemporaries. One of the largest problems many other scientists found with his theory was that the fossil record did not appear to support it; the "Cambrian Explosion" seemed to be evidence that species appeared suddenly and in their present form. There remained scant fossil records that indicated the ancestral or transitional fossils necessary to substantiate Darwin's theory. Darwin wrote this criticism into *The Origin of Species*, saying:

> " The abrupt manner in which whole groups of species suddenly appear in certain formations has been urged by several paleontologists—for instance, by Agassiz, Pictet, and Sedgwick—as a fatal objection to the belief in the transmutation of species. If numerous species, belonging to the same genera or families, have really started into life all at once, the fact would be fatal to the theory of descent with slow modification through natural selection.

Other scientists argued there was no reason to believe that micro-changes in genetics had ever led to the formation of a wholly new species. After all, the Galapagos finches, despite their differences, were all still distinctly finches. Additionally, the contemporary theory of "blending inheritance" posed a significant problem to Darwin's theory. The predominant theory of genetics at the time was that an offspring is the average, or blend, of its parents' characteristics. If this were true, then all positive mutations would be halved with each generation, and the advantageous trait would dwindle. However, Gregor Mendel's later genetic theory addressed this objection. Mendel proved that offspring are not simply the average of the two parents, but rather that positive mutations could be dominant genes that would not be offset by the second parent's gene.

Religious Opposition

Darwin's ideas sparked immediate controversy from the religious community. Not only did his theory regard humankind as merely another variation in the progression of animal development, but his ideas also conflicted with Biblical creationism, which said God created all the animals at once in their present forms. Neither did his theory line up with orthodox ideas about the age of the earth. Theologians who traced genealogies in the Bible maintained that humankind was merely thousands of years away from Adam and the seven days of creation, but Darwin's theory propounded an earth that has taken billions of years to reach its current state. Arguments about the truth of Darwin's theory became pivotal in the debate between atheists and creationists, and remain so for many.

Annalisa Galgano, 2013

WILLIAM M. THACKERAY, 1811–1863, *British Satirical Novelist*

> " All is vanity, nothing is fair.
>
> —*Vanity Fair*

- Was an important British Victorian novelist and journalist
- Started life in Calcutta, India, the child of English civil servants
- Rivalled Charles Dickens throughout his writing career
- Loved writing historical novels, although he was known for writing with a whimsical sense of humor
- Succeeded because of his sharp, meaningful satire with intentions to increase human sympathy
- Crafted novels that showed elements of domestic realism without idealization

Key Works

Catherine, 1839–1840
The Book of Snobs, 1846–1847
Vanity Fair: A Novel Without a Hero, 1847–1848
Pendennis, 1849–1850
The History of Henry Esmond, 1852
The Newcomes, 1853–1855
The Virginian, 1857–1859
The Adventures of Philip, 1861–1862

Biography

William Makepeace Thackeray was an English Victorian novelist of the 19th century. He was born in Calcutta, India, to British parents who had moved there as civil servants. When his father died, Thackeray sailed for England to attend the prestigious Charterhouse boarding school and then matriculated at Trinity College in Cambridge, where he met Alfred Lord Tennyson and Edward Fitzgerald, but was unsuccessful in attaining a degree. As a wealthy young man, he toured Europe and then studied law. His privileged life was not without suffering as his second daughter died and his wife developed incurable insanity, which meant institutionalizing her. His suffering served to make him less cynical, and he sought to understand the life of common humanity. *Vanity Fair*, which was published in parts, was Thackeray's key to a popularity that rivalled Dickens', as it depicts the breadth of human experience. He wrote *Pendennis* and *Rebecca and Rowena* as he was getting over cholera. Thackeray then took on a historical topic, and proved to be an excellent historical novelist in *The History of Henry Esmond*. After a tour of the United States, he published *The Newcomes*, his satire about a family of social climbers. Then came two more historical novels, including *The Virginians*. Thackeray continued a friendly rivalry with Dickens as magazine editor for *Cornhill Magazine*. He died suddenly on Christmas Eve in 1863.

Literary Style

As a historian, Thackeray depicted imperfect people and times. In *Vanity Fair*, he satirized specific settings and situations, such as his own difficult years at boarding school where he had experienced "the sadistic discipline and teaching methods that characterized such institutions." He wrote of snobbish people and of unconventional characters, for example, an appealing Jewish woman rather than the traditional fairy-tale heroine. Another heroine, Becky Sharp, rebels against marriage and the woman's customary passive role. Likewise, a character in *The History of Henry Esmond*, Lyndon, is a mercenary who treats his wife cruelly and dies in prison. *The Virginians* depicts the plight of two boys in the same family who oppose each other in the American Revolution. Thackeray expresses no sentimentality in criticizing "social climbing, romantic delusions, and commercial calculation," a critique that reappears in the work of 20th-century novelists.

CHARLES DICKENS, 1812–1870, *The Giant of Victorian Literature*

> " Suffering has been stronger than all other teaching, and has taught me to understand what your heart used to be. I have been bent and broken, but—I hope—into a better shape.
>
> —*Great Expectations*

- Was an English novelist, playwright, and satirist of the Victorian period
- Infused his novels with many autobiographical elements from his own childhood, which included time as an impoverished laborer in a debtor's workhouse
- Popularized the expression "Merry Christmas" with the publication of *A Christmas Carol* in 1843; the wild success of this book earned him the nickname "The Father of Christmas"
- Wrote often about the need for social reform, particularly concerning the issues of class struggle and debtors' prisons
- Funded and oversaw the operation of a safe house for reformed prostitutes in England
- Set a sales record: *A Tale of Two Cities* has sold over 200,000,000 copies and remains the bestselling novel of all time

Key Works

The Pickwick Papers, 1836–1837
Oliver Twist, 1837–1839
A Christmas Carol, 1843
David Copperfield, 1849–1850
Bleak House, 1852–1853
Hard Times, 1854
Little Dorrit, 1855–1857
A Tale of Two Cities, 1859
Great Expectations, 1860–1861

Biography

Charles John Huffam Dickens was born in 1812, the second child of John and Elizabeth Dickens, a pair who lived above their means and encouraged their son's early writing talent. When Dickens was 12, his family experienced a drastic reversal of fortune: his father was incarcerated in debtors' prison until he could pay off his many loans. Dickens's mother and younger siblings were sent to live with John Dickens in prison, but Dickens himself ended up in a workhouse where he labored in a boot-blacking factory for 12 hours every day. This dismal period of his life sparked his passion for various social reforms and influenced his later writing. Many of his books, including *The Pickwick Papers, Oliver Twist, Little Dorrit,* and *David Copperfield,* include commentary on labor laws, workhouses, and debtors' prisons. After completing an unremarkable education, Dickens worked as a law clerk for several years, which gave him insight into how England's legal system regularly disadvantaged the lower class.

He soon transitioned to a position as a newspaper writer, which gave him a platform to publish his writing in monthly installments. The first episode of *The Pickwick Papers*, Dickens's earliest work, was published the day he married Catherine Hogarth in 1836. He enjoyed immediate popularity as an author and soon published many more works in newspapers, including the well-known *Oliver Twist*, *A Christmas Carol*, and the autobiographical *David Copperfield*. In 1851, Dickens was shattered by the death of his father and one of his daughters. For the next few years, his publications came to be known as his "dark novels." No longer so merry or sentimental, *Bleak House*, *Hard Times*, and *Little Dorrit* put a much greater emphasis on grim social issues and personal disappointment.

Due to his immense popularity, Dickens was a remarkably busy figure. In addition to extensive philanthropic work, he also went on domestic and international reading tours, wrote daily, and oversaw the production of many of his own plays. In 1857, Dickens fell passionately in love with the 18-year-old Ellen Ternan, an actress in one of his productions. Dickens scandalously separated from Catherine, who had borne him 10 children, and bought a separate house for Ellen. His frequent public appearances soon affected his health, but Dickens maintained his rigorous schedule in spite of his sickness. He died in 1870 after suffering a brain aneurysm while writing in his study. His last novel, *The Mystery of Edwin Drood*, has since been published but remains unfinished. Though he had expressed his wish to be buried in the Rochester area of his childhood, Dickens was eventually buried in the Poets' Corner of Westminster Abbey alongside the likes of Shakespeare and Chaucer. Dickens's works have been constantly in print, and he remains a prominent figure in English literature.

Writing Style

A keen satirist, Dickens often communicates his most passionate appeals for social change through the absurdities of his villains. For example, in *Oliver Twist*, the "fat, healthy" master of the workhouse explodes with anger at the young, starving orphan who meekly requests more food. Dickens knew that the cruelty of the master would be far more effective in stirring outraged audiences to action than a description of a poor boy. His nasty caricatures of villains sharply contrast with the idealized heroes in his stories. Dickens illustrates the sharp dissonance between the innocence of his young protagonists and the injustices of society. For example, a young street girl in *Oliver Twist* explains her pitiful predicament: "Thank Heaven upon your knees … that you were never in the midst of cold and hunger, and riot and drunkenness, and—and—something worse than all—as I have been from my cradle. I may use the word, for the alley and the gutter were mine, as they will be my deathbed." Though some later authors criticize Dickens for over-idealizing his characters and leading nearly all of his protagonists to a happy ending, this sentimental literary device is characteristic of most Victorian writing and was well-received by his audiences. Since Dickens published most of his works episodically in newspapers, he was able to respond to the feedback of readers after each passage before writing the next installment. His attentiveness to his audience, as well as the easy accessibility of his writing, made him popular in all social groups.

"Virtue in Rags": Dickens's Social Commentary

Many of the social issues that Dickens commonly addressed in his writing were partially autobiographical. His personal experience with debtors' prisons, the legal system, and class struggle gave him a compassionate lens that he strove to impart to the Victorian elite. His novel *Little Dorrit* is the story of a young girl who grew up in a debtors' prison alongside her spendthrift father. Like Dickens himself, the young Dorrit was responsible for providing for her family and siblings. He writes, "She took the place of the eldest of the three, in all things but precedence; was the head of the fallen family; and bore, in her own heart, its anxieties and shames." Likewise, Dickens is found again in the lonely David Copperfield, who cries, "I had no advice, no counsel, no encouragement, no consolation, no assistance, no support, of any kind, from anyone, that I can call to mind." Dickens's sympathies were not limited to impoverished children; though he was quite wealthy as an adult, he remained attentive to the marginalization and abuse faced by the adult working class. In *Hard Times*, Dickens exposes the dehumanizing treatment of factory owners towards their workers, who were called "hands" rather than "people." His main objective in his social commentary was to demonstrate to those in the upper echelons of society the humanity of those below. During his time in the United States, Dickens was very disturbed by the treatment of slaves, an issue he addressed in his novel *Martin Chuzzlewit*. While giving a speech in New York, Dickens emphasized, "Virtue shows quite as well in rags and patches as she does in purple and fine linen."

His writings succeeded in inspiring social change; for example, his descriptions of debtors' prisons in *The Pickwick Papers* were influential in closing down the Fleet Prison in England. Before Dickens's death, all debtors' prisons in the country were officially abolished. George Bernard Shaw once said that Dickens's *Great Expectations* was more seditious than even Karl Marx's *Das Kapital*. Marx himself wrote that Dickens "issued to the world more political and social truths than have been uttered by all the professional politicians, publicists, and moralists put together." One suspects Dickens would have been proud to be known as a purveyor of social truths.

Annalisa Galgano, 2013

SOREN KIERKEGAARD, 1813–1855, *A Radically Committed Christian*

" Prayer does not change God, but it changes him who prays.

- Broke his engagement to Regine Olsen, a woman he loved his whole life, believing both that he was unworthy of marriage and that God had placed a higher call on his life
- Inherited the family tendency toward "melancholy" (depression)
- Refused to live in an ivory tower; a man of the people, he conversed with fellow Danes for hours daily in the streets of Copenhagen
- Worked to distinguish true Christianity—the suffering following of Jesus Christ—from Christendom—the established order of the Church—which he loathed
- Is often appropriated by 20th-century existentialists and postmodern thinkers as a precursor to their own views
- Wrote under pseudonyms rather than explicitly identifying ideas with his own beliefs

Key Works

Either/Or, 1843
Fear and Trembling, 1843
Philosophical Fragments, 1844

The Sickness Unto Death, 1849
Practice in Christianity, 1850

Biography

Soren Kierkegaard was born into one of the wealthiest families of Copenhagen in 1813. His father Michael was a self-made man, rising out of relative poverty in west Jutland to take over his uncle's merchant business in the capital. Michael married his servant, Anne Sorensdatter Lund, and they had seven children. Soren was the youngest. Struggling with depression, Michael Kierkegaard enforced a "strict and severe form of Christianity" for his children. While Soren moved away from his father's extremism, he carried the tendency toward depression that his father experienced. One of the formative events of young Soren's life was his broken engagement to Regine Olsen. Though loving Regine deeply until his death, Soren felt incapable of entering into the covenant of marriage. The precise reason for breaking off the marriage is unknown and the cause of some speculation. Whatever the case, the freedom from marital union freed up substantial time in Soren's schedule, and, after completing his doctoral dissertation in 1841, he made his mark on the philosophical and religious world of Denmark with such works as *Either/Or, Repetition,* several of the *Upbuilding Discourses, Philosophical Fragments,* and other writings. His final years were marked by a sustained attack on the church of Denmark, before his death in 1855.

Pseudonymity and Existentialism

One of the most notable aspects of Kierkegaard's writings is his use of pseudonyms. Apparently, he used the pen names to present opinions he might not hold himself. While Kierkegaard contends that "the whole of my authorship relates to my Christianity," this face value assertion has come under fire. C. Stephen Evans explains that some call this the "*myth* of Kierkegaard," claiming instead that Kierkegaard's "self-understanding … was essentially a literary expression of how Kierkegaard wanted to be understood by history rather than an accurate account of his true intentions." Others suggest that the proliferation of pseudonyms—he used more than 14 different names—should make us wary of trusting someone who, as Louis Mackey puts it, "fabricates as many masks to hide behind as Kierkegaard does."

Nevertheless, this postmodern reading of Kierkegaard is not the only reading. C. Stephen Evans, in his *Kierkegaard: An Introduction,* contends that distancing the actual Kierkegaard from his words "allows a person to enjoy the style and literary techniques of Kierkegaard without fear of being challenged by Kierkegaard as one human person speaking to another about issues of ultimate importance." He further maintains that the pseudonymity of the authorship enables Kierkegaard to write from different perspectives in the way of a novelist. The pseudonyms "embody" the multiple answers to life's questions.

Kierkegaard did not believe that knowledge was something that could be systematically transmitted from one person to another, nor did he believe with Socrates that the truth is buried within each of us and merely needs to be excavated. A teacher can lead students to a contemplation of the good, but he cannot make the student love the good. For Kierkegaard, life is a process of becoming more of a defined self, Our growth as humans "requires the development of the appropriate passions, and cannot be achieved simply through knowing propositions." It is our very passions that require education and the pseudonyms help convey this truth.

The Three Stages of Life: the Aesthetic, the Ethical, and the Religious

While Kierkegaard refers to the three terms above as "stages," it is important to note that he does not mean this in the sense that everyone has an aesthetic stage followed by an ethical and then a religious stage. Think of this more in terms of engaging with the world. The aesthetic self is all about gratification of desire, whether it be through arts and culture, or even religion. The ethical self feels duty-bound to certain institutions and organizations. The religious self is subdivided into two categories that Kierkegaard calls Religiousness A and Religiousness B. Religiousness A is the law-based state of belief in which the believer feels his or her guilt before God. Religiousness B is a state that transcends the self by radical commitment to Christ. For Kierkegaard, this state of life is the highest end of a human, channeling both our aesthetic and religious stages into the proper channel.

"Truth is Subjectivity"

Kierkegaard is perhaps best known for his statement in *Concluding Scientific Postscript* that "subjectivity is truth and truth is subjectivity." Although some might call this relativism, Kierkegaard does not mean that truth is whatever we make of it, but rather that "all truth must be *appropriated* individually." Thomas Flynn helpfully notes that "Kierkegaard was more concerned with combating lukewarm or purely nominal religious belief than with apologetics." In other words, Kierkegaard's audience were not skeptics looking for answers but fellow Christians looking for a kick in the pants. And, indeed, Kierkegaard relished the opportunity to kick comfortable believers in the pants. Much of his philosophical ire was directed against the state church and the ways in which Christendom—the status of the church as almost equal to or even above the state in terms of power—has been horrible in the long run for Christianity, enervating believers and helping church functionaries get fat and happy. Kierkegaard devoted the last years of his life to attacking the lukewarm nature of the state church. Notably, Kierkegaard never actually attacked Christianity itself, merely its marriage to the state.

Toby Coffman, faculty

CLAUDE BERNARD, 1813–1878, *Provocateur of Physiology*

> " The doubter is a true man of science; he doubts not only himself and his interpretations, but he believes in science.
>
> —*An Introduction to the Study of Experimental Medicine*

- Discovered the function of the pancreas and the liver along with pioneering experimental methods of medical research like the blind experiment
- Laid the base for the later ideas of homeostasis with his *milieu intériuer*, or internal environment
- Used vivisection, or the dissection of live animals, to derive many of his medical discoveries; unfortunately, both his wife and daughter were strongly opposed to vivisection and his wife separated from him after he refused to stop
- Wanted to be a playwright, but after he showed one of his early plays to a critic, the critic encouraged him to continue on the path of medicine
- Helped to find the root cause of diabetes via his work concerning the pancreas and liver and the discovery of glycogen
- Discovered the vasomotor nerves, which alter the diameter of blood vessels in response to outside factors

Key Works

Introduction to the Study of Experimental Medicine, 1865

Biography

Claude Bernard was at the forefront of the study of physiology. Born in 1813 in France, Bernard began his collegiate studies at the College of Thoissey. Only a year later he left, not finishing his degree, to go to Lyon as a pharmacist's assistant. During his free time he wrote plays, which eventually led to him leaving Lyon for Paris, play in hand, in 1834. Eventually a major drama critic advised him to take up physiology instead of literature. Bernard followed the advice and worked as an intern for his most influential predecessor, François Magendie. While Bernard maintained this position, he was able to start running his experiments in physiology. In 1847, he became Magendie's substitute professor, and in 1855 superseded him as the primary professor of medicine at the Collège de France. During this period, Bernard did extensive research on the nervous system as well as on toxins and medical substances. He was elected to the Academy of Science in 1854 and the Academy of Medicine in 1861. Under Napoleon III, Bernard built an official laboratory in 1864 and was elected as senator in 1869. Even in the last years of his life, he continued to work on his studies. He died on February 10, 1878, and was the first scientist to have a national funeral, an honor generally reserved for military and political figures.

Homeostasis (*Milieu Intérieur*)

Bernard coined the idea of *milieu intérieur*, or internal environment, which has developed into the theory of homeostasis. He concluded that "the fixity of the internal environment is the condition for free life." There is a distinction between the outside environment and the interior; the interior can regulate itself in order to maintain a temperature and state that is good for the organism. Also, the "tissues are in fact withdrawn from direct external influences and are protected by a veritable internal environment" that facilitates homeostasis mostly by circulating fluid throughout the body. His prolific investigations into homeostasis built the foundation for later research of the "nervous action with the control of metabolism, circulation, and respiration," as well as the function of feedback control loops with regard to homeostasis. Building on his work, scientists made breakthroughs with feedback control loops, discovering how internal sensors could detect change—such as a cooler environment or increased blood pressure—and then regulate steps to maintain homeostasis. He is most famous for his idea that "the maintenance of the stability of the internal environment is the prerequisite for the development of a complex nervous system."

Blind Experiments

Bernard was a firm believer that scientific "medicine, like the other sciences, can be established only by experimental means." For this reason, he was a prominent figure in experimenting with animals and, most especially, medical trials. Bernard is often thought of as the "founder of modern experimental physiology" and he instituted the idea of a blind experiment. A blind trial can be used when knowledge of the experiment could create bias in the results. In a single blind trial, the groups studied, including the control group, do not know what group they are in, eliminating bias in the results of the survey. Although Bernard worked with only a single-blind experiment, his ideas have extended to double-blind experiments in which the researcher also does not know into which group the patient has been placed. This intentional ignorance prevents the researcher from inadvertently providing clues to the patient about what group he or she is in, or from manipulating the data to include more positive or negative results. Bernard's idea of a blind experiment includes the placebo effect: if the patient believes he is getting a drug, even if the "drug" is only a sugar pill, his condition may improve or alter. With blind experiments, researchers can see which results are from the medicine and which are psychological.

The Digestive System

Although many doctors had attempted to discover the secret of the pancreas and liver, Bernard was the first to establish that the pancreas has an important role in the digestion of fat. He realized that fluid in the pancreas, which he called the "pancreatic juice," is "capable of emulsifying and saponifying neutral fats." In other words, this pancreatic juice is capable of breaking down larger fat molecules into smaller, evenly distributed particles. Bernard also did major work with sugars in the body. He found that even when animals were not being fed sugar they produced sugar in their livers. After doing experiments with sugars and their effect on the human body, Bernard realized that animals synthesized their own sugar, which he named glycogen. Today we know that glycogen is an important chemical used to store energy in animals; in humans, glycogen is mostly produced in the liver and the muscles, and the body converts the glycogen to glucose when needed.

Caroline Fuschino, 2015
Jackson Howell, 2015

CHARLES MACKAY ◊ 1814–1899, *The Crowd's Economist*

> We find that whole communities suddenly fix their minds upon one object, and go mad in its pursuit; that millions of people become simultaneously impressed with one delusion, and run after it, till their attention is caught by some new folly more captivating than the first.
>
> —*Extraordinary Popular Delusions and Madness of Crowds*

- Was a Scottish writer, journalist and poet
- Contributed to *The Daily News*, a newspaper established by his associate Charles Dickens
- Wrote several hit songs in his day, including "Cheer, Boys, Cheer"
- Did pioneering work with the concept of financial bubbles
- Demonstrated the economic effects of "herd mentality"

Key Works

Extraordinary Popular Delusions and Madness of Crowds, 1841
Gaelic Etymology of the Languages of Western Europe, 1877

Biography

Charles MacKay was born in Perth, Scotland, on March 26, 1812, to George MacKay, a bandmaster in the Royal Artillery, and his wife, Amelia, who died shortly after Charles's birth. As a child, MacKay was sent to live with a retired veteran, whose wife taught him many Scottish songs. At the age of 10, he was sent to London to continue his education. There, a friend of the family encouraged MacKay's writing, having a famous preacher read his verses aloud; MacKay described the experience, saying it "moulded my future career, and made me a man of letters."

MacKay studied languages both in London and Brussels, mastering French, German, Italian, and Spanish. He wrote in both French and British newspapers and, after his schooling, worked as a tutor. Eventually, he found work at various newspapers throughout Britain and Scotland, including *The Sun*, *Morning Chronicle*, and the *Glasgow Argus*. He visited the United States during the Civil War, acting as a correspondent and meeting such writers as Henry Wadsworth Longfellow, Ralph Waldo Emerson, William Hickling Prescott, and Oliver Wendell Holmes. MacKay had three wives and two known children; his daughter became the novelist Marie Corelli. He returned to England and died in London on December 24, 1889.

Economic Bubbles

In his book, *Extraordinary Popular Delusions and Madness of Crowds*, MacKay describes a number of different financial bubbles. Three are especially notorious: the Dutch tulip bubble (17th century), the South Sea Company bubble (1711–1720), and the Mississippi Company bubble (1719–1720). In each, various groups fell prey to a series of bad investments. In the South Sea Company bubble, an English joint-stock company held a monopoly on trade and government debt during the War of Spanish Succession. There was no hope of the company turning a profit since the civil war prevented international trade, yet its stock rose in value. The company's illicit operations (dealing in government debt) were exposed, causing the stock to crash. The crash ruined many people, and the national economy shrank. In the Mississippi Company bubble, there was wide speculation over an exaggerated claim of wealth in the Louisiana Territory, leading to inflation. The French government did not have the gold necessary for investors wishing to exchange their banknotes, causing a stock market crash in the Louisiana Territory. The Dutch tulip crisis occurred in the Dutch Golden Age, when the price for planting tulips was 10 times that of the annual income of a skilled worker. This led to a debasing of the currency similar to that which occurred in the Mississippi Company bubble.

MacKay's main observation was that rational individuals sometimes act irrationally in crowds. Investments they would otherwise not buy into become so irresistible in a crowd that warning signs are often ignored. Speculation leads to more speculation, and once rationality is re-introduced into the situation, the consequences can be extreme. The pursuit of riches, or tulips, can drive crowds, even countries, into detrimental situations.

Legacy

In *Extraordinary Popular Delusions and Madness of Crowds* MacKay wrote, "Men, it has been well said, **think in herds**; it will be seen that they **go mad in herds**, while they only recover their senses slowly, and one by one." Today one might call that the mob mentality. Though many of the financial figures he uses in his book have been discredited, the observations that he made about how individuals act in a crowd remain valid. The observations of the Beanie Baby craze of the 1990s, in which the price of Beanie Babies went up dramatically, can be attributed to what MacKay proposed in *Extraordinary Popular Delusions and Madness of Crowds*. Indeed, one could even study the housing bubble in the late 2000s using MacKay's insights.

Toby Coffman, faculty

GEORGE BOOLE, 1815–1864, *The TRUE Logician*

> " Of the many forms of false culture, a premature converse with abstractions is perhaps the most likely to prove fatal to the growth of a masculine vigour of intellect.
>
> —Preface to *A Treatise on Differential Equations*

- Was born to a poor family, but quickly learned five languages and became brilliant in mathematics
- Began teaching to support his family
- Refused a position at Cambridge because it would cost too much
- Became friends with De Morgan, who would later expand the Boolean algebra theories with De Morgan's laws
- Published *On a General Method of Analysis*, which introduced his Boolean algebra
- Reduced logic to a series of true and false relations and the operations that change the values
- Died in 1864 after a relatively short life after he walked to his lecture in the pouring rain and taught in soaked clothing

Key Works

An investigation into the Laws of Thought, on Which are founded the Mathematical Theories of Logic and Probabilities, 1854

On a General Method in Analysis, 1844

Biography

Born a frail child to an English shoemaker and a maid, George Boole's origins were certainly not prestigious. At 2, he attended a school for tradesmen's children. His father became the primary source of his instruction in mathematics. However, young George quickly became more interested in languages and began to learn many. His first, Latin, he learned from a tutor, but Boole taught himself Greek, French, and German. Eventually, his father's business collapsed, and Boole was forced to become a teacher in order to support his family. Although he earned an invitation to study at Cambridge, he could not do so, needing instead to financially support his family. After several years of teaching, he was given the opportunity to run a school, Hall's Academy.

During this time Boole began to correspond with De Morgan, another logician, and wrote *On a General Method in Analysis*, which he gave to De Morgan for comments before publishing it. This work brought him fame and a position as the chair of mathematics at Queen's College, Cork, and eventually the Dean of Science. While chair of mathematics, he met Mary Everest and married her, despite an age gap of 17 years. In 1854, he published his most important work, *An investigation into the Laws of Thought, on Which are founded the Mathematical Theories of Logic and Probabilities*. In this, Boole explained Boolean algebra, which brought him widespread popularity. He went on to publish prodigiously concerning differential equations and probability, and was highly decorated as a mathematician. He died in 1864 after catching a feverish cold from getting rain-soaked. His wife may hastened his death by throwing buckets of water over him on his sickbed in the belief that a remedy should resemble the cause.

Boolean Algebra

Boole's most prominent achievement was his creation of Boolean algebra. Boolean algebra is a form of logic; the catch is that the logic is reduced to basic algebra, simplifying it and making it easy to use in many applications. As a result, it has modern-day uses, ranging from basic computer construction and programming to switching circuits. Boolean algebra is formally defined as a set B of elements a, b. There are two basic binary operations, one that represents a logical AND (^) and one that represents a logical OR (v). With an AND, both elements must be true to return true. An OR requires only one element to be true to return true. For example, if A is true and B is false, and the formula A ^ B is given, the result is false, as A AND B are not true. On the other hand, if the formula is A v B, then the result is true, as A OR B is true. Additionally, this logic follows basic algebra rules, such as the law of commutativity (A ^ B = B ^ A) and the law of associativity ((A ^ B) ^ C = A ^ (B ^ C)). Furthermore, symbols were eventually added to give more functionality, such as ¬, which means negation. This can turn a false into a true or a true into a false when placed next to any element.

Boolean algebra follows some basic algebraic rules, which, though different from the ones used in regular algebra, are consistent. For example, the phrase A ^ 0 will always return 0, regardless of what A is. Following more of these rules, the complex phrase ¬A ^ (A v B) v (B v A ^ A) ^ (A v ¬B) can be simplified to only A v B. This has many practical applications, such as in the construction of computers. If one has a wide array of inputs and only one output that needs to be different depending on what the inputs are, a "logic gate"—a series of AND, OR, and NOT operators—can be constructed. So, depending on what all of these inputs may be, the output will be different. Computers amplify this concept millions of times, as there are potentially millions of inputs and needed outputs per computer. Simplifying the algebra also simplifies the computer, making it smaller and more efficient.

Trisha Rouleau, 2015

HENRY DAVID THOREAU, 1817–1862, *The Hermit in the Wilderness*

" The mass of men lead lives of quiet desperation.

—*Civil Disobedience*

- Was an ardent and outspoken abolitionist and conductor on the Underground Railroad.
- Was imprisoned for refusal to pay his poll tax
- Censured society's oppressive conventions and lauded the individual's free spirit
- Fell in love with and proposed to Ellen Sewall, as did his brother; her father turned them both down due to their liberal religious views
- Prized simplicity and independent thought and censured society for enslaving men's minds
- Derived his epistemology from a quote by Confucius: "To know that we know what we know, and that we do not know what we do not know, that is true knowledge."
- "Responded "I don't know that we ever quarreled," when asked, "Have you made your peace with God?"

Key Works

On the Duty of Civil Disobedience, 1849
Walden, 1854
Walking, 1862

Biography

As a child, Henry David Thoreau would stay "awake at night looking through the stars as if he could see God behind them." This fascination with nature and the observations he could draw from the natural world set the tone for Thoreau's life and works. Essayist, poet, and author, Thoreau centered his works on simple living in nature, and transcendentalism.

Thoreau was born in Concord, Massachusetts in 1817, where he resided for most of his life. He attended public Concord school and private Concord Academy where he was an excellent student. He then attended Harvard. Because Thoreau was "temperamentally unsuited" for a job in law, ministry, or medicine, fields that many Harvard graduates worked in, he decided to pursue teaching. He originally started teaching at a public school in Concord but resigned after two weeks because of conflict with the superintendent.

Thoreau had always been close to his brother, John, and in 1838 they decided to open a school together. In 1841, John cut himself while shaving, developed lockjaw, and died in 25-year-old Thoreau's arms. Thoreau closed the school and moved in with Ralph Waldo Emerson, his neighbor and the author of Thoreau's favorite book, *Nature*.

Emerson and Thoreau developed a "turbulent relationship due to serious philosophical and personal differences" but always considered themselves good friends. Reversing the typical six-day work cycle, Thoreau built a house on Emerson's property in Walden and began to work only one day of the week in order to devote the other six days to transcendental concerns. The notes he took on this experiment turned into his famous work, *Walden*. Throughout his career, he recorded impressions on his frequent nature walks and developed more than 20 volumes of essays, poems, and books. In May of 1862, Thoreau died of a recurring bout of tuberculosis he had been battling since college. At his funeral, Emerson remarked, "The nation knows not yet … how great a son it has lost … wherever there is knowledge, wherever there is virtue, wherever there is beauty, he will find a home."

Walden Or; Life in the Woods

Henry David Thoreau's most prominent work is *Walden Or; Life in the Woods*. In contrast to his first book, *A Week on the Concord and Merrimack Rivers*, *Walden* was semi-successful; over 2,000 copies were printed. Critics, however, attacked Thoreau's character and lifestyle, accusing him of "crankiness and irresponsibility. Despite this, his book and ideas garnered more success as time went on, and six editions of *Walden* were published in 1948, 11 in 1958, and 23 in 1968, along with many editions of his other works.

E.B. White, heavily influenced by Thoreau, writes, "Henry went forth to battle when he took to the woods, and *Walden* is the report of a man torn by two powerful and opposing drives—the desire to enjoy the world and the urge to set the world straight." Thoreau moves away from society because he yearns "to learn what are the gross necessaries of life and what methods have been taken to obtain them." He wants to rid himself of all the inessential aspects of life, so he lives off of the land and all it has to offer. Simplicity frees Thoreau from the shackles of society that keep him from truly knowing himself. He explains that he "turn[s his] face more exclusively than ever to the woods, where [he is] better known"; in the woods he finds peace, knowing that "public opinion is a weak tyrant compared with [his] own private opinion."

He begins *Walden* by worrying about what it means to find happiness and meaning in life and how to impose those values on the rest of the world; however, later in the book, he admits that "we are acquainted with a mere pellicle of the globe on which we live … I am reminded of the greater Benefactor and Intelligence that stands over me the human insect." Living in seclusion, Thoreau ceases to concern himself with the burden of fixing others; instead he embraces his own smallness and acknowledges a power more suited to stand over the world. He writes *Walden* to demonstrate that living by self-reliance rather than by society's influences leads to simplicity, which makes for a better life. Just like his transcendental counterpart Emerson, Thoreau transcends the values and opinions of society and finds peace in self-reliance.

"On the Duty of Civil Disobedience"

Setting the stage for Thoreau, Emerson writes in "Politics" (1844) that "the less government we have, the better." Years later, after spending a night in jail for not paying a poll tax, Thoreau pens his famous essay "Resistance to Civil Government," now known as "Civil Disobedience," wherein he declares that "the government itself, which is only the mode the people have chosen to execute their will, is equally liable to be abused and perverted before the people can act through it." Although the government is the machine by which citizens can exercise their will, the machine, according to Thoreau, can pervert justice before the citizens even have a chance to voice their will. And if government fails to act in accordance with its citizens, what is the use of obedience to such a machine? An opponent to slavery and The Mexican-American War, Thoreau felt compelled to argue for a society in which citizens use "friction" to stop the political machine from perpetuating "a great evil." For him the evils of government were all too apparent in the forms of oppression and injustice that beset antebellum America. While these ideas lend themselves to anarchy, Thoreau does not seek friction for friction's sake; the essay clarifies that his stance is not a matter of whim but a demanding moral principle. He expects civil disobedience to stem from a man's thoughtful reaction to injustice. This kind of resistance promotes the creation of a government that recognizes man's intellectual and physical independence. He writes, "There will never be a really free and enlightened State until the State comes to recognize the individual as a higher and independent power, from which all its own power and authority are derived, and treats him accordingly." No man can submit to a law that goes against his conscience and still remain a man. Thoreau concludes: "If a plant cannot live according to its nature, it dies; and so a man."

Wesley Mott, in his essay, "Civil Disobedience," affirms the longevity and impact of Thoreau's ideas: "Over the years, Thoreau's essay has had a profound influence on reformers worldwide, from Tolstoy in Russia and Gandhi in South Africa and India; to Martin Luther King, Jr's Civil Rights movement and the opposition to the Vietnam War in the United States; to recent demonstrations for civil rights in the former Soviet Union and China."

Caroline Fuschino, 2015
Jessica Goeser, researcher
Briauna Schultz, 2013

KARL MARX, 1818–1883, *The Master of False Premises*

" The proletarians have nothing to lose but their chains. They have a world to win. Working Men of All Countries, Unite!

—The Communist Manifesto

- Lived much of his life in self-imposed poverty in London, after being born into the wealthy German middle class and being expelled from German, France, and Belgium multiple times
- Saw the injustice of his "enlightenment" father forced to convert to Christianity
- Raised in a repressive absolute monarchy (until 1776, true almost everywhere)
- A usurper, distorter of G.W.F. Hegel's philosophies
- Wrote for several newspapers including the *New York Tribune*
- Published *The Communist Manifesto* with Friedrich Engels in 1848; published *Das Kapital* in 1867
- Was a radical socialist, communist, and atheist who preached for a dictatorship of the proletariat
- Led the communist International Workingmen's Assocation, organized to encourage underprivileged workers to carry out revolutionary action
- Probably the most physically destructive ideas in the history of civilization
- One of the most influential and divisive figures in history
- Is the impetus behind all major communist revolutionary movements of the past century (Lenin, Stalin, Mao Tse-Tung, Fidel Castro, Khmer Rouge, untold millions of deaths by forced starvation, mass execution, and invasion, not to mention billions living through generations of extreme poverty, severe censorship of speech and ideas, secret police raids and confiscations of property, and lives lived in general fear and paranoia)
- Is perceived positively even today by progressives, socialists, and liberal popular culture in general, due in part to the universalization of "free" public schooling (one of Marx's proposals), but negatively by reality—considering experiences such as the fall of communism and Nazism
- Developed his materialist dialectic as a direct reversal of Hegel's idealist dialectic; rather than reason unfolding itself through History by means of logic, Marx had the "classless" worker's state unfolding itself through history by means of economic laws related to control of the means of production
- History moved by class struggle, gradually evolving toward a dictatorship of the proletariat, as the precursor to a true classless society in which the state "withers away" (a dialectical model which seems not to correspond to the realities of any actual communist dictatorship that has been tried)
- Believed "property is theft", and that a just society would be structured according to the principle "From each according to his ability, to each according to his need" (two famous "Marxist" expressions, incidentally, which Marx actually swiped from two French socialist writers); these two ideas fundamentally contradict the basic modern political premise that individual human beings are the primary political realities, have a right to self-determination, and own themselves (the foundation of property rights)
- His theory of surplus value, a centerpiece of his critique of capitalism, postulates that capitalist control of the means of production is inherently designed to keep workers at subsistence wages, so that no upward mobility is possible, but the workers will continue to work out of physical necessity, because the owners will never raise wages beyond the level required to keep the workers minimally alive, regardless of profit—a theory contradicted by the single example of

398 · Chapter 6

Henry Ford's famous Five Dollar Day wage doubling, a fact which did nothing to discourage Marxists from adhering to the fantasy

- Criticized religion as the "opiate of the masses" which distracts the poor with an idea of heaven so that they don't try to change their actual living conditions on earth
- Proposed ten planks of communist revolution in the Communist Manifesto—almost all of which have been instituted worldwide today, with barely a raised eyebrow from people who would scoff if you told them they shared many Marxist premises about the role of government
- Viewed himself as a man of scientific, or deterministic, thought, but built his vision on numerous flawed premises (see section below)

Key works

The German Ideology, 1846
The Communist Manifesto, 1848
Das Kapital: Volume 1, 1867

Biography

Karl Marx, who was born in 1818 and died of bronchitis on March 14, 1883, is best known for advocating the abolition of private property through revolutions that would overthrow capitalism and lead to greater human freedom. Marx's parents were Jewish, but they converted to Lutheranism in order to make it easier for Marx's father, Heinrich, to practice law in Trier, the German Rhineland. Heinrich wanted young Karl to study law, too, but when Karl was imprisoned for drunkenness and mildly wounded in a duel while (allegedly) studying law at the University of Bonn at age 17, his father ordered an end to his "wild rampaging" and sent him to the University of Berlin. There, Marx focused on philosophy and wrote his doctoral thesis comparing the philosophies of Democritus and Epicurus.

Marx started writing for newspapers when he couldn't get a university job. Many of his politically radical articles angered the Prussian government enough that he had to leave the country. This pattern would continue, whether in Paris, Belgium, or Prussia, until he finally moved his family to London after he had tried to stoke the fires of the 1848 revolution in Germany by starting a radical newspaper.

In London, they initially lived in deep poverty, and Marx's ideas spread very slowly. Marx complained of being able to afford only bread and potatoes, and he frequently visited pawnshops. Four of his children died early. They were too poor to afford a coffin for their little 1-year-old Franzisca, and his wife Jenny wrote, "Our three living children lay down by us, and we all wept for the little angel whose livid, lifeless body was in the next room." Jenny received two inheritances in 1856 and, coupled with Karl's weekly writings for the *New York Tribune*, they became more financially secure.

Marx's ideas slowly spread through writings like *The German Ideology*, *Das Kapital*, and the famous *Communist Manifesto* that he published with his friend Friedrich Engels. His wife passed away in January of 1883, and on March 14, at the age of 65, Karl Marx died.

Flawed Premises

Marx fundamentally misunderstands and mischaracterizes human nature. (Find an expanded definition of human nature in Appendix A.) These flawed premises lead to a defective worldview and to not only ineffective, but distastrously destructive social and political systems. Among his dangerously mistaken ideas, Marx:

- Sought, as a central principle, to eliminate private property
- Theorized "dialectical materialism"—that societies progress through class struggle
- Saw government regulation as better than free markets
- Believed man was evolving morally through history and becoming more civil
- Saw class conflict over the unity represented by America's "E Pluribus Unum" (out of many, one)
- Saw government, not God or nature, as the source of our human rights
- Saw government as good and more government as even better
- Saw government as the source of all charity
- Saw government power over the people as a good thing
- Sought statism and oversight above free choice
- Saw servitude and subordination (elite governance) over liberty
- Preferred dependence and hand-outs over earned success and self-sufficiency
- Saw labor, not intellect, as the producer of wealth
- Held to total atheist materialism

Losing Yourself in Work

One of Marx's fundamental criticisms of capitalism is the way it strips value from labor. He thinks work should express the workers' creativity and human powers, as well as meet the needs of others. Instead, laborers under capitalism are "alienated" in their work. Think of the difference between, say, building a dresser for your brother's wedding that you "pour yourself into," and sharpening pins at a factory job. Sharpening pins on a factory line doesn't express one's passions or fulfill one's potential for excellence as a human being, and the worker loses control of the product he made when the capitalist owner snatches it away. Marx thinks such labor reduces humans to animals, since he believes an important distinction between humans and animals is creative work. But under the industrial capitalism that Marx is criticizing, human labor is done simply to make money to live; the worker doesn't receive fulfillment from her labor, nor does that work express her powers and creativity. For the alienated laborer under capitalism, work is simply misery.

Marx also argues that capitalism is based on exploiting the impoverished working class. As Peter Singer explains in *Marx: A Very Short Introduction*:

> He wanted to show why the enormous increase in productivity brought about by the industrial revolution had made the great majority of human beings worse off than before. He wanted to reveal how the old relationships of master and slave, lord and serf, survived under the cloak of freedom of contract. His answer to these questions was the doctrine of surplus value.

In a capitalist society, the rich exploit the poor because of what Marx calls "surplus value." Since the bourgeois capitalist owns the factory and materials, once the owner has paid the worker a wage, any extra profit that the worker produces belongs to the owner. The worker is selling his labor to the owner. For example, if the worker agrees to work for $50 for eight hours of work, the worker will often do $50 worth of labor for the owner within a couple hours. What does the worker produce for the other hours of labor? Profit for the capitalist. The owner skims that extra productivity away from the worker as profit. Meanwhile, according to Marx, the worker's life isn't improved, and he continues as an exploited slave laborer for the capitalist.

Religion: The Drug That Gives People Fake Happiness

Marx sees a link between alienation and the creation of religion. In his "Contribution to a Critique of Hegel's Philosophy of Right, Introduction," Marx says, "Religion is the sigh of the oppressed creature, the heart of a heartless world, and the soul of soulless conditions. It is the *opium* of the people." Marx is an atheist; he accepts Ludwig Feuerbach's view that humans created God in their own image, and worship of that God prevents them from realizing their true humanity. Thus, religion doesn't come from God; instead it is both an expression of and a protest against the suffering of workers who hope things will be better in a future life. Religion is like alcohol: it numbs you to the injustice that you experience as a worker. It goes even farther by promising future happiness, and so it keeps people content and peacefully "drugged." For Marx, this is a harmful illusion: it allows the rich to keep their powerful positions and seduces the poor into accepting their horrible lot in life. If a true community of human equality could be reached, Marx thinks religion would simply wither away. Stop hoping for paradise in the future, he wants to say to the poor. Take what is yours *now* through revolution.

Workers of the World, Unite!

Most people know that Marx's solution to this situation is communism: getting rid of private property. However, the possibility of communism depends on the Marxist view of history, which is historical materialism. Peter Singer writes:

> According to Marx's view of history, as the economic basis of society alters, so all consciousness alters. Greed, egoism, and envy are not ingrained forever in the character of human beings. They would disappear in a society in which private property and private means of production were replaced with communal property and socially organized means of production. We would lose our preoccupation with our private interests.

Marx believes that when studying history, if you investigate the different systems of property ownership (common property, slavery, private property, feudalism, etc.) in particular eras, you'll have the key to understanding that society. Notice that the key to understanding society isn't the *ideas* or philosophies of that society; instead, one needs to understand the material conditions in which people live. The conditions we live in make us think in certain ways. This is why Marx's view of history is called "materialistic."

History often focuses upon the role of leaders and heroes, or perhaps the important role of ideas—but not Marx. He sees history as a series of struggles between different classes—the rich and the poor, or more famously, the "bourgeoisie" and the "proletariat." The bourgeoisie are the property owners, or capitalists, and the proletariat are the working class who own very little property. The bourgeoisie, in the name of "Free Trade," have engaged in "naked, shameless, direct, brutal exploitations" of the proletariat, and the cause is ultimately private property. History is the story of a small number of rich oppressing a large number of poor, but this will change once the proletariat revolt and take over the factories. Marx believes that the new communist system will transform greedy, exploitive relationships into relationships of equality where all people have dignified work.

Joshua E. Fernalld, 2016
Kurt Gutschick, faculty
Daren Jonescu, advisor

HERMAN MELVILLE, 1819–1891, *The Whaling and Sailing Romantic*

" Many sensible things banished from high life find an asylum among the mob.

—White-Jacket

- Spent his childhood in poverty after his father died bankrupt
- Deserted a whaling ship he had signed to sail upon, and then wrote his first trilogy of romances
- Underwent a transition from realistic narratives to extremely imaginative romances, then found a medium after receiving negative responses to his unrealistic pieces
- Sold only 3,797 copies of *Moby Dick* during his lifetime
- Withdrew from the world of prose after 1857 and wrote poetry for the last half of his life
- Spoke these last words (as did his famous character, Billy Budd): "God bless Captain Vere."

Key Works

Typee, 1846
Omoo, 1847
Mardi, 1849
White-Jacket, 1850
Moby Dick, 1851
Bartleby, the Scrivener, 1853
Billy Budd, written 1888–1891 and was left unfinished, published in 1924

Biography

Herman Melville was born in New York City in 1819; his father was an importer and merchant who moved the family to Albany to branch into the fur trade. The business did not prosper, and when he died two years later, the family had to declare bankruptcy in 1832. Herman clerked at a bank to help make ends meet, and attended Albany Academy and Albany Classical School where he discovered his gift for writing. He tried many professions before deciding to become a sailor. At 18, he embarked upon his first voyage, and at 22 sailed on the whaler *Acushnet*. His voyages aboard this ship inspired him to write a trio of romances about his experiences. The first, *Typee*, is the most realistic of the three; it details a time he and a friend abandoned ship to escape the intolerable conditions, and lived with a tribe of alleged cannibals to survive. The second, *Omoo*, recounts his adventures on Tahiti, addressing themes such as the destructiveness of humankind. The final book in the trio, *Mardi*, represents a change from realism to fantasy, transforming Melville's style gradually throughout the story. This was the least popular in the series, and its bad reviews convinced Melville to write with more realism in *Redburn* and *White-Jacket*. This thematic transition foreshadowed the coming of *Moby Dick*. Neither *Moby Dick* nor his similar work, *Pierre*, yielded a positive response, so Melville turned to magazine writing and later poetry. He is also known for the short story "Bartleby, the Scrivener," which is regularly anthologized. He published an important review of close friend Nathaniel Hawthorne's work, and continued to write poetry until a heart attack ended his life in 1891. Another of Melville's most famous works, *Billy Budd, Sailor*, was published posthumously in 1924. Although he lacked fame during his life, today he is recognized as one of the great American writers of the 19th century.

Melville's Romanticism

Herman Melville is often lauded as a central literary figure in 19th-century romanticism. Many of his recurrent themes—emotional introspection, religious musings, the immense power of the natural world, and reflections on free will and fate—are trademarks of traditional romanticism. However, Melville, like his friend Nathaniel Hawthorne, also explored darker themes in his works. Though he often depicted the sublime beauty of nature, Melville also understood the sinister and violent aspects of the natural world. Likewise, many of Melville's religious musings abandoned pure exaltation and began to question the goodness and truthfulness of Christianity itself. In his books, he challenged the traditional romantic idea that man is a "noble savage." Central to many of Melville's works are dark themes such as humanity's corruption, evil, and capacity for sin. This new American branch of the romantic movement is often called dark romanticism, and it focused less on the nobility of humankind and more on man's inherent capacity for evil.

In fact, many of Melville's characters personify wickedness itself. One example of this can be found in the character of Claggart, the master-at-arms in *Billy Budd, Sailor*. Melville describes Claggart's total, inexplicable hatred and cruelty towards the virtuous Billy Budd:

> For what can more partake of the mysterious than an antipathy spontaneous and profound such as is evoked in certain exceptional mortals by the mere aspect of some other mortal, however harmless he may be, if not called forth by this very harmlessness itself?

In the novel, Claggart is the embodiment of evil; he despises Billy Budd because of Billy's innocence and goodness. Claggart is not the only wicked character in Melville's works. Captain Ahab of *Moby Dick* is perhaps the most famous of Melville's villains. Through him, Melville explores the evil that man will commit to accomplish his own ends. Throughout the story, Captain Ahab becomes the physical manifestation of the devil, baptizing his weapons in blood so that he may gain revenge on Moby Dick, the infamous white whale.

However, it is not only Melville's villains who discredit the idea of the "noble savage"; Melville deliberately reveals the sinfulness of most of his characters. For example, he describes Captain Ahab's entire crew as a depraved bunch:

> Here, then, was this grey-headed, ungodly old man, chasing with curses a Job's whale round the world, at the head of a crew, too, chiefly made up of mongrel renegades, and castaways, and cannibals—morally enfeebled also, by the incompetence of mere unaided virtue or right-mindedness in Starbuck, the invulnerable jollity of indifference and recklessness in Stubb, and the pervading mediocrity in Flask. Such a crew, so officered, seemed specially picked and packed by some infernal fatality to help him to his monomaniac revenge.

This picture of humankind is hardly flattering or noble. Though Melville's dark romanticism marks a definite departure from traditional romantic ideas, his groundbreaking style helped distinguish and propel American romanticism towards the age of Realism that would define the next several decades.

Faith and Doubt

Melville's struggle to understand religion plays out in some of his novels. Melville's mother baptized her children and taught them the fundamentals of the Reformed Church. However, Melville fell into doubt and disbelief during his years as a teenager; he reflects on this in Chapter 114 of *Moby Dick*, where he states that we all go "through infancy's unconscious spell, boyhood's thoughtless faith, adolescent's doubt (the common doom), then skepticism, then disbelief, resting at last in manhood's pondering repose of If." The "If" represents an uncertainty about God, as most questions of doubt start with "If." For example, "If God is good, then why … ?" However, this doubt does not reflect total disbelief, as it shows that one is still pondering the existence of a god. For Melville, the "If" represents an acceptance of man's inevitable death; he finds peace in doubt by relinquishing the power to find truth. Melville seems to have gone through the cycle himself, embracing and losing the faith of his boyhood, resting at the final question of "If."

In *Moby Dick*, Melville uses his characters to portray his feelings about faith and his doubts about organized religion. One of his characters, Ishmael, is "someone caught midway between belief and unbelief," indicating that he is "not the disbelieving antagonist" but rather an uncertain wanderer. In the end, according to Bruce Lockerbie in *Dismissing God: Modern Writers' Struggle against Religion*, he "has reached no final theological opinion about the universe and his place in it." Thus, Melville's book tells a story of a man who was born a Christian but at some point in his teen years loses his faith and is now searching to discover his place in the world. Both author and character are wanderers, unsure of their place and apprehensive of their creator. Additionally, Melville shows his skepticism of total belief and total unbelief by critiquing both. He never creates "a reputable representative of Christian orthodoxy," with the exception of Father Mapple; instead, he makes "wild-eyed prophets, Shaker fanatics, or moral weaklings," revealing his disillusionment with Christians. At the same time, however, he attacks total unbelief, separating Ishmael from Ahab, who is "in cahoots with the devil." Ahab, as an atheist and a fanatic, represents the extremes of total belief and total unbelief. Ahab's fanaticism alienates Ishmael, a skeptic, who is caught between the two. Perhaps this is indicative of Melville's religious views; both Melville and Ishmael are doubting souls, seeking their place in the world of absolutes.

Benjamin Rocklin, 2017

GEORGE ELIOT, 1819–1880, *Mistress of Realism*

> " Women who are content with light and easily broken ties do not act as I have done. They obtain what they desire and are still invited to dinner.
> —Referring to her life with George Lewes

- Received more critical acclaim than any author of her day, outshining even Charles Dickens
- Was wary of the strict Victorian social order and the restrictions it placed on women
- Wrote under the pen name George Eliot, even thought she was born Mary Ann Evans
- Used a realistic style, uniquely metaphorical and didactically moral, for which she is both criticized and praised
- Was admired by Virginia Woolf and Queen Victoria
- Depicted the struggle between living a good life and a selfish life
- Took four years to write *Middlemarch*, totaling an impressive 800 pages

Key Works

Adam Bede, 1859
The Mill on the Floss, 1860
Silas Marner, 1861

Middlemarch, 1871–72
Daniel Deronda, 1876

Biography

Fated to a life as a social pariah, George Eliot, born Mary Anne Evans on November 22, 1819, eventually conquered societal disdain through her critically acclaimed prose. Her father was an estate agent in Warwickshire, and with the death of her mother in 1836, Eliot took on the role of dutiful daughter and housekeeper, caring for her father and siblings. Although raised a traditional Christian, Eliot seriously questioned the faith when she was exposed to religious free-thinkers, yet when her father demanded that she continue to attend church, she submitted until his death in 1849.

Thirty years old and without prospects, Eliot sought ways to support herself, adding to the £100 annuity left to her by her father. She moved to London and began writing, eventually becoming editor of the *Westminster Review*. There she met and moved in with a married man, George Henry Lewes. Even though his wife was already living with another man, the common-law couple was scorned for living together. Despite the scandal surrounding them, their relationship proved invaluable as Lewes' encouragement prompted Eliot to write fiction. She took the pen name George Eliot—George after her lover and Eliot because she said it was "a good mouth-filling word." Her first novel, *Adam Bede*, met with immediate critical and financial success. A flourishing and prolific career swept aside the scandal that had plagued her early life. After Lewes' death in 1878, Eliot married John Walter Cross in 1880; she was 61 at the time, he 41. The marriage was short-lived, as Eliot died that same year after catching a cold. Due to her impious lifestyle, her body was forbidden burial in Westminster Abbey's Poet's Corner. Instead, her husband chose a plot near where George Lewes lay in Highgate Cemetery.

Middlemarch

Eliot's seminal work of fiction records the transformation of two young idealists, Dorothea Brooke and Tertius Lydgate. Subtitled as "A Study of Provincial Life," *Middlemarch* is one of the most critically acclaimed books of the Victorian era. Eliot created what one critic claims is "probably the greatest novel ever written in the English realistic tradition"; it is often considered the peak of her artistic efforts and philosophical concepts. The novel depicts the conflict between living an egotistical and insensitive life, or a life of understanding and sympathy. Focusing on the real-life challenge of choosing to live a good life, the novel emphasizes how fulfilling it can be to pursue goodness, stringing Eliot's Christian ethics throughout the story's web.

Eliot referred to her work as "this particular web" because throughout the text, all of her characters connect one way or another—forming a twisted yet realistic web of human interaction and emotion. She speculates on this web in her narration: "But any one watching keenly the stealthy convergence of human lots, sees a slow preparation of effects from one life on another, which tells like a calculated irony on the indifference or the frozen stare with which we look at our unintroduced neighbour. Destiny stands by sarcastic with our *dramatis personae* folded in her hand." Whether her characters recognize it not, their lives are inextricably connected. A.S. Byatt, the novelist, elucidates, "All are held together by one of the most complicated and brilliantly worked metaphors anywhere in fiction. It is a metaphor of a web. ... It is both a field of force, a trap like a spider web, and a pattern of invisible connecting links between humans meeting each other's eye." Eliot weaves this twisted web, shaping a passionate tale of village life and family conflict, and offers what Virginia Woolf said is "one of the few English novels written for grown-up people." Although romantically comedic, *Middlemarch* portrays the gravity of submitting to convention. Eliot conveys the laws of a "social order and principles of moral conduct" to which her characters must submit or suffer the consequences, thus illustrating, as Deborah Felder puts it in *A Bookshelf of Our Own*, that "the growing good of the world is partly dependent on unhistoric acts; and that things are not so ill with you and me as they might have been, is half owing to the number who lived faithfully a hidden life, and rest in unvisited tombs."

Style

Eliot differs from many other writers of her time in that her novels do not rely on dialogue but on her narrative style. She writes with original metaphors that "encapsulate her characters and foreshadow their destinies." In *Middlemarch*, she describes Dr. Casaubon's wooing "as sincere as the bark of a dog or the cawing of an amorous rook," portending the dry romance that would follow. These metaphors, rife in her work, paint a striking picture of the disasters and triumphs of her characters, allowing readers to identify with them. Eliot's phrasing also follows a pattern of relishing the character's own self-delusion only to end on a deflating note. In *Felix Holt*, she writes, "Some attributed [Mrs. Sampson's] reticence to a wise incredulity, others to a want of memory, others to simple ignorance." Here, Eliot almost sniggers at her own character's pretense. In *The Mill on the Floss*, she provides the same kind of incisive description: "Mrs. Glegg paused, for speaking with much energy for the good of others is naturally exhausting."

She also felt free to interrupt the narrative to moralize or philosophize about the themes or events surrounding her characters. This famed excerpt from *Middlemarch* epitomizes her narrative insight:

> The element of tragedy which lies in the very fact of frequency has not yet wrought itself into the coarse emotion of mankind; and perhaps our frames could hardly bear much of it. If we had a keen vision and feeling of all ordinary human life, it would be like hearing the grass grow and the squirrel's heart beat, and we should die of the roar which lies on the other side of silence. As it is, the quickest of us walk about well wadded with stupidity.

In relating her opinion of the twofold tragedy of human emotion, Eliot ceases to narrate and begins to teach. Although Henry James considered the technique intrusive, others say it elevates her writing "from ingenious storytelling to divine comedy."

Realism

Eliot's realism, while dominant, was not definitive. She believed that writing should be a portrayal of reality and yet admitted that reality would always elude the writer. She explained, "Approximate truth is the only truth attainable, but at least one must strive for that, and not wade off into arbitrary falsehood." Consequently, she was less focused on making her writing seem realistic than she was on relating the world as she really saw it. Her fiction was honest and, therefore, realistic.

Addressing the common issues of her day, *The Mill on the Floss* can be read as Eliot's analysis of the struggles readers would be dealing with. The novel describes the life of a young woman who is forced to choose between the fantasy she finds in books and the harsh reality of the real world, clearly advocating for the real world by rewarding rational and dutiful behavior. Eliot's works focus not only on personal struggles but also on the greater societal issues. In *Middlemarch*, Van Doren Charles Lincoln says in "Critics and Seers," Eliot investigates the social structure and inner workings of English society;

it is "as complete an account of the kind of lives that people live as we can find anywhere in fiction." Real life societal expectations and class regulations govern Eliot's characters' actions. This conflict between obligation and desire manifests in failed marriages, stolen goods, secret rendezvous, and other such struggles for her characters. Although she is a realist, she would acknowledge that her works are fictional accounts of reality—not truth but near truth.

Samantha Sherwood, 2015
Lauren Wade, 2015

HENRY THOMAS BUCKLE, 1821–1862, *History in Terms of Science*

" I am deeply convinced that the time is fast approaching when the history of man will be placed on its proper footing; when its study will be recognized as the noblest and most arduous of all pursuits; and when it will be clearly seen that, to cultivate it with success, there is wanting a wide and comprehensive mind, richly furnished with the highest branches of human knowledge.

—*History of Civilization in England*

- Hated education from an outside source, dropping out of school at 14 to become largely self-educated
- Was sickly and delicate throughout his entire life
- Traveled throughout Europe in search of acquiring knowledge from many cultures
- Could read and write in 19 different languages
- Went from his family's Calvinist beliefs to acceptance of Darwinism
- Sought to address the question of the science of history
- Saw history as the study of a physical process following set patterns, something he saw supported by Darwinian evolution
- Sought out the regularities of history like a scientist and thought that historians not doing this were inferior to both scientists and the history they were studying
- Died at the age of 40, preventing the publishing of further volumes of his *History of Civilizations in England*

Key Works
History of Civilization in England Vol. 1, 1857
History of Civilization in England Vol. 2, 1861

Biography
Born on November 24, 1824, in Kent, England, Henry Thomas Buckle was delicate, caring little for games and childhood activities. As a boy, he was more interested in Shakespeare and other literature. His parents thought it best for him to receive a school education, but Buckle loathed his education and at 14, after demonstrating a thorough knowledge of mathematics, asked his parents to take him out of school. Buckle then resumed a life at home as a result of his bad health. Around this time, his father's health began to decline and in 1840 he died, which traumatically affected Buckle. The family left England to travel abroad, and when Buckle returned to England he was a different man. Previously a devout Calvinist, he returned to England as a Darwinist. He began to study and research on his own—

never attending a university or having a tutor, but relying solely on his own intellect. He later traveled throughout Europe, desiring to acquire knowledge by directly engaging with various cultures and people. During this time, Buckle consistently read and wrote about historical literature.

When he suddenly fell ill with rheumatic fever, Buckle began to contemplate his profession and his purpose. He considered several options, eventually settling on devoting his entire life to his reading and writing of history. For 14 years Buckle worked on his History. He documented the history of the civilization of England, being most interested in the cultural aspect of nations. In 1857, Buckle published the first volume of his *History of Civilizations in England* and the second volume in 1862. He approached history scientifically, a radical method for the time period. His approach derived from the influence of John Stuart Mill's empiricism and Auguste Comte's belief that history exemplifies a pattern of progress and improvement. Buckle traveled the world, but contracted another fever and died while touring the Middle East in 1862. His early death ended the project that had become his life work. Still, he left behind a significant impact on the study of history.

Legacy

Henry Thomas Buckle's influence is primarily as a historian who changed the focus of the study of history. During his time, historical study was subject to a reverence for the past and to the subjectivity of the historian's intent, often to the detriment of rational and scientific analysis. Historical study in his day also placed an emphasis on religion, the morals of civilization, literature, government, and a providential expectation, each as "prime movers of human affairs." Buckle denied all of this. He sought to represent history as "a physical process that followed set patterns, a view that was reinforced by the analogy of Darwinian evolution." He searched and connected the facts of human history with the realities of their geographic and natural environment.

Buckle's denial of the historical method of the time led to much criticism, especially in response to his *History of Civilization in England*, which had minimized free will through its focus on empirical evidence. One such criticism found in an original book review from 1857 says, "Buckle has more aptitude for the chronology, than the history of civilization, as his ponderous display of learning but too plainly proves." The reviewer suggests Buckle's greatest offence was his claim to have brought history into the age of science, making traditional forms of history obsolete by bringing the past under general laws similar to scientific laws. Consequently, Buckle deemphasized the impact of civilizations' moral, religious, and governmental ideals on which historians traditionally focused. Henry Thomas Buckle receives much credit for this shift and the results in the study of history.

Nate Kosirog, faculty
Nathaniel Whatmore, 2015

GUSTAVE FLAUBERT, 1821–1880, *Father of French Realism*

> " Human speech is like a cracked kettle on which we tap crude rhythms for bears to dance to, while we long to make music that will melt the stars.
>
> —*Madame Bovary*

- Suffered seizures from epilepsy

- Spent five years on his most famous novel, *Madame Bovary*
- Was sued after the release of *Madame Bovary* for insulting the Catholic Church and women, with his explicit and realistic portrayal of a woman's desires
- Exposed the persistent gap between societal expectations and societal reality
- Ended a long-term affair with Louise Colet because she was persistent about meeting his mother, but Flaubert did not believe she was worthy of the introduction
- Based much of his writing on his own life and his own experiences, including his sickness and the effects it had on him
- Inspired many authors, such as Joseph Conrad, Thomas Hardy, Ivan Turgenev, F. Scott Fitzgerald, Henry James, and Mario Vargas Llosa

Key Works

Madame Bovary, 1857
L'Education Sentimentale, 1869

Biography

Gustave Flaubert was born in Rouen, France on December 12, 1821. As a child he feared his father, an intimidating surgeon, and so spent much time with his mother. A lifelong epileptic, Flaubert never wrote an epileptic character into his novels but did make several characters vulnerable to hallucinations. At 15 he fell in love with Elisa Sclésinger, who was married and years older. When the reality of their incompatibility became clear, he decided to never pursue another woman with marriage in mind. Hence, he traveled to Paris to study law, with not much success. During this time he visited prostitutes, eventually contracting venereal diseases from which he would never recover. This experience shaped his spiteful view of women, which would later be expressed through his writing. Flaubert linked sexuality to immorality, which "brought him notions of doom, death, and annihilation." In 1845 he experienced his first attack of temporal-lobe epilepsy and constantly suffered from seizures after this event. The next year marked the death of his father and sister, causing Flaubert to stop studying law and dedicate himself to his writing. After he wrote *The Temptation of Saint Anthony*, he left on a 20-month trip through the eastern Mediterranean. He returned through Greece and Italy, which inspired some of his work. For the next few years Flaubert had a romantic relationship with Louise Colet; his letters to her expressed his struggles in composing *Madame Bovary*. This novel would be the source of his enduring literary reputation. After years filled with pain, Flaubert died of a brain hemorrhage at the age of 58.

Inspiration and Style

Gustave Flaubert, famously referred to as the martyr of style, rebelled against fictional trends of the day and introduced modern realistic narration. Influenced by his environment, Flaubert included popular romantic undertones in his novels, but blended them with realism. His works expressed the ideals of the romantic era through an objective and scientific lens, resulting in his explicit and astonishingly realistic portrayal of society at the time. In fact, the explicit nature of *Madame Bovary* led the Catholic Church to institute a lawsuit against him; it ultimately failed to prevent the book's release.

While it was not uncommon during the 19th century for an author to publish a book a year, Flaubert took five years to finish writing *Madame Bovary* in order to perfect it. His perfectionism earned him a reputation in the writing community for always searching for what he called "*le mot juste*," or the right word. As a result, he would take, on average, a week to finish one page.

Writers such as Charles Baudelaire, from whom he drew his questions of morality and religion, inspired Flaubert's themes. Flaubert's *Madame Bovary* and Baudelaire's famed *Les Fleurs du Mal* both landed in court for offending public morals and the church. In addition to realism, Flaubert's use of irony expresses a hatred of the middle class and French culture. He is also known for investigating the difference between everyday life and the life portrayed by romanticism. This theme is displayed throughout his works, but perhaps best in *Madame Bovary*, as his protagonist, Emma, is never fully satisfied by her love affairs due to her overly romantic expectations. His writing was often considered morbid, pessimistic, and unemotional, perhaps reflective of his lifelong battle with epilepsy and the constant disappointments he faced with women.

Madame Bovary

When *Madame Bovary* was released, Flaubert was sued for his realistic and highly insulting portrayal of the bourgeois life. Gustave Flaubert crafts a female character who exhibits values contrary to society's ideal—an unrepentant adulteress, a vain female, and an absent mother. Emma is not a romantic heroine, yet she remains a compelling protagonist. As Kathryn Harrison writes in her article "Desperate Housewives," readers "cannot like Emma Bovary, and yet they follow her with the kind of attention reserved for car wrecks, whether literal or metaphorical."

The popularity of this story goes beyond its explicit content; the true appeal is in Flaubert's compelling confrontation of humanity's existential emptiness, according to Harrison. Emma was a self-absorbed middle-class woman who was always looking for love in all the wrong places, and yet, despite these failings, or maybe because of them, Flaubert admitted, "Madame Bovary, c'est moi," meaning, "Madame Bovary is me." *Madame Bovary* was written in the midst of his stylistic struggle, as he was caught between romanticism and realism. This mix typifies Emma's internal struggle, connecting Flaubert to his character. Perhaps driven by his own disillusionment, he began as a romantic and moved towards realism as he grew artistically and became more and more cynical. And perhaps this can be attributed to the life events that shaped his works: left by the women he loved, bored with the women of his affairs, and crippled by his epilepsy. Perhaps, in the end, life never measured up to his romantic expectations.

Savannah Cressman, 2011
Trisha Rouleau, 2015

FYODOR DOSTOEVSKY, 1821–1881, *The Underground Man*

> " What is hell? I maintain that it is the suffering of being unable to love.
>
> —*The Brothers Karamazov*

- Was a Russian novelist whose most famous works—*The Idiot, Crime and Punishment,* and *The Brothers Karamazov*—are still being read and translated worldwide
- Graduated from the St. Petersburg Academy of Military Engineering as sub-lieutenant but soon resigned to become a fiction writer
- Published a damning account of the penal system in *The House of the Dead* after being imprisoned in Siberia for political dissidence; he narrowly escaped with his life
- Converted to Christianity and subsequently rejected the nihilism and rationalism of his time

- Explored the human experience through the themes of depravity and love, shame and pride, triumph and defeat

Key Works

Notes From Underground; Or Letters from the Underworld, 1864
Crime and Punishment, 1866
The Idiot, 1869
Demons or *The Devils* or *The Possessed*, 1872
The Brothers Karamazov, 1880

Biography

Fyodor Mikhailovich Dostoevsky was born in 1821 in Moscow. After his mother died when he was 16, Dostoevsky moved to St. Petersburg with his father and was sent to the School of Military Engineers. Shortly after serfs killed his negligent father, the orphaned Dostoevsky had his first epileptic seizure, a condition that would plague him throughout his life. In 1844, he became a second lieutenant in the military, but he had to leave school because of his debt. He decided to make money as a writer, and he finished his first book, *Poor Folk*, in 1846.

A political radical, Dostoevsky joined a group of intellectuals that discussed the possibility of socialist reform. The group was arrested for dissidence in 1849, and Dostoevsky was sentenced to death by firing squad. At the last second, the tsar commuted the sentence, and Dostoevsky was instead exiled to a penal colony in Siberia. The deplorable conditions of the prison would become the crucible for his first great work, *The House of the Dead*. While in Siberia, Dostoevsky married Maria Dmitrievna Isaev. In 1864, Dostoevsky's wife and brother died within three months of each other, evoking frequent epileptic seizures. Dostoevsky remarried in 1867 to Anna Grigorievna Snitkin, the secretary of a publishing house. While the couple traveled throughout Europe, Dostoevsky published *The Idiot* and *Demons*. In 1880, he released his magnum opus—*The Brothers Karamazov*—a novel about the murder of an immoral patriarch and the conflicts between his three surviving sons. Though he planned to write a sequel, he suffered a pulmonary hemorrhage and died before he could accomplish this task. Dostoevsky ranks with Leo Tolstoy as one of the greatest Russian novelists of all time. His works, particularly *Crime and Punishment* and *The Brothers Karamazov*, continue to be translated and read worldwide.

Nihilism

Dostoevsky uses many of his characters to explore the devastating consequences of the nihilism of 19th-century Russia. Nihilism propounds that there is no divine nature, no higher purpose, no absolute good; man merely exists, and even that is debatable. For the nihilist, Dostoevsky writes, "The whole work of man really seems to consist in nothing but proving to himself every minute that he is a man and not a piano key." Dostoevsky argues that this conception of life as an existential crisis wherein man must accept his meaninglessness results in an ultimately utilitarian morality. Raskolnikov, the protagonist in *Crime and Punishment*, actually acts on his nihilism by killing an old pawnbroker. He justifies this murder through utilitarian reasoning, arguing that people would benefit more from her death than from her miserly life. In the same novel, another character, Svidrigailov, recognizes that he could pursue a nihilist agenda and rape Raskolnikov's sister, but decides not to because the intercourse would not fulfill his desire for love. His inner turmoil ultimately drives him to commit suicide.

For Dostoevsky, human emotion continually spars with nihilism, and many of his characters experience intellectual suffering as they try to mesh nihilist beliefs with their clashing emotional responses. Facing the possibility of a meaningless existence, "everyone is striving to … find at least some general sense in the general senselessness," he writes in *The Brothers Karamazov*. Dostoevsky argues that this inner conflict can be resolved only through a belief in God. Even Raskolnikov is "renewed by love." As the nihilism that had ruled his mind succumbs to the love in his heart, Raskolnikov relies upon the New Testament and strives toward gradual regeneration, "passing from one world into another."

Human Nature

"Man is a mystery. It must be unraveled and if you spend your whole life unraveling it, do not say that this was a waste of time; I am preoccupied with this mystery because I want to be a human being." Most of Dostoevsky's characters take a fairly dim view of human nature, but not all are nihilists. Many of his religious characters express their belief in original sin, the baked-in depravity of every human. However, unlike their nihilistic counterparts, Dostoevsky's religious characters stress that love can overcome this inherent wickedness. In *The Brother Karamazov*, the elder monk Zosima explains, "Brothers, love is a teacher; but one must know how to acquire it, for it is hard to acquire, it is dearly bought, it is won slowly by long labor, for one ought to love not for a chance moment, but for all time. Anyone, even the wicked man, can love by chance." Dostoevsky suggests that the corruption of human nature cannot be overcome through force or alternative philosophies, but rather through loving humility grounded in the Christian faith.

Christian Faith from the Underground

Dostoevsky's religious beliefs were heavily influenced by his upbringing. Growing up in a devout, Orthodox household and during his years in school and the military, Dostoevsky was regarded as a quiet, yet passionate Christian. He spent many hours each day reading and praying, and according to his peers, he often spoke about his love for Christ.

Dostoevsky was very aware of the many powerful arguments against Christianity, and he refused to shy away from them. He would not forsake his philosophical integrity to embrace faith. Much of Dostoevsky's writing is "a process of rethinking Christianity in dialogue, a process which reached no final conclusion in his novels, whatever may have been the case with his own spiritual pilgrimage" writes Malcom Jones in "Dostoevsky and the Dynamics of Religious Experience." Though Dostoevsky often entertained doubts about his faith, philosophical challenges could never ultimately sway him from his love of Christ. In a letter to Natalia Fonvizina, Dostoevsky writes:

> " I confess that I am a child of my age, a child of unbelief and doubt up to this very moment and (I am certain of it) to the grave. What terrible torments this thirst to believe has cost me and continues to cost me, burning more strongly in my soul the more contrary arguments there are. Nevertheless, God sometimes sends me moments of complete tranquility. In such moments I love and find that I am loved by others, and in such moments I have nurtured in myself a symbol of truth, in which everything is clear and holy for me.

Succinctly put, Dostoevsky's faith in Christianity is not "rational," but experiential. He does not believe that Christianity is a compelling argument but a compelling way of life. Though he would agree with the nihilists of his time that life was fraught with unavoidable suffering, Dostoevsky proposes that the way of faith and love is the only viable response to this reality.

Many 19th-century rationalists believed that people commit wrongs simply because they don't know better. In *Notes from Underground*, Dostoevsky expresses his frustration with this belief, explaining that human beings often act irrationally by intention. The protagonist of this novel struggles (and fails) to understand his place in society and to rationally sort out his conflicting thoughts and feelings. *Notes from Underground* is not an explicitly Christian text; rather it is a refutation of rationalism that "displays the dreadful consequences for the individual and for society of such ideas taken to their logical conclusion, and just hints that there is another way." In other words, by displaying the impossibility of rationalism, Dostoevsky gently implies that Christianity is a more consistent worldview.

Cole Baker, 2012
Toby Coffman, faculty
Ryan Russell, 2015

FRANCIS GALTON, 1822–1911, *Divider of Races*

> Man is gifted with pity and other kindly feelings; he has also the power of preventing many kinds of suffering. I conceive it to fall well within his province to replace Natural Selection by other processes that are more merciful and not less effective.
>
> —*Memories of My Life*

- Founded eugenics, a science that tries to improve the human race by controlling which people become parents
- Was a child prodigy, and read Shakespeare for pleasure at age 6
- Inherited great wealth from his father; he never had a job
- Traveled extensively in Africa as a young man
- Believed everything could be qualitative
- Saw genetics as determinative of intellect and social standing
- Was convinced that some races were superior to others
- Used a survey for research—the first person to do so
- Studied just about every scientific subject, but especially genetics, statistics, and meteorology
- Created a system for analyzing fingerprints and the first weather map

Key Works

Narrative of an Explorer in Tropical South Africa, 1853
Meteorographica, 1863
Hereditary Genius, 1869
English Men of Science, 1874
Inquiry into Human Faculty and Its Development, 1883
Natural Inheritance, 1889
Memories of My Life, 1908

Biography

Francis Galton was a wealthy genius whose fatal flaw was arrogance. Born near Birmingham, England to an eminent family that included the likes of Charles and Erasmus Darwin, he had an easy childhood. His intelligence was apparent from the beginning; by age 4, he could multiply, tell time, and read English, Latin, and some French. At 16, Galton entered medical school, but "he used it partly as a chance to systematically sample the pharmaceuticals cabinet, in alphabetical order," as the compendium *Science and Its Times* notes. He stopped at C when a dose of Croton oil made him throw up.

Galton was not a fan of the workload of medical school, and when his father died, leaving him with, as Galton phrased it, "a sufficient fortune to make me independent of the medical profession," he promptly quit school and set out to travel the world. He explored virtually unknown lands in Sudan, Syria, and Southwest Africa, and wrote two books on his travels. Both the Geographical Society and the Royal Society recognized him for his efforts.

On returning home, Galton decided to become a scientist by hobby. He started with meteorology, but on the publication of his cousin Charles Darwin's *On the Origin of Species*, Galton became fascinated with heredity and genetics. Strongly convinced that everything is quantifiable and could be proven mathematically, he was one of the founding members of the biometric school, a school of thought in which scientists use statistics to prove ideas in genetics.

Galton's study of genetics led him to a conclusion that would earn him much attention and even infamy: he was convinced that "pre-eminence in various fields was due almost entirely to hereditary factors." In other words, intelligence, ability, and ultimately social rank were determined at birth. It was around this time that Galton coined the term "eugenics" and became heavily invested in the science.

Although genetics and heredity were the subjects Galton favored, he also dabbled in many other sciences, including physics, astronomy, geography, cognitive psychology, anthropology, evolutionary biology, music, meteorology, and criminal detection. So extensive were his scientific endeavors that he even investigated the power of prayer, the optimal method of making tea, and the body weights of British nobles. For his efforts, he was knighted in 1909. Ironically, considering his own concept of selective breeding, he died childless in 1911.

Born Great

Galton's reputation changed from "bored English gentleman" to "great calamity of traditional thought" thanks to his studies in genetics. The publication of his cousin Darwin's *On the Origin of Species* got the ball rolling. As Galton himself recalls:

> The publication in 1859 of the *Origin of Species* by Charles Darwin made a marked epoch in my own mental development, as it did in that of human thought generally. Its effect was to demolish a multitude of dogmatic barriers by a single stroke, and to arouse a spirit of rebellion against all ancient authorities whose positive and unauthenticated statements were contradicted by modern science.

The idea of natural selection started him thinking that intelligence and general ability were hereditary. This conclusion is not so surprising when one considers how brilliant and prominent his own family was; nonetheless, it deviated from the common belief at the time, which held that everyone was born with essentially equal ability. Darwin himself was repulsed by Galton's ideas, writing to Galton that: "You have made a convert of an opponent in one sense for I have always maintained that, excepting fools, men did not differ much in intellect, only in zeal and hard work." Nonetheless, Galton attempted to prove his theory. He reviewed newspaper obituaries and traced the lineage of England's most prominent families, arriving at the conclusion that intelligence and eminence were in fact hereditary.

Scholars have long been perplexed by Galton's seeming dismissal of the role environment plays in human development. Galton, however, would claim that he *did* consider the role that environment played in shaping the individual, going as far as to study genetically similar twins raised in different environments and children adopted into families of a different race other than their own. His studies, he insisted, only proved that intelligence stemmed more from nature than from nurture.

Galton's work became even more controversial when he started working in eugenics, which was essentially the study of how to better the human race by selective parenthood. It involved "'breeding in' desirable traits of the human population, such as talent and healthiness, and 'breeding out' undesirable traits, such as stupidity and weakness." Of course, this train of thought led to some races (Europeans) being recognized as genetically superior and more intelligent than the rest of the world, an idea which would have lasting effects on social conduct between races and groups of people.

Other Theories in Genetics

Galton made several other important findings in the field of genetics that were of greater scientific credibility than his work in eugenics. For example, he proved Darwin's theory of pangenesis incorrect. Darwin had proposed that traits were passed on from one individual to the next via particles called "gemmules." These gemmules moved throughout the body copying physical traits and eventually ended up in the reproductive organs so that they could be transferred to the offspring. Galton concluded that if such particles existed, then they must travel through the bloodstream. This led him to set up an experiment where he transfused the blood of a common lop-eared rabbit into a purebred silver-gray rabbit. He then bred the silver-grey rabbit with another of its kind, but the offspring were still silver-grey, disproving Darwin's theory. Darwin, upon publication of Galton's results, argued that he never said blood was involved in the transfer of gemmules.

Galton's other significant contribution to genetics was his theory of ancestral heredity. It stated that each parent "contributes one half of the traits to the offspring, each grandparent one-fourth, and so on. With each generation, the traits become more diluted and the offspring begin exhibiting the average of race, not the average of the parents." Galton believed that traits blended together and that therefore, if one flower were red and the other blue, the offspring would be purple. Gregory Mendel would prove this part of the theory wrong with his concept of particulate heredity. Mendel's theory held that particles (later identified as genes) carried traits to the offspring and came from both parents. Because these particles did not "blend" together, as Galton had proposed, the offspring of a red and blue flower may be simply red or blue, depending on which trait was dominant. However, it is important to note that Galton's idea was mathematically correct insofar as each parent supplies half of a child's genes.

Statistics

Galton's natural curiosity about the world around him led him to his discoveries in statistics. While studying heredity, he realized that there was no way to calculate the probability of passing certain traits from generation to generation. A firm believer that everything could be quantified, Galton experimented with sweet-pea seeds to compare diameters of parent generations with the next generations to see if there was a correlation. He used 100 seeds of seven different diameter sizes, and when he viewed the results through a two-way plot, found that "the median diameter of the offspring of the large seeds were less than that of their parents while the median diameter of the offspring of the small seeds were greater than that of their parents." This experiment showed Galton that the offspring tended to regress to a relatively middle size, rather than the larger seeds giving rise to larger offspring and vice versa. Little did he know, this discovery of "regression" wasn't just a coincidence.

Galton moved on to study humans and their offspring. He constructed a device that allowed him to measure the heights and weights of parents and their grown children to test his theory of regression. This time, however, Galton made his second major discovery in statistics, noting that among the sizes of the adult children and their parents, there was a common regression line in which the children always reverted back to a mean or average. He called this a "normal curve" which he used "to describe measures of human attributes." Galton's discoveries allowed him to create the statistical notion of correlation which led to his understanding of how generations were related to each other and allowed further exploration in the study of heredity and genetics.

Galton took this work and became the first man to use surveys for research. He asked English scientists to fill out a questionnaire on which he based his book, *English Men of Science.* The survey consisted of questions regarding their height and weight, family medical history, interest in science itself, as well as their merit. Galton said, "the intent of this book is to supply what may be termed a Natural History of the English Men of Science of the present day." Galton knew that the scientists had a well-rounded mix of traits, and thought they were "well fitted for statistical investigation." He was able to incorporate his earlier work in both genetics and statistics to investigate and refine his theories through the studies of the men in his survey.

Other Scientific Contributions

Galton was a man with way too much time on his hands. As a result, he made several other significant scientific findings in various fields. His earliest work was in meteorology, where he introduced to the world the modern weather map, publishing the first one in *The Times* on April 1, 1875. Galton also coined the term "anticyclone" to describe high pressure systems.

Later in his life, Galton did a significant amount of work concerning fingerprinting because he thought "it might be a way to track differences in families, race, morals, and intellect." Although he was never able to find a connection between one's fingerprint and one's intelligence, he did identify common patterns in fingerprints (plain arch, simple loop, and so on), and he introduced a fingerprint classification system still used today.

Seemingly obsessed with comparing people to one another, Galton also created the technique known as composite photography or, using the language of the day, composite portraiture. It involved superimposing multiple portraits of various people in order to produce an "average face." Continuing with his comparisons, Galton devised several tests to gather data on an individual's reaction time, range of hearing, vision, and even strength because he believed reaction time and sensory ability were linked to intellect. He tested more than 9,000 people, and the mass of anthropometric data gathered from such tests was not thoroughly analyzed until the 1980s.

BERNHARD RIEMANN, 1826–1866, *The Hypotheses of Geometry*

> " Einstein's theory, more especially the second part (the general theory), is intimately connected with the discoveries of the non-Euclidean geometricians, Riemann in particular. Indeed, had it not been for Riemann's work, and for the considerable extension it has conferred upon our understanding of the problem of space, Einstein's general theory could never have arisen.
>
> —d'Abro, *The Evolution of Scientific thought from Newton to Einstein*

- Was a gifted mathematician from an early age
- Explained the original Riemann surface
- Lectured on a new geometry of many dimensions and situations
- Contributed to analysis, number theory, and differential geometry
- Provided the framework for Einstein's theory of relativity
- Died of tuberculosis at 39
- Published only one volume, yet profoundly affected modern mathematics

Key Works

"On the Number of Primes Not Exceeding a Given Bound," 1859
The Collected Works of Bernhard Riemann, 1892

Biography

The young Georg Friedrich Bernhard Riemann was taught by his father and a village schoolmaster until he surpassed his teachers' knowledge. At that point, Riemann went to Hanover to enter the Lyceum and then the Johanneum. There, too, the headmaster encouraged him in his mathematics studies. At 19, Riemann went to Gottingen University where he embarked on the study of mathematics. While studying under famous scientists, Riemann submitted his doctoral dissertation. The paper explained complex function theory and Riemann surfaces. Hoping for work at Gottingen, Riemann applied for the only available opening, a lecturer paid by his students. His qualifying lecture was an argument for a new concept of geometry operating in many dimensions. While Riemann had truly broken new ground, no one really understood or appreciated his innovations until 50 years later when Albert Einstein declared that Riemann's theories gave an authentic description of the universe. In fact, Einstein used Riemannian geometry to uncover his general theory of relativity and what was later called Riemann space. Einstein used Reimann's theories when developing his concepts of the "fourth dimension," and the "curvature of space."

Riemann lived at a time that provided very little income even for gifted educators, so he spent 10 years in "honored starvation" which resulted in his poor and worsening health. Yet he continued to write on complex functions and the foundations of geometry, as well as mathematical physics.

Riemann died on a trip to Italy where he had gone to recover from tuberculosis that had bothered him for years. He had previously married Elise Koch and fathered a daughter Ida. Suffering from the deaths of his mother and three sisters (also from tuberculosis), and exhausted from overwork, he succumbed to the disease while resting under a tree.

HENRIK IBSEN, 1828–1906, *The Provocative Norwegian Victorian*

> " HELMER: I would gladly toil day and night for you, Nora, enduring all manner of sorrow and distress. But nobody sacrifices his *honor* for the one he loves.
> NORA: Hundreds and thousands of women have.
>
> —*A Doll's House*

- Was a Norwegian playwright known for social satire and unusual topic selections
- Wrote in three different stylistic phases: poetic, satiric, and psychological
- Drew attention to women's rights with *A Doll's House*, and earned unintended fame from feminists
- Sparked conversation and debate with his plays, which were often banned
- Is often associated with the rise of "independent theaters"
- Professed his dramatic purpose by stating, "I do but ask, my call is not to answer"

Key Works
Peer Gynt, 1867
A Doll's House, 1879
Ghosts, 1881
Hedda Gabler, 1890

Biography
Revolutionary in the world of modern theatre, Henrik Ibsen distinguished himself with his bold satires and controversial approach to the hot topics of his era. Born March 20, 1828, in Skien, Norway, Ibsen moved around the country in the wake of his father's business failures. The industrial landscape of Skien would long find expression in his plays. Unable to achieve success in his homeland, Ibsen moved to continental Europe and there released his first two well-received plays, *Brand* and *Peer Gynt*. These works are written in verse and contain early traces of his criticism of late-19th century social mores in Norway. Ibsen soon moved away from verse plays to incorporate more controversial satirical and psychological themes. Ibsen's plays—notably *A Doll's House* and *Ghosts*—were often banned from production, which contributed to a rise in private and so-called independent theaters throughout Europe. Introducing avant-garde topics through heavily developed and realistic characters, Ibsen provoked a new, realist form of drama. He was a progressive in a non-progressive era, defined by what Eric Bentley calls a "genuinely radical attitude to life in general." Ibsen suffered two strokes in his later years and died in Christiania, Norway in 1906.

A Doll's House and Ibsen's Unintended Feminist Heroism
Ibsen's most remembered work, *A Doll's House*, relays the story of Nora Helmer, the smiling, submissive "little singing bird" wife of Torvald Helmer. Over the course of the play—and facing the prospect of financial ruin—Nora comes to recognize the superficiality of her marriage with Torvald. She realizes that she has been a "doll wife" in the same way she "was Daddy's doll child." Nora concludes that she needs to educate herself in order to make something of her life, so that she is not defined by her

marriage or motherhood. She gives her wedding ring back, saying, "Oh, Torvald, I don't believe in miracles any more." Thus, she leaves Torvald alone with a legendary offstage door slam that critics have called "the slam heard around the world."

Like most of his works, Ibsen's *A Doll's House* received criticism for its bold social statements—questioning and discussing gender roles, marriage, healthy relationships, and independence—but it gained high praise from the feminist community as revolutionary for women's rights. When Ibsen was invited to speak at the Norwegian Women's Rights League, he admitted "[I] must disclaim the honor of having consciously worked for the women's rights movement. I am not even quite clear as to just what this women's rights movement really is. To me it has seemed a problem of humanity in general. … True enough, it is desirable to solve the problem of women's rights, along with a[ll] the others; but that has not been the whole purpose. My task has been the description of humanity."

Elizabeth Palms, 2014

LEO TOLSTOY, 1829–1910, *Existential Russian*

    " Without knowing what I am or why I am here, life is impossible.

—*Anna Karenina*

- Focused primarily on Russian society, war, and the meaning of life and death in his works
- Wrote two enduring novels, *War and Peace* and *Anna Karenina*, which are still widely read
- Is considered so influential that a style of writing was dubbed "Tolstoyan" in his honor; it is characterized by abundant, repetitive phrases, each one slightly different than the original, adding new meaning in waves
- Underwent an extreme religious conversion in his later years and sparked a religious movement

Key Works

War and Peace, 1869
Anna Karenina, 1877
My Confession, 1879
The Death of Ivan Ilych, 1884

Biography

Leo Tolstoy (Count Leo Nikolayevich Tolstoy), heralded by many as the greatest writer of all time, was born in August 1828 in the Russian town of Yasnaya Polyana. Orphaned at the age of 6, Tolstoy was raised by his aunts and enlisted in the army as a young man. Though he soon grew disenchanted with military life, Tolstoy's experience in war informed and inspired some of his greatest fiction, including the novel *War and Peace*. After returning to his estate in Yasnaya Polyana with his new wife Sophie Behrs, Tolstoy made a point of educating peasant children in his town. Tolstoy's first two novels, *War and Peace* and *Anna Karenina*, earned him instant fame and fans. Though controversial, his messages about Russian society, warfare, time, life, and death were met with public and critical acclaim. During this time, Tolstoy underwent a radical religious conversion that resulted in the ire of both his family and the Russian Orthodox Church. Despite being excommunicated from the church in 1901 for his controversial religious publications, Tolstoy resolutely continued living and teaching his radical doctrines until his death in 1910. His religious life and publications gained him a vast number of disciples around the world. Today, Tolstoy's personal diaries, fictional works, and religious teachings give readers insight into his grappling with morality, death, and meaning.

On *War and Peace*

Many critics regard Tolstoy's *War and Peace* as the greatest literary work of all time. This masterpiece is considered at once a work of historical fiction, philosophical literature, a romance, and a war drama. Drawing from extensive research, interviews with veterans, and his own military experience in the Crimea, Tolstoy explores the meaning of war, the accuracy of history, the origin of power, and the state of Russian society through the lens of Napoleon's 1812 campaign in Russia. In his description of the war, Tolstoy emphasizes that scholars wrongfully attribute the movement of history to a few, "powerful" people. Tolstoy argues instead that history is driven by the masses. He writes:

> There are laws directing events, and some of these laws are known to us while we are conscious of others we cannot comprehend. The discovery of these laws in only possible when we have quite abandoned the attempt to find the cause in the will of some one man.

Tolstoy ridicules the idea that military "leaders" actually influence anything. He compared Napoleon to "a child who, holding a couple of straps tied inside a carriage, thinks that he is driving it."

Another prominent theme of the book is the existential dread of death. In the face of death, Tolstoy writes that men discover the meaninglessness of their past values and understand the true meaning of life. This theme is most famously expressed when Prince Andrei, lying feverish and critically wounded on the battlefield, meets Napoleon. Although Napoleon had previously been Prince Andrei's greatest hero, Andrei's near-death experience triggers a spiritual realization about the meaninglessness of the war and of Napoleon himself:

> [Prince Andrei] knew that it was Napoleon—his hero—but at that moment, Napoleon seemed to him such a small, insignificant man compared with what was now happening between his soul and this lofty, infinite sky with clouds racing across it … he only wished that those people would help him and bring him back to life, which seemed so beautiful to him, because he now understood it so differently.

Tolstoy himself struggles with the meaning of life and the dread of death throughout *War and Peace*. It seems that Tolstoy, like Prince Andrei and another character, Pierre Bezukhov, gradually comes to recognize the futility of war and the immense meaning to be found in everyday life.

On Life and Death

In his works, Tolstoy frequently fixates on the themes of seeking the meaning of life and confronting the fear of death. In his renowned *Anna Karenina*, Tolstoy seems chiefly preoccupied with understanding life, while *The Death of Ivan Ilych* is principally a story about dying.

The first line of *Anna Karenina* is perhaps Tolstoy's most well known aphorism: "All happy families resemble one another. Each unhappy family is unhappy in its own way." This line sets the tone for the rest of the novel, which is the intertwined stories of three Russian families during the Russo-Turkish war. Tolstoy's drama is not only a critical examination of Russian society, but also a philosophical exploration of the purpose of life and the ideal of love. Anna Karenina begins the novel as a devoted wife and mother. She leaves her family to pursue a romance with another man and eventually drives herself mad with guilt over her decision. Just as she commits suicide by throwing herself under a train, Anna realizes too late that she had been living for all the wrong things. Though Anna's life ends tragically, the novel ends with Levin's realization that the purpose of his life is to "live for his soul" by finding meaning and fulfillment in his own estate and family.

In contrast to Anna Karenina, Tolstoy's novella, *The Death of Ivan Ilych*, is about the meaning of death. In the story, Ivan Ilych is a middle-aged man suffering from a terminal illness. His dying months are miserable. Ilych is abandoned by his co-workers, ignored by his family, and hardly comforted by his doctors. Only Gerasim, one of Ilych's peasant servants, offers Ilych any compassion or perspective. Though he tries to deny his life's failures, Ilych eventually comes to realize that his entire life had been lived senselessly. The last three days of Ilych's life parallel the agonizing death of Christ. At one point, Ilych pleads, "Why, why do you torment me so horribly?" In his final moments with his family, Ilych finally realizes that he can end his suffering and that of his family by dying. In sudden relief, Ilych breathes his words, "Death is finished. It is no more." With this enigmatic phrase, Tolstoy ends his story.

Religious Works

Tolstoy's later years were nearly entirely characterized by his religious conversion and code of ethics. In his new faith, Tolstoy rejected most of the traditional doctrines of his orthodox upbringing. He disbelieved the doctrine of the Holy Trinity, the existence of miracles, the immortality of the soul, and the divinity of Jesus. Instead, he published his own "corrected" version of the gospels that focused on the moral teachings of the Sermon on the Mount. Tolstoy himself strove to fulfill this new gospel; he abandoned his wealth, denounced all forms of state authority, and lived a life of austerity, abstinence, and self-discipline. Forsaking the church of his birth and the approval of his loved ones, Tolstoy advanced his new worldview through his many religious publications. Tolstoy documented his previous spiritual struggles in *Confession* (1882). He followed this work with *What I Believe* (1884), *What Then Must We Do?* (1886), *On Life* (1887), and *The Kingdom of God is Within You* (1893). Through his religious works, Tolstoy gained a large following of disciples from around the world. This movement came to be called "Tolstoyism," and its doctrines emphasized poverty, charity, and hard manual work.

Nikki Brandon, 2016
Julianne Swayze, 2016

RICHARD DEDEKIND, 1831–1916, *Infinitely Important Mathematician*

> " That which is provable, ought not to be believed in science without proof.
> —*Was sind und was sollen die Zahlen?*

- Was born into a family with three siblings in Brunswick, Germany, where he would stay for most of his life
- Studied at a local technical university and then the University of Göttingen, with Carl Gauss, the famous mathematician, as his doctoral advisor

- Became good friends with Riemann, Gauss, Cantor, and Dirichlet, among others
- Made major contributions to mathematics, mostly in the fields of number theory and abstract algebra
- Created a way to define the real numbers, through his Dedekind cut
- Invented the first precise definition for infinity, the set similar to a subset of itself
- Became a professor at Brunswick (after two positions at Göttingen and Zurich), where he stayed for the rest of his life
- Died in 1916, 20 years after his retirement and an astonishing mathematical career

Key Works

Stetigkeit und irrationale Zahlen, 1872
Was sind und was sollen die Zahlen? 1888

Biography

Richard Dedekind was born on October 6, 1831, in Brunswick, Germany, to a family with three siblings. He lived in Brunswick for most of his life. After attending primary and secondary school in the city, he studied at the local technical university for two years until his transfer to the University of Göttingen. The accepted hub for scientific research in Europe at the time, Göttingen was where Dedekind met his doctoral teacher, Carl Gauss, one of the best mathematicians of all time. Under Gauss, Dedekind wrote both his doctoral thesis on mathematics by 1852, and the customary second thesis, called *Habilitation*, by 1854. *Habilitation* was written alongside Bernhard Riemann, the rising mathematics star of the time and his good friend. After his graduation, Dedekind stayed at the University for another four years as an unsalaried lecturer, where he met and became friends with P.G. Lejeune-Dirichlet. Later in his life, Dedekind edited and reviewed all three of these mathematicians' works. In 1858, he moved to Zurich, Switzerland, where he took his first salaried position at the Polytechnic there, one he held for only four years before moving back to Brunswick. From 1862 until his retirement in 1896, Dedekind held a professorship at the local university, staying in Brunswick for the rest of his life. Near the end of his career, he published the majority of his work, causing him to come into contact with many important mathematicians of the time, including Georg Cantor and Leopold Kronecker.

Number Theory

Dedekind made a variety of contributions to mathematics, mostly in the field of number theory. He invented another way to define rational real numbers, a problem mathematicians had attempted to solve for centuries. In the Dedekind cut, one picks an arbitrary real number, irrational or rational, and then defines the remaining numbers in an ordered set, relative to this "cut." So, in his example, one can pick the number $\sqrt{2}$, an irrational number, and then define every rational number relative to it: $(-\infty, \sqrt{2}) \cup (\sqrt{2}, \infty)$, in standard set notation. This means that all the rational numbers went from negative infinity up to, but not including, the square root of 2, as well as from the square root of 2, exclusive, to positive infinity. This same method can then be used with a cut of a rational number, like 5, 7/3, or -4.8, which would then partition the real numbers in the same way. This time, however, the latter set (the one that in the previous example was from the square root of 2 to infinity) would include said "cut," such as 5. To non-mathematicians, this system seems rather pointless, as almost everyone intuitively knows what real numbers are, but it was more useful in an abstract sense. Since some cuts can be made from irrational numbers, such as the square root of 2, with the resulting set $(-\infty, \sqrt{2}) \cup (\sqrt{2},$

∞), still representing every rational number, it proves that the rational numbers are not continuous. In other words, since one can partition the set of all real numbers into two parts, the number that splits the two sections cannot be a part of either group. This number, therefore, causes the set of all rational numbers to be split at every irrational number.

Dedekind also made a major contribution relative to the properties of infinite sets. He defined an infinite set (in fact, he gave the first definition for it), as a set that is similar to its own subset. Similarity, as Dedekind explained it, was a property equivalent to one-to-one correspondence today. In other words, if within some set of numbers every number has one and only one "partner" in another set, then it is similar. For example, the equation $y = x$. For any and every value of y, there is exactly one value of x that corresponds to it. The value $y = 3$ will correspond to only $x = 3$, and vice versa. A subset, also, is a set that is a part of another set, such as the set of all numbers from 1 to 100, and the set of all numbers from 50 to 60. Every number within the latter set is also within the former set, but there are also numbers within the former set that are not in the latter set. The latter set, then, is a subset of the former set. Therefore, if somehow there is a set that has a one-to-one correspondence with a subset of itself, both sets are infinitely big. The set of every natural number (1, 2, 3, …) is similar to the subset of every natural number that is also a square (1, 4, 9, …), because there is only one natural number that can be squared to result in 1 or 4 or 9, for example. Therefore, both the set of every natural number and the set of every natural square are infinitely large.

McCarthy Nolan, 2016

WILHELM WUNDT, 1832–1920, *Father of Experimental Psychology*

" The more we are inclined today, and rightly, to demand that experience shall have an influence on philosophy, so much the more is it in place to emphasize that precisely in our time philosophy must assert its old influence among the empirical sciences.
—Chair of Philosophy Inaugural Address at Leipzig

- Taught physiology/philosophy at the University of Leipzig
- Founded experimental psychology and Völkerpsychologie
- Established the first recognized experimental psychology laboratory, in which students from all over the world worked and studied
- Combined physiological examination with psychology theory to revolutionize the study of human behavior
- Believed that "the exact description of consciousness is the sole aim of experimental psychology"
- Spent the last 20 years of his life writing a 10-volume work on the cultural influences on psychology

Key Works

Lectures on Human and Animal Psychology, 1863
Principles of Physiological Psychology, 1873
Outlines of Psychology, 1896
Völkerpsychologie (Elements of Folk Psychology), 1900–1920

Biography

Wilhelm Max Wundt was born on August 16, 1832, near the lively port city of Mannheim, Germany, but he grew up in the smaller, more tranquil village of Heidelsheim. Most of Wundt's childhood was spent in solitude. he was not very social with his peers, spending most of his time with older, wiser people who would challenge him intellectually. His relationship with his tutor and mentor, Friedrich Müller, was closer to a father-son relationship than his relationship with his actual father. There was relational disconnect in his home life, as well as pressure to continue the family practice of medicine.

As a young adult, he struggled with finding his place in school and, unable to handle boarding school, eventually became a troubled teen. Wundt's mother, in an attempt to give him a second chance, moved her son to a relative's house so that he could attend a better-suited school. Later, to his surprise, he was accepted to the University of Heidelberg. In university, Wundt studied mathematics and science with a private tutor, as he needed extra help due to his less-than-sufficient grades in preparatory school. Because of his professors and influences in university, Wundt became enthusiastic about chemistry, although he remained on the medical track. Wundt was never fully satisfied with his medical pursuits, yet continued anyway. After graduating, he worked in a local city hospital, seeing traumatic wounds, injuries, and illnesses. He was exposed not only to physical trauma, but also to the patients' psychological "wounds," which intrigued him. He opted to further explore the psychological facets of the medical world. Leaving the hospital, Wundt taught at the University of Heidelberg. He started as an assistant and apprentice of the notable Herman von Helmholtz who had shown that many aspects of conscious sensation and perception could be accounted for via mechanistic analysis of the physiological systems involved in seeing and hearing. During this time, Wundt's first writings were published, one of them being *Contributions to the Theory of Sensory Perception*.

In 1872, Wundt married Sophie Mau, and they had one daughter. In 1875, he accepted an offer from the University of Leipzig. There, he instituted an experimental psychology lab which became a thriving, world-renowned center for research and study. Wundt's revolutionary theories and mixture of anatomical, psychological, and philosophical concepts inspired the future of psychology as a science. International scholars came to Wundt's lab for study, research and observation. He wrote many books based on his research, including the very first textbook relevant to experimental psychology. Towards the end of his life, Wundt shifted his research methods, and began focusing on the cultural and sociological aspects of psychology because he recognized that not all human functions could be observed scientifically. He wrote the 10-volume edition of *Völkerpsychologie* during the last 20 years of his life, and finished his autobiography in 1920, not long before he died.

Consciousness and Introspection: Experimental Psychology

Wundt developed the theory that every living organism has a level of consciousness; therefore, every organism's action or motivation is a result of physiological and psychological stimuli, and these mental occurrences can be measured. For Wundt, the ultimate goal of studying the relationship between physiological functions and human behaviors was to understand human consciousness, and to understand human consciousness and the mental processes that composed its elements, he used the psychological tool of introspection.

A biography of Wilhelm Wundt says that, "Wundt made the point that psychology, before tackling metaphysical problems, should start by trying to understand the simplest experiences, and that this should be done using the methods of physiology." Therefore, Wundt's method was to observe the elements and senses individually in the laboratory based on a subject's reactions to differing circumstances. Wundt trained all of his experimental subjects in the introspective way of thinking before testing, and then exposed them to standard stimuli (such as a metronome or light), and asked them to report their sensations. The results of these psychological experiments enabled him able to break down consciousness into three categories: representations, willing, and feeling. These are the three ways Wundt believed one can be aware of and connected to the world. "Representations" signify visual perceptions including imagining and seeing. The "willing" category of consciousness refers to how the mind interacts with the surrounding world, and it involves desires, decisions, and details. Finally, the third category, "feeling," can be measured through physical reactions such as relaxation, tension, and excitement in experiments. The Stanford Encyclopedia of Philosophy describes the fundamental idea of experimental psychology as the study of the way the exterior world affects the inner being. By combining the understanding of physical, observable reactions and exercising introspection, Wundt was able to synthesize human consciousness more fully than ever before.

Social Analysis: Völkerpsychologie

A less recognized, but nonetheless significant, portion of Wundt's work was his focus on the cultural influences and expressions of psychology: religion, language, myths, history, art, laws, and customs. Although the former portion of his career was methodically and experimentally based, according to Thomson Gale in *Psychologists and Their Theories for Students*,

> He did not believe that his experimental methods were applicable to most areas of psychology. This shift in direction returned him to his first loves of literature, arts, and the ritualistic practices common among various ethnic and cultural groups that he believed revealed the true essences of cultural psychology.

Wundt recognized in particular that a fundamental area of consciousness unique to humans is the elevated ability to communicate. This fascination with language and how a person's language might reveal many aspects of his psychological make-up triggered a research topic of "psycholinguistics." Wundt primarily posed this idea, which ignited interest for future studies of higher mental processes such as language. Wundt's vision was that understanding the development of such mental processes could lead to understanding the framework for a better society.

Elise Kemp, 2016

DMITRI MENDELEEV, 1834–1907, *Father of the Periodic Table*

> It is the function of science to discover the existence of a general reign of order in nature and to find the causes governing this order. And this refers in equal measure to the relations of man—social and political—and to the entire universe as a whole.
> —*Mendeleev on the Periodic Law: Selected Writings, 1869–1905*

- Developed the periodic table, which organized known chemical elements
- Had element 101, "Mendelevium," named for him
- Taught Chemistry as a professor at the Technological Institute and University of St. Petersburg

- Developed the Periodic Law that says when elements are arranged in ascending order, there exists a recurrence of chemical and physical properties
- Anticipated the discovery of gallium, scandium, and germanium
- Wrote *Principles in Chemistry*, a classic textbook
- Invented the spectroscope and pyrocollodion, founded the first oil refinery in Russia, and introduced the metric system to Russia

Key Works

A Discourse on the Combination of Alcohol and Water, 1865
The Dependence between the Properties of the Atomic Weights of the Elements, 1869
The Principles of Chemistry, 2 vol., 1871

Biography

Dmitri Ivanovich Mendeleev had a challenging upbringing in Tobolsk in western Siberia. He was the youngest of 14–17 children (records are uncertain), whose father became blind and lost his job. When he was 16, his mother lost her income when the glassoworks she managed burned down, and his father died of tuberculosis. Fortunately, Mendeleev's mother was committed to his education and took him to Central Pedagogical Institute in St. Petersburg. He did well and continued in graduate study in chemistry. He became a professor of chemistry and later Director of the Bureau of Weights and Measures. Mendeleev married twice and had six children. At his funeral in 1907, his students carried a large copy of the periodic table to honor his achievements.

Known for developing the periodic table, Mendeleev was not the first scientist to try to classify the elements. Before Mendeleev, that is before 1860, Stanislao Cannizzaro discovered how to calculate atomic weights using vapor density, which allowed scientists to classify the elements. Mendeleev expanded on Cannizzaro's work, making a small two-dimensional grid in 1868. From this he determined the larger pattern of periodicity for the elements, a periodic law. In 1869, Mendeleev arranged all the known 65 elements in a table and revised it until 1871 to a chunky rectangle with intersecting groups and periods. He created the chart putting the elements in order of atomic weight, then organized the chart to place elements with similar chemical properties "periodically" in vertical columns. The rows were "periods." This table was a standard in every textbook, lecture room and museum for a century.

Mendeleev's Periodic Table

Mendeleev reserved blanks in the table for unknown elements, feeling confident that one could predict them by studying the elements around the space. In this way he saw the discovery of gallium become part of the chart, and then scandium and germanium. In 1890, the inert gases were discovered and clearly formed a precise periodic group. So Mendeleev added a Group 0 because the gases have a valency of zero. During this time, Mendeleev was an important scientist throughout Russia, well known for writing the popular chemistry text *The Principles of Chemistry*.

Scientists continued to build their understanding of the elements after Mendeleev's death. Ernest Rutherford realized that the atom is structured like a tiny solar system with a nucleus surrounded by weightless electrons. Bohr and Rutherford, too, contributed to the Periodic Table by confirming it used the "invisible world of chemical atoms." Their electronic table is a replica of Mendeleev's table that had been based on chemical grounds.

Mendeleev received international recognition for his contributions to the field of chemistry, including honorary awards from Oxford and Cambridge, and a medal from the Royal Society of London. Element 101 was named "Mendelevium," and a crater on the moon was named Mendeleev, both in his honor.

MARK TWAIN, 1835–1910, *The Lincoln of American Literature*

> " Now I can only pray that there may be a God—and a heaven—or something better.
> —*The Autobiography of Mark Twain*

- Was a Missouri-born journalist, humorist, and writer whose adventures throughout the United States and Europe provided ample material for his creative works
- Used biting wit and venomous sarcasm to humorously illustrate the iniquities, cruelties, and suffering of human life
- Is typically classified as a realist

- Captured the wide variety of dialects found throughout 19th-century United States, contributing to the creation of a distinctly American literary style
- Believed that people were doomed to moral failure, and he resented God for having created man with immoral impulses while demanding his moral uprightness
- Disdained the hypocrisy and impracticality of religion and other sources of morality
- Thought that man was essentially a machine, his thoughts and behaviors determined according to his biology and external influences
- Used the antics of the title character in *Huckleberry Finn* to satirically demonstrate the injustice and deception of societal mores, in particular slavery and racism, and the individual's inability to truly escape them
- Gained fame as "the father of American literature"

Key Works

Roughing It, 1872
The Gilded Age: A Tale of Today, 1873
The Adventures of Tom Sawyer, 1876
The Prince and the Pauper, 1881
Life on the Mississippi, 1883
Adventures of Huckleberry Finn, 1884
A Connecticut Yankee in King Arthur's Court, 1889
Autobiography of Mark Twain, 2010

Biography

Without a doubt, the works of Mark Twain rank amongst the very best in American literature. Born Samuel Langhorne Clemens in Florida, Missouri, Twain grew up in the nearby town of Hannibal. After the untimely death of his stern and professionally unsuccessful father, Twain's formal education was cut short, and he bounced around various occupations and enterprises in his early life. In the spring of 1857, while on his way down the Mississippi towards South America, he met Horace Bixby, a steamboat captain, for whom he served as an apprentice over the next two years. Sailing up and down the Mississippi, Twain developed an acute understanding of the importance of the river as an American economic and cultural lifeline, an experience that provided ample material for his creative works. Joining a Confederate militia during the Civil War, Twain saw no combat and eventually left for the Nevada gold rush. "Speculation fever" proved unfruitful, but he eked out a living by submitting humor pieces to a nearby newspaper, adopting the pen name "Mark Twain," a reference to an expression frequently used by riverboat crews to indicate a given location's depth and navigability.

Twain's literary career took off when he returned home, with the publishing of "The Celebrated Jumping Frog of Calaveras County." In 1867, he took a long tour of Europe and the Middle East, and the satirical and sarcastic letters he penned during his voyage won him wide popularity and acclaim on both sides of the Atlantic. Twain married in 1870 and settled with his new wife in Hartford, Connecticut, where he wrote a memoir of his travels out west entitled *Roughing It*, followed by other novels and essays in a wide variety of genres, including *The Gilded Age, The Prince and the Pauper, Life on the Mississippi, The Adventures of Tom Sawyer*, and his most famous work, *Adventures of Huckleberry Finn*.

The latter portion of Twain's career witnessed a sharp change in his humor, from charming burlesque to "venomous satire." His published works, particularly *A Connecticut Yankee in King Arthur's Court*, began to take on a more socially critical tone, a trend that was not well received by the public in America or Europe. His finances also soured and, during a series of European lecture tours he took to bolster his economic position, his favorite daughter died at the age of 24. Twain's other daughter also fell ill, as did his wife, who remained weak and bedridden for several years before dying of cardiac disease. As a result, Twain fell into a "fatalistic despair" that began to infect his work, and his writing became increasingly pessimistic and bitter.

Twain lived his final decade in New York City, where he became a socialite and a spokesman for the Progressive Movement. His last publications were mostly attacks on the work of others and pessimistic in nature, particularly the essay *What Is Man?*. Twain's last few years were plagued with poor health and, after dictating a long, meandering, and rancorous autobiography, he suffered a heart attack and died in Redding, Connecticut, in 1910.

Twain's Sarcastic and Satirical Humor

Twain's most beloved literary trait is his humor, which pervades the vast majority of his writing and has made him one of the most distinctive voices in American literature. His early short stories feature a "wild, extravagant, masculine humor typical of the western frontier," which he adopted from the folk tales and jests that surrounded him during his time in Nevada and California. As his career progressed, Twain developed a highly realistic sense of satire that consistently targeted gentility, elitism, and pomposity, though his "merciless" mockery was "always intended to reveal the foibles and follies of human nature and the human tendency to mistreat one another." The deterioration of Twain's personal life, beginning with the collapse of his finances and the death of his daughter, led to a darkening of his sense of humor that pervades his later writing. His sometimes prickly bitterness aside, however, the later Twain is just as perceptive and witty as the Twain of *Roughing It* and *Huckleberry Finn*, and on politics and social issues, perhaps even more so.

The Complex Realism of Twain's Fiction

Twain is typically categorized as a literary "realist," an author who rejects the heavily idealized presentation of romantic work in favor of "realistic" depictions of everyday, commonplace society as it truly is. The humor of Twain's work relies in large part on the accuracy of his illustration of late-19th-century American life, for without this attention to the "color, the relief, the expression, the surface, the substance of the human spectacle," his socially conscious, mocking sense of humor would lose both focus and relevance, according to Tom Quirk in "The Realism of Huckleberry Finn."

This attention to realistic detail does not, however, preclude Twain's narratives from inconsistency or even absurdity of plot. As Roger Lathbury notes, "any and all of the events recorded [in *Huckleberry Finn*] conceivably could have happened along the Mississippi ... but they indicate no definite narrative direction," and sometimes border on inconceivable. For example, events in *Huckleberry Finn* often seem to have a just-so quality. A long dormant feud roars to life a few days after Huck arrives on the plantation; of all of the small farms in Arkansas, Jim and Huck wind up on the one owned by Tom Sawyer's aunt and uncle. Nonetheless, Twain's great strength lies in his ability to humorously, if sometimes hyperbolically, capture the spirit of the richly varied America in which he lived. Twain's "attachment to the announced principles of literary realism" may be "tenuous at best," but at the very least, his approach of mocking the pretensions and iniquities of the world required a certain realism, a certain "enchantment," a certain "atmosphere ... too pleasing, too hypnotic, to permit skepticism."

Twain's Ear for Folk Idiom

The success of Twain's humor is in large part a result of his genius for authentically capturing the wide variety of speech patterns found throughout the 19th-century United States. Much like Charles Dickens, Twain had a masterful ear for dialect, and his ability to articulate on the page the colloquialisms and mannerisms of various social, economic, and regional subcultures lends a sense of realistic plausibility to his humor. In *Huckleberry Finn*, a text populated by characters as richly textured as Jim, the King and the Duke, and Pap, Twain is credited as having "raised the rendition of native dialect and idiom, among both whites and blacks, to a high art," providing the world with the first authentically American piece of literature. The readers of the post–Civil War period discovered new enjoyment in listening to native voices with accents different from their own, and Twain's fresh and unique idiomatic ingenuity allowed the writer to capitalize on this newfound fascination. Twain's skill in engagingly rendering the vernacular of the countryside has influenced every subsequent literary generation in the United States, but no author before or after Twain has been able to so authentically capture on the page the distinctively American, democratic "poetry of the common people."

Twain's Religion and the Human Machine

Twain's pessimism regarding the nature of man and the future of society does not lie far beneath the humorous surface of his work. Throughout his life, but particularly after his personal and financial calamities of the 1890s, Twain was "disgusted with his fellow humans and found the world intolerable." His disdain was particularly acute for traditional morality and religion, which he found odiously hypocritical and impractical. As an unorthodox Calvinist, Twain "hated God for his malice toward humanity, especially his duplicity in commanding humans to be moral, when he had predestined them to be as they were, and in urging humans to seek salvation, when he had predestined most of them to Hell."

To Twain, man was "the butt of God's rather grim, practical joke or hoax ... preprogrammed to fail from the beginning of creation by a Catch-22 system." This harsh predestination Twain saw "repeated in nature, history, society, and individual human beings," and his writings frequently deal with issues of determinism. Just as he is predestined theologically, man, according to Twain, is predestined morally and behaviorally, unable to completely resist or defy the "constraints of social convention," in particular racism, classism, and the delusional hypocrisy of religion.

Twain articulates this worldview in a Socratic-style dialogue entitled *What Is Man?* In it, an old man and a young man debate human nature and the self-gratifying impulses that determine thought and behavior. They arrive at the cynical conclusion, consistent with Twain's unorthodox but still quasi-Calvinist worldview, that man is an "impersonal machine" which owes its existence and its nature to its "MAKE, and to the INFLUENCES brought to bear upon it by his heredities, his habitat, his associations." Regarding the human machine and the notion of free will, Twain's Old Man—a fitting metonym for the elderly Twain himself—declares that "not only did [you] not make that machinery yourself, but you have NOT EVEN ANY COMMAND OVER IT." This shows Twain's decidedly skeptical worldview, and showcases his doubt about humanity's wisdom and the possibility of social progress.

Adventures of Huckleberry Finn: Twain's Magnum Opus

Twain's most famous novel, *Adventures of Huckleberry Finn*, is often praised as an artful examination of the determinism Twain explores in *What Is Man?* The novel's title character is frequently preoccupied with the complicated clash between social norms and individual expressions of morality. The overcoming of racial, religious, and regional stereotypes in favor of "practical" morality is a common theme threading together the various narratives that make up the text, as is a general skepticism for traditional sources of authority, among them one's elders, the Bible, and even one's conscience as cultivated by society.

The antics of Huck are humorous and satirical, but they are masterfully designed to demonstrate the "injustice and deception" of societal mores, in particular slavery and racism, and the individual's inability to really escape them. For Twain, *Huckleberry Finn* and similar writings were to be devoted to "describing existence as he saw it in the forlorn hope that [it] could expose its cruelty" and impracticality. Twain's articulation of his worldview is often just beneath the surface in *Huckleberry Finn*. His devotion to pragmatism in place of traditional morality comes through in Huck's cheeky response to a lesson from Scripture, one that summarily but unintentionally dismisses the epistemological core of Christianity: "Moses had been dead a considerable long time; so then I didn't care no more about him, because I don't take no stock in dead people." Given his insistence that "None of us can be as great as God, but any of us can be as good," it is likely that Twain himself would agree.

Brandon Martinez, researcher

HENRY BROOKS ADAMS, 1838–1918, *America's First Modern Historian*

> " Society in America was always trying, almost as blindly as an earthworm, to realize and understand itself, to catch up with its own head, and to twist about in search of its tail. Society offered the profile of a long, straggling caravan, stretching loosely toward the prairies, its few score of leaders far in advance and its millions of immigrants, Negroes, and Indians far in the rear, somewhere in archaic time.
> —*The Education of Henry Adams: An Autobiography*

- Was descended from two American presidents, John Adams and John Quincy Adams
- Graduated from Harvard University in 1858 and attended law school in Berlin until 1860
- Served as secretary to his father, appointed Minister to Great Britain by Abraham Lincoln
- Worked as a political journalist in Washington DC, especially focusing on the corruption of the Grant administration
- Served as an assistant professor of history at Harvard and the editor of *North American Review*
- Viewed education skeptically; in his experience, it was of no value
- Sought to define history through analyzing individual emotions and opinions
- Grew increasingly cynical and pessimistic in his writings

Key Works
Democracy: An American Novel, 1880
Esther: A Novel, 1884
History of the United States of America, 1888
Mont-Saint-Michel and Chartres, 1904
The Education of Henry Adams: An Autobiography, 1908

Biography

Henry Brooks Adams was born in 1838 to an American family with a prestigious legacy and great wealth. Both his great-grandfather and grandfather were American Presidents, and his father was a prominent politician. After completing his studies at Harvard, Adams decided to study law at the University of Berlin in 1858. He then joined his father in London and became his secretary. His father had transitioned from being a congressman to the Minister of England during the American Civil War. Upon his return to the states, Adams worked as a journalist in Washington DC, where he became disillusioned with the scandals of Washington politics. The 1870s found Adams returning to his alma mater as an assistant professor of history while also serving as an editor for the *North American Review*. In the decade to follow, Adams experienced both tragedy and success: his wife committed suicide in 1885, and he completed his most extensive work, the nine-volume *History of the United States of America* in 1888. He lived in solitude after retiring from his post at Harvard, and spent most of his time researching, traveling, and writing. Near the end of his life, Adams completed his best-known work, *The Education of Henry Adams, an Autobiography*. The book was originally meant to be given only to friends, but was widely published after his death in 1918.

Writings on History, Education, and Technology

In his nine-volume *History of the United States of America*, Adams compiled research that helped readers understand the beginnings of the nation. He devoted a large portion of his *History* to the presidencies of Jefferson and Madison, focusing on their foreign policy towards Europe. While his method was primarily scientific, he incorporated a form of narrative, which is one of the most attractive characteristics of his work. His autobiography, *The Education of Henry Adams*, used some of the same scientific methods that lent credibility to his larger *History*, but it also included his social criticisms more blatantly. One of his main frustrations concerned education, and he boldly claimed that he had learned nothing from his studies at Harvard. From Adams's perspective, his education had failed to prepare him for the Gilded and Industrial Ages. As a result, he was deeply frustrated by the rise of technology, perceiving that it would result only in chaos and dysfunction. He wrote that man "simply absorbs and complicates forces." Adams warned that within the rise of technology loomed "the ultimate possibility of man's self-destruction." The changes around him led Adams to conclude that "society in America was always trying, almost as blindly as an earthworm, to realize and understand itself."

Adams's works each reflect different periods in his life. His *History* was written at a time when he was undoubtedly critical, but somehow optimistic about the future. His autobiography, written after his wife's suicide, reveals his deep pessimism and despair about the fate of humankind. Still, this did not detract from his significance, and he was eventually called "America's first modern Historian."

Legacy

Often considered a philosopher in his journalism and historical writings, Henry Brooks Adams left a mark on American and world history through the publication of his two major works—*History of the United States of America* and *The Education of Henry Adams: An Autobiography*. In some ways, Adams's legacy survives through his narrative style of documentation joined with social commentary, which helped readers to better understand the early stages of the United States.

Nate Kosirog, faculty
Nathaniel Whatmore, 2015

CHARLES SANDERS PEIRCE, 1839–1914, *The Logical Pragmatist*

" All nature abounds in proofs of other influences than merely mechanical action, even in the physical world.

—Pragmatism and Pragmaticism

- Graduated from Harvard University with degrees in Philosophy and Chemistry
- Worked as a scientist, as Professor of Logic in Mathematics at Johns Hopkins University, and at the US Coast and Geodetic Survey and the astronomical observatory at Harvard
- Teetered on the brink of poverty
- Separated his work into three groups—cosmology (matter), psychology (mind), and theology (God)—because of the extensive subject matter and quantity of his writing
- Developed the Theory of Signs, central to his peculiar version of idealism
- Was highly critical of Kant's and Hegel's logic; being primarily a logician, he regarding both as sloppy; nevertheless, in his mature thinking he must clearly be classed among the large group of neo-Hegelians that dominated late 19th and early 20th century Anglo-American philosophy
- Regarded the world of appearances (which he called "the phaneron") as a complex collection of "signs" (properties, events, laws), each sign existing in a three-part relation with an object represented by the sign and a subject or mental apprehension of the sign; and this world of signs is both strictly logical/ideal and continually evolving—hence the Hegelianism
- Coined his own explanation of pragmatism regarding things and meaning: "what a thing means is simply what habits it involves," which is to say how a thing is habitually used determines what its sign represents, i.e., there are no "objectively" true meanings in the world, only typical uses or interpretations

Key Works

"On a New List of Categories," 1867
The Architecture of Theories, 1891
The Law of Mind, 1892
Pragmatism and Pragmaticism, 1903
A Neglected Argument for the Reality of God, 1908

Biography

Charles Sanders Peirce was born September 10, 1839, in Cambridge, Massachusetts. His father was a professor of mathematics at Harvard (many believe that he was integral to the building and success of the program), one of the founders and director of the US Coast and Geodetic Society, and a founder of the Smithsonian Institution. Charles was the second of his parents' five children, and his lifelong love of reason and logic began when he was only 12, when he read Immanuel Kant's *Critique of Pure Reason*. He graduated from Harvard in 1859 after studying philosophy, and received his Masters from Harvard in 1862. During this time he began a lifelong friendship with philosopher and psychologist William James.

Although Peirce desired to devote his life to the study and research of logic, his father firmly believed that one could not make a living as a research logician. Therefore, from 1859 to 1891 he worked as a scientist for the US Coast and Geodetic Survey. He married Melusina Fay and worked a second job from 1879 to 1884 teaching logic at the Department of Mathematics at Johns Hopkins University. However, this teaching job was suddenly terminated due to his cohabiting with a gypsy, Juliette Annette Froissy, before divorcing his wife. He waited only six days after divorcing Fay to marry Froissy.

Soon after, his job at the US Coast and Geodetic Survey ended abruptly in 1891 because Congress cut the funding for the program. Because of his chaotic employment, he often lived on the edge of penury, eking out a living doing intellectual odd-jobs and consulting work. He worked at Harvard as an assistant at the astronomical observatory from 1869 to 1872. In 1867, he became a member of the Academy of Arts and Science, and in 1877, he became a member of the National Academy of Sciences.

After his teaching jobs ended, he purchased property in Milford, Pennsylvania where he lived until he died of cancer on April 19, 1914.

Philosophical Ideas

Peirce was a renowned philosopher and logician, writing exhaustively on the subjects of epistemology, scientific method, semiotics, metaphysics, cosmology, ontology, and mathematics. Because his study of philosophy was so extensive and could not be seen as one entity, he divided his work into several sections in order to separate the developments in his thinking.

His first section included his work from 1859–1861, and was the foundation for his later work. During this time, he "derived a threefold ontological classification of all there is into matter (the object of cosmology), mind (the object of psychology), and God (the object of theology)." He separated everything in the world into these three categories in order to better understand them. However, as he created these categories, he realized that they had no correlation, and he sought to connect the three ideas in some way.

With the second section, which he worked on from 1866–1870, he set out to connect his three categories of mind, matter, and God. To do this, he formulated his Theory of Signs, in which he concluded that everything in the world represented a sign. Peirce states, "I define a sign as anything which is so determined by something else, called its Object, and so determines an effect upon a person." This could be anything from someone waving hello, to the factors that affect where a person lives. He "depicted thinking as essentially the interplay of signs, generalizing even that the individual human mind is a sign." Using this thinking, he connected his three ontological categories by specifying what each signified. His first section, Matter, he describes as anything that falls under an emotional experience. His second part of his system, Mind, he shows is anything that is a practical experience. Mind and logic go hand in hand. His God section is any intellectual experience, as he spent time researching how people were able to comprehend the concept of God. After he made these distinctions, Peirce referred to these three categories as the It (the sense world), the Thou (the mental world), and the I (the abstract world). Peirce's distinctions in these categories allowed him to further his philosophical studies.

The third section, which he worked on from 1870–1889, included his famous work on pragmatism. Although Peirce did not popularize the word, he is credited with coining the term "pragmatism." After studying Kant's definition of pragmatism, he created what he called his pragmatic theory of meaning. This theory states that "what the concept of an object means is simply the set of all habits involving that object." This means that instead of defining an object only in terms of its innate, visual qualities, Peirce also took into account its interaction with other objects. This was a new way of thinking for his time, and he became famous for creating this definition of pragmatism.

Peirce spent the rest of his philosophical career studying in the field of logic, furthering his key ideas of pragmatism, and cementing his ontological system. The majority of his work was not published before he died, but his countless papers were condensed and eventually published in several volumes as *The Collected Works of Charles Peirce* after his death. He is still known today for his work on his system and his refined definition of pragmatism.

Jack Beebe, 2012
McCarthy Nolan, 2016
Daren Jonescu, advisor

WILLIAM SUMNER, 1840–1910, *Lover of Free Trade*

> " The greatest folly of which a man can be capable ... is to sit down with a slate and pencil to plan out a new social world.
> —"Proceedings of the First American Congress of Liberal Religious Societies"

- Coined the now popular economic term "Folkways"
- Spent his career as a sociologist at Yale, although he studied for the Episcopal ministry
- Was an enthusiastic advocate for laissez-faire economics
- Is known as a Social-Darwinist, but this does not accurately reflect his views

Key Works

The Forgotten Man, 1876
What Social Classes Owe to Each Other, 1883
Folkways, 1906

Biography

William Graham Sumner was born in New Jersey in 1840 to recent British immigrants. He graduated high school in Hartford, and went on to attend Yale University with a full academic scholarship. He graduated in 1863 and left for England, Germany, and Switzerland to refine his knowledge and practice of Episcopal ministry, and worked as a minister from 1868–1872. He returned to the United States when he found that Episcopal ministry "conflicted with his wider interests." In 1872, he was offered the chair of political and social science at Yale University, and gladly accepted. Upon returning to Yale as a professor of political economy, he acquired popularity as a teacher, but it was his work in social development that made him well known among his peers. He taught at Yale until 1883, when he took leave due to a decline in his health. Sumner returned to teaching in 1899, and became Vice President of the Anti-Imperialist League. Throughout his career, he published many books and papers that explained his support of the ideas of "free-market capitalism, minimal government, and individualism." He taught at Yale until his death in 1910.

Folkways

When Sumner transitioned into the study of sociology, he found that there were topics he had previously touched upon in lectures that needed better definition. However, this was a large task and Sumner felt "I could not do justice to it in a chapter of another book." This prompted him to write a treatise, *Folkways*, in order to "introduce [his] own treatment of the 'mores.'" Published in 1906,

Folkways is Sumner's most well known work. He believed that folkways are essentially the habits of a group of people, and studying them is foundational to sociology. In his treatise, Sumner said, "The folkways, at a time, provide for all the needs of life and then and there. They are uniform, universal in the group, imperative, and invariable." He explained that they are not made purposely and they are a societal force. The other term he addresses in *Folkways* is "mores." Sumner considered mores to be the implied moral rules of a society. They are not coordinated by anyone in power, but are unspoken rules that nonetheless pressure the populace into conformity. They force members of society to live accordingly since they are grounded in what that society considers to be morally or ethically right, or at least necessary for proper etiquette.

Classical Liberalism

Sumner argued for nearly absolute individual liberty. Although many think of Sumner as a social Darwinist, embracing the idea that "human society is marked by the same sort of 'struggle for existence' that characterizes the animal world, and that the victors of this struggle emerge according to the rule of 'survival of the fittest,'" he actually believed that this survival of the fittest is a constraint of the world, not a goal that politics should strive for. Some called him cold-hearted for opinions such as, "it would have been better for society and would have involved to pain to them, if [the certain classes of troublesome and bewildered persons] had never been born." However, he argued his policies would protect the "common working people *against* the economic and political 'elite.'" His hero was this "Forgotten Man," as he termed it, an ordinary working man who would work hard for the good of himself and his family and would support the nation.

Sumner was also a proponent of "extreme laissez-faire policy, opposing any governmental actions that obstructed natural economic affairs," including social reform and the harmful monopolies created by labor unions. He tried to say to those with legislative power: "*Laissez-faire* means: Do not meddle; wait and observe. Do not regulate; study. Do not give orders; be teachable. Do not enter upon any rash experiments; be patient until you see how it will work out." He also believed that laws tend to be "rigid, arbitrary, hard to change, dictated by some dogma or ideal, and not such as the development of trade and industry would from time to time call for." Therefore, he opposed large-scale legislation and argued for men and women managing themselves. He was a huge proponent for the gold standard of American currency, or the concept that all of the money printed in America is backed by gold that the government has in the US Treasury, because he believed that it would prevent inflation. He concluded laissez-faire was the best way to create a powerful economy and protect the common working man, his Forgotten Man, from inequity and exploitation.

Caroline Fuschino, 2015
Julianna Swayze, 2016
Alexi Wenger

OLIVER WENDELL HOLMES, JR., 1841–1935, *The Great Dissenter*

" The life of the law has not been logic; it has been experience.

—*The Common Law*

- Was one of the longest serving Supreme Court justices

- Graduated from Harvard, and returned there to teach as a professor in a spot created specifically for him, only to leave and join Massachusetts's judicial branch a few weeks later
- Was the son of Oliver Wendell Holmes Sr., an influential writer
- Earned the title "The Great Dissenter" because of his influential contrarian opinions, which would shape future laws and judicial decisions
- Founded a law school in England as well as multiple firms in America
- Presided over many court cases; rather than his concepts being written in books, the majority of his work and opinions derive from his court cases
- Was a founding member of the Metaphysical Club, a pragmatist society that included Peirce, William James, and other prominent thinkers of the day
- Did not consider himself to be a pragmatic philosopher; however many scholars put him into this category because of his sharp transition from legal formalism to legal realism; for example, he said that:
  - The sovereign's will does not make the law, but rather the judges' interpretation of that will, i.e., the meaning of the government's will is determined by how it is applied by judges
  - A legal duty is merely a man's prediction that certain behavior will lead to punishment by the court, i.e., "duty" is not a natural truth, but defined by what men happen to fear enough to act a certain way

Key Work
The Common Law, 1881

Biography
Wealth and culture ran through Oliver Wendell Holmes Jr's blood. He was born in Boston, Massachusetts in 1841. His father was a successful writer, and his mother, Amelia Lee Jackson, was a well-respected abolitionist. His father's influence in society opened doors both educationally and personally, giving him connections with people like Ralph Waldo Emerson. Holmes's early life was uneventful until his enrollment in Harvard University, which was interrupted by the Civil War. His greatest learning experience was his part in the Civil War, where he received three battle wounds and gained a new outlook on the world. He originally joined as a volunteer, but with rising tensions, he became fully employed and participated in multiple campaigns, leaving the ranks as a colonel. He returned to Harvard and graduated with a law degree. Shortly after, his alma mater hired him as a professor, but a few weeks later he left the position to become a state justice. He held this position until Theodore Roosevelt nominated him to the Supreme Court. As a Supreme Court Justice, Holmes made many controversial decisions that differentiated him from the other justices. Justice Holmes held "firmly to his faith in the process of trial and error." This, and his unprecedented work ethic, led to his fame in the United States and abroad.

Legal Realism
With the turn of the century, Holmes's service as a Supreme Court justice began. His staunch, skeptical jurisprudence marked a new strain of thought within the Unites States judiciary branch, and his dissenting opinions and writings in *The Common Law* heralded a new era of legal theory. Holmes's pragmatic legal realism manifested because he believed that law and its purpose evolve as culture changes. He pulled from the depths of his own experiences, especially the Civil War. In *The Common*

Law, Holmes states that "the life of the law has not been logic: it has been experience." He saw the law itself as ever-changing, an evolving state of nature reflecting the ever-changing culture and perspective of its people. This philosophy was also a nod to his perception of natural law. Rather than a moral code binding people to one another by a religious authority, he posited "that men make their own laws." He went on to say, "the common law is not a brooding omnipresence in the sky," but rather, "the law is the witness and external deposit of our moral life. Its history is the history of the moral development of the race." Holmes adored the idea of culture always being in motion. Ideas and perceptions were fluid for him, always changing their shapes. As scholars of his work have stated, "he believed all the world and everything in it to be in a state of transition." Culture is not founded solely on tradition but is also shaped by the experience and perspective of the people living within its social boundaries. Consequently, as this perspective guided Holmes in many of his court cases, he set a precedent of practicing legal realism for the decades to come.

Liberty

Holmes's decisions hinged upon his belief in the Bill of Rights and the Amendments. Rather than a rigid set of statutes, Holmes believed them to be a "framework within which the most significant issues of the day could be determined, addressed, and, with a little patience, quite possibly resolved." The Constitution was a guiding principle. Through this work, Holmes set many precedents related to freedom of speech and unreasonable seizures.

Holmes's most famous cases on the first amendment are *Schenck v. United States* and *Abrams v. Parker*. In both of these cases, Holmes helped outline the extent and limits of freedom of speech. In the first case, *Schenck v. United States*, a socialist was passing out leaflets telling people not to abide by the draft. He was found guilty of "causing and attempting to cause insubordination." The court decided unanimously that he was guilty because of what would later become known as "clear and present danger." Holmes describes the limits of speech:

> Stringent protection of free speech would not protect a man in falsely shouting fire in a theatre and causing a panic. It does not even protect a man from an injunction against uttering words that may have all the effect. The question in every case is whether the words used are used in such circumstances and are of such a nature as to create a clear and present danger that they will bring about the substantive evils that Congress has a right to prevent.

This decision defined the boundaries for freedom of speech for years, yet later, in the *Abrams v. Parker* case, Holmes took a very different approach. His dissenting opinion on the case is known to be "his most passionate defense of free speech." Holmes was adamant that freedom of speech should not easily be given up and that "we should be eternally vigilant against attempts to check the expression of opinions that we loathe and believe to be fraught with death, unless they so imminently threaten immediate interference with the lawful and pressing purposes of the law that an immediate check is required to save the country." He recognized that freedoms, once given up, are not easily gained back.

In *Silverthorne Lumber Co. v. United States*, Holmes coined the phrase "fruit of the poisonous tree." This case set down precedents for the fourth amendment rather than the first. At issue was the police unlawfully seizing evidence and taking pictures of it before returning it. In a previous case, *United States v. Woods*, primary evidence was declared unusable in court if it was received unwarrantedly, but the case didn't rule on information gathered through unlawful seizures. Holmes wrote:

> The essence of a provision forbidding the acquisition of evidence in a certain way is that not merely evidence so acquired shall not be used before the Court but that it shall not be used at all. … If knowledge of them is gained from an independent source they may be proved like any others, but the knowledge gained by the Government's own wrong cannot be used by it in the way proposed.

This decision led to the term "the fruit of the poisonous tree" because any evidence or information gained without a warrant would be inadmissible in court.

Eugenics

Despite his eminence and erudition, Holmes was not perfect. One of his most widely criticized decisions is the *Buck v. Bell* case in 1927. This court decision manifested the common view of eugenics at the time. The Supreme Court ruled (with one dissenting vote) that Carrie Buck, a woman diagnosed with a mental disorder, should be sterilized. Holmes, the majority opinion writer, founds his opinion on the belief that it is best that "instead of waiting to execute degenerate offspring for crime or [to] let them starve for their imbecility" that "society can" and should "prevent those who are manifestly unfit from continuing their kind," even going as far to say that "three generations of imbeciles are enough" in reference to Carrie Buck. This is a dark spot for American culture. Only a decade later, the Nazi party used this case as a reason for killing Jewish ethnic groups.

Jackson Howell, 2015
Daren Jonescu, advisor

WILLIAM JAMES, 1842–1910, *The Father of American Psychology*

> Knowledge about life is one thing; effective occupation of a place in life, with its dynamic currents passing through your being, is another.
> —*The Varieties of Religious Experience*

- Was born into a wealthy New York family in New York City's most luxurious hotel, Astor House
- Engaged in heated family debates at dinner, even with company present
- Received an MD from Harvard, concentrating his studies in physiology
- Taught at Harvard for 35 years, writing his seminal works while there and teaching students like Gertrude Stein and George Santayana
- Wrote his first major work, *Principles of Psychology*, which became a standard text in the field for 70 years and is still widely read
- Treated religion as admirable and necessary, even if empirically false *in The Varieties of Religious Experience*, which he based on the Gifford lectures at the University of Edinburgh
- Laid out the philosophy of Pragmatism in *Pragmatism*, his last major work; he is considered both a founder and a leading voice of the movement

Key Works

The Principles of Psychology, 1890
The Varieties of Religious Experience, 1902

Biography

William James was born to the wealthy James family on January 11, 1842, at Astor House in New York City. The James children were raised in a freethinking home and received a broad education in Europe as well as in the US. His brother, Henry, went on to become a famous novelist. The old saying is that Henry was a novelist who wrote psychology, and William was a psychologist who wrote novels. After briefly training to become a painter, James enrolled at Harvard University in 1861, graduating with an MD in 1869. He struggled with depression throughout the late 1860s and early 1870s before being stabilized by two major life events. In 1872 he began teaching physiology at Harvard, and in 1878 he married Alice Howe Gibbens, who would become the mother to James's four children.

James held his position at Harvard for 35 years, fusing physiology with psychology and philosophy in a trademark way that flattened the differences between disciplines and would be horrifying to a professor in the current climate of university specialization. His concerns were broadly humanistic, and he had profound influence on a number of students, among them Gertrude Stein, the novelist and poet, and George Santayana, a Harvard professor of philosophy and compatriot with James in the pragmatist school of philosophy. While at Harvard, James published *The Principles of Psychology*, a major work in the field that would exert influence for decades.

The Varieties of Religious Experience, based on the Gifford lectures at the University of Edinburgh, is his best-known major work. It presents, in keeping with the family tradition (his father was a follower of the Swedish theologian Emanuel Swedenborg) and James's own inclinations, a hodge-podge view of religious affections that attempts to smooth over the differences between competing faiths. He aims to amalgamate the core of the belief systems and not their particulars. *The Varieties* outlived the typical range of influence for a book of religious reflections, and it continues to be standard fare in the curriculum of psychology majors, often to their chagrin. Before his death in 1910, James published *Pragmatism*, his final major work, and one that did its part to shape the influential philosophical school of Pragmatism, of which James is a figurehead. William James died of heart failure at his summer home in New Hampshire on August 26, 1910. His place in American letters and thought is indisputable, and his philosophy of pragmatism still appeals to many within our multicultural setting.

Pragmatism

James was one of the earliest and most forceful proponents of a philosophical school he called pragmatism. Simply defined in one of his lectures on the topic, the pragmatic method of philosophy "is primarily a method of settling metaphysical disputes that otherwise might be interminable." James goes on to say that the key to philosophical validity is not objective truth but the "practical cash-value" or instrumentality of a particular claim. Therefore, opposing sides in a debate should not come into conflict over their differences, but each should acknowledge that the other receives practical benefits from adhering to their school of thought. By arguing for the contingency of all truth, while simultaneously affirming the dignity and coherence of these contingent truths, James was attempting to avoid the harm that can come from vigorous disagreement. As such, pragmatism acts as "a mediator and reconciler. She has in fact no prejudices whatever. She will entertain any hypothesis, she will consider any evidence."

The concept of God, and other theological claims, is not ruled out of this generous epistemology. Clearly, belief in God has had practical and instrumental value for humans throughout history, and it is outside the purview of pragmatism to condemn what has been "pragmatically so successful." Unlike pure empiricism, pragmatism can accommodate abstractions alongside empirical fact, or can follow both logic and the senses. A purely scientific view of the world—one that takes into account only empirical observations and disparages, for example, religion for its egocentrism—is a false bill of goods. A purely scientific account of the world is a bit like, as James phrases it in *The Varieties of Religious Experience*, being offered "a printed bill of fare as the equivalent of a solid meal." As the word suggests, pragmatist philosophy must also be grounded in action and, indeed, the aim of the philosophy is to inspire one toward action. E. Paul Colella notes, that for the philosopher, "while he cannot avoid some technicalities, he must remain in effective touch with the practical concerns" of his audience. There is an individualist element to such a philosophy as well. Colella notes that one of James's many shifts in the direction of Pragmatism was to "treat the intensely personal experiences of real individuals as philosophically legitimate."

James's influence on the development of pragmatist schools of thought can hardly be overstated. The editors of the *Great Books* series claim that "Pragmatism owes its fame as a movement" to James, and that, moreover, the school of pragmatism is the "most original contribution that the United States has made in philosophy." For James, pragmatism was the proper end of all philosophy. As the great uniter, it has the power, as he tells it in "Philosophical Conceptions & Practical Results," his first major lecture on pragmatism, to "bring theory down to a single point. … It would solve all the antinomies and contradictions, it would let loose all the right impulses and emotions; and everyone on hearing it would say, 'Why, that *is* the truth!—*that* is what I have been believing, that is what I have really been living on this whole time, but I could never find the words for it before.'" Dogs and cats would live together; the lion would lie down with the lamb.

As should be clear, there was a utopian element in James's pragmatism that opens it to the charge of glibness. It is difficult to reduce all human difference—in religion or any other matter—to mere misunderstanding that can be paved over by goodwill. People believe things strongly and often to the precise exclusion of other beliefs. In the end, though, pragmatism has become the defining philosophy of contemporary America. The creed "live and let live," a pragmatic notion in a nice aphorism, essentially defines the individualist ethos of the United States.

Religion

In *The Varieties of Religious Experience*, James demonstrates the theory of pragmatism as it touches on the subject of religion, and fulfills a promise to his religiously curious father to deal in a sustained way with the issue of religion. The lectures are wide-ranging, covering subjects such as "The Reality of the Unseen," "Conversion," and "Mysticism," before culminating in James's own thoughts on the subject in the concluding lecture and the postscript to the text, in which he commends the "pragmatic way of taking religion to be the deeper way."

What exactly constitutes this "pragmatic" view on religion is unfolded throughout his conclusion. For James, the varieties of religious beliefs can be summed up in a few principles: (1) the visible world draws its significance from a spiritual world; (2) union with that spiritual world is our goal; (3) prayer, or communion, with that spiritual world is both possible and the means of entry for the spiritual into the physical; (4) psychologically, religion adds either "lyrical enchantment" or an "appeal to earnestness and heroism" to life; and finally (5) an assurance of ultimate peace, and a directive to love others. James's own religious views, such as they can be discerned, tended toward the syncretic, or blending of beliefs. In his lectures on pragmatism, he credits the method with "unstiffening" our theories. James believed that if he could make people recognize that their rigid belief systems had broad similarities with competing worldviews, then people would be less "stiff" in their understanding of religion.

Utilitarianism

At the heart of James's philosophical pragmatism, and the way in which pragmatism comes to bear on his treatment of religion, is the principle of utility. Utility, and its school of thought, utilitarianism, is a philosophy of action popularized by John Stuart Mill and Jeremy Bentham that argues a proper course of action is the one that provides for the most good and the least harm. James dedicated *Pragmatism* to Mill and was forthright in declaring the similarities between utilitarianism and pragmatism. Trygve Throntveit labels James's utilitarian ethics as "a practical guide to conduct proceeding from an apprehension of the good combined with "an *ideal* of private and public interests converging." It is easy to see how the principle of utility—ethics in action—buttresses James's religious sensibilities, and supports his declaration in *The Varieties of Religious Experience* that it is best for "each man to stay in his own experience, whate'er it be, and for others to tolerate him there."

The inescapable caveat of utilitarianism in the religious sphere is this: to be extended tolerance one must of course be tolerant. In his Gifford lectures, James discusses how to regard those with "over-beliefs," or those who could be called fundamentalists of their faiths. James states that "over-beliefs in various directions are absolutely indispensable, and that we should treat them with tenderness and tolerance, so long as they are not intolerant themselves." Though James never defined what constitutes "intolerance," Throntveit writes that in James's view, "The purpose of ethics was to help people reflect upon, test, and revise their freely embraced ideals to accord with the republican reality of moral life, while also helping them alter that reality to accommodate as many ideals as possible." In other words, all individual beliefs and religious practices are permissible unless they interfere with the beliefs and practices of others. The ultimate aim of this approach is to create a "tolerant" society that maximizes the comfort of as many people as possible.

Toby Coffman, faculty

HENRY JAMES, 1843–1916, *The Psychological Novelist*

> We work in the dark—we do what we can—we give what we have. Our doubt is our passion, and our passion is our task. The rest is the madness of art.
>
> —"The Middle Years"

- Founded and led the literary school of Realism
- Wrote his later works in a style which critics compared to Impressionist painting styles
- Completed 20 novels, 112 stories, 12 plays, and over 3,000 pages of criticism
- Used third person point of view in his novels to experiment with different viewpoints
- Emphasized the difference between who people are and who they express themselves to be
- Received the Order of Merit from King George V in 1916

Key Works

Daisy Miller, 1879
Washington Square, 1881
Portrait of a Lady, 1881
The Bostonians, 1886
The Turn of the Screw, 1898
The Ambassadors, 1903
The Golden Bowl, 1904
The Wings of the Dove, 1909

Biography

Born on April 15, 1843, in New York City, Henry James was immediately thrust into American aristocracy. His father, Henry James Sr, was a follower of philosopher Emanuel Swedenborg and was associated with Henry David Thoreau, Margaret Fuller, and Ralph Waldo Emerson. His older brother, William James, became a well-known philosopher and psychologist, and his sister a published writer. Henry James's privileged upbringing provided for elite education and extensive travel, usually through Europe with his father. When he was 12, he and his family left New York City and moved to Europe. There he was privately tutored in London, Geneva, and Paris.

In 1862, James enrolled in Harvard Law School, where he lasted for one year. Leaving law to focus on his writing, he remained in Cambridge, Massachusetts. In 1865, James's work began appearing in the *Atlantic Monthly*, and many of his writings and criticisms were featured in reviews and journals. After four years, he journeyed back to England, France, and Italy and over time became more and more "disengaged from America," finally moving to London in 1876. Between 1879 and 1882, he wrote his first series, and in 1886 and for the next five years he focused on writing drama. As an unmarried man, he was able to devote himself to what he called the "sacred rage" of his art. In 1909, he suffered from a long nervous illness. Years later he was disturbed by WWI and started working in hospitals and writing for charities, even becoming a British citizen because of his disgust with America's refusal to come to England's aid. In 1915, he had a stroke and came down with pneumonia, dying months later in 1916. Before his death, he received the Order of Merit. Many of his novels, including *The Europeans, The Bostonians, The Golden Bowl, The Wings of the Dove, Washington Square*, and *The Portrait of a Lady*, have been made into movies, which, along with the enduring popularity of the works themselves, keep his ideas alive.

Early James: Old World Meets New

Because Henry James produced so many works, it is easy to see how much he grew both thematically and stylistically. In fact, his works can be categorized into three stages: the early period (1876–1881), characterized by his own life experiences and often centering on an intellectual American in Europe; the middle period (1882–1889), which saw an increase in metaphor and symbolism and a focus on greater social complexities; and the late period (1900–1916), characterized by far more elaborate works and the flourishing of James's literary style. His earlier and later works deal thematically with the difference in cultures, usually through the lens of either American foreigners in Europe or European foreigners in America. James drew from his own life experiences to describe the gap between new world morals and old world knowledge.

Using individual characters to represent whole cultures, James portrays the complex relationship of nations; for example, a recurring motif is that of a naive, innocent girl from young America being taken advantage of by an older, more experienced, and deceitful man from Europe. By creating a character representing the New World and having her innocence corrupted by a deceitful man representing the Old World, James demonstrates that the history he loved in Europe also resulted in corruption. The corruption of innocence through European deception was a major theme in his early and final periods. His works also explores the difference between desire and love; almost all of his main characters who pursue love end up disappointed. While desire lives in one's perception of reality and not reality itself, love is the recognition of truth and the ability to see people for who they are. Perception is a theme that Henry James plays with as well, and since an individual's perception of another can cloud who he or she really is, love is a constant struggle in James's stories.

Later James: The Rise of the Psychological Novel

In this period, Henry James began to move toward an increasingly metaphoric style and opted for subtlety over simplicity. By his final phase, his style had risen to a much higher level of complexity than in previous works. His sentences were marked by long, elaborate imagery and elevated syntax. James also firmly believed in telling stories that readers could relate to and did this through realism in his novels. Nonetheless, he also experimented with perspective and how reality is altered by the perspectives of each character. He used third person point of view, so readers could only see what the characters saw; this allowed readers to experience the confusion in James's characters that results from having limited perspective. This element made Henry James's writing more introspective and personal, and as he grew into this style, he also explored more personal themes. His works often centered on personal relationships and exhibited as much of an interest in the interaction between characters as in the characters themselves. He perfected this structure in the works of his later stage. While themes of love, morality, and class structure of the day still exist in these works, James expressed them through the thoughts of his characters while staying objective as a narrator.

The Paradox of Publicity

According to Henry James's philosophy, everyone has two figures—a public, empty figure, and a private, real person. This is most clearly described in his essay published in *The Atlantic* entitled "The Private Life." In this tale, a writer is found to be two figures. One can exist only in the public's eye and is little more than an image to be upheld, while the other can exist independently and works alone in his study.

In *The Bostonians*, Henry James slowly works to flip the characters' private and public lives. He explores the effects of publicity in this novel by allowing those who have spent too much time in the public eye to lose the privilege of privacy. The private person is the one with his or her own ideas, thoughts, and secrets, so by losing privacy, a character essentially loses himself. This is displayed best in *The Bostonians* with Miss Peabody, someone who has spent too much time in the public eye and has gradually lost herself. Even her face had been "made vague by exposure to some slow dissolvement. The long practice of philanthropy had not given accent to her features; it had rubbed out their transitions, their meanings." Miss Peabody has devoted herself to her cause and put it first in her life, but because of this she has become impersonal and dull: "as the novel's most extreme altruist, Miss Peabody suffers from a loss of self." In this text, publicity exploits the private person by making the person's life the object of the public's eye rather than the person's object (i.e., their art or mission); "the paradox of publicity is that it enacts a reversal between the private and the public." It is not difficult to see these same issues in our own culture, and James in some ways anticipates the excesses of celebrity culture.

Trisha Rouleau, 2015

FRIEDRICH NIETZSCHE, 1844–1900, *The Godless Wanderer*

> " The world seen from within, the world described and defined by its "intelligible character"—it would be "will to power" and nothing else.
> —*Beyond Good and Evil*

- Was the son of a Lutheran pastor; while young, he considered the same vocation
- Was a professor of philology, but persistent health problems forced him to retire very young
- Composed music, and was a close personal friend and protégé of Richard Wagner; they had a falling out; Nietzsche wrote a major work of aesthetics, *The Case of Wagner*, condemning Wagner's appeal to decadence
- Often wrote very harshly of the historical "cunning" of the Jews, but had a Jewish best friend; when his sister announced her engagement to an anti-Semite, Nietzsche threatened never to speak to her again
- Suffered a complete mental breakdown at age 44, 11 years prior to his death
- Defined himself as an amoralist and despiser of traditional morality, yet lived a very ascetic life:
  - Typically walked alone in the mountains with a notebook every day
  - Had few serious social relationships, with a reputation for politeness and thoughtfulness as a friend
  - Proposed marriage a few times, mainly out of loneliness, but the women all turned him down
  - Criticized the German obsession with beer, regarding it as a collectivizing, will-weakening vice
- The underlying force of the world's continual change, similar to Schopenhauer's Will, is "will to power": All life is ultimately an expression (strong or weak) of will to power, i.e., the desire to expend one's primal energy, to command; life is a continual struggle for influence, intellectual or practical
- Said "God is dead"; Christianity "Platonism for the people"; saw himself as *the* rival of both Plato and Jesus
- Believed Socrates and Jesus were men who felt powerless, and took revenge by promoting philosophies of moderation and humility, ultimately undermining the powerful civilizations in which they lived
- Disapproved of the West's philosophical and religious tendency to create systems aimed at unearthly, eternal ends (Plato's "Forms," Christianity's "Heaven"); believed such thinking was anti-life, since there is no realm of eternal truth, but only continual becoming and the subtle influences of physical conditions
- Called the body "the great reason," as opposed to rational thought itself, which he dubbed "the little reason"; strongly influenced Freud with his views about the relationship between body and mind

- Espoused perspectivism: truth and goodness are defined by the situation and needs of the people judging
- Believed that Western metaphysics ("Platonism") and religion have played themselves out, that the old "idols" are dying, which leads to what he perceived as the West's great danger, nihilism (belief in nothing)
- Frequently spoke of late modern man as standing at the edge of the abyss (nihilism), and having to make a choice: succumb to the nothingness (life without values or meaning), or *create new values*; the first leads to "the last man" (bourgeois middle class life), and the second requires an *Übermensch* (overman or superman)
- The *Übermensch*, like other Nietzschean ideas, was later coopted by the Nazi Party, thanks to the efforts of Nietzsche's estranged sister Elisabeth, who took control of his works and legacy for her own purposes after his mental collapse, and who was a proto-Nazi (and later an actual one)
- The creation of new values (i.e., new standards of good and evil) demands men strong enough to face life's meaninglessness, and to overcome it by an act of sheer *will*
- Nietzsche, who suffered debilitating headaches and practical failure throughout his life, introduced the ancient Greek notion of "eternal return": the ultimate act of life-affirmation is to be able to say that, knowing what you know about the pain and disappointment of life, you would wish your life to repeat cyclically, exactly the same way, eternally; this is his psychological test of one's devotion to life on earth
- Has had enormous (often harmful) influence over the past century's philosophy, art, and popular culture

Key Works

The Birth of Tragedy, 1872
Thus Spoke Zarathustra, 1885, 1892
Beyond Good and Evil, 1886
The Will to Power, 1901

Biography

Friedrich Nietzsche was born October 15, 1844, in the German town of Röchen bei Lützen. His father, a Lutheran minister, died of a brain disease when Nietzsche was only 5 years old. Six months after the death of his father, his brother died as well at the age of 2. After moving to Naumburg an der Saale, the 14-year-old Nietzsche began his schooling at a very distinguished German boarding school, Schulpforta. After one year of study at Bonn, Nietzsche moved to the University of Leipzig and became immersed in the ideas of Arthur Schopenhauer. Schopenhauer and his atheism soon became a very influential part of Nietzsche's beliefs. Nietzsche also befriended the famous composer, Richard Wagner; he acknowledged their friendship as the most important achievement in his life.

After graduating with a degree in philology, Nietzsche started his professional career as a professor at the University of Basel, where he taught philology and wrote his first book, *The Birth of Tragedy*. Though his work was not well received, an undaunted Nietzsche went on to publish a series of studies on contemporary German culture called the *Unfashionable Observations*. Throughout the 1880s, Nietzsche became a nomadic philosopher, wandering around Europe, writing most of his major works, and never staying in one place for more than a few months. During this time he most famously wrote *Thus Spoke Zarathustra* and *Beyond Good and Evil*. This nomadic period proved successful for Nietzsche and lasted until the beginning of 1889. On January 3, 1889, while walking along the streets of Turin, Italy,

Nietzsche suffered a mental breakdown which left him an invalid for the rest of his life. The reason for Nietzsche's breakdown is unknown; however, the most widely accepted hypothesis is that his wide assortment of medications and fragile nervous system clashed and the result was insanity. He continued to live with his mother until her death in 1897. His sister then took care of him until his death in 1900.

"God Is Dead"

Through his declaration "God is dead," Nietzsche recognized the declining religiosity of his day and the increasing atheism in his culture. Despite this departure from faith, Nietzsche noted that traditional moral values did not seem to fade from society. Nietzsche felt compelled to awaken the world to the fact that society had already killed God through its indifference to faith, so the moral conventions of faith were now obsolete and without any grounding. In his work, he sought to articulate how society can remain moral and functional without a religious foundation.

Perspectivism

Nietzsche operated under the theory that "that there is no absolute, 'God's eye' standpoint from which one can survey everything that is." In contemplating human values and ethics from this nihilistic stance, Nietzsche sought a new way to measure values, one that did not assume the existence of an absolute good and evil. How does one measure values without referencing some absolute? Nietzsche's answer in *Beyond Good and Evil* started with perspectivism. Perspectivism, "the basic condition of all life," contends that there is no knowledge independent of one's perspective; for Nietzsche, one's culture, education, lifestyle, etc., colored the lens through which knowledge is gleaned and values created. Consequently, beliefs about absolute truth are fictitious, "the purely invented world of the unconditional," and yet, he acknowledged, society needed this invention. Although one cannot disassociate his perspective from his interpretation of good and evil, Nietzsche wrote that it was necessary "to recognize untruth as a condition of life." Lest one assume his perspectivism invites a chaotic relativism in which all viewpoints stand equal, Nietzsche was quick to point out that just because all truth is rooted in interpretation, it does not mean that some interpretations are not stupid or false; there are gradations, it seems, to perspectives.

Revaluation of Values

In light of the "death of God" and the birth of nihilism, Nietzsche proposed "that the logic of an existence lacking inherent meaning demands, from an organizational standpoint, a value-creating response." This meant that "because values are important for the well being of the human animal, because belief in them is essential to our existence," humanity cannot abandon morality; rather, for the sake of our flourishing, we must move beyond dogmatic morality. Nietzsche engaged in a radical questioning of the value and objectivity of truth; he explored where our values come from, and wanted to know *why* we value what we do.

We can move beyond good and evil by recognizing that our moral beliefs are subject to our perspective, not fixed in absolutes. We are value-creators, morality-makers. At the highest level of humanity, there is not good and evil; there are perhaps only good and bad judgments, which promote or destroy life as we interpret it. Consequently, a revaluation of truth takes places in the heart of the post-moral man; he does not see ethical dilemmas couched in absolutes, but rather he embraces his limited perspective and acts accordingly. He conceives of value differently, which leads to immense freedom and moral possibility. For Nietzsche, "there are no moral phenomena at all, only a moral interpretation of phenomena." Suddenly, things that were once seen "as a source of sin and error" are now open to interpretation and alteration.

The Übermensch and the Will to Power

Although only briefly mentioned in Nietzsche's work, the Übermensch (literally, the overman or superman) stands as the culmination of much of his philosophy. Unfortunately, the convoluted nature of his work taints this seminal notion with confusion. Commentators often disagree as to the significance of the concept, asking: "Is the notion presented to establish a set of character traits as most desirable, or does it represent instead an ideal attitude? Is the Übermensch an attainable goal? Is it a solipsistic goal? Is it an evolutionary goal in the Darwinian sense?" Regardless, it is clear that Nietzsche regarded the Übermensch as the ideal man, one whose revaluation of morality leaves him free to promote the will to power.

In the face of nihilism, Nietzsche suggested there were two main responses available to man: the way of the herd or the way of the Übermensch. The distinction between the two can be discovered through the way in which they each conceive of freedom: "For the hopeless, human freedom is conceived negatively in the 'freedom from' restraints, from higher expectations, measures of rank, and the striving for greatness. While the higher type, on the other hand, understands freedom positively in the 'freedom for' achievement, for revaluations of values, overcoming nihilism, and self-mastery." This higher type is the Übermensch. He does not relinquish his identity in the face of an ultimately meaningless existence; instead, he harnesses the will to power to make himself master of himself.

Nietzsche further elucidated: "Only where there is life is there also will: not will to life but—thus I teach you—will to power." The will to power is the positive answer to nihilism; it is not an empty drive for satisfaction but is a vibrant energy of creation. Since life as the Übermensch is the chief end of humanity, all that is good affirms the will to power. All that is good creates meaning. And so, "from within the logic of will to power, narrowly construed, human meaning is thus affirmed. 'But to what end?' one might ask. 'To no end,' Nietzsche would answer." Ultimately, the will to power allows man to break free from traditional values through self-assertion, originality, and imagination, yet even the Übermensch cannot answer, "Why?"

At times, confusion over this idea led to perversions of Nietzsche's theories. Most significantly, Nazi Germany used the notion of the Übermensch as a philosophical foundation for the cultivation of an Aryan master race (via the annihilation of lesser races). However, Nietzsche himself criticized anti-Semitism and did not present the Übermensch as a racial delineator.

Jessica Goeser, researcher
Daren Jonescu, advisor

GEORG CANTOR, 1845–1918, *Mathematician of Infinite Set Theory*

   " A set is a Many that allows itself to be thought of as a One.
—Quoted in Rucker's *Infinity and the Mind*

- Received the Sylvester Medal in 1904 for mathematics
- Was essential in the work of infinite sets of numbers

- Had chronic nervous breakdowns
- Was an accomplished violinist
- Spent his life proving that his theories were eventually proved correct
- Became a full professor at the University of Halle at age 34
- Laid the foundation for all modern math

Key Works

"About a characteristic of the essence of all real algebraic numbers," 1874

Biography

Georg Cantor was born in St. Petersburg, Russia in 1845. From his earliest years, Cantor was exposed to his parents' Christian faith. His mother was Catholic and his father Lutheran. Cantor grew to firmly believe the faith his parents espoused; his religious beliefs would significantly influence his work. Both parents were also quite musical, a trait Cantor inherited—he was a phenomenal violinist. His father fell ill in 1856, forcing the family to move to Germany. It was there, at a private school in Darmstadt, that Cantor first distinguished himself in math. He then spent a brief period at the University of Zurich before transferring to the University of Berlin, to continue to study math, philosophy, and physics. Cantor also attended the University of Göttingen for a semester before writing a doctoral thesis in 1867 on an unanswered question that appeared in Carl Gauss's 1801 paper.

After completing his education, Cantor worked at the University of Halle. He started as an unpaid lecturer but progressed to a full professorship by age 34, a post he kept until his death in 1918. Cantor's first significant contribution to mathematics was in the field of mathematical analysis. He solidified mathematical understanding of the real number system through his work with fundamental sequences. After this work, Cantor was determined to discover whether or not there could be one-to-one correspondence between a set of natural numbers, also called whole numbers, and a set of real numbers. He discovered this could not be done, leading to the subsequent discovery that there are infinite transcendental numbers.

Looking for a greater challenge, Cantor set out to prove that it was also impossible to assign one-to-one correspondence between a line segment and a square. However, he ended up proving the exact opposite. That discovery was so firmly against traditional mathematical thought that it received much criticism from highly respected mathematicians of the day. Most notably, Leopold Kronecker said, "God made integers; all else is the work of man." He was so deeply offended by Cantor's ideas he adamantly opposed Cantor's attempts to secure a position at the University of Berlin, successfully preventing Cantor from ever working there. This was not an isolated occurrence; throughout his lifetime, Cantor faced numerous setbacks and much condemnation for his theories, especially the theological and philosophical implications he recognized. He believed that his math did not disprove God, but even linked the idea of infinity and God. Also, he believed God appointed him to reveal his mathematical beliefs to the world.

Despite these criticisms, Cantor made notable contributions to the mathematical community and received many honors for his works. He founded and presided over the Mathematical Society and received honorary degrees from numerous universities. Also, the Royal Society presented him with the Sylvester Medal in 1904. During his tenure at Halle, Cantor married Vally Guttmann, and they had six children together. He also published a paper, entitled "About a characteristic of the essence of all real algebraic numbers" which explained all of his fundamental work. After he established these more fundamental principles of modern math, he extended his study of infinity, attempting to prove the continuum hypothesis. Cantor was never successful in finding a proof, and the stress of the problem, along with recurring depression, forced him to stop working. He was eventually hospitalized in the psychiatric clinic of the University of Halle where he died on January 6, 1918.

Infinite Set Theory

Galileo, long before Cantor's time, had hypothesized that concepts such as "less than, equal to, and greater than" could be applied only to finite numbers; these concepts broke down as soon as they were applied to infinity. Cantor disagreed, believing that if it "was possible to add 1 and 1, or 25 and 25, etc, then it ought to be possible to add infinity and infinity." One of the examples he used to establish this new notion is that the number of points (which are infinitesimally small) on the side of a square is "no more 'numerous' than the number of points" within the square. Therefore, some subsets of infinity can also be infinity. Another prominent example to prove Cantor's idea is the diagonal argument, which proves there are different sizes of infinity.

Caroline Fuschino, 2015
Julianna Swayze, 2016
Alexi Wenger

HENRI POINCARÉ, 1854–1912, *The Last Universalist*

> " It is by logic that we prove, but by intuition that we discover. To know how to criticize is good, to know how to create is better.
>
> —*Science and Method*

- Was born in Nancy, France, to a professor of medicine
- Studied engineering, mathematics, and physics in order to become a mining engineer, but eventually received a doctorate with his dissertation on differential equations
- Wrote over 500 papers and 30 books on myriad topics, across 34 years of a distinguished career as a professor at the University of Paris
- Made major breakthroughs across all the sciences, causing his biographer to call him the "last universalist"
- Devised a way to integrate differential equations, which he saw could allow him to study the solar system and the orbits within it with more depth, and later led him to the development of chaos theory
- Formulated a rough idea of the principle of special relativity years before and without knowledge of Einstein's work on the same topic
- Held that math wasn't true based on how it defined terms, but that it reflected knowledge of the real world (in contrast to some who believed that math could be reduced to logic)
- Believed that all geometries (Euclidean and non-Euclidean) were just different ways of looking at the same facts, some easier than others for different problems

Key Works

Science and Hypothesis, 1901

The Value of Science, 1905
Science and Method, 1908

Biography

Henri Poincaré was born into an influential family on April 29, 1854. His father was a professor of medicine, his brother-in-law a philosopher, and his cousin a president and prime minister-to-be. He was raised Catholic but later renounced his faith and criticized the religion, especially in its mixing of science and faith. He studied at the Lyceé in Nancy and graduated top of his class in nearly every subject with a bachelor's degree in science and letters. He served in the Ambulance Corps in the Franco-Prussian war alongside his father. Once the French lost and life returned to normal, he returned to his education.

After working as a mine inspector, he earned a doctorate, submitting a dissertation on partial differential equations. After obtaining his degree, he became a junior lecturer in mathematics at the University of Caen. He quickly gained renown, not least through his creation of a new branch of mathematics in the field of qualitative differential equations, and was offered a position at the University of Paris and then the Ecolé Polytechnique. He also continued his career in the mines as the head engineer responsible for northern development, then the chief engineer, and finally the French inspector general, all while holding three different department chairs at the universities. He was elected to the French Academy of Sciences in 1887, voted its president in 1906, and then elected to the elite Académie Française in 1909. He intervened in the famous Dreyfus Affair, defending Dreyfus from the army which accused him of treason, and attacking some unfounded probabilistic claims by the prosecution. He died on July 17, 1912, and was buried in the family vault. He was 58 years old and had accomplished a remarkable amount of work in his life across a dozen fields, and had advanced mathematics, philosophy, and science in groundbreaking ways.

Philosophy of Mathematics

Poincaré was by self-identification an intuitionist and a conventionalist, two ideals that would shape his mathematical and scientific pursuits and philosophy for his entire career. During this period, the study of mathematics was floundering. Mathematical foundations had recently been upturned, and different schools of thought had emerged to try and fill this gap: logicism, formalism, set theory, and intuitionism. Poincaré himself spearheaded the latter. To him and the rest of the intuitionists, the world—and math specifically—was based on a system of intuitive principles. Most of the other schools of logic were attempting to prove those principles, but for Poincaré, since a child intuitively knows two plus two equals four, there was no need to try and prove it. This simplified the whole matter and allowed mathematicians to continue innovating without spending years proving the commutative property of addition.

He also believed that Euclidean and non-Euclidean systems of geometry were simply different ways to look at the universe, each perfectly valid, each easier to use in certain instances than others. For example, students learn Euclid's ancient system of a flat plane to learn the coordinate system (and this is more often than not easier to use than more complex systems). On the other hand, in the formulation of general relativity, Einstein found it best to use a form of non-Euclidean geometry. Hence, Poincaré thought that the decision of which system to use was purely a matter of "economy and simplicity." At the same time though, he did not believe that the different forms of geometry were purely arbitrary and meaningless. He believed that the world was a certain objective way; different geometries or scientific theories used different language to describe it.

Philosophy of Science

Poincaré's philosophy of science can most simply be termed "conventionalism." He believed that the principles of science were conventions—that is, chosen by definition—but they were not arbitrary. As he said, "Are the laws of acceleration … nothing but arbitrary conventions? Conventions, yes; arbitrary, no; they would seem arbitrary if we forgot the experiences which guided the founders of science to their adoption." Once a definition, such as Newton's definition of gravity, was chosen, then certain conclusions and results would follow that could be either true or false. Further, every hypothesis, every theory, constantly had to make predictions about the world, and if it were unable to make predictions, or did so incorrectly, it should be put away and moved past in favor of a better one. This, to Poincaré, was the central aim of science: prediction.

While he firmly believed that scientific theories arise from experience, he also pointed out they cannot be verified by experience alone. To predict the world, one must first see a pattern in it, and these patterns arise from the interpolation of data. Imagine a graph of data points, where the points roughly form a curve. There is an obvious pattern, one that a child could see, but in order to create the curve that one sees in the data, one must inevitably generalize. By generalizing the data, one has to make the decision of how accurate or general to make the line, creating the disconnect between the experience of gathering the data points and creating the curve that comes from them. Therefore, there will always be a difference between facts and theories, proving the need for prediction-based science.

Poincaré noted the need to continue using, in a different manner, outdated theories. If a hypothesis that previously held true, such as the predictions of the planetary orbits before Galileo, were suddenly proven false, scientists must have missed something important. In this example, the missing element would be the existence of a non-geocentric solar system. By looking at the differences between the new data and the old theory, scientists can and should determine the missing piece of the puzzle, enabling them to formulate a new theory.

Achievements

Beyond his extensive philosophical writings, Poincaré also contributed substantially to advancements across nearly a dozen disciplines in math and science. In his doctoral dissertation, he made groundbreaking progress in the area of differential equations, solving the challenge of integrating those equations and determining their difficult geometric properties. In overcoming this obstacle, he used a form of non-Euclidean geometry that allowed him to cross fields into celestial mechanics, where he made significant progress on the famous three-body problem, a question that asked how to determine the orbits of three bodies, usually planets, given their masses and initial velocities.

The problem initially arose when astronomers attempted to predict the orbits of the sun, earth, and moon, a basic three-body system, and later gained traction when the King of Sweden offered a prize to anyone who could solve it. Poincaré won the prize. In solving this problem, he also became the first to discover and explain chaos theory, a system crucial to determining the orbits of planets and the movements of storm systems on Earth. Chaos theory is more commonly known as the butterfly effect, a grossly oversimplified analogy wherein a butterfly flaps its wings in China and creates a hurricane years later on the other side of the world. In the same way, Poincaré found that if the initial velocity or mass of just one of the planets in the three-body problem were changed ever so slightly, the entire orbits of all the planets will be altered significantly.

Although his work was largely dismissed at the time, by the close of the 20th century meteorologists would find that it was nearly impossible to determine the weather patterns to any long-term degree, for much the same reasons. Poincaré sketched out the theory of special relativity a decade before Einstein became famous for it, and from that derived precisely the Lorentz transformations, a set of equations necessary for any insight into quantum mechanics. He developed the Poincaré Recurrence Theorem, which states that every isolated system (like the universe) will eventually return to its original state. This theorem proved essential to discussions of entropy and the end of the universe. Finally, he created the Poincaré Conjecture, a theory about topology that proved crucial to the field of topology, but was unsolvable for more than 100 years. It states that any and every three-dimensional container could, after any number of simple algebraic transformations, be turned into a sphere. The theory is one of the Millennium Prize problems, a set of seven questions and theories created at the turn of the millennium, each with a $1,000,000 award attached to them. It was the first and (to date) only problem solved, by Grigori Perelman in 2002.

Jeff Culver, faculty
McCarthy Nolan, 2016

JAMES GEORGE FRAZER ◊ 1854–1941, *Undertaker of Religion*

> At least it is a remarkable coincidence, if it is nothing more, that the Christian and the heathen festivals of the divine death and resurrection should have been solemnized at the same season and in the same places.
>
> —*The Golden Bough*

- Wrote a particularly influential book on religion, and was the best known anthropologist of his time
- Emphasized (in his most famous work, *The Golden Bough*) that the human mind evolved through stages: magic, then religion, and finally science or reason
- Began his career in anthropology when a friend who was the editor of *Encyclopaedia Britannica* asked him to contribute articles on "Taboo" and "Totem"
- Popularized comparative studies of religion, using data from many different cultures and religions from around the world to show their similarities
- Was concerned with the workings of the "primitive mind," like many others of his day
- Considered himself to be an "undertaker of religion," showing that religion belonged to a primitive state of mankind
- Believed one could understand religion by discovering its origins, which are in agricultural themes of death and resurrection
- Was knighted in 1914 by King George V
- Inspired the works of Sigmund Freud, George Bernard Shaw, and T.S. Eliot, among others
- Promoted religion as a subject worthy of intellectual discourse and helped legitimize anthropology as a science

Major Works

The Golden Bough, 1890

Biography

James George Frazer was born in Glasgow, Scotland in 1854 to a middle-class family. He attended Glasgow University in 1869 and entered Trinity College in Cambridge in 1874, where he trained as a lawyer and a classicist. In 1896 he married Elizabeth "Lilly" Grove, a French widow with two children. She actively promoted Frazer's work and arranged for it to be translated into French. Frazer's interest in the then sparsely populated field of anthropology—the study of cultures—began when his friend, the religion scholar William Robertson Smith, asked him to write entries beginning with the letter 'P' and beyond for his *Encyclopedia Britannica*. Writing the entries for "totem" and "tattoo," Frazer was hooked.

In 1890 he published what would become his most famous work, *The Golden Bough*, which eventually ran to 13 volumes and multiple editions and is still in print today. *The Golden Bough* garners special attention as Frazer's best-known work; however, he also contributed other works to the anthropological study of primitive religion. Among these are *Lectures on the Early History of the Kingship, Totemism and Exogamy, Totem and Taboo*, and *Folklore in the Old Testament*. His writings were particularly noteworthy because they offered an academic analysis of religion in the classical world that used largely non-technical language. Knighted in 1914, he enjoyed wide popularity in the early 20th century. Though his works influenced the likes of George Bernard Shaw, Sigmund Freud, and T.S. Eliot, today they are generally considered unscholarly, as he rarely conducted field research in other cultures and was criticized for doing "armchair" anthropology. He went blind in 1931 and died in 1941.

The Evolution of the Human Mind

What made Frazer's work so powerful and compelling was the explanation he provided for the evolution of the human mind through different cultures. He believed that comparing religions and cultures throughout history would reveal a pattern in which human thinking evolved from simple to complex. He explained the patterns of reasoning and logic of "primitive" cultures in three stages. Initially, humans attempt to effect changes in nature and account for unexplained events by relying on spells, incantations, totems, and the like. This is the stage Frazer called "magic," in which humans try to control the impersonal forces of nature like rains, storms, and drought by commanding the gods to do their bidding.

Magic evolves into religion, the second stage, according to Frazer. Instead of trying to tame the impersonal forces of nature by magic, humans—or more specifically, the priests—beg and beseech the gods through religion. This is how Frazer explains cultural belief in a deity figure, as humans inevitably recognize the inherent limitations of their own bodies.

Finally, religion evolves into what Frazer considers the highest stage: reason, or science. As Robert Ackerman describes this stage of the evolution of the human mind, "Educated persons came to understand that they no longer needed priests, or indeed anything supernatural, to understand the wholly natural workings of the world; reason, in its highest form, science, would suffice." At the most advanced stages, humans no longer need magic and religion: science and reason replace such "primitive" ways of thinking. Frazer concluded that "savages," or tribal peoples living apart from industrialized civilization today, are survivors of the same primitive cultures from which present-day man has evolved, but he shocked his readers by including the revered ancient Greeks and Romans as participants in such primitivism.

The Golden Bough

The title of Frazer's most famous work comes from a sacred oak tree that had a yellow branch and was the site of an odd sort of ritual combat outside ancient Rome. In *Fifty Key Thinkers on Religions*, Gary Kessler explains:

> The rule was that any runaway slave who managed to kill the "priest" who guarded the shrine would gain his freedom. … The victorious slave would now become the guardian and either kill or be killed in turn. He watched over a temple and a sacred oak tree that had a yellow branch or "golden bough." This guardian was called the "King of the Wood" and, although obviously human, was also regarded as a divine lover of Diana and the animating spirit of the sacred oak tree. A "sacred marriage" was annually celebrated between the "King of the Wood" and a female spirit in order to induce fecundity.

This is how *The Golden Bough* begins—almost like a murder mystery—and it was immensely popular in its day. It showed that even among the revered Greek and Roman cultures there was backwards primitivism, which was still present in the lives of contemporary peasants, as well as the "savages" that European colonialism was discovering. By comparing the practices of several ancient Mediterranean religions, Frazer tried to show that all were rooted in agricultural dying and reviving, and readers quickly saw the connection he made between "primitive" religions and Christianity.

He drew parallels between the major tenets of so-called primitive religions and Christianity, stating that, "while they differ from each other in many particulars, the resemblances between them are numerous and fundamental." Christianity, he implied, was just one of the many primitive fertility religions. Though he was fascinated with religions and their similarities, Frazer rejected belief in the supernatural. He stated that Christianity had an "origin in savagery, and [it] naturally appealed to peoples in whom the savage instincts were still strong." Frazer's theories, although undermined by the accusation that he was an "armchair" anthropologist, inspired many writers and thinkers and are still discussed today.

Tyler King, 2016
Trisha Rouleau, 2015
Cole Watson, 2018
Daren Jonescu, advisor

Chapter 7
The 20th Century

*We must make the building of a free society
once more an intellectual adventure,
a deed of courage.*

Friedrich Hayck

> " The attempt to procure a certainty of happiness and a protection against suffering through a delusional remolding of reality is made by a considerable number of people in common. The religions of mankind must be classed among the mass-delusions of this kind. No one, needless to say, who shares a delusion ever recognizes it as such.
>
> —*Civilization and Its Discontents*

- Was an Austrian neuropsychologist, atheist, and critic of spiritualism, who believed that science and religion were "mortal enemies"
- Developed methodology for psychoanalysis, by which the roots of mental illness could be identified and then treated through free conversation
- Theorized that man's "psychic energy" was derived from the dynamic interaction of two primal drives, one for sexual gratification, the other for destructive aggression
- Divided the mind into the ego, id, and superego, the dynamic interactions of which shape the movement of mental forces between the conscious and unconscious
- Believed that the drive of Eros (libido) led individuals to organize into civilization, while the death wish (aggression) led them to resent it
- Theorized that the "Oedipus complex" causes male children to resent their fathers and be sexually drawn to their mothers
- Suggested that the adult man projects his feelings about his father onto nature, a process that culminates in the invention of an imaginary, divine father and the birth of theistic religion
- Believed that religion acts as an antidote to the "helplessness" of daily life, regulating relationships between individuals and enforcing moral standards
- Is acknowledged as one of the most influential thinkers of the 20th century, particularly in clinical psychology, even though his methods and results have been largely discredited

Key Works

The Interpretation of Dreams, 1900
A General Introduction to Pyscho-Analysis, 1915–17
Beyond the Pleasure Principle, 1920
The Ego and the Id, 1923
The Future of an Illusion, 1927
Civilization and Its Discontents, 1929

Biography

Frequently cited as the father of psychoanalysis, Sigmund Freud was an Austrian neuropsychologist whose primary works concerned the origins, structure, development, and treatment of human mental health. He was born in the Austrian town of Freyberg in 1856 and moved with his family to Vienna when he was 4. He earned his medical degree in 1881 and married soon after. He and his wife had six children. He went into private practice and started treating psychological disorders. Many of his contemporaries thought he placed too much emphasis on sexual causes of disorders and it wasn't until he was invited to give a series of talks in the United States in 1909 that he became famous. He fled

Austria in 1938 to escape the Nazis and died the following year in England, committing suicide after a battle with oral cancer.

The Basis for Freudian Theory

Broadly speaking, Freud approached his studies scientifically, with an emphasis on rationalism, logic, and data-based analysis. Rigidly empirical and disdainful of philosophy, he based his theories of psychoanalysis and the mind largely on the results of his experiences with actual patients. He speculated that mental irregularities could be the result of psychological rather than physiological forces, a hypothesis that led to the development of a host of theories that continue to influence the field today. His clinical experiences produced plentiful raw material for his studies of the mind. The atrocities of the First World War traumatized Freud, and the profound human costs of the conflict reinforced his theories regarding the self-destructive aggressiveness inherent in the human psyche. An avowed atheist and a critic of spiritualism of any sort, he consistently allied himself with naturalism and believed that all phenomena, especially the mental, were born of natural processes, whether chemical or physical. To Freud, religion and science were "mortal enemies."

Freud's most important contribution to modern psychology is arguably his methodology for psychoanalysis, a therapeutic process for identifying the emotional roots of mental illness and alleviating them through conversation. Practitioners of psychoanalysis encourage their patients to speak freely on whatever comes to mind, while their therapist remains out of sight. Through analysis of their statements, their verbal mistakes (now called "Freudian slips"), and even their dreams, a psychoanalyst can attempt to stir up forgotten and repressed thoughts, memories, and feelings, so that the patient may rationally work through them and thereby alleviate mental illness. While the practical points of the method have evolved since Freud began his studies into the subject, the fundamental theory behind the "talking cure" has been extremely influential in the development of modern psychology and psychiatry.

The Freudian Anatomy of the Human Mind

To Freud, man is a highly impulse-driven creature, primarily ruled by instinct and desire rather than rationality and self-control. Chief amongst man's primal drives, Freud believed, are those for sexual gratification and destructive aggressiveness, the interplay of which provides the "psychic energy" that gives rise to personality, behavior, and, eventually, social relationships. Ruled by greed and self-interest, men are "creatures," said Freud, "among whose instinctual endowments is to be reckoned a powerful share of aggressiveness," in no small part focused on the obtainment of sexual gratification. Humans "strive after happiness; they want to become happy and to remain so."

Freud divided the human psyche into the conscious and the unconscious. In the psychoanalytic sense, the conscious refers to all those feelings, emotions, sensations, thoughts, and desires about which an individual can be aware. The unconscious—a concept that predated Freud but upon which he radically improved—refers to all those impulses, drives, desires, and energies about which an individual is unaware, and which have been repressed into the hidden depths of the psyche since childhood. According to Freud, the mental health of the individual depends primarily on the successful repression or release of unconscious desires and impulses, such that equilibrium can be maintained between the urges of the unconscious and the demands of social decency, which act to restrict the drives for sex and aggression. If this equilibrium is not achieved—if negative, unconscious impulses are not successfully repressed, or not allowed to be fulfilled—then neurosis, or mental illness, will result.

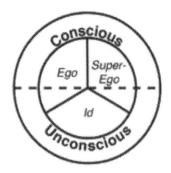

The Freudian Mind: Consciousness

Later in his career, Freud further divided the human mind into the ego, superego, and id. The id refers to the basic, unchecked impulses and drives of the unconscious (the two are not equivalent; the id is entirely unconscious, but the unconscious is not entirely composed of the id). The ego refers to the rational, thinking part of the psyche that confronts, processes, and interacts with reality. The ego is partially conscious and partially unconscious. The superego refers to a distinct component of the ego, that which contains the moral or ethical norms imposed by and internalized through the individual's relationship with his parents during the course of infancy and adolescence (see figure above). According to Freud, the superego—sometimes conceptualized loosely by other scholars as the conscience—and the id both exert pressure on the ego in a kind of tug-of-war, in which the id drives for the satisfaction of the basic instincts while the superego's moral strictures push for their containment (see figure below). This dynamic interplay shapes the contours of the individual's personality and behavior and is responsible for determining whether he or she will suffer from mental neurosis, and to what extent.

The Freudian Mind: Personality

Individual Psychology and Social Development

This eternal battle between the id and the superego lays not only the foundation for individual psychology, but also the basis for human society generally. In *Civilization and Its Discontents*, Freud argues that social organization—what he called "civilization"—is the result of the two competing primary drives, those for sexual gratification and aggressive destruction. Freud claimed that the innate instinct for sexual connection, community, and creativity—called Eros or the libido—leads humans to associate with one another socially. By doing so, said Freud, these individuals are forced to give up some of their liberties, particularly their ability to freely act on their sexual and aggressive urges, for the improved, mutual security of all. This shedding of freedoms is reinforced across generations through the development of the superego, which encapsulates the moral, ethical, and behavioral commands of society and checks the sexual and aggressive instincts of the id. This process yields great anxiety for the individual, for he has "exchanged a portion of his possibilities of happiness for a portion of security."

This uncomfortable transaction is not without its consequences, Freud argues, for "no doubt [man] will always defend his claim to individual liberty against the will of the group," seeing civilization "as a yoke which must be shaken off." This assertion of independence springs from the second of the basic drives, that for aggressiveness and the inflicting of pain, which Freud broadly labels the "death drive" or "death instinct." Building upon his original theory, Freud argues that the death drive is unavoidably aimed at the external world—that is, the society that dictates—as well as the individual himself, even to the point of self-destruction. The superego acts aggressively to check this instinct and transform it into more positive forms of energy and behavior. This battle between Eros and the death drive rages continuously, generating a tremendous amount of anxiety and neurosis for the individual caught between them.

The Oedipus Complex and the Development of Theistic Religion

Likely the most famous Freudian theory is that of the Oedipus complex. This theory posits that every male child is unconsciously resentful of his father and sexually drawn to his mother. This erotic identification with the mother results from the physical and psychological intimacy experienced with the mother throughout infancy and adolescence. Because of this sexual attachment, according to Freud, the young male is unconsciously extremely jealous of his father, who not only wields power over him, but also possesses sexual authority over the mother to the exclusion of all others.

Based on the universality of this psychological trend, Freud postulated that "primal man"—a sort of fictional metonym representing human social communities of the distant past—banded together with his brothers to murder his father, to avenge their jealousy of his strength and sexual primacy over the maternal figure. The guilt and shame of this "impious deed," springing from primal man's consequent loss of his father's comfort, protection, and provision, continues to fester across generations. Modern man does not murder his father, but he does internalize the shame, fear, and jealousy experienced during the Oedipal phase of childhood, eventually projecting these feelings towards an imaginary, omnipotent, divine being, so that he may "respect [the father's] will thenceforward."

The Oedipus complex is essential, Freud argued, to the development of theistic religion, which he believed to be an ancient, unconscious response to the anxiety and neurosis that spring from the oedipal relationship and the existential complications of living in a dangerous world. From "man's need to make his helplessness tolerable," Freud says, it "became the task of the gods to even out the defects and evils of civilization, to attend to the sufferings which men inflict on one another in their life together, and to watch over the fulfillment of the precepts of civilization, which men obey so imperfectly." For Freud, the Judeo-Christian god was little more than the imaginary product of an unconscious substitution, in which the comfort and protection of a real, living father was displaced by the comfort and protection of a divine, immortal one: "The recognition that ... helplessness lasts throughout life made it necessary to cling to the existence of a father, but this time a more powerful one." Religion, then, is the unfortunate result of the shame, guilt, and anxiety caused by the oedipal murder, combined with the existential "helplessness" induced by the intolerable realities of daily life. While modern males do not generally commit patricide, Freud would argue that the Oedipal complex continues to plague adolescent males even today, giving rise to the continued need for psychological relief in the form of a divine father.

Caroline Fuschino, 2015
Matt Horn, 2015
Brandon Martinez, researcher

GEORGE BERNARD SHAW, 1856–1950, *Playwright, Eugenicist, Socialist*

> " We are all dependent on one another, every soul of us on earth.
>
> —*Pygmalion*, Act V

- Wrote more than 60 plays and won the Nobel Prize for Literature in 1925
- Was an atheist turned mystic
- Was an avid member and founder of the Fabian Society, a peaceful socialist movement, and edited *Fabian Essays of Socialism*, a collection of essays on Fabian ideas
- Approved of communism and Joseph Stalin, but not the violence associated with them
- Advocated for eugenics—a truly Nazi idea—as population control, and called for a lethal, but humane, gas that later came about (Zyklon B), and was used in the Holocaust
- Saw WWI as evidence of the corruption of the capitalistic system and was deeply troubled by the waste of life; counter to public sentiment, he never compromised his opposition
- Founded the London School of Economics
- Valued only labor, not intellect, as the proper source of individual income, believing that poverty could be eliminated by giving equal pay to all
- Was a tough but fair critic of the arts, admitting to some mistakes of his own
- Criticized the smallpox vaccine, even though he almost died of the disease
- Never consummated his lifelong marriage, despite having a number of affairs with married women
- Lived until he was 94, perhaps because he never smoked or drank and was a vegetarian for the majority of his life
- Was known for his wit, and once remarked, "My way of joking is to tell the truth—it's the funniest joke in the world"

Key Works

Fabian Essays of Socialism (editor), 1889
Man and Superman, 1903
Major Barbara, 1907
Pygmalion, 1912

Biography

Avid playwright, music critic, theatre critic, and actor, Shaw has been compared to Shakespeare for his remarkable and enduring plays. George Bernard Shaw was born July 26, 1856, in Dublin, Ireland. He hated the "George" and never used it either personally or professionally. Shaw also strongly disliked organized school; he attended only sporadically and accumulated an irregular education. Shortly before he turned 16, his mother left his father to live with another man in London. This household turmoil is likely at the root of the problematic parent-child relationships that featured in most of his works. Despite the struggles of his childhood, he persevered to success in his adult life.

In 1876, Shaw moved to London where he became a renowned, but broke, music and theatre critic. In his early time in London, he would often stand on soapboxes at Speaker's Corner at Hyde Park and socialist rallies in order to overcome his stage fright and his stammer. Although he began his literary career as a critic and novelist, he published his first play, *Widower's Houses*, in 1891 to demonstrate his criticism of the English stage and to "turn the stage into a forum of ideas."

With Beatrice and Sidney Webb, he helped to found the Fabian Society, an organization that he passionately and actively participated in his entire life. In 1898, he married Charlotte Payne-Townshend, an Irish woman, in what was possibly an unconsummated marriage, and lived off of her finances until he received royalties for his plays in 1904. After 1904, he was quite wealthy in his own right. Later, he won the Nobel Prize for Literature in 1925, accepting only the title and not the monetary reward. He enjoyed international fame and spent his time traveling for the rest of his life.

In 1950, at 94 years old, he fell off of a ladder while trimming a tree and died a few days later of complications. Throughout his career, he wrote over 60 plays and is the only person to have been awarded both the Nobel Prize in Literature and an Oscar (for the adaptation of *Pygmalion*).

Pygmalion

Shaw wrote the play *Pygmalion* in 1913, and it opened in London in 1914; it is by far his most popular work, transcending the ages and inspiring the Audrey Hepburn movie *My Fair Lady*. As it opens, Professor Higgins, a teacher of phonetics, and his friend Colonel Pickering strike a wager: can Higgins take poor flower girl Eliza Doolittle, who speaks with a thick and unrefined accent, and teach her to speak formally enough to convince high society that she is a duchess? Under the tutelage of Higgins, Eliza continues to refine not only her language, but also her broader level of social sophistication; however, Higgins seems only interested in his bet and, when it seems he has won and is done with her, Eliza becomes enraged and remarks: "What am I fit for? What have you left me fit for?" Higgins realizes, with the help of Pickering, that he has mistreated Eliza; the play ends with Higgins asking her to continue to work with him, though her final response to this invitation is left ambiguous.

Throughout this play, Shaw explores the complexities of social class and wealth. He highlights the detriments of wealth, showing how money oppresses and controls man. When Eliza's father receives a large endowment, he bemoans the money, telling Higgins that before he "was happy. [He] was free," and now he is "worried; tied neck and heels; and everybody touches [him] for money." Rather than embrace the new money, Mr. Doolittle finds it oppressive. Shaw criticizes the desire for money through those characters that have come into great wealth or nobility and ultimately regret their new place.

He also depicts characters that ascend the social ladder quickly as snobbish toward their former class. When she realizes her father is going to marry the common woman he was dating, even though he has now attained wealth, Eliza exclaims, "You're going to let yourself down to marry that low common woman!" She is offended that he is even considering marrying a woman of such low upbringing—despite her own common birth and upbringing that she had escaped only a few months prior. Shaw shows that great wealth makes people quickly forget their roots and ignore or even antagonize the lower classes. This conclusion supports his fundamental belief that the class system is corrupt and that the upper class frequently takes advantage of those under them.

Pygmalion is titled after the Greek myth in which a sculptor creates a statue of an ideal woman so beautiful that he marries her once Aphrodite brings her to life. Shaw seems to draw a comparison between the objectification of Pygmalion's woman and her modern contemporary; although separated by centuries, these women lack independence as well as a true voice in society. While both desperately crave independence, they are never able to truly be separate from men and live as they please. Eliza decides that if no man can be kind to her, she'll "have independence." However, at the end of the play, she must either marry Freddy, a silly, high-born young man who romances her; move in with Higgins, who has offered her a job but is a misogynist and treats her poorly; or stay with her own father, who is now able to support her but does not want her. Though Liza may have more freedom than Pygmalion's statue, Shaw observes that a woman's future still hinges on men. Shaw illustrates that manners do not a free woman make.

Eugenics

Shaw asserted that, if a person could not justify his existence or does not provide more than he consumes, he should be terminated; such people are a detriment and a burden to society, and their termination should be seen as bettering society. This process of selective breeding and extermination is called eugenics and was a popular movement in the early 20th century. Shaw sought, in his eugenics, to "remove bad or deleterious genes from the population, increasing the genetic fitness of humanity as a result." In other words, he believed eugenics would develop a stronger and better community. While he never outwardly advocated killing people, he did strongly argue for population control, and he concluded that the population "cannot use the organizations of our society for the purpose of keeping [the fruitless individual] alive."

It is not difficult to see the potential for disaster in eugenic theory. In WWII, the Nazi Party took Shaw's and others' ideas on eugenics to the extreme: they killed those deemed genetically inferior and allowed only the genetically gifted to reproduce. However, it is likely that Shaw never intended for eugenics to go this far or become this violent, for after the tremendous loss of life he saw during WWII, he became depressed and lost all faith in the capitalist system. Paradoxically, Shaw recognized that if eugenics had been instituted generations earlier his existence would have happened only by a slim chance because of his own genetic unfitness. Ironically, he who claimed to come from a "poor gene pool" himself gave so much to literature and society.

The Fabian Society

On January 4, 1884, a splinter group of the English socialists formed the Fabian Society at 17 Osnaburgh Street in London. This group defined themselves as a "socialist political organization, dedicated to transforming Britain into a socialist state." They desired to pursue this through systematic and progressive legislation promoted through education and persuasion rather than a bloody revolution. On October 5, 1884, Shaw became a member of the Fabian Society after reading the first Fabian tract and attending a meeting.

In 1889, he published *Fabian Essays of Socialism*, which combined eight essays outlining the Fabian Society's beliefs. Shaw advocated for collectivism over individualism and the "elimination of privately owned land and the establishment of community ownership of the means of production." He strongly believed that the "most striking result of 19th-century capitalism in Britain had been to divide society into hostile classes." Because he believed equality was the key to a successful society, Shaw was strongly against the current class system, as the upper and middle classes essentially won while the greedy employers ruthlessly exploited the lower class. With the Fabian Society, Shaw was instrumental in founding both the London School of Economics and the English Labor Party.

Over the course of his life, Shaw met the dragons of this earth (poverty, war, sex and irresponsibility) and honored them with gloriously sloppy thinking.

Joshua E. Fernald, 2016
Caroline Fuschino, 2015

JOSEPH CONRAD ◊ 1857–1924, *Originator of Modernist Literature*

> " I don't like work—no man does—but I like what is in the work—the chance to find yourself. Your own reality—for yourself not for others—what no other man can ever know. They can only see the mere show, and never can tell what it really means.
> —*Heart of Darkness*

- Was christened Jósef Teodor Konrad Korzeniowski; Joseph Conrad is actually his pen name
- Believed in the strength of a story and thought that fiction carries more truth than history
- Thought that writers were historians in a sense because they recorded human experience in their own, artistic way
- Spent much of his life before he started writing as a seaman working for private companies before joining the British Navy
- Was among the first writers to start the modernist movement in literature
- Used a narrator in his many of his stories in order to add a human perspective on certain topics
- Explored the separation of the individual and community in his novels
- Published *Heart of Darkness*, his most famous work, in 1899 and it remains one of the most recognizable novels of modern literature

Key Works

The Nigger of Narcissus, 1897
Heart of Darkness, 1899
Lord Jim, 1900
Nostromo, 1904
The Secret Agent, 1907
The Secret Sharer, 1909
Under Western Eyes, 1911

Biography

Joseph Conrad is one of the most influential writers of the Modern literary era because of his beautiful prose and gripping stories. Conrad was born Jósef Teodor Konrad Korzeniowski on December 3, 1857, in Berdichev, Ukraine. After his father, a poet and political dissident, was exiled into Russia, Conrad had his first exposure to English literature. Both of his parents died in his youth, and after living with and being educated by his uncle, Conrad took to the sea, sailing with a French ship to Martinique before joining the British Navy. His time at sea provided the inspiration for much of his later writing. He eventually captained a riverboat up the Congo River in Africa, an experience that formed the direct material of his most famous work, *Heart of Darkness*. Suffering from physical and psychological damage from his experiences, Conrad retired from the navy and lived out his life writing and spending time with his wife and children before his death in 1924.

Style and the Power of Fiction

Joseph Conrad's style, while not always elegant, at times rises to great heights. Since English was not his native tongue, he brought inventive qualities to his writing in English. Though his writing can be dense and convoluted, it is also praised for being "swift, sensuous and cinematic." Conrad's style served the purpose of driving home his deep belief in the power of fiction. In his essay on Henry James, he makes the bold claim that "fiction is history." He believes this because fiction is "based on the reality of forms and the observation of social phenomena, whereas history is based on documents, and the reading of print and handwriting—on second-hand impression." In other words, fiction comes straight from the first-hand observation and thinking of the writer, but history is based off the writings of others that may be based off the writings of even more others; therefore, "fiction is nearer to truth." This idea that Conrad himself was a historian writing truth about human nature guaranteed an honest, tell-it-how-it-is approach to his novels.

Conrad and Modernism

A main contributor to the modern movement in literature, Joseph Conrad sometimes receives credit as its originator. Conrad drew his inspiration to write in a more impressionist form, using a narrator, from the French writer Guy de Maupassant.

One of Conrad's oft-revisited themes was the relation of the individual to society. Conrad believed that individuals are naturally drawn to community but find it hard to connect and therefore form these communities. This lack of connection is due to the fact of people's individual personalities. Each man and woman has different, individual personalities, and the values of the individual will always clash with the values of the community. Because of this, man is inherently lonesome. Conrad shows this constant battle between solitude and the desire for connection in his novels. Though the action might take place on boats or on adventures, when the necessity to come together is pertinent to success, personalities frequently clash, aborting any attempt at community. This back and forth is the reason why many characters in Conrad's novels turn insane. Tension between the individual and community is another defining feature of literary modernism.

Heart of Darkness

Conrad's *Heart of Darkness* is a potent combination of imperialism and insanity, and a cornerstone of modernist literature. Conrad wrote the book in the midst of the colonization of Africa, and it is an ode to the atrocities that the Congolese faced due to Belgian imperialism. Due to his time as captain of a riverboat that worked on the Congo River, Conrad used personal experience and first-hand observation as a foundation for this story. Conrad uses his narrator, Marlow, as an agent to criticize Belgium's poor treatment of the country. At the beginning of the story, Marlow shares his thoughts about colonizing, and it is the basis of good and bad imperialism. Marlow notes that to have a "just" colony, you need "the devotion to efficiency" and the "idea … an unselfish belief in the idea, something you can set up, and bow down before."

Conrad condemns the colonization of Congo throughout the novella via Marlow's observations of the system's inefficiencies. First, Marlow notices a lack of efficiency within the currency system. Congolese currency, as decided by Belgium, consisted of "pieces of brass wire, each about nine inches long," and the natives were supposed to "buy their provisions with that currency." Marlow remarks, "You can see how that worked." Conrad then condemns the colonization by displaying Marlow's observation of slavery. So-called criminals were being forced to work for free, even though they might have been accused of something that should merit only a minor fine. Marlow sarcastically notes, "It might have been connected with the philanthropic desire of giving the criminals something to do." Conrad uses Marlow as an agent to describe his observations of the inefficient Belgian colonization of Congo.

Heart of Darkness continues to be required reading in many high school and college classes, and inspired the film classic, *Apocalypse Now*.

Cole Baker, 2012
Toby Coffman, faculty

THORSTEIN VEBLEN ◊ 1857–1929, *Critic of Conspicuous Consumption*

" It is extremely gratifying to possess something more than others.
—*The Theory of the Leisure Class*

- Was raised on a farm in Minnesota by Norwegian-American immigrant parents
- Began his academic career in philosophy but switched to the more lucrative field of economics
- Believed that economics should be treated as an evolutionary science and infused his economic research with anthropology and sociology
- Was a prolific writer but a notoriously bad professor who could scarcely hold down university positions at the University of Chicago, Stanford University, and the University of Missouri
- Published his most famous book, *The Theory of the Leisure Class*, in 1899
- Rejected traditional economic assumptions, notably of the rational consumer and marginal utility
- Criticized the Gilded Age's consumer culture and businessmen's hold on industrialization and academia
- Coined the term *conspicuous consumption* and is the namesake of the related microeconomic term *Veblen good*

Key Works

Why Is Economics Not an Evolutionary Science? 1898
The Theory of the Leisure Class: An Economic Study of Institutions, 1899
The Theory of Business Enterprise, 1904

Biography

Thorstein Bunde Veblen was born and raised in a Norwegian immigrant family in Wisconsin and Minnesota. Norwegian was his primary language until beginning school. Attracted to economics, Veblen majored in philosophy at Carleton College before a brief stopover at Johns Hopkins en route to doctoral work at Yale. Unable to find employment in his chosen field, he eventually returned to school, studying economics at Cornell. Plucked from Cornell by one of his professors, Veblen went to the newly formed University of Chicago where he edited the *Journal of American Economy*, was made a full professor, and wrote his famous *The Theory of the Leisure Class*.

Though a brilliant, prolific researcher, he proved to be a subpar teacher and was a thorn in the side of faculty and staff. He was notorious for "announcing that he would give no examination and would give each student a grade of 'C.'" Eventually this tendency—combined with his extramarital romantic escapades—led to his removal from the University of Chicago, and later, Stanford. Veblen's "caustic criticism of academia" made him few friends in the university world. He ended his career in New York City as an editor for *The Dial*, a political literary magazine, and taught at the New School for Social Research. Veblen died in 1929 of a heart attack, having left New York.

Economics As an Evolutionary Science

Nonconformist is a fitting word to describe Veblen as he contemplated classical economics. Monmouth University economics professor Steven Pressman writes that Veblen "sought to broaden and enrich economics with the insights from other disciplines." The standout of Veblen's earliest articles, "Why Is Economics Not an Evolutionary Science?" highlights his unorthodox approach to economics. He asserts that "[E]conomics is helplessly behind the times, and unable to handle its subject-matter in a way to entitle it to standing as a modern science." Seeking to outline a future for the field, he established himself as a countercultural economist through his preoccupation with human culture. The article laid out some of the ideas that he would more thoroughly develop the following year in *The Theory of the Leisure Class*. Most salient is his rejection of the idea of "natural law"; this sharply separates him from conventional economists. According to Veblen, economics meets some criteria to be an evolutionary science because it is factual and constitutes a "close-knit body of theory," but it falls short in "the interest from which the facts are appreciated." Natural law theory states that people behave in normal or natural ways; in economics, actions that fall outside of natural law are "disturbing factors" that upset the natural direction of the economy. Veblen further feels that natural law economics is didactic and tries to control human behavior.

One of the principal errors of natural law economic theory is that it inaccurately views man as constantly seeking pleasure. This impulse, called hedonism, makes of each individual an "isolated, definitive human datum" that would remain in "stable equilibrium" if not for outside forces. Instead, Veblen asserts that man has an "instinct" for constantly doing an activity, and his habits and interests, shaped by his culture, determine his activity. To be evolutionary, economics must be concerned with "economic action," *why* and then *how* the dynamic man utilizes a fixed amount of resources, bringing them into the "economic life process." This combination of culture and economics is what will, according to Veblen, liberate economics to become an evolutionary science.

Business versus Industry

One sphere that Veblen observed through his evolutionary, culture-concerned lens was the industrial environment of his day. He analyzed consumerism, most notably in *The Theory of the Leisure Class*, but expressed his criticism of the pandemic Western capitalism at the turn of the century in later publications such as *The Theory of Business Enterprise*, *The Instinct of Workmanship and the State of the Industrial Arts*, and *Absentee Ownership and Business Enterprise in Recent Times: The Case for America*. He believed there to be a severe lack of traditional industry in the late 19th-century industrial revolution, and he criticized how businessmen seemed to be the not-so-invisible hand controlling, and thus suppressing, industry in its organic form. Veblen is consistent in drawing a distinction between business, which means making money, and industry, which means making goods.

Holding fast to his rejection of natural law, he denounced "the inability of moral systems to control the power of modern business, severe business cycles, and the rise of powerful monopolies like US Steel and Standard Oil." Veblen refused to shrug such phenomena off with the assurance that things would autocorrect back to "equilibrium." Perfect competition, Veblen asserts, allows an inefficient, money-obsessed system to supersede the naturally occurring, naturally productive making of goods. Veblen calls for a return to an industrial revolution of engineers producing goods, not businessmen producing money.

The Theory of the Leisure Class

Veblen's magnum opus is *The Theory of the Leisure Class*, a work that sets forth a cultural theory of consumption. Veblen begins the work explaining the origins of ownership, which he directly associates with the development of a leisure class. The existence of a leisure class depends upon a separation between "worthy" and "unworthy" employments. Those comprising the leisure class are marked by their non-industrial jobs: politicians, lawyers, and priests. Tracing a gradual shift in human culture from the "peaceable and sedentary" primitive savages to the "barbarian culture" that allows for a leisure class, Veblen argues that in this transition people become more individualistic and predatory rather than communal and mutually beneficial.

Humans naturally desire to be builders, but barbarian culture rewards only wealth acquisition, which incentivizes people to instead become exploiters. Classical economists, he accuses, do not properly recognize how the struggle for wealth has evolved from the struggle for subsistence to a "competition for an increase in the comforts of life," and incorrectly classify consumption as "the end [goal] of acquisition and accumulation." As the predatory nature of barbarian culture gains ground, it motivates us to emulate people around us. Suppose you buy the latest model iPhone. Before long, a newer, supposedly better, phone comes to market that your best friend buys. You feel inadequate now. Such a phenomenon is what Veblen would call "pecuniary emulation," in which there is an ever-changing standard of luxury. Man will live "in chronic dissatisfaction" until achieving the standard, and thereafter work to widen the gap between himself and his fellow men. With his theory of "pecuniary emulation" in hand, Veblen moves to his capstone theory of conspicuous consumption.

Conspicuous Consumption

Veblen's most challenging assertion in *The Theory of the Leisure Class* is that consumption makes people happy. Concurrent with this challenge is the idea that consumers are not rational, but irrational agents, consumed not only with what they need but also with what will make them look good. This latter tendency—consumption for the purpose of show—Veblen calls "conspicuous consumption." Now a buzzword in economics, conspicuous consumption is the classic "keeping up with the Joneses" idea of economics. We don't buy because we need; we buy to look better than the family next door.

Interestingly, Veblen points to conspicuous consumption as the origin of "good manners" and refined education, for "[c]losely related to the good requirement that the gentleman must consume freely and of the right kind of goods, there is the requirement that he must know how to consume them in a seemly manner." Consumption is not a carefully calculated buying decision but a showy act of pecuniary emulation according to cultural standards. After the economic crash of 2009, conspicuous consumption became the explanation for the housing bubble and the gleeful acquisition of bad debt, which led to the crash.

MAX PLANCK, 1858–1947, *Father of the Quantum Theory*

> " Science cannot solve the ultimate mystery of nature. And that is because, in the last analysis, we ourselves are a part of the mystery that we are trying to solve.
>
> —*Where Is Science Going?*

- Studied the scientific anomaly of black-body radiation and was a professor at the University of Berlin
- Didn't agree with the Nazis, but was very conservative and didn't want to make waves
- Enjoyed a friendship with Einstein, who discovered special relativity, which, along with quantum theory, was fundamental to physics in the 20th century
- Originated the idea of the existence of a quantum world that followed a different set of physics than the world we know
- Won the Nobel Prize in Physics in 1918 for his discoveries
- Created the equation (known as Planck's Law) that relates the quantum of light and its frequency using the Planck Constant
- Conducted experiments which led to the invention of transistors, lasers, and the discovery of the special theory of relativity

Key Work

Treatise on Thermodynamics, 1904

Biography

As a theoretical physicist, Max Planck made tremendous progress in the field of quantum mechanics and is considered by many to be the founder of the quantum theory. Born into an intellectual family in Kiel, Germany, on April 23, 1858, he was the fourth child of Johann Planck and his second wife, Emma Patzig. While a professor of theoretical physics at the University of Berlin, he published his *Treatise on Thermodynamics* in 1904, including his new discoveries in black-body radiation and a new idea, Planck's Constant, which described the inverse relationship between a particle's energy and wave frequency. This discovery revolutionized physics forever and is considered the birth of quantum physics, as it was incompatible with classical physics. The groundbreaking revelation earned Planck the 1918 Nobel Prize in Physics.

Soon after, WWI ended, and Planck and his fellow German researchers did their best to take advantage of the many new innovations that came with it. The terrible post-WWI German economy made it hard for him to even do research. In 1933, the Nazis rose to power in Germany and began to remove Jewish scientists from their positions in universities and laboratories, exiling and humiliating them. Planck believed the political turmoil would die down, saying, as he had in WWI, "persevere and continue working." He secretly managed to keep many Jewish scientists in their positions, making the suspicious Third Reich pressure him to leave the KWG, a leading scientific institution at the time. Meanwhile, the leadership of the country was advocating newly created "Deutsche Physik," Aryan Physics, which tried to remove all ideas of special relativity and quantum theory as being too "Jewish." He was forced into the countryside, not by the German police, but by the increasing number of Allied air raids, which would destroy his house and all scientific records he kept there in 1944. By then, his first wife and four children had all died, leaving him with little will to live, and he died in 1947 in a countryside home in Göttingen. He had revolutionized physics forever, having created an entirely new branch of study, which, along with Einstein's special relativity, was the fundamental theory behind physics for almost 100 years.

Quantum Theory

In the 19th and 20th centuries, scientists were discovering the atomic world and making major breakthroughs into its nature. This led to the discovery of neutrons, electrons, nuclear fission, radioactivity, and other characteristics of atoms that are used in hundreds of practical applications today. But scientists were running into a problem. They were finding that, on the atomic level, physics stopped working. Phenomena, such as the photoelectric effect, did not follow the rules of the ordinary physics of that time.

Physicists, including Max Planck, had begun to write new rules that explained the ways that atomic particles behave. These rules became known as Quantum Mechanics. The word "quantum" refers to the minimum amount of electromagnetic energy (light) that can be absorbed or released by an atom. This minimum is what is used to transition between classical and quantum physics. One of Planck's major contributions to this field was developing a way to calculate this minimum amount of energy. To determine this value, Planck had to incorporate a value known as the Planck Constant. This constant allows the calculation of the minimum amount of energy (E) using the frequency of the light (v) multiplied by Planck's Constant (h). This equation, $E=hv$, was able to make the quantum world a little more understandable; however, there was still a problem.

Scientists found that, at the quantum level, trying to take any measurements of the particles affected the particles in unpredictable ways, leading to inaccurate results. This dilemma, named almost 30 years after Planck's discoveries, is known as Heisenberg's Uncertainty Principle, the inability to simultaneously measure both the position and the momentum of a particle. Planck's work created a transition between the empiricism of a classical clockwork universe and the abstract and theoretical ideas of the quantum world.

Scientific Impacts Today

Planck's discoveries in quantum mechanics opened a new field for physicists to explore. This field has led to numerous theories and observations critical to invention and operation of many common objects today. Quantum mechanics led to the invention of the transistor, an essential component of modern personal computers. Quantum mechanics are necessary in the function of lasers, which are used in medicine, welding industries, CDs, spectroscopy, missile guidance, skin treatments, and more. Using quantum mechanics, scientists have developed a way to turn thermal energy into electricity.

Planck's work also led to the discovery of quantum entanglement. Quantum entanglement is a phenomenon that occurs between two "entangled" particles. These particles, no matter how far apart, are able to respond instantaneously to change in the spin of the other. Theoretically, even if the particles were an infinite distance apart, they would still be able to instantly communicate with one another. This is problematic, because for them to be able to communicate, they would have to send information traveling faster than light. Scientists explored this phenomenon, and it led to the development of the special theory of relativity. Overall, Planck's foundation of the quantum theory has not only provided a strong basis for current research and theories, but has also been responsible for the many current inventions that incorporate quantum mechanics.

Jack Beebe, 2012

HENRI BERGSON, 1859–1941, *A Professor of Intuition*

> " The idea of the future, pregnant with an infinity of possibilities, is thus more fruitful than the future itself, and this is why we find more charm in hope than in possession, in dreams than in reality.
>
> —*Time and Free Will*

- Was born the second of seven children to a wealthy Jewish family in Paris
- Published the correct solution to one of Pascal's mathematical problems (that had been solved wrongly for years) when he was only 17
- Caused the first traffic jam on Broadway as people crowded in to see him when he spoke at Columbia University in 1913
- Was condemned for his philosophy that adhered to the theory of evolution by the Catholic church in 1914
- Served as a diplomat during WWI and worked with Woodrow Wilson to create the League of Nations
- Received the Nobel Prize for literature in 1928
- Instructed his wife to burn all of his papers upon his death
- Expanded on Darwin's theory of evolution and ruled out Darwin's mechanistic approach in his most famous work, *Creative Evolution*
- Redefined time as a continuous duration of progress and change
- Sought to prove that memory is spiritual by explaining the science of how people lose and regain memory
- Became the first notable philosopher to address humor with his essay "Laughter"
- Is rumored that his interpretation of multiplicity was the basis for Einstein's theory of relativity

Key Works

Time and Free Will, 1889
Matter and Memory, 1896
Creative Evolution, 1907
The Two Sources of Morality and Religion, 1932

Biography

Henri Bergson was a renowned philosopher, scientist, teacher, and politician. He was born the second of seven children to a wealthy Jewish family in Paris in 1859. He was an exceptional student from a very early age. He especially excelled in mathematics; at 17, Bergson won a prize for his solution to a complex problem and solved one of Pascal's most misunderstood and complex problems. In 1888, he published his first prominent philosophical work, *Time and Free Will*, followed eight years later by *Matter and Memory*, which led to his appointment as the chair of ancient philosophy at the Collége de France.

His influential article "Introduction to Metaphysics" marked the beginning of a philosophical movement known as "Bergsonism."

He published his most famous work, *Creative Evolution*, in 1907. This work stirred controversy by questioning many of Darwin's theories, and it catalyzed the rise of the "Bergsonian cult." When Bergson spoke at Columbia University in 1913, people flocked from all across New York to hear him, causing the first traffic jam on Broadway. At the start of WWI, Bergson began his political career as a diplomat and worked with Woodrow Wilson on a "league of nations." In 1922, he retired from teaching and was elected president of the International Commission for Intellectual Cooperation, where he is remembered for his heated debate with Albert Einstein. In 1928, Bergson received the Nobel Prize for literature. He retired from public life a few years later due to severe arthritis. Toward the end of his life, he converted to Christianity and published his final work, *The Two Sources of Morality and Religion*. This book is the basis for much ongoing debate about the specifics of his religious and philosophical beliefs. Upon his death, Bergson asked his wife to burn all of his unfinished and unpublished papers, so now only Bergson's personal library is available for study.

Concept of Multiplicity

Bergson's concept of qualitative multiplicity served as the basis for most of his theories. His most prominent example of multiplicity is that of sympathy, which consists in a "transition from repugnance to fear, from fear to sympathy, and from sympathy itself to humility." It is a continual flow of feelings and is termed qualitative multiplicity because it is transitory and constantly changing, yet it remains in perfect alliance. He believed a true multiplicity to be inexpressible, demonstrating it using his concept of duration. Duration is what he also refers to as "pure time"; it is concrete, active, and immeasurable. It "involves the succession of conscious states in an immeasurable flow. And real time therefore is apprehended by intuition, time perceived as indivisible."

Bergson uses three illustrations of duration. First, he portrays duration as two spools with a tape between them—one constantly unwinding while the other is winding up. He uses this to demonstrate that time is continuous and progressing but can never be the same because of the ever-increasing presence of the past. His second illustration is the color spectrum; while there are a variety of colors, they naturally flow together, maintaining continuity. While the spool depicts constant difference, the image of the color spectrum illustrates multiplicity through different shades. Third, he compares duration to a rubber band being stretched in which focus is placed on tracing the movement; it is continuously changing, but indivisible. "Bergson compares all three images: 'the unrolling of our duration [the spool] in certain aspects resembles the unity of a movement which progresses [the elastic], in others, a multiplicity of states spreading out [the color spectrum].' Now we can see that duration really consists in two characteristics: unity and multiplicity." Duration is particularly influential to Bergson's theory on memory, and his concept of multiplicity is the root of his theories on memory, intuition, and evolution because of its focus on continuity within change.

Theory on Memory

For Bergson, there are two types of memory. First, there is habitual memory, the record of automatic behavior gained by repetition, and it constitutes our routine. The second type is what Bergson calls "pure memory." It is the unconscious, spiritual remembrance of personal events. Bergson uses the illustration of losing and regaining word memory, independent of brain traces, to show that pure memory is not physical. He describes memory with his memory cone illustration: an inverted cone intersecting with a plane (see figure). The point of intersection between the tip of the cone and the plane represents the present and physical, while the base of the cone represents past memories. Like a telescope, memory takes the wide array of past memories and narrows them to specific memories, but it may require a bit of rotation to receive the memory with perfect clarity. Still, the memory as recalled in the present is not the same experience as it was originally. The past is always larger for the present moment than it was for a past moment, so the two moments can never be the same.

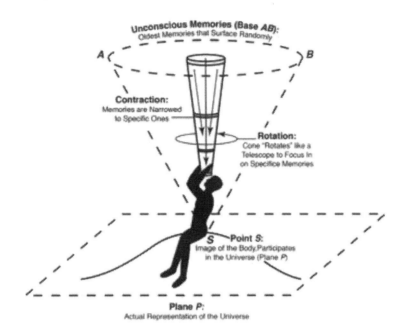

Henry Bergson's Memory Cone: How Certain Memories Surface

Intuition

To Bergson, intuition is a form of memory; it is an experience. It is instinct that has developed the capacity to act separately from the demands of action and social life. Like a separate mode of thinking, intuition is instinct with a conscience that requires one to turn from action to concentration. Bergson describes it as entering into oneself to find absolute knowledge. He elaborates by using the example of the color spectrum; if the color spectrum were simply the color orange, entering into it would reveal different shades of orange. One would be more red and one more yellow, and by way of this revelation, the entire color spectrum would be found. He calls intuition a method because it is a series of acts that correspond to degrees of duration.

Creative Evolution

In his work *Creative Evolution*, Bergson challenged Darwin's theory of evolution, claiming the mechanistic approach untenable. He argued that it would make real change and creativity impossible because each stage would contain all previous stages. He described evolution through his doctrine of the vital impetus. Because Bergson believed that evolution needed a creative consciousness to direct it, he invented the vital impetus, which he defined as "a current of consciousness" that permeates all living bodies and determines their direction of evolution and is passed on through reproduction. He believed that the vital impetus created the variety that causes evolution. The original, created variety then separated along three different paths—plants, insects, and vertebrates, by which all living things have come to be. The vital impulse found its best expression in humans and so embodies our intelligence. It has also instilled in all living things instinct, but because of a necessity of intelligence, humans have broken free from instinct. He believed that humans are the purpose of evolution. In *The Two Sources of Morality and Religion*, Bergson likened the vital impetus to God and claimed that "evolution is nothing less than God's undertaking to create creators, that he may have, beside himself, beings worthy of His love."

Morality and Religion

Morality and religion work together in Bergson's philosophy He discusses their linkage in *The Two Sources of Morality and Religion*. Two types of societies emerge from differing approaches to morality and religion. The first is one of closed morality and static religion. Closed morality comes from the reality that some species cannot exist on their own and need others; it is concerned with the survival of personal society and therefore results in war. Closed morality pairs with static religion. This is based on the "fabulation function," which causes people to imagine that there is a "presence" watching over them. They fabricate gods who protect them on the basis that they follow a strict set of rules. This closed morality system predominates among societies worldwide. The opposite of this system is one of open morality and dynamic religion; such a society prioritizes creativity and progress rather than social cohesion. Open morality is based on "creative emotion," which does not result in the doctrines and organization typical of closed morality. The emergence into dynamic religion allows the vital impetus to manifest itself in a person, creating mystics, who achieve contact with the creative effort and aspire to help complete the development of man.

Samantha Sherwood, 2015

JOHN DEWEY, 1859–1952, *Socialist, Atheist, Education Reformer*

" A democracy is more than a form of government; it is primarily a mode of associated living, of conjoined communicative experience.

—*Democracy in Education*

- Is considered the most significant educational thinker of the 20th century by some, and the worst thing that ever happened to American education by others
- Was an atheist and secular humanist with the goal of driving religion from public education
- Led the progressive movement as a promoter of socialism and collectivism, and was a primary figure in the philosophy of pragmatism
- Developed the Laboratory School at the University of Chicago to test experimental educational theories, and was later fired from there
- Co-founded the New School for Social Research, a modern, progressive school
- Was a teachers' union organizer and a close friend of Bertrand Russell, another atheist rebel
- Got caught up in the May Fourth Movement, a student anti-imperialist protest, while visiting China, and extended his visit to two years in order to help with the cause and give over 200 lectures to Chinese students
- Died of pneumonia at the age 92

Key Works

Democracy and Education, 1916
Human Nature and Conduct, 1919
Philosophy and Civilization, 1931
Experience and Education, 1938

Biography

John Dewey is perhaps most famous for his educational reforms, work he diligently pursued throughout his life, but he was also a philosopher and a theorist who researched and wrote on a variety of topics, from logic and psychology to fine art and religion. By one count, a bibliography of his printed works amounted to 150 pages of citations.

Dewey was born on October 20, 1859, in Burlington, Vermont. Fascinated by philosophy, he earned his undergraduate degree from the University of Vermont before attending the newly founded Johns Hopkins graduate school in 1882. He completed his doctorate in 1884 and went to the University of Michigan for a decade as an instructor. At Michigan, he became more interested in psychology and education, lamenting the slowness at which educational practice adapted to reflect changes in psychology. In 1886 he married Harriet Chipman, and they had six children together. They were married for 41 years, until Chipman's death in 1926.

In 1894 he was hired by the new University of Chicago, where he attained recognition for his work in educational theory. He administered the Laboratory Schools (which came to be called the Dewey Schools), where he tested his theories in the experimental classrooms. In 1904 he left Chicago over a disagreement concerning the education program and settled at Columbia University in New York until his retirement in 1930. He remained active as a researcher and writer after his retirement. In New York he became actively involved in progressive politics, holding office with the American Civil Liberties Union and playing a leading role in advocating peace. On traveling to China, he became involved in an anti-imperialist movement and remained in China for two years. Dewey was awarded honorary degrees from 13 universities and lectured throughout the world in the 1920s. He died of pneumonia in 1952 at the age of 92.

Educational Theory and Reform

John Dewey passionately advocated for educational reform and maintained, "All of philosophy is a philosophy of education." He chiefly believed that "the central task of education is to develop the capacity of every individual for intelligent deliberation and balanced consideration of alternatives through mutual communication." In his *Experience and Education*, he outlined the tenets of traditional and progressive education, but criticized both the conservatives and radicals of educational thought because this either/or viewpoint did not take into account that "circumstances compel us to compromise." Dewey was wary that progressive education might "develop its principles negatively rather than positively or constructively." Therefore, the progressives needed to reform the traditional method of education, not do away with it entirely.

Experience, in his opinion, was the very height of education. Experience leads to growth, and both growth and experience are continuous features of human life. All growth and experience, however, are not necessarily good; if the experience leads towards growth as a thief, for example, this negative growth hampers later experiences that the student could have had. It is because of this cumulative cycle of experience and growth that all experience "cannot be directly equated to" education. It is the educator's job, then, to know "how to utilize the surroundings … that exist so as to extract from them all that they have to contribute to building up experiences that are worth while."

Though wary of progressive overreach, Dewey argued for an education progressive in its structure, one that allows children some autonomy over their own education. Children already exhibit social control, as is evidenced by young children playing games such as tag. Even though without explicit leaders in this game, each child adheres to rules, and parents or authority figures rarely have to step in. In schools, this social control could also be used to create a school "in which all individuals have an opportunity to contribute something" and the teacher becomes less of an all-powerful dictator and more of a "leader of group activities." Dewey argued for a compromise between these two extreme positions, where development would occur "through reciprocal give-and-take, the teacher taking but not being afraid to also give." He suggested that students study "anything which could be called a study" such as arithmetic, history, geography, or natural sciences that can also be applied to ordinary life experience. Dewey's educational theories helped shape the American educational system, and his work and example are still highly influential with contemporary reformers.

Progressivism

Much of Dewey's educational and philosophical program was motivated by a devotion to a progressive ideal of human development. Briefly, progressivism is a school of thought that believes in an upward trajectory for human culture. Though the word is not universally popular, it was an extremely popular movement in the early 20th century and can count among its numbers diverse thinkers and politicians. Progressivism can be brought to bear on any concept. Even God was not exempted from Dewey's progressive vision. For Dewey, God was not a transcendent being, but rather a signifier of the relationship between ideals and their realization. In *A Common Faith*, he stated the matter clearly: "It is this *active* relation between ideal and actual to which I would give the name 'God.'"

For the progressive, at least in the mold of Dewey, history is moving in a specific direction, generally toward a higher degree of whatever a particular progressive happens to value. In other words, we approach "God" as we achieve progressive social values. Dewey thought of history as linear, progressing from savagery and barbarism to enlightened civilization. He wrote in *Democracy and Education*, "With increased culture, progress takes place." Early in the book the "savage" is negatively compared to the "democratic" or the "scientific," two words which Dewey used as synonyms for the civilized world. The development of an individual child was viewed through this same linear progression: savage to civilized. Dewey's experimental school at the University of Chicago put this concept on display. Laura Runyon, a teacher at the school, described it as follows: "For [the student] is primitive man, striving to find out by tracing how he may control nature, and in this experimentation discover nature's laws."

The Darwinian theory of biological evolution undergirded the belief in linear progression; the progressives merely adapted the evolution of species to include evolution of culture as well. Such a view is highly ethnocentric and gives primacy of place to developed western cultures, placing native or African cultures farther back on the road from savagery to civilization. Fallace argues that Dewey disposed of the "linear historical" view of history and replaced it with a "cultural pluralistic" view sometime before the 1920s. In that period, evolutionary biology began losing steam to the burgeoning schools of behavioral psychology and cultural anthropology. Thus Dewey began moving toward a more pluralistic view in both his philosophical and educational views.

Pragmatism

Like William James, Dewey was a member of the philosophical school of pragmatism. Pragmatism is, unsurprisingly, a philosophy that assesses ideas and beliefs based on their pragmatic or instrumental effects. In *Philosophy and Civilization*, Dewey defined it simply as "the doctrine that reality possesses practical character." In other words, reality is contingent on human experience of reality. Dewey gives the example of a carpenter seeing his tools and materials only "in reference to what he wants to do to them and with them."

Commenting on the practical nature of pragmatism in his *Introduction to Philosophy*, Dewey claims: "We are at root practical beings, beings engaged in exercise. This practice constitutes at first both self and the world of reality. There is no distinction." Dewey's pragmatism is differentiated from James's in a number of ways—Dewey's focus tends to be more social when compared to James's individual focus— but the essentials of the school hold. Pragmatism is at its core progressive, believing that positive social change can happen. The route to such change is what Mark Uffelman calls "self-cultivation," a process of developing one's own abilities and social awareness in order to serve the common good. Pragmatism had a definite moral edge for Dewey as well. As he writes in *Human Nature and Conduct*, his goal was to bring "morals to earth, and if they still aspire to heaven it is to the heavens *of* the earth, and not to another world." The "pragmatic lesson" is to "liberate and liberalize action." There is an unmistakable utopian element to such a belief. Dewey's desire was for a realized change. Alan Ryan finds Dewey's pragmatic utopia to be neither a "distant goal nor a city not built with human hands." Rather, "he was a visionary about the here and now, about the potentiality of the modern world." Dewey did not believe that progress was inevitable, only probable, and he worked fiercely to see the social changes he desired enacted.

Toby Coffman, faculty
Joshua E. Fernalld, 2016
Caroline Fuschino, 2015

ANTON PAVLOVICH CHEKHOV ◊ 1860–1904, *The Russian Realist*

> " I am writing a play not without satisfaction although I sin terribly against the conventions of the stage. It is a comedy, three female parts, six male, four acts, a landscape (view of a lake); much conversation about literature, little action, tons of love.
> —Letter to Aleksey Suvorin discussing *The Seagull*

- Was a Russian playwright celebrated for bringing realism to drama in an era characterized by melodrama
- Departed from conventional theatre by integrating seemingly meaningless details of everyday life and removing active events from plotlines in favor of dialogue-based plot
- Wrote four plays—*The Seagull, Uncle Vanya, Three Sisters*, and *The Cherry Orchard*, which are considered the true "Chekhovian" plays

- Collaborated with famous director and actor Konstantin Stanislavski and the Moscow Art Theater, where he met his wife Olga

Key Works

Platonov, 1881
Ivanov, 1887
The Wood Demon, 1889
The Seagull, 1896
Uncle Vanya, 1897
Three Sisters, 1901
The Cherry Orchard, 1903

Biography

A czar of Russian letters, Anton Pavlovich Chekhov was born in January 1860 in Taganrog, Russia. He attended the local Greek school and then the local high school, learning in the classical style he would grow to hate. His father was a freed serf who fled to Moscow, leaving behind a pile of bad debt. The family eventually followed, and Chekhov attended classes at the medical school of Moscow University. Chekhov, despite the fervor of the times, remained apolitical. This neutral tone often led to criticism. He published comic pieces in magazines before stepping into the world of drama with 1887's *Ivanov*. His big break was *The Seagull* in 1896, followed immediately by *Uncle Vanya* in 1897. He quietly married an actress from his plays in 1901; he only informed his mother of his marriage via a short telegram. Chekhov was only 44 when he died of tuberculosis in 1904.

Drama

Though he was later lauded for bringing realism to contemporary drama, Chekhov had a rough start, and it took a stylistic progression for him to get his footing in the theatrical world. His first plays, *Platonov*, *Ivanov*, and *The Wood Demon*, were largely unsuccessful. Critics complained that Chekhov's attempts to capture human psychology were overshadowed by excessive melodrama and moral didacticism.

Chekhov's turning point came with *The Seagull*; its success was followed by *Uncle Vanya*, *Three Sisters*, and *The Cherry Orchard*. In these later plays, he developed his unique style of drama that, at first glance, appears quite undramatic. In his attempt to capture the flow and rhythm of everyday life, Chekhov portrays drama in nuanced dialogue rather than in direct action. The most "dramatic" events of his plays—love affairs, suicides, and other unusual occurrences—take place offstage. Chekhov's heroes are typically rather ordinary characters who find themselves stuck in the mundane routines of everyday life. Chekhov does not rely on traditional villains or heroes; instead, his characters are plagued by unrequited love, unmet dreams, and unfulfilling careers. Though his complex work was initially criticized for its seeming lack of plot or purpose, its meaning is found in the subtle contradictions and subdued struggles of everyday life. This dramatic realism is often resolved in an understated comedy. Richard Gillman of Yale University asserts that Chekhov did not intend to be outright hilarious, but rather to "liberate, to relieve, and to heal" in the midst of the often seriousness of life.

The Seagull

One of his most celebrated plays, *The Seagull*, depicts events on a Russian country estate. The romantic and artistic struggles of *The Seagull*'s four main characters are revealed principally through dialogue. The audience is not privy to the play's major events, such as Treplyov killing a seagull or his later suicide attempts. Instead, viewers must divine these events from dialogue. In addition to various romantic subplots, another major theme in *The Seagull* is the examination of theater itself. Chekhov seems to be explaining his own vocation through the words of Nina Zarchnaya, who tells Treplyov:

> I know now, I understand. In what we do—whether we act on the stage or write—the most important thing isn't fame or glory or anything I used to dream about—but the ability to endure. To know how to bear your cross and have faith. I have faith, and my pain is less, and when I think about my vocation I'm not afraid of life.

The Seagull undoubtedly portrays the trademark Chekhovian "flow of life." Dialogue and subtext, rather than direct action, reveal the play's themes. Gillman writes that the main characters of the play, Nina, Arkadina, Trigorin, and Treplyov, represent "selves seeking, or failing, to reconcile the various modes of living." Through his understated plot, Chekhov explores the contradictions of romance and the tensions of the literary and dramatic worlds.

Uncle Vanya

Neither a comedy nor a tragedy, *Uncle Vanya* stands as one of Chekhov's greatest—and most complex—works. The story follows the disenchantment of Voynitsky, widely called Vanya, with his brother-in-law and former role model, Professor Serebyakov. Vanya becomes depressed and disgusted with Serebyakov, and he accuses Serebyakov's young second wife, Yelena, of wasting her life with the old, sick man. Through the unfolding of several love triangles, the play's characters reveal a quiet obsession with making up for wasted time. Despite Vanya's many years of working to support Serebyakov and the estate, Serebyakov suggests selling the property. Vanya flies into a rage and shoots at Serebyakov twice while the two are offstage. Vanya misses both times and slumps into a chair in despair. In typical Chekhovian fashion, the characters soon return to the mundane activities of their ordinary lives, and the play ends rather anticlimactically This work about wasted time, latent resentment, and passive dissatisfaction with life is a realist masterpiece that perfectly captures Chekhov's unique style.

Elizabeth Palms, 2014

ALFRED NORTH WHITEHEAD, 1861–1947, *Founded Process Theology*

> It is as true to say that God creates the World, as that the World creates God.
> —*Process and Reality*

- Was a British mathematician whose first experience with philosophy came while attending his own lectures on the subject at Harvard
- Encouraged students to develop their own method of learning and never inhibited students in their pursuits; such a notoriously easy grader that an A-minus in one of his classes was considered failure

- Collaborated with a former student, Bertrand Russell, to publish the highly influential *Principia Mathematica* in 1910
- Believed the underlying foundation of reality was events and processes instead of atomic bits of matter
- Rejected determinism and believed that all processes in the world have creative power and do not abide by universal laws alone
- Created a metaphysical system which was used as the foundation for process theology
- Viewed God as a relational being that is not outside of time but experiences the present in the same manner as humanity
- Believed that God is capable of being emotionally affected by his creation and that humanity is capable of free will, since God does not know which decisions humans will make
- Thought of religion as a deeply personal matter that instills meaning and significance into the individual, but he personally refrained from joining any specific church
- Said that the history of Western philosophy may be characterized as "a series of footnotes to Plato"

Key Works

Principia Mathematica, 1910
Science and the Modern World, 1925
Religion in the Making, 1926
Process and Reality, 1929
Adventures of Ideas, 1933

Biography

Alfred North Whitehead was born on February 15, 1861, in Kent, England. As a young boy, Whitehead excelled at mathematics and began his collegiate studies at Trinity College, Cambridge a year ahead of his peers. While at Cambridge, he discovered his passion for teaching and was offered a professorship at Trinity, where he taught mathematics for the next 30 years. During this time, he collaborated with a former student, Bertrand Russell, and the pair published the highly influential *Principia Mathematica* in 1910. In the same year, a close friend and fellow colleague of Whitehead's indulged in a marital affair that became a local scandal. In response, Trinity fired the professor, and Whitehead, outraged at the severity of Trinity's sentence, resigned his professorship in public protest.

After leaving Trinity, he moved to London and in 1914 was appointed professor of applied mathematics at the Imperial College of Science and Technology. Ten years later, facing mandatory retirement, he decided to accept a professorship at Harvard, arriving there at 65. During this period he produced his three most profound and lasting works: *Science and the Modern World*, *Process and Reality*, and *Adventures of Ideas*. His biggest influence on philosophy is found in the creation and refinement of process theology. Whitehead was universally praised as a teacher, and his ex-students described him as a gentle and soft-spoken man: "He was always benign, there was not a grain of ill will anywhere in him; for all his formidable armament, never a wounding word." Whitehead died peacefully in his bed in 1947 and, according to his wishes, all of his unpublished papers were burned.

Opponent of Scientific Materialism

Although Whitehead spent the vast majority of his academic career as a logician and mathematician, his contributions to metaphysics are considered his most lasting works. He believed that advancements in scientific theory had inadvertently clouded the minds of scientists and made them believe that speculative philosophy (or metaphysics) was unimportant since it could not be empirically tested. According to Whitehead, many of the scientific theories in use during his time were relying on an incorrect metaphysical system that was inhibiting them from properly describing the world. He opposed scientific materialism, the view that the universe is composed of "an irreducible brute matter, or material, spread through space in a flux of configurations." Whitehead claimed that scientific materialism did not account for teleological (or purpose driven) aspects of the universe and was incapable of fully incorporating human perception and experience into the universe as a whole. He proposed a radically different method of viewing the universe: the philosophy of organism.

Philosophy of Organism

Whitehead believed that the basic units of reality are not small bits of matter but processes or events. According to this picture of reality, there are no such things as points of time or space. All things are defined by events, not by microscopic objects of matter (like electrons or quarks). Whitehead didn't deny that atoms or microscopic things exist; he claimed that they are abstractions of reality that have retained a stable meaning but can ultimately be reduced down to the events that define them. Imagine it this way: it is a commonly held belief that people are fundamentally the same through time, that the changes that do occur within an individual are secondary to their core identity as a person. However, according to Whitehead's view, a person's "core identity" is only the result of overlapping experiences that share important features with one another. So, when someone talks about a person's identity, they are not referring to an unchanging nature in that person, but are recognizing similar features of multiple events and making generalizations based off these similarities. Therefore, identities do not define people, but people define identities.

Process Theology

Though never using the term "process theology" himself, Whitehead presented a robust metaphysics and a view of religion that were later refined and used as the foundation of process theology. He defined religion as "what the individual does with his own solitariness," and viewed God as a more personal co-participant in the creative process of the universe than what would be traditionally found in orthodox religion. Process theology takes these claims and further develops them into an entire theological system of belief.

What is process theology exactly? Remember that according to Whitehead's metaphysics the world is made up of events, and he stressed the importance of creativity in these events. Process theology uses this as a foundation for the belief that although God is the supreme or eminent creative power, he is not the only creative power; God and creatures are co-creators. In order to understand this principle, it is important to understand the nature of time according to process theology. In traditional theism, God views all of time as being spread out like a canvas with an eternal and omniscient vantage point that allows him to see every event simultaneously. Process theism challenges this view and claims that there is no eternal perspective that allows God to view the universe or creation as complete. Every moment is a new creation of time, and God is not outside of time but experiences each moment similar to the way we do. Process theologians argue that traditional theism, insofar as it places God outside of time, presents God as not being pleased, surprised, disappointed, or affected in any manner by any event that occur, since God already knows what will happen. They argue that this view of God is not in line with scripture, where God is seen as loving and caring for his creation and being affected by what happens to his followers. Process theology solves this by viewing God on a more relational level with his creation since He is affected by what occurs in the world.

God's Relationship with Humankind

These claims have three tremendous impacts on the relationship between God and humanity as Whitehead sees it. To begin with, God is sensitive to the lives and outcomes of his followers. Whitehead viewed God as "the great companion—the fellow-sufferer who understands." First, God is no longer impassive or the unmoved mover, as Thomas Aquinas argued, but is capable of feelings, emotions, and being affected by the suffering of his creation. Accordingly, God is not responsible for the evils and sufferings in the world, since he did not know which future would be actualized by humanity. Second, process theologians argue that traditional theism views God's choice to create the world as valueless; there is nothing gained or lost in the creation of the world, since God is the only creator and the ultimate value. God existing without the world has the same amount of infinite value as God existing with the world. According to process theology, traditional theism is wrong. The world and creation have value since they have the power to create things and operate alongside the ultimate creator to bring about new creation. Lastly, God operates according to his love for his creation and does not coerce or force things to occur in the world.

God leads and guides creation towards the best possible future, and it is a man's choice whether to follow God's calling. This means that humankind and God's relationship is not unilateral, but relational, and an active process. God's intentions for his creation are pure, objectively good, and based on love. Accordingly, being a Christian is an active process and "leads to a recognition that one's own life is worth living only to the extent that it is merged with the essential rightness of the objective universe. Such loyalty to the world expresses the intuition of sacredness underlying an appreciation for the interrelatedness of everything and for the significance of every detail to the total picture of the universe." All events and all processes of creation have value from both their own creative power and God's creative power.

Toby Coffman, faculty
Tyler King, 2016
Tatjana Scherschel, 2015
Daren Jonescu, advisor

GEORGE SANTAYANA, 1863–1952, *The Dreamer*

> " The world is not respectable; it is mortal, tormented, confused, deluded forever; but it is shot through with beauty, with love, with glints of courage and laughter; and in these, the spirit blooms timidly, and struggles to the light amid the thorns.
> —"Platonism and the Spiritual Life"

- Was a Spanish-American philosopher who claimed his aim was to celebrate life through his intellectual studies
- Became disenchanted with modern universities, which he saw as being too focused on money
- Was convinced that matter alone made up all reality

- Believed firmly in naturalism: that knowledge and belief are not the product of abstract reasoning, but of personal and environmental material conditions which make certain beliefs inescapable; the true is whatever it is essential to believe given one's natural (material) circumstances
- Preferred to study all philosophies, religions, and other products of human thought from an outside, naturalistic perspective—not "What is the truth value of what those people believe?" but rather "What conditions make it necessary for them to believe that?"
- Believed that religion, like poetry, is an artistic expression of human experience
- Held that mankind could only ever understand essences, the distinguishing features of different facts, which are variable and many, derived from variable material conditions
- Thought that humanity could never obtain true knowledge in the sense of a single certainty about any given thing, since there is no stable "correct" understanding of anything, taken out of its personal and environmental context
- Was a kind of moral relativist: believed that what was morally "good" for one individual may not be good for another individual in a different circumstance (naturalism again); self-realization (the proper human goal) is not universalizable in its content
- Held that happiness comes from self-knowledge, which means not knowledge of a universal notion like "human nature," but rather knowledge of one's actual interests in all their contextual permutations
- Emphasized the self-realization of the idiosyncratic individual, which led him (unlike some of his American intellectual peers, who were typically men of the progressive left) to a conservative political position, with the state as insurer of the social space for individual development, rather than imposer of artificial collective social structure, as in the case of the socialist John Dewey

Key Works

The Sense of Beauty: Being the Outline of Aesthetic Theory, 1896
Interpretations of Poetry and Religion, 1900
The Life of Reason: The Phases of Human of Human Progress, 1905–1906
Character and Opinion in the United States, 1920
Scepticism and Animal Faith: Introduction to a System of Philosophy, 1923
The Realms of Being, 1927–1940
The Last Puritan: A Memoir in the Form of a Novel, 1935
Persons and Places, 1944

Biography

George Santayana, originally Jorge Augustín Nicolás Ruiz de Santayana, was born in Madrid but is considered one of the great American authors and philosophers. As a result of his parents' separation, the young Santayana spent the first eight years of his life living with his father in Spain. Although his father tried to move to Boston in an attempt to reconcile with Santayana's mother (who was keeping her pledge to her first husband to raise their children in America), his father could not bear the climate. He returned to Europe after only a few months and left Santayana with his mother.

Santayana's early education was both rigorous and thorough, but he had no love for Boston Latin School, the school that he attended. His autobiography gives insight into his childhood loneliness: "I know I was solitary and unhappy, out of humor with everything that surrounded me, and attached only to a persistent dream-life." During this time Santayana developed a love of poetry and reading. By the time he was an undergraduate at Harvard, Santayana had shed all of his childhood shyness. He was a member of 11 organizations on campus, and, after receiving his doctorate, taught philosophy to the likes of T.S. Eliot, Robert Frost, and Walter Lippmann.

Santayana soon became disenchanted with American University life, believing that it had become too corporate in nature and cared more about money and political clout than celebrating intellectual freedom and ideas. He began to alter his lifestyle from "that of an active student turned professor to one focused on the imaginative celebration of life." He semi-retired, traveling back and forth between the US and Europe to please his Harvard friends. Before long he stopped trying to fit into a sterile academic world and took full advantage of his independence from any intellectual organization. He settled in Rome and produced some of his greatest masterpieces, including *Scepticism and Animal Faith* and a collection of four volumes called *Realms of Being*. Nearing the end of his life, Santayana began writing his three-part autobiography, *Persons and Places*, in 1944. He succumbed to cancer in 1952.

"On Both Sides of the Atlantic": Aesthetics and Culture

Santayana titled the second section of his autobiography "On Both Sides of the Atlantic" to reflect his travels between the United States and Europe. During this time Santayana developed his philosophical beliefs concerning aesthetics and became something of a cultural critic.

Santayana held the conviction that "religion and poetry are expressive celebrations of life." Born from the interaction of the human psyche and the physical environment, religion and poetry were naturalistic subjects through and through. Attempting to apply science to either would destroy both their beauty and expressive nature. In Santayana's words, "poetry loses its frivolity and ceases to demoralise, while religion surrenders its illusions and ceases to deceive" when science and so called rational thought are used to analyze them.

Considering his sensitivity to the more beautiful things of the world and his developing naturalism, it should surprise no one that Santayana soon became disillusioned with American culture, which he viewed as being too focused on work and too dependent on old Puritan ideologies. He wrote in *Character and Opinion in the United States*:

> You must wave, you must cheer, you must push with the irresistible crowd; otherwise you will feel like a traitor, a soulless outcast, a deserted ship high and dry on the shore. … This national faith and morality are vague in idea, but inexorable in spirit; they are the gospel of work and the belief in progress. By them, in a country where all men are free, every man finds that what most matters has been settled beforehand.

Perhaps no work describes his cultural critique of America better than his only novel, *The Last Puritan*. In it, Santayana sets up a vivid contrast between the young European character, Mario, who is carefree and, by American standards, "appears too focused on the peripheral aspects of life: travel, opera, love affairs, and architecture," and the tragic American youth, Oliver Alden, who is the last Puritan. Oliver is a dedicated student and football star, but cannot escape the slow grind of never-ending obligations and tasks that make up his life. Denying obligation and duty are just not something he can do, given his Puritan upbringing constantly tugging at his conscience. As a result, he ends up dying tragically.

An Intellectual Vagabond

When Santayana moved back to Europe his philosophy began to mature. He acknowledges that he was always a realist, writing that despite "my religious and other day-dreams, I was at bottom a young realist; I knew I was dreaming, and so was awake." As he grew older, he began to develop a viewpoint in which all the grand and eloquent philosophies and religions of the world were nothing more than "the soliloquies and the ghosts" of the play of nature and humankind. He saw himself as an outsider looking in, an "intellectual vagabond or tramp, not isolated in the specific perspectives of an ideology." In setting out to define his philosophical beliefs, Santayana also made it clear that he was practicing philosophy not to be engaged in society and culture, but rather to celebrate life as the original philosophers of Greek and Roman tradition set out to do. With this mindset he developed his materialist and naturalist philosophies.

Naturalism

Santayana's naturalism was rooted in materialism, which formed the basis of his philosophy. According to Santayana, matter was the source of all things. He held that "there are purely natural or materialistic causes of all the phenomena of existence." This meant that even human thought was the product of the interactions of the psyche with the material environment. Essentially, our animal life and its interactions with nature produce thought and reason. According to Santayana's philosophy, the mind could not affect nature because it was a creation of nature, not the other way around. In fact, Santayana believed that the mind did not really understand much (or any) of nature or truth at all.

This important feature of his philosophy comes into better light when one considers Santayana's concept of essences vs. existence. He believed that the essences are "the obvious features that distinguish facts from each other." Essences have no true existence, but yet they are all that the mind can conceive. What this boils down to is that there is not necessarily any connection between what is perceived and what actually exists. Santayana was skeptical about one's ability to ever achieve true knowledge.

This conviction in humanity's lack of genuine knowledge also explains Santayana's belief that the works of the imagination "alone are good; and [that] the rest—the whole real world—is ashes in its mouth." For Santayana, these products of the imagination included religion, and he did not believe in any god. Santayana simply saw all forms of religion as expressive art forms resulting from human experience and not actually depicting anything that actually existed.

Ethics

Many authorities on Santayana's moral philosophy hold him to be an "extreme moral relativist who maintains that all individual moral perspectives have equal standing and are based on the heritable traits and environmental circumstances of individuals." In other words, there is no absolute definition of good and bad that applies to everyone. Santayana's ethics were deeply rooted in his naturalism philosophy and consisted of two basic tenets: "the forms of the good are diverse, and the good of each animal is definite and final." Santayana included humans in his definition of "animal."

The first tenet describes the belief that all animal interests and goods are equal. These goods depend on the creature's inheritable physical traits and the environment. What is good for an animal in one circumstance may be different than what is good for a different animal in a different circumstance. Furthermore, what is good for an animal may change as time and environment change. Santayana's second point simply maintains that what is good for an individual is the final and definitive good for him personally. This puts a lot of weight on self-knowledge. The extent to which a person can understand his own interests and needs determines the extent to which he can live a good life of contentment. This requires a knowledge and appreciation of one's culture and physical traits.

Tyler King, 2016
Tatjana Scherschel, 2015
Daren Jonescu, advisor

MAX WEBER ◊ 1864–1920, *Father of Sociology*

" After industry and frugality, nothing contributes more to the raising of a young man in the world than punctuality and justice.
—*The Protestant Ethic and the Spirit of Capitalism*

- Was one of the most influential sociologists in the general culture
- Suffered from severe depression brought on by a nasty fight with his father, who suddenly died two months later
- Argued that social scientists needed to consider the meanings that actors *themselves* assign to their own experiences and actions
- Wanted to separate the worlds of politics and science, since science can tell us nothing about values (this is an example of what is called the fact-value distinction)
- Pondered different ways people justify the right to rule; thought modern times are characterized by bureaucratic authority and belief in legal order and rules
- Explored questions about how to obtain objective knowledge when we study the subjective, personal values held by people in history
- Formulated the concept of an "ideal type" as a tool for sociology (an abstract, hypothetical concept or "typical case")
- Volunteered in WWI at age 50 and became a hospital administrator
- Tried to explain how we choose certain historical phenomena as worthy of our attention over other historically important phenomena
- Thought that modern science and technology had dismissed religious values as irrational and superstitious and thus "disenchanted" our world
- Analyzed the various ways we justify authority—written rules and procedures, unwritten rules from long ago, or the authority of the extraordinary person
- Analyzed American capitalism, famously and highly questionably, as essentially a product of the "Protestant work ethic"; in general, Weber (and sociology) open to the criticism that in his zeal to find the social phenomena underlying major political and moral decisions, he overlooks or dismisses the role and influence of individual human reasoning, particularly philosophical and political reasoning; in other words, he dismisses the historical significance of individual great minds who led movements and inspired change

Key Works

Economy and Society, 1921–22
Protestant Ethic and the Spirit of Capitalism, 1904–1905

Biography

Karl Emil Maximilian Weber was born in 1864, the eldest of seven children, to a wealthy industrialist and merchant family in northwestern Germany. He received a doctorate in law and obtained a university job when he wrote a report for *Verein für Sozialpolitik*, the leading social science association, on the struggles of German agricultural workers who were losing jobs as a result of Polish migrant workers. The success of this report landed him a University of Freiburg professorship at age 30. He married Marianne Schnitger in 1893, though the marriage was likely never consummated, and he later had extramarital affairs.

Weber's reputation continued to grow, and he took a prestigious professorship at the University of Heidelberg in 1896. Shortly thereafter his father died, partly as a result of a heated argument he'd had with Weber. This led to deep depression, insomnia, and even a nervous breakdown for Weber, and at age 33 he was forced to stop teaching. His absence from the classroom lasted for the 16 years. He continued to research and write, and participated in many academic and public groups. During WWI, Weber grew disillusioned with war and became a vocal critic of the Kaiser government. By the time the war ended in 1918, he was viewed as an intellectual and leader, helping to draft the Weimar Constitution as well as serve as an advisor to the German delegation to Versailles. He ultimately became frustrated with day-to-day politics and returned to his scholarly pursuits. In 1920, at 56, Max Weber died of pneumonia.

How "Predestination" Made People Work Harder

Weber thought that people did not always crave wealth, money, and profit the way they do in modern capitalistic society: "A man does not 'by nature' wish to earn more and more money, but simply to live as he is accustomed to live and to earn as much as is necessary for that purpose," Something changed and, for Weber, the roots of the change are in the Protestant Reformation. This is the focus of his famous work *The Protestant Ethic and the Spirit of Capitalism*.

Weber singled out two ideas from the Reformation: Luther's idea of "calling" and Calvin's doctrine of "predestination." Before Luther, if one had a calling, it was typically a religious vocation like a priest or a monk. Protestantism expanded this idea of calling to include "worldly" vocations: everyday work was a calling from God. The doctrine of predestination provided the motivation to complete that work as well as possible, since it taught that God has "elected" or chosen some people for salvation. You can't know if you're elected, unfortunately, and that uncertainty inevitably produces anxiety, even terror. However, if you obey God by being frugal, refraining from luxury and frivolous pleasures, and being devoted to your work, that *might* be a sign that God has chosen you for salvation. Hence, according to Weber, Protestantism produced a certain type of person: the early capitalist businessman who was ascetic and frugal. These traits thrive in capitalism. Benjamin Franklin was one of Weber's favorite examples: "We shall nevertheless provisionally use the expression 'spirit of capitalism' for that attitude which, in the pursuit of a calling strives systematically for profit for its own sake in the manner exemplified by Benjamin Franklin."

Thus, Protestantism, particularly Calvinism and its doctrine of predestination, played a major role in creating the conditions necessary for capitalism to flourish. Luther preached about one's worldly calling, and thus worldly activity took on a religious character. Calvin's idea of predestination—and the uncertainty and anxiety produced by taking the doctrine to heart—resulted in Protestants valuing profit and material success as an indication of God's blessing.

We've Been Disenchanted

In *The Protestant Ethic and the Spirit of Capitalism*, Weber emphasized how religious and cultural values played a crucial role in the rise of modern capitalism. However, once capitalism "gets going," and modern people become habituated to it, the religious elements fall away, much like the early stages of a rocket going into space.

The calculable processes of production in modern capitalism are just one of many instances of what Weber called "rationalization," or "a historical drive towards a world in which 'one can, in principle, master all things by calculation.'" Rationalization makes things more predictable and easy to master; it also increases our knowledge of causes and effects, increases our control over our lives, and impersonally reduces workers to mere numbers in an accounting book. Rationalization brings benefits to society, but Weber saw reason for concern. He closed *The Protestant Ethic and the Spirit of Capitalism* with the arresting metaphor of a "shell," or what has often been called "an iron cage":

> No one yet knows who will live in that shell in the future. Perhaps new prophets will emerge, or powerful old ideas and ideals will be reborn at the end of this monstrous development. Or perhaps—if neither of these occurs—"Chinese" ossification, dressed up with a kind of desperate self-importance, will set in. Then, however, it might be truly said of the "last men" in this cultural development: "specialists without spirit, hedonists without a heart, these nonentities imagine they have attained a stage of humankind never before reached.

The rationalization of our modern world brought on particularly by modern science has robbed the world of gods. We've been "disenchanted," according to Weber. Magic and mystery no longer permeate our sense of the world, and if we *do* happen to encounter mystery we try to solve it, not embrace it.

Jeff Culver, faculty
Daren Jonescu, advisor

LUIGI PIRANDELLO ◊ 1867–1936, *Absurd Playwright Challenging Reality*

> The capacity for deluding ourselves that today's reality is the only true one, on the one hand, sustains us, but on the other, it plunges us into an endless void.
> —*One, No One, and One Hundred Thousand*

- Was a Sicilian writer, who was awarded the Nobel Prize in Literature in 1934
- Invented "new theater" in the 1920s
- Was obsessed with expressing the differences between reality and appearance, madness and sanity
- Contributed to the theater style of the grotesque and absurd
- Held membership in the Italian Fascist Party

Key Works

Six Characters in Search of an Author, 1921

Henry IV, 1921
The Late Mattia Pascal, 1904

Biography

Luigi Pirandello was born in 1867 to a wealthy, mine-owning Sicilian family. After a move to Palermo, Pirandello began his studies at the University of Palermo—a hotbed of future fascists—before transferring to Rome. He completed his doctorate in philology in 1891. Financial tragedy struck the family with the flooding of their sulfur mine, forcing Pirandello into more practical work. His first novel, *The Late Mattia Pascal*, was a commercial and critical success. However, his wife Antonietta was mentally unstable; her jealousies often brought on physical violence, and Pirandello was forced to place her in asylum care in 1919. It was during this period, before and after the First World War, that Pirandello wrote many of the plays that made him famous, including 1921's controversial *Six Characters in Search of an Author*. The play's unusual take on chronology and progression helped make it an example of literary modernism. Though a one-time member of the Italian fascist party, his relationship with fascist politics was uneasy. He was awarded the Nobel Prize in Literature in 1934, just two years before his death.

Six Characters in Search of an Author

Pirandello's play, *Six Characters in Search of an Author*, centers on a family of six characters. The play was instantly polarizing, with some in attendance even labeling it a play of madness. Dreamt up by an author while at the same time denied the right to live on the stage, the titular six characters leave the author in search of someone who will write their story—a tragedy that slowly unfolds throughout the play. Pirandello's unique style acts as an origin point for modernist theater and incorporated many of his most characteristic themes and motifs. His use of "play in production" or a play within a play allows him to speak to the nature of the theater, which he believed incapable of perfectly capturing the story because it simply was not the story. The theater inherently seeks to reflect the real world; Pirandello confronts this in his "mirror theater" style as well. In *Six Characters*, the actors mirror the characters while the characters realize their inability to do so properly: "it isn't possible to live in front of a mirror which not only freezes us with the images of ourselves, but throws our likeness back at us with a horrible grimace." Questions of identity became a hallmark of modernist drama.

Absurdism and Relativism

Pirandello was a major contributor to the Theater of the Absurd, as well. *Six Characters* compares illusion and reality in order to flip the audience's preconceived perspective on its head. While the actors and manager (voicing the audience's perspective) believe that their lives are real and the characters and their story simply illusion, the characters argue that their reality is more real than their human counterparts'.

Life and art contrast in that life is spontaneous and limited by death, unlike art, which is still and eternal. The father gets upset at the manager for calling his reality an illusion when in fact his "reality doesn't change: it can't change! It can't be other than what it is, because it is already fixed for ever … your reality is a mere transitory and fleeting illusion, taking this form today and that tomorrow." For humans, the spontaneity of life means a constantly changing story.

Pirandello argues that humans change masks day to day to accommodate their changing environments and therefore hold no single identity. Characters, on the other hand, are eternally the same, always in the same story. Therefore, the characters are fixed at all times while a human's "self" is fickle and unstable, so "a character, sir, may always ask a man who he is. Because a character has really a life of his own, marked with his especial characteristics; for which reason he is always 'somebody.' But a man—I'm not speaking of you now—may very well be 'nobody.'" The absurdism is brought to a climax in the last act when the characters show the actors the death of the child and a boy; the actors react thinking that they are actually dead—letting go of their distinction between their reality and the characters' illusion in favor of the reality of the art shown to them. These themes are seen throughout Pirandello's works, especially *Naked Masks* and *Henry IV*, but they came together in *Six Characters in Search of an Author* to ignite a new style in 20th-century theater.

Trisha Rouleau, 2015

VLADIMIR LENIN, 1870–1924, *Leader of the Bolshevik Revolution*

> " Politics begin where the masses are, not where there are thousands, but where there are millions, that is where serious politics begin.
> —Report to the Seventh Congress of the Russian Communist Party

- Was a Russian revolutionary who strongly supported the Communist ideals of Karl Marx
- Co-founded the Marxist newspaper, *Iskra*, which effectively spread communist propaganda all over Russia
- Traveled across Europe to spread the idea of a proletariat revolution
- Was imprisoned multiple times by the Russian government for his revolutionary acts
- Created the Bolsheviks, who ended up taking control of the Russian government in 1917
- Ruled over the Russian government alongside Leon Trotsky for seven years
- Advocated for communism because it established the proletariat class as equal to the aristocracy
- Spearheaded the revolution through the opposition's many provisional governments until October
- Staged a coup on the Winter Palace, taking over the government in October 1917

Key Works
The April Theses, 1917

Biography
The revolutionary ideals of Vladimir Lenin were hugely influential in paving the way for communism to take hold of the Soviet Union. Born into late-19th-century Russia, Lenin grew up surrounded by revolution. Before he was 20 years old, Lenin already resented the autocratic government of Russia and admired Karl Marx. In 1895, Lenin began traveling around Europe to spread enthusiasm among the already committed Marxists. Back in Russia, he attempted to initiate a proletariat uprising, but was quickly caught and imprisoned before being exiled to Siberia. When his exile ended in 1900, Lenin began writing a newspaper called *Iskra*, which disseminated pro-communist propaganda across the country. Eventually, Lenin wrote a bold book that outlined his plans for a Marxist revolution. He and his associates fled to England to avoid being arrested for the controversy. In 1905 Lenin stirred his Bolshevik party to attempt a revolution, but Tsar Nicholas II held the chaos at bay for several years

with promises such as the "October Manifesto." In 1914, the beginning of WWI sparked another uprising in Russia. Lenin was forced into hiding, but it wasn't long before he resumed urging the Bolsheviks to stage a rapid coup. This time, the insurrection succeeded and Lenin gained control of the Russian government. The Bolsheviks renamed themselves the Communist Party, and Lenin consolidated party rule over Russia. Over the next several years, Lenin confronted the Russian Civil War, multiple assassination attempts, and the famine of 1921. Ruling with an iron fist, Lenin crushed those who opposed the Bolsheviks, and his reign became known as the "Red Terror." He died in 1924.

Communism

Lenin, an ardent believer in Marxist ideals, was the first to implement communism in the Soviet Union. Communism is a political system that entails removing all private property and implementing state control over all production systems. Lenin believed that possessing property led to greed and social unbalance and that the removal of property would result in perfect equality. He argued that communism would end oppression and division based on social class, which would result in a heavenly society: one with no economic classes, no war or oppression, and full freedom with light work. This utopian idea excited many workers of the day, who formed Communist parties all around Europe and caused Marxist revolutions in Russia and, eventually, China. These societies ultimately failed, however, as each state that attempted to control societal and economic activity became a regime more oppressive than the last. Both the Soviet Union and China eventually abandoned socialism and communism for other systems.

Bolshevik Revolution

World War I was a terrible time for the Soviet Union, with Czar Nicholas II sending 15 million untrained workers and farmers to the front lines. More than half of the men died in battle or from famine. Back in Moscow, Czar Nicholas decided to lead his armies from the front lines, so he transferred his power to his wife, who later let the monk Rasputin take control. Rasputin's rule led to the collapse of the economy and mass famine. His assassination by Nicholas's cousin and nephew-in-law was met with widespread relief.

Soon, proletariat workers began a bloody but mostly leaderless riot known as the February Revolution. Since no political or rebel leaders were able to regain control, Lenin mustered the support of the Bolsheviks and rose to informal power over Russia. Within his first month, Lenin won the trust of the people after implementing reforms and advocating for peace negotiations that would help Germany win the war. Lenin's popular support led to the downfall of every provisional government that attempted to take power over the next three months. By the end of October, the Bolsheviks gained control of Petrograd and Moscow in a bloody coup outside the Winter Palace. They removed the previous leader, Kerensky, and placed Lenin in charge of the Council of Commissars as the head of the new government. The country was still heavily divided, however, and Lenin knew he needed to end Russia's involvement in the World War in order to make any domestic progress, so he began peace negotiations with Germany. He eventually succeeded in pulling Russia out of the war, which gave Trotsky and Lenin the time to put the country back together before Lenin's death and Stalin's rise to leadership.

Jack Beebe, 2012
Joshua E. Fernalld, 2016
McCarthy Nolan, 2016

MARCEL PROUST, 1871–1922, *The Discoverer of Lost Time*

> " It is inconceivable that a piece of sculpture or a piece of music which gives us an emotion that we feel to be more exalted, more pure, more true, does not correspond to some definite spiritual reality, or life would be meaningless.
>
> —*The Captive*

- Wrote *Remembrance of Things Past* or *In Search of Lost Time*, his magnum opus and autobiography, which consists of seven volumes and 1,267,069 words
- Called to mind a childhood memory by tasting a madeleine cookie that prompted him to write *In Search of Lost Time*
- Focused on memory and time as prominent themes in his writing
- Explored involuntary memory and the subconscious quality of memory
- Wrote in a room lined with cork in order to block out the roar of Paris
- Worked constantly during the last 10 years of his life, hardly leaving his bedroom

Key Works

Remembrance of Things Past or *In Search of Lost Time*
Volume One: *Swann's Way*, 1913
Volume Two: *Within a Budding Grove*, 1919
Volume Three: *The Guermantes Way*, 1920/1921
Volume Four: *Sodom and Gomorrah*, 1921/1922
Volume Five: *The Captive*, 1923
Volume Six: *The Fugitive*, 1925
Volume Seven: *Time Regained*, 1927

Biography

Proust was born on July 10, 1871, in Auteuil, France. As a young boy, he and his family spent summers in his father's family home in Illiers and also in Normandy. By the age of 9, he started to suffer from chronic asthma attacks, which plagued him his entire life.

Following a brief military service, Proust entered École des Sciences Politiques where he received licentiates in law (1893) and literature (1895). At the same time, he studied memory and time lectures by French philosopher Henri Bergson. Because he spent his free time in drawing rooms for the aristocratic and wealthy, some considered him a wealthy snob and his early writing went unacclaimed. Following the death of his parents, he moved away from his family home and into a cork-lined bedroom where he secluded himself for years as he wrote. He penned parodies of his favorite French authors that were published in the newspaper *Le Figaro*.

Over the years, he wrote three versions of *Swann's Way* (*Du côté de chez Swann*), the first from 1905 to 1906, the second from 1907 to 1908, and the third in 1909. The third version became the final product, and in 1912, he searched for a publisher. None of the large publishing houses would adopt the piece; however, a newer publishing house agreed to work with him. WWI delayed the publication of the second volume, *Within a Budding Grove* (*À l'ombre des jeunes filles en fleurs*) to 1919. Volumes three and four, *The Guermantes Way* (*Le Côte de Guermantes*) and *Sodom and Gomorrah* (*Sodome et Gomorrhe*), were published shortly before his death. Proust died in Paris on November 18, 1933. The last three volumes—*The Captive* (*La Prisonniére*), *The Fugitive* (*Albertine disparue*), and *Time Regained* (*Le Temps retrouvê*)—

were edited by his brother. His magnum opus spanned 4,000 manuscript pages, and it is still widely read with translations in multiple languages.

Time

In Search of Lost Time, quite naturally, examines the mysteriousness of time. Proust explores the quickness of time and the lack of awareness and appreciation people have for time. In *Swann's Way* the narrator recognizes that past time is lost: "and in [himself], too, many things have perished which [he] imagined would last forever, and new ones have arisen, giving birth to new sorrows and new joys which in those days [he] could not have foreseen, just as now the old are hard to understand." Throughout the volumes, he explores the time he has lost, and in *Time Regained*, "he divulges a way to recover the whole of our lives." He learns to appreciate the moment, and that "an hour is not merely an hour. It is a vase full of scents and sounds and projects and climates." He becomes aware of everything around him through the full use of his senses. The time that has passed can be found in sensory experiences and involuntary memory.

One way in which man defies time is through art. For Proust, art survives beyond its maker and, in a way, allows the creator to discover a life more real than that of this world. In *Time Regained*, he writes, "Real life, life at last laid bare and illuminated—the only life in consequence which can be said to be really lived—is literature." However, creating this real life comes at the cost of this life for the artist. Not only does Proust believe that the artist must withdraw from the world's particulars, he suggests that the true artist must continually face his death as he creates. Artists "who believe that their works will last … form the habit of placing them in a period when they themselves will have crumbled into dust. And thus, by obliging them to reflect on their own extinction, the idea of fame saddens them because it is inseparable from the idea of death." Art has the power to endure through time, a feat no man has yet to accomplish.

Memory

Memory is another major theme in *In Search of Lost Time*, and Proust "is as all-inclusive as literature can get; what normal people filter out of memory the narrator channels in." There are 1,200 allusions to memory throughout the seven volumes. Proust emphasizes involuntary memory and examines the process of involuntary memories catalyzed by sensory experience (such as sight). The most iconic example of this occurs in *Swann's Way* where the narrator involuntarily recalls childhood memories while eating a madeleine cookie: "And suddenly the memory returns. The taste was that of the little crumb of madeleine. … The sight of the madeleine had recalled nothing to my mind before I tasted it." Proust believes that most of our past is lost. Involuntary memories usually are "shifting and confused gusts of memory [that] never lasted for more than a few seconds" and they are so sudden they lead to overwhelming euphoric emotions. He continues to study the relationship of the memory and sensory experience throughout all seven volumes. The connection between the senses and our memories has been examined in modern psychology since Proust's day and has confirmed with science his suggestions with fiction.

Marcel Proust's *In Search of Lost Time* continues to enrapture readers with its "complexity, its depth, its inexhaustible richness." Proust felt that books were the best of friendships, and in reading his work "you are going to find that he is both more friendly and more alien than you ever imagined. … His capacity for thinking things through is going to seem almost infinitely great."

JOHAN HUIZINGA ◊ 1872–1945, *Developer of the Future from the Past*

- Led the Dutch resistance during the Nazi takeover
- Focused on cultural history rather than just political history
- Was exiled by the Nazis in WWII
- Knew Dutch, Sanskrit, Arabic, Greek, Latin, Middle High German, and Old Norse
- Wrote his doctoral thesis on court jesters in ancient Sanskrit drama
- Had membership and office in the Royal Netherlands Academy of Science

Key Works

The Waning of the Middle Ages, 1919
Homo Ludens, 1938
The Outraged World, 1945

Biography

Johan Huizinga was a historian and prominent professor who, unlike many of his peers, approached history not only from a political perspective but also a cultural one. Huizinga was foremost a storyteller. Born in Groningen, Netherlands, on December 7, 1872, his father was a professor of physiology at the University of Groningen, where Huizinga would later work. When he was a child, Huizinga witnessed the reenactment of a medieval procession in Groningen, which sparked his insatiable appetite for history. In 1891, Huizinga entered the University of Groningen, where he studied psychology and learned Sanskrit, Middle High German, and Old Norse. In 1893, he started his studies of comparative linguistics at the University of Leipzig. He returned to Groningen for his doctoral degree, which he received in 1897 after writing his thesis on the role of the court jester in ancient Sanskrit drama.

Huizinga spent the majority of his career at the University of Leiden. There he wrote his most famous works, including his magnum opus: *Herfsttij der middeleeuwen* or *The Waning of the Middle Ages*. The idea for this book came to him when he was on a Sunday stroll in Groningen in 1907 where he had an epiphany that the late "Middle Ages were not so much a prelude to the future as an epoch of fading and decay." He became professor of general history at Leiden in 1915, and held the post until 1942. At that time, he spoke critically about the country's Nazi occupiers, and was held in detention in a small parish in the eastern Netherlands where he lived out his days. He died on February 1, 1945, barely missing the news of liberation from Nazi rule.

Waning of the Middle Ages

In *The Waning of the Middle Ages*, also called *The Autumn of the Middle Ages*, Huizinga focused on the history and culture of the late Middle Ages. He classified that time as a period of decline and weariness, saying "the 14th and 15th centuries [are] regarded as a period of termination." After an exhaustive study of the art and philosophy of the period, he concluded that many of the thinkers commonly believed to have sparked the Renaissance actually mark the closure of the Middle Ages. In other words, this period marked the end of an era, and not the beginning of the Renaissance.

Huizinga was fascinated with the patterns of history and espoused the idea that history is similar to a living being, occurring in cycles. Cultures rise and fall only to be replaced by new ones. The periods of time between those cycles intrigued Huizinga, and the end of the Middle Ages was the perfect example of the end of and beginning to just such a cycle. He prefaced the English translation of his work with an explanation: "It occasionally happens that a period in which one had, hitherto, been mainly looking for the coming to birth of new things, suddenly reveals itself as an epoch of fading and decay."

Though noteworthy mainly because it took a contrarian position about the period to that commonly accepted, *The Waning of the Middle Ages* was one of the earliest works to clearly articulate the concept of history being a series of repetitive cycles. Although some doubt has since been cast on Huizinga's research practices, the impressive literary style and its importance in advocating historical cultural research still make the work an impressive read.

Homo Ludens

Huizinga's other famous work, *Homo Ludens*, was written later in his career, and focused on what makes a person human. It was a culmination of his lifelong studies of cultural history, in which he made the case that "play can be seen in almost every facet of civilization." He argued that play drives all facets of society and is the essence of human nature. For example, in Chapter Four, he demonstrated that even law is play, since legal procedures are games, and lawsuits resemble contests; they embody a passion for argument and counterargument, and a desire to win. The thesis of his book surrounded this idea that "all forms of human cultures emerged out of playfulness, which was the fundamental drive of human existence." Through his studies of cultural history, Huizinga found that the development of civilization and the function of society are founded on the element of play.

Caroline Fuschino, 2015
Julianna Swayze, 2016
Alexi Wenger, 2016

BERTRAND RUSSELL, 1872–1970, *A Maverick Genius*

" Can human beings know anything, and if so, what and how? This question is really the most essentially philosophical of all questions.
—Letter to Lady Ottoline, December 13, 1911

- A British aristocrat, the ultimate silver spoon intellectual and a very free spirit
- An atheist from an atheist family
- His father consented to his mother's love affair
- Had John Stuart Mill, an atheist, as his godfather
- Contemplated suicide often as a lonely child
- Did not believe in free will, nor, therefore, in personal responsibility
- Had four marriages and numerous affairs; was a social renegade who felt that men and women shouldn't be restricted by thwarting "healthy" sexual desires

- A "celebrity philosopher"
- Philosopher, logician, mathematician, historian and social critic
- Endured jail twice due to courageous anti-war and anti-nuclear activism—a liberal, a socialist, and a pacifist
- Was awarded the British Order of Merit and the Nobel Prize in Literature, 1950
- Wrote over 60 books on topics of religion, epistemology, science, ethics, philosophy of mind, and philosophy of science; his most important contributions are in symbolic logic and mathematics
- Held originally, like most of his relevant contemporaries, to Hegelian idealism
- Helped to initiate a revolution in 20th-century Anglo-American philosophy with his rejection of idealism, as others became willing to separate themselves from the academic generation that had identified all problems and possible answers in neo-idealist terms
- Held that logic is the essence of philosophy as well as the foundation for all mathematics
- Wanted to design a logically perfect language that would be more precise than clumsy, conventional languages
- Taught Ludwig Wittgenstein, one of the most important philosophers of the 20th century
- A highly educated, very intelligent man, lacking in wisdom and unfit to teach at Valor Christian High School

Key Works

Principia Mathematica, 1910
The Problems of Philosophy, 1912
Why I Am Not a Christian, 1927
A History of Western Philosophy, 1945

Biography

The beliefs of Bertrand Russell, regarding everything from logical atomism to sexual morality, have stirred the thoughts of the philosophical community for years. In the beginning, Russell was just another young Englishman. Both of his parents died when he was very young, and his grandmother raised him. He attended Cambridge University for his undergraduate studies. A self-proclaimed pacifist, Russell was prosecuted during WWI for his involvement in actions protesting Britain's involvement. After serving his sentence, he went to America to teach at the University of Chicago, UCLA, and City College in New York. While at City College, Russell wrote the book *Marriage and Morals*. The book outlined his belief regarding the role of sex: "The desire for sex is precisely analogous to the desire for food and drink." His liberal outlook as expressed in his book resulted in his being fired from his teaching position. He returned to Cambridge as a professor. Seventeen years later, however, he was again prosecuted for anti-war activities; this time, he was protesting nuclear weapons. Following Hitler's atrocities during WWII, Russell no longer considered himself a pacifist, but he still protested America's role in the Vietnam War. By the end of his life, Russell had won many awards, including a Nobel Prize in Literature. He was hugely influential in the field of philosophy and his works are still widely discussed today.

Mathematics and Logic

Russell reacted to the idealism of Hegel that prevailed in England in the early 20th century, which held that all reality is unified and wholly based in Mind. Russell's important objection to idealism was that "it saw everything as interrelated" and thereby, according to Russell, made mathematics impossible, since in mathematics each unit must be identified and known before its relations with other units can be considered. Russell and his friend G.E. Moore rejected the doctrines of idealism that saw reality as ultimately one mental unity. Instead, they argued for an atomic view of reality that viewed things as less interrelated and more individualistic. This rejection of idealism paved the way for Russell's and Alfred North Whitehead's 10-year work, *Principia Mathematica*, in which they attempted to show that all of mathematics could be derived from a handful of logical axioms.

The Problems of Philosophy

Contrary to its title, Russell's book, *The Problems of Philosophy*, does not actually address many of philosphy's commonly mentioned faults. Instead, Russell breaks down different philosophical arguments and responds to them. One of the first topics he discusses is the meaning of philosophy. Russell acknowledges that many people study philosophy in an attempt to receive answers to deep questions regarding the universe; however, this is a false hope, as often philosophers are left with more questions than when they started. Russell maintains that philosophy is nonetheless a beneficial study because it promotes curiosity and allows people to see that there is more to the world than what we perceive. Another important aspect of philosophy is the effect it has on the world. Contrary to a subject such as science, philosophy can directly benefit only those who study it. With science, even though one may never study it, he can still greatly benefit from its effects through new products, procedures, or results of scientific research. In the field of philosophy, the products of research are ideas and concepts that affect the thinking of those who stumble upon them; therefore, whoever fails to study philosophy won't receive any direct benefits.

One important concept that Russell illustrates is the idea of knowledge. Russell suggests that knowledge can be broken into two components. One, the sense datum, is what we directly perceive. An example that Russell gives is a table that he is observing. Had he used only the sense data that he was able to perceive with his eyes, then his reality of the table would change every time a shadow was cast upon it or the sun shifted its reflection. In order to form an accurate depiction of reality, we must infer data based on past knowledge and experiences. Although the sense data may be saying that the table has a bright white stripe in the center, we are able to understand that the white stripe is simply a reflection of the window behind it. This is called an instinctive belief. Because the sense data is only what we perceive, and what we perceive can be altered by everything around us, we can never truly understand what anything truly is. In addition to instinctive belief, Russell explains another form of knowledge that he refers to as "a priori." This is knowledge that can be obtained only through logic and reason. Russell's viewpoints on perception and reality have intrigued philosophers for years.

Logical Atomism and the Theory of Descriptions

One of Russell's more important ideas was that ordinary, plain language must often be translated into logical statements in order to properly evaluate its truth. This is called his "Theory of Descriptions"; all proper nouns and sentences can be rewritten in terms of logic. He was frustrated with the imprecision and clumsiness of language, not least because of the many paradoxical and contradictory sentences possible. Because of this, he tried to simplify all language into chains of logical reasoning and math equations. This effort, along with his broader idea of logical atomism, was the eventual cause of a new form of logic, predicate calculus, that irrevocably linked mathematics and logic. A common example of logical atomism and the theory of descriptions is the sentence, "The present king of France is bald." As there is no king of France at the moment, it would be false, but the sentence, "The present king of

France is not bald" is false as well, leading to an impossible paradox. He solved this by simplifying the sentence down to three logical phrases, which if any were false, would make the sentence false: there is a present king of France, he is bald, and anyone else who is the present king of France is also bald. This revolutionized logic and language alike, as he had essentially created analytic philosophy.

Russell's overarching goal was his logical atomism theory, which was an extension of the Theory of Descriptions. He believed everything can and should be broken down into simple facts for analysis, and that any complex idea could be described in these simple facts. To determine the truthfulness of the philosophy was thus to examine the logically simple parts and compare them. This was, for many thinkers of the day, the central thesis to analytical philosophy. Furthermore, he thought that philosophy itself could be diluted not to the search for knowledge, but to whether humans could possess knowledge at all. He famously asked, "Can human beings know anything, and if so, what and how? This question is really the most essentially philosophical of all questions." He thought this was the purpose of philosophy, to comprehend a perfect and logical language that used only one word for each object and described every complex object with relationships between simple ones, mathematically, so that they could determine the truth behind difficult topics.

Views on Christianity

Russell spent his life searching for definite answers, and, indeed, this was much of the reason he became a philosopher: to answer his troubling questions. He started in mathematics and his logical atomism followed from that, making it reasonable to assume that he found the answers, or at least thought he did, in logic and reason. This placed him at odds with most of the religious community, not least because he believed religion couldn't be proved with science or fact, and that it, therefore, couldn't be held with certainty. When asked what he would say if God questioned him about why he had no faith, Russell answered, "Not enough evidence, God, not enough evidence."

He later compiled his arguments against Christianity into a book, *Why I Am Not a Christian*, where he listed the charges against Christianity: the moral objections to Christianity, a disbelief in the moral excellence of Jesus, and finally an insufficient number of facts supporting it. He argued that the church, and Christianity in general, had slowed progress significantly, citing such examples as the Catholic Church banning Galileo's cosmic findings and the Crusades. Furthermore, he noted that Jesus was not fully a good man and thus not perfect, including evidence like the cursing of the fig tree, the condemnation of his enemies, and the teaching about the unpardonable sin. Finally, he leveled accusations that there was not enough evidence for God according to empirical science and rational doubt. These all provoked many responses from Christians around the globe, making him well known as a strong apologist for atheism.

Jack Beebe, 2012
Jeff Culver, faculty
McCarthy Nolan, 2016
Daren Jonescu, advisor

WILLA CATHER ◊ 1873–1947, *Pioneer of American Fiction*

" Art is a concrete and personal and rather childish thing after all—no matter what people do to graft it into science and make it sociological and psychological; it is no good at all unless it is let alone to be itself—a game of make-believe, or re-production, very exciting and delightful to people who have an ear for it or an eye for it.

—Light on Adobe Walls

- Was an American novelist known for her stories of Midwest settler life, more specifically, of her hometown in Nebraska
- Won the Pulitzer Prize in 1922 for her novel *One of Ours*
- Wrote about simplified subjects, but was known for "portrait writing" of the people and places she knew well
- Was considered an unconventional and revolutionary fiction writer
- Was lauded by literary critic Eleanor Hinman: "Whatever she does is done with every fibre. There is no pretense in her, and no conventionality. … She has ideas and is not afraid to express them. Her mind scintillates and sends rays of light down many avenues of thought"

Key Works

Alexander's Bridge, 1913
O Pioneers! 1913
My Ántonia, 1918
One of Ours, 1922
A Lost Lady, 1923

Biography

Willa Sibert Cather, the oldest of seven children, was born on December 7, 1873, in her grandmother's home near Winchester, Virginia. When she was 9 years old, her family decided to join the a wagon train heading west, and eventually they settled on a ranch in Red Cloud, Nebraska. This lifestyle shift and change of pace shaped Cather's perspective of the world, which she would eventually pour into her imaginative, prairie-inspired fiction. Her grandmother tutored Cather in English classics and Latin before Cather attended the University of Nebraska.

Upon arriving at college, she took on a masculine persona with a boyish haircut—she even went by the name "William" Cather on occasion. She originally hoped to become a physician, but following the success of her essay, "Some Personal Characteristics of Thomas Carlyle," she refocused her aspirations on writing. After a brief period teaching, she moved to New York City as an editor for *McClure's*. After the success of her novel *O Pioneers!* in 1913, Cather found her distinctive style and trademark focus on the West. *My Ántonia*, a memoir inspired by an immigrant neighbor and comprised of unconventional narratives and commentary, is considered her masterpiece In her later years, Cather had to deal with the deaths of her mother, her brothers Douglass and Roscoe, and her friend Isabelle McClung, the person for whom she said she had written all of her books. The outbreak of WWII occupied her attention, and problems with her right hand impaired her ability to write. Still, there were some bright spots in these final years. She received the gold medal for fiction from the National Institute of Arts and Letters in 1944, an honor that marked a decade of achievement. Three years later on April 24, 1947, Cather died of a cerebral hemorrhage in her New York residence.

Frontier Life

With her "gift of infusing [her] own abundant vitality into the speaker[s]" in her novels, Cather was able to put the humble state of Nebraska on the literary map. At the time, there was an unspoken, but generally assumed ideal setting for fiction. Only places that would clearly inspire were the subjects of fiction, such as the cosmopolitan cities of Europe. Cather attempted this approach in her first novel, *Alexander's Bridge*, which she wrote following a short visit to London. When she returned to her America, reflecting on what she had written, Cather remarks, "the longer I stayed in a country I really did care about ... the more unnecessary and superficial a book like *Alexander's Bridge* seemed to me."

Therefore, she decided to direct her focus to the familiar, which marked the birth of *O Pioneers!* It was in this novel that Cather's true voice finally came to fruition, and it was because of its publishing that Cather was able to launch into true freelance writing. Like most of her writing, *O Pioneers!* sprang out of Cather's life in Nebraska. The characters of *O Pioneers!* were inspired by Cather's Swedish farmer neighbors that held a place very dear to her heart. Cather is most well known for her awe-striking detail and ability to portray such inspiring beauty of a place that appears desolate to the unknowing eye. On her experience of writing this novel that she calls "novel of the soil," Cather notes, "there was no arranging or 'inventing'; everything was spontaneous and took its own place, right or wrong." Her keen memory of her bare-footed, grass-stained, and mud-covered childhood forever inspired her stories of life on the frontier.

The recurring themes of Cather's novels are man versus nature and the beauty of simplicity. Discussing her simplistic writing style that shaped the famous prairie life stories, Cather once said, "Too much detail is apt, like any other form of extravagance, to become slightly vulgar; and it quite destroys in a book a very satisfying element analogous to what painters call 'composition.'" Contemporary reviews of *O Pioneers!* said that "the novel has great dramatic power; it is deep, thrilling, intense–and this intensity comes through the simplicity–one might almost say severity, of treatment." David Stouck, a literary critic exploring the importance of landscape in writing, commented that "much of our instinctive pleasure in reading *O Pioneers!* must derive from our sharing in that wish to find a sheltered place, a refuge carved out of a hostile terrain." Cather takes a very specific, ordinary place, and beautifies its importance, ultimately showing the truth of America's past.

Idealized Past

Cather claims that all of her inspiration was imprinted into her storytelling before the age of 15. The memories of her childhood remained her key inspiration for a lifetime of works. The lens through which Cather saw the world was always one of memory. On the writing style of *My Ántonia*, literary critic Maria Ornella Treglia comments, "Another interesting aspect of how Cather treats the theme of memory is that the past and the present are intertwined: While memories bring solace to the disappointments of life, they, in turn, are colored by the present." Part of Cather's appeal is that her appreciation of the past and her vibrant memory colored her writing all the way through her career. Cather uses her vivid perception of beauty to romanticize even common items of a pioneer lifestyle. For example, this passage from *O Pioneers!* exemplifies her idealized view and portrayal of the past:

> " Telephone wires hum along the white roads, which always run at right angles. From the graveyard gate one can count a dozen gayly painted farmhouses; the gilded weather-vanes on the big red barns wink at each other across the green and brown and yellow

fields. The light steel windmills tremble throughout their frames and tug at their moorings.

Cather personifies the ordinary objects of the farm atmosphere with cheerful, active phrases such as "telephone wires hum" and "big red barns wink," illuminating the life that she sees despite its ordinary nature. She juxtaposes unlikely word pairings, such as "gilded weather-vanes," to embellish the object, making it seem much more significant and wonderful than it really is on its own. In this specific passage, these diction choices create the romantic atmosphere. And as is her typical style, Cather crafts her writing to fluidly match her awe of past experiences. However, sometimes Cather's impulse to glorify frontier life has the effect of smoothing over the rough edges of pioneer existence. By focusing on the beauty, the real struggle and privation often experienced by settlers is overlooked. Because of this, it can be tempting to view Cather as more sentimental in her fiction, praising an idealized frontier, rather than a realist, recounting life as it actually was.

G.K. CHESTERTON ◊ 1874–1936, *The Prince of Paradox*

66 The mass of men have been forced to be gay about the little things, but sad about the big ones. Nevertheless (I offer my last dogma defiantly) it is not native to man to be so. Man is more himself, man is more manlike, when joy is the fundamental thing in him, and grief the superficial. Melancholy should be an innocent interlude, a tender and fugitive frame of mind; praise should be the permanent pulsation of the soul.

—Orthodoxy

- Wanted to reform English government and society, particularly England's injustices to its dependents
- Criticized progressives and conservatives
- Converted from Anglican to Catholicism and defended the Christian faith
- Presented a "defense of the common man" in many of his writings
- Was a prolific poet, novelist, journalist, and essayist
- Wrote with humor, logic, laughter, and paradox
- Developed priest-detective Father Brown in a popular series of mysteries
- Harbored anti-Semitic sentiments, according to some

Key Works

Orthodoxy, 1908
The Everlasting Man, 1925
Heretics, 1905
St. Francis of Assisi, 1923
St. Thomas Aquinas: The Dumb Ox, 1933
The Man Who Was Thursday, 1908

Biography

Gilbert Keith Chesterton, known as G.K. Chesterton, was born in 1874 to a middle-class Kensington couple. As a young man, Chesterton became fascinated with the occult and experimented with Ouija boards. Because of a lackluster performance as a young student at St. Paul's School, he ended up attending the Slade School of Art instead of Oxford, intending to become an illustrator. He also studied literature, but left school without a degree in either subject. When he wanted to marry Francis Blogg, Chesterton knew he needed a career, so he began as a journalist, committed to write against the "Decadents and Pessimists who ruled the culture of the age." He wrote in a style that appealed to readers of *London's Daily News* and began publishing books, 10 of them by 1906, and many more in the following years. In 1931, the BBC asked him to do a radio talk; this turned into a series of perhaps 40 talks per year until his death in June 1936. This took place at his home in Beaconsfield, England. A large man (6'4" and almost 300 pounds), he died of congestive heart failure.

Writings and Criticism

Time magazine observed of Chesterton's writing style: "Whenever possible Chesterton made his points with popular sayings, proverbs, allegories—first carefully turning them inside out." Through paradox he communicated his philosophical convictions for orthodoxy and tradition as the necessary order of society.

Chesterton hoped for sweeping reform to bring about the forgotten traditions of Christianity. Yet he wrote essay after essay on minutiae rather than delving into his deep philosophical opinions. Some critics felt he frittered away his writing gift with superfluous weekly columns rather than writing important fiction. He used his love of everyday details to write the Father Brown mysteries and the successful *The Man Who Was Thursday*. He liked to read the greatest writers to contrast their ideas with his own. His outstanding criticisms of Charles Dickens and George Bernard Shaw are still read and admired today.

But Chesterton felt that religion and politics were the worthiest writing subjects, and he railed against the lack of effectiveness of the English political process. Cecil Chesterton, G.K.'s brother, and his friend Hilaire Belloc shared his interests and established a newspaper to use for a political platform. Early on, Cecil became vocal about an insider trading scandal focused on Liberal Party leaders buying stock in the American Marconi Company. Cecil accused the Jewish officials who had been involved in the corruption. G.K. had even more opportunity to advertise his views when took over as editor of *The New Witness* after Cecil died in WWI. In the paper, Chesterton criticized a number of Jews, especially those who had been involved in the Marconi scandal. Chesterton denied that he was prejudiced toward all Jews, yet he pointed to the "international Jew" (stateless, secularized) as the cause of the breakdown of English culture.

Chesterton became discouraged with the condition of man's soul under industrial capitalism and was disillusioned by WWI. His "shrill tone" turned readers away, and he lost popularity. Writing for his own *G.K.'s Weekly*, Chesterton produced essays on the evils of capitalism, and wrote often about his perspective on religion and morals.

Chesterton died as a result of overindulgence in food and drink, as well as overwork. H.G. Wells wrote about Chesterton's abilities and passions: "He was hampered by enormous ignorance, but at least he had courage. He was ready to attack the rich and the powerful, and he damaged his own career by doing so." Lionel Trilling characterized both Chesterton and Orwell as "men who have considerable intellectual power but who are not happy in the institutionalized life of intellectuality; who have a feeling for an older and simpler time, and a guiding awareness of the ordinary life of the people, yet without any touch of the sentimental malice of populism; and a strong feeling for the commonplace; and a direct, unabashed sense of the nation, even a conscious love of it."

ROBERT LEE FROST ◊ 1874–1963, *A Beloved American Poet*

66 To be a poet is a condition, not a profession.

- Was a teacher and poet-philosopher who published poetry starting at age 39 for 50 years
- Depicted American rural life in New England with his accurate and beautiful use of colloquial speech
- Attended but never graduated from Dartmouth and Harvard, yet he was later given 40 honorary graduate degrees
- Married and adored his high school sweetheart who became "the unspoken half of everything" he wrote; he dedicated all but one book to her
- Had six children and lost all but two
- Approached a publisher in England and initially became popular there
- Was the first poet to recite a poem at a presidential inauguration, (John F. Kennedy's), as well as the first to hold a poet-in-residence position at a college
- Received four Pulitzer prizes and the Congressional Gold Medal
- Met with Soviet Premier Nikita Khrushchev in a cultural visit with President Kennedy to Russia
- Founded and was deeply involved with Bread Loaf School of English in Vermont, associated with Middlebury College

Key Works

A Boy's Will, 1913
North of Boston, 1914
"Mending Wall," 1914
"The Road Not Taken," 1916
Mountain Interval, 1916
"Stopping by the Woods on a Snowy Evening," 1923
Introduction to King Jasper, 1935
A Further Range, 1937
A Witness Tree, 1942
Collected Poems, 1969

Biography

To Americans, Robert Frost was a farmer who wrote simple poetry about rural life. Although he was born in San Francisco in 1874, he and his mother and sister moved to Massachusetts after his father died of tuberculosis when Frost was 11. After Frost graduated from high school in Massachusetts, he attended Dartmouth for just one term and worked as a mill worker, reporter, and teacher, before trying school again at Harvard. He again left without a degree. He married Elinor, his love since high school, after she graduated from Sarah Lawrence. They moved to New Hampshire where they spent

12 years and experienced multiple failures (as poultry farmers, for instance) and tragedies. Their eldest son died of cholera in 1900, and their youngest daughter died in 1907. The fates of their other children were also unfortunate: their son Carol committed suicide, their daughter Irma became mentally ill, and their daughter Marjorie died in childbirth in her late 20s. In 1912, the Frosts sold their farm and moved to England where they remained until shortly after the outbreak of WWI. By the time they returned to America, Frost's work was being well-reviewed (by the likes of Ezra Pound and Edward Thomas). He and Elinor bought another farm in New Hampshire and Frost settled into writing and teaching at several colleges, including Amherst and Middlebury. When Elinor died of cancer in 1938, Frost left his teaching position at Amherst. He continued to have a prolific writing career, receiving many awards, until his mid-80s. Frost died of complications related to prostate cancer in 1963.

At a Crossroads

Just as the narrator in Frost's "The Road Not Taken" stands at a fork in the road, so too does Frost himself. In a sense, he stands at the intersection of 19th-century poetry and modern verse. His works encapsulate many 19th-century traditions and themes, but also include elements common to modernist poetry, especially his use of modern idioms and his directness. He mostly eschews rhyme and the flowery language common to 19th-century romantic poets. Yet scholars note Frost was not an innovator, and his poetry was never experimental. Frost, unlike many of his contemporaries, never completely ditched conventional metrical forms for free verse. He preferred a standardized meter and line length, averring that the poet's "first commitment [was] to metre and length of line," and that the tone, mood or atmosphere of a nascent poem dictated those choices.

He was thoughtful about his poetry, in the sense of reflecting on why and how he composed. He maintained that a poem is "never a put-up job. … It begins as a lump in the throat, a sense of wrong, a homesickness, a loneliness. It is never a thought to begin with. It is at its best when it is a tantalizing vagueness." In a 1932 letter to literary critic and professor Sydney Cox, Frost explained his conception of poetry: "The objective idea is all I ever cared about. Most of my ideas occur in verse. … To be too subjective with what an artist has managed to make objective is to come on him presumptuously and render ungraceful what he in pain of his life had faith he had made graceful."

Even though his use of new England vernacular was criticized during his day, it is the hallmark of many of his poems, and what makes them "speak" to people of today like they did when he first wrote them. They are accessible. Frost's poetry held so much appeal for the common man, that John F. Kennedy, during his presidential campaign, often concluded a speech by quoting the final lines of "Stopping by Woods on a Snowy Evening" about promises he had to keep. At 86, Frost recited "The Gift Outright" at Kennedy's inauguration. Although a very enigmatic and private man, Frost left opportunities to get to know him personally through his many letters, immortalized in Selected Letters of Robert Frost and his recorded talks at Bread Loaf School of English, Middlebury College.

CHARLES BEARD ◊ 1874–1948, *American Historian, Radical Revisionist*

" All the lessons of history in four sentences: Whom the gods would destroy, they first make mad with power. The mills of God grind slowly, but they grind exceedingly small. The bee fertilizes the flower it robs. When it is dark enough, you can see the stars.

- Wrote studies on the development of US political institutions
- Saw socioeconomic conflict and motivational factors
- Married Mary Ritter, historian and student of women's roles
- Was a leader of the Progressive movement and American liberalism
- Developed his idea that the Constitutional framers were chiefly motivated by finances
- Believed that economics motivated governmental action
- Wrote a synthesis of US history, in conjunction with his wife
- Realized the subjective nature of a historian's selections of facts
- Attacked President Franklin D. Roosevelt for bringing about America's participation in war with Japan
- Was criticized as an isolationist

Key Works

An Economic Interpretation of the Constitution, 1913
Economic Origins of Jeffersonian Democracy, 1915
The Economic Basis of Politics, 1943
The Rise of American Civilization (in collaboration with Mary Ritter Beard), 1927
America in Midpassage (in collaboration with Mary Ritter Beard), 1939
The American Spirit (in collaboration with Mary Ritter Beard), 1942
Beards' Basic History of the United States, 1921
President Roosevelt and the Coming of the War, 1941, 1948

Biography

Charles Austin Beard was born in Indiana in 1874. Reared in a prosperous family, he attended DePauw University and then Oxford where he helped found a workingman's school in 1899. Beard returned to the Sates briefly and married Mary Ritter in 1900, before taking up residence in England again. He didn't return to the US permanently until 1904 when he took up a teaching position at Columba University in New York City. Beard subsequently became one of the leaders of the progressive movement and American liberalism. While teaching at Columbia, he became very interested in the delegates at the Federal Constitutional Convention, especially with respect to their economic interests. He portrayed the framers of the Constitution as motivated by self-interest. He founded the New School for Social Research (after resigning from Columbia to protest the firing of several professors on charges of disloyalty and subversion), and became the director of the Training School for Public Service in New York City. He wrote *A Charter for the Social Science in the Schools* in 1932, which became a very important book for teaching history. His most popular books were *The Rise of American Civilization* and two sequels (*America in Midpassage* and *The American Spirit*) that he wrote with his wife, also a learned historian. These books, too, continued to approach history with the broad strokes of social science. Beard explained that he was "surveying life as a whole, as distinguished from microscopic analysis by departments." He died in 1948 in New Haven, Connecticut.

Criticism of FDR

Beard was criticized initially as a radical for his new ideas in approaching historical study and later for condemning Franklin D. Roosevelt for America's foreign policy. He wrote that Roosevelt had given in "to the material and moral forces of Hitler and Mussolini by fighting them." He felt Roosevelt provoked America's involvement in WWII. In "The Myth of Rugged American Individualism" he discussed the deplorable state that Western civilization was in. Beard was called as an isolationist because of these views, and his reputation declined somewhat after the publication of his last works, but he is still considered to be one of the most influential American historians of the 20th century.

THOMAS MANN, 1875–1955, *Godfather of the Conservative Revolution*

> " Tolerance becomes a crime when applied to evil.
>
> —*The Magic Mountain*

- Resisted authority and their demands, and thus didn't learn much at school
- Won the Nobel Prize for Literature in 1929
- Wrote literature with religious aspects but was not necessarily Christian
- Sympathized with communist aims and criticized those who attacked it although he was not personally a communist
- Claimed to be an "unpolitical man"
- Wrote *Reflections of a Nonpolitical Man,* which was considered a big part of the conservative revolution
- Created characters who are isolated or struggle with the normality of life

Key Works

Buddenbrooks, 1901
Tonio Kroger, 1903
Tristan, 1903
Death in Venice, 1912
Reflections of a Nonpolitical Man, 1918
The Magic Mountain, 1924
Doctor Faustus, 1947
The Holy Sinner, 1951

Biography

Born in Lübeck, Germany, on June 6, 1875, Thomas Mann was considered one of the most important German writers of his age. Like many genius writers, he was not fully appreciated or understood in his younger years. The second son of a merchant a senator of the city, he did not fare well in school since he had, as he termed in, an "innate and paralyzing resistance to any external demands." Anything of significance that Mann learned, he taught himself. He was supposed to take over his father's grain firm, but when his father died young, when Mann was 15, the firm was liquidated, and after Mann finished school he became a clerk in a Munich insurance company. He published his novel *Buddenbrooks* (which went on to win the Nobel prize for Literature), a naturalistic saga about his own family, in 1901 and married in 1905. He and his wife had six children. He wrote prolifically, producing primarily short stories and novels, but also essays and drama. Distrusting the Nazis from the start, Mann and his wife moved to California in 1933 and he became an avid supporter of Franklin D. Roosevelt and outspoken critic of the Nazis and fascism. He supported the Allies through what he wrote during this time, and became an American citizen in 1940. In 1955, Thomas Mann died at age 80, of atherosclerosis in a hospital in Zurich.

Forgiveness

Mann makes it clear that he believes forgiveness is an important quality to have. He spends a fair amount of time on this concept in his texts (*Joseph and His Brothers*, *Young Joseph*, *Joseph in Egypt*, and *Joseph the Provider*) about the biblical patriarch Joseph, explaining the forgiveness Joseph showed his brothers. During the seven lean years, Joseph's brothers come to him for grain, and he not only forgives them but also asks for their forgiveness for his foolishness as a child. In this way, Mann shows the value of forgiveness, although not for everyone. While he believed we should forgive and reconcile with our friends and family, Mann stood by the belief that we should not forgive those who "make deals with the devil," for they deserve hell. He felt this way about the Nazis, and that while most people can be reasoned with peacefully, they could not.

The Conservative Revolution

The Conservative Revolution was a radical movement in which Thomas Mann was closely involved. This group of Germans had conservative tendencies of some sort, but were disappointed with the state into which Germany had been put by its loss of WWI and sought to advance ideas that were both conservative and revolutionary in nature. Although many of the participants in the Conservative Revolution did not agree on much, they agreed on the rejection of a parliamentary democracy, liberalism, and Marxism, on the idea of "*Volksgemeinschaft*" (folk community), and on the importance of *Volk* ("people"). Mann's *Reflections of a Nonpolitical Man* had an influence on the Revolution unmatched by any other, and Mann himself was viewed as something of a "godfather" of the movement. Though Mann's thoughts on government were revolutionary at the time, his writing itself was very traditional.

Reflections

Ironically, in claiming to be "unpolitical," Mann seemed to seal his fate as a noted political figure; however, his changing political views indicate that his beliefs were more circumstantial than absolute. Although he apparently held no political views, he claimed that if he did alter his opinion that he did not alter his purpose, which remained throughout his life a vindication of an unpolitical, spiritual Germany. Mann believed that *Reflections* was an essential part of his development as a writer, and if he changed during or after it, it was because he was developing intellectually throughout the novel. During his time writing *Reflections*, considered essential to the Conservative Revolution, Mann moved away from a radical pro-war, anti-Western stance and toward a more loose and hands-off perspective.

Isolation and Struggle

In three of Mann's stories, he emphasized the idea that an artist needs to give up the joys of ordinary life. For writers, this generally means they have to give up any type of personal life in order to give themselves wholly to their work. Mann also emphasized that an artist must suffer to create. In *The Holy Sinner*, Mann writes from the point of view of a monk who observes the goings-on of a royal family and all that they enjoy and struggle with. The monk had to give up ordinary pleasures in life to live a life of solitude for God. Although the monk is watching a family struggle, he himself struggles watching it and knowing he can't experience the same kinds of experiences because he has given up a normal life. In many of Mann's books, his heroes are isolated, do not carry out a normal life, and are unable to love.

Legacy

Thomas Mann was a prominent writer in his time, well-regarded internationally, and with a desire to not be distracted from his writing by political battles. Despite his desire to remain "unpolitical," Mann took up his pen to fight for the causes of democracy and freedom. In WWI, Mann was an active German nationalist, and the "godfather" of the Conservative Revolution. By WWII, he had become an advocate for American democracy and had influential political connections. Lecturing and writing at Princeton, he made the case against despotic totalitarianism and stated the case for freedom against despotism. He won the Nobel Prize for literature in 1929 principally for his novel *Buddenbrooks*, which had "won steadily increased recognition as one of the classic works of contemporary literature."

Moriah Thompson, 2018

G.H. HARDY ◊ 1877–1947, *Champion of Pure Mathematics*

" It is not worth an intelligent man's time to be in the majority. By definition there are already enough people to do that.

—A Mathematician's Apology

- Avoided applying his work to the real world; was a "pure" mathematician
- Despised the role mathematicians played in instigating WWI
- Contributed inadvertently to genetics and quantum mechanics
- Explored analytical number theory, divergent series, and prime numbers

Key Works

A Mathematician's Apology, 1940
A Course of Pure Mathematics, 1908
Divergent Series, 1948

Biography

Hardy was born in Cranleigh, Surrey, in 1877. He demonstrated early promise in mathematics and attended Winchester College, a school renowned for its mathematics, at age 13. Despite his genius, Hardy was painfully shy, and he actively avoided all occasions for ceremonies and awards. Due to his promising skills in math, he attended university at Trinity College, Cambridge, and published his first textbook, *A Course of Pure Mathematics*, in 1908. Hardy's innovative work with pure mathematics established him as the greatest pure mathematician in England, which attracted the attention and collaboration of several other contemporary thinkers. During WWI, Hardy co-championed an English anti-war movement with his close friend Bertrand Russell. Though Hardy achieved notable success for his many publications, he remained unmarried and childless until his death in 1947.

Pure Mathematics

Hardy did not want to change the world. In fact, he did not want any of his mathematical work to be applied to any real world problems. He boasted of "never having produced a mathematical result that served any useful purpose." In this way he was a "pure" mathematician, one who contributed only to the abstract world of numbers. Hardy's devotion to pure mathematics stemmed from his hatred of war and of the role that mathematicians and scientists had played in provoking and escalating WWI. In his autobiographical *A Mathematician's Apology*, Hardy notes that "science works for evil as well as for good," but that mathematicians should take comfort in the fact that their subject's "very remoteness from ordinary human activities should keep it gentle and clean." In lieu of studying applied mathematics, Hardy explored analytical number theory, divergent series, prime numbers, and similar topics.

Though Hardy rejected the use of his mathematics for practical purposes, he believed that his work could still bring pleasure to humanity, much like art, music, or literature. Hardy wrote, "It may be very hard to define mathematical beauty, but that is just as true of beauty of any kind—we may not know quite what we mean by a beautiful poem, but that does not prevent us from recognizing one when we read it." Furthermore, Hardy believed math to be a higher form of creative expression than art, music, and the like. He saw the latter subjects as being based off of ideas but being expressed through media such as paint and words. Math, however, required no medium and was simply the purest form of an idea; its beauty was inherent in its existence.

Accidental Scientific Applications

For all his aversion to practical application, Hardy inadvertently made a few significant contributions to applied science. His most famous theory is known as the Hardy-Weinberg Principle; through his use of simple algebraic principles, Hardy illustrated that allele and genotype frequencies in a population will remain the same in the absence of evolutionary forces. This illustration was an important breakthrough in the field of Mendelian genetics in the early 20th century. He made another notable scientific contribution with the Hardy-Ramanujan Asymptotic Formula, used by Bohr in his studies of atomic nuclei and which later formed the foundation of modern understandings of thermodynamic functions within the field of quantum mechanics.

Collaborative Work

While acclaimed for his individual works, Hardy is also well known for his collaborative work with other mathematicians. In 1913, he began mentoring Srinivasa Ramanujan, an Indian mathematician who impressed Hardy with his impeccable theorems. Ramanujan would later join Hardy at Cambridge, where the two enjoyed a flourishing six-year partnership. Hardy's longest collaboration, a 35-year partnership with mathematician J.E. Littlewood, has been considered by many as one of the greatest partnerships between two popular thinkers of all time. As C.P. Snow writes in the foreword to *A Mathematician's Apology*, this pairing was "the most famous collaboration in the history of mathematics. There has been nothing like it in any science or in any other field of creative activity." Littlewood and Hardy even co-published "The Four Axioms of Collaboration," a set of guiding principles to maximize collaborations between other great thinkers.

MARGARET SANGER ◊ 1879-1966, *A Pioneering Feminist*

> " When motherhood becomes the fruit of a deep yearning, not the result of ignorance or accident, its children will become the foundation of a new race.
>
> —*Woman and the New Race*

- Crusaded for female reproductive rights; cared deeply about women having the right to control their bodies and make decisions about the size of their families
- Was influenced by her own family's poverty and her mother's death at 48
- Became a nurse
- Wrote a column on birth control for *The New York Call*, a socialist newspaper
- Ran her own newspaper, *The Woman Rebel*, which resulted in her arrest because of the anti-obscenity Comstock Laws
- Directed the printing of *Family Limitation* on conception prevention during her self-imposed exile to England
- Had her trial called off suddenly after three days because of growing support from the public
- Convinced her sister to open the first birth control clinic in America
- Established The American Birth Control League which became known as the Planned Parenthood Federation of America
- Asked scientist Gregory Pincus to develop an inexpensive oral contraceptive which resulted in the "Pill"
- Shaped the eugenics movement and advocated the sterilization of "the mentally and physically defective"; as a result, sterilization was legalized in 30 states and 60,000 people were sterilized

Key Works

Family Limitation, 1914

Biography

Margaret Sanger forever changed the landscape of women's lives by working for reproductive rights. Born Margaret Higgins, one of 11 children from very poor Irish immigrants, she lived the life of poverty, toil, unemployment, drunkenness, cruelty, quarreling, fight, poverty, debts, and jails that plagued many large families. Her mother died at 48 after seven miscarriages and 18 pregnancies. Sanger rebounded by becoming a nurse, ministering to the poor of New York City where she saw women who had little or no medical care. She married William Sanger in 1902 and they had three children together. The Sangers moved to New York City in 1912, and Margaret Sanger began her career as a reproductive activist by writing a column called "What Every Girl Should Know." She was arrested for what was seen as "obscene, lewd, lascivious, and filthy" content. In order to avoid jail time, Sanger fled to England under an assumed name. She returned to the US in 1915, after the charges were dropped, and she and William divorced. She continued to teach about birth control and advocate for it throughout her life. She died in a Tucson nursing home in 1966.

Reproductive Rights and the "Pill"

Driven by her mother's experience and what she saw as a nurse in New York City, Sanger spent her life advocating for women's access to birth control knowledge and methods. From writing essays, she moved to smuggling diaphragms into the country when she returned from her brief exile in England.

In Britain, Sanger had gained the support of many British radicals and her worldwide following had grown. She began lecturing, and convinced her sister to begin the first birth control clinic.

Laws began to change and doctors were eventually allowed to give contraceptive advice. Sanger began *The Birth Control Review*, which she gave to her organization The American Birth Control League, which became Planned Parenthood Federation of America.

Sanger lectured throughout the United States, Japan, and India, sharing her knowledge of contraception. In 1950 she asked scientist Gregory Pincus to invent an inexpensive oral conception with minimal side effects. Then Enovid produced the first oral contraceptive, "the Pill" in 1957 through Pincus's work. Prescribing the Pill as a contraceptive was illegal, so doctors prescribed it for menstrual disorders with the side effect of preventing conception. In 1965 the Supreme Court ruled in Griswold v. Connecticut that married couples could use birth control. Sanger is still regarded with mixed feelings, venerated by those who appreciate her determination and her contribution to women's reproductive rights, and reviled by those who label her as a radical feminist who changed women's attitudes forever, and those opposed to her views on eugenics.

ALBERT EINSTEIN, 1879–1955, *Locksmith to Mysteries of the Universe*

" Wisdom is not a product of schooling but of the lifelong attempt to acquire it.
—To J. Dispentiere: March 24, 1954

- Was a German physicist, outspoken pacifist, humanitarian, democrat, and supporter of Jewish Zionism
- Believed that scientists had a moral responsibility to humanity
- Discovered that the speed of light remains constant
- Wrote the 1905 *Annus Mirabilis* papers, consisting of four articles that profoundly changed scientific views on space, time, mass, and energy
- Confirmed the existence of atoms and molecules by observing the relationship between water and air
- Disagreed with Newton and proved that a dynamic, rather than static, universe existed
- Developed his "Theory of Relativity" that changed the public's idea of space and time
- Penned his "Theory of Relativity," and afterwards was so drained that he stayed in bed for two weeks
- Created the famous equation $E=mc^2$ which led to the creation of the atomic bomb
- Rejected Father Georges Lemaitre's Big Bang Theory
- Died in 1955 still believing in a "Steady State" universe

Key Works

"On a Heuristic Point of View Concerning the Production and Transformation of Light," 1905
"On the Motion of Small Particles Suspended in a Stationary Liquid, as Required by the Molecular Kinetic Theory of Heat," 1905
"On the Electrodynamics of Moving Bodies," 1905
"Does the Inertia of a Body Depend upon its Energy Content?" 1905
"Cosmological Considerations of the General Theory of Relativity," 1917

Biography

One of the most influential scientists of all time, Einstein made huge strides in scientific knowledge. His "legendary mind revolutionized our understanding of nature; ... [his] theories opened the door to possibilities as bizarre as time travel ... [and] he made a great contribution to our perspective of space, time, matter, and the universe." His work inspired not only other physicists and cosmologists, but also artists, writers, and philosophers. Born on March 14, 1879, in Ulm, Germany, Einstein was the first child of his Jewish parents. Though formally educated, he received his primary education through his own readings and studies under the guidance of his uncle, Jakob, and family friend, Max Talmud. After Einstein's parents moved to Italy, leaving their son to complete his schooling in Germany, he dropped out of school and denounced both his faith and German heritage. He struggled in Italy to go back to school or even to acquire a job. His employment was inconsistent until 1902, when he was hired as a clerk in a Swiss patent office in Benn. This new job paid well and allowed him to support and marry Meliva Maric on January 6, 1903. The couple soon had two children, Hans Albert and Eduard.

In 1905 he published a series of four papers in the *Annalen der Physik*, all of which proved enormously important in the physics community and drew the attention of influential physicist Max Planck, the father of quantum theory. Although his work became popular, Einstein was still unhappy with his theory, as it did not incorporate gravity's effect on relativity. He would continue to work on his General Theory of Relativity for the next ten years, announcing its completion in 1915. To prove his theory, Einstein funded two expeditions in May 1919 that focused on the bending of starlight. During this time he also divorced his wife and married Elsa Lowenthal. In 1921 he won the Nobel Prize in Physics for his explanation of the photoelectric effect in the first of his 1905 papers. Between 1921 and 1929, Einstein applied his Theory of Relativity to all space and discovered that the universe was indeed dynamic, which would be proved by astronomer Edwin Hubble at the end of 1929. During the rise of the Nazis in Germany, Einstein relocated to New Jersey and continued his work at the Institute for Advanced Study at Princeton. During this same time, Einstein faced sadness at home when his son, Eduard, was diagnosed with schizophrenia and his second wife passed away.

As the prospect of war ramped up in the late 1930s, Einstein realized that his famous equation $E=mc^2$ could be helpful theoretically in the technology needed for an atomic bomb. An outspoken pacifist, he was not asked to work on the Manhattan Project, but instead participated by reviewing weapon designs. After the bomb was dropped on Hiroshima, he formed a group to oppose the use of the bombs his equation had helped conceive, calling this activist group the Emergency Committee of Atomic Scientists. Toward the end of his life, he continued theorizing about black holes and even time travel, but he fell gradually out of contact with the physics community until his death on April 18, 1955.

Annus Mirabilis Papers

Although between 1900 and 1905 Einstein did not have a consistent job, 1905 was termed his "Miraculous Year" as he was able to publish several scientific papers explaining his theories in detail. The first of these papers was called "On a Heuristic Point of View Concerning the Production and Transformation of Light," discussing the photoelectric effect. In researching the photoelectric effect, he concluded that "energy is not distributed continuously over ever-increasing volumes of space, but consists of a finite number of energy quanta localized at points of space that move without dividing, and can be absorbed or generated only as complete units." In other words, Einstein realized that light consists of individual photons, an insight which enabled him to develop the quantum theory of light.

The second paper Einstein published was titled "On the Motion of Small Particles Suspended in a Stationary Liquid, as Required by the Molecular Kinetic Theory of Heat." This paper explained Brownian motion, how particles move at random when suspended in a fluid. This paper was pivotal in the history of science as it confirmed the existence of atoms and molecules. Einstein's next publication, "On the Electrodynamics of Moving Bodies," explained the relationship between space and time, which later became known as the Principle of Relativity. The last paper, "Does the Inertia of a Body Depend upon its Energy Content?" was proved that the energy of an object affects the mass of the object. After more research on special relativity, Einstein formulated the famous equation: $E=mc^2$. With this he demonstrated that the speed of light affects the equivalence of energy and mass. The influence of these articles can hardly be overstated as they set the stage for all of modern physics.

Theory of Relativity

In The Theory of Relativity, Einstein proposed that "the gravitational attraction between masses could be understood as resulting from a curvature of space and time." Einstein continued studying his theory, which he broke into two parts: the special theory and the general theory. The special theory relates to space and time and claims that "things are at rest or in relative uniform motion." It also shows that the laws of physics are the same for all inertial systems. The general theory contains Einstein's claim on gravity. He believed that an accelerating system is no different than a system that is at rest in a gravitational field. He also claimed that it is possible for light to be curved when it is in a gravitational field in space. The general theory also led him to predict the possibility of black holes and the continuous expansion of the universe. These predictions and discoveries paved the way for scientists to enter a new "dimension."

Cosmology

Though cosmology, the study of the origin and structure of the universe, has existed for centuries, the cornerstone of modern cosmology is Einstein's 1917 paper "Cosmological Considerations of the General Theory of Relativity." He first applied his theory of general relativity to all matter in space in 1917, theorizing that gravity doesn't link matter, but instead bends time and space around it to attract other matter. This groundbreaking theory of gravity became his model for the universe and inspired cosmogonists such as Karl Shwarzschild, Arthur Eddington, and Willem de Sitter. After further exploring his model, however, Einstein discovered that his equations would lead to a dynamic universe that expands and contracts. Since all evidence of the universe at the time confirmed Newton's static universe theory, Einstein added what he called a cosmological constant to his equations.

In 1929 astronomer Edward Hubble confirmed Einstein's theory that the universe was indeed dynamic. Hubble, after observing a distant star, discovered that its light was changing over time. It soon became evident that the light was changing due to the star's movement away from earth. This observation proved that Einstein's static model would not work unless applied, as it originally had been, to a dynamic universe. Einstein's equations prove that space is constantly expanding around us, and at one point it was much smaller than it is today. Such a view suggests that it will have a beginning and an end. This theory became the basis for present-day cosmological studies and led to contemporary views such as the Big Bang theory.

Jewish Physics

Einstein's approach to science was neither realist nor positivist, but somewhere between the two. He looked at science with a philosopher's eye that allowed him to see beyond what had already been done and to ask new questions. His view on the study of physics was creative and imaginative; he even remarked that while "knowledge is limited, imagination circles the world." However, though his approach may have enabled his formulation of the Theory of Relativity, it made him the target of a popular science movement called Deutsche Physik. The followers of this movement pushed classic scientific methods over the imaginative Jewish work, especially after being influenced by the rising Nazi movement. Einstein's work was denounced as Jewish Physics and burned throughout Germany. It soon became clear that Einstein was not safe in his home country, and he was forced to relocate to the United States of America, where he settled at the Institute for Advanced Study at Princeton.

Around that time physicists first discovered the immense power that could come from splitting the uranium atom. Because Einstein was a renowned pacifist, German physicist, and partial socialist, the United States government refrained from asking him to participate in the Manhattan Project. They instead recruited his closest colleagues for the assignment. Einstein, after changing his pacifist views in 1933, joined the war effort by analyzing weapon designs for the US Navy and selling the original copy of his paper on special relativity for $6.5 million. His newfound beliefs didn't last long. After Einstein heard about an atomic bomb being dropped on Japan, he immediately returned to his pacifist beliefs and founded the Emergency Committee of Atomic Scientists to endorse the end of the bomb.

Savannah Cressman, 2011
Trish Rouleau, 2015

JAMES JOYCE, 1882–1941, *The Obfuscated Genius*

> " By his monstrous way of life he seemed to have put himself beyond the limits of reality. Nothing moved him or spoke to him from the real world unless he heard it in an echo of the infuriated cries within him.
>
> —*Portrait of the Artist of a Young Man*

- Proclaimed himself to be an Irish-Italian journalist; although he grew up solely in Ireland, he spent the remainder of his life abroad
- Set many of his stories in his home town of Dublin
- Brought a new stream of consciousness style of writing to the literary world
- Spoke 17 different languages
- Was a talented singer who won awards for his voice
- Saw his most famous work, *Ulysses*, banned because it was considered pornographic
- Suffered from ocular illness; at times, he was able to write only with a red crayon on large sheets of paper
- Struggled financially until *Ulysses* became popular
- Endured heartbreak when his daughter was diagnosed as an incurable schizophrenic; Joyce never stopped searching for a cure, feeling that he had failed her as a father

Key Works

Dubliners, 1914
A Portrait of the Artist as a Young Man, 1916
Ulysses, 1922

Finnegan's Wake, 1939

Biography

Born in Dublin, Ireland, on February 2, 1882, James Joyce was the eldest of 10 children born to John and Marry Joyce. Joyce attended a Jesuit school until his family could no longer afford the tuition, and he was forced to drop out. In 1893 he enrolled at Belvedere College (with a scholarship), later matriculating to University College, Dublin. Fostering his creative talents, Joyce wrote literary reviews during this time; one such review of Ibsen's play received a positive personal response from Ibsen himself. Upon graduation, Joyce moved to Paris to study medicine; however, the sudden illness and eventual death of his mother recalled him home. Despite her pleas, Joyce rejected her fervent Catholicism. Back in Dublin, he met Nora Barnacle, who became his muse and wife. After leaving Ireland in 1904, he returned to Ireland only four times. The couple bounced around Europe, residing in Zurich, Switzerland; Trieste, Italy; and Pola, Croatia, in an effort to find stable work for Joyce, all the time living in near squalor as Joyce worked on *Ulysses*.

After years as a struggling artist, Joyce enjoyed the minor critical success of *Portrait of the Artist as a Young Man*, which his supporter Ezra Pound got printed in serial form in 1914. He, Nora, and their two children, Giorgio (born 1905) and Lucia (born 1907), moved to Paris after WWI, but they fled to Zurich before the invasion of the Nazis in WWII. His anxiety high (living on handouts from patrons), his eyesight failing (eventually leading to an iridectomy), Joyce attempted publication of the controversial *Ulysses*. Released in serial form in 1918, *Ulysses* was quickly banned in the UK and the US as obscene and pornographic. Eventually, Sylvia Beach of Shakespeare & Co. in Paris published the novel in 1922. Whether attracted to the controversy or intrigued by the style, American readers bought bootlegged copies of the novel until 1933, when the Supreme Court lifted the ban and consumers could buy the book outright. The UK lifted the ban in 1936.

Finally receiving the critical and financial success that had eluded him, Joyce started work on *Finnegan's Wake*. Having "lived remotely and in poverty to perfect his style," Joyce was "uncontaminated by commercial influences," and readers flocked to his prose. The most esoteric and acclaimed of his works, *Finnegan's Wake* was published in 1939 to immediate success. Unfortunately, Joyce did not enjoy his success long. After an intestinal operation, he died on January 13, 1941, and was buried in Fluntern cemetery in Zurich.

Portrait of the Artist as a Young Man

Based upon the short story "Stephen Hero," *Portrait of the Artist as a Young Man* traces the life of Stephen Dedalus from childhood to college and is in many ways autobiographical. This novel does not follow traditional plot arcs but simply meanders through a boy's struggle for identity. As readers, we know from the outset what fate awaits Stephen Dedalus, for the novel is a portrait of an *artist*; however, the protagonist is unsure of his destiny and must wade through the complex emotions of discovery. *Portrait* commences Stephen's journey with a lullaby:

> Once upon a time and a very good time it was there was a moocow coming down along the road and this moocow that was coming down along the road met a nicens little boy named baby tuckoo…

> His father told him that story: his father looked at him through a glass: he had a hairy face.
>
> He was baby tuckoo.

The perspective of the young boy ("moocow") is important to the design of the novel, as Stephen narrates appropriately to the season of his life. From here, we learn more of Stephen's religious mother, drunk father, and impoverished home. Constantly set apart from his surroundings—a Jesuit boarding school, Belvedere College, a brief and zealous religious phase—Stephen feels that his isolation and independence must indicate a unique fate for him, but what? Offering a prescient hand, Joyce confirms his protagonist's heroic nature, naming him after Christianity's first martyr and mythology's cleverest inventor; clearly, Stephen Dedalus is destined to suffer for the glory of art.

In addition to tracing the theme of identity, *Portrait* provides overt discussion about the nature of art, illuminating perhaps Joyce's own explanation for his literary style. "The object of the artist is the creation of the beautiful," yet discerning "what the beautiful is is another question." For Stephen and for Joyce, literature is the "highest and most spiritual art," and as such the artist must seek ways to purify his narrative, thus preserving the beauty of it. Lower forms of narrative start in first person and devolve into third, about which Stephen concludes that "the narrative is no longer purely personal. The personality of the artist passes into the narration itself, flowing round and round the persons and the action like a vital sea." To purify his prose, an artist must not let the reader reflect on the sea and instead plunge him into the stream of consciousness of the characters, so that "the artist, like the God of creation, remains within or behind or beyond or above his handiwork, invisible, refined out of existence, indifferent, paring his fingernails."

In shaping himself as an artist, Stephen discloses a fervent distrust of tradition and society through the two themes of nationalism and religion. Increasing his alienation, Stephen rejects the rising Irish nationalism of his contemporaries and its associated Catholicism. Stephen's rejection of his homeland is necessary because unless he relieves himself of the "burden of impressions" imbibed in his youth "he will have no future." According to Stephen, to be a nationalist is to adopt "the attitude of a dull-witted loyal serf." His nation's past weighs upon him, keeping him from the independence of mind necessary to the artist. He admits, "When the soul of a man is born in this country there are nets flung at it to hold it back from flight. You talk to me of nationality, language, religion. I shall try to fly by those nets." Through this metaphor, Stephen contends that the very background of an Irish artist entraps him—in defining him, it confines him.

Ulysses

The "damned monster-novel," as Joyce called it, takes readers through June 16, 1904, in Dublin for three main characters: Stephen Dedalus, Leopold Bloom, and Molly Bloom, Leopold's wife. *Ulysses* serves as a modern retelling of Homer's *Odyssey*, without fantastical creatures or mythical gods, adopting the epic plot—a man overcoming many obstacles in order to get home. Rather than 10 years like Odysseus, Leopold's journey lasts for only one day. Each of the 18 episodes in *Ulysses* reflects the interactions and observations designed to emulate a corresponding situation in *The Odyssey*, turning physical exploits into internal challenges. Presented through free indirect discourse, Bloom "becomes both an Odyssean wanderer and a representative of 'everyman' as the novel develops, and the workings of his mind perhaps reflect his modern, mundane and yet 'universal' status." Since Joyce presents the story of an average day, the routine temptations and blasé struggles his characters experience are seemingly insignificant, such as being tempted by an attractive woman on the beach or finding a place to eat lunch. Indeed, the entirety of the novel's plot cannot be construed as *epic* in nature. The action consists of a funeral, a fight, political discord, an act of seduction, one of adultery, the birth of a child, a drunken orgy, the rupture of friendship and the loss of a position. However, these obstacles reveal deeper themes, such as love, nationalism, and paternity, which breathe life into human existence. Discussing the novel with a friend, Joyce explained, "I want … to give a picture of Dublin so complete that if the city one day suddenly disappeared from the earth it could be reconstructed out of my book."

Joyce's Style

Joyce's unique style lends itself to both obfuscation and revelation. Although free indirect discourse had been used before and certainly after Joyce, none have mastered it so completely. Pulling nearly any excerpt from *Portrait* reveals the seamless blending of narration and inner monologue:

> Towards dawn he awoke. O what sweet music! His soul was all dewy wet. Over his limbs in sleep pale cool waves of light had passed. He lay still, as if his soul lay amid cool waters, conscious of faint sweet music. His mind was waking slowly to a tremulous morning knowledge, a morning inspiration. A spirit filled him, pure as the purest water, sweet as dew, moving as music.

Although not yet reaching the level of stylistic complexity that emerged in *Finnegan's Wake*, *Portrait* introduced free indirect discourse to the modern reader. Using the psychological content of the novel to shape the style of the prose, Joyce's "prose follows and reflects the stages of his [Stephen's] intellectual development, whether imitating the childlike simplicity of his earliest memories, or the thrilling awareness of his artistic awakening." Gibberish starts the journey and exalted prose ends the *Portrait*. In this way, content and form symbiotically create the novel for Joyce. There is no narrator guiding the reader's reactions or evaluations; thus, the reader experiences life alongside the character, not separated by a third-party, omniscient narrator.

Describing *Ulysses*, Joyce explains in a letter, "My intention is not only to render the myth *sub specie temporis nostri* but also to allow each adventure (that is, every hour, every organ, every art being interconnected and interrelated in the somatic scheme of the whole) to condition and even to create its own technique." Again, Joyce verifies his belief that the content, or what he's writing about, cannot be separated from form, or the way in which he writes about it. When Joyce was struggling to write *Ulysses*, he admitted to a friend that while he already had the right words, he was seeking "the perfect order of words in the sentence. There is an order in every way appropriate." Considering Joyce's narrative style, it is no wonder that not only the words, but also their order were paramount to him. Far more than being unique, Joyce's style dramatized the very plight of humanity. His free indirect discourse allows for a multiplicity of meanings and a conflagration of wordplay that ultimately reflects the "futility of every analytical attempt to provide a singular and absolutely coherent explanation of the meaning of human existence." Joyce's style essentially transcribes life as we experience it, the beauty and the stupidity in one slurred sentence.

Madison Thompson, 2015

JACQUES MARITAIN, 1882–1973, *The Powerful Authority on Aquinas*

> " Authority and power are two different things: power is the force by means of which you can oblige others to obey you. Authority is the right to direct and command, to be listened to or obeyed by others. Authority requests power. Power without authority is tyranny.
>
> —*Man and the State*

- Was known as an interpreter of Thomas Aquinas, his inspiration
- Influenced the United Nations Declaration of 1948, the Canadian Charter of Rights and Freedoms, the Constitution of the Fourth French Republic, and other national declarations with his human rights views
- Was honored by the University of Notre Dame which created a Jacques Maritain Center in 1958 to encourage philosophical research
- Vowed to commit suicide with his wife if they did not find the meaning of life
- Believed that democracy was the only way to bring morality into politics, and that true democracy must be influenced by the Gospel
- Wrote *Creative Intuition in Art and Poetry*, which he based on the lectures he gave at the National Gallery of Art

Key Works

The Degrees of Knowledge, 1932
The Range of Reason, 1952
The Person and the Common Good, 1947
Art and Scholasticism with other Essays, 1947

Biography

The French philosopher Jacques Maritain influenced 20th-century philosophy through his interpretation of St. Thomas Aquinas, and through his own exposition of political and social philosophy. Maritain was born on November 18, 1882, in Paris, France, to Paul Maritain, a lawyer, and Geneviève Favre, the daughter of a French statesman. He received a license in philosophy and the natural sciences at Lycée Henri IV and the Sorbonne. At Sorbonne, Maritain met Raïssa Oumansof. They were both frustrated with the dryness of French intellectual life and made an oath to commit suicide if they did not "find some answer to the apparent meaningless of life." They fell in love and so broke their oath to suicide and were married in 1904. Shortly after, they attended a lecture by Henri Bergson, where they converted to the Roman Catholic faith. In 1921, Maritain became a philosophy professor, and, in 1928, was appointed to the Chair of Logic and Cosmology. He focused on expanding Thomistic philosophy and defending Catholic thought; however, in the early 1930s, he shifted his focus to Christian humanism and natural rights, writing books on religion and culture, the science of epistemology, and political philosophy. After an 18-year gap, Maritain returned to the world of academia, teaching at Princeton, the Pontifical Institute of Mediaeval Studies, Columbia University, Notre Dame, and the University of Chicago. In 1960, his wife Raïssa Oumansof passed away, and he spent the remaining 13 years of his life secluded with a religious order where he continued to write.

Theory of Knowledge

Maritain believed in two orders of knowledge. The first is the order of rational knowledge, which includes the knowledge of sensible nature. Within this order, there are three degrees of abstraction. The first degree includes knowledge that does not deal with the physical, but with the essence and definition of an object. The second is of mathematical objects, such as quantity and number. These exist only in material objects, but can be discussed without relation to those objects. The third degree consists of metaphysical knowledge, that which exists independent of the physical. The higher an object is in its immateriality, the higher its degree of abstraction. The second order is of knowledge that transcends rationality; it includes theological wisdom, knowledge of the divine from both reason and faith, and mystical theology, known through nature or discipline in meditation. Maritain also believed that there are different realities: a material reality that is regarded by the senses and through reason, and a subconscious reality that holds a "universe of concepts, logical connection, rational discursus, and rational deliberation."

Moral Philosophy

Maritain's moral philosophy is based on natural law. The natural law is innately discovered and "prescribes our most fundamental duties," but rather than being founded in experience, it is known by reason. Because people have differing capacities to reason, the natural law is not fully known. As man develops, his knowledge of the natural law is progressively developing as well. This is the cause of the variations in customs and standards from culture to culture. He concludes that natural law is not universal in that it is not known, understood, and respected in the same way by all. But while it can never be completely known, it remains "objective and binding."

Religious Philosophy

Reason and faith are not at odds, claimed Maritain, but they work together to prove the existence of God. Using the five ways of Thomas Aquinas, he felt that the existence of God was certainly proved. He developed a sixth way in addition to the original five. There is an intuition that makes it impossible for humans to understand, as thinking beings, that at one point they did not exist, but they also could not have existed in their own body for eternity, so there must be a "being of transcendent personality" within whom a person has always existed. Because we all recognize our humanity as separate from a divine reality, we must realize that there is a being that oversees and directs everything from this divine reality. People also come to the realization of God through metaphysical intuition. A man can unknowingly come to God by turning to a morally good life and choosing to do good. When a man realizes that he is part of a "being-with-nothingness," he comes to realize the probable existence of a transcendent "being-without-nothingness."

Political Philosophy

Maritain's political philosophy is rooted in his definition of a human being as both an individual and a person. He defines an individual as that "which derives from matter," and a person by his "subsisting spirit." Put simply, the individual is the body while the person is the soul. As an individual, man needs society because of his weak physical state, but, while a person may contribute to society because of his generous spirit, a person has an end higher than the physical world. A person, the spiritual side of man, has the ultimate goal of becoming one with the metaphysical being Maritain refers to as the "transcendent Whole." Maritain describes man, being a person, as "above and superior to political society" because the soul is "destined for an eternal union with the transcendent Whole"; because the soul has this high, spiritual end that goes beyond society, society, then, can be placed in authority over the individual, but not the person. Instead of relying on society-made laws, Maritain encouraged a democracy combining eternally minded inspiration with both secular freedoms and political doctrines rooted in the natural moral conscience. He also believed that the church should be concerned less with obtaining social power and more with providing spiritual inspiration, claiming that this political arrangement would allow those of different religions to cooperate, ultimately creating the most successful government.

Philosophy of Art

Well educated in the arts, Maritain was considered to have the finest aesthetic sensibility among major figures of modern philosophy. He viewed art as the human continuation of divine creation; art is "a virtue of the practical intellect that aims at making." Although rooted in the natural world, successful art transforms something earthly into something divine. By doing so, art makes something beautiful. The aim of art, it follows, is beauty. Maritain claimed that poetic knowledge, which is the foundation for poetry, is co-natural, non-conceptual, and non-rational; it comes from the intellect and is awakened in a poet through revelation by emotion. Thus, poetry is directed by emotion—it "is directed toward concrete existence as connatural [sic] to the soul pierced by a given emotion." In these ways, art creates a world in itself.

Legacy

Jacques Maritain is known as the most influential Catholic philosopher of the 20th century. Driven by his disgust towards the materialism of the French bourgeois, Maritain searched for the cause of materialism and questioned whether society had more to offer than material pleasures. His dissatisfaction with the bourgeois influenced his efforts in leading Catholic thought towards political democracy. Although Maritain's early philosophy focused on defending the Catholic faith against its secular opponents and expanding Thomistic philosophy, he shifted his focus to social issues such as liberal Christian humanism and defense of natural rights. Combining his work in political philosophy and social philosophy, Maritain made significant contributions in drafting the United Nations Universal Declaration of Human Rights.

Makayla Dahl, 2016
Samantha Sherwood, 2013

VIRGINIA WOOLF ◊ 1882–1941, *Modernist and Feminist*

“ Lock up your libraries if you like; but there is no gate, no lock, no bolt that you can set upon the freedom of my mind.

—*A Room of One's Own*

- Struggled with depression all her life and had several nervous breakdowns
- Participated in the Bloomsbury group—an informal gathering of modernist intellectuals and artists in Bloomsbury, London, who met to discuss ideas, form friendships, and maximize creative energy
- Was an atheist
- Read and wrote constantly to compensate for her lack of a university education

- Spoke out about women's lack of access to education and learned professions, and saw marriage inequality as keeping women from doing what they are capable of
- Wrote daily journals extensively—she penned more than 500,000 words from 1915 to her death in 1941
- Married Leonard Woolf, a member of the Bloomsbury group who was an author, publisher, and political theorist
- Founded her own publishing company—Hogarth Press
- Concentrated on the psychology of the characters in her novels
- Is famous for her extensive use of a stream of consciousness writing style
- Committed suicide by drowning in the River Ouse in Sussex, England

Key Works

Mrs. Dalloway, 1925
To the Lighthouse, 1927
Orlando, 1928
A Room of One's Own, 1929
The Waves, 1931

Biography

Born in London in 1882, Woolf hailed from a family of intellectuals. Her mother, Julia Jackson Duckworth, was an heir to the Duckworth publishing family; her father, Sir Leslie Stephen, was a Victorian critic, scholar, philosopher, and biographer. Although well read as a child, Woolf's young life was also wrought with tragedy. Throughout her childhood, her brother sexually abused her, and when she was 13 years old, her mother died. These two events led to her first mental breakdown, and her struggle with depression was only exacerbated by the following events: in 1897, her half-sister, whom she loved dearly, died during childbirth; in 1904, her father died of cancer; and in 1906, her brother died of typhoid. After her father's death, she moved to the section of London known as Bloomsbury with her sister and two brothers. This is where the Bloomsbury group was established.

Such luminaries as E.M. Forster, T.S. Eliot, Clive Bell, and Leonard Woolf were associated with the group. She married Woolf in 1912. A bisexual, Woolf fell in love with another married woman, Vita (Victoria) Sackville West, an affair that inspired one of her biographies, *Orlando*. Throughout her literary career, she wrote many novels, short stories, non-fiction, and biographies. Woolf struggled with severe depression that tended to intensify upon completion of a literary work. In addition to writing, she was a critic for the *Times Literary Supplement* and established Hogarth Press, which published all of her books. Her most notable works are *Mrs. Dalloway*, *To the Lighthouse*, *A Room of One's Own*, and *The Waves*. In March 1941, Woolf committed suicide by drowning herself in the River Ouse in Sussex, England. The suicide was "an act influenced by her dread of World War II … and her fear that she was about to lose her mind and become a burden to her husband, who had supported her emotionally and intellectually." In her suicide note, she reveals that her greatest happiness in life came from her husband: "I feel certain I am going mad again. I feel we can't go through another of those terrible times. And I shan't recover this time. You have given me the greatest possible happiness. … I owe all the happiness of my life to you." Despite the titillating nature of her suicide, Woolf is best known today for her contributions to modern literature and her influence on 20th-century literature.

Woolf's Complicated Feminism

While Woolf is undoubtedly and rightly described as a feminist thinker, her concerns in gender equality are not purely those of female advancement. For most women of Woolf's era, formal education was neglected. Responding to this unfair situation, "Woolf wrote extensively on the problem of women's access to the learned professions, such as academia, the church, the law, and medicine, a problem that was exacerbated by women's exclusion from Oxford and Cambridge."

Beyond a concern for equal access to education, other feminist ideas animate Woolf's work. In *Orlando*, she questions the idea of gender roles and serves as an "elaborate love letter" to Vita Sackville-West, "rendering Vita androgynous and immortal, transforming her story into a myth." This quality of androgyny is central to Woolf's critique of gender roles and inequities. *To the Lighthouse*, perhaps Woolf's best-known work, takes aim at the gender disparities within marriage. The main characters in the novel are a married couple, Mr. and Mrs. Ramsey, who work as a thinly veiled reference to Woolf's parents. In the novel, Mr. Ramsey embodies intellect over emotion, while Mrs. Ramsey attempts to adopt the traditional female role of caregiver and housewife. In *A Room of One's Own*, Woolf famously imagines Judith Shakespeare, sister to the Bard, who is equally talented yet, due to the oppressive nature of gender roles, is not allowed to let her talent flourish in the manner of her brother. Woolf imagines that, unable to give free rein to her talent, Judith would kill herself in despair.

Woolf sees all thinkers and writers as inherently limited by their gender. She called for an "androgynous mind" that is "resonant and porous; that [transmits] emotion without impediment; that [is] naturally creative, incandescent and undivided." A fatal flaw in any writer is to "think of their sex." Believing each mind to have a male as well as a female side, she argues that "some collaboration has to take place between the woman and the man before the act of creation can be accomplished. Some marriage of opposites has to be consummated." Woolf, then, seems every bit as intent on liberating the minds of men as changing the circumstances of women.

The Modern Novel

Woolf was a member of the modernist school of fiction writing, a movement that eschewed the "conventions of the traditional novel," ignoring elements such as plot. Modern novels focus more on the analysis and psychology of individual characters. One way in which this is achieved is through stream of consciousness, where the reader is transported into the mind of the character, able to hear his or her uninterrupted impressions. Here is an example from one of Woolf's best-known novels, *Mrs. Dalloway*:

> That girl, thought Mrs. Dempster (who saved crusts for the squirrels and often ate her lunch in Regent's Park), don't know a thing yet; and really it seemed to her better to be a little stout, a little slack, a little moderate in one's expectations. Percy drank. Well, better to have a son, thought Mrs. Dempster. She had had a hard time of it, and couldn't help smiling at a girl like that. You'll get married if you're pretty enough, thought Mrs. Dempster. Get married, she thought, and then you'll know. Oh, the cooks, and so on. Every man has his ways. But whether I'd chosen quite like that if I could have known, thought Mrs. Dempster, and could not help wishing to whisper a word to Maise Johnson; to feel on the creased pouch of her worn out face the kiss of pity. For it's been a hard life, thought Mrs. Dempster.

The way thought bounces to thought is indicative of our own mental patterns and the true-to-life feel Woolf and other modernists strove for. Indeed, the stream of consciousness technique allows for her narratives to go "beyond being 'about' the very nature of reality, it is itself a vision of reality." Woolf's ability to transcend merely describing reality into essentially writing reality itself gives her novels a poetic feel, stylistically. The psychological emphasis of her famous novels, such as *To the Lighthouse* and *Mrs. Dalloway*, are indicative of this style and place Woolf in the pantheon of great modern authors.

Toby Coffman, faculty
Briauna Schultz, 2013

SIR ARTHUR EDDINGTON ◊ 1882–1944, *A Stellar Man*

" Proof is the idol before whom the pure mathematician tortures himself.
—*The Nature of the Physical World*

- Was knighted in 1930 and received the Order of Merit in 1938
- Refused to fight during WWI because he was a strong Quaker and pacifist, and was denied when he volunteered to drive an ambulance or help with other frontline non-combat duties
- Received honorary degrees from 12 universities
- Won every prize in math that Cambridge's Trinity College offered
- Dominated stellar astronomy through sheer originality and insight
- Remained a bachelor his whole life, living at the observatory with his mother and sister

Key Works

Stellar Movements and the Structure of the Universe, 1914
The Nature of the Physical World, 1928
Science and the Unseen World, 1929
The Expanding Universe, 1933
Relativity Theory of Protons and Electrons, 1936
Fundamental Theory, 1946

Biography

Sir Arthur Stanley Eddington was the premier astrophysicist of his time, pioneering the propagation of Einstein's theory of relativity and revolutionizing knowledge of stellar astronomy. He was born in northwestern England on December 28, 1882, the only son to strong Quaker parents. A precocious child, Eddington memorized the 24x24 multiplication table before he could read. In 1902, he entered Trinity College of Cambridge and concentrated in mathematics, winning every prize on offer. He became the chief assistant at the Royal Observatory in 1906 and remained at the position until 1913, when he was appointed the Plumian Professor of Astronomy at Cambridge. A year later, he was appointed the director of its observatory and remained in this position until his death.

Throughout his life, he took part in many astrological expeditions, including watching an eclipse in Brazil, establishing the longitude of Malta, and originally verifying Einstein's theory of relativity in 1919 while watching a solar eclipse in Príncipe, West Africa. Refused a non-combat role during WWI, Eddington was freed to work on Einstein's theory of relativity. He was the only one in England to receive a copy of Einstein's paper of 1915 during the war, and Einstein himself considered Eddington's translation the best presentation of the theory in any language. In fact, Eddington became known for his remarkable ability to explain advanced scientific concepts in relatively simple terms. He had a wry sense of humor but was plagued by shyness.

Eddington, despite the severe pain of cancer, worked without complaint at the observatory, where he resided with his mother and sister, until his death in 1944. He was much admired and awarded for his efforts; he was knighted in 1930, given the Order of Merit in 1938, and served as the President of the Royal Astronomical Society, Physical Society, Mathematical Association, and International Astronomical Union. His contributions to the worlds of astronomy and physics, especially as it related to Einstein's theory of relativity, paved the way for future developments in the field.

Stars

When it came to stellar astronomy, Eddington's brilliance shone as bright as the stars he studied. One of his greatest contributions was illustrating how stars did not collapse in on themselves as a result of gravity. Eddington reasoned that the internal heat of a star increased as its matter was compressed due to gravity. The extreme heat of the star's interior caused an increase in internal radiation pressures, serving to counterbalance gravity. Although all scientists understood that the interior temperature of stars was around 40 million degrees, several argued that this was not hot enough for Eddington's theory to work. In response Eddington replied: "If any physicist tells you that 40 million degrees is not hot enough for the generation of stellar energy, tell him to go and find a hotter place."

Eddington's research on the temperature and stability of stars led him to the discovery of the mass-luminance law. This "implies that the size of a star is directly proportional to its luminosity, making the mass of a star to be decided upon its intrinsic brightness." He believed that there was a limit to how bright and how large a stable star could get, and today this maximum is known as Eddington's Limit.

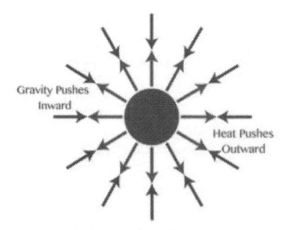

Gravity Pushes Inward

Heat Pushes Outward

The opposing forces of gravity and heat on the star balance each other out, preventing the star from collapsing.

Why Stars Don't Collapse from Gravity

Eddington theorized that any star nearing this limit would pulsate. Sure enough pulsating stars called Cepheids were soon discovered. They served as important measurement-markers because their distance from Earth could be calculated using the mass-luminance law.

Still focusing on the masses of stars, Eddington siphoned his research into the practice of measuring the diameter of nearby gas giants. Using an interferometer (an apparatus that utilizes the interference of waves for precise determinations) and some concepts from relativity theory, Eddington realized that he could calculate the density of white dwarfs, a class of star existing only in theory.

Of his contemporaries, Eddington was one of the first to envision a larger universe. Most scientists saw the spiral clouds of the night sky as being nebulae, but Eddington theorized, correctly, that they were actually whole galaxies lying outside the Milky Way. He could not, however, wrap his mind around the idea of black holes and argued against their existence.

Relativity Theory

Eddington was a fervent advocate of the relativity theory and was largely responsible for its acceptance. Not only did he write extensively about it, but he set out to prove its validity. Eddington subscribed to Einstein's theory of relativity after reading his paper during WWI. Einstein's theory stated that the sun's gravitational field should warp space-time to such an extent that light is bent passing through it, making the stars' positions seem to shift to an observer standing on the Earth. In 1919, Eddington traveled to West Africa to observe a solar eclipse. This expedition was the first to confirm "that gravity will bend the path of light when it passes near a massive star." Eddington's expedition made Einstein a celebrity overnight, and precipitated the eventual triumph of general relativity over classical Newtonian physics. Eddington is largely credited for the popularity of Einstein's theory.

Eddington possessed the rare ability to explain complex scientific ideas in uncomplicated terms. He put this talent to work, writing books on relativity and the mathematics for the general public. Even Einstein himself wrote that Eddington's *Mathematical Theory of Relativity* was "the finest presentation of the subject in any language."

However, Eddington was not content to merely explain another physicist's theory. Towards the end of his life, he sought to link quantum theory with relativity. He paid special attention to constants such as "Planck's constant, the velocity of light, the mass ratio of proton to electron, and the gravitational constant," all of which remained definitive and unchanging across the entire universe. He thought that these numbers signified something greater in the universe and were key to connecting the abstract theories of his day. However, his work on the subject was "not as lucid as his earlier work" and didn't receive the same level of critical acclaim.

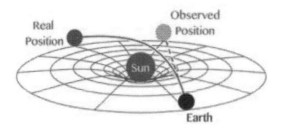

Eddington proved that a star's light was affected
by the sun's gravity, making its observed position
different from its actual position.

Confirming Relativity: Eddington's Support for Einstein's Theory

Caroline Fuschino, 2015
Julianna Swayze, 2016
Alexi Wenger, 2016

FRANZ KAFKA, 1883–1924, *Master of Dreamy Absurdity*

> One morning, when Gregor Samsa woke from troubled dreams, he found himself transformed in his bed into a horrible vermin.
>
> —*The Metamorphosis*

- Started life in Prague, Czechoslovakia, part of a Jewish minority within a larger German community.
- Worked as a lawyer, where he learned of the suffering of the working class
- Experienced social alienation from both other minorities and from the Czechs
- Suffered from intense hypochondria and lifelong depression, which are reflected in his writing
- Was tortured by his ambiguous, fearful relationship with his father
- Returned to common themes in his texts: familial strife, powerlessness, chaos, and deep guilt
- Showed via his parables "that the incomprehensible cannot be comprehended"
- Wrote of average men portrayed realistically in bizarre situations of crisis and their defeats
- Asked his friend, Max Brod, to destroy their correspondence, but it was posthumously published

Key Works

The Metamorphosis, 1915
"In the Penal Colony," 1919
"A Hunger Artist," 1922
The Trial, 1925
The Castle, 1926

Biography

Franz Kafka was born on July 3, 1883, to Hermann and Julie Kafka. As the eldest of six siblings, Kafka spent his childhood as part of the isolated German-speaking Jewish minority in Prague. Kafka himself was ambivalent about his Jewishness; he often expressed outright racism and hatred towards the Jewish race, yet also went through several short obsessions with Jewish literature, history, and the Hebrew language. Franz Kafka not only experienced social alienation but also felt isolated by his immediate family. These feelings perhaps contributed to his intense hypochondria and lifelong depression. From his early childhood, Kafka's relationship with his father was famously fraught with feelings of awe, guilt, and dread. Whether Hermann Kafka genuinely mistreated his son is unclear, but Franz's lifelong perception of inferiority and familial isolation became a private obsession and a central theme in most of his writing. Kafka's biographer later wrote that Kafka "cultivated his fear of the father with obsessive pleasure, because it was for him the very condition of his existence." Kafka did not discover his passion for writing until his university years, where he fell into several literary circles and met fellow author Max Brod. Apart from Brod, Kafka did not maintain many close relationships in his life. His longest romance was a five-year, long-distance engagement with Felice Bauer. Their turbulent relationship ended in 1917 when Kafka was diagnosed with tuberculosis. His illness forced him to move back home with his parents until he found solace in 20-year-old Dora Diamant. The couple lived together in Berlin, Prague, and later in a sanatorium near Vienna until Kafka finally succumbed to his illness in 1924. After Kafka's death, Brod became the guardian of Kafka's writings and legacy. Ignoring his friend's dying request that all his unpublished works be burned, Brod organized, compiled, and published many of Kafka's private writings.

Style

Kafka is perhaps best known for the strangeness of his writing style. His writing is at once dream-like and lucid, austere and rich. Kafka's tendency for describing bizarre and surreal situations through matter-of-fact language disorients readers and characters alike. His characters seem to react to absurd events with mundane acceptance, in a style that has come to be known as magical realism. For example, in *The Metamorphosis*, Gregor Samsa reacts to his transformation into a giant bug by wondering if he still might catch the morning train. In *The Trial*, protagonist Josef K.'s response to his inexplicable arrest is to inquire about his breakfast; when he learns it will not be provided, he eats an apple instead. When the townspeople in *A Country Doctor* force the doctor into a bizarre healing ritual, the doctor accepts this absurd turn of events as though it were wholly unremarkable:

> I am stripped of my clothes and, with my fingers in my beard and my head tilted to one side, I look at the people quietly. I am completely calm and clear about everything and stay that way, too, although it is not helping me at all, for they are now taking me by the head and feet and dragging me into the bed. They lay me against the wall on the side of wound. Then they all go out of the room. The door is shut. The singing stops. Clouds move in front of the moon.

Kafka's style is primarily characterized by his matter-of-fact tone in describing dreamlike and ominous events. The popular term "Kafkaesque" is still commonly used to describe surreal, bizarre, or disorienting situations or feelings of impending danger.

Themes

Many of Kafka's recurrent themes echo his own mental fixations. He often describes the tortured relationships between tyrannical fathers and their submissive sons. Both *The Metamorphosis* and *The Judgment* end with sons dying at the wish of their fathers. Kafka also often emphasizes the impossibility of redemption or success. Saul Friedländer writes, "In Kafka's fiction all main characters, humans or animals, try to reach some unattainable goal, and all such hopes are dashed." Kafka's characters are condemned to endure senseless trauma in a world governed by incomprehensible absurdities. For example, Josef K. in *The Trial* mildly endures arrest, trial, and capital punishment for an unknown crime at the ruling of an unknown authority. Kafka's characters most often accept their powerlessness and passively submit to the chaotic forces that govern their fate.

Another common theme throughout Kafka's work is a deep, unnamed, and implacable sense of guilt and shame. The officer in Kafka's short story "In The Penal Colony" is obsessed with punishing guiltiness, and he declares, "My guiding principle is this: guilt is never to be doubted." Gregor Samsa, the protagonist in *The Metamorphosis*, feels guilty for his very existence. After he is transformed into a giant bug, Gregor is no longer able to work or provide for his family. He senses that his family sees him as a terror, a burden, and a disappointment; he responds by hiding himself and wallowing in shame. Kafka writes,

> Gregor was now cut off from his mother, who was perhaps nearly dying because of him; he dared not open the door for fear of frightening his sister, who had to stay with her mother, there was nothing he could do but wait; and harassed by self-reproach and worry he began to crawl to and fro.

These same themes—familial strife, powerlessness, chaos, and deep guilt—plagued Kafka himself throughout his life. Most often, Kafka's characters are unable to overcome their obstacles, and they must passively submit to the chaos and power of circumstances beyond their control.

Lloyd Isaac, 2017

NIELS BOHR ◊ 1885–1962, *A Physicist with Electron Affinity*

> We are all agreed that your theory is crazy. The question that divides us is whether it is crazy enough to have a chance of being correct.
> —Spoken to Wolfgang Pauli and Werner Heisenberg

- Was a genius undaunted by quantum physics and abstract ideas
- Earned recognition for his wit and kindness
- Came from an intelligent and athletic family of Nobel Prize winners and Olympic competitors
- Created a new model for the atom
- Understood how energy and quanta were involved in atomic structure
- Believed electrons to be both a wave and a particle with only one characteristic manifesting itself at any given time
- Gained world-renowned fame and acknowledgement
- Won the Nobel Peace Prize in 1922

- Advanced nuclear physics by identifying U-235 as an isotope capable of fission
- Helped Jews and scientists escape Nazi Germany
- Worked on the Manhattan Project reluctantly
- Foresaw the consequences of building the atomic bomb
- Spoke against keeping the science of nuclear fission secret

Key Works

The Theory of Spectra and Atomic Constitution, 1924
Atomic Theory and the Description of Nature, 1934
Atomic Physics and Human Knowledge, 1959
Essays, 1958–1962, on Atomic Physics and Human Knowledge, 1963

Biography

Genius was commonplace in the Bohr family. Niels's father taught physiology at the University of Copenhagen, his brother was a well-known mathematician, and his son, Aage, followed in his father's footsteps and won the Nobel Prize. Growing up in Denmark, Bohr engaged in philosophical conversations with his father's friends, conversations that would inspire him to pursue an academic and intellectual life. As a young adult, Bohr attended the University of Copenhagen, where he switched from studying philosophy to physics. Fascinated with electrons, he soon realized that "electron phenomena had features difficult, if not impossible, for classical physics to explain."

So Bohr left classical physics and began to explore the new, unknown world of quantum physics. He partnered with Ernest Rutherford, and together they changed our knowledge of the structure of the atom. Working in England, Bohr became more theory-oriented, devising several theories on the opposing nature of matter. Soon, Denmark began to worry that their prized physicist was spending too much time in England and enticed him into going home with several awards and honors. Bohr even had an Institute for Theoretical Physics established for him at the University of Copenhagen. In the 1930s, Bohr began to study nuclear fission. With WWII approaching, this change in direction proved to be both a blessing and a curse. During the war, Bohr stayed in Europe helping Jewish scientists escape persecution until he no longer had any choice. He ended up in Los Alamos, reluctantly helping with the Manhattan Project and the development of the atomic bomb. He regretted his involvement and dedicated the rest of his life to responsible nuclear energy policy.

Atomic Structure

The atom was a mysterious and foreign concept to most people in the early 20th century. Scientists of the day believed it to have little shape. To them, the atom was essentially a small blob of matter with electrons interspersed like "raisins in a pudding or like seeds in a watermelon." Through experimentation and prodigious brainpower, Bohr and his friend, Ernest Rutherford, revolutionized how the world saw the atom.

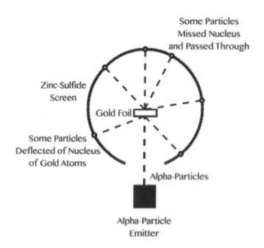

Rutherford's Gold Foil Experiment: Discovering the Nucleus

Rutherford began with an experiment involving radiation. He sent a stream of alpha particles through a thin sheet of gold foil. While most of the particles passed right through the foil, a few "bounced back as though [they] had hit something solid." Rutherford had stumbled upon a secret hidden deep in the heart of the atom: the nucleus. He discovered that most of the matter in the atom fit into "a very small, extremely dense region." The rest of the atom consisted of empty space in which electrons orbited this dense center or nucleus. Most of the particles passed through the gold foil because they were simply passing through this empty space. The few particles that reflected happened to strike the nucleus.

The traditional "plum pudding" model had been shattered, but Bohr was not satisfied with Rutherford's vision for the atom. If electrons orbited the nucleus, they should, according to classical physics, "continually lose energy by emitting electromagnetic radiation" until they spiraled into the nucleus. Clearly this did not happen. So Bohr abandoned the prevailing laws of physics in his quest to discover what exactly happened within the boundaries of an atom.

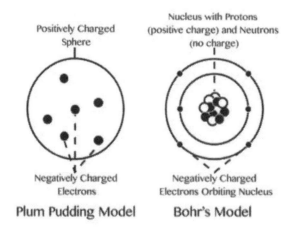

Neils Bohr's Atomic Model

Considering the idea that energies are quantized (meaning that energy comes in little packets, not a steady stream), Bohr postulated that electrons could be found only in orbits of certain "allowed" energy levels for each atom. They couldn't just orbit willy-nilly anywhere at all. If an electron was orbiting in one of these permitted energy levels, it would not emit or absorb any radiation, and it would therefore not spiral into the nucleus. However, Bohr did believe that an electron could jump to a higher permitted energy level by absorbing exactly the required amount of energy. It could also drop to a lower level by emitting the required amount of energy to enter that level.

Although there were some flaws with Bohr's concept of the atom, his model pointed future scientists in the right direction. The two most important takeaway ideas for future scientists were that electrons could exist only in definite energy levels and that energy was involved in moving electrons to and from different levels. For his efforts he received the Nobel Peace Prize in 1922.

Theory of Complementarity and the Correspondence Principle

Prior to Bohr, energy and matter within classical physics were characterized separately, with energy being represented as waves and matter as particles. However, in the 1920s, the physics world began to note that light and electrons exhibited properties of both a wave and a particle. To account for this, Bohr formulated a new theory, the theory of complementarity, which rationalized that light could be viewed as either a wave or a particle, but both could not be observed simultaneously. With this discovery, many physicists were stumped by the prospect that it was not one or the other. Bohr introduced a different point of view, which he called the Copenhagen Interpretation in 1922. Instead of thinking of light particle/waves as contradictory, Bohr thought, "they expressed different aspects of a single unitary phenomenon that could not be described completely as either a wave or a particle, but instead exhibited the properties of both." He gave people a new way of viewing the world—not only physics, but in life in general—as this new idea of duality was a profound discovery that had not yet been explored.

Nuclear Physics

With physics legends like Albert Einstein, Werner Heisenberg, Ernest Rutherford, and Niels Bohr bouncing ideas off one another, physics experienced its Golden Age in the 1930s. The discovery of the neutron at the beginning of the decade prompted this elite club of scientists to look away from the electron and to focus on the nucleus instead. This led to one of the most fateful coincidences in history: the development of the theory of nuclear fission on the eve of WWII.

In 1939 Bohr was leaving for the United States when he learned of two successful nuclear fission experiments in Germany. He had reservations about where nuclear fission could lead, but Bohr firmly believed that "it would take the entire efforts of a country to make a bomb." Because such a tremendous effort seemed unlikely to ever happen, Bohr set about working on splitting the nucleus for the sake of science.

He discovered that "the rare U-235 isotope was the isotope that made uranium fissionable, and which made a chain reaction theoretically possible." He also thought up the droplet theory, in which the nucleus was viewed as being similar to a droplet of water. It could theoretically be split, if the drop was elongated long enough. By the time WWII broke out in Europe, Bohr had already cemented himself as a leading figure in nuclear physics.

His expertise in nuclear matters made him a natural fit in the Manhattan Project, to which he became attached after leaving Europe. Though ultimately successful in creating the atomic bomb, Bohr was fearful of the long-term consequences of such an invention. His son, another Nobel winner, would later write: "My father's thoughts … constantly dwelt on the serious consequences of the atom bomb, on the terrifying perspectives opened, and on its profound effect on post-war problems."

Tatjana Scherschel, 2015

ERWIN SCHRÖDINGER ◊ 1887–1961, *Quantum Physicist*

" The present is the only thing that has no end.

—*My View of the World*

- Was a quantum physicist famous for his illustration of "Schrödinger's cat"
- Derived a groundbreaking formula for tracking and predicting the positions of subatomic particles
- Won the Nobel Prize in Physics in 1933
- Taught as a professor at eight different universities

Key Works

What is Life? 1944
Nature and the Greeks, 1954
Expanding Universes, 1956
Mind and Matter, 1958
Meine Weltansicht (My View of the World), 1961

Biography

Erwin Schrödinger was one of the foremost quantum physicists of his time, helping form quantum theory in the 1920s. Schrödinger was born in Austria on August 12, 1887. An avid student, he had a wide range of interests, including the "severe logic of ancient grammar and the beauty of German poetry." In 1910, after obtaining his doctorate in math and physics, Schrödinger briefly worked in a physics lab before being drafted to fight in WWI. During his service as an artillery officer, Schrödinger entertained himself by studying philosophy. After the war, he married Anna Maria Bertel and held teaching positions at Stuttgart, Breslau, the University of Zürich, and the University of Berlin. His work on wave mechanics during this time earned Schrödinger the Nobel Prize in Physics in 1933. Later that year, Schrödinger resigned from his post at the University of Berlin in protest of the Nazi regime's persecution of Jews. Over the next two decades, he moved around various universities in Austria, Italy, and Ireland. After his retirement in 1955, he returned to the University of Vienna to become a professor emeritus until his death in 1961. Schrödinger is still considered one of the most exceptional physicists of the 20th century.

Schrödinger's Equation

In the early 20th century, physicists were puzzled to discover that the physical laws governing the behavior of objects did not seem to apply to the behavior of subatomic particles. It appeared that light, electrons, and other subatomic particles behaved as *both* waves and particles, yet physicists of the time could not detect a pattern or reason for this behavior. Moreover, subatomic particles could not be tracked through both space and time. The field of quantum physics was created to study this phenomenon. Schrödinger played a key role in the development of this new field. His largest contribution to quantum mechanics was Schrödinger's equation, which could accurately track—and predict—the changes in a quantum system over time. Schrödinger's research is still considered some of the most important work in modern physics, and he received the Nobel Prize in physics in 1933 for the formation of his equation. Many scientists still use his formula as the basis for more complex and nuanced quantum theories.

Schrödinger's Cat: Alive or Dead?

Schrödinger is perhaps most famous for his theoretical illustration of a cat in a box. In Schrödinger's time, the most common understanding of quantum mechanics was the Copenhagen interpretation, which involved the theory of superposition. This is the idea that while no one is observing an object, the "object can be in more than one state at once" and, if no one observes how an event happened, it "happened in all possible ways." In other words, scientists believed that as long as subatomic particles were left unobserved, they would occupy multiple physical states at once and cause multiple, even conflicting, outcomes. Once the particles were observed, however, scientists believe that the particles' state and activity would immediately collapse into a single, knowable reality.

To illustrate how ridiculous he considered this theory, Schrödinger invented his famous cat thought-experiment. He applied contemporary quantum theory to a hypothetical cat in a steel box. Inside the box would also be a flask of poison and a radioactive monitor. If the monitor detected radioactive decay, it would automatically shatter the flask of poison and kill the cat. According to the Copenhagen interpretation, the cat in the box would be both alive *and* dead until an observer looked inside. At that point, the cat's reality would collapse into just one option, and it would be either alive *or* dead.

Schrödinger believed that this illustration would make others realize the absurdity of the theory of superposition, but it had the opposite effect. Though no one ever attempted to actually put a cat in a deadly box, this experimental design was used with smaller particles to prove the veracity of the theory. Ironically, Schrödinger's "ridiculous" illustration, intended to argue against the Copenhagen theory, actually inspired successful experiments that confirmed subatomic superpositioning.

Alexi Wenger, 2016

EUGENE O'NEILL ◊ 1888–1953, *Playwright in the Spirit of the Greeks*

> " The tragedy of life is what makes it worthwhile. I think that only life, which merits living, lies in the effect to realize some dream, and the higher the dream is, the harder it is to realize.
>
> —*The Unknown O'Neill: Unpublished or Unfamiliar Writings of Eugene O'Neill*

- Was the only American playwright to be awarded a Noble Prize for Literature (1936)
- Wrote more than 20 full-length plays between 1920–1943, the height of his career
- Won four Pulitzer Prizes for drama
- Achieved the most translations and productions for a playwright, after William Shakespeare and George Bernard Shaw.
- Wrote that "in all [his] plays sin is punished and redemption takes place"

- Helped raise American theatre into a medium that has equaled the best in US fiction, painting, and music

Key Works

Beyond the Horizon, 1920
The Emperor Jones, 1920
Anna Christie, 1922
Desire Under the Elms, 1924
Strange Interlude, 1928
Mourning Becomes Electra, 1931
Ah! Wilderness, 1933
The Iceman Cometh, 1939
Long Day's Journey into Night, posthumously 1954

Biography

Eugene O'Neill was born in a hotel room in New York City in 1888. His Catholic father was a fairly successful actor, exposing O'Neill to the theater early in his life. Kicked out of Princeton after his freshman year due to a prank he pulled, O'Neill entered the newspaper industry. After a bout with tuberculosis, he became interested in the theater and, following his treatment, took a playwriting course at Harvard.

He published a succession of notable and popular plays throughout the 1920s and 1930s: *Beyond the Horizon, Anna Christie, Strange Interlude, Mourning Becomes Electra, Ah! Wilderness*, and *The Iceman Cometh*. He won four Pulitzer Prizes over the course of these two decades, and he worked to create plays that invoked "the inner drama of his characters more than their physical or social world." His influence on the succeeding generation of great American playwrights—Arthur Miller and Tennessee Williams notable among them—is undeniable. In 1943, his health started to decline, and his writing career came to an end when it became impossible for him to hold a pen. He spent the final two years of his life in a Boston hotel room, and as his death approached, he declared to the doctor: "Born in a goddamn hotel room and dying in a hotel room!"

Recreation of Greek Tragedies

Many of O'Neill's plays were inspired by ancient Greek tragedy, beginning with *Desire Under the Elms*. Greek tragedy inspired him because it was "the first theatre that sprang, by virtue of man's imaginative interpretation of life, out of his worship to Dionysus." His most esteemed recreation of Greek tragedy is *Mourning Becomes Electra*, based on Aeschylus's trilogy *Oresteia*, and first produced in 1931. Similar to *Oresteia*, its structure is in three separate plays comprising 13 acts: "Homecoming, A Play in Four Acts," "The Hunted, A Play in Five Acts," and "The Haunted, A Play in Four Acts."

Just as the structure of O'Neill's play resembles that of the Greek tragedy, so does the plot: O'Neil "retained the forms and the conflicts of the Greek characters; the heroic leader returning from war; his adulterous wife who murders him; his jealous, repressed daughter, who avenges him through the murder of her mother; and his weak incestuous son, who is goaded by his sister first to matricide and then to suicide." *Mourning Becomes Electra* is set during the Civil War at the Mannon family home, where Ezra, the father, his wife, Christine, and their children, Lavinia and Orin, reside. As the play is a tragedy, it is filled with matricide, suicide, and homicide. In the final act of the final play in the trilogy, only one Mannon survives—the daughter, Lavinia. She ends with this somber reflection: "I've got to punish myself! Living alone here with the dead is a worse act of justice than death or prison! I'll never go out or see anyone! I'll have the shutters nailed closed so no sunlight can ever get in. I'll live alone with the dead and keep their secrets, and let them hound me, until the curse is paid out and the last Mannon is let die!" *Mourning Becomes Electra* captures powerful tragedy, while it represents the playwright's most complete use of Greek forms, themes, and characters.

Toby Coffman, faculty

T.S. ELIOT ◊ 1888–1965, *Modernist Poet*

66 No poet, no artist of any art, has his complete meaning alone. His significance, his appreciation is the appreciation of his relation to the dead poets and artists. You cannot value him alone; you must set him, for contrast and comparison, among the dead.

—*The Sacred Wood*

- Considered himself "classical in literature, royalist in politics, and Anglo-Catholic in religion"
- Was well known as a dramatist, a critic, and a poet
- Received the Nobel Prize in 1948 for Literature and the British Order of Merit
- Alluded to more than 35 different authors, such as Shakespeare, Baudelaire, Spenser, and Dante, in one of his greatest poems, "The Waste Land"
- Published "The Four Quartets" originally as four separate poems but later unified them to create one long poem

Key Works

"The Love Song of J. Alfred Prufrock," 1915
The Sacred Wood, 1920
"The Waste Land," 1922
Murder in the Cathedral, 1935
"The Four Quartets," 1943

Biography

Thomas Stearns Eliot was from a well-to-do St. Louis family. After finishing his PhD at Harvard, he moved to Europe, studying in Paris before landing at Merton College in Oxford. While at Oxford, he met the poet Ezra Pound, who helped edit two of his most prominent poems, "The Love Song of J. Alfred Prufrock" and "The Waste Land." In 1915 he married Vivien Haigh-Wood, whose mental instability plagued their marriage until their separation in 1933. From 1917 until 1925, Eliot worked at Lloyd's Bank in the colonial and foreign department.

During this time he pursued his literary career, publishing his first work of critical prose, *The Sacred Wood*, and "The Waste Land" in 1922. He edited a quarterly review, *The Criterion*, from 1922 to 1939. After leaving Lloyd's, he became the director at the publishing firm, Faber and Faber, until his death. An anglophile, Eliot renounced his American citizenship and joined the Anglican Church in 1927. His most famous religious poems, "Ash Wednesday" and "Four Quartets," were published in this period. He is credited with "broaden[ing] the base for a discussion of literature into philosophy and theology and thereby claimed that to be judged as truly great any poetry must be tested by more than pure literary standards." In 1948 he was awarded the Order of Merit by George VI and the Nobel Prize in Literature. He died in London on January 4, 1965.

"The Love Song of J. Alfred Prufrock"

"The Love Song of J. Alfred Prufrock" was published in Eliot's first volume of poetry, *Prufrock and Other Observations*. The poem is narrated from the perspective of an aging, pensive, and somewhat socially detached man caught in the tension of his own desire for companionship and his distaste for idle conversation. J. Alfred Prufrock, Eliot's protagonist, yearns for meaningful companionship as he introduces the poem with a hope for relationship: "Let us go then, you and I."

Eliot's use of poetic rhyme scheme provides a repetition that mirrors the theme of musical and relational harmony. It resembles that of the waltz, a two-person dance, showing the protagonist's deep-rooted desire for intimacy and companionship. Yet despite this desire, he lacks the social adequacy to participate in "a world of decaying traditions." His parenthetical interjections of his thoughts—"with a bald spot in the middle of my hair"—suggest concern for the way others view him, yet he has a repugnant attitude towards his companions' superficial small talk. This tension leaves him fearful and completely immobile in the society he belongs to. Frustrated by the vacuous nature of his tea-time conversations, the narrator illustrates most of the poem through sensory images. Prufrock is a "dramatic, lyrical, ironic, and brilliantly discontinuous" poem used to reveal the isolation and dehumanizing nature of Modern society.

"The Waste Land"

"The Waste Land," Eliot's most celebrated poem, was written in 1922, and the original text spanned more than 800 lines. His friend, Ezra Pound, a modernist poet and critic, revised and edited Eliot's poem, cutting it to around 400 lines, in five sections—"The Burial of the Dead," "A Game of Chess," "The Fire Sermon," "Death By Water," and "What the Thunder Said." Written before Eliot's conversion to Anglicanism, scholars allege "The Waste Land" suffers from a dearth of love and faith.

One example (of many) in which Eliot suggests a religious decline is in part one: "To where Saint Mary Woolnoth kept the hours / With a dead sound on the final stroke of nine." The dead sound of Saint Mary Woolnoth signifies the death of the church. There are a number of biblical allusions, and the spiritual drought that is realized in the poem leads to an intellectual and spiritual death of the modern person: "He who was living is now dead / We who were living are now dying." In addition, the poem overflows with allusions to authors such as Baudelaire, Chaucer, Spenser, Shakespeare, and Dante, a reminder to the reader "of the pieces of a once great culture that are scattered around."

Eliot found modern culture and art to be intellectually vapid and therefore placed allusions to French, Spanish, and Hindi cultures, and included references to different eras and texts in "The Waste Land." The effect of these allusions is it "allows [the poem] to be read in the context of any age and place," making the poem timeless. In terms of structure, throughout the entirety of the poem, new speakers and new scenes are presented without any obvious transitions; this is due partly to Pound's cuts and revisions, but it is also due to Eliot's style which reflects modernism's emphasis on non-representational art and non-linear narrative. "The Waste Land" is a thought-provoking and intellectually arduous poem and, because of this poem, Eliot is considered to have founded modernism in poetry.

"The Four Quartets"

"The Four Quartets" consists of four poems published separately—"Burnt Norton" (1936), "East Coker" (1940), "The Dry Salvages" (1941), and "Little Gidding" (1941). They were collected into one poem in 1943. As Eliot's final published poem, it is regarded by critics and poets alike as his magnum opus. Each of the four "quartets" is a reference, an ode to a specific place that was personal to Eliot, and represents his spiritual findings in that place. Eliot strived, even in his most meditative, spiritual, and abstract poem, to keep his ideas rooted in concrete subjects, resulting in a poetic compilation of these four distinct places of revelation. It is "something of a summing up of his experiences" at this point of his life, which had included becoming a British citizen, joining the Anglican church, and separating from an emotionally unstable wife. They quartets alternate in tone between lyrical, meditative, and prosaic, offering stark contrasts of sound and symbol, as well as frequent repetition of words, phrases, and images.

"Burnt Norton," is the name of a manor in southwest England that Eliot visited with his childhood friend, Emily Hale, only a few years prior to the poem's publication. Together they wandered the rose gardens of the manor, and in the poem he hears and wanders after the voices of children playing there. The theme central to part one of "The Four Quartets" is man's position between time and timelessness, "what might have been," and "perpetual possibility." Eliot speculates on eternity, history, and how the two intertwine.

Part two, "East Coker," is named after a small village to which the Eliot family could trace its origins to the 1400s. Upon his pilgrimage, Eliot reflects on the legacy of his ancestry. He acknowledges that most historical remnants are now redesigned, destroyed, or overlooked—a thought that disturbs him, as the legacy left by his ancestors appears nonexistent. His disappointment propels him to further question "the vacant interstellar spaces, the vacant into the vacant." He ultimately lands on the truth and purpose that he finds in his understanding of the Bible, exemplified through Eliot's "rhetoric of traditional mystical paradox … permeated by a profoundly nostalgic and Anglican vision of history."

Subsequently, "The Dry Salvages" refers to another place from Eliot's past. As the beginning of the section notes, the Dry Salvages "is a small group of rocks, with a beacon, off the N.E. coast of Cape Ann, Massachusetts," which is located near Eliot's childhood hometown. Writing at a time of worldwide uncertainty and destruction, WWII, Eliot highlights the tempestuous, untamed nature of water through the vivid imagery of shipwreck and wave-tousled chaos.

Fluidly tying together ideas from the previous sections, Eliot masterfully illustrates man's helplessness yet hints at the hope he has discovered. *Boston Globe* journalist, James Parker, says, "the poem's religiosity springs from its confrontation with wastage, shipwreck, destruction—the broken net and the bone on the beach, and the terrible anxiety of the sailor's wife. 'Where is there an end to the drifting wreckage?' For Eliot … the end was beyond—with God."

And finally, the grand finale of the quartet, "Little Gidding," refers to an Anglican monastery that Eliot uses to capture the idea of lives being renewed. Eliot strongly employs his modernist voice by calling his audience to a new way of thinking. For example, he writes, "Then fools' approval stings, and honour stains / From wrong to wrong the exasperated spirit / Proceeds, unless restored by that refining fire / Where you must move in measure, like a dancer." Eliot signals his urgent desire for a changed mindset in his noticeably more dramatic and directly conversational tone, closing his divinely contemplative reverie with a worldly, tangible application.

LUDWIG WITTGENSTEIN ◊ 1889–1951, *Philosopher of Language*

> " The limits of my language are the limits of my world.
>
> —*Tractatus Logico-Philosophicus*

- A giant of 20th-century philosophy; he produced two very different and incompatible philosophies that are both considered masterpieces
- Gave away one of the largest inheritances in Europe, designed and built a house for his sister, but he himself lived a simple life in a hut in Norway
- Focused on the role of language in human life and understanding; the classic "analytic" philosopher, believing that all meaningful philosophical questions (questions that philosophy can answer) are questions about language and how it is to be used, rather than about the extra-linguistic world, per se
- There's no essential nature that all of language shares—we should not look for the essence of "justice" or "beauty" but look for resemblances in how we use words
- Wrote his first book, the *Tractatus Logico-Philosophicus*, after volunteering for the front lines in the Austrian army in WWI, during which he was decorated for bravery and taken prisoner
- After he wrote the *Tractatus*, he believed he had solved the major problems of philosophy, and thus turned to the "useful" work of teaching elementary school
- The early Wittgenstein tried to clarify the limits of language—what could be meaningfully said; believed most philosophical problems result from confused talk
- Thought ethics and religion *show* themselves to be meaningful in a mystical way, but that nothing philosophically informative can be *said* about them
- The later Wittgenstein argues that sentences get their meaning from how they're used in language, *not* from matching up with objects outside language (again, the key element of true linguistic analysis)
- Early Wittgenstein sees language as a picture, while the later Wittgenstein sees language as a tool with many different uses
- How we use language is best thought of as a game: just as there are different rules for football and soccer, so distinctive uses of language use different rules
- The later Wittgenstein held that different forms and ways of life yield different concepts, rules, and logics of language

Key Works

Tractatus Logico-Philosophicus, 1922
Philosophical Investigations, 1953

Biography

Ludwig Wittgenstein was the youngest of eight children and was born into one of the wealthiest families in Austria on April 26, 1889. His father made much of his fortune in the iron and steel industry, and his mother was a cultured lover of music who invited Brahms and Mahler into their home. One of Wittgenstein's unusual talents later in life was the ability to whistle entire musical scores from memory; however, he primarily delighted in machines and engineering in his youth. As a child, he constructed a working model of a sewing machine, and was working on designing a propeller when the mathematics of the problem piqued his interest in the nature of math, and thus philosophy. He discovered the work of philosopher Bertrand Russell and then studied with him at Cambridge in 1912.

Wittgenstein was a creative genius, and his personality was so powerfully intense that John Maynard Keynes often referred to him as "God." When he began work on his first masterpiece, the *Tractatus Logico-Philosophicus*, he left Cambridge and built himself a hut in Norway. When the First World War began, he refused entry as an officer and insisted on enlisting. He volunteered for dangerous missions, continued writing philosophy, and was captured by the Italians in 1918. After the war he gave away his inherited fortune (which had made him one of the richest single men in Europe at the time), and lived simply for the rest of his life.

He believed that his *Tractatus* had solved the problems of philosophy, so he turned to teaching peasant children in a poor alpine village and later became a gardener. He repeatedly contemplated becoming a monk, but eventually found his way back to philosophy. In the second stage of his philosophical career, he rejected much of his thinking in *Tractatus* and produced a second masterpiece, his *Philosophical Investigations*. He died of cancer in 1951. When the doctor informed him that the end was near, he reportedly replied, "Good." It is said that his last words were, "Tell them I've had a wonderful life."

The Early Wittgenstein

Wittgenstein's *Tractatus Logico-Philosophicus* (usually called the *Tractatus*) is part of his "early" thought. In it, his goal is to demonstrate the limits of meaningful language; he wants to distinguish talk that makes sense from simple nonsense. As he says in the preface, "The whole sense of the book might be summed up in the following words: what can be said at all can be said clearly, and what we cannot talk about we must pass over in silence. Thus the aim of this book is to set a limit to thought, or rather—not to thought, but to the expression of thoughts."

One of the keys to understanding the *Tractatus* is the "picture" theory of language. Wittgenstein gives an example of a car accident being enacted by lawyers in a courtroom using dolls and toy cars. The dolls and toy cars "picture" the facts of the accident, and for Wittgenstein, that's what language does, too. Language gives us a picture of the world, and that picture may or may not correctly represent the "facts" of the world. The sentence, "The cat sat on the mat," pictures the world by sharing the "same logical form" with the world. This idea takes some unpacking. What does it mean to share the same logical form? Think of taking a picture at a concert with one's cell phone. When looking through the camera, the image on the camera screen shares the same logical form as the object one is photographing at the concert. Or think of a map: a map shares the same logical form as the city that it represents when the streets, parks, and buildings on the map "match up" with the actual streets, parks, and buildings. Consider one last example that Wittgenstein uses, involving a symphony. As Buckingham et al., put it, "The sound waves generated by a performance of a symphony, the score of that symphony, and the pattern formed by the grooves on a gramophone recording of the symphony all share between the same logical form."

Using the picture theory of language, Wittgenstein can explain what makes some language meaningful, and other language meaningless: any assertion that cannot picture the facts is meaningless. If our language does not picture anything then it is not meaningful. This has the interesting implication that religious and ethical values are *meaningless*. After all, consider how many religious and ethical statements are formulated with statements like "should" or "ought": "You *should* sell all you have and give it to the poor." How exactly, wonders Wittgenstein, could this possibly be pictured? We can use language to picture someone doing that very action, but how can one picture that someone *should* do that action? This is why Wittgenstein concludes that, "It is clear that ethics cannot be put into language."

Here, however, Wittgenstein becomes somewhat mystical, for he doesn't believe that ethical and religious issues are nonsense. Rather, he believes that they simply cannot be put into words. As he says, "They are like the steps of a philosophical ladder that helps us to climb altogether beyond the problems of philosophy, but which we can kick away once we have ascended."

The Later Wittgenstein

If the controlling metaphor in Wittgenstein's early work is language as a picture, the controlling metaphor in his later work is language as a tool. In *The Philosophical Investigations*, the meaning of a word doesn't come from how well it pictures the facts, but from how it is *used*. How does the word function in our lives? How is it used? Thus, "For a *large* class of cases—though not for all—in which we employ the word 'meaning' it can be defined thus: the meaning of a word is its use in the language."

If the meaning of language comes from how it is used rather than what it "pictures," the variety of ways we use language suggests that words like "justice," or even "game," don't have a fixed essence. In contrast to Plato, who thought that there was an ideal, perfect form of "justice," Wittgenstein argues that there is what he calls a "family resemblance," among instances of things like justice or games. "Just as we can see similarities in the face, walk or voice of family members without being able to specify the precise character of the family resemblance, so words and games can be similar in different words without having an abstract essence." Searle asks us to think of the variety of games: board games, Olympic games, gambling games, ball games, etc. They don't share a single essence, but there are crisscrossing and overlapping similarities. Wittgenstein calls these "family resemblances." There is no one thing that the word "game" stands for, and the same goes for much of our language.

People use words in an incredible variety of ways depending on situation and context, and Wittgenstein labels these wider senses of language and meaning "language games." We talk very differently about football than we talk about mathematics, chess, or religion, and these are examples of different language games. Among the many examples that Wittgenstein mentions are reporting an event, speculating about an event, forming or testing a hypothesis, making up and/or reading a story, play-acting, guessing riddles, making a joke, translating, asking, thanking, and so on. Notice that how we use language depends upon the particular activity we are engaged in. This is why Wittgenstein says that the concept "is meant to bring into prominence the fact that the *speaking* of language is part of an activity, or of a form of life." In contrast to the *Tractatus*, where he claimed that words have meaning by simply representing objects, in the *Philosophical Investigations*, Wittgenstein views language much more broadly as a tool to be used in the varied contexts of our daily lives.

Jeff Culver, faculty
Daren Jonescu, advisor

LEO STRAUSS ◊ 1889–1973, *German-American Political and Classical Philosopher*

- Briefly trained to be a Jesuit priest and studied theology; broke with Catholicism in 1919
- Was born in Kirchhain, Germany to conservative/orthodox Jewish parents
- Trained in the neo-Kantian tradition, later immersed in the work of the phenomenologists Edmund Husserl and Martin Heidegger
- Focused his research on the Greek texts of Plato and Aristotle
- Served in the German army during WWI
- Joined a Jewish fraternity and worked for the German Zionist movement
- Identified as a theist
- Resigned his position at the Academy of Jewish Research in 1932
- Adopted his wife's son, Thomas, and later his sister's child; he had no biological children
- Left Germany just ahead of the Nazi take-over
- Chose not to return to his native country because of the Nazis; found temporary employment at the University of Cambridge in 1935
- Moved to the United States in 1937 because he couldn't find permanent work in England
- Spent most of his career as a professor of political science at the University of Chicago, where he taught several generations of students and published fifteen books
- Became a US citizen in 1944
- Believed politics and philosophy were necessarily intertwined, and regarded the trial and death of Socrates as the moment when political philosophy came into existence
- Distinguished "scholars" from "great thinkers" and considered himself a mere scholar
- Studied the natural rights of man through Thomas Hobbes and John Locke and relied heavily on Plato, Aristotle, and Cicero
- Critiqued Jean-Jacques Rousseau and Edmund Burke and was opposed to the works of Martin Heidegger who "sanitized and politicized Nietzsche"
- Wrote that Friedrich Nietzsche was the first philosopher to properly understand historicism, an idea grounded in a general acceptance of Hegelian philosophy of history
- Studied Al-Farabi and Maimonides
- Called for a distinction between exoteric (or public) and esoteric (or secret) teaching, arguing that serious writers write esoterically
- Proposed that the classical and medieval art of esoteric writing is the proper medium for philosophic learning
- Suggested philosophy must guard itself especially against those readers who believe themselves authoritative, wise, and liberal defenders of the status quo
- Believed in questioning established opinions or in investigating the principles of morality

MARTIN HEIDEGGER ◊ 1889–1976, *Philosopher of "Being"*

- Briefly trained to be a Jesuit priest and studied theology; broke with Catholicism in 1919
- Joined the Nazi party in 1933 and spoke in favor of Hitler and the Nazi cause; resigned from his office and politics in 1934
- Wrote prolifically: his collected works comprise around 100 volumes
- Used many neologisms (made-up words) in his writing, seeking to take the reader into a thought-world suited to his new ideas, a kind of poetic process of suggesting with evocative language rather than directly describing with mundane, prosaic language
- Aristotle's discussion of the various senses of being in his *Metaphysics* was a major inspiration of Heidegger's lifelong focus on the meaning of Being as such
- "Beings" are things like tables, desks, school buildings, animals, and storms, but Heidegger instead was fascinated by "Being" (singular) itself, not those other beings or "entities"; in other words, the standard introductory questions of philosophy, such as "How do we know the table exists?" give way in Heidegger to the more fundamental but often overlooked question, "What does 'to exist' mean?"
- Thought almost all of Western philosophy was at a dead end because it had forgotten to focus on Being itself and instead focused on beings or things; forgetting to focus on Being (the "forgetting of Being") is *nihilism*
- Started his own investigations not with consciousness and the mind in abstraction from everyday experience (like Descartes), but in the Greek style, by examining how humans actually live in the world
- Thought that the pre-Socratic philosophers somehow naïvely experienced Being as it was and didn't overanalyze it
- His human focus, however, even from the beginning of his most famous work, *Being and Time*, is on *Dasein*, not simply humans, but a human collective, human life as a social structure; that is, Heidegger largely ignores the truly naïve perspective on Being, which is the Being (existence as such) of the real, biological individual, in favor of the somewhat speculative human-as-community abstraction of *Dasein*; this seems to artificially load the deck towards a *social* conception of Being (a bias which may help to explain Heidegger's flirtation with Nazism)
- Viewed our modern 20th-century technological culture as nihilistic, since it doesn't ponder the meaning of Being but simply uses beings and things as instruments

Key Works

Being and Time, 1927
What Is Metaphysics? 1929
On the Essence of Truth, 1930
The Origin of the Work of Art, 1935
Letter on Humanism, 1946
Building Dwelling Thinking, 1951
The Basic Problems of Phenomenology, 1954
The Question Concerning Technology, 1954
What Is Called Thinking? 1954

Biography

Martin Heidegger was born in Germany's Black Forest region in 1889, and he remained attached to the area and its people all his life. He began his academic studies at the University of Freiburg in Germany, studying theology to become a priest, but he was discharged within a month due to heart trouble. His poor health made him unsuitable for combat duties in 1915, and he was assigned to the postal and meteorological services during WWI. He decided to study philosophy after meeting Edmund Husserl. He served as Husserl's assistant for a few years, and ultimately succeeded him at the University of Freiburg. In 1917, Heidegger married a Protestant, Elfriede Petri, and shortly after the birth of his son in 1919, he announced his break with Catholicism.

In 1933, the Nazis came to power and ousted the director at the University of Freiburg. Heidegger was a member of the Nazi party, and he became the new director. His involvement with the Nazis remains controversial. As director "depending on whose account one believes, he either enthusiastically implemented the Nazi policy of bringing university education into line with Hitler's nauseating political programme … or he allowed that policy to be officially implemented while conducting a partially underground campaign of resistance to some of its details, especially its anti-Semitism." He resigned a year later, and though he remained a member of the Nazi party, he didn't participate in politics. He was under surveillance by the Gestapo in the 1940s, was humiliatingly sent out from the university during WWII to dig trenches, and the French banned him from teaching for five years after the war. He ultimately settled into a secluded life of scholarship in the Black Forest and died there in 1976.

Dasein

Philosophy courses often ask questions about existence: Does God exist? Does free will exist? Do minds exist separately from brains? Heidegger wants to back up a bit: Are we sure we know what it means to "exist?" What does it mean "to be?" As a 17-year-old, Heidegger read Franz Brentano's book *On the Manifold Meaning of Being According to Aristotle*, and his life-long project was begun: he wanted to uncover the meaning of "Being" or existence.

He decided to investigate Being in a very particular way—by investigating what it is like to be a *human being*. After all, there are many types of beings—tables, mountains, stars, puppies, and candy corn are all beings or entities that exist—but humans are the only type of being that actually ask questions about Being or existence. This fact about humans is so important that Heidegger identifies humans with the word *Dasein*—that being who frets about the nature of "Being." Or as Heidegger himself puts it in *Being and Time*: "*Dasein* is … distinguished by the fact that, in its Being, that Being is an *issue* for it."

Heidegger insists that exploring what it's like to be human is the best way to explore the meaning of Being in general. He also insists that this must be done from the *inside*. Heidegger doesn't want to treat humans as objects viewed from the outside. Instead, he believes that to understand humans, one has to start by looking from the inside: what is it like to be human? This is what he calls his "existential analytic" of Dasein: analyzing human existence from within the perspective of existence, and it is his main project in his most influential work, *Being and Time*.

Investigating the Meaning of Being through Dasein

Heidegger wrote around 100 volumes on many topics, and his thought is often divided into the "early" and "later" Heidegger. His most famous work, *Being and Time*, is among his early work. Later in life, he explored the meaning of Being through his writings on topics as varied as technology, art, poetry, architecture, and language. *Being and Time* is a notoriously difficult book. This is partly because Heidegger was trying to critique most of Western philosophy before him, and to do so, he had to create a brand new vocabulary. Learning Heidegger is often like learning a new language.

Heidegger's approach is called phenomenology, and it might be illustrated by the example of tools. For Heidegger, if you want to understand tools and they way they exist, you don't do it by examining them scientifically, taking them apart, and abstractly thinking about the tools as objects. Instead, the way to understand a tool is to *use the tool*. Pick it up; don't just stare at it. This, in a much-simplified nutshell, is Heidegger's phenomenological approach: the way to understand what it means "to be" is by exploring experiences in our everyday, non-theoretical, immersed, busy lives. Heidegger is focused primarily on the practical, and only secondarily on the theoretical.

Famously, this is also the reason he doesn't think the distinction we typically make between ourselves as "subjects" and the rest of the world as "objects" is very helpful. When someone plays a video game, there's no experience of oneself as a subject and the controller or the game as an object. When one is in the flow of a game, there's no distinction between one's hand and the controller, nor between ourselves and the world of the game. We are completely immersed in the world. Heidegger thinks this applies not just to tools and video games, but also to the way we exist in our everyday lives; this is why he calls us *Dasein*, which literally means "being-there." Our existence is "being-in-the-world."

Notice the contrast between Heidegger and the skeptical Descartes. Descartes goes into a room by himself and comes up with the famous *cogito ergo sum*: "I think, therefore I exist." Heidegger leaves his room and tries to examine what our experiences of working and living in the world are like before we taint them with fancy words and jargon. His point is not that the fancy words and philosophical jargon aren't important. His point is that those insights *depend* upon and are rooted in our experiences in the world that take place *before* we consciously think about them. This is why Korab-Karpowicz says, "The starting point of philosophy for [Heidegger] is not consciousness, but Dasein in its being."

Heidegger thinks our existence is most fundamentally wrapped up in time, or, as he would call it, "temporality." "Dasein … exists historically and can so exist only because it is temporal in the very basis of its Being." Our sense of time as a sequence of "nows"—or one moment after another—is not our most fundamental sense of time. We're not beings *in* time; Heidegger thinks even that way of putting it separates us from time. Instead, time is part of the most basic way we live. At birth, we find ourselves with a past—without any choice, we're thrown into a specific time period, culture, and family. But as we live our lives, each choice and action is projected toward some future possibility: getting to class, going to lunch, applying for college, etc., and these are "ways to be," as Heidegger puts it. For Heidegger, my most authentic existence comes when I realize and take to heart the understanding that I myself will die: all my possibilities will end.

Jeff Culver, faculty
Daren Jonescu, advisor

> " The greatest question of our time is not communism vs. individualism, not Europe vs. America, not even the East vs. the West; it is whether men can bear to live without God.
>
> —*On the Meaning of Life*

- Was an American writer, historian, and philosopher
- Began to study to become a priest but was excommunicated in response to his lecture "The Origins of Religion"
- Taught school at Ferrer School and later Columbia University
- Was discovered by Max Schuster, cofounder of Simon and Schuster
- Approached history as an amalgamation of art, science, religion, politics, literature, and economics, rather than history as a separate entity
- Produced with his wife *The Story of Civilization*, an 11-volume work that was translated in many languages, written to popularize history
- Shared with his wife the Pulitzer Prize for General Non-Fiction in 1968
- Received the Presidential Medal of Freedom in 1977
- Wrote 21 volumes of a 23-chapter book, *Heroes of History*, that was published 20 years after his death

Key Works

The Story of Philosophy, 1926
The Story of Civilization, 11 vols. (with his wife Ariel Durant), 1935–1975
The Mansions of Philosophy, 1929
A Program for America, 1931
The Tragedy of Russia, 1933
Heroes of History: A brief History of Civilization from Ancient Tribes to the Dawn of the Modern Age, 2001

Biography

William James Durant was born into a large working class family in North Adams, Massachusetts. Neither his father nor mother could read or write, but they educated their children with the help of French Canadian Sisters of Charity. The children attended public school and then a parochial school with St. Cecilia's Church. Influenced by James Mooney, a priest, Durant decided to enter the priesthood. While studying at St. Peter's college, Durant lost his faith and became a socialist. Hoping to continue to become a priest who could help unite socialism to the Catholic Church, in the meantime Durant taught school and became a librarian. Finally he gave up on the priesthood, but he continued to teach and lecture on his convictions. Durant ran up against the Catholic Church with his lecture "The Origins of Religion," and was excommunicated by the Church. Leaving home temporarily, he began teaching at the Ferrer School where he met a new student, Ariel, whom he married. She became a valuable partner in his pursuits. At that time, Durant began graduate studies and teaching at Columbia University. Will Durant and his wife both died in 1981.

A Remarkable Writing Career

Speaking regularly in the city and across the US, Durant got the attention of Max Schuster, cofounder of Simon and Schuster, who encouraged him to rework his lectures into something that could be published. *The Story of Philosophy* was the result, a very successful beginning to a prolific writing career.

While continuing to teach and lecture, Durant wrote volume one of *The Story of Civilization, Our Oriental Heritage.* The next year he wrote the book's introduction, *The Foundations of Civilizations.* The entire work encompasses milestones in art, science, religion, politics, literature, and economics. Working with his wife, Durant wanted to make history accessible to the ordinary reader. Elaborating on the scope of Durant's goals, Bernard A. Weisberger said that the key to the book's popularity was Durant's revealing "patterns and structures, tides and movements in history." In fact, the volumes were so popular that they were translated into many languages, and the Durants worked on the project together for the rest of their lives. To prepare for the writing, Will read more than 500 books, recorded notes, and then organized his notes for formal manuscripts. The couple even traveled to the places they read and wrote about. The last volume was finished when Will was 90 and Ariel was 77. Nothing like the *Story of Civilization* had ever been written before: a reference book in narrative style for ordinary men and women that includes the major events of the entire history of western civilization and details of the lives of common people.

Will Durant's other writing accomplishments include *The Mansions of Philosophy, A Program for America,* and *The Tragedy of Russia.* Together with his wife Durant wrote *The Lessons of History* (conclusions about the changes in humans throughout history,) *Interpretations of Life* (descriptions of noteworthy 20th-century writers) and *A Dual Autobiography (*details of their life together). As a result of their work in *The Age of Louis XIV,* volume 8 of *The Story of Civilization,* they were awarded the Huntington Hartford Foundation Award for Literature. Later the Pulitzer Prize for nonfiction literature in 1968 honored them for Volume 10, *Rousseau and Revolution,* also from *The Story of Civilization.* They received the Medal of Freedom in 1977.

Twenty years after Durant's death, Simon & Schuster published *Heroes of History: A Brief History of Civilization from Ancient Tribes to the Dawn of the Modern Age.* Durant wrote 21 of what he had outlined for a 23-chapter book before his death. The book summarizes part of the material from *The Story of Civilization,* with the addition of philosophers, poets, and statesmen and Biblical figures.

ARNOLD JOSEPH TOYNBEE, 1889–1975, *Philosopher of History*

> " [The Historian] can help his fellow man of different civilizations to become more familiar with one another, and, in consequence, less afraid of one another and less hostile to one another, by helping them to understand and appreciate one another's histories and to see in these local and partial stories a common achievement and common possession of the whole human family. ... And it is one family; it always has been one family in the making.
>
> —*How the Book Took Shape*

- Described himself as a "meta-historian"
- Was considered a representative of speculative philosophy of history
- Served in the Political Intelligence Department of the War Office during WWI
- Was a member of British Delegation to the Paris Peace Conference
- Worked as a professor of Byzantine and modern Greek language, literature, and history at London University from 1912–1915

- Was appointed Director of Studies at the Royal Institute of International Affairs and professor of international history at London University for 30 years
- Directed the Research office of the Foreign Department from 1943 through 1945 when he served on the British delegation to the Paris Peace Conference after WWII
- Believed that the past and the future had a parallel structure where the future was shaped by the past
- Believed that civilizations were doomed to extinction if they did not respond as his analysis determined they should
- Conceptualized ideas for world peace, believing it could originate in China if the United States and the Soviet Union were not able to maintain peace
- Emphasized the religious aspect of civilizations, leading critics today to challenge his interpretation for its reliance on religion's influence in shaping a civilization

Key Works

A Study of History, 1939–1961
A Historian's Approach to Religion, 1956
Change of Habit: the Challenge of Our Time, 1966
Cities on the Move, 1970
Constantine Porphyrogenitus and His World, 1973

Biography

The philosophical historian Arnold Joseph Toynbee was born in London in 1889 to an upper middle class family. He was raised with a proper English education and attended Balliol College, Oxford, from 1912 to 1915, where he learned Greek History and Literature, and was a fellow and tutor. When WWI began, Toynbee enlisted and served in the Political Intelligence Department of the War Office where, among other duties, he edited accounts of atrocities. Toynbee became prominent in the war effort, including being selected as a member of the Middle Eastern section of the British delegation to the Paris Peace Conference. After the war, he became a professor of Byzantine and Modern Greek literature, history, and language at London University through 1924. In 1925, he became Director of Studies in the Royal Institute of International Affairs, and Professor of International History where he remained until his retirement in 1955. Toynbee died in York, England on October 22, 1975, but not before completing his 12 volumes of *A Study of History* and other significant works.

Historical Analysis

Arnold Toynbee distinguished himself among modern historians primarily as a philosopher of history. Mortimer Adler goes so far as to claim Toynbee was the "greatest philosopher of history in the world today." Being a philosopher of history, Toynbee used his expert knowledge of civilizations, their trends, and tendencies to explain their significance to modern civilizations as well as to predict the future. In this, he is unlike many of the earlier historians who focused their analysis of history on the past, merely recording what happened. Toynbee's emphasis of studying history in this way originated from a conversation about the similarities between WWI and the sequence of events in early Greco-Roman history. It is said that after this conversation, "it occurred to him that similar parallels might be discernible elsewhere, that there is as he puts it, 'a species of human society that we label "civilizations"' and that the representatives of this species which have thus far appeared on this planet may exemplify in their various histories a common pattern of development." While Oswald Spengler had adopted this method previously, Toynbee believed the Spengler's analysis was lacking the historical evidence necessary to support his conclusions. For this reason, Toynbee set out to analyze more civilizations and create a clearer framework for why civilizations rise and fall. As a result, Toynbee's *A Study of History* included analysis of 26 civilizations from the last 6,000 years.

He put special emphasis on the philosophy, religion, soteriology, sociology, and teleology of each civilization, probably receiving the most criticism for his assessment of the religious and moral standing of civilizations. Through this analysis Toynbee showed the cyclical progression and decline of each civilization and eventually used his criteria to predict similar outcomes for more modern civilizations, such as he did for the United States and Soviet Union in his text *Change and Habit: The Challenge of Our Time*. Even though he saw the eventual decline of civilizations as the most likely outcome, his analysis did allow for the possibility that civilizations could avoid decline if they responded appropriately in light of the criteria he laid out for the rise and fall of civilizations. The view that civilizations could prevent their eventual decline led to Toynbee's belief that world peace was inevitable.

Toynbee met with much criticism for approaching history as a means of predicting the future of civilizations using the criteria he had established for their rise and fall. In his *A Study of History*, Toynbee claims that the growth of civilizations tends to occur when they "become [their] own environment and [their] own challenger and [their] own field of action." In this statement he is elaborating on a theme that civilizations rise out of challenges, responding to and rising above them. Toynbee also claims that "dynamic movements" in society are created by "creative individuals." These creative individuals or "transfigured personalities" can lead to the downfall of a civilization. Toynbee proclaims that "a failure of the creative power in the minority, an answering withdrawal of mimesis (imitation) on the part of the majority, and a consequent loss of social unity in the society as a whole" are what can eventually lead to the downfall of a civilization. His last explanation for the decline of civilizations is "a loss of self-determination," primarily through the inability of institutions to evolve with the times. Probably his most clear example of this would be how the institution of slavery was not eliminated but only morphed into a different form in the Industrialization period and its labor force. Toynbee believed that all of his criteria point to potential causes for the eventual breakdown of civilizations typically "evidenced by a [breakdown] of social classes which are no longer articulated by an overarching set of cultural ideals." All of this points to Toynbee's unusual metahistorical approach through his emphasis on cause and effect, through rational explanations for the rise and fall of civilizations, and through his debunking of "theories which ascribe civilizational decline to cosmic forces beyond human control."

Toby Coffman, faculty
Nate Kosirog, faculty

> " The mathematicians, the astronomers and the physicists, for example, have been very religious men, with few exceptions. The deeper they penetrated into the mystery of the universe, the deeper was their conviction that the power behind the stars and behind the electrons of atoms was one of law and goodness.
>
> —In an interview with *The New York Times*, 1933

- Studied civil engineering at a Jesuit school and Catholic University of Louvain, Belgium
- Became a priest after serving in the Belgian artillery in WWI
- Was educated in theology, theoretical mathematics, and astrophysics at Harvard and MIT
- Became professor of astrophysics at Catholic University in Louvain for 37 years
- Saw the simplest solution to Einstein's theory of relativity is a universe expanding in all directions
- Wrote his first paper about expanding universe even as Einstein supported the idea of a static universe in 1927
- Accumulated data for support of his expanding universe idea from Edwin Hubble's recent discovery of galaxies moving away
- Theorized that Einstein's theory of relativity could mean a moment of birth for the universe, two billion years ago
- Speculated that a single primordial atom (called "the big bang") disintegrated, sending radioactive energy everywhere

Key Works

A Homogeneous Universe of Constant Mass and Increasing Radiation, Taking Account of the Radial Velocity of Extragalactic Nebulae, 1927
Revue des Questions Scientifiques, 1929

Biography

Monseigneur Georges Henri Joseph Édouard Lemaître, born in Belgium to a deeply religious family, became a brilliant astronomer who was accomplished in astrophysics as well as Catholic theology. He understood both worlds, that of a priest and a scientist, to be completely compatible. Having decided to be a priest as well as a scientist at age 9, Lemaître said, "I was interested in truth from the standpoint of salvation, you see, as well as truth from the standpoint of scientific certainty." Lemaître studied civil engineering at Louvain University until joining an artillery unit in WWI. Later, he earned a PhD even as he was an ordained priest. Cambridge University offered him a fellowship in astrophysics, which led to further study at Harvard and Massachusetts Institute of Technology. Finally returning to Belgium, Lemaître taught at the University of Louvain for many years. Lemaître was honored in his lifetime by the Prix Francqui, Villanova University's Mendel Medal, and an honorary degree from McGill University in Montreal.

The Expanding Universe

Lemaître became interested in Einstein's theory of relativity, which was founded on a series of mathematical calculations. (Einstein later called these faulty and the "biggest blunder" of his career.) Lemaître questioned Einstein's work on gravity, which led him to his understanding of an expanding universe. This theory opposed the current belief, including Einstein's, in a static universe. Lemaître didn't know that Soviet meteorologist Alexander A. Friedmann had also arrived at that same conclusion five years earlier, yet no proof for the idea existed. Then Edwin Powell Hubble showed data demonstrating that the galaxies were moving with great speed away from the Earth, providing foundation to Lemaître's ideas. Einstein finally accepted Lemaître's work as the most reasonable conclusion to his equations of gravity.

Lemaître concluded further that if one looks at expansion, one can also go backward in time, to envision a "cosmic egg" that exploded, dispersing matter in all directions. In other words, if galaxies are moving outward, once they must have been closer and closer until they came together in a single point. He postulated, using Hubble's data, that this "Big Bang" would have been about two billion years ago, exploding an atom about 30 times the size of the sun and very dense. The explosion would have kept going until the universe was a billion light-years wide. Lemaître also speculated that something, perhaps background "noise" should be left over and discernible today. When German astronomer Walter Baade reworked Hubble's calculations, scientists saw the Earth's origin occurring even farther in the past. Today, scientists postulate that the "primeval atom" burst 13.8 billion years ago. In 1965, American astronomers Arno Penzias and Robert Wilson detected leftover noise, which gave more support to Lemaître's theories.

WORLD WAR I, 1914–1918, *THE GREAT WAR*

WWI was the product of a series of accidents and alliances. It could almost be said to have been fought over "Nothing" but happenstance. When Serbian rebel Gavrilo Princip shot Austrian Archduke Franz Ferdinand, a number of diplomatic failures and choking alliances ensured that the entire world was dragged into war. WWI saw a new rise in military technology, with tanks and airplanes, trench warfare, and gas. When the dust settled, it was hard to say who'd won and who'd lost. Vengeance ruled the day at the peace conferences, dooming any peace to be sadly short-lived.

Though WWI began with shots ringing out in Sarajevo in July 1914, the conflict's roots can be traced back to decades of tension between the European powers. The aftermath of the Franco-Prussian war; the revolts in Austria-Hungary, Russia, and the Ottoman Empire; the formation of an alliance between Britain, Russia, and France known as the Triple Entente; Germany's unrest and formation of their own alliance with the Ottomans and Austria-Hungry—all were instrumental in setting the stage for a major diplomatic collapse within Europe. The tipping point came on a summer day in 1914. On June 28, a Serbian nationalist assassinated Archduke Franz Ferdinand, heir of the Austro-Hungarian Empire, in the streets of Sarajevo. As a result, Austria-Hungary declared war on Serbia on July 28 and set in motion the conflict that would soon engulf Europe. Declarations of war cascaded from this point, with Germany declaring war on both Russia and France. After Germany invaded Belgium in its assault on France, England entered the conflict in favor of France, Russia, and Belgium. The Ottoman Empire and Bulgaria sided with Germany and Austria-Hungary. In 1915, Italy joined sides with the Triple Entente, and finally, after much consideration and reflection, the United States joined forces with the Entente in 1917, playing an integral part in ending the war.

World War I ranks as one of the deadliest wars in human history, and its repercussions threw Europe into turmoil. In total, around 65 million troops were deployed; of those, 37 million were injured and 8.5 million died over the course of the four-year war. In the first major conflict of the war in September 1914, the horrific battle of the Marne, three days of fighting between two million soldiers resulted in more than 500,000 dead and wounded. The armies used trenches to create battle lines, leaving soldiers to live in holes in the ground alongside rats and diseases that plagued all armies. New advancements in military technology allowed for gas attacks, bombings from overhead planes, precise artillery strikes, and the efficient use of machine guns. Because of the nature of the battle lines, an open field was all that lay between the two opposing forces. Soldiers trying to overtake the enemy trench repeatedly rushed across this "no man's land." This field was covered by mines, barbed wire, and deep holes made by artillery. While the men tried to avoid these obstacles, they were also under fire from riflemen, machine guns, snipers, and gas attacks. All these factors combined to make WWI one of the deadliest.

The Treaty of Versailles ended the conflict and was signed by all participants on June 28, 1919. The treaty led to German occupation by the French, British, and Americans. Germany lost its right to an army and was not allowed to join the League of Nations that was also created by the treaty. A few years later, a Germany broken by the reparations payments demanded by the Treaty of Versailles elected Adolph Hitler to power. Hitler blithely ignored the treaty of Versailles and set Germany's feet on the path to WWII.

Caroline Fuschino, 2015
Julianna Swayze, 2016
Alexi Wenger, 2016

THE RUSSIAN REVOLUTION, 1917

In the midst of the cries of WWI, the Russians at last had their own long-awaited revolution. With the secret support of Germany (who wished for Russia to withdraw from the war), Vladimir Lenin would return to his homeland from exile in order to overthrow the Czar and usher in the era of Communism. Russia became the Soviet Union, and would rise in time to become the other great superpower to challenge the United States in the post-war period.

ALDOUS HUXLEY ◊ 1894–1963, *The Pleasure Dystopian*

> But I don't want comfort. I want God, I want poetry, I want real danger, I want freedom, I want goodness. I want sin.
>
> —*Brave New World*

- Is most famous for his dystopian novel, *Brave New World*, which imagines a future not where people are prisoners of the state (*1984*) but prisoners of pleasure
- Both sides of his family included famous figures, most notably his paternal grandfather, T.H. Huxley, also known as "Darwin's bulldog"
- Suffered from a crippling eye disease that left him with barely any sight
- Taught George Orwell while a French professor at Eton
- Moved to America and worked as screenwriter, writing early film versions of *Pride and Prejudice* and *Jane Eyre*
- Adopted the use of psychedelic drugs later in life, writing about his experiences, and had his wife administer LSD on his deathbed

Key Works

Brave New World, 1931
The Doors of Perception, 1954

Biography

Aldous Leonard Huxley was born in Surrey, England in 1894. Amply displaying the sometimes cloistered nature of the British islands, Huxley descends on his father's side from T.H. Huxley, coiner of the term "agnostic" and popularly known as "Darwin's bulldog," and on his mother's side from the scholar and poet Matthew Arnold. Huxley's early life was marked by the tragic deaths of his mother when he was 14 and his brother, by suicide, two years later. He also contracted a rare eye disease when he was young that blinded him for a period of 2–3 years and left his sight irreparably damaged for the remainder of his life. After graduating from Oxford, Huxley taught French for a brief and inauspicious time at Eton College, where George Orwell numbered among his students. Huxley then took up writing in earnest, publishing a series of well-reviewed but modestly successful novels before publishing *Brave New World* in 1932. The novel established Huxley as a dystopian writer and he would take up the theme in later, and less successful novels. Huxley moved with his wife and son to Hollywood in the late 1930s where he was exposed to and developed an affinity for Eastern religious traditions. Huxley also worked as a screenwriter during this time. Towards the end of his life, he experimented with psychedelic drugs, including LSD, and wrote about his experiences in *The Doors of Perception*. Huxley died of laryngeal cancer while being administered LSD as a sedative on November 22, 1963. Huxley's death was overshadowed by the assassination of John F. Kennedy in Dallas that same day. The English fabulist and scholar, C.S. Lewis, also died on that day. Huxley's legacy continues on in his best known work, *Brave New World*, which ranks with his student George Orwell's own dystopian novel, *1984*, as a master of the genre and a warning of the world that could be.

The Dystopia of Happiness—*Brave New World* and Dystopia

Huxley's dystopian vision of the future is not one where all conduct is aggressively policed by an omnipresent martial force, a good percentage of the population is malnourished, a dictator rules autocratically from an impenetrable lair, or any of the other popular fantasies. Huxley's dystopian vision is marked by a World State that promotes casual sexual relationships, non-taxing work, unlimited entertainment, and, if you ever need a break, a *soma* holiday that helps you forget you were ever distressed (*soma* is the drug without a comedown that everyone in this vision of the world takes at least daily—"one cubic centimeter kills ten gloomy sentiments"). The governing principle of this new world order is happiness. One of the main characters, Mustafa Mond, is the Director for Western Europe, one of ten such directors in the world. Though revealed to be quite knowledgeable about the old world, Mond believes that art, science, beauty, and love all ultimately stand in the way of happiness. Therefore, the tendency toward each has been destroyed in the elaborate social conditioning process of the state. People within the World State are conditioned to desire endless consumption and to fear solitude and thought that falls outside of the tightly structured, nightly, "hypnopedic" conditioning they have received since infancy. The product, Mond admits in the book's denouement, is a hollowed-out happiness but one that keeps the populace placated and manageable.

Community, Identity, Stability—The Tenets of the World State

Happiness is contingent on the three tenets of the World State being fulfilled: community, identity, stability. Anything that threatens those pillars threatens the health of the World State. Individualism is verboten. Identity outside of the community is heresy. Stability must be maintained at the price of all individualism, thought, and desire for anything apart from pleasure. As such, the social order is highly controlled and stability seems to be the chief goal of the World State. In the Central London Hatchery and Conditioning Centre, where newborns are methodically created in a laboratory and shepherded through their prenatal term by thoughtless technicians, each child is placed within a social class from the moment of the sperm fertilizing the egg. Epsilons and Gammas, the lower orders, are denied oxygen at specific intervals, stunting their growth and intelligence and making them desirous of the life of service they are destined to live. Once the children are born, they are conditioned to enjoy their place in the caste system and never rebel against their destiny (decided by technicians called Predestinators).

The Doors of Perception—Huxley and Psychedelic Drugs

One of the central ironies of Huxley's thought life, noted by Christopher Hitchens in his introduction of *Brave New World*, is that Huxley was deeply inconsistent when it came to living out what his writerly convictions. Though *soma* is straightforwardly an obstacle to humane living in *Brave New World*, by the end of his life Huxley was an avid experimenter in psychedelic drugs, including peyote and LSD. His 1954 philosophical treatise, *The Doors of Perception*, chronicled his experience with peyote (mescaline). In the work, Huxley claimed that his use of the drug allowed him to participate in "common being" with other creatures. The book was highly controversial but was influential in the development of the Beat movement, which transmogrified into the Hippie movement of the late 1960s. Jim Morrison, lead singer of *The Doors*, named his band as a tribute to Huxley's philosophical exploration. Morrison died at the age of 27, addicted to alcohol, amongst other substances.

Legacy

The major questions raised by Huxley's work are as important and disputed today as they were when the book was first published. Questions of drug legalization, elderly care, physician-assisted suicide, casual sex, class divisions are still present. Huxley's enduring contribution might best be summed up in the contrast that Neal Postman, the NYU professor and intellectual gadfly, drew between Huxley's vision and Orwell's contrasting warning: "In short, Orwell feared that what we hate will ruin us. Huxley feared that what we love will ruin us." This is the fear that is alive and well today: that the very things we think will make us comfortable and happy might, in the end, destroy our humanity.

F. SCOTT FITZGERALD ◊ 1896–1940, *The Poet Laureate of the Jazz Age*

❝ I was within and without. Simultaneously enchanted and repelled by the inexhaustible variety of life.

—*The Great Gatsby*

• Is often called the voice of the "lost generation" who came of age during WWI

- Was romanticized by the American press as a man of Roaring Twenties glamour
- Became a heavy partier and battled alcoholism later in life, which hindered his ability to produce decent literature
- Moved to Hollywood to write movie scripts
- Explored the darker side of affluent society in his works, despite his glitzy 1920s public life
- Published short stories in magazines to test the waters for themes and plot lines he would later use in major novels
- Questioned the American Dream, a term that was popular during his lifetime
- Contrasted idealism with realism by juxtaposing unrealistic, rose-colored ideas with bleaker, albeit more realistic turnouts (i.e., love at first site versus blind infatuation)

Key Works

This Side of Paradise, 1920
The Great Gatsby, 1925

Biography

Born in 1896 in St. Paul, Minnesota, Fitzgerald discovered his writing skills fairly early in life when he began contributing to his college newspaper, *The Princeton Tiger*. Despite his success in journalistic and dramatic life, academic struggles prompted Fitzgerald to drop out of college and join the army in 1917. While stationed in Montgomery, Alabama, he met Zelda Sayre, a beautiful and wealthy Southern debutante, whom he married after the success of his first novel, *This Side of Paradise*, in 1920.

The Fitzgeralds were both blessed and cursed with an overwhelming amount of publicity. The couple was seen as the embodiment of 1920s glamour, and Fitzgerald, his novels his mouthpiece, was seen as the voice of the generation. In order to support his extravagant lifestyle, Fitzgerald began writing short stories for an array of magazines. The couple had their only child in 1921, and after the success of his second novel, *The Beautiful and the Damned*, the family moved to Long Island, which would serve as the backdrop for his most successful novel, *The Great Gatsby*.

By the mid 1920s, Francis and Zelda Fitzgerald's fame shifted to infamy as they were documented traveling between America and Europe as notorious partiers. Their relationship grew shaky; Zelda was institutionalized sporadically for the rest of her life, and the now-alcoholic Scott struggled to produce any literature of merit. His final completed novel, *Tender Is the Night*, was a modest success, seen today as little more than a relic of the Jazz Age. He moved to Hollywood to become a freelance scriptwriter, where he met Sheilah Graham, with whom he would carry on an affair for the rest of his life. He died of a heart attack on December 21, 1940. His final novel, the half finished *The Love of the Last Tycoon*, was published posthumously. Several of his published works saw new life in the 1950s and beyond as successful movies, which served to revive his popularity after his death.

The Great Gatsby and the American Dream

The 1920s was a time of renewed optimism in the wake of WWI, and the pursuit of the American Dream captivated the country. Perhaps nowhere in literature is the American Dream so firmly rebuked as in *The Great Gatsby*. The nature of the American Dream appears innocent: a hard-working and honest man can achieve his goals and attain prosperity. However, while Nick Carraway, the book's narrator, and Jay Gatsby, the book's protagonist, move from the Midwest to pursue this dream, neither truly find it.

Though he renounces his old life and even his name to recreate himself as Jay Gatsby, Gatsby is nothing more than a criminal profiting from illegal alcohol trade. Consumed with his invented picture of himself, Gatsby loses touch with reality and falls victim to the flawed optimism of his age. In his reckless pursuit of the married Daisy Buchanan, Gatsby becomes more attached to this idea than he is tethered to any sense of reality. The book argues that the rich stay rich (and are protected by their wealth) while the poor who try to get rich never quite succeed (and most often die). Nick fails in the bond trade; Gatsby is exposed and wrongfully murdered; and Myrtle Wilson, the ambitious wife of a gas station owner, is run over by a symbol of the wealth she so desires, Gatsby's lavishly extravagant car. Nick Carraway's belief in the dream dies with Gatsby. While he may have had reason to believe in the American Dream and the power of money before, the downfall of his friend proves that money cannot fix everything and that the innocent dream so many hold dear is flawed and corrupt.

However, with his full command of both language and the American psyche, Fitzgerald ends the book on this haunting note: "Gatsby believed in the green light, the orgastic future, that year by year recedes before us. It eluded us then, but that's no matter—to-morrow we will run faster, stretch out our arms farther. … And one fine morning—So we beat on, boats against the current, borne back ceaselessly into the past." Though in many ways serving as a warning about the perils of the American Dream, the novel acknowledges in the end that the belief is so deeply ingrained in who we are that no amount of warning will cause us to call off our pursuit.

Old Money versus New Money

Another enduring theme of the novel is the contrast between people of old money, those who may not know from where their wealth comes, and those of new money, the newly rich whose numbers were greatly swelling in the 1920s. To symbolize the contrast, they are even put into two different towns in *The Great Gatsby*: the old money lives in East Egg and the new in West Egg (the geographical symbolism here is noteworthy, as Fitzgerald is contrasting the "old" east and the "new" west). Many of the conflicts of the novel come down to the encounter between these two different ways of being wealthy.

Though similarly morally bankrupt, Daisy (who comes from old money) reflexively judges the immorality of the new money crowd at one of Gatsby's famous parties. Tom Buchanan, Daisy's husband and noted womanizer, laments at the party, "By God, I may be old-fashioned in my ideas, but women run around too much these days to suit me." Daisy is likewise appalled by the crowd. In the end, old money is clearly victorious over the new. As mentioned, all of the strivers for wealth and old money status are either dead or returning to the Midwest licking their wounds. Nick sums up the luxuries afforded Tom and Daisy by their wealth in perhaps the second most haunting passage of the novel: "They were careless people, Tom and Daisy—they smashed up things and creatures and then retreated back into their money or their vast carelessness, or whatever it was that kept them together, and let other people clean up the mess they had made." Unprotected by wealth to the degree of the Buchanans, every other character in the novel is "smashed up." Old money wins.

Natalie Hathcote, 2017
Trisha Rouleau, 2015

> " "Some people say they can't understand your writing, even after they've read it two or three times. What approach would you suggest for them?"
> Faulkner replied, "Read it four times."
>
> —*The Paris Review*

- Never graduated high school; instead he opted to read books at home
- Was heavily involved in the Southern Renaissance, a rejuvenation of Southern literature
- Invented his own county, Yoknapatawpha, and set much of the action of his books there
- Won the Nobel Prize for Literature in 1949 and the Pulitzer Prize for fiction in 1955 and 1963
- Helped popularize, along with Virginia Woolf, the "stream-of-consciousness" style of writing
- Created layered and confusing stories that frequently required multiple readings
- Wrote stories that focused heavily on the thoughts of characters, making them seem human

Key Works

The Sound and the Fury, 1929
As I Lay Dying, 1930
Sanctuary, 1931
Light in August, 1932
Absalom, Absalom! 1936
Go Down, Moses, 1942

Biography

Raised in a family with a past rooted in American history, William Falkner (later stylized to Faulkner) was born in New Albany, Mississippi in 1897. Along with a family friend, he created an individualized educational plan. After a slow start to his literary career, Faulkner first met fame with *The Sound and the Fury*. Following this, he published a "stream-of-consciousness" series of novels as well as the dark comedy, *As I Lay Dying*. Prior to writing *Dying*, he had written another work, *Sanctuary*—a serious work that, while it may have been motivated by purely financial needs, was nonetheless another success. He later published collections of short stories and of poems. In 1932, he published *Light in August*, a complex and moving piece of literature, centering on the search for personal identity and personal destiny.

With a semblance of wealth provided by his publications, Faulkner took up flying and bought a plane. He then wrote another novel, *Pylon*, about racing pilots. He gave his plane to his younger brother, Dean, and prompted him to begin a career in flight. But to Faulkner's great anguish, Dean died in a plane crash. The emotional impact this had on Faulkner was immense, and his next publication, *Absalom, Absalom!*, was one of his most passionate books. In 1950 he was awarded the Nobel Prize in Literature, an award that brought him unsought fame. His writing is oftentimes considered to have declined following his Nobel Prize, though he was awarded two Pulitzer Prizes in the twilight of his life. He began to focus more on his personal life, and died of heart attack at 64 in 1962.

Stream of Consciousness

William Faulkner was one of the great American writers, a fact evidenced by his works. He had a unique way of capturing the human element, writing the thoughts and actions of his characters in "stream-of-consciousness" style. This mode of writing focuses on transcribing the thoughts of the characters onto the pages of the book, oftentimes giving readers a glimpse into the most raw form of consciousness, not the filtered and wisely selected words that frequently compose dialogue, the most common method through which the inner workings of the main players are seen. Through this, true candor can be provided, and true honesty gained. An example from *As I Lay Dying* shows how stream of consciousness works: "I have done no wrong to be cussed by. I am not religious, I reckon. But peace is my heart: I know it is. I have done things but neither better nor worse than them that pretend otherlike, and I know that Old Marster will care for me as for ere a sparrow that falls." Here the raw, unfiltered thoughts of the character can be seen, flowing organically in the manner of human thought. Faulkner's writing provides some of the most elegant examples of this style.

Yoknapatawpha County

Yoknapatawpha County, a mash-up of Chickasaw words, is a fictional county invented by Faulkner. Though he did little research to establish his literary world, it is based heavily upon Lafayette County, Mississippi, where Faulkner lived and worked for most of his career. He took aspects of it from personal experiences and family stories that had been passed down to him. Rather than considering it a fictionalized version of his home, he considered it to be an independent fictional entity, with geography, residents, and history all its own. He used Yoknapatawpha County as a setting for several of his novels and short stories, from the 1929 novel *The Sound and the Fury*, to his final published work, *The Reivers*, in 1962. Four of his most influential works, *The Sound and the Fury*, *As I Lay Dying*, *Light in August*, and *Absalom, Absalom!* are set in this county.

The Southern Renaissance

Late 19th- and early 20th-century Southern authors generally focused on the Civil War, heavily idealizing the "lost paradise" of the antebellum South and detailing the heroism of the Confederate cause. In many ways this is understandable; defeat in the Civil War left many aspects of Southern culture in shambles. Many of these authors remembered the war vividly and therefore obsessed over it and reflected upon it with bias.

In the 1920s, however, a new generation of authors began to take over. These authors had been born well after the Civil War, and so were able to avoid the biases that came with the misguided nostalgia of those before. These authors wrote about the concept of Southern identity in a deeper way, thinking more objectively. During this period, which took place primarily in the 1920s and 1930s, New Orleans emerged as a hub for these various writers, paralleling Florence in the Italian renaissance, if to a much lesser degree. This melting pot of different authors gave new direction to the stylings of many, at the time fledgling, writers who are prominently recognized and acclaimed today. Faulkner visited New Orleans for six months during the outset of his writing career, and there began his first foray into fiction. These two times proved quite influential for Faulkner. He later went on to write *Mosquitoes*, his own satirical take on aspects of the New Orleans creative environment. Faulkner would come to be seen as the leader of this renaissance, often on the forefront of innovation and creative styles.

Natalie Hathcote, 2017

BERTOLT BRECHT ◊ 1898–1956, *Playwright for Politics*

> " For art to be "unpolitical" means only to ally itself with the "ruling" group.
> —*A Short Organum for the Theater*

- Exhibited a harsh Marxist agenda in his plays
- Plagiarized unapologetically in his works, claiming it enhanced the play's satirical effects
- Let the women he had affairs write parts of his plays
- Used an "alienation" technique in performances of his plays so the audience would take away his message rather than a vague feeling of being entertained
- Had his works banned in Germany during WWII
- Won the Stalin Peace Prize in Moscow in 1955
- Invented "epic theater," which is still a style used today

Key Works

The Threepenny Opera, 1938
Mother Courage, 1941
The Caucasian Chalk Circle, 1944

Biography

Born in Germany in 1898, Bertolt Brecht showed a precocious nature for theater, writing his first play at age 16. Though a German citizen, Brecht avoided the first World War by studying medicine and philosophy in Munich. After moving to Berlin to work for the Deutsches Theater, he gained popularity as well as criticism for his experimental "Marxist theater" as well as his "alienation" technique. Brecht believed that his plays were not only meant to be entertaining but to awaken his audience to the darkness that lurks in this world and, through that, to inspire social change. His most famous and most widely produced play was "Die Dreigroschenoper" (The Threepenny Opera), which satirized John Gay's already 200-year-old play, a "Beggar's Opera." However popular his plays, his Marxist agenda made him a target for the rising Nazi party; when they took power in 1933, Brecht and his family were forced to flee—first to Scandinavia until 1941, and then to California until 1948. All of his writings were banned in Germany and his citizenship was revoked. He continued to write for the stage while in the United States, but his political opinions were no more welcome in the United States than Germany. After being interrogated by the House Unamerican Activities Commission under suspicion of being a communist, Brecht moved back to Berlin. He was awarded the Stalin Peace Prize in Moscow in 1955, and died the next year.

Epic Theater

Brecht created a new kind of drama, exemplified in his plays and cemented with his theater group— The Berliner Ensemble. This style is still practiced and referred to as "epic theater," which centers around the idea of the audience's alienation. Brecht saw how drama attempted to draw the audience into the story so that they felt transported into a new world. However, this Aristotelian way of producing a play contradicted what he was trying to do in theater. He believed audiences tended to get too attached to characters, which clouded their vision and warped their ability to critically analyze the situation without bias, encouraging them to "hang up their brains with their hats in the cloakroom." Therefore, Brecht wanted to do everything he could to keep his audience acutely aware of where they were—in a theater watching normal people act out characters. To purposely distance them from the story, Brecht had actors break character on stage, talk in third person, and read stage directions out loud; he kept stage lights visible and stage sets basic; he kept curtains up for set changes and used music to disrupt the reality of a scene. This "alienation effect" allowed the production to be more thoughtful and less emotional, advancing the purpose of every show to promote action and social change.

Irony, Wit, and Plagiarism

Though his plays could hardly be called comedy, Brecht used humor to get across his message. Audiences are meant to laugh at the characters and cry at their laughing; however, "His biting satires, grotesque parodies, and sharp irony may be aimed at eliciting laughter, but the emotional registers of shock, astonishment, and embarrassment are more likely to accompany the mockery, sarcasm, and ridicule one finds in his stage plays." Brecht used satire to point out the publically accepted evils of his time in hopes of raising attention and igniting social change. He also employed irony to call attention to problems and contradictions in society.

Brecht poked fun at other writers, other works, other styles, reality norms, historical stories, and stereotypes in order to allow a clear message to shine through. His use of parody bordered on plagiarism, partially due to his anti-individualist take on art, and partially because he wanted to make connections between serious works to point out their faults. *The Threepenny Opera* rips off John Gay's *Beggar's Opera*, and Brecht's *Round Heads and Pointed Heads,* retells Shakespeare's *Measure for Measure.* He saw this reworking of other plays as perfectly acceptable, radical revision. Later, he moved towards farce as a weapon against political enemies during his exile from Germany.

Competitive Nature of Capitalism

Keeping with his Marxist beliefs as well as his political activist theatre style, Brecht used his plays to accusingly point out the competitive nature of capitalism. He thought it dangerous for allowing money to take center stage. Brecht's anti-capitalist bias can be seen in all of his works. This is especially evident in *The Rise and Fall of the City of Mahagonny* which takes place in the United States where capitalism is cutthroat. The city is like a net cast out to snare edible birds. But by the end of the opera, the city itself is destroyed. *The Threepenny Opera* is another take on the topic, where theft is justified in a capitalist society. Brecht explored contradicting definitions of justice in *The Threepenny Opera,* wherein a common thief, who the audience is purposely set up to disapprove of, is saved and goes on to rob more. The play essentially asks "Why not?," satirizing a capitalist society where only those who can't make money are condemned. Brecht emphasized the way money skews our moral sense and makes every man fend for himself: "Though the rich of this earth find no difficulty in creating misery, they can't bear to see it." While Brecht's endings are purposely meant to spark discussion, they are pointed towards inspiring anti-capitalist and pro-Marxist social change.

Toby Coffman, faculty
Trisha Rouleau, 2015

JOHN R.R. TOLKIEN ◊ 1892–1973, *The Lord of the Rings*

> " It's a dangerous business, Frodo, going out your door. You step onto the road, and if you don't keep your feet, there's no knowing where you might be swept off to.
>
> —*The Lord of the Rings*

- Loved the English countryside, the inspiration for the setting Middle Earth
- Was a linguist and Oxford scholar who was fascinated by languages, even inventing his own
- Became concerned about technological "progress," due to experiencing industrialization in Birmingham
- Was deeply religious with a faith in God's providence
- Befriended C.S. Lewis and was part of the Inklings, a literary discussion group
- Lived through two wars and experienced the loss of many friends
- Received the honor of having his magnum opus, *The Lord of the Rings*, voted the greatest book of the 20th century in a British poll
- Feared for humanity's potential to destroy the earth and our misuse of power
- Was made Commander of the Order of the British Empire by Queen Elizabeth II
- Is generally considered the father of modern fantasy literature

Key Works

Oxford English Dictionary (part of the staff in 1919 and 1920)
"Beowulf: The Monsters and the Critics," 1936
The Hobbit, 1937
On Fairy Stories, 1947
The Fellowship of the Ring, v.1 The Lord of the Rings, 1954
The Two Towers, v.2 The Lord of the Rings, 1955
The Return of the King, v.3 The Lord of the Rings, 1955
The Silmarillion, 1977

Biography

John Ronal Reuel Tolkien was born in South Africa but spent most of his life in England after his father's early death. In a country village near Birmingham, his mother Mabel began educating her sons in languages, botany, and drawing. Tolkien accepted wholeheartedly his mother's conversion to Catholicism, and his time in the village nurtured a love of the English countryside and a love of the Lord. When he was just 11, his mother died, forcing the children to move to Birmingham, a dirty, industrial city. Here he met his future wife, Edith Mary Bratt.

Studying for an Oxford scholarship, Tolkien because fascinated with languages, teaching himself Old English and an extinct German language, Gothic. At Oxford he pursued philology, the study of the development of languages. In 1916 he was at last able to marry Edith, and shortly thereafter had to join the British Army as WWI began. He had four children in the next 12 years, but was deeply hurt by what he had seen in combat and the deaths of many of his friends. Not until after the war was he moved to write again, and so taught at Oxford and began working on the *Oxford English Dictionary*.

Along with his scholarly writing, Tolkien created the history of Middle Earth where his invented languages live. Writing for his children, he produced *The Hobbit*, which was the spark for his next the three volumes, which became *The Lord of the Rings*. Again, war provided the background for Tolkien's

560 · Chapter 7

thinking, and although he said his trilogy was not an allegory about WWII, he was clearly fearful of encroaching technology and its power to destroy. Consequently some literary critics spurned his work, but the world liked it, and the book became a best seller. Tolkien renewed his creative efforts with *The Silmarillion*, developing the prehistory of Middle Earth, which wasn't published until after his death by his son Christopher. He also wrote several critical pieces, which bring together his scholarship, creativity, and ethical opinions.

Tolkien's Themes

1. Absolute Power Corrupts Absolutely—The ring represents man's desire to dominate. Expressed as an addiction, it damages him and sets him apart from his best self and others.
2. Providence—while Tolkien doesn't mention God, Providence covers the story and works as a force for averting evil. Providence provides good conclusions, yet it doesn't produce "happily ever after endings."
3. Mercy and Pity—Mercy is given again and again as characters understand and sympathize with one another.
4. Death and Deathlessness—Tolkien said that Lord of the Rings is about death and deathlessness. He contrasts the immortal elves with mortal men. The Middle Earth characters refer to death as a "gift" which leads to joining one's creator. The elves don't have this opportunity.
5. Moral Absolutes—Tolkien presents moral absolutes, but he presents man's imperfections and his intellectual limitations.

Tolkien's Legacy

No other fantasy writer has had such a strong influence as Tolkien, whose writing created unparalleled archetypes. He developed themes that appear in modern fantasy, as well as mythological races such as dwarves, goblins, orcs, and hobbits. In addition, the source of the kindly wizard and a band of heroes on a quest to save the world, which is a staple of contemporary fantasy novels and films, comes from Tolkien's high fantasy. The heroes use their brains and their strength to combat evil in a world where moral certainty is strong. His legacy lives on, as the dozen volumes about the history of Middle Earth continue to be best sellers.

C.S. LEWIS ◊ 1898–1963, *Enchanting Writer and Apologist*

" I have found a desire within myself that no experience in this world can satisfy; the most probable explanation is that I was made for another world.

—*Mere Christianity*

- Was a British professor, critic, novelist, poet, essayist, and Christian apologist
- Spent most of his career working at Oxford in English/Medieval and Renaissance English
- Converted to theism and then to Christianity
- Created fiction that often contained deep religious themes
- Valued science and scientific reason as just one kind of reasoning and actually criticized Scientism, the deification of science that glorifies a naturalistic worldview without God
- Held that biological evolution is compatible with Christian creation accounts

- Married Helen Joy Davidman, who was dying of cancer.
- Wrote nonfiction with a gift for logic, metaphor, and analogy
- Insisted on reason and experience as faith's foundation
- Has inspired generations of Christians

Key Works

The Pilgrim's Regress: An Allegorical Apology for Christianity, Reason and Romanticism, 1933
Screwtape Letters, 1942
Mere Christianity, 1952
The Great Divorce, 1945
Miracles, 1947
"An Obstinacy in Belief" (originally "Faith and Evidence"), 1953
Till We Have Faces, 1956
A Grief Observed, 1961
Letters to Malcolm, 1964
The Space Trilogy:
    Out of the Silent Planet, 1938
    Perelandra, 1943
    That Hideeous Strength: A Modern Fairy-Tale for Grownups, 1945
The Chronicles of Narnia:
    The Lion, the Witch, and the Wardrobe: A Story for Children, 1950
    Prince Caspian, The Return to Narnia, 1950
    The Voyage of the Dawn Treader, 1952
    The Silver Chair, 1953
    The Horse and His Boy, 1954
    The Magician's Nephew, 1955
    The Last Battle, 1956

Biography

Clive Staples Lewis, born in 1888 in Belfast, Ireland, experienced a difficult childhood. His mother died of cancer when he was 9, taking with her Lewis's sense of security. His father, equally devastated, sent him to an English boarding school. Shortly after Lewis began at Oxford, he was called into service to join WWI. Wounded at the Battle of Arras, he spent some time at the hospital before returning. Then Lewis attended Oxford where he was influenced by the poet William Butler Yeats and hoped to create a similar career as a poet himself. Lewis studied the classics and English literature with a concentration on medieval and Renaissance writers. He wasn't successful, though, at his attempt to publish his first poetry collection, *Spirits in Bondage: A Cycle of Lyrics*. He found that he was very good at teaching English, which directed him to a 30-year career as a Fellow of Magdalen College, Oxford. During his tenure at Oxford, Lewis developed a friendship with another medieval scholar, J.R.R. Tolkien, in weekly meetings of the literary group calling themselves the "Inklings." Later, the department of Medieval and Renaissance Literature was created especially for him at Cambridge, where he served until 1963. Lewis was respected and popular, well known for his literary scholarship. In Cambridge, Lewis married Helen Joy Davidman Gresham, an American writer who had been influenced by reading his books and converted to Christianity. After a long correspondence with Lewis, she moved to England. Their friendship grew and they married when he was 60. Soon after, Joy was diagnosed with cancer; mercifully, a brief remission allowed them three happy years together. Lewis, upon her death, wrote *A Grief Observed*, a personal account of his feelings. He resigned from Cambridge shortly before his own death in 1963.

Lewis and God

Lewis wrote of how he met God one night in his room at Magdalen College. Each night as he studied, he felt God approach him, and although he didn't want to meet him, he finally gave in to God's call, knelt, and prayed. His initial reluctance was changed and his faith strengthened through conversations with the Inklings; as a result, he eventually joined the Anglican Church. Lewis lived out his faith by continually contemplating and writing about his thoughts of God. He wrote books, lectures, and radio broadcasts that reached the general public who could relate to his conversational style, comparisons, and logic. He gave the public a moral and intellectual leader by sharing his faith in writing and speaking.

Lewis and Science

Lewis saw himself as a rationalist with scientific impulses. He appreciated that science could be used to benefit mankind, yet he was aware of the its limitations. He felt strongly that truth, value, meaning, and ideals were essential, although not part of pure science. Lewis criticized Scientism, which he assessed to be a popularizing and deifying of science. Scientism was any circumstances in experimentation when a naturalistic worldview overcomes any possible notion of a non-quantifiable reality such as God.

In Lewis's thinking, the Genesis account of creation was a folk tale. He thought evil itself had been around even before Adam. He also maintained a theistic view of evolution. All of these beliefs stemmed from Lewis's reasoning that science is ever changing in a world of changing opinion. He insisted that biological evolution is compatible with Christian stories of creation, and was always trying to place science where it properly belonged to encourage recognition that God is behind everything and is the power of the universe, not just a scientific calculation. Lewis wrote a trilogy of space novels after reading Olaf Stapledon's *Last and First Men* and Cambridge Biochemist J.S.S. Haldane's essay "Man's Destiny." Both of these writings show interplanetary travel in a world without God. Lewis criticized Stapledon's creation because science is shown to be the greatest good. He thought Stapledon's *Star Maker* portrayed a people who value only power through technology without ethics.

Through the Wardrobe Door

As Lewis reflected on what to teach through his writing, he decided to write children's fantasy, which he believed could reveal in a unique way the things he knew to be true. He imagined fascinating animals, mythical creatures, and representatives of evil to tell his stories. One of his remarkable creations, Aslan, is a Christ-like figure who Lewis describes this way: "Let us suppose that there were a land like Narnia and that the son of God, as He became a Man in our world, became a Lion there, and then imagine what would happen." His first fantasy, *The Lion, the Witch, and the Wardrobe*, tells of the land of Narnia and the Pevensies. One of the children finds a wardrobe that opens to an enchanted forest. One reviewer said that as the children free Narnia, "Lewis gives life to the deepest principles of his Christian faith." The story shows us an evil world peopled with weak men who can achieve great heights through the love of the Redeemer. The saga is one of the most cherished writings in all of children's literature. Lewis is admired for his amazing fantasy, the incorporations of techniques he had learned from methods of other writers, and his wisdom in the telling. Reading the last page of the seven books of the saga, M.S. Crouch remarks, "With deep satisfaction mingled with regret … It has been a memorable experience and a privilege to visit the great magical world of Narnia."

Lewis produced outstanding literary criticism as well, especially *English Literature in the Sixteenth Century, Excluding Drama*. He wrote a last novel in 1956, *Till We Have Faces: A Myth Retold*. Within the new Cupid and Psyche tale, Lewis explores all his important themes: "the problem of evil, the relation of the natural to the supernatural, the efficacy of prayer, the nature of sacrifice, the place of poetry in the life of the mind, the foreshadowing of Christian revelation in pagan religion." Similar to the conclusions Lewis reaches in his later works, he acknowledges that life is a preparation for seeing God.

Lewis's legacy still gives ordinary people knowledge of Christianity and strong reasons for faith. His example, too, delineates for us "the feel, the quality, of a life truly lived before God."

ERNEST HEMINGWAY ◊ 1899–1961, *Papa*

> " The world breaks everyone and afterward many are strong in the broken places. But those that will not break it kills. It kills the very good and the very gentle and the very brave impartially. If you are none of these you can be sure it will kill you too but there will be no special hurry.
>
> —*A Farewell to Arms*

- Popularized the use of terse prose, especially in short stories
- Won the Pulitzer Prize and Nobel Prize for Literature in 1952 for *The Old Man and the Sea*
- Spoke Italian, French, English, and Spanish due to his work as a journalist in Europe
- Survived two plane crashes, though he was mistakenly reported dead after the first
- Received an award for bravery from the Italian government during WWI after carrying an injured soldier on his back to a medical center while badly injured himself
- Was good friends with F. Scott Fitzgerald and other literary Americans of the "lost generation"
- Experimented as an amateur boxer and bullfighter and popularized the running of the bulls in Pamplona in *The Sun Also Rises*, which was banned in Boston due to profane language

Key Works

The Sun Also Rises, 1926
A Farewell to Arms, 1929
For Whom the Bell Tolls, 1940
The Old Man and the Sea, 1952

Biography

As a child in Illinois, Ernest Hemingway learned a love for adventure and the outdoors from his father. Though he pursued his love of writing and journalism from his youth, working on his high school newspaper and then for the *Kansas City Star*, his budding career was interrupted by WWI. He was an ambulance driver for the Italian Army and won the Italian Silver Medal for Bravery before being wounded. In the hospital he met a nurse who accepted his proposal of marriage but then left him. Only 20, he returned from war, found another newspaper job, and married his first wife. They moved to Paris, where Hemingway worked as a foreign correspondent. In 1925, he published his first major work, *The Sun Also Rises*, which drew on his experiences in Europe as a part of "the lost generation" of artists and intellectuals unmoored by the events of the Great War.

Hemingway's fictional characters famously embody many of his own traits, including his love of drinking, boxing, hunting, womanizing, and bullfighting, as well as his obsession with violence and strength. Later in life, his work as a war correspondent earned him the enduring nickname "Papa" and inspired *For Whom the Bell Tolls*. This novel's success was followed by a decade of near literary silence until Hemingway, by then well into his fourth marriage, published *The Old Man and the Sea*. This last novella won the Pulitzer Prize in 1953 and the Nobel Prize for Literature in 1954, and many consider it to be Hemingway's greatest success. In his last years, Hemingway's health deteriorated due to his age and old injuries from a plane crash in Africa. After upcoming leader Fidel Castro forced Hemingway and his wife to leave Cuba for Idaho, Hemingway committed suicide on July 2, 1961. Hemingway's remarkable fame for his classic works, his plain prose, and his adventurous lifestyle have led some to conclude that perhaps "Hemingway's greatest fictional character was Hemingway."

Style

Most evident in his short stories, Hemingway's straightforward prose acts as a rebellion against the more frilly and descriptive writing that characterized earlier 20th-century authors. His style was terse and concise, describing only observable action and dialog, and leaving the reader to understand the meaning of the events and the emotions that inspired them or resulted from them. In *Death in the Afternoon*, Hemingway writes, "If a writer of prose knows enough about what he is writing about he may omit things that he knows and the reader, if the writer is writing truly enough, will have a feeling of those things." A typical example of this style is found in *The Sun Also Rises*:

> It was hot and bright. Up the street was a little square with trees and grass where there were taxis parked. A taxi came up the street, the waiter hanging out at the side. I tipped him and told the driver where to drive, and got in beside Brett. The driver started up the street. I settled back. Brett moved close to me. We sat close against each other. I put my arm around her and she rested against me comfortably. It was very hot and bright, and the houses looked sharply white.

Hemingway describes no emotion, and supplies no interpretation of this scene, yet readers understand quite a lot about the relationship between Jake (the narrator) and Brett.

Hemingway once described his writing style as the "Iceberg Theory," which was his term for leading readers to a deeper understanding of his work by revealing very few details, just as the bulk of an iceberg is hidden below the surface. Similarly, the art of omission, or describing only the surface details of deeply meaningful events, actually gives more weight and draws more attention to the story's unstated themes. The short story "Hills like White Elephants" exemplifies this technique, consisting mostly of banal dialogue that entirely avoids the story's central subject: abortion. About another of his short stories, Hemingway explained, "'Big Two-Hearted River '... is about a boy coming home from the war. ... So the war, all mention of the war, anything about the war, is omitted." Hemingway's revolutionary Iceberg Theory signified a major turning point in American literature.

Themes and the Code Hero

Ernest Hemingway unapologetically drew inspiration from his own life experiences. His heroes were based on himself, their adventures drawn from his own exploits, and many other characters inspired by people he had encountered along the way. Frederic Henry, the hero of *A Farewell to Arms*, is an ambulance driver for the Italian army in WWI, a role Hemingway performed himself. Robert Jordan, the protagonist of *For Whom the Bell Tolls*, fights for the anti-Franco guerillas, a conflict Hemingway covered as a journalist.

Most Hemingway heroes embody Hemingway's own famous masculinity, and the values that Hemingway himself idealized were tested in his characters as they encountered deadly situations. As one scholar notes, Hemingway's major characters are all either resilient men already accustomed to living in the tough world or young men learning to adapt to the difficulties of life. Hemingway's hunters, bullfighters, and soldiers display valor, honor, and strength in their grace under pressure and in their courage in the face of death. Many of Hemingway's stories are expositions of human conflict, and his heroes often encounter the meaninglessness of violence, death, and war. Hemingway called these characters "code heroes": strong men who overcome the difficulties of the world by firmly abiding by their code of values.

Annalisa Galgano, 2013
Trisha Rouleau, 2015

JOHN MAYNARD KEYNES ◊ 1883–1946, *An Interventionist Economist*

" The ideas of economists and political philosophers, both when they are right and when they are wrong are more powerful than is commonly understood. Indeed, the world is ruled by little else. Practical men, who believe themselves to be quite exempt from any intellectual influences, are usually slaves of some defunct economist.

—*The General Theory of Employment, Interest and Money*

- Was a British interventionist economist
- Started a new trend in economic thinking different from that of classical economists, favoring government economic controls and intervention, especially greater government spending and debt during economic downturns
- Believed that free markets would do more harm than good if left unattended by government
- Popularized the idea that demand drove economic growth and that consumer spending, not business expansion, was key to a healthy economy
- Believed government could use both monetary and fiscal policy to steer markets to greater economic growth
- Was one of the most influential figures of the 20th century, whose writings have influenced a number of governmental policies since the 1940s—notably FDR's New Deal and LBJ's Great Society

Key Works

Economic Consequences of the Peace, 1919
The General Theory of Employment, Interest and Money, 1936

Biography

John Maynard Keynes was born into an upper middle class English family. His father was a lecturer at the University of Cambridge and his mother was a social reformer. Keynes was educated at both Eton College and Cambridge and showed interest in mathematics, history, and the classics before landing on economics. After a brief stint in the India office, he worked as a lecturer at Cambridge in economics. He was appointed to the Royal Commission on Indian Currency and Finance. A homosexual, he never married.

During WWI Keynes took a position in the English Treasury Department, where he designed terms of credit payments between England and its allies. He was appointed as the Treasury's financial representative to the Versailles peace conference at the end of WWI. Believing that high war reparations levied against the Germans would bring dire consequences, Keynes warned:

> The policy of reducing Germany to servitude for a generation, of degrading the lives of millions of human beings, and of depriving a whole nation of happiness should be abhorrent and detestable,—abhorrent and detestable, even if it were possible, even if it enriched ourselves, even if it did not sow the decay of the whole civilised life of Europe.

He was unable to convince even the British to adopt lower reparations from the Germans.

During the Great Depression he published a number of papers arguing the connection between unemployment, wages, and aggregate demand. He wrote in *The General Theory of Employment, Interest and Money* that government spending and deficits during downturns in the business cycle were necessary to boost the amount of money being spent throughout the economy. This is known as the multiplier effect. His work was not taken seriously until after his death. He was a main advisor for the British as WWII was coming to an end, and argued for a single world currency and a single central world bank. Though his recommendations were rejected, he was happy overall with the peace treaty that ended WWII. He passed away in 1946.

Aggregates

Keynes's work started with refining and building upon the work of the business cycle. This idea is founded in the assumption that economies go through times of expansion, boom, recessions, and troughs (sometimes known as depression, depending on the length). He believed that it was the demand for goods and services in the economy that drove economic growth, writing in *The General Theory*, "All production is for the purpose of ultimately satisfying a consumer." This idea on aggregate demand was an argument against Say's law of supply driving economic growth.

Keynes believed that aggregate demand was made up of three parts: 1) consumer spending, 2) investments, and 3) government spending. He believed that an increase in spending in any of these areas would lead to increased demand, and thus, increased overall output in the economy, or what he saw as economic growth. In addition, this would have a multiplier effect, meaning that as one would spend money on a good, that money would be taken by the business and spent on something else, which would then be spent on something else by another business. Therefore, it did not matter which one of these aspects of aggregate demand increased; so long as one aspect increased, it would be a benefit to overall output and the economy as a whole.

Given his belief in the multiplier effect, he argued that governments should spend more during times of economic downturns and recessions. Even paying people to perform menial tasks would be more beneficial than simple unemployment. In some ways this revisits the ideas of Thomas Malthus, who saw savings as hindering economic growth. The more money saved, the less spent, the less aggregate demand and economic output. Keynes also believed there was a correlation between interest and unemployment. Aggregate supply, the total supply of goods and services in an economy, could be increased by low interest rates. The savings of individuals would be loaned out to businesses to increase output. Since he believed prices, including the cost of labor, were sticky, he thought that wages would remain constant, as would the prices of these goods and services. He believed that whatever the government could do to boost the spending, both in a monetary and fiscal sense, it should do while output was low.

Government Intervention

When the business cycle led to unemployment, Keynes argued it was the government that should help to steer the economy back to a period of economic growth. He did not believe, as classical economists did, in leaving the market to re-equilibrate by itself. He believed that doing so would prolong suffering.

Keynes criticized the classical economists' idea of a laissez-faire approach to economics, stating in *The General Theory*, "Thus, the weight of my criticism is directed against the inadequacy of the *theoretical* foundations of the *laissez-faire* doctrine upon which I was brought up and for many years I taught." Instead man should be subject to act on what he called the "animal spirits." He describes them in *The General Theory* as, "Most, probably, of our decisions to do something positive, the full consequences of which will be drawn out over many days to come, can only be taken as the result of animal spirits—a spontaneous urge to action rather than inaction, and not as the outcome of a weighted average of quantitative benefits multiplied by quantitative probabilities."

Keynes applied that rationale to most of his writing on government action during economic downturns. He argued that in times of decreased output, government should increase spending to boost aggregate demand. If this meant that governments had to deficit spend, they should do so, and increase taxes in times of increased output to pay for it. The idea that governments would stop spending on politically popular programs, then turn around and raise taxes, is not how governments throughout history had operated. He felt that governments should use both fiscal and monetary policy to increase aggregate demand. Fiscal policies included the lowering of taxes so people would have more to spend, and increased government spending, or stimulus.

He was critical of the fact that most economists before him focused on economics in the long run and ignored current affairs. He stated, "But this long run is a misleading guide to current affairs. In the long run we are all dead. Economists set themselves too easy, too useless a task if in tempestuous seasons they can only tell us that when the storm is long past, the ocean is flat again." Thus it was up to government to do something to fix problems in the present, even to the point of deficit spending. These ideas had their first real world application in the New Deal policies of Franklin Delano Roosevelt. Though these programs cannot be directly attributed to Keynes, his arguments inherently support many of the policies. There is still debate as to whether those programs or other factors got the United States out of the Great Depression. Regardless, the idea of government spending to increase aggregate demand remains a popular prescription to economic downturns.

Kurt Gutschick, faculty

FREIDRICH AUGUST HAYEK ◊ 1899–1992, *Blocking the Road to Serfdom*

> " The virtue of the Free Market is that it gives the maximum latitude for people to use information that only they have. In short, the market process generates the data. Without markets, data are almost nonexistent.

- Taught at the London School of Economics and the University of Chicago
- Joined Milton Friedman in attacking government intervention in economics
- Contended that government meddling eventually leads to totalitarianism
- Served as economic adviser to Margaret Thatcher and Ronald Reagan
- Moved to England in 1938 to the faculty of the London School of Economics, where he stayed for 18 years and became a British citizen
- Wrote *The Road to Serfdom* to warn his fellow British citizens of the dangers of socialism; John Maynard Keynes praised the book highly, and the book remains a bestseller today
- Shared the 1974 Nobel Memorial Prize in Economic Sciences with Gunnar Myrdal
- Was appointed a member of the Order of the Companions of Honour by Queen Elizabeth II on the advice of Prime Minister Margaret Thatcher for his "services to the study of economics"
- Received the first Hanns Martin Schleyer Prize in 1984
- Received the US Presidential Medal of Freedom in 1991 from President George H.W. Bush
- Was a major social theorist and political philosopher of the 20th century, and his account of how changing prices communicate information that enables individuals to coordinate their plans is widely regarded as an important achievement in economics
- Had his article "The Use of Knowledge in Society" selected as one of the top 20 articles published in *The American Economic Review* during its first 100 years

Key Works

Prices and Production, 1931
The Road to Serfdom, 1944
"The Use of Knowledge in Society," 1945

Biography

Friedrich Hayek has been called the "most consequential thinker of the mainstream political right in the twentieth century." Born in Austria in 1899, and second cousin to the philosopher Ludwig Wittgenstein, Hayek's education was interrupted by brief service on the Italian front in WWI. After the war Hayek pursued his studies and eventually earned doctorates in both law and political science. He was famously a polymath, making contributions to political theory, psychology, and economics. It is the latter of which that secured him lasting recognition, as well as the Nobel Prize for Economics in 1974. Hayek's early academic career was spent at the London School of Economics. He left for the University of Chicago in 1950, serving on the same staff as Milton Friedman, and finished his career at the University of Freiburg in West Germany. Hayek counseled Margaret Thatcher on economics in the late 1970s, was honored by Queen Elizabeth II by being appointed a member of the Order of the Companions of Honour, and received the Presidential Medal of Freedom by President George H.W. Bush in 1991. Hayek died shortly after, in 1992 at his home in Freiburg. He remains broadly influential within the field of economics to this day.

Austrian School of Economics

Most of Hayek's early work, and what he remains most notable for today in the field of economics, was his groundbreaking explorations in the 1920s and 1930s on what came to be called the Austrian School of Economics. The Austrian school combined Hayek's passions for exploration of the business cycle, capital theory, and monetary theory. Like Adam Smith, Hayek saw the invisible forces shaping the market as remarkably efficient yet the market nonetheless contained flaws. What to account for this?

One of the factors cited in *Prices and Production* is government meddling in the money supply. When the government increases the money supply interest rates decrease and credit becomes artificially cheap. Cheap credit allows businesses to make decisions—financing projects that would be beyond their means in a true interest situation—they otherwise would not make in a genuine market leading to long-term failures.

Debates With Keynes

Outside of the esoteric world of academic economics, Hayek is also known for his debates with his economic rival, John Maynard Keynes, who was famous for arguing that government intervention could help forestall economic depressions. The two debated each other in a series of letters to the *London Times*. While they agreed on many matters, disagreement on government's role in easing economic crises drove a wedge between the two men. Hayek's contention, which is largely the same as that made by Milton Friedman, was that government intervention would exacerbate inflationary pressure and eventually lead to a state of mutual inflation and high unemployment. Historical data that has emerged from succeeding economic crises justifies Hayek's position.

The Road to Serfdom and Against Socialism

Hayek and his school also combated the growing influence of socialism in economic circles. Hayek pointed out in "The Use of Knowledge in Society" that among the many shortcomings of socialist economics, a central flaw is that data required for the type of central planning that socialism hinges on are simply not possible. The "data," such as they exist, are spread out amongst many actors in a market and cannot be systematized. Market forces generate the data; in lieu of market forces, there is no data to analyze, and the socialist central planner will be shooting in the dark. This same reasoning caused Hayek to reject other darling causes of the economic left: he rejected unions as privileging the unionized at the expense of the nonunionized; he argued that rent control decreases the housing supply; that subsidies for agriculture decrease the general welfare and incentivize politicians to privilege the farming class over other forms of labor.

Hayek's most famous work attacking socialism was *The Road to Serfdom*, published in 1944. Citing parallels between the economic policy of Nazi Germany and socialist efforts in British politics, Hayek argued that government intervention in the economy ultimately leads to totalitarianism. He contended that economics is not a field that be abstracted from other facets of life: "Economic control is not merely control of a sector of human life which can be separated from the rest; it is the control of the means for all our ends."

The Road to Serfdom established Hayek as the "world's leading classical liberal," a label he proudly bore. He would later balk at being called a conservative, a political stance that he associated with religious pressures and nationalism, but he was proud to defend a classically liberal position. Hayek's emphasis on personal freedom, most stridently from government control, dictated his economic, political, and social thought and served as the backbone of the rest of his life's work.

MILTON FRIEDMAN ◊ 1912–2006, *Free Market Bulldog*

" Well first of all, tell me, is there some society you know of that doesn't run on greed? You think Russia doesn't run on greed? You think China doesn't run on greed? What is greed?

—from an interview with Phil Donahue, 1979

- Is revered as the most lucid free-market economic communicator ever and the most influential economist of the second half of the 20th century
- Adhered to the famous Chicago School of economic thought
- Won the Nobel Prize in Economics in 1976
- Won the John Bates Clark Medal in 1951 for economists under the age of 40
- Argued, in his book, *Capitalism and Freedom*, that government intervention in the economy is usually harmful and ineffective
- Challenged what he later called "naive Keynesian" theory in his magnum opus, *Free to Choose*
- Predicted what would come to be known as stagflation
- Served as an economic adviser to Richard Nixon, Ronald Reagan, and Margaret Thatcher
- Blamed the government (the Fed) for the severity of the Great Depression
- Advocated radical freedom for individual and corporate actors, free from government interference, including such policies as: a volunteer military, freely floating exchange rates, abolition of medical licenses, a negative income tax, and school vouchers

Key Works

Capitalism and Freedom, 1962
Free to Choose, 1980

Biography

Milton Friedman has been called the "twentieth century's most prominent advocate of free markets." Friedman was born in Brooklyn in 1912, the son of Jewish immigrants, and went on to attend Rutgers University before receiving his MA from the University of Chicago and his PhD from Columbia University in 1946. Penning a series of influential economic treatises in the mid-twentieth century— including *A Theory of the Consumption Function* and *Capitalism and Freedom*—Friedman was honored for his work with both the John Bates Clark Medal, given to superlative economists under the age of 40, and the Nobel Prize for Economics in 1976. He also served in Richard Nixon's economic counsel and taught at the University of Chicago until 1977. After retiring from Chicago, Friedman worked at the Hoover Institution at Stanford University as a senior research fellow. He then served as an advisor to Ronald Reagan, incessantly promoting a free market system with limited government interference. Friedman died of heart failure in 2006, still a diligent economist. *The Wall Street Journal* published his final article the day after his death.

Defense of Free Markets

Free market economics had dominated the English-speaking world until John Maynard Keynes published *The General Theory of Employment, Interest, and Money* in 1936 and questioned this orthodoxy, arguing for government intervention in monetary policy. Friedman directly and fervently attacked the notion that it was the role of the government to meddle in economic affairs. Government intervention was, for Friedman, often ineffective and, perhaps more perniciously, usually permanent. In other words, once a government policy is established it is nearly impossible to remove or modify it even when the situation that motivated the intervention changes. Friedman was also careful to link, particularly in *Capitalism and Freedom*, economic freedom to personal, political freedom more broadly. Free markets provide the consumer with choice, and government intervention serves only to hamper the choices on offer.

Friedman, and the school of thought that he influenced and directed, served as a midcentury response to the swing towards Keynesianism. Friedman went after the Keynesian school by reasserting in *A Theory of the Consumption Function* the classical notion of *homo economicus*, or economic man. Economic man is a rational, self-interested market entity who will make the most rational decision over the long run. While there are obvious flaws in this view—nearly every player in the free market has made economic decisions that are anything but rational; people in Colorado *own* jet skis, for example—but in the aggregate the notion of economic man is useful in making monetary policy.

Friedman also took aim at the Keynesian link between inflation, or a general increase in the price of goods, and unemployment that associated high inflation with low unemployment. Keynes contended that the best way for a government to manage its money was through direct government intervention—taxing and spending. Friedman warned that a government policy that intentionally raised inflation in order to combat unemployment would in the long run lead to a condition called "stagflation," or the pernicious combination of both high inflation and high unemployment. Friedman's rationale was that over time people would factor high inflation into their future predictions and therefore lessen business owner's benefit in hiring new employees and increase new employees desire to secure a higher wage, the end result being increasing unemployment. His predictive thesis bore tangible fruit in the 1970s as persistent inflation brought on persistent unemployment. The monetary policy of the Reagan administration—with Friedman as a key influence—was able to arrest this slide after a painful period of high unemployment.

Finally, Friedman was a long and tireless advocate for profound and sweeping changes in governmental monetary policy. Friedman long argued for the abolition of the US Federal Reserve, thinking it better to "replace its control over interest rates and the money supply with a mechanical rule for monetary growth." Friedman's preferred monetary policies are most obvious in *Capitalism and Freedom*. In this work he argues for the abolishment of the following: price supports, tariffs, licensing, minimum wage, Social Security, housing subsidies, the draft, toll roads, the post office, and national parks. While some of those examples may strike a modern reader as extreme, Friedman believed earnestly that private entities could better protect and better facilitate these services than the heavy hand of government. The same notion caused Friedman to focus much of his energy later in his life on voucher programs for education. Often lambasted as a ploy of the religious right, an agnostic Jewish economist was perhaps the most vocal advocate of a once crazy position that is now seriously debated. So it was for many of Friedman's ideas: what seemed like heresy turned out to be prophecy.

THEODOSIUS DOBZHANSKY ◊ 1900–1975, *Mutator of Evolution Theory*

> " Nothing in biology makes sense except in light of evolution.
> —Response to a petition of the King of Saudi Arabia to repress heresies on science

- Invented the field of evolutionary biology
- Studied organisms and perform clinical research outside of the laboratory, one of the few researchers to do so
- Worked with Nobel Prize winner Thomas Hunt Morgan to study ladybugs and "garbage flies"
- Published more than 400 research papers

Key Works

Genetics and the Origin of Species, 1937
The Modern Synthesis, 1942
The Biological Basis of Human Freedom, 1956
Mankind Evolving, 1962
Ultimate Concern, 1967

Biography

Theodosius Dobzhansky was born Feodosy Grigor'evitch Dobzhansky in Russian Ukraine in 1900 to Polish parents. His father was a math teacher. After graduating from the University of Kiev, Dobzhansky received a Rockefeller grant to attend Columbia University, where he began his partnership with Thomas Hunt Morgan. When Morgan eventually left Columbia to pursue his genetic research at the California Institute of Technology, Dobzhansky accompanied him. Dobzhansky and Morgan performed notable experiments on fruit flies and what Dobzhansky christened "garbage flies." Through these experiment and others, Dobzhansky substantially merged the fields of genetics and evolution for the first time; he published these findings in his 1937 book *Genetics and the Origin of Species*. Perhaps due to his clear and simple writing style, Dobzhansky soon became a widely appreciated public figure. Also in 1937 he became an American citizen. During his later years as a professor at Columbia, Dobzhansky often travelled internationally to test his theories on a greater variety of species and specimens. He died in late 1975, leaving behind a new field of biology, and perhaps even more impressively, more than 400 succinct papers that opened this new field to the public.

Genetics and Evolution

Dobzhansky is renowned for combining the fields of genetics and evolution to create evolutionary biology. Early in his research career, he realized that the genetic variation within and between populations of ladybugs could be explained by the same mechanisms as evolution. That is, he believed that evolutionary changes could be understood by studying minor genetic changes in a single species over time.

At the time of Dobzhansky's research, the scientific community believed that a species was defined as a group of plants or animals that had identical genes. However, in his research, Dobzhansky observed genetic differences and mutations *within* species as well. He demonstrated through his experiments that chromosome inversion leads to significant amounts of genetic variety; this in turn leads to a reproductive advantage. Owing to the short life cycle of the flies he used for his experiments, Dobzhansky could witness a quick process of evolution by observing many successive generations of flies. The genetic differences he observed enabled species to evolve and adapt to changing environments as they reproduced. In other words, over time, slight genetic mutations increase a species' ability to adapt, and thus ensure a species' long-term survival. Dobzhansky argued that "the more genetic diversity is contained in a particular population, the more chance that population has to survive environmental changes." Across thousands or millions of years, species had mutated and adapted until they were no longer genetically compatible with other species.

This knowledge led Dobzhansky to his theory of isolating mechanisms. Dobzhansky theorized that over the course of evolution, species had genetically changed so much that these genetic differences now prevent different species from successfully reproducing with one another. He called these genetic reproductive barriers "isolating mechanisms." According to Dobzhansky, isolating mechanisms take the form of physical or genetic traits that inhibit gene exchange between species.

Dobzhansky believed that his genetic research and his theory of isolating mechanisms could be used to understand evolution: "There is no way toward an understanding of the mechanisms of macro-evolutionary changes … other than through a full comprehension of the micro-evolutionary processes observable within the span of a human lifetime." He is still credited with reinvigorating the scientific study of evolution with his groundbreaking systematic, paleontological, and botanical theories.

Caroline Fuschino, 2015
Julianna Swayze, 2016
Alexi Wenger, 2016

MARGARET MEAD ◊ 1901–1978, *The Mother of Multi-Culturalism*

> " Never believe that a few caring people can't change the world. For, indeed, that's all who ever have.

- Was an American anthropologist who studied and popularized culture, psychology, and personality
- Studied anthropology at Columbia with Franz Boas at the beginning of WWI
- Worked in Samoa to study young girls (against the advice of colleagues); wrote *Coming of Age in Samoa*, with the final chapter "Education for Choice"
- Became curator of ethnology at American Museum of Natural History in NYC
- Traveled to New Guinea with her second husband to study the thought of young children
- Studied schizophrenia in culture in Bali
- Wrote *Balinese Character* with her third husband, Gregory Bateson, using new field techniques, particularly film
- Helped craft public policy related to anthropology during WWII and after
- Emphasized culture as the foundation for personality development
- Taught anthropology at Columbia, Fordham, Cincinnati, and Topeka universities
- Was a key participant at the first UN forum on human settlements
- Was awarded the Presidential Medal of Freedom posthumously

Key Works

Coming of Age in Samoa, 1928
The Social Organization of Manu'a, 1930
Growing Up in New Guinea, 1930
Sex and Temperament in Three Primitive Societies, 1935
Balinese Character, 1942
Male and Female, 1949
The Study of Cultures at a Distance, 1953
New Lives for the Old, 1956
Culture and Commitment, 1970
A Way of Seeing, 1975

Biography

Margaret Mead came by her intellectual curiosity and drive partly because of her own family culture—her father was a professor at the Wharton School of Finance and Commerce, her mother a sociologist and women's rights advocate, and her grandmother a child psychologist. A lover of tradition and ritual, she joined the Episcopal church when she was 12, and her religion was a source of support and comfort throughout her life. She entered DePauw, contemplating careers in painting or English, but transferred to Barnard to study psychology. In her senior year, she decided to become an anthropologist after a course with Franz Boas; she graduated in 1923, married Luther Cressman, and entered Columbia as a graduate student. Mead's initial fieldwork was a trip to Samoa where she defied her peers by ignoring their cautions on the dangers of a woman alone on a Pacific Island. Her lifelong interest in children flourished there as she studied the lives of young girls. Returning to America, Mead became curator of ethnology at the American Museum of Natural History in New York. She married twice more, continued to conduct field research and write and educate, and died in New York City in 1978.

A New Anthropology

Mead wanted to help Americans understand cultural anthropology and its importance to public policy. She worked with close friend Ruth Benedict, during and after WWII, to influence public policy with knowledge gained from anthropology. Mead believed that cultural understanding was key in assessing the needs and motivations of the allies, enemies, and individuals involved in the conflict, and in structuring post-war refugee policy. Other policy arenas where anthropology was useful included a study of American food habits, which aided with newly instituted rationing. Going to England, Mead helped the British understand the American soldiers stationed there. After the war, she became director of Research in Contemporary Cultures, to lead the study of complex modern cultures.

Mead branched out to study psychology, learning theory, and psychoanalysis. She saw the importance of culture in personality development. She wrote *Coming of Age in Samoa*, ending the book with "Education for Choice," clearly the focus of much of her later work. Mead concluded that the stress Westerners have given to the period of adolescence are unique to western society, not part of all societies. In that vein she went to New Guinea with Reo Fortune, her second husband, also an anthropologist. She wanted to study the thoughts of young children in their social worlds and to test some of her latest ideas on that subject. Mead believed that a person matures within his cultural context of ideological systems, others' expectations, and socialization techniques.

Mead also studied psychiatry within the cultural contest of schizophrenia. She went to Bali, where some of the manifestations of that condition are acceptable to the culture. She went with her third husband, Gregory Bateson, a British anthropologist. The two used new field techniques, including film, to perceive details not observable any other way. Of the 38,000 photographs they took, they used 759 for a joint writing of *Balinese Character*, significant for its ethnological detail presented.

As a professor at Columbia, Fordham, Cincinnati, and Topeka University, Mead continued to educate students and the general public about cultural anthropology. She is appreciated as a leading scholar of the 20th century and shared her beliefs through her writing, lecturing, and a column in *Redbook* magazine. Margaret Mead created a new outline for American women, who can have careers as well as families. Her daughter, Mary Catherine Bateson, became an anthropologist who wrote *With a Daughter's Eye: A Memoir of Margaret Mead and Gregory Bateson*.

THE CHINESE CIVIL WAR, 1928–1949

Long since weakened by European interference and trampled underfoot by the march of the Japanese, the Chinese too would ultimately turn to Communism under the leadership of Mao Zedong. Sometimes assisting, sometimes challenging acting ruler and autocrat Chiang Kai-shek, Mao's communists resisted the imperial Japanese forces until they could seize control of the government. Once installed, Mao's vision of Communism consumed China, changing the country in a number of ways, many of them painful. Today China has taken Russia's place as the United States' biggest rival. Who knows what the future will hold.

WORLD WAR II, 1939–1945, *THE WAR OF THE TWENTIETH CENTURY*

World War I was supposed to be the "war to end all wars," but in its conclusion the Treaty of Versailles held the seeds of yet another world conflict. The harsh terms of the Treaty, including backbreaking reparations from Germany to the Allies, crippled the German economy and resulted in starvation and chaos. These conditions paved the way for the rise of Adolf Hitler and the Nazi party. The Germans, desperate for someone to turn their economy around and restore national pride, elected Hitler their "Fuhrer" in 1934. Hitler was not the first dictator to come to power in Europe due to economic crises resulting from the aftermath of WWI. Francisco Franco took over Spain and established the first fascist dictatorship. Mussolini followed suit in Italy, and invaded Ethiopia in 1935 in an attempt to expand Italy's sphere of influence and income streams.

On the other side of the world, Japan, an island nation with little in the way of national resources, sought to procure the resources to fuel the country's growth by invading Manchuria in 1931 and China in 1937 in pursuit of a Japanese-headed Asian sphere, free of Western influence. Together, Germany, Japan, and Italy three formed the Axis, which would threaten the safety of the world. What followed was a battle between democracy and autocracy, in which honor and horror stood vigil over the battlefield.

More or less simultaneously with these Axis advances, the Great Depression was wreaking havoc on economies around the world. With millions of people out of work, countries struggled to maintain production and feed their people, resulting in unstable governments, worldwide turmoil, and the rise of political movements and leaders that promised to make a difference. France and Great Britain, for instance, both experienced strong fascist and communist movements in the years leading up to WWII.

Finally, due to populations drained by WWI and its aftermath, Britain and France tried to avoid war with Hitler rather than confront him, and practiced a policy of appeasement. They ignored his early breaches of the Treaty of Versailles, allowing Germany to remilitarize and invade the Rhineland in pursuit of Hitler's goal of reuniting the German people. They took no decisive action over the annexation of Austria, and facilitated the German dictator's annexation of Czechoslovakia via the Munich Agreement. It wasn't until Hitler invaded Germany in 1939 that Britain and France declared war on Germany on September 3, 1939, pitting the Allies (Britain, France, USA (from 1941), USSR, Australia, Belgium, Brazil, Canada, China, Denmark, Greece, Netherlands, New Zealand, Norway, Poland, South Africa and Yugoslavia) against the Axis powers (Germany, Japan, Italy, Hungary, Romania and Bulgaria).

Where WWI was a static war fought mainly in trenches, WWII introduced new styles of warfare, including "blitzkrieg" (lightning attack), fast advances by tank units to overwhelm an enemy's opposition. Using this tactic, Germany quickly invaded and occupied Norway, Netherlands, Belgium, Luxembourg, France, Denmark, Yugoslavia, Greece, and Western Poland. Aerial warfare and strategic bombing came into their own during WWII, beginning with the Battle of Britain, and ending with the Allied bombardment of the German means of production, which crippled the Germans' ability to wage war, and the firebombing and then dropping of two nuclear bombs on Japan which had brought the US into the war on December 7, 1941, with their would-be preemptive attack on Pearl Harbor.

Notable Battles

The Battle of Britain, 1940

Also known as the Blitz, the Battle of Britain encapsulated the ongoing struggle of the British Royal Air Force against the German Luftwaffe over England during WWII, culminating in a period of 57 nights in a row during which the capital city of London was bombed repeatedly and extensively. The British endured, avoiding defeat and disgrace, and demonstrated their air superiority over the Germans. Although planes were still a relatively recent invention, they proved instrumental across both World Wars.

The Bombing of Pearl Harbor, 1941

The Japanese attack which "Roused the sleeping giant," pulling the United States into WWII. Desperate to disrupt United States control of the Pacific, the Japanese navy hatched a plan to sink the main Pacific fleet at Pearl Harbor, assuming they could dominate the region during the ensuing window for repairs. Although the attack was a success, which took Pearl Harbor by surprise, a number of United States aircraft carriers were away at the time, sparing them from destruction and allowing America to continue its Pacific operations.

The Battle of Midway, 1942

The turning point of the Pacific theater of WWII, the Battle of Midway demonstrated the importance and effectiveness of aircraft carriers in modern naval warfare. Like planes, aircraft carriers were recent additions of the global war machine, and both Japan and the United States took note of their power. Ultimately, however, the United States' superior manufacturing capacity allowed them to construct and send out many more carriers than the Japanese could manage, turning the tide in favor of the Americans.

The Battle of Stalingrad, 1942–1943

Although D-Day and the Battle of the Bulge are typically more celebrated, the Battle of Stalingrad was perhaps the single most crucial clash of WWII. Mired in the snow and poorly supplied, the Russians nevertheless managed to wear down a significant fraction of the German army, weathering the enemy's enthusiasm for war and killing a startling number of their soldiers. Unfortunately, even when compared with other battles of the time, the cost was dreadful. Far more Russian soldiers and civilians died than German ones, Russia's success due more to its excess population than its tactics or technology.

The Bombing of Hiroshima and Nagasaki, 1945

More an event than a battle, the development and dropping of two atomic bombs over Japan marked the end of WWII and the start of the nuclear age. The ethics of this act are still hotly debated even to this day, as is the paradigm shift that followed, delivering to the world the ideas of manmade Armageddon and mutually assured destruction.

More than 60 million people, 3% of the world's 1940 population, died in WWII, including approximately 6 million Jews exterminated by the Germans. The war in Europe ended on May 8, 1945, and the Japanese formally surrendered on the USS Missouri on September 2, 1945.

WERNER HEISENBERG ◊ 1901–1976, *A Man on the Edge of Uncertainty*

❝ What we observe is not nature itself, but nature exposed to our method of questioning.
—*Physics and Philosophy: The Revolution in Modern Science*

- Was a pioneer of early quantum mechanics
- Created a new model of the atom based on matrix algebra
- Discovered the uncertainty principle
- Debated with Einstein, Bohr, and others
- Won the Nobel Peace Prize in 1932
- Defended quantum mechanics in the face of Nazi harassment
- Worked on the German atomic bomb unwillingly
- Served as spokesperson for German science after the war

Key Works

About the Quantum-Theoretical Reinterpretation of Kinetic and Mechanical Relationships, 1925
Physics and Philosophy: The Revolution in Modern Science, 1956
Physics and Beyond, 1969

Biography

Werner Heisenberg showed early signs of genius, and his early interest in math and science was fostered by his father, a professor of middle and modern Greek. As a teenager, Heisenberg studied

Einstein's relativity theory on his own, perhaps never realizing that he himself would one day debate physics with the legendary genius. He even taught himself calculus, which was not offered at his school, and did music on the side. He attended the University of Munich and quickly received his doctorate. At age 25, he was given a professorship at the University of Munich and then later at Leipzig. He went on to study under the likes of Arnold Sommerfeld, Max Born, and Niels Bohr. Heisenberg spent a great deal of time working with Bohr in Copenhagen, research that would lead to his famous uncertainty principle and the "Copenhagen Interpretation."

His famous matrix mechanics, which predicted subatomic behavior, earned Heisenberg the Nobel Peace Prize just as WWII was breaking out. Although encouraged by his peers to flee Germany, he believed it was his duty to stay and to protect German physics, which had come under Nazi attack as a "Jewish science." For years, he defended himself against Nazi harassment, but with the advent of nuclear fission he was suddenly in high demand. Recruited—one might say forced—to work on the atomic bomb, Heisenberg was a reluctant participant. Before a German bomb was created, the Allies won the war. For the rest of his life, Heisenberg worked to revive German science, and advocated the use of nuclear energy. He died from cancer in 1976.

The Beginning of Quantum Mechanics

Heisenberg had a tendency to go out on a limb with a radical theory, but ultimately he would be proven right, or at least on the right track. He was a math prodigy and often devised mathematical models to explain his reasoning. While working under noted physicist Niels Bohr in 1925, he observed some flaws with Bohr's atomic model, which failed to work for an atom with more than one electron. Furthermore, it did not account for the wave-like properties of electrons. Heisenberg undertook the daunting task of creating another model for the atom. He believed that the "the approach of trying to visualize a physical model of the atom was destined to fail because of the paradoxical wave-particle nature of electrons." So his model would not be a physical model, but one based on math. Heisenberg also vowed to do away with the idea of basing electron energies on their orbits, proclaiming, "All of my meagre efforts go toward killing off and suitably replacing the concept of the orbital path which one cannot observe." Instead of focusing on what cannot be observed, Heisenberg looked to what could be observed and measured, specifically the energy that electrons emitted and absorbed.

Soon Heisenberg created a mathematical model of the atom based on matrices (arrays of numbers), but the math was so abstract that "he was not sure it made any sense." He had another physicist, Max Born, look at it. Born recognized the math as corresponding to matrix algebra and gave Heisenberg the green light. Heisenberg refined his work, and his matrix mechanics accurately described subatomic behavior for atoms with several electrons. While physicists of the day were impressed, even they "were repelled at the obscure nature of the mathematics involved."

At around the same time, another scientific genius, Erwin Schrödinger, came up with an alternative theory to explain the energy associated with electrons. He concluded that this energy did not correspond to fixed orbitals, as Bohr had stated, but to the vibrational frequencies of the electrons themselves. Known as wave mechanics, Schrödinger's theory used simpler math and was also easier to visualize than Heisenberg's matrix mechanics. However Heisenberg's work was still correct. When combined, the two theories formed the basis of quantum mechanics and gave a much more accurate, if more abstract, idea of how energy and quanta relate to subatomic particles.

The Uncertainty Principle

As the physics world discussed the concept of quantum mechanics, Heisenberg realized that both Schrödinger's theory and his own were inadequate. Their math was correct, but something was amiss. Heisenberg finally found the problem when looking over a set of equations that other physicists had created using the quantum mechanics concept. He saw that whenever "one tried to measure both the position and velocity of a particle at the same time, the results were imprecise." It dawned on him that this uncertainty was not due to a problem with the math or poor measuring devices, but was simply an inherent part of the subatomic world.

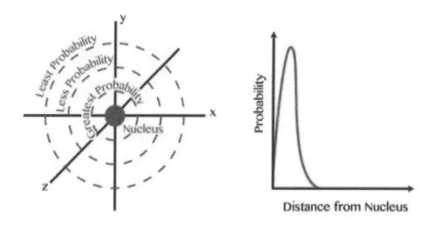

For a Hydrogen Atom, Electrons have a Greater
Probability of being located closer to the Nucleus.

The Heisenberg Uncertainty Principle

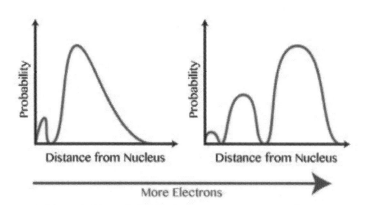

As the number of Electrons increases, Electrons are
more likely to be found farther away from the Nucleus

Changing Locational Probabilities

He postulated a new theory, known as the uncertainty principle, to describe this phenomenon. In Heisenberg's own words: "The more precisely the position is determined, the less precisely the momentum is known in this instant, and vice versa." One cannot know the position and momentum of a particle at the same time; there is always some level of uncertainty. As Heisenberg realized, the reason for this had to do with the dual nature of subatomic particles. Every subatomic particle has an associated wave. The particle's position "can be precisely located where the wave's undulations are most intense. But where the wave's undulations are most intense, the wavelength is also at its most ill-defined, and the velocity of the associated particle is impossible to determine." Furthermore, the simple act of measuring the momentum of a particle will change its position, making any simultaneous measurement of the position invalid. Subatomic particles are so small that it is impossible to observe them without interfering with either their position or momentum.

Heisenberg's work on the uncertainty principle was closely related to Bohr's complementarity theory, which postulated how one can observe a particle as either a wave or a particle, but not both at the same time. Together, these two interpretations became known as the Copenhagen interpretation, which became a crucial concept in quantum mechanics. For example, it meant that no chemist or physicist could ever know the exact location of an electron. Thus, any atomic model had to be based on the probability that an electron would be found at a certain spot and not on well-defined circular paths. The result was seeing electrons as inhabiting a region in which they were most likely to be found, known today as an orbital. Heisenberg's theories and experiments still influence physicists today.

Tatjana Scherschel, 2015
Julianna Swayze, 2016

MORTIMER ADLER ◊ 1902–2001, *A Lover of the Classics*

" The purpose of learning is growth, and our minds, unlike our bodies, can continue growing as we continue to live.

- Created the first Great Books course with mentor John Erskine at Columbia University
- Saw reading great books (profound and lasting) as a vehicle for discussing eternal questions
- Edited a 54-volume set of 443 great books with *Encyclopaedia Britannica*
- Produced an index (syntopicon) of 102 great ideas
- Founded the Aspen Institute in Colorado
- Hoped to reform public schools with his Paideia Project
- Published popular books on philosophy
- Debated with Leo Strauss, Allan Bloom, and William Bennett over the role of great books as the beginning of questioning
- Declared himself to be a socialist, working for "a future in which the ideals of democracy and socialism will be more fully realized"

Key Works
How to Read a Book: The Art of Getting a Liberal Education, 1940
The Revolution in Education, 1944 (with Milton Mayer)
The Capitalist Manifesto, 1958 (with Louis O. Kelso)
Great Ideas from the Great Books, 1961
The Common Sense of Politics, 1971
Philosopher at Large: An Intellectual Autobiography, 1977
Reforming Education: The Schooling of a People and Their Education Beyond Schooling, 1977

The Paideia Proposal: An Educational Manifesto, 1982
Reforming Education: The Opening of the American Mind, 1988
The Great Ideas: A Lexicon of Western Thought, 1992
How to Prove There is a God, 2011

Biography

The hallmark of Mortimer J. Adler's philosophy is self-directed reading. Born to a teacher and a jewelry salesman in New York, Adler had a brilliant mind and a burning love of reading and writing. His first job was working as a copyboy at the *New York Sun,* but when he read the autobiography of John Stuart Mill, he was so inspired that he quit high school to continue reading Plato. He attended Columbia University and completed the philosophy degree.

Adler's first graduate work, a dissertation on how to measure music appreciation, resulted in a published book and a degree in psychology from Columbia. During this period he married twice and had four sons. Adler continued to examine the ideas he encountered at Columbia, including those of the educational philosopher John Dewey, and when he began teaching psychology himself at the University of Chicago, he argued against Dewey's philosophy.

Also at Chicago University, Adler wrestled with his faith. Born of Orthodox Jewish immigrants, Adler had a lot to think about upon reading the classics. He finally was baptized as an Episcopalian. In a 1990 article in *Christianity* magazine, Adler stated, "My chief reason for choosing Christianity was because the mysteries were incomprehensible. What's the point of revelation if we could figure it out ourselves? If it were wholly comprehensible, then it would just be another philosophy."

Adler authored an amazing number of books, appealing to the ordinary reader to appreciate philosophy. He wrote about the philosophies important to thinking about economics, racism, law, science, theology, and many other crucial topics, in an effort to stamp out skepticism, subjectivism, and relativism. Adler served as a consultant to the Ford Foundation and joined commentator Bill Moyers for a PBS-TV series *Six Great Ideas.* He founded the Center for the Study of Great Ideas and directed the Institute for Philosophical Research at Chicago's Institute. He was the chairman of the editorial board of *Encyclopaedia Britannica* for years. Because he cared about student learning so earnestly, he was awarded the Aquinas Medal from Columbia and the Wilma and Roswell Messing Award from St. Louis University Libraries. He died in San Mateo, California, in 2001.

Absolute Truths through Great Books

For Adler, the epitome of education was studying the great writings of the western world. He believed we are as enlightened by Aristotle's ethics today as were those who listened to Aristotle's lectures when they were first delivered, because the ethical problems that human beings confront in their lives have not changed over the centuries. Moral virtue and the blessings of good fortune are today, as they have always been in the past, the keys to living well, unaffected by all the technological changes in the environment, or those in our social, political, and economic institutions. He believed that the moral problems facing individuals are the same in every century, though they appear to us in different guises, and held that Dewey's harmful methods of experimentation and fluctuating values created a climate of social unrest. Adler preferred Aristotle and Thomas Aquinas, who articulated absolute truths and values for all time. He expressed this in *How to Read a Book: The Art of Getting a Liberal Education.*

Adler's mantra, "philosophy is everybody's business," saw him through criticism from some educators. He had to convince Robert M. Hutchins, president of the University of Chicago, of a new way to learn. He recommended throwing out textbooks and lectures and replacing them with a schedule of reading and discussion of great books, one per week. The goal, he believed, was an understanding of logic and the importance of choosing honesty and goodness. Hutchins allowed Adler to oversee a program off campus where a coordinator gathered readers of a variety of ages and background for reading on moral issues. Only the Catholic scholars applauded his new idea, so his Great Books program became just another educational trend. The most significant criticism directed against him claimed that Adler had omitted many worthy writers, especially non-white and female.

Adler had a lifelong concern that America's educational system was too oppositional and politically charged. He wanted to create understanding among educational theorists through his Paideia Project. His long-term hope was to persuade all educators to include Great Books seminars in elementary and high schools with the help of a series of books, conferences, and outreach program. The result of these initiatives was his increasing importance in educational circles as a man who spoke publicly about education issues and wrote accessible books on philosophy.

Adler changed his own philosophical focus over the course of his life, first following Aristotle and then the Scholasticism of Thomas Aquinas. He liked combative discussion, which brought him into conflict over university curricula. He became more and more liberal, arguing with Leo Strauss's belief that the classics taught an eternal truth. Adler believed that in a democracy, great books should start the discussion, not end it. He questioned whether capitalism is democratic and he advocated for property redistribution. Adler finally announced that he was a socialist, and felt he was following a path similar to that of his childhood idol, John Stuart Mills—the path from classicism to liberalism to socialism.

Adler didn't value student-centered elective programs and vocational training; as a result, his ideas elicited praise from 20th-century educational analysts. Those who support Adler's Great Books curricula have changed from textbooks and homework to Socratic learning and argue that more learning takes place in their classrooms. Some scholars, however, continue to disapprove of Adler's whites-only selections. Yet even now, Adler's insistence on in-depth reading has inspired educators to encourage charter, magnet, and home schools.

GEORGE ORWELL ◊ 1903–1950, *Novelist and Satirist*

" War is peace. Freedom is slavery. And Big Brother is watching you.

—1984

- Was a British novelist, essayist, journalist, and critic, and author of *1984*, his magnum opus
- Studied English and French under Aldous Huxley, the dystopic author of *Brave New World*, at Eton; they corresponded about their dystopias
- Saw the direct effects of English imperialism upon India, gaining sympathy for oppressed locals
- Soured on the communist project of the Soviet Union, although he was a socialist

Key Works

Down and Out in Paris and London, 1933

Burmese Days, 1934
Animal Farm, 1945
1984, 1949

Biography

Eric Arthur Blair—he would later adopt the pen name George Orwell—was born in 1903 on June 25, to Ida Mabel Limouzin and Richard Walmesley Blair in India while his father served as a minor official in the British Indian government. When he was 1 year old, they moved back to England where he was raised. Starting at age 8, he attended a private boarding school. He did well and later received scholarships for a few higher educational institutions. From 1917–1921, he attended Eton where Aldous Huxley, the author of *Brave New World*, taught Orwell English and French.

During this time he had some of his articles published in the school newspaper. In 1922, he joined the imperial civil service. After his training, serving in the Indian Imperial Police of Burma as an assistant district superintendent, "he became increasingly disenchanted with imperial practices and more sympathetic with the natives, who he considered to be unjustly oppressed." He left his position in 1928 and wrote a novel about his experiences there—*Burmese Days*. For the following five years, he worked and lived with criminals and people in poverty in both London and Paris, which prompted him to write *Down and Out in Paris and London*. This time encouraged Orwell in his socialism, though he rejected Marxism and the extremes of Soviet communism. His first financially successful work was his novella, *Animal Farm*, which was followed by his last and greatest novel, *1984*. He died of tuberculosis in 1950.

Animal Farm

The novella *Animal Farm* is an anti-Soviet satire and allegory. Orwell said this about his work: "Every line of every serious work that I have written since 1936 has been written, directly or indirectly, against totalitarianism; *Animal Farm* was the first book in which I tried, with full consciousness of what I was doing, to fuse political purpose and artistic purpose into one whole." Comrade Napoleon, the leader of the animals on the farm, is a thinly veiled stand-in for Joseph Stalin. Mr. Jones, the original owner of the farm, represents the hapless Czar Nicholas II, the pre-Russian revolution leader. The book begins with Old Major, the old boar on the farm and the allegory's Karl Marx figure, declaring the principles of Animalism, essentially the equality of all animals and the parasitic nature of humans:

> " In fighting against Man, we must not come to resemble him. Even when you have conquered him, do not adopt his vices. No animal must ever live in a house or sleep in a bed, or wear cloths, or drink alcohol, or smoke tobacco, or touch money, or engage in trade. … Above all, no animal must ever tyrannize over his own kind. Weak or strong, clever or simple, we are all brothers. No animal must ever kill any other animal. All animals are equal.

Though Old Major dies, two pigs, Snowball and Napoleon, lead the revolution, overthrowing man, and adopting seven maxims of Animalism that are to be followed on the farm. Snowball is the Trotsky figure, an idealist who genuinely believes in the principles of Animalism; however he is eventually deceived and overthrown by Napoleon. During his time as leader over the animals, Napoleon did everything that Old Major warned against; one by one, he changed the maxims to allow himself and the other animals with high authority to break the maxims that every animal was supposed to follow.

Eventually, instead of the final maxim being "All animals are equal," it became "All animals are equal but some animals are more equal than others."

By the end of the novella, through deceitfulness, Napoleon and the pigs under him became indistinguishable from the human farmers such as Mr. Jones, if not worse, just as Stalin and his followers became indistinguishable from the tyrannical czars: "The creatures outside looked from pig to man, and from man to pig, and from pig to man again; but already it was impossible to say which was which." Orwell could not be clearer in arguing that Soviet overreach had damaged the principles of communism, creating a form of government even more totalitarian than the one overthrown.

1984

Orwell wrote *1984* as another warning of the oppressive and nightmarish qualities of a totalitarian government, a fear made greater by the actual totalitarian regimes that flourished in Europe in the first half of the 20th century. The novel follows Winston Smith's journey of disobedience against Big Brother and the Party of the Republic of Oceania. Telescreens, which monitor people's every movement and listen to their every word, are eveywhere—there is no escape from observation. Oceania is "a world of fear and treachery and torment, a world of trampling and being trampled upon, a world which will grow not less but more merciless as it refines itself. … In [this] world there will be no emotions except fear, rage, triumph, and self-abasement."

Throughout the course of the novel, Winston, despite working for the Ministry of Truth, partakes in a love affair with a girl named Julia in the fiction department, and then they join a secret brotherhood that works against the Party. No one is able to hide from the subjugation of the Party forever, and eventually everyone in defiance is caught and subject to physical torture and mental conditioning. So strong is the Party's control that "[i]n the end the Party [will] announce that two plus two made five, and you would have to believe it." In the end, the Party has won even Winston over, as the novel ends on this horrifying narration: "But it was all right, everything was all right, the struggle was finished. He had won the victory over himself. He loved Big Brother."

Toby Coffman, faculty
Briauna Schultz, 2013

JEAN-PAUL SARTRE, 1905–1980, *The French Father of Existentialism*

> " Hell is other people.
>
> —*No Exit*

- Is commonly referred to as the Father of Existentialism
- Received the Nobel Prize for Literature, but refused the award
- Was a sporadic supporter of the Communist Party
- Believed that the individual alone should determine his identity and morality
- Believed that everyone is inclined to find his/her identity through those around him, which is the gravest sin one can commit; calls this tendency "bad faith"
- The first step toward self-determination is the refusal to identify oneself with ego, as ego constitutes a flight from freedom, a predetermined identity that lacks the freedom of

"authenticity" (a word now commonly used in popular psychological language, but actually introduced as an obscure and almost indefinable alternative to the ego by Sartre and other twentieth century theorists)

- The key to the ego vs. "authentic selfness" divide is that the ego lacks freedom and is self-regarding, whereas the authentic self is generous and giving; that is, the goals of authenticity and overcoming alienation have a moral and political dimension, and are part of an implicit critique of Western liberty
- Authenticity, in one of Sartre's formulations, is thwarted in capitalist societies by systemic exploitation and oppression; only socialism and/or communism inherently mitigates the harmful effects of ego and inauthenticity; thus, the freedom we gain from determining our own identity is not the freedom of Thomas Jefferson, but of John Dewey or Karl Marx: the freedom to "express yourself" openly while placing your time and energy voluntarily at the mercy of the collective, i.e., of the social system or state

Key Works

Nausea, 1938
Being and Nothingness, 1943
The Flies, 1943
No Exit, 1944
Existentialism Is a Humanism, 1946
Critique of Dialectical Reason, 1960

Biography

Jean-Paul Sartre is commonly regarded as the father of existentialist philosophy. Born in Paris in 1905 to a naval officer and his wife, Sartre received a prestigious education, including his four-year study at the École Normale Supérieur. There, he met Simone de Beauvoir (who went on to become a celebrated philosopher, writer and feminist), and the two became life-long companions. At the conclusion of WWII, Sartre played a central role in advancing the existentialist movement. His philosophy is most clearly elaborated in the transcript of his lecture "Existentialism is a Humanism," first delivered in Paris, 1945, and published in 1946. Sartre subsequently launched into his role as the Existentialist movement's poster boy. His writing reached international acclaim by 1946, and he was awarded the Nobel Prize in Literature in 1964 for his autobiography, *The Words*. However, he refused to accept the award. Always an advocate of far-left-wing politics, Sartre had an on-again-off-again relationship with the Communist Party, and it was his interest in the political sphere that prompted him to cease his writing of fictional literature. In the 1970s, Sartre experienced a number of strokes that rendered him nearly blind. His last publication, *L'espoir maintenant*, was a series of interviews with Benny Lévy, a former Mao supporter for whom he also served as secretary. Sartre's death, on April 15, 1980, catalyzed a massive demonstration in Paris, which was a testament to Sartre's influence on the creative, intellectual, and political lives of the public.

No Exit

No Exit is probably Jean-Paul Sartre's most famous work. It concerns three individuals who find themselves in a bland hotel room that turns out to be Hell. The characters, Garcin, Estelle, and Inez, are all dead, and they have residual guilt requiring healing. Garcin was a pacifist journalist who was shot by firing squad for deserting. He is ashamed of his death, in addition to his constant unfaithfulness

586 · Chapter 7

to his wife, so he expresses a deep need to be recognized as courageous, since he cannot accept his identity as a coward. Estelle is a young, beautiful, and foolish woman who died of pneumonia. She was unfaithful to her husband and became pregnant with the baby of her lover. When the baby was born, Estelle murdered the baby in front of the father, who then committed suicide. Estelle wanted the baby out of her life because she did not want to share her lover's affection with it. After the man killed himself, Estelle became distraught and her desperation for male companionship and affirmation only increased until her death. Lastly, Inez is a bright, snarky lesbian who was murdered by her partner. Inez fell in love with the wife of her cousin, whom she then seduced and subsequently entered into a relationship with. Inez regularly manipulated and emotionally abused her companion, who became so depressed that she killed both herself and Inez by breaking a gas line in their apartment. Though Inez is the most "pragmatic" of the three protagonists, and though she is the only one willing to accept her shame and inadequacies, she still struggles with a feeling of isolation. Her identification as a lesbian is socially unacceptable. Thus, she suffers with loneliness and a need for love.

Each of these characters has personal and specific wounds and shortcomings, but not one of them is able to fix these problems alone. Garcin needs affirmation that he is not a coward, even though he believes, deep down, that he is. Thus, he looks to Estelle and Inez for reassurance. Estelle will not give him an honest answer because she'll say anything for male attention. Inez will not appease him because she's convinced he is a coward and, also, enjoys watching him suffer. In short, Garcin seeks a new identity for himself but cannot come by it in a satisfactory way. Both Estelle and Inez have the same problem. Estelle wants to be regarded as a beautiful woman, and she desires affirmation in the form of a man's complete love and devotion. Since Garcin is the only man in the room, she flings herself on him but receives no genuine love. Garcin entertains her for a brief moment, but does so out of lust and spite. Garcin has no affection for Estelle, but uses her for the sake of sexual pleasure, as well as a means of revenge against Inez (who refused to affirm Garcin and is romantically interested in Estelle). Thus, Inez suffers because she desires affection from Estelle, but will not get it because Estelle is interested in Garcin. Each character's desire for, and rejection by, the others inspires the most famous quote and conclusion of the play, "Hell is other people."

"The Human Project"

According to Sartre, there is one fundamental desire shared by all people: the desire to be God, a deity capable of free-consciousness and self-identification. The act of fulfilling this desire is what Sartre called "The Human Project." Sartre believed that individuals are naturally free in that they have the power of free-consciousness. While this free-consciousness allows people to examine and define the world around them, it means people easily self-identify. As a result, the nature of human consciousness compels individuals to create identity outside themselves.

No Exit is so famous in part because of how expertly it captures Sartre's philosophy. The statement, "Hell is other people," expresses several key tenets of Sartrian thought: one, the human individual possesses a free consciousness that allows him to identify and define himself and others; two, the individual is contrarily compelled to seek identity through others, thereby denying his characteristic qualities of free consciousness and self-identification. The subsequent torture that follows this conflict between independence and dependence is the very "Hell" Sartre writes about in *No Exit*.

Jean-Paul Sartre's existentialism affirms that the human individual is, and ought to be, responsible for his own fate and beliefs. To the greatest extent possible, the individual should conduct his own destiny.

Through the character Inez, Sartre expresses this precise belief, stating, "A man is what he wills himself to be," and "It's what one does, and nothing else, that shows the stuff one's made of ... one's whole life is complete at that moment ... you are—your life and nothing else."

Human beings are rare because of the nature of their consciousness. Though people are composed of physical matter, there is an element of them that is, seemingly, immaterial: consciousness. Unlike plants and other animals, human beings can analyze surroundings, apply definitions, and create meaning. A person can look out on a landscape and divide it into various, distinct elements according to the unique characteristics of the objects he observes. He can look out on a plain and identify rocks, trees, and bushes, which are separate from one another based upon their individual qualities (as observed and determined by the viewer) and purposes. His ability to distinguish and categorize the myriad forms of existence distinguishes him as a "for-itself" being.

"Bad Faith"

Sartre called a being incapable of this sort of free consciousness an "in-itself," as it is unable to change or consider its own existence or the existence of others. It remains the essential being/thing it was upon origination. By contrast, human beings—though bound by many innate conditions outside their choosing—are able to select much of their identity "for" themselves. This element of freedom separates the human individual as a "for-itself."

For Sartre, the gravest sin one can commit is degrading himself or herself to the status of an in-itself. By attempting to find one's existence outside himself, he commits "bad faith," a phrase capturing the movement from a "for-itself" to an "in-itself." Though the human consciousness is capable of identifying and qualifying the objects and beings around him, he is less capable (or inclined) to identify himself. Rather, the individual most often succumbs to seemingly insurmountable elements of reality, which he falsely perceives as formative of his personality. For example, a human being has many natural traits that are outside of his control. Hair color, eye color, sensory abilities, and even intelligence, are all such traits. These characteristics are what Sartre calls elements of "facticity." According to Sartre, many people falsely believe that facticity dictates who they are and what they can do. He expresses this idea very clearly in his play, *The Flies*.

The Flies: "Existence before Essence"

Sartre's play, *The Flies*, is a modern imagining of the ancient Greek play, *The Libation Bearers*. *The Libation Bearers* is the second part of the three-part tragedy called the *Orestaia*, a story about a banished son, Orestes, who returns to his home city of Argos to avenge the death of his father, Agamemnon, who was killed by Orestes' mother, Clytemnestra, and her lover, Aegisthus. The final play of the *Orestaia* focuses heavily on the question of justice, asking whether Orestes was justified in his act of revenge. Should he be punished for murdering his mother and her lover, or should he be applauded?

Sartre invents his own rendering of *The Libation Bearers* precisely because of the moral questions inherent in the story. However, instead of focusing on the question, "What is justice?" Sartre asks, "How does/should one determine justice?" The distinction here is a crucial one, as Sartre concludes that right and wrong have less to do with *what* one does, and more with *how* one chooses to do it.

In Sartre's play, Orestes secretly returns to the city of Argos after many years of exile and finds that the city is infested with flies. Because the citizens of Argos allowed Clytemnestra and Aegisthus to kill king

Agamemnon, they are plagued with flies as a constant punishment and reminder. This punishment is a pleasure to the god, Jupiter, who travels the city disguised as an old man. Throughout the story, Orestes endures a moral struggle in which he ultimately decides that ethics are decided by the individual. Jupiter threatens and frightens the Argives into believing and following his moral codes, forcing them to wear sackcloth and ashes, as well as partake in the annual Dead Man's Day, wherein corpses rise from the dead to torment the living for their sins one day out of the year. However, the Argives practice contrition so regularly that it becomes habit. Consequently, their displays of remorse are not genuine, but merely cultural. Witnessing these empty displays of guilt, wherein individuals wear black simply because "everyone wears black," Orestes begins to question the presiding moral authority. While Jupiter has immense power, and can severely punish people for disobeying him, he cannot force anyone to do his will. This revelation inspires Orestes to not only avenge his father, but also remove any guilt from the act, as he is ultimately responsible for what he does and feels.

Orestes's revelation is an application of Sartre's axiom, "existence precedes essence." The "Jupiters" of modern existence, which include presiding governments, religious beliefs, and cultural or ethical norms, falsely instill the belief that there is some power outside themselves which forces them to act and be a certain way. However, to Sartre, this power is merely a show of force and has no actual authority in itself. These cultural norms, as well as the many inherent traits people possess, do not dictate who they are. Rather, they are objects and tools that the individual, through her free consciousness, can use to determine who she wishes to be. Thus, it is not the "essence" of the individual that determines her identity. Rather, it is her sheer existence, her conscious being, which dictates the nature of her personhood. For if one allows her essence to dictate her identity, she is no better than the plants and animals who are merely beings "in-themselves," and not "for-themselves."

David Eschrich, researcher
Daren Jonescu, advisor

CONRAD H. WADDINGTON ◊ 1905–1975, *Birth-giver of Epigenetics*

"" Dig down to nothing and come up with everything.

- Created the field of epigenetics and popularized the model of the epigenetic landscape
- Contributed to modern genetic understanding through his popular theory of canalization
- Served as a scientific advisor to the Commander in Chief, Coastal Command, and Royal Air Force during WWII; he was later named Commander of the Order of the British Empire

Key Works
Introduction to Modern Genetics, 1939
Organisers and Genes, 1940
The Scientific Attitude, 1941
The Ethical Animal, 1960
The Epigenetics of Birds, 1952
Principles of Embryology, 1956
The Strategy of the Genes, 1957

Biography

Though he was born in England in 1905, Conrad Waddington spent the early years of his childhood in India before returning to England to study science. In 1926, Waddington married his first wife (with whom he had a son) and graduated from Cambridge with first class honors in the natural sciences. Waddington's later research of bird and mammal embryos in the Cambridge research library gave him new insights into the links between traditional Mendelian Genetics and the embryonic development of organs and tissues. By publishing his findings in *Organisers and Genes,* Waddington merged the fields of embryology and genetics for the first time.

Waddington's extensive travels earned him multiple appointments as a travelling fellow of the Rockefeller Foundation. In WWII, he was recruited as a scientific advisor to the Commander-in-Chief, the Coastal Command, and the Royal Air Force. He developed better methods for tracking U-boats using mathematical modeling. After the war, Waddington moved with his second wife (with whom had had two daughters) to take up his new position as the chair of genetics at the University of Edinburgh. Here, he published some of his most well known research on genetic assimilation and embryology. Widely recognized as the father of epigenetics, he received many honors for his work, including the Albert Brachet Prize for embryology, and he was named the Commander of the of Order of the British Empire in 1958. Waddington continued publishing his research regularly until his death in 1974.

Epigenetic Landscape

Waddington's greatest contribution to his field was his discovery of the science of epigenetics and the "epigenetic landscape." Waddington wanted to create a visual model to represent the ways embryonic stem cells may differentiate, or specialize into a specific type of cell. He began studying competence, chemical induction, and gene expression and regulation in order to understand how cells differentiate; he called this field of study "epigenetics," which he defined as "the branch of biology which studies the causal interactions between genes and their products, which bring the phenotype into being." Waddington encapsulated his insights into the differentiation process in his model of the epigenetic landscape. He described the process of differentiation as "a series of ridges and valleys a cell can traverse on its way to a final tissue type." He pictured the cells as little marbles that roll down a mountain with ridges and valleys, each taking a different pathway. Each cell's individual path determines whether that "marble" becomes a nerve, a red blood cell, a bone cell, or any other type. This visual model revolutionized the understanding of epigenetics, and it has since formed the foundation for all subsequent epigenetic research.

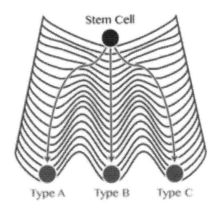

Waddington imagined a stem cell as a marble that could
roll down different valleys to become different cells.

Waddington's Epigenetic Landscape

Genetic Assimilation and Canalization

One of Waddington's most famous experiments, which led to his definition of canalization, involved *Drosophila melanogaster*, a wild-type fly. A large stock of these flies was exposed to an environmental shock—a high temperature or an ether vapor—when they were still in the early developmental stages as eggs or pupae. Survivors of the shock were visibly damaged: "aberrant in appearance and sub-normal in vitality." Waddington then selected a number of flies whose environmental shock had caused them to be crossveinless, or lacking the small veins that run between the major veins of an insect's wing. Even though the flies in this group looked like genetically mutated flies, it is highly unlikely that the flies' genes would have actually mutated from the shock in such a short time. Waddington allowed these crossveinless flies to mate with one another, and then he exposed half of the new generation of flies to the same environmental shock and allowed half of the new flies to develop naturally.

Waddington continued this process for many generations and realized "from the sixteenth generation [of wild-type flies] onwards, the frequency of phenocopies rose again and attained a value four times as high as it had been at its lowest point." In other words, as the generations went on, a higher proportion of flies began to exhibit crossveinlessness as a result of environmental shocks. In addition to this increase in the proportion of phenocopies, the flies actually began to resemble genetically mutated flies. The phenocopies could no longer fly, and, most notably, after 15 generations of breeding, there was no longer a need for the environmental shock to produce the crossveinlessness trait. Waddington's careful selection of flies had led to "a strain in which the abnormal phenotype comes to be produced in the absence of any abnormal environment"; crossveinlessness had become hereditary, an acquired trait. This seemed a great mystery, as the non-genetic damage to the flies seemed to gradually become a hereditary genetic trait, despite the fact that previous experiments had proven that generations do not pass on acquired traits. Even more a mystery was the fact that the control group flies, related to the original flies but never exposed to any environmental stress, began to produce crossveinless offspring as well, even though none of their ancestors were ever exposed to environmental shocks in development.

Waddington explained these mysteries through his idea of canalization. He believed a species is "buffered … so that approximately the optimum end-result is attained in spite of minor variations, both genetic and environmental in origin." Waddington argued that species would tend to one phenotype, even with diverse genetic information, because natural selection favored that configuration. The effects of naturally occurring genetic variations were "masked by the effects of other genes" in order to guarantee the greatest chance at survival. Waddington used the term "canalization" to explain this phenomenon. The genetic variations within species were like different canals in a valley; no matter which genotype the organism has, its observable traits will settle at the "bottom of the valley."

As a result, even genetically different organisms will appear to share all the same traits. These "bottom of the valley" traits are the genetically dominant shared advantages that were passed on by natural selection. However, in the face of a strong environmental shock, organisms will de-canalize and expose their underlying genetic variations. In his wild-type fly experiment, Waddington simulated "natural selection" by repeatedly breeding the most damaged flies with one another. In doing this, he artificially made crossveinlessness a naturally selected trait. Waddington forcibly re-routed the "canals" of the flies' traits by breeding only damaged flies. Though Waddington never altered the genes of the flies, his experiment did alter which genes dominantly expressed themselves over time. After a long time, crossveinlessness became the more dominant trait for survival, and it became the new "bottom of the valley" for Waddington's flies.

Caroline Fuschino, 2015
Julianna Swayze, 2016
Alexi Wenger, 2016

AYN RAND ◊ 1905–1982, *Russian Immigrant, Economic Novelist*

> " Freedom (n.): To ask nothing. To expect nothing. To depend on nothing.
> —*The Fountainhead*

- Lived through the Russian Revolution
- Immigrated to America in 1926 at age 21
- Was a staunch free market capitalist
- Believed in reason as the only means of acquiring knowledge
- Rejected faith and religion, an atheist
- Advocated self-interest, equating the invisible hand of the free market to the "common good"
- Argued that rational thought (reason) is humanity's noblest virtue

Key Works

The Fountainhead, 1943
Atlas Shrugged, 1957

Biography

Alisa Zinovyevna Rosenbaum's philosophies are debated today as she supported capitalism, criticized collectivism, and questioned the power of government. She was Jewish, born in Russia to a pharmacist and his wife, and lived through the Russian Revolution. During the Revolution, her father's pharmacy was seized by the Bolsheviks, and the family moved to the Crimea and lived in poverty. This may be the source of Rand's strong feelings about government intrusion into individuals' livelihoods. She left

Russia in 1926 to visit relatives in Chicago and never returned. After a few months in Illinois, she headed to Hollywood and became a screenwriter, using the name Ayn Rand. She married actor Frank O'Connor and became an American citizen. While working on her writing, Rand got a job as a clerk at RKO Pictures and landed in the wardrobe department, eventually becoming its head. She achieved success as a writer with *The Fountainhead*, which became a movie starring Gary Cooper, and then *Atlas Shrugged*. She was adapting the latter book for television when she died of heart failure in 1982.

The Capitalist Novelist

In "The Objectivist Ethics," Rand defines her terms: "When I say "capitalism," I mean a full, pure, uncontrolled, unregulated laissez-faire capitalism—with a separation of state and economics, in the same way and for the same reasons as the separation of state and church." Perhaps because of her family's encounter with the Bolsheviks, Rand embraced and advocated pure capitalism with single-minded focus. Once she came to American, she criticized the similarities between the New Deal and the central planning of the communists. She saw governments as greedy, seeking power in every situation, even when in the seemingly altruistic hands of intellectuals. All bureaucrats were empire builders very different from Rand's heroes, the men of business just trying to give life to their dreams. She argued, in "What Is Capitalism":

> The *moral* justification of capitalism does not lie in the altruist claim that it represents the best way to achieve 'the common good.' It is true that capitalism does—if that catch-phrase has any meaning—but this is merely a secondary consequence. The moral justification of capitalism lies in the fact that it is the only system consonant with man's rational nature, that it protects man's survival *qua* man, and that its ruling principle is: *justice*.

Politically, she believed government should be reduced to a minarchism or minarchy, operating only very essential functions, letting the laissez-faire free market provide other necessary operations.

Objectivism

Her philosophies came to be known as objectivism. Craig Biddle, writing for *The Objective Standard*, explains the logic of objectivism this way:

1. The Nature of Reality—the universe has no creator. Existence is the only given thing. Everything acts according to its nature. Because there is nothing apart from man himself, nothing has authority over man. Nothing is higher than the democratic consensus or social convention.
2. Man's Means of Knowledge—man learns by reason alone.
3. The Standard of Moral Value—whatever man requires for life on earth, things we need to live and prosper are good.
4. The Proper Beneficiary of Values—the beneficiary is the person who earns the values. He can keep it, use it, sell, it, as you please.
5. Moral Virtue—the total of the values that direct his actions. Being moral is going after whatever your life depends on (as long as it harms no one else), never sacrificing for someone or something else. Virtue is "perfectly self, non-sacrificial, and thus moral."
6. The Nature of Rights—a man must be free to act on his own opinions. Since physical force is the only thing that could stop him, people must never use physical force against another.

7. The Proper Purpose of Government—Force is so evil and antithetical to individual liberty that the government must ban its use except against those who initiate force. Government isn't needed to impose any control on the economy or speech, because that would take away liberty. The society would be completely free to every person to behave as he determines is best for himself, except to initiate force.

Objectivists continue to create momentum within academic settings and inspire both libertarians and conservatives.

Atlas Shrugged

Atlas Shrugged, published in 1957, earned Rand great wealth and brought to (fictional, at least) fruition her philosophical system of objectivism. The story of *Atlas Shrugged* unfolds to an exciting climax which finds all the nation's creative entrepreneurs living in Galt's Gulch in Colorado, including the novel's railroad tycoon protagonist, Dagny, and the man she loves, John Galt, who has organized a "strike of the mind" against government regulations and interference. Galt, Rand's hero, testifies in court to the many evils of collectivism. The politicians of the nation give up even the pretence of working for the people's good, and John Galt takes over the airwaves and speaks to the people, describing why he organized the strike. The government decides to make Galt their economic dictator, and take him prisoner. Galt, of course, refuses to cooperate, even though they torture him. Dagny and the strikers rescue Galt and Dagny finally joins the strike. Soon, the country's collapse is complete. Throughout, the novel celebrates the accomplishments of entrepreneurs and inventors, while vilifying government officials and politics. While writing critics have described Rand's writing "cardboard characters and tabloid style," suitable for adolescents, she had a knack for creating hypnotizing myths.

SAMUEL BECKETT ◊ 1906–1989, *The Absurdista*

> 66 We always find something … to give us the impression we exist.
>
> —*Waiting for Godot*

- Endured a difficult family life which affected his view of life, making him a very negative man
- Was part of the Resistance against the Nazis in Paris until he and his wife were forced to flee during WWII
- Revolutionized drama by writing plays that did not follow conventional plot sequences
- Spoke three languages—French, Italian, and English—and generally wrote in French and then translated his own works back into English
- Won the Nobel Prize in Literature in 1969 for his absurdist works
- Did not like his Nobel Prize fame, and was antisocial throughout his whole life

Key Works

Murphy, 1938
Waiting for Godot, 1948
Endgame, 1957

Biography

Perhaps the most reluctant recipient of the Nobel Prize in Literature in the award's history is Samuel Beckett. Born in 1906 in Ireland to a construction worker and a nurse, Beckett's childhood was plagued with illness and depression, which made him a withdrawn and antisocial child. He developed his trademark pessimism from an early age. Picking up French and Italian while at Trinity College, he traveled the Continent before settling in Paris, and had a number of brief teaching stints before embarking on his writing career. In Paris, he met Suzanne Dechevaux-Dumesnuil, a piano student, who was his companion and lover and whom he married in 1961. His Irish citizenship allowed him to remain in France as a neutral after WWII broke out, and he worked as a courier in the French underground resistance. The French government awarded him the Croix de Guerre for bravery after the war. *Waiting for Godot*, Beckett's most famous play, was first produced in 1953 and established Beckett as a powerhouse playwright. He received the Nobel Prize for Literature in 1969 for his contributions as a novelist, poet, playwright, and critic. For the quiet, unsociable writer, it was not an honor but rather a catastrophe to have so much attention for his work, and despite the popularity he gained from this, he remained a highly private man. He ignored the fame and continued writing until the end of his life in December 1989, mere months after his wife's death.

The Theatre of the Absurd

Shortly before Beckett's time, the German philosopher Friedrich Nietzsche had shocked the world with his controversial thesis that "God is dead." This assertion was part of a larger philosophical move away from religion and meaning and toward a world of atheistic absurdity. Western man, who had long "turned to love, courage, and God for the strength to go on," realized that there is another "way of coping … one lacking all dignity, heroism, and nobility: accepting the comic, the absurd." Beckett joined this new generation of writers. His plays fit into a genre popularly known as Theatre of the Absurd. Absurdity, at its core, is the idea that there is no meaning at all in our existence. As such, absurdist plays portray characters who live life for its own sake in a universe no longer making sense because there is no God. These plays "portray a purposeless, absurd world" where little happens and little makes sense.

Much of Beckett's dialogue throughout his play calls attention to this meaninglessness. In *Endgame*, the character Hamm fearfully asks Clov, "We're not beginning to … mean something?" a question which Clov ridicules. In *Waiting for Godot* the two main characters wait for a man named Godot—who will bring salvation with him but never comes. Many critics have pointed out that Godot could stand for God, and the fact that he never appears symbolizes the absurdity of sitting and waiting for a deity to come and save humankind. Late in *Godot*, the characters themselves point out the futility of life:

> Estragon: No use struggling.
> Vladimir: One is what one is.
> Estragon: No use wriggling.
> Vladimir: The essential doesn't change.
> Estragon: Nothing to be done.

Estragon and Vladimir see the purposeless world in this dialogue, and they seem to realize that this purposelessness is inevitable. Rather than fight against the irrational life, this dialogue suggests there is nothing to do but accept it. Later, Estragon poses that mankind will "always find something … to give us the impression we exist." But even with this glimmer of hope that may come with creating a meaning for oneself, Vladimir portends that in "an instant all will vanish and [mankind will] be alone once more, in the midst of nothingness." In the tradition of absurdist plays, *Waiting for Godot* portrays the feeble struggling of insignificant man facing meaningless oblivion without hope from any god.

The absurdist plays can be best summed up in a quote from one of these plays: "Nothing happens, nobody comes, nobody goes, it's awful!" In fact, as in most absurdist plays, not "much happens . . . there is little plot, little incident, and little characterization." A popular critic once described a two-act Beckett play as a story where "nothing happens, twice." In *Waiting for Godot*, two characters talk while they wait for a man who never arrives. In *Endgame*, a couple of characters wait to die. In *Happy Days*, a woman and her husband sit and talk in a waist-deep, growing mound. These plotless plays recognize the lack of purpose in real life; there is no great story or interesting twist, just as there is also no great story or overarching purpose in life.

The dialogue of absurdist plays has evolved into nothing more than meaningless exchanges, and the action is repetitive. In *Waiting for Godot*, Vladimir and Estragon argue about thinking:

> " Estragon: That's the idea, let's contradict each other.
> Vladimir: Impossible.
> Estragon: You think so?
> Vladimir: We're in no danger of ever thinking any more.

The dialogue in this scene makes little sense; in other words, it is completely absurd. Actions in absurdist plays are repetitive to represent the lack of "a fixed center, meaning, or purpose in lives," even though the characters go on living these cyclical and meaningless lives. In *Endgame*, for example, Clov constantly threatens to leave although he never really does. Through this repetition, Beckett, along with other absurdist playwrights, underscores the cyclical stasis of the existence.

The settings of Beckett's plays in particular are desolate and dark. *Waiting for Godot* is set with simply a rock and a tree along a deserted country road. *Endgame* takes place in an almost bunker-like room, decorated with only two small windows and two trash cans that house Hamm's parents. *Krapp's Last Tape* shows a man at a desk, only the center of the stage illuminated to depict his imprisonment in his own mind due to his deafness and partial blindness. These isolated settings likely emphasize the hopelessness of mankind in the face of lack of purpose.

Dark Comedy

Many of Beckett's notable works are dark comedies. Dark comedy is characterized by gallows humor, making light of typically serious topics such as death and illness. Although Becket classifies *Waiting for Godot* as a "tragicomedy," it has many elements of a dark comedy. *Godot* features whimsical characters that seem funny in the beginning of the play but who sour into parodies and mockeries of the human existence as the play wears on. Their antics are amusing until the observer realizes the characters are weak and depraved. They are worthy of pity, not laughter, and that changes the play from something light to something dark and gloomy. The play ends without any validation for the characters; their waiting has been in vain. Thus, despite allowing the audience to laugh through most of it, the play leaves the audience with a scarcely acknowledged fear that maybe Beckett's take on human nature is correct, which is no laughing matter.

Endgame also shows elements of dark comedy and functions the same way *Waiting for Godot* does, expressing Beckett's deep, often depressing thoughts in a manner that evokes laughter. Beckett believed "nothing is funnier than unhappiness." *Endgame* represents the final moments of a chess game, when all the extraneous pieces have been played but both kings are still in play. At that moment, both sides see the futility of the situation; neither can win and both parties know that, yet they both continue to play. The whole situation is a large metaphor for life. Without all the other pieces left in the game, the chess players can no longer pretend there is any hope of a winner. It is much the same in life. Only when all the props and extra players are stripped away will an individual accept the hopeless situation of his life. The play itself is at times amusing, but there is an undercurrent of hopelessness that is slightly too relatable to really be joked about. Although *Endgame* is not truly a dark comedy in the strictest sense of the term, it still evokes a certain morbid laughter while it highlights ideas that are both too deep and dark to typically find their way into comedies.

Elizabeth Palms, 2014

CLAUDE LÉVI-STRAUSS ◊ 1908–2009, *Influential Modern Anthropologist*

> " I therefore claim to show, not how men think in myths, but how myths operate in men's minds without them being aware of the fact.
> —*Mythologiques 1: The Raw and the Cooked*

- Was born in Brussels in 1908, and became one of the most influential anthropologists of the 20th century
- Fled before the Nazi regime in 1941; settled down as a professor of sociology and later the cultural attaché in the United States
- Thought culture was similar to language: both are controlled through hidden rules, patterns, and structures that humans unconsciously use
- Believed the whole is greater than the sum of its parts: thought the relationships *between* people and cultures are far more important than the individuals themselves
- Saw the concept of "exchange" as fundamental to how culture spreads, particularly the exchange of women in marriage
- Explained the fundamental cultural rule against incest as a way to create alliances with others and marry outside of one's family
- Believed all the hidden rules and complex systems of a culture can be discovered and identified through analogies he called "binary oppositions"
- Analyzed the importance of myths in culture: argued that while myths seem to differ, they share fundamental similarities and have a common structure
- Suggested that all myths have parts that are opposite or contradict one another, but also have parts that attempt to resolve these oppositions

Key Works

The Elementary Structures of Kinship, 1949
Tristes Tropiques, 1955
The Savage Mind, 1962
Mythologiques, The Origin of Table Manners, 1968

Biography

Claude Lévi-Strauss was a world-renowned anthropologist and important contributor to the idea of structuralism that was particularly influential in 1950s and 1960s France. Lévi-Strauss was born in Brussels, Belgium, in 1908 to a French-Jewish family. Early in his youth, his family moved to Paris where he would spend the entirety of his childhood. During his high school years, Lévi-Strauss became involved with the socialist party and joined the Groupe d'Études Socialistes (Socialist Study Group), eventually becoming its secretary. After high school, he earned a law degree and went on to obtain a PhD in philosophy from the Sorbonne.

While teaching high school philosophy, Lévi-Strauss received a phone call that he would later describe as decisive for his vocation as an anthropologist. The director of one of the most important schools in France offered him a teaching position at the University of São Paulo in Brazil. There, he did his only fieldwork with his wife Dina, an ethnographer, eventually publishing his research as *Elementary Structures of Kinship*. In 1939 he moved back to France; however, he was forced to flee the country due to the start of WWII; Dina remained to fight with the Resistance. He migrated to New York City where he began to teach at the New School for Social Research.

Lévi-Strauss moved back to France at the end of the war and became a professor at the Collège de France—the highest distinction in French higher education. As a professor, he published the important *The Savage Mind*, along with a best seller, *Tristes Tropiques*, a book that influenced people in so many different fields that the committee for France's premier literary prize apologized that they couldn't award it to Lévi-Strauss since the book wasn't technically a novel. He died in France on November 1, 2009, at age 100.

Structural Anthropology

Lévi-Strauss thought that language—specifically linguistics—was a perfect analogy for studying cultures. For him, language consists of sets of oppositions and differences. No term has meaning entirely by itself, and since terms gain meaning through contrasts with other terms, the anthropologist should follow the linguist in examining the relationships *between* objects, ideas, and traditions, rather than just the objects or traditions themselves. This is a form of "linguistic structuralism," and Lévi-Strauss was heavily indebted to the ideas of the linguists Ferdinand de Saussure and Roman Jakobson, adding the aspects of structuralism found within linguistics to his theories about culture.

Linguistic structuralism is the idea that speakers of any language are unconsciously controlled by distinct syntactical rules. Lévi-Strauss applied this idea of unconscious human structuring to the formation of society itself. Just as meaning is not derived from a spoken sentence without the structures and rules of language, culture acquires meaning only through its structures. These structures are found within families; the dynamic of a family (having a mother and a father and those parents having children) is a structure. Lévi-Strauss believed that, just as meaning is acquired with structures within spoken language, without the structure of a family, the father and mother would just be two random people and the brother and sister would just be two random people. The cultural structure gives meaning to a family.

Lévi-Strauss is famous for his structuralist explanation of the almost universal laws against incest. In the same way that the linguist must not study a term without examining the broader context, the anthropologist must not look simply at the prohibition against incest, but the broader function that the idea of "exchange" plays. He finds that the prohibition against incest also serves to direct social groups toward intermarriage (if a youth can't marry his sister, he has to marry a woman from another family), creating an obligation to return the favor and, thus, social cohesion. Lévi-Strauss thinks of this exchange of women between groups as the passage from nature to culture, since it is the foundation for lasting bonds between peoples.

Lévi-Strauss explains that all of culture's structures can be simplified into analogies called "binary oppositions." A person knows a steak is best when it is cooked, not raw. The person knows this only because she understands that a meat cannot be both cooked and raw, and she is familiar with the different eating experience that each state implies. These binary oppositions are everywhere: man and woman, nature and culture, love and hate, war and peace. Culture's structures are made through these oppositions. Lévi-Strauss states in *Tristes Tropiques* that, "cultural types occur in all societies, because they result from straightforward antitheses; but their social function may differ widely from society to society." In applying this statement to the idea of binary oppositions, Lévi-Strauss is not saying that raw meat and cooked meat are the exact same in every culture, but he believes that the distinction of "raw" versus "cooked" exists in every culture. He was able to come up with these cultural insights because he looked past the individual and focused on the world's cultures as a whole.

Myth: Stories about the Fundamental Contradictions in Life

It is perhaps not surprising to learn that Lévi-Strauss uses linguistic methods to analyze myths. While he believes that myths are a completely different form of language, one can still use the analogy of a language to explore the structure of myths, which is just what Lévi-Strauss does. Myths are an easy window into the thoughts behind the culture, as the creators import their own beliefs into the myth. Therefore, as structuralism teaches that culture and life are made up of binary oppositions, myths are, too; however, these oppositions are, by definition, unresolvable. In Lévi-Strauss's own words, "mythology confronts the student with a situation which at first sight appears contradictory."

The point of the myth, then, is to resolve dilemmas, or at least give the semblance of a resolution. Myths resonate with us because we have been given a solution to a problem, one that we didn't consciously know we had. To prove this, Lévi-Strauss gives examples of nearly 200 stories from cultures around the world and across time. A more recent example, however, can be found in J.K. Rowling's *Harry Potter* series. In it, the world is divided into two parts, a simple binary opposition: a magical world, inhabited by the wizards including the titular character; and the non-magical, or "muggle" world. Conflict arises between the two, as the antagonist of the series turns against the muggles and attempts genocide. This seemingly polar contrast is resolved at the end of the series with the hero, a half-blood mix of muggle (Harry's mother Lily came from a muggle family) and magical, defeating the villain. There are hundreds of other examples throughout this series alone, and in nearly all popular myths and stories.

Cole Baker, 2012
Jeff Culver, faculty
McCarthy Nolan, 2016

ALEKSANDR SOLZHENITSYN, 1918–2008, *A Man of Courage and God*

- Was arrested for making disparaging comments about Stalin and sentenced to eight years of manual labor within the Soviet prison system, which he termed the "gulag"
- Published *One Day in the Life of Ivan Denisovich* about the brutality of labor camp life in the Soviet system; the book was, surprisingly, endorsed by Nikita Khrushchev and printed in Russia
- Won the Nobel Prize in Literature in 1970
- Survived an assassination attempt by the KGB in 1971, prior to his exile
- Was honored by *Time* magazine, which named *The Gulag Archipelago* the best nonfiction book of the 20th century
- Accepted banishment from Russia and remained in exile from 1974–1994, returning after the fall of the Soviet Union
- Spoke out passionately against the excesses and decadence of Western culture, claiming that it had the same spiritual emptiness at its core as the socialist East

Key Works

One Day in the Life of Ivan Denisovich, 1962
The First Circle, 1968
Cancer Ward, 1968
Nobel Prize acceptance letter, 1970
August 1914, 1971
The Gulag Archipelago, 1974
Harvard commencement address, 1978

Biography

From an obscure and inauspicious birth, Aleksandr Isayevich Solzhenitsyn became the greatest chronicler of the atrocities of the Stalinist prison system of Soviet Russia. He was born in Russia on December 11, 1918, at the beginning of the Leninist revolution that dislodged the czar and turned Russia into a socialist state. His father Isaakiy died in a hunting accident months before his birth. His mother, Taisia, encouraged him academically and taught him about the Russian Orthodox faith. Before the outbreak of WWII, Solzhenitsyn studied math at Rostov State University and took correspondence courses from the Moscow Institute of Philosophy, Literature, and History. During the war he served as a captain and was well decorated, receiving both the Patriotic War medal and the Red Star medal. He ran afoul of authority when the military confiscated his personal correspondence and found disparaging remarks about Stalin. Along with many others, he was sentenced to eight years in a labor camp, with the specter of permanent exile looming upon release. He was shuttled to many camps and had numerous jobs at each, such as miner, foundry supervisor, and bricklayer. After his release in 1953, he was sent into exile in Kazakhstan where he almost died from cancer. After treatment the cancer went into remission, and Solzhenitsyn survived more than another 50 years.

His experiences in the prison system form the lynchpin for his two most influential works, *One Day in the Life of Ivan Denisovich* (hereafter *One Day*) and *The Gulag Archipelago*. His experience in his struggle with cancer influenced his 1968 book *Cancer Ward*. In 1956, he was exonerated of his crimes and allowed to stay in Russia. He spent much of his time writing and teaching at a local secondary school. In 1962 he managed to have *One Day* printed in Russia, given Nikita Khrushchev's relative liberality when compared to Stalin. The poet Anna Akhmatova enthused, "Every single citizen of the 200 million inhabitants of the Soviet Union has the duty to read this text and commit it to memory." *One Day* proved immediately popular, both within Russia and abroad and established Solzhenitsyn's reputation.

The sliver of freedom that allowed for *One Day*'s publication ended when Khrushchev was removed from power in 1964. Harassed by the KGB, Solzhenitsyn was forced into hiding to complete works like *The Gulag Archipelago,* staying at the cabin of a friend in Estonia during the harsh winter months. His productivity was incredible: nearly 1,800 pages of writing in the space of 110 days. In 1970, he was awarded the Nobel Prize for literature, and around the same time KGB agents attempted to assassinate him with poison. He managed to elude death, though not without injury. After seizing a manuscript version of *The Gulag Archipelago* in 1974, the KGB arrested Solzhenitsyn, stripped him of his Russian citizenship, and put him on a plane to Frankfurt, West Germany. He lived in Cologne, Zurich, Stanford University in California, and Vermont during his 20-year exile. Finally, in 1990, after the fall of the Soviet Union, Solzhenitsyn's citizenship was restored and he returned to Russia in 1994, living in Moscow until his death in 2008. He died on August 3, 2008, of heart failure. Today, works like *One Day* and excerpts from the massive *The Gulag Archipelago* are mandatory reading in Russian schools.

Good and Evil

Solzhenitsyn's best-known quote is likely this line from *The Gulag Archipelago*: "The line dividing good and evil cuts through the heart of every human being." In many ways, this tension is the core theme of the work. Daniel Mahoney has called *The Gulag Archipelago* "an epic poem chronicling the evils of ideology and the prospects for good and evil within the human heart." Hannah Arendt, in observing the trials of Nazi war criminals at Nuremberg, observed what she termed "the banality of evil." The men she saw in the courtroom weren't monsters out of a medieval morality play, but ordinary men who were convinced to commit atrocious crimes against humanity by their unwillingness to say no.

This same conviction corresponds with Solzhenitsyn's moral sense, for the line dividing our hearts does not remain static over time, but shifts, so that "even within hearts overwhelmed by evil, one small bridgehead of good remains. And even in the best of all hearts, there remains ... an uprooted small corner of evil." In a Harvard commencement address, Solzhenitsyn noted that part of the reason for the shocking amount of evil perpetrated in the 20th century stems from a misconception at the heart of humanism: "Man—the master of this world—does not bear any evil within himself, and all the defects of life are caused by misguided social systems, which must therefore be corrected." By refusing to acknowledge the intrinsic evil inherent in every person, modern man is trying to fix the problem of evil by pulling up weeds rather than by digging out the roots.

Lest all this focus on evil seem too dour, it should be noted that underlying *the Gulag Archipelago* and Solzhenitsyn's entire body of work is a sense of hope. Solzhenitsyn's wife, Natalia, in a new introduction to the book for use in Russian schools, writes that "the book is about the ascent of the human spirit, about its struggle with evil. That is the reason why, when readers reach the end of the work, they feel not only pain and anger, but an upsurge of strength and light." We must acknowledge and confront our intrinsic evil in order to choose the good. Only then can we hope to effect positive change within our culture.

Food

On the surface, something as simple as "food" hardly seems like a key theme for a Nobel-winning author. However, given the forced elemental state of the gulag prisoners, food is of great importance in both *One Day* and *The Gulag Archipelago*. "Every bit of bread and piece of meat becomes a cherished symbol of life. Every meal of oatmeal, thin stew, or bread ration is the vehicle one needs to reach the end of the day." The paltry food issued to the prisoners each day fails to provide the nourishment necessary to allow for higher order needs (think Maslow's hierarchy), forcing the prisoners to remain almost animalistic in their desires. Especially within *One Day*, the very act of eating is slowed down and described in detail. Ivan Denisovich Shukhov, the titular character, eats his cold stew with "slow concentration," lingering over the few moments of freedom every day his meager ration affords him. Acknowledging the centrality of food to the prison experience, Dongmei Xu argues that "the prisoners are ready to compromise, acquiescing in the deprivation of their human rights for the mere sake of food." Xu goes on to connect the prisoner's overpowering desire for food to a tangible expression of their longing for freedom and home. Deprived of any contact with home and relatively little hope for freedom, the prisoners focus on the one thing within their immediate context that provides a bit of freedom and familiarity: their time spent in eating.

Religion and the West

Solzhenitsyn, once the darling of American liberals, had a falling out with the group when he gave the commencement address at Harvard in 1978. He had ruffled feathers before with his "Letter to the Soviet Leaders" in 1974, when he forcefully asserted, "I myself see Christianity today as the only living spiritual force capable of undertaking the spiritual healing of Russia." This was bad news for his former cheerleaders, a sort of the-way-forward-is-through-the-past message to American liberals. Edward E. Ericson notes that Solzhenitsyn's greatest sin in the eyes of his disenchanted western fans was to not offer unadulterated praise of humanism and progressivism. He quotes Mary McGrory in a comment that is shocking for its blunt ethnocentrism: "The unspoken expectation was that after three years in our midst, he would have to say we are superior, that our way is not only better, but best." Solzhenitsyn's Harvard commencement address had, as Malcolm Muggeridge points out, the temerity to claim that a right view of freedom is better derived from "the New Testament rather than from such impeccable sources as the American Declaration of Independence and the judgments of the US Supreme Court." Importantly for Solzhenitsyn, the force of his literary accomplishment and the effectiveness of his barrage against Soviet barbarism is rooted in and made possible by the tenets of the Christian faith.

Alexander Schmemann, an Orthodox theologian, pointed out this truth when he saw in Solzhenitsyn's writing "a deep and all-embracing … perception of the world, man, and life, which, historically, was born and grew from Biblical and Christian revelation, and only from it." Schmemann found Solzhenitsyn's writing centered on "the triune intuition of creation, fall, and redemption." Solzhenitsyn found this view of his own writing salutary, professing gratitude to Schmemann for "formulat[ing] important traits of Christianity which I could not have formulated myself." Solzhenitsyn's Harvard speech made manifest what was latent in the works written under the eye of the Soviet censors. To his audience, he boldly declared that despite the enormous amount of freedom in the West, western culture was languishing: "The West has finally achieved the rights of man, and even to excess, but man's sense of responsibility to God and society has grown dimmer and dimmer." Like Soviet Russia, Solzhenitsyn perceived that the West needed not some grand new idea, but a return to the force capable of spiritual healing that would lead to civic restoration: the Christian religion. The advice was met with as much approval in Cambridge as it was in Moscow.

Courage

"Every man always has handy a dozen glib little reasons why he is right not to sacrifice himself," Solzhenitsyn declares, indicting even himself, in the opening chapter to *The Gulag Archipelago*. At the heart of this declaration is the idea that if more of those arrested on trumped-up charges had resisted vocally and in public, then the capriciousness of the system would not be so overlooked. The problem with such a claim is that it is almost impossible to validate. How many people would have to shout at their accusers in the street in order to promote change? Various nonviolent movements of the past century, including those that eventually dismantled communism in the Soviet Union (like the Solidarity movement in Poland) demonstrate amply that courage is not synonymous with physical resistance. Part of Solzhenitsyn's indictment of Western culture in his Harvard address emanates from what he views as a basic lack of courage in contemporary Western life. He told his audience, "A decline in courage may be the most striking feature that an outside observer notices in the West today. The Western world has lost its civic courage." But the cure for the malady was not as easily discerned as the diagnosis. If Solzhenitsyn personally missed an opportunity to display courage upon his arrest, he certainly showed the virtue abundantly in the clandestine authorship of many of his works of the 1960s, refusing to bow before a Soviet system without checks and balances. Solzhenitsyn lamented his chosen path as chronicler of the gulag system, wishing that "I could go away from it all, go away many years to the back of beyond with nothing but fields and open skies ... and nothing to do but work on my novel at my own pace." However, Solzhenitsyn saw before him what needed to be done, and with courage, persisted in his task.

Toby Coffman, faculty
Ryan Russell, 2015

JACQUES DERRIDA ◊ 1930–2004, *The Deconstructor*

> " We are all translators, mediators.
>
> —quoted in an interview in *Points...: Interviews*

- Was born in French-controlled Algeria to Jewish parents
- Avoided military service in the Algerian War by working as a teacher
- Was educated at the Ecole Normale Superieure and received a grant to study at Harvard for his accomplishments in France
- Taught at the Ecole Normale Superieure for 20 years and began writing in earnest during this time
- Began articulating his theories about the nature of language, the impossibility of valid interpretation, and the ways in which power guides interpretation
- Was best known for his contributions to the idea of *deconstruction*, which was refined under his philosophical guidance
- Deconstructed works by questioning the structures of language and interpretation of texts
- Became a leading figure in the post-structuralist and postmodern movements
- Built theories on language and power that were crucial to the French strikes of 1968

- Split his time between France and the United States for the remainder of his life after a brief stint at Yale
- Espoused a philosophy that has become dominant in the American university system, with subjectivity and deconstruction the default modes of literary analysis
- Spoke out passionately against the excesses and decadence of Western culture, claiming that it had the same spiritual emptiness at its core as the socialist East

Key Works

Of Grammatology, 1967
Writing and Difference, 1978
Aporias, 1993
Ethics, Institutions, and the Right to Philosophy, 2002

Biography

Jacques Derrida was born in 1930 to Jewish parents in French-occupied Algeria. As part of his adolescent rebellion, Derrida began reading philosophers such as Nietzsche, Rousseau, and Camus. Eventually admitted to the Ecole Naturale Superieure (ENS) in 1952, he completed his Master's degree on the existentialist philosopher Edmund Husserl and was awarded a fellowship at Harvard. There, he met and married his wife, the psycho-analyst Marguerite Aucouturier. The couple moved to Paris where Derrida had a brief stint at the Sorbonne before settling permanently at ENS. It was in this period that Derrida's philosophical career flourished, including the banner year of 1967 in which he published three works. After a brief stint at Yale, Derrida found he liked the American scene and split the remainder of his life between France and the United States. Most prominently, he taught at UC-Irvine from 1986 until his death in 2004 from pancreatic cancer. His philosophical legacy lives on in university Humanities departments which remain under the sway of deconstruction.

"There is nothing outside the text"

Derrida's most famous contribution to the history of ideas came in his early work, *Of Grammatology*, when he famously said, "There is nothing outside the text." This idea has often been interpreted to mean that Derrida believed that nothing really exists as a thing in-itself but exists only as a linguistic reality. If there is nothing real outside of these texts, then most everything we believe about the world is a fiction. A reading more consistent with Derrida's broader project has to do with his focus on interpretation. In short, everything requires interpretation. There is no such thing as a bare fact. A desk is not a desk in some sense of Platonic idealism, but a "desk," a socially constructed artifact that we read meaning into. As James K.A. Smith writes, "interpretation is an inescapable part of being human and experiencing the world." But this goes deeper for Derrida, as Smith explains: "When Derrida claims that there is nothing outside the text, he means there is no reality that is not always already interpreted through the mediating lens of language."

Everything we experience is channeled through the linguistic tools at our disposal and even the nature of our language affects the way we "read" or interpret an event. On a certain level, this is obvious to us from experience. If you have been moved to tears by a film that your friend found boring, you know that interpretation is not a simple matter. Which one of you was "objectively" right in your response? A car accident will be "read" differently depending on whether you are the party that did the T-boning or the party who was T-boned. In the same way, a parent's cancer diagnosis will be read differently depending on one's previously held metaphysical and eschatological beliefs.

At a later point in his career, Derrida attempted to clarify his position by noting that perhaps a better way of articulating the idea is by saying there is nothing outside of "contexts." Our place in this world—time period, educational background, socioeconomic background, philosophical first principles—constitutes our context and narrows our field of interpretation. Derrida's argument contextualized (pun intended) in this way removes some of the glaring subjectivity from his famous line.

Derrida, the Author, and Texts

In the words of Kevin Vanhoozer, "Derrida is an unbeliever in the reliability, decidability, and neutrality of the sign." He tried to liberate readers from slavish conformity to the written word. He encouraged them to "play" with a text. He sought to undo the notion that philosophy was a purely rational affair by attacking the bifurcation between rationality and subjectivity. As Vanhoozer notes, for Derrida "what appears to be reasonable is actually only persuasive." Moreover, it appears reasonable and therefore persuasive only to people already predisposed to agree with the "rational" position. For Derrida, language (or the "sign") is about opposing ideas. This is a desk, not an automobile. That is a dog, not a cat. Writing is not a clear act, then. It actually can work to "displace" meaning.

Therefore, Derrida subscribed to the "death of the author." By this he meant that an interpreter (reader) doesn't have to make authorial intention the supreme hermeneutical principle; instead, the reader is free to play with the text. In such creative play, there is no need to read for "truth." Readers are now able to "read freed from the urge to truth." Similarly, readers are freed from any inherent meaning within the text itself. Everything one reads—if there is nothing outside the text—is to some degree metaphorical and therefore open to multiple interpretations. Derrida and other deconstructors have given lip service to the idea that this freedom necessarily leads to interpretive anarchy, but in this no-holds-barred world it is hard to see how one interpretation could be privileged above the next. Vanhoozer claims that such an hermeneutic is only possible in a world in which a higher authority is absent. If there is nothing out there to confer meaning, then we quickly lose ourselves in a multiplicity of interpretations.

THE COLD WAR, 1946–1989, THE SUPERPOWERS AND PROXY WARS

Despite the hopes of many, neither WWI nor WWII succeeded in being the war to end all wars. Shortly after the defeat of the Axis powers, the world prepared for a new kind of war: the battle between Freedom/Free Markets and Communism/Socialism, the United States and the Soviet Union. This war never actually broke out, at least not as wars classically do, but was instead spent developing weapons and stockpiling bombs, waging proxy wars (Korea, Vietnam, Afghanistan) and manipulating global politics. With the advent of the atomic bomb, open war might have meant the end of humanity. Instead things simmered, and eventually dispersed.

Cuban Missile Crisis, 1962

After the Bay of Pigs invasion of 1962, Nikita Khrushchev supported the Cuban military by supplying missiles to Cuba. Meanwhile, the United States prepared to invade Cuba off the Florida coast. The conflict came to a head when the Soviets shot down an American U-2. The Kremlin sent two letters to the United States warning them to desist their interference in Cuban affairs. Despite pressure to retaliate, President John F. Kennedy chose to reply with cool and rational thought rather than an immediate airstrike against the island. He and Attorney General Robert Kennedy engineered a blockade of Cuba that brought about a peaceful solution to the possible nuclear disaster. Kennedy was able to force Khrushchev to withdraw the missiles from Cuba after the 13-day confrontation without war, and at the same time restore world stability.

The Vietnam War, 1959–1975

One of several proxy wars waged indirectly between the great powers, the Vietnam War ended in defeat for the United States, its first great loss since the War of 1812. Vietnam was lost to Communism, and the faith of the American people in their military was visibly shaken. Arguably it has still not recovered, even to this day.

THE WAR ON TERROR, 2001 TO THE PRESENT

On September 11, 2001, several Islamic terrorists hijacked four commercial airliners and crashed them into the twin towers of the World Trade Center in New York and the Pentagon military headquarters in Washington DC. Neither the first nor the last Islamic terrorist attack, it was the first time since WWII that American blood had been spilled on American soil by foreign enemies, and lead to the War on Terror—currently in progress, with no end in sight.

Andrew Ryan McElrath
Coronado, California

Made in United States
Troutdale, OR
09/14/2023

12895359R00350